SOCIAL SCIENCE

in question

The Challenge of the Social Sciences

The Open University Course Team

Sally Baker, research librarian

Pam Berry, compositor

John Blunden, critical reader

David Calderwood, project controller

Lene Connolly, print buying controller

Margaret Dickens, print buying co-ordinator

Jessica Evans, critical reader

Jennifer Gove, critical reader

Celia Hart, picture researcher

Jonathan Hunt, copublishing advisor

Kate Hunter, research methods editor

Caroline Husher, designer

Sophie Jowett, rights editor

Mike Levers, photographer

Martin Le Voi, critical reader

Val Kirby, course secretary

Christine Meeks, course secretary

Peter Redman, study guide writer,
 staff tutor

Professor Andrew Sayer, Department of
Sociology, University of Lancaster,
external assessor

Ros Shirley, course secretary

Lynne Slocombe, editor

Mark J Smith, course chair, writer

Paul Smith, research librarian

Deborah Steinberg, Department of Sociology,
University of Warwick, tutor panel member

Keith Stribley, course manager

Alison Tucker, BBC OUPC producer

Christine Tucker, BBC OUPC production
assistant

Tony Walton, tutor panel member

Andrew Whitehead, graphic artist

Kathryn Woodward, critical reader,
staff tutor

Simeon Yates, research methods writer

This book is part of The Open University course D820 *The Challenge of the Social Sciences* in the Master's Programme in the Social Sciences. Details of this and any other Open University course can be obtained from the Courses Reservations Centre, PO Box 724, The Open University, Milton Keynes MK7 6ZS, United Kingdom: tel. (00 44) (0)1908 653231. For availability of other course components, contact Open University Worldwide Ltd, The Berrill Building, Walton Hall. Milton Keynes MK7 6AA, United Kingdom: tel. (00 44) (0)1908 858585, e-mail ouwenq@open.ac.uk. Alternatively, much useful information can be obtained from the Open University's website http://www.open.ac.uk.

SOCIAL SCIENCE
in question

Mark J Smith

SAGE Publications
London • Thousand Oaks • New Delhi
in association with
The Open University

The Open
University

SAGE Publications Ltd
6 Bonhill Street
London EC2A 4PU

SAGE Publications Inc
2455 Teller Road
Thousand Oaks
California 91320

SAGE Publications India Pvt Ltd
32, M-Block Market
Greater Kailash - I
New Delhi 110 048

British Library Cataloguing in Publication Data

A catalogue record for this book is available from
The British Library

ISBN 0 7619 6040-6 (cased)
ISBN 0 7619 6041-4 (pbk)

Library of Congress catalog card number 98-061247

Edited, designed and typeset by The Open University

Index compiled by Isobel Mclean

Printed in Great Britain by Scotprint, Haddington

1.1

SOCIAL SCIENCE
in question

Contents

Preface		vii
Chapter 1	Social Science as a Situated Practice	1
Chapter 2	The Story of Science	25
Chapter 3	The Emergence of the Social Sciences	73
Chapter 4	Imagination and Complexity in the Social Sciences	127
Chapter 5	Paradigms, Conventions and Relativism	181
Chapter 6	Language, Discourse and Culture: Rethinking Representation in the Social Sciences	229
Chapter 7	Situated Knowledges: Rethinking Knowledge and Reality	277
References		331
Acknowledgements		337
Glossary of key words		339
Index		354

Mark J Smith

Preface

This book is designed as an introduction to the debates on knowledge construction for social scientists at a time when the philosophies of the social sciences are in discord and open contestation. It provides a guide to the approaches to knowledge construction from positivism to postmodernism and tackles many of the key concepts with which social science is familiar. So much has been questioned and problematized in the late twentieth century that social scientists have to tread very carefully when charting new pathways in knowledge construction. This book attempts to map the ways in which social scientists have travelled in the past in order to highlight some of the problems and obstacles they faced as well as some of the mistakes they made.

The book starts from the presumption that all knowledge is situated in a specific historical and social location – and that approaches to knowledge construction are not exempt from this. As a result, it asks you to carefully think through your own assumptions about what social scientific knowledge is like or should be like and what it means to engage in social scientific practice. To help you along the way, the book has a range of devices for charting your path through the approaches, arguments and applications developed by social scientists. These devices include:

- Comments in the margins which draw your attention to some of the key teaching points – although you should also make your own notes as you work through the material in each chapter. Some marginal notes remind you to look back at relevant sections to refresh your memory or let you know when key approaches are coming up. Each significant section of material ends with a brief summary to aid understanding and provide general reminders of the themes developed throughout the text.

- Diagrams in the margins which either remind you where you are in the development of the chapter or, instead, offer opportunities for you to strengthen your understanding of the connections between different approaches. This process of comparing and contrasting approaches is an important step in developing your own evaluative strategy.

- Each chapter contains a series of activities and associated readings which will help you to interpret and apply the approaches considered. Occasionally we ask you to revisit readings from earlier chapters to demonstrate how textual evidence can be read and (re-)evaluated in different ways.

- Many of the key words in social science are also defined in a glossary which you can find at the end of the book. The glossary is not a dictionary but a brief guide to some of the most frequently used social scientific concepts. Like *Keywords* by Raymond Williams, the purpose is to pinpoint the different ways in which such concepts are taken up and articulated with different sets of assumptions about what it means to practise social science.

As with all Open University texts, this book is the product of many collective discussions and a constant process of thinking through the different ways in which approaches to social scientific knowledge have been developed – we have drawn from a range of social scientific disciplines to highlight the ways in which different disciplinary domains have often faced the same problems and issues (although, frequently they resolved them in different ways).

Thanks are due to many friends and colleagues at the Open University for their comments and support during the writing of this book. Particular thanks are due to Simeon Yates, who battles with spirit against the same problems in social scientific research methodology, as well as to John Blunden, Jessica Evans, Jennifer Gove, Martin Le Voi, Peter Redman, Keith Stribley and Kath Woodward for their careful and considered reflections and criticism and for many, many imaginative suggestions. Since this book highlights the importance of the production of meanings through active engagement with the texts which make up the social sciences, I am grateful to Deborah Steinberg, Tony Walton and the external assessor Professor Andrew Sayer for consistently reminding me about the different ways in which this book can be read.

This book attempts to do many things which have been long overdue in the debates on the philosophies of the social sciences, both in terms of presentational style and in content. This would not have been possible without the support of the creative energy and attention to detail of the editor Lynne Slocombe, who participated in the process of working through the interconnections between visual and written text in a way which gives dedication a new meaning. I am also especially grateful for the help of Sally Baker, Pam Berry, Caroline Husher, Mike Levers, Christine Meeks, Paul Smith and Andrew Whitehead for their long labours on the design, text and artwork. Finally, the themes throughout this book sprang from something much more intimate – I dedicate this book to my mother, Sheila, and to the memory of my father, Peter, who consistently taught me that if social science had no strong connections with the everyday lives of the people that social scientists study, then it wasn't worth doing.

Mark J. Smith

Chapter 1
Social Science
as a Situated Practice

Contents

1	Introduction	3
2	Facing the challenges in the social sciences	5
2.1	The challenge of change	5
2.2	The challenge of methods	6
2.3	The challenge of terminology	8
2.4	Thinking through the challenges	11
3	What does it mean to practise social science?	12
3.1	What does it mean for knowledge to be situated?	12
4	Connecting the social sciences to everyday life	15
4.1	The perspective of the stranger	16

Reading A
  Owning and renting houses *Peter Saunders*   21

Reading B
  The homeless woman: a documentary photograph *Jacky Chapman*   21

Reading C
  The homeless *Jean Conway*   22

Reading D
  The meaning of home *Annabel Tomas and Helga Dittmar*   23

1   Introduction

Why study the philosophy of the social sciences? Before we can answer this question we need to ask briefly a whole series of preliminary questions, such as:

- Why do we study social phenomena?
- How do we study social phenomena?
- How does theory help us to deal with complex evidence?
- Which theory is the most appropriate?
- Which concepts are most useful for the task?
- How do we generate hypotheses?
- What makes our evidence and arguments plausible?

The philosophy of the social sciences provides a range of alternative ways of thinking through the questions involved in social research.

In short, social research involves a great number of choices and we need to use some kind of criteria in order to judge which are the best ones to make. This is what the philosophy of the social sciences offers, a way of making sense of these complex and difficult choices. Now, before you think the philosophy of social science is 'the best thing since sliced bread', that it solves all the problems you will normally encounter as you prepare to engage in actual research, there is another issue that you must consider. The philosophy of the social sciences encompasses a whole series of competing standards and criteria that offer different ways in which the above choices can be understood and assessed. This diversity of rules and standards of scientific knowledge is a product of the variety of actual research in both the natural and the social sciences. The philosophy of the social sciences contains as much disagreement as any of the areas of social research with which it comes into contact.

Much depends on what you want to achieve in your research. Do you want to establish objective knowledge? Do you want reliable or valid data? Do you wish to communicate your research to a wide audience or a specific scientific community? Your answers to such questions will have an impact upon which perspective within the philosophy of the social sciences most closely relates to your own research strategy. This chapter begins to explore these diverse choices, while subsequent chapters introduce the different perspectives and provide examples of how they have been applied. So you will encounter quite a wide range of positions in the philosophy of social science as well as social theories. Each chapter is associated with a definite approach or with a range of positions which contain some common foundational assumptions. The purpose of this book as a whole is to introduce you to the problems and issues involved in social research. The specific purpose of Chapter 1 is not to provide any answers but to set out a range of questions and debates that are relevant to social researchers.

Now, with these issues in mind, let's turn to the structure of this chapter. Following this introduction, there are three sections:

As societies change and social problems are redefined, the social sciences have to respond to be effective.

- Section 2 deals with the challenges facing social scientists in their attempts to understand and explain what is going on around us. As social scientists, we are faced with the task of coming to terms with a complex dynamic world. This means that social researchers have to ensure that their theoretical tools and assumptions are appropriate to the tasks they face.

- In section 3, we look at social science as a 'situated practice', that is, embedded in the very social relations it attempts to explain and understand. This leads us to assess how situational factors influence research practice. At this stage, it is sensible to highlight two aspects of what it means to be situated: **social situatedness** (in terms of a particular culture with its own distinctive values and debates) and **historical situatedness** (in terms of the particular tradition of thought). Understanding social science as a situated practice is a theme that is emphasized throughout this book as we address the context in which the various approaches in the philosophy of the social sciences emerged. This is related to their arguments about the character of knowledge and the rules of scientific method.

- Section 4 acknowledges the important connections between the changing social world, which we all have to cope with, and the development of concepts and theoretical frameworks in the social sciences. We explore how it is possible to bridge the gap between detached scientific knowledge and the human component of the relations and processes which social scientists attempt to represent. In particular, we draw upon the arguments of Alfred Schütz, whose approach also recommends that social science should attempt to find ways of communicating its ideas and evidence widely to all members of society.

Situated knowledge – each form of social knowledge is located within a historically specific culture. Scientific knowledge is no exception.

The relationship between social scientists' knowledge and everyday life raises questions about how detached social research should attempt to be.

The relationship between the researcher and those being studied thus becomes a dialogue, rather than the social scientist simply imposing an authoritative voice upon the object in question. In this way, social scientific practice not only opens up new options for how we study the social world but also provides an opportunity for drawing upon a wider range of human knowledge and experience. Figure 1.1 illustrates the three main themes of this chapter.

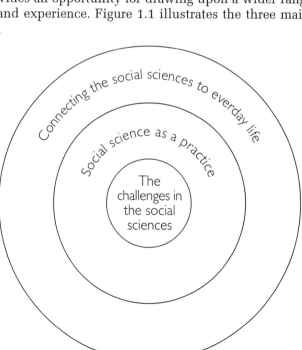

This marginal diagram will help you keep track of where you are as you read through this chapter.

Figure 1.1   Working your way through the chapter.

This chapter begins to explore what 'science' means, in relation both to contemporary social science and everyday life. Scientific knowledge is often described as **objective knowledge**, which means that it can be taken as a true account of something and that scientific explanations can be applied universally, that is, in all situations. In addition to being universal in scope, if knowledge is considered to be objective then it is also assumed to be detached from subjective experiences in any one situation. In this way, objective knowledge is detached from the specific object under investigation at any point in time. In such instances there is the possibility that these objects are treated as manifestations or examples of a more general scientific law or an underlying causal process.

Objective knowledge is universal in scope and detached from subjective experiences.

As you work though this chapter, think very carefully about what it means to be scientific when studying social relations and processes. In particular, think about whether it is possible and desirable to try to create objective knowledge. Consider also whether social science should involve an explicit attempt to make the concepts used in research connect to the lived experiences of the people being studied. In Chapters 2 and 3 we look at why objective knowledge and the study of hard facts have come to occupy such a prominent place within the social sciences.

2   Facing the challenges in the social sciences

We are living in a very complex and rapidly changing world. Social science does not exist in a vacuum: by its very nature, social scientific study directly considers those things in life which are close to our concerns as human beings – how we produce things, communicate with one another, govern ourselves, understand our varied environments, and how to solve the problems we face in the organization of social relations and processes. The social sciences offer a way of dealing with all of these issues. However, the ways in which we produce, communicate, organize and so on vary enormously as well, and they are themselves constantly undergoing processes of change. Social scientists need to produce convincing explanations for these changes and identify appropriate responses to them. To do this we have to deal with the wide range of theories and methods available. In short, studying social existence with some degree of success involves recognizing and responding to a series of challenges.

2.1   The challenge of change

The challenges facing the social sciences as bodies of knowledge and as practical guides to action are much more difficult today than previously. The institutions and social processes (such as the state, the national economy, the human personality, the environment and societies) which served as traditional objects of analysis have all undergone or are presently undergoing dramatic transformation, and in some cases are being superseded by new objects and new ways of investigating them. To demonstrate this challenge, let's consider briefly three interrelated processes: globalization, environmental change and the communications revolution.

- The precise character and dimensions of globalization are still open to dispute. However, the spread of networks between businesses, academics, political movements and so on seems to operate without respect for national boundaries. This raises questions about attempts to explain these changes in terms of concepts which are focused upon national environments in isolation from wider patterns of human activity.

- The relationships between social and physical environments are also barely understood, which makes understanding environmental change even more difficult. The problems which have emerged, from global warming and ozone depletion to acid rain pollution, have led many social scientists to forge new interdisciplinary links and to reassess the role of the natural sciences in contributing to the study of environmental problems. In addition, environmental ethics have led some social scientists to think more carefully about the instrumental attitudes to natural things.

- The transformations in communications (the Internet, interactive television, electronic information and transnational media companies using satellite technology to transmit programmes beyond the control of any particular nation-state) are notable for their global impact and for forcing us to rethink the relationship between technology, language and social relations, as well as opening up new opportunities for communicating over vast distances.

These three processes are clearly interrelated, for globalization would make little sense if it did not involve consideration of global communications and environmental problems. These examples illustrate just three of the many significant challenges to the social sciences in defining the things which should be studied.

2.2   The challenge of methods

The methodological challenges facing the social sciences are best outlined in the form of a series of questions about how we should engage in research and what kind of research attitude is appropriate.

- Should social scientists look to the assumptions and methods developed in the natural sciences or develop their own assumptions and methods?

- Do the objects which we study in the social sciences, such as the self, society, the economy, ideology or democracy, really exist or are they convenient fictions we have grown to trust?

- Can social life be reduced to simplified relations where it is possible to say that x may be related to or cause y, or is everyday social life more complex than this?

- Is it possible for social scientists to bridge the gap between attempts to build general explanations, that hold good across a range of similar situations, and attempts to understand the complexity of one concrete situation?

In this chapter we begin to define these questions and problems, and recognize their importance rather than formulate any definite answers. All of these questions are closely related to one another and stem from an underlying problem with the scientific study of social relations. In the natural sciences it is assumed that the objects of analysis (for example, atoms, DNA, forests, mountains, planets) are clearly separate from the researcher. For the time being, we will not challenge this assumption but instead concentrate upon its implications for studying people. The treatment of objects of analysis as separate from the researcher is more problematic in the social sciences. For example, when we study the family, education or culture, we are part of these things, for we live, think and communicate within them. Social science has to wrestle with the problem of human beings creating explanations about themselves and their society when they are part and parcel of that society. Even when social scientists think about and describe their theories and findings they use words, analogies and metaphors whose meanings are tied to the society of which they are a part.

Social scientists are part of their own object of analysis.

These issues provide problems for a social scientist who wishes to be separate from the object of study, in the manner of natural scientists. Social scientists who attempt to do this can be said to be detached but they can never be fully separated from the object. Clearly, when we study a rock or a tree we are not actually part of these things although we can act upon them. This conundrum is often referred to as the **subject–object problem.** Conventionally, the researcher is seen as the subject and the thing being researched is taken to be the object, but in social science we are both the subject and object of our own knowledge. When we study social life we are also studying ourselves. So, we have to find a way of assessing evidence from everyday experience. Either we can dismiss everyday experience as irrelevant in the pursuit of hard facts and objective **scientific laws,** or we can self-consciously embrace it and use it fruitfully in order to gain insights into aspects of social existence which would otherwise remain unnoticed. When we study social institutions and cultural forms, in quite a fundamental way we are studying ourselves, and social scientific practice should acknowledge this.

These problems become even more acute when we study an institution with which we are all intimately familiar. Imagine you wished to study the family as your object, you would be faced with a range of research choices, of which we shall consider two:

- How do you define the family?
- What exactly is it about the family that you wish to study?

The problems in defining clearly what a family is, and what is the most appropriate form of research method to study an aspect of the family, provide a useful illustration of the subject–object problem. Studies of family life in the mid twentieth century tended to assume that the nuclear family (with two parents of the opposite sex and their offspring) should form the basic unit of analysis. Many of the social researchers involved in this field drew upon their own experiences of family life to define their object of analysis. In so doing, forms of family life which did not conform to this criterion were defined as abnormal or deviant and placed within the broader category of social problems. This form of distinction was very much in line with the moral and cultural discourses in the West during this period. Contemporary researchers accept a greater plurality of family forms (single parent, gay and lesbian families and so on) and generally avoid the particular formation of concepts of the 1950s and 1960s. All social researchers have experienced some form of socialization, so that when they identify their objects of analysis as 'conjugal roles' or 'sibling rivalry' these concepts have a personal and subjective dimension. Even the language used has an inescapable symbolic content.

Social researchers, then, view the family in various ways. For some, it is the basis of a strong and stable social order, as in some branches of sociology which focus upon the functions of the family. For others, it is the mechanism for reproducing power relationships in society more generally, as well as distorting personality development. This was illustrated by feminist analyses such as Kate Millet's *Sexual Politics* (1970) and by radical psychiatrists such as R.D. Laing. In *The Divided Self* (1960), Laing identified conflictual family relationships as the cause of schizophrenia. In the cases he examined, he discovered that children who 'interiorized' the conflict between parents were more likely to experience mental illness in their subsequent lives. Furthermore, it is worthwhile considering for a moment how Laing came to fix upon this relationship. In childhood, he experienced such relationships within his own family environment. These may have had an impact on his choice of research topic as well as on his subsequent line of argument. Such personal experiences could have provided a unique perspective on such relations, but they could also have narrowed his consideration of alternative explanations of schizophrenia. This example serves to highlight the way in which social science cannot and should not be separated from subjective experiences. By recognizing the relationship between the construction of scientific concepts and social relations we can develop a better understanding of human existence.

Personal experiences and participation in social institutions all affect the practice of social research.

You may wish to study issues around which there is considerable public controversy. Moreover, you face a choice of research techniques. These choices can have a considerable effect upon the outcome of your research. For instance, if you ask for responses to standardized questions from a large number of families you may be able to compare the results between one group and another. However, if you spend a greater amount of time with a smaller number of families you may produce richer and more revealing insights into family lives. But you may also encounter problems in trying to generalize to other situations. These choices reveal how difficult it is, in practice, to separate the **context of discovery**, where we decide what it is we want to study and how it should be studied, from the **context of justification**, where we attempt to interpret the evidence we have collected and explain the social processes involved.

2.3   The challenge of terminology

Probably the biggest challenge that you will encounter is acquiring a command of the terms and concepts of this field of knowledge – even the words 'philosophy' and 'science' can seem off-putting. In this book you will come into contact with a wide range of '-isms', '-sophies' and '-ologies', some of which you may have encountered in previous studies. Actually, these terms are best seen as shorthand for groups of assumptions and ideas about the way the social world is organized and the most appropriate methods for studying it. Although they save us from repeating the same assumptions over and over again, there are dangers in becoming over-dependent on these shorthands. In sticking rigidly to a set of methodological principles, we can become inflexible. Some of these concepts have become so widely established that they have the same status as articles of faith – they are taken for granted as true. The following chapters open up the possibility of seeing social research as a diverse set of options rather than one appropriate way to study the social world. As social scientists you will encounter unexpected social phenomena for which conventional approaches are no longer adequate in providing a plausible explanation. In such situations you will have to innovate with your existing theoretical assumptions and research methods and you may decide that even the fundamental assumptions need to be rethought.

The existence of specialized terminology and language poses a significant challenge to anyone trying to study a social science. Over the last hundred years, each social scientific discipline has carved out its own space and, in defining its own distinctive object of analysis, has equipped itself with a specific set of concepts and references which hold meaning only for those who work or hope to work within it. Most of the key concepts are open to disagreement and, as you read through this book, you will begin to identify the ways in which science itself is a contested concept and can mean very different things to different approaches in the philosophy of social science. In addition, frequently used concepts, such as experience, causality, theory, models and scientific method, may have very different meanings in each social scientific discipline. These may also vary from everyday uses of the same terms. Everyone who has studied in the social sciences has encountered this problem at some point and most of us still do. Another good reason for using shorthand concepts for collections of assumptions and ideas is that they provide a shared language for the discussion of complex ideas.

Activity 1.1

Now turn to the first four readings, which are all from recent social research on housing and homelessness. Reading A, 'Owning and renting houses', an extract from *A Nation of Home Owners* by Peter Saunders, concentrates on empirical trends in housing. In Reading B you are asked to 'read' a documentary photograph of a homeless woman. In Reading C, 'The homeless', Jean Conway adopts a more campaigning approach in this extract from *Capital Decay, An Analysis of London's Housing*. Finally, Reading D, 'The meaning of home', from 'The Experience of Homeless Women' by Annabel Tomas and Helga Dittmar, considers responses to in-depth interviews with women in Brighton conducted by Tomas.

Compare and contrast these examples in order to make a short list of the similarities and differences between them:

● Make notes on how they define their objects of analysis.

● What do you think they are attempting to achieve?

- Can you identify the audiences for each of the examples of social research?
- Which of these studies would you consider to be scientific?

Which of these examples attempt to take sides and provide a voice for powerless individuals? Whose voice is most audible in each of the extracts? Is it that of the researcher or that of the people being studied?

You should also consider whether any of these readings demonstrate political bias and, if they do, what political values are involved.

Keep these examples in mind when you work through Activity 1.2 later in this chapter.

These four brief examples of research on homelessness demonstrate how varied social research can be, but also how important it is to be careful in one's own choice of research techniques. Some social researchers attempt to keep their distance from the object in question in order to remain objective or to gain an overall picture. Nevertheless, this does not prevent cultural values and even moral judgements from entering the research process in fundamental ways. A great deal of policy-oriented research on topics such as housing or poverty have political objectives built in. For instance, Peter Saunders in Reading A develops a case for the operation of the free market as a way of satisfying housing needs. This account of the problem and proposed solution is founded upon 'neo-liberal' political and social values, which view individual freedom as a central part of a smoothly functioning market economy. This approach assumes that human beings can and should act in terms of their own self-interest, and that if all individuals are left to their own devices the consequences will be the best possible outcome for everyone. In particular, Saunders recommends that all council house tenants should take out mortgages or loans and enter the private housing market. According to the 'neo-liberal' position, 'homelessness' and 'poverty' are personal troubles rather than social problems and, therefore, not the responsibility of the state. For Saunders, state intervention distorts the housing market and produces unsatisfactory outcomes, such as the growth of inadequate state housing schemes. If we contrast this with Jean Conway's account of homelessness in London, in Reading C, we can see a very different approach which reaches the opposite conclusions on the role of the state in housing policy. For Conway, 'homelessness' is a social problem rather than a personal lifestyle choice. This approach raises the need for a social policy response by the state authorities. So we can see that each of these examples suggests a very different view of where the boundary between private choices and public responsibility lies. This has demonstrable consequences on the nature of the research practices in each case.

Other social researchers become much more involved with those being studied and try to provide a personal and vivid account of the everyday experiences of the homeless and what their situation means to them. These are not mutually exclusive options and some social researchers have shown themselves to be inventive in combining a range of research strategies. In Reading D, the empirical research carried out by Annabel Tomas attempts, much more explicitly, to understand the gendered dimensions of

Social scientific knowledge is shaped by the values and aims of researchers, and the choice of research methods can reflect this.

research on homelessness by focusing upon what home and homelessness mean to homeless women. Actually, most existing research concentrates upon homeless men, or treats the experiences of homeless men as universal, so that homeless women are invisible. The photographic representation of a homeless woman (Reading B) has the appearance of a close and personal representation, but we also need to address the control of the documentary researcher over the representation. The image is designed to tell a particular story and may reflect the presumptions and prejudices of the researcher rather than offering an authentic account of the experiences of the homeless woman depicted.

2.4 Thinking through the challenges

In addressing the challenges of the social sciences, we have emphasized the ways in which social researchers are themselves located within a particular social and cultural context and that it is worthwhile to consider the implications of this for social science. This leads us to consider if, and how, our own position in society has an impact upon the way that we produce social scientific knowledge. In short, we should consider how much we draw upon our own values, assumptions and identities when we develop concepts, formulate arguments and collect empirical evidence. One way in which social scientists can deal with this problem is to adopt the methods of the natural sciences and attempt to be detached from their object of study. But how detached should we be? As you saw in Activity 1.1, a more detached perspective, like that of Saunders (Reading A), does not provide the same kinds of understanding that a more involved method provides, like that of Tomas (Reading D). Yet both have useful and interesting things to say. In section 3 we explore in more detail what it means to be part of the object we are attempting to study. In other words, what does it mean to be situated in a social or historical context?

Summary

In a rapidly changing world, the objects of analysis with which the social sciences are familiar (such as the state and the national economy) no longer seem to operate in the same way and are possibly becoming redundant. New problems and issues are emerging which demand innovation and flexibility.

The jargon of the disciplines in the social sciences can become a barrier to understanding. As a starting-point, you should simply treat terms as labels for sets of assumptions and ideas and compare different uses of the concepts.

The last challenge, or rather a set of choices, relates to theory and method in the social sciences. Should we continue to assume that it is desirable to study social objects in the manner of the natural sciences (traditionally defined), or reject scientific procedures in the study of social life, or redefine what we mean by science?

3   What does it mean to practise social science?

This chapter explores the processes through which we comprehend the world around us. When it comes to understanding and explaining the way that social life operates, social scientists draw from a conceptual tool kit, just as we possess a conceptual tool kit for watching a movie or as a spectator at any sports event. There are times when all human beings feel that something appears to be plausible or appears to be false and we are quite aware that others would disagree with our own point of view. We may wish to comment critically on the story-line of a film or make comparisons between a sports team's performance now and a similar event five or thirty years previously. In both of these everyday situations, we are using the same conceptual skills which are present in effective social scientific research. Theory is an essential part of the social sciences. Charles Lemert suggests that theory is a 'basic survival skill' (Lemert, 1993, p.1) and perhaps it is best seen in this light, as a multifaceted Swiss army knife with a variety of uses and the possibility that we may use a particular tool in a new way to resolve a problem or meet a new challenge.

Although theory works at a whole series of levels, there are common characteristics which can be identified in the things we do, from the most abstract to the most ordinary everyday levels. For instance, when you awake every morning you engage in a complex series of tasks of varying levels of complexity, ranging from brushing your teeth to finding your way to work. This means that you have to initiate a series of reflections about the world around you. Let's take the example of making your way to work. Generally, we do not see this as complicated or problematic until normality comes to a halt when you leave your means of payment at home by mistake or a public transport strike prevents you getting from A to B. When routines break down we have to theorize the situation we are in and plan our actions more carefully. All activities can have the appearance of being routine and untheorized but they still have a theoretical dimension. We simply take our theories of how the world works for granted, as unquestionably true. Similarly, the activities engaged in by social scientists can be just as habitual and routine, whether these involve the construction of an experiment in child psychology, the preparation of a list of questions for an interview, or the processing of data within a theoretical model of the economy or voting behaviour. Usually, it is only when these research tools no longer work that social scientists begin to rethink the assumptions behind them – and sometimes, not even then. In other words, social science involves a wide range of tacit assumptions which become so deeply embedded that it is hard even to identify them.

Theory is an important component of all human practices, from mundane tasks to social scientific research.

3.1   What does it mean for knowledge to be situated?

Scientific knowledge has been frequently portrayed as universally true. If this were the case then there would be no fundamental disagreements, for what counts as true would never change. However, what has been considered scientific in the past is now often seen as archaic or simply odd. The opposite approach would be to say that truth is relative – no one view is superior to any other. Both of these positions are simplistic. Contemporary defenders of science would argue that science is improving and that the misinterpretations and flaws of the past were simply 'poor science'.

The approach adopted in this section is that we should take seriously the issue that science has changed over time and varies across cultures. This approach tries to establish why certain views of science are taken to be plausible at certain points in time in particular societies. For instance, you may have used alternative health therapies. One of these, Chinese medicine, includes sets of assumptions about the holistic relationship between mind and body. This is at odds with the mechanical approach of Western medicine, which clearly separates physiological disorders from mental states. This does not mean that what we consider to be scientific is a fad or fashion but that we need to consider what makes a particular conception of scientific method plausible and privileged. Western medical science is founded upon the assumption that the mind and body are separate things and that the body can be understood as a complex machine made up of tissues, cells, bones, fluid and so on. In such a view, illness is a mechanical malfunction which can be remedied with appropriate treatment. Unlike this mechanistic view of the body, Chinese medicine rests upon the assumption that mind and body are intimately connected. This means that treatment should not only involve a recognition of emotional and mental states but also work with the body to repair itself. The practitioners of both mechanistic and holistic medicine consider their knowledge systems to be scientific and each claim in the West and in China is plausible within its respective cultural location.

To situate science is to establish its location. By situating the traditions in scientific method we can begin to have a clearer insight into contemporary approaches. We can also make more informed judgements about which assumptions and methods are most appropriate for our own social research. In order to understand the ways in which knowledge is produced and communicated at any point in time and place, you should consider the ways in which scientific knowledge is situated. Science, as a social practice, is situated in two ways:

- knowledge is situated socially through the cultural and institutional life of a given community;
- knowledge is situated historically by examining the shared traditions of knowledge production.

In the search for the universal principles of scientific method, one feature of the history of science, the context within which knowledge is produced, is often neglected. This does not mean that we have no control over scientific knowledge, for, as a human product, the form and the content of social science are very much the product of the assumptions and methods of social scientists and will change accordingly.

This book focuses upon approaches towards the natural as well as the social sciences. This is a reflection of the extent to which social scientists have drawn upon the philosophy of natural science to justify their own work. You will also have your attention drawn to the way in which we establish criteria as to what constitutes scientific or non-scientific knowledge.

All such criteria are grounded in human practices and the academic and commercial institutional environments in which natural and social science take place. In the following chapters you will encounter a range of examples which address how social scientists behave and make sense of their own existence. By identifying the cultural assumptions upon which the social sciences have developed, it is possible to begin to identify the impact of social science in society. In addition, by being sensitive to the way in which research is produced, we can also begin to spot the assumptions and values which are often left unstated in social scientific research. Not all researchers make their value positions as explicit as Saunders or Conway in Readings A and C. Scientists are often seen as remote and detached from everyday experience, a view that they themselves have often been quite happy to promote. The desire to be **objective** in social science can create a distance between the researcher and the object under consideration (in this case, human beings and the relations between them). This distance can lead to the mental constructs of the researcher being imposed upon the object rather than account being taken of the complex existence of human actors and their own institutional environments.

While all models in the social sciences simplify social life in order to make it understandable, there are also dangers in providing a one-sided or partial account, especially where the experiences of those being studied are distorted or even ignored. There is an implicit danger in any attempt to attain objective knowledge, that what appears to be obvious to one group of researchers at a particular point in time is often treated as matter of fact. Indeed, what we take as objective truth has changed so much and so frequently that it is worthwhile regarding all such claims with suspicion. For example, if we take the treatment of women's experience in social scientific research, we find that the concerns of women have been primarily defined in terms of masculine perceptions of women's role in society. So, for instance, in studies of social mobility and educational attainment the class position of women has often been defined in terms of the occupational position of the father or husband. More subtly (and very rarely challenged) theories of female voting behaviour are packed full of assumptions about the traditionalist and religious orientation of women, concluding that women are more conservatively inclined than men. Similarly, the discussion of 'race' and ethnicity in the 1960s and 1970s was largely conducted in the voice of those who were not part of the cultural groups identified as an object. In this way, crude stereotypes often go unchallenged in the social sciences. Black identities are frequently expressed through the concepts and terms of reference of white ethnocentric social science. The problem of ethnocentric knowledge is the way in which we do not often acknowledge how our own cultural location shapes our ideas. As tacit knowledge, ethnocentricity is hard to identify. This can be seen in the ways in which broad umbrella labels such as 'black', 'white' and 'Asian' have attained a factual status in many areas of social science. There is a danger that we end up treating such labels as nouns rather than adjectives. By identifying a group of people as 'blacks' or 'Asians' you fix the identity of the people involved as manifestations of an objective category and ignore cultural differences.

Always ask yourself what values underpin the choice of concepts and the way in which an object of study is defined. Values are a key component of any investigation of the social world, even if there remains a tendency to

All forms of social scientific knowledge are based upon human practices within institutional environments.

Social scientists simplify the complexity of social life to make it more understandable – but it could also mean that they make biased/ misinformed judgements in social science.

When defining social identities, social scientists have often translated prejudices into objective categories.

hide one's own value position. In the next section, we consider an approach which acknowledges the cultural location of knowledge and turns it around to good use. We explore one attempt to build a bridge of understanding between our everyday experiences of the events around us and the detached scientific knowledge of specialists. This approach allows us to move closer to the meanings of the people being studied and how they understand their own activity, while at the same time maintaining a critical distance from the unreflective habits of everyday life.

Summary

Social scientific inquiry, like all human practices, operates through a set of taken-for-granted assumptions and draws upon the same skills we use in everyday life. It is difficult to separate the treatment of facts in social science from deeply embedded cultural values.

Social scientific knowledge is situated in two ways: *historically* in terms of the shared values and guidelines transmitted from previous studies in the social sciences, and *socially* within a specific cultural and institutional context.

4   Connecting the social sciences to everyday life

In the previous sections we considered the challenges facing the contemporary social sciences and the issues raised by thinking of social research as a situated practice. You will already have identified the ways in which the social sciences are complicated by the problem of researchers attempting to know and understand the social world they inhabit. At this point it is useful to develop a checklist of the ways that this has affected social research practice.

- The definition of objects of analysis reflects the taken-for-granted assumptions of the social researcher (as we saw when considering gender and ethnicity within social science).

- Social researchers select research methods (ranging from surveys to in-depth interviews) in order to fulfil certain purposes (such as the interviews with homeless women in Reading D).

- Political values can affect the purpose and character of social research (as in the examples of the policy implications of research in Readings A and C).

- Personal experiences are often involved in research in quite subtle ways (such as R.D. Laing's motivations for considering family relations as a cause of mental illness, discussed in section 2.2).

- Social researchers often enter into the activity of gathering evidence on the basis of a particular conception of what is a normal or abnormal state of affairs (such as a 'normal family').

This is not an exhaustive list, but simply sensitizes us to the importance of thinking through what we do when setting out on a research project. We should always consider why we are doing social research in a particular way and why we have rejected other ways. It is important to reflect upon the way in which we define objects of analysis and select a particular problem to investigate, and why we consider one approach to be more useful than another in providing the ideas and evidence we need.

4.1 The perspective of the stranger

One way in which it is possible to build links between everyday experience and social scientific research is to adopt the approach recommended by the philosopher and sociologist Alfred Schütz (1899–1959). As a refugee from Austria in the late 1930s, he found himself transported to America and encountered considerable difficulties in reorienting himself to new conditions and a new culture. This personal experience of not having familiar bearings, and of encountering the impact of cultural differences, sensitized him to the problems of how we perceive and understand social life as well as how we communicate our understandings to others. Schütz argued that in both social science and in everyday life we use 'types' or mental constructs, which allow us generally to predict how others around us are likely to behave. By stereotyping the behaviour and motivations of others, we are able to identify predictable patterns around us which enable us to think through a situation and act.

In the social sciences, we also use types to make sense of empirical evidence but we deny that these types are based upon our commonsense stock of knowledge and treat them as objective things (as if they really do exist in the way that we imagine them). Schütz recommended that we should follow the 'postulate of adequacy' whereby ideas had to link lived experience with scientific knowledge. Each concept or idea in a 'scientific model of human action', if it is to be considered as adequate, must be constructed in such a way that it is understandable in terms of the taken-for-granted assumptions of everyday life. A scientific statement is considered to be adequate when it accounts for everyday experience and is understandable to those who live in the relations being studied (Schütz, 1953, p.34). To illustrate, Schütz provides an account of how this form of social analysis can produce insights into the events and relations around us. He asks us to imagine the built environment of a city as our chosen object of analysis and imagine three viewpoints about this urban setting and city life.

Stereotypes are useful in the organization of evidence, but they hold dangers if they are seen as real things.

Types are one-sided exaggerations or simple conceptual devices (stereotypes) for comparing our experiences.

- *The person on the street,* someone who is simply at home in a particular place, operating through tacit knowledge, getting by without the need for much deep reflection.

- *The cartographer,* someone with the expertise to map urban environments, but who maintains a degree of detachment from the object and is unable to comprehend what it is like to live in such a place. We can treat this as a metaphor for the problems of much of social scientific practice.

- *The stranger,* someone who is passing through, but who needs to establish an adequate grasp of existing social relationships in order to get by. The stranger is neither unreflective like the person on the street nor trapped within the narrow vantage point of an academic specialism (Schütz, 1943).

These three 'types' help us to understand the relationship between everyday language and experiences and the terminology of scientific study. 'Strangers' have a unique vantage point, able to participate in everyday life yet still maintain a degree of detachment. Indeed, Schütz was drawing upon his own commonsense experiences as an Austrian refugee (a stranger) in New York, where he had to acquire enough working knowledge to survive without ever really fitting in (Schütz, 1944). While the person on the street has a 'working knowledge' of the situation and can follow the vague rules which have worked well before, the social scientist tends to have a specialized knowledge limited to a particular aspect of urban life, such as housing distribution, traffic flows, population movements, or even waste disposal systems. One of the issues you will encounter when doing social research is whether to be detached from or involved in the processes, relations and institutions with which social scientists are concerned.

For instance, economists who attempt to develop models of the economy using computer simulation programs (that is, econometrics) do not actually go and find out about the purchasing decisions of all members of a society. They do depend on existing statistical information which at some point will have been constructed through contact with consumers, producers and government officials. The point of econometrics is to develop a big picture of the economy and to make predictions about what will happen if the present situation continues or when some of the relationships change. Like all other kinds of social scientific practice they have uses, but they also have limitations. Econometric models are used to establish broad patterns of economic activity and, at the end of the day, this is what governments need to make policies. However, they cannot account for the complex ways in which people behave in real markets. Just as there are difficulties if you become too detached, if you become too involved in the lives of the people and social relations you are studying, you can lose sight of the aims and objectives of your research. In such situations, where the researcher is unable to stand back from the taken-for-granted assumptions of the people involved, the research will not really convey what is actually happening. This is not simply a product of the choice of research technique, for even an econometric forecast can be detached in one sense but still be based upon the taken-for-granted assumptions of a particular set of cultural values. So, as a social scientist, the attitude you will have towards finding out about people's lives will be just as important as your choice of research method.

The 'stranger' sees beyond the lived experiences of everyday life, but is not so detached as to lose contact with the people being studied.

Social scientific research could, however, bridge the gap between the level of detached and often obscure scientific terminology and the level of everyday practical knowledge by adopting the vantage point of the 'stranger'. This acts as a bridge between social scientific accounts and the everyday experiences of those being studied. In this way, Schütz suggested, a wider audience could also use social science research and social scientists could avoid preaching to the converted. This example itself addresses this concern to make scientific practice connect to everyday life. By using the three types – the person on the street, the cartographer and the stranger – and by asking us to be strangers, Schütz is actually demonstrating the technique of communicating complex ideas to a broader audience. In this case, the types are instantly recognizable in everyday language and Schütz's approach draws from this to build those bridges of understanding to social scientific knowledge (Schütz, 1943, 1946, 1953).

Activity 1.2

Compare and contrast the three illustrations reproduced below and make
notes on what they tell you about the situation they represent.

Figure 1.2   The stranger in a crowd.
A busy morning in a mainline London train station, with lots of people heading in
various directions, each with a sense of purpose. This displays the habitual and largely
tacit knowledge which we use in environments that are intimately familiar and where
we 'feel at home'.

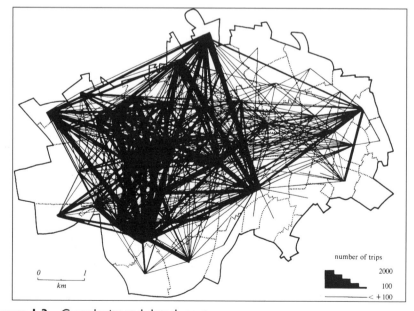

Figure 1.3   Complexity and detachment.
Complexity can be overwhelming. A geographical representation of transport links
with a confusing and complex array of factors and movements which are difficult to
decipher for anyone untrained in advanced cartography.

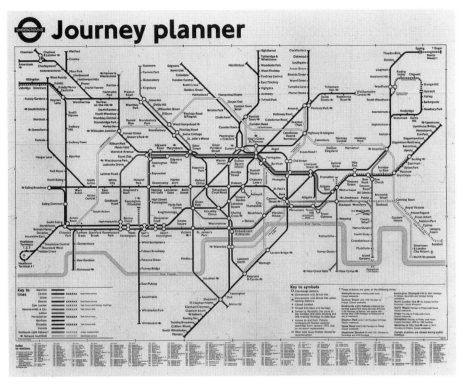

Figure 1.4   The London tube map.
The London tube map, designed as a comprehensible and reasonably accurate guide (in term of its function) which makes sense to transport users and to social scientists.

Now that you've had a chance to compare and contrast these illustrations, here are some points you may want to think about. In Figure 1.2, the 'stranger', in the centre of the picture, has to stand back from lived experience in order to understand what is happening and, in the process, constructs a more detached viewpoint. Figure 1.3, by Schütz's criteria, is too complex and detached for us to make sense of what it means to travel in the space represented. Although it provides a detached account of transport flows which is technically accurate, it does not attempt to connect with the human experiences of the people involved in these processes. In addition, it is very difficult to interpret even if you are trained in the social science involved. Figure 1.4, however, provides an example of how it is possible to bridge the gap between everyday life and social science. In terms of its capacity to convey information accessibly, the tube map offers a model of good social scientific practice.

Compare and contrast these three examples in Activity 1.2 with the three ideal types identified by Schütz. Now return to Activity 1.1 and reconsider the four examples of research on housing and homelessness. Do any of the readings in Activity 1.1 find ways of making connections between everyday life and social scientific knowledge?

These examples remind us of the importance of making social scientific knowledge accessible to people beyond the narrow group of social scientists who no longer need to be convinced in any case. It also reminds us that effective social science can convey complex relationships without baffling the audience, while at the same time providing an effective guide to action. The London tube map is often regarded as a masterpiece of design because it is able to convey so much information in such an accessible way. Social scientists should have similar aspirations in the design of their research and the presentation of their evidence.

The preference for 'detachment' and 'objective' characteristics in many areas of social science raises another important question about the social sciences. Why is there such a strong desire to adopt the label of science when studying social objects of analysis? Part of the answer lies in the legitimacy social researchers acquire when they are seen as scientific. Science is often strongly associated with truth and progress which is a legacy of the Enlightenment belief in the power of human reason since the eighteenth *See Chapter 2.* century. Research institutions which can convincingly portray themselves as scientific appear to do well in securing government funding for research. When the Social Science Research Council was reorganized as the Economic and Social Research Council by Keith Joseph (then Education Secretary in the first Thatcher administration), the loss of status was also reflected in reduced funding. Science is more than just a name, for it holds connotations of authoritative knowledge. To describe a statement as scientific is to indicate that it is 'true' or at least that it is as close to 'truth' as we can achieve. In order to understand how this came to be, we need to examine the emergence of scientific ideas in history, the application of these ideas to the study of social life and human relationships, and the character of scientific knowledge itself. This is our task in Chapter 2.

Summary

If social researchers are to be effective in understanding people, they need to be detached from common sense (the perspective of the person on the street). However, they should not be so detached that they fall into the trap of imposing their own categories upon the object without regard for the experience of those involved (the perspective of the expert).

The standpoint of the 'stranger' provides a way of mediating between the detached position of the scientist and the personal experiences of everyday life. This serves as a way of grounding social science in human processes and relationships rather than treating scientific knowledge as though it is divorced from subjective experiences.

READING A
Owning and renting houses

Peter Saunders

All studies of council house sales show that buyers have higher incomes than other tenants – ... the mean income for the heads of households who bought was twice that of those who continued to rent. Studies also show that buyers are disproportionately middle aged and are often drawn from households with more than one earner. In Aberdeen, for example, 75 per cent of sales have been to multiple-earner households ... and sales have been concentrated among households where the principal earner is in secure employment, where he or she is in a skilled manual or a non-manual occupation and where the family is of a conventional nuclear type. ...

There is in Britain a worrying gap opening up between what have been termed the 'middle mass' and the 'underclass'. This division is, of course, generated by factors other than the housing system, but it is coming to be most vividly expressed through housing differences and it is reproduced through tenure-based inequalities. However it is defined, the underclass appears to be concentrated in the least desirable parts of the council housing sector. State rental has today become associated with low incomes, high dependency on state benefits, high rates of unemployment and disproportionate numbers of single parents and single elderly people. When council tenants do have jobs, they are increasingly likely to involve unskilled or semi-skilled employment.

The residualization of the low paid and the economically inactive on what remain of the nation's council estates (for much of the best housing has been sold into owner-occupation) does not simply reflect existing economic inequalities but actually contributes to new ones. While home owners of all social classes share in the expansion of the country's wealth by virtue of their ownership of domestic property, those who remain in the council sector (many of whom would like to buy) are deprived of the chance to benefit from the rising value of the house or flat they live in. Instead, they face the prospect of indefinite rent payments (subsidized where necessary by housing benefit). As the home-owning middle mass gets wealthier, those who are trapped in state housing stay exactly where they are. Socialist defenders of state housing call this 'rent pooling'. Tenants themselves call it 'money down the drain'.

Source: Saunders, 1990, pp.320, 369.

READING B
The homeless woman: a documentary photograph

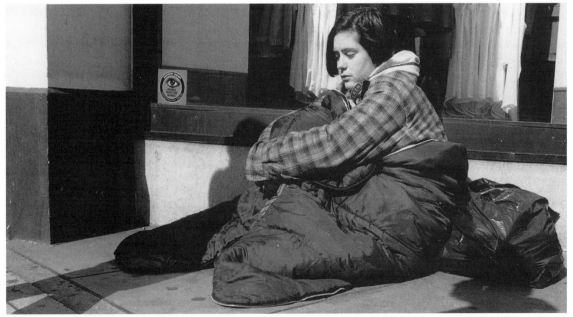

Source: Photograph by Jacky Chapman, Format.

READING C
The homeless

Jean Conway

While some homeless people actually sleep on the streets, thousands more do not have a permanent home and move between various types of unsuitable and insecure housing. There is no measure of the scale of this housing need. The number of homeless households accepted by the London boroughs has been steadily rising over a long period – from 4,000 in 1971 to over 12,000 in the mid 1970s and over 24,000 in 1983.

The incidence of recorded homelessness is far greater in London than elsewhere, with 4.6 households per 1,000 resident households accepted in London compared with an average of 2.3 for England; for Inner London the figure was even higher at 6.6 households per 1,000 resident households.

But these figures only show those whom the authorities were obliged to accept under the Homeless Persons Act, notably excluding most single people and childless couples. Thousands more do not apply because they know they will not be accepted, and do apply but are rejected. ... This suggests that there is a massive problem of homelessness in London, only a small proportion of which is officially measured or dealt with by the statutory agencies.

Yet these agencies are overwhelmed. In spite of giving one in three lettings to the homeless, over three quarters of the boroughs resort to using bed and breakfast accommodation for some homeless people because they are unable to give them council housing. In December 1983 there were over 3,000 homeless households in temporary accommodation in London, including nearly 2,000 in bed and breakfast hotels. This is obviously a highly unsatisfactory response to the problem, both for the family and for the boroughs ... It may be cheaper for a borough to build or acquire a house for letting than to keep a family in bed and breakfast.

The London boroughs are clearly swamped by the scale of homelessness and are unable to cope with the problem. At the same time, they are failing to rehouse many people from the waiting list, to carry out adequate decanting programmes for modernization schemes, and to meet other pressing housing needs. The continuing housing shortage and consequent difficulty in obtaining accommodation suggests that London will be unable to provide a decent home for many of its residents for the foreseeable future. ...

Examination of London's housing situation suggests that there must be a London-wide authority to deploy London's resources effectively in order to meet needs which are unevenly spread. This function is vital because:

- the scale of housing need remains beyond the abilities of individual boroughs to tackle alone;

- need is unevenly distributed across London, as are the resources to tackle the problems;

- by their very nature, some housing problems and activities cannot be effectively tackled on a borough basis;

- each borough programme needs to be fitted into a co-ordinated approach for the metropolis as a whole.

Source: Conway, 1984, pp.59–61, 72.

READING D
The meaning of home

Annabel Tomas and Helga Dittmar

The need for a practical understanding of homeless women's lives motivates and underpins the life historical and experiential approach adopted in this study. Homelessness is seen as a life process and the lives of homeless women, and the stories they tell about their lives, are examined and specified in terms that are appropriate to a social understanding (Blasi, 1990). There is a concern in this approach to frame the issue of homelessness in terms of an agent, contending with a set of social problems, rather than as an individual entrapped in history, or borne along by an unspecified disease process. People are viewed as active participants in the experience, negotiation, and (re)creation of their personal and social histories. They are understood to be purposive, resilient and goal-directed in their creative use of symbols, space, language, and ritualised behaviour, even as these activities are seriously curtailed (Fiske, 1991; Glasser, 1988; Jackson, 1988; Snow *et al.*, 1988). Furthermore, whether people are constrained or enabled, they experience, negotiate and are creative, not only in practice, but also in the stories told about this practice. The stories homeless women tell *about* their experiences *of* housing are considered especially important, since we understand them as 'going beyond' the event, offering an evaluation of it. Thus, a life history narrative offers an important source of data (Bruner, 1990), and a useful resource to an understanding of homelessness, and by implication, the meaning of 'home'. ...

In our study, interview data are seen as displaying cultural realities (Silverman, 1985), neither true nor false, but simply 'real'. Interview data, from this point of view, are not one side of the picture to be balanced by observation of what respondents actually do, or with what an observer may say. Instead, realism implies that such data reproduce and rearticulate cultural particulars in given patterns of social organisation. It is in these patterns of social organisation, expressed in a life history narrative, that the experience of housing and the meaning of home for homeless women is sought. ...

One difference between 'home' and 'ideal home' spontaneously expressed by eight of the securely housed women, but not expressed by the homeless women at all, was the probability of attainment. For example, "I know what I want, but I don't know if I'll get it", and "Well, that's what I would like". This suggests that these women were differentiating in their definition between home and ideal home. In their responses to the question 'What would be your ideal home?', all 12 securely housed women said that their ideal home would be a place of warmth and belonging surrounded by family and friends. In addition, a number of material attributes were highlighted, such as a desirable location (e.g. "a cottage in the country"), more space indoors and outdoors (e.g. "somewhere with a big garden and plenty of room"), or a greater level of material wealth (e.g. "the usual – roses in the garden, honey in the cupboard"). In the definitions of 'ideal home' given by securely housed women such material features are foremost, and the 'ideal home' is therefore more than 'a place (house) of warmth and belonging (home)'. In the same way that the defining features of 'house' (safety and security) had been assumed in their definition of 'home', so too, was 'warmth and belonging' (home), assumed in their definition of 'ideal home'.

The hierarchical and progressive nature of securely housed women's distinctions between house, home and ideal home are consistent with the current theoretical proposition of there being an intimate link between the experience of housing and the meaning of home. The positive connotations attached to the concept home as a place of psychological significance dependent on, yet over and above, the safety and security of four walls and a roof, was clearly expressed. The psychologically meaningful home appears to have arisen from the reality of their housing histories – safety and security in housing. ...

However, turning to the homeless women, it is apparent from their responses, that the distinction in meaning between a 'house', a 'home' and an 'ideal home' is not so easily rendered. Only three of the 12 homeless women could confidently define any difference in meaning between a house and a home. Nine of the 12 homeless women had great difficulty. Unlike the securely housed women who readily understood the question, most of the homeless women responded with uncertainty by asking such questions as "What do you mean?", "A place to stay?", "Is there a difference?", or "Um ... I don't know ... Do you mean a children's home?". They appeared to have difficulty with the question itself, as well as finding it hard to provide an answer. Those three who did define a difference did so as follows (the names given here are pseudonyms):

1. A house is just a house ... it's where people live with you. A home is somewhere I can

go that doesn't close the door at 10 pm ...
somewhere that's mine. Ideal home ... no-one
... I don't want no-one living there. (Daphne,
31 years)

2. If you have your own home you can come
    back when you want ... um ... somewhere I
    can be alone. (*and a house?*) It's not
    mine. At the moment where I am it's
    full of people. Ideal home ... A mansion
    of course! ... it would be far away ...
    (*laughing*) ... a different country if possible.
    (Pat, 37 years)

3. A home is where you can stay, you have
    the run of the place. A house I imagine
    you don't. It's not yours. A home is
    somewhere nice. (*Ideal home?*) would be a
    four-bedroomed house. (Mandy, 33 years)

Whereas for securely housed women, the house is
defined in terms of its neutral independence, and
home as dependent on the social relations contained within it, for homeless women, a house is
someone else's house where other people live
with you (dependence). Home is a place of your
own where you can be alone (independence).
With the exception of "somewhere nice", expressions such as 'warmth' and 'belonging' were
not mentioned at all by homeless women.

Again, as could be expected, and in line with current theorising, the relationship between a homeless woman's experience of housing (abuse and
relocation) and her definition of 'home' (safety
and security) is clearly expressed. However, whilst
the securely housed women's definition of home
appears to reflect their experiences *of* housing,
the definitions of home given by homeless women
appear to reflect their umnmet needs *for* housing.
The house of safety and security that securely
housed women had assumed, homeless women
had not yet achieved, neither in the reality of
their housing histories, nor in their definitions of
house and home. ... For homeless women, the
identity-related concerns of 'home' were not so easily abstracted from the physiological requirements
of a place of safety. The fact that nine homeless
women could not articulate any difference in meaning between a house and a home may also suggest
that the relationship between 'housing' (as a place
of safety and security) and 'home' (as psychologi-
ally meaningful) has been severed completely. In
this case the definition of 'home' as meaningful
would be expected to be confused with the experience of housing as abusive, suggesting that the
house/home distinction is not so easily rendered
in the absence of safety and security. ... Finally,
homeless women did not consider themselves to

be homeless. None of the 12 women would accept
being called homeless. They said they were not
homeless because they lived somewhere. Thus,
they were neither 'homed' according to the housed
women's definition nor 'homeless' according to
theirs.

References

BLASI, G. (1990) 'Social policy and social science research on homelessness', *Journal of Social Issues*,
46, pp.207–19.

BRUNER, J. (1990) *Acts of Meaning* (MA, Harvard
University Press).

FISKE, J. (1991)'For cultural interpretation: A study
of the culture of homelessness', *Critical Studies in
Mass Communication*, 8, pp.455–74.

GLASSER, I. (1988) *More than Bread: Ethnography of
a Soup Kitchen*, Tuscaloosa, AL, University of
Alabama Press.

JACKSON, P. (1988) 'Street life: The politics of carnival. Environment and planning', *Society and
Space*, 6, pp.213–27.

SILVERMAN, D. (1985) *Qualitative Methodology and
Sociology*, London, Gower.

SNOW, D., BAKER, S. and ANDERSON, L.(1988) 'On the
precariousness of measuring sanity in insane contexts', *Social Problems*, 35, pp.281–8.

Source: Tomas and Dittmar, 1995, pp.497–8, 503–5.

Chapter 2
The Story of Science

Contents

1	Introduction	27
1.1	Science as authentic knowledge	28
1.2	Science and the circuit of knowledge	32
2	**Representing science**	**33**
2.1	Science and its metaphors	34
2.2	Closed systems and open systems	41
3	**Science and modernity**	**46**
3.1	Science, observation and experimentation	47
3.2	The historical context of the Enlightenment	55
3.3	The Enlightenment, progress and social science	58
4	**Conclusion: questions from the Enlightenment**	**64**

Reading A
The development of emotions: using experimental methods
Keith Oatley and Jennifer M. Jenkins   66

Reading B
The *Encyclopédie*
Michael Bartholomew, Stephanie Clennell and Linda Walsh   69

Reading C
What is the Enlightenment?
Robert Hollinger   71

1 Introduction

In Chapter 1 we began to explore the impact of the 'idea of science' on the way in which social scientists engage in the practice of research. In particular, we highlighted the way that 'scientific knowledge' has often been seen as detached from the object of analysis which it attempts to represent. We explored the possibility that scientific knowledge could attempt to establish connections with the everyday lived experience of those being studied and, at the same time, help to ensure that the results of social scientific research were much more accessible to a wider audience. In this way, it was argued, social scientists could avoid the tendency to impose their own ideas, models and theories upon the objects of analysis within the social sciences. This leaves a fundamental question unanswered: why did this idea of science, as the most authoritative form of knowledge, come about in the first place? When we begin to unravel how this happened, it is possible to identify many of the issues and problems currently facing social scientists today.

The scientific method, as we understand it, emerged in the seventeenth century. This chapter explores the story of science in order to shed some light on the reasons why social scientists have adopted versions of the methods and assumptions of the natural sciences when constructing scientific explanations of social relations and processes. We explore three dimensions which are central to seeing how science has come to be understood by communities of scientists and wider audiences: knowledge systems, social structures and social agents in the production and transmission of knowledge.

- **Knowledge systems** involve a complex series of assumptions and methodological rules about what counts as appropriate knowledge in a given time and place. The idea of science is part of a complex set of relationships encompassing the ideas of truth, reason, progress and humanity. We begin to explore these relationships in section 1.1.

This is the elaborate treatment of these key concepts. Later on, when you see this sign **g** again, use the glossary – but if you want to think through these concepts in more detail come back to this section.

- **Social structures** involve relations and patterns of behaviour which have become so well established across time and space that they provide the (largely unquestioned) conditions for human action and thought. It is important to identify the transformations of the social structure which knowledge systems inhabit and help to construct. By doing this, we can examine the way in which the institutions associated with the transmission of knowledge, from the monasteries to the academies, relate to the wider social context.

- **Social agents** involve the groupings and associations which are actively engaged in the development and transmission of knowledge. More specifically, social agents are the scientists, teachers, researchers and administrators who are involved in the representation of knowledge to each other as well as wider audiences.

Focusing upon the interaction of these three dimensions helps us to make sense of how knowledge systems change. First, by looking at the relationship between knowledge systems and the social structure, we can begin to think about why some forms of knowledge appear to be more plausible or authoritative in different times and places. Second, by exploring the connections between social agents and knowledge systems we can begin to understand the processes through which ideas come to be accepted and contested. Finally, by exploring how social agents draw from and challenge the social structures which they inhabit, we are able to examine the ways in which knowledge systems such as science are reproduced, modified and transformed. Examining these ideas, relationships, institutions and people enables us to identify some of the significant differences in the ways that authoritative knowledge has been subject to change, and to question those things which we take to be self-evidently true today. Sensitivity to these factors will provide us with useful ways to respond to the challenges identified in Chapter 1, that are facing social scientists now.

This will enable us to explore what scientific inquiry actually involves and to trace its emergence in the modern period of human history (roughly the last five hundred years). Scientific knowledge is often distinguished from traditional ways of thinking, such as religion and spiritualism, as well as popular culture and folklore, magic and superstition, political ideologies, or crystal healing and other forms of contemporary New Age thinking. From the standpoint of many scientists, all of these ways of thinking are fictitious, whereas science produces factual knowledge. This is not to say that 'non-scientific' forms of knowledge have no use but that each attempts to create an order, in which human beings can anticipate and predict the behaviour of others and thus engage in interaction with confidence. Without some degree of predictability in everyday life, social relationships would certainly be difficult to establish. For the scientist, however, this should not be the basis of scientific knowledge – that scientific knowledge should be free of bias, universal in scope and reliable in application. In opposition to fictitious ways of thinking, the scientist, it is argued, is simply concerned with truth and falsehood, in describing what can be observed in a factual way and explaining how things work in accordance with scientific laws which apply to all situations. In short, defenders of the scientific standpoint suggest that scientific knowledge is superior to other forms of knowledge because it can deliver a true account of reality rather than just being a belief system. Clearly this is open to challenge, since it is also possible to think of science as a very effective form of story-telling. This raises issues which are addressed throughout the following chapters. In this chapter we concentrate on how this approach emerged and how this model of superior knowledge came to prevail over other forms of knowledge.

Scientific knowledge aspires to be universal and provides a reliable account based upon the application of rational thought to empirical evidence.

For scientific accounts, the key question is: is it true or false?

1.1 Science as authentic knowledge

Science is a very powerful and evocative word or idea in Western culture. It conveys legitimacy and authenticity upon the people, ideas and institutions with which it is associated. A claim to authenticity means that a statement is 'true to life', the real thing, rather than an imitation. Let's explore what appears to be a simple example.

Statement A   It is plainly the case that poverty is the cause of crime.

Statement B   Scientific research reveals that poverty is the cause of crime.

Statements A and B, at first sight, claim to be telling us the same thing. However, when we look closely at them we can identify substantial differences in the authority they carry. Statement A involves an attempt to assert a causal relationship as if it were a matter of fact. Irrespective of how assertive the person may be in making this statement, it still sounds like an opinion, based on personal values. Statement B, on the other hand, has the 'ring of truth'. Including the idea of being 'scientific' provides additional meaning and a sense of truth, authenticity and the stamp of authority, which is lacking or more ambiguous in Statement A. Perhaps this is partly because Statement B brings into view the idea of research and suggests a process of 'revelation', an act of discovery, the notion that only science can dig beneath the level of surface appearances and provide concrete evidence of what is really happening. Ultimately, the weight we place upon statements such as these is simply a matter of trust – we seem, in Western culture, to trust science. In addition, the way in which such statements are meaningful for the general public, as well as a specialist academic audience, plays a part in the authentication of such causal explanations.

> The label 'science' provides a statement with a degree of authority and authenticity it would not otherwise possess.

Let's take a recent example of a controversial 'scientific discovery' where science has been used to explain social identity. Research in the biological sciences into the genetic structure of human beings has produced the possibility that 'sexual preference' may be indicated by a particular configuration of genetic material in human DNA. This remains only a possibility and scientists have been keen to stress the tentative nature of their hypotheses, although they point to the recorded differences in the genetic structure of heterosexual and homosexual males in the USA. However, the public understanding of this 'discovery' was mediated largely through representations of the scientific 'event' in the mass media, which focused upon the discovery of the 'gay gene'. In this case, we are concerned with how science is represented rather than whether such representations involve an example of the misuse of scientific knowledge. Let's translate these media reports into a version of Statement B.

Statement C   Scientific research reveals that there is a genetic cause of homosexuality.

Perhaps the most significant feature of this example is the extent to which this 'discovery' was accepted across the broad spectrum of opinion on the issue of gay identity, at least initially. A great deal of scientific research into gay identity has been focused upon socialization patterns. This research placed a strong emphasis upon 'homosexuality' as an acquired condition. It was argued that, if this was the case, then gay identity could be resolved through programmes of re-education and, in some cases, the use of aversion therapies to discourage behaviour considered to be unacceptable to social norms and values (Bancroft, 1974). The 'discovery' of the 'gay gene' therefore shifted the ground upon which these debates were based. The identification of a gay gene was applauded by many of the advocates of 'gay rights' on the grounds that, if sexual preference is inscribed in our genes, there is little or no possibility of changing someone's basic nature through the techniques of re-education.

However, this coincided with a change of tack within those groups devoted to removing 'homosexuality' from contemporary society. They shifted their approach from re-education towards the idea that this 'discovery' opened the way for genetic engineering. It is also important to stress the context of this debate, particularly in the USA, where the association of AIDS with ideas of a 'gay plague' expressed by powerful moral movements had created a situation of hostile debate between gay rights activists and morals campaigners. In each case, although the evidence was tentative, the 'discovery' of a gene for sexual preference was to have a profound effect upon how this debate was understood and conducted. In effect, scientific thinking and evidence were used by both sides in this debate to legitimize and authenticate their respective viewpoints.

Scientific knowledge can be used to support any argument or opinion and provides authoritative weight for a particular standpoint.

We have to be very careful here, for even the term 'homosexuality' is not neutral or innocent. It was invented in the late nineteenth century to indicate a mental and physiological disorder and, in so doing, already implies the assertion of the need for treatment and cure (Weeks, 1989, pp.96–121). In this debate, even the language used to describe this sexual identity conveys something of the meaningful character of the words used: 'gay' has more positive and less stigmatized associations than 'homosexual' (Plummer, 1975). Indeed, it is now open to question whether the categories of heterosexuality and homosexuality serve any useful role in scientific research. Ideas such as these are part of complex ways of thinking which rest upon moral judgements as to what is normal and abnormal; that is, scientific thought tends to reflect such cultural values.

So what does this tell us about science? Certainly 'science' can be used to justify a wide range of approaches, explanations and even opinions. In the case of the 'gay gene discovery', a discovery in natural scientific research was taken up and reinterpreted in various ways by different interests in society. Similarly, when we try to understand and explain a particular problem or issue there is a tendency to search for some underlying or basic cause. Again, this implies that causes, once diagnosed, can be treated and cured. In the case of poverty and crime, raised in Statements A and B, poverty is described as a definite observable and measurable condition. Poverty is given 'factual' status, even though the definitions of poverty change, while crime statistics, although they are a product of the criminal justice system, are seen to provide measurable variables such as recorded crimes and the number of convictions. In the case of both natural and social causes, we can see a common feature in the way that scientific explanations are constructed, whether this is about sexual preference or criminality. The 'scientific' label provides a level of authenticity which conveys the status of truth.

Activity 2.1

Before you read on, consider carefully the representations of scientists in Figures 2.1 to 2.4. Make a note of the ideas, things and processes which come to mind when you think about science. Then spend about five minutes making a list of all the positive contributions and negative effects of science, especially practical examples.

This may throw up meanings and associations which you would not have expected. You are likely to encounter similar evaluations throughout this book.

Figure 2.1   The extraordinary scientist.
Albert Einstein, the 'father' of contemporary physics.

Figure 2.2   The mad scientist.
Peter Cushing as Dr Frankenstein – the 'Hammer horror' version of the dark side of science.

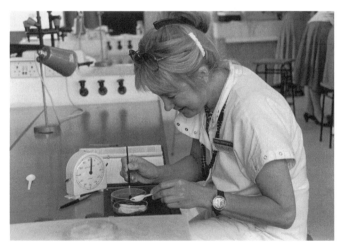

Figure 2.3   The diligent scientist.
A student working with care and precision in the laboratory.

Figure 2.4   Imagining the scientist of the future.
Leonard Nimoy as Mr Spock, the science fiction version of the logical scientist.

1.2 Science and the circuit of knowledge

One way to address the issues highlighted in the introduction to this chapter is to explore the way in which science is defined in relation to a limited number of associated ideas. I will argue that science, in the sense identified above, is important for modern Western societies because of its association with the ideas of truth, reason, progress and humanity. Here is an example of how this works.

> The success of the *scientific method* is explained in terms of its ability to reveal the *truth* and so implies the use of the capacities of human *reason* to do so. It is assumed that this search for the truth is an intentional activity which reflects the needs of *humanity* and, as a consequence, secures human *progress*.

This is just one descriptive way of demonstrating the relationship between science, truth, reason, progress and humanity. These five concepts exist in a complex circuit of knowledge, represented in Figure 2.5, whereby each idea is explained through its interrelationships with the other ideas.

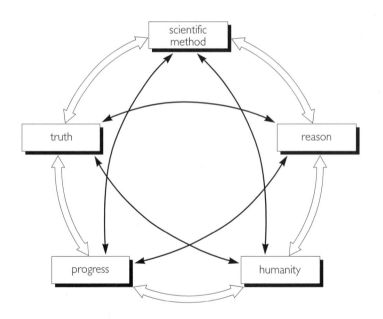

As you read through the chapter, this marginal diagram indicates where the connections are being made between the ideas in the circuit.

Figure 2.5   The scientific circuit of knowledge.

Taken from another starting-point, we can see how each of the parts of the circuit only makes sense in relationship to the others. For instance, in order to achieve *progress* we should deploy our capacity for *reason* within the methodological rules of *scientific method,* in order to establish the *truth* of a situation and use this as means of serving the needs of *humanity*. So, to emphasize again, each part of the circuit is defined through its relationships with other parts of the circuit.

This way of thinking locks us into a particular set of criteria for evaluating knowledge and deciding what is, and what is not, useful knowledge. This chapter identifies how these ideas came to be seen as authoritative knowledge. First, in section 2 we limit ourselves to a consideration of the ways in which science has been represented and understood by examining some of the analogies and metaphors involved in the communication of the idea of science. In particular, we focus upon the assumption that studying society is in some way similar to studying a living organism and the idea that the assumptions and methods of the natural sciences can in some way inform social scientific practice (a position we define in Chapter 3 as **naturalism**). We explore two well known examples of the experimental method in practice and see how it involves the technique of constructing closed systems. **Closed systems** exist when it is possible to identify a simple causal relationship between two (or a limited number of) observable things without any recognition of external complexity or any consideration of the internal properties of the thing in question. Finally, we also consider some of the implications involved in using closed systems when we study people and their relationships. Your concern throughout this book should be to think through what it means to be a social 'scientist' or social researcher – these are not neutral descriptive labels, they are packed full of meanings and associations. To make sense of social scientific practice, we need to think about what science means.

Summary

Knowledge systems make sense within the institutions which comprise the social structures of a particular society and are developed through the social agents (the scholars, teachers and researchers) who inhabit these institutions.

The idea of scientific method is part of a complex integrated circuit of knowledge and makes sense through its relationships with the ideas of truth, reason, progress and humanity. The authenticity of a scientific viewpoint is based on the way in which it draws upon this circuit.

2   Representing science

A system of representation is a way of organizing and arranging a series of concepts in order to produce a version of the world. When you study the world scientifically, whether you are looking at rocks, plants or people, you are nevertheless engaged in representing that world through language, and through the concepts, words and associations which make up a linguistic system. We are always at least one step removed from the thing we attempt to represent, for the words we use express the concept or the idea of that thing, never the thing itself. Effective communication is dependent upon getting across these concepts and ideas in a way which makes sense to the audience within our own community, whether this is the immediate social group, an academic community or the wider society. Successful ways of thinking about science, that convey the authenticity of any account of the natural or social world, have to speak the language of the intended audience. In this section, which focuses on the role of analogies and metaphors, we explore some of the most successful ways in which science has been represented, and we begin to understand the legacy of scientific thinking for the social sciences. Rather than looking straightaway at what science is, we first examine the ways in which scientific thought and method have had an impact on studying people, concentrating upon those aspects of science which are most pertinent to the ways that social scientists conduct themselves. This is to emphasize the way in which science is as much an attitude to inquiry as it is a definite set of principles, concepts and methodological procedures.

2.1   Science and its metaphors

In the nineteenth century the social sciences adopted the procedures and methods of the natural sciences. Given the increasing importance and success of natural scientific ideas, there were good reasons for doing so. In attempting to encourage a sceptical audience to see the relevance of any new set of ideas, it helps if you can draw their attention to a way of doing things which is both familiar and respected. By this time, the natural sciences had been widely disseminated and were well regarded. The adoption of well established principles ensured a more sympathetic reception from the academic audience concerned. More important, when amateur scholarship gave way to the professionalization of scientific research in the nineteenth and twentieth centuries, along with the institutional spread of respected centres of learning there was an increased likelihood of research funding from public and private bodies. Scientific work, in the study of the natural and social worlds, became more career oriented and institutionalized, as well as male dominated.

Early social scientists drew upon the representations of scientific practice established in the study of natural things in order to persuade their audiences of the truth of their ideas.

For social scientists, a range of possible models for scientific inquiry was on offer, providing some flexibility for interpretation and adaptation to human beings as objects of analysis. Some social scientists opted for assumptions and methods which were derived from physics or chemistry, others for the more closely related life sciences of biology and, in particular, physiology and anatomy. The types of analogies and metaphors adapted from the natural sciences for social scientific use had a strong effect upon the character and development of each social science discipline. In Figure 2.6, you can see how the affinity of society and nature was expressed through representations such as this satirical cartoon of Darwin and his next of kin. These associations in the public imagination reinforced the belief that the social and natural worlds could be studied in the same way. In addition, the boundaries between studying natural things and studying people were not as fixed as they are today. For instance, it was common to refer to 'natural philosophy' and the 'moral sciences' allowing for greater flexibility and innovation.

Figure 2.6   Charles Darwin and the origin of the human species.

The organic analogy, the treatment of society as if it resembled the functioning of the human body, has been one of the most effective stories ever told in the social sciences.

These themes are taken further later on in Chapter 3, section 3 on normality and pathology.

In the nineteenth century the comparisons with biology, and especially Charles Darwin's account of evolutionary biology in *The Origin of Species* (1859/1872), were influential as well as more widely popular in explaining processes of social change and the internal social structures of western Europe and North America (see the cartoon in Figure 2.6). For some, social science represented a form of anatomy (an early anatomy class is illustrated in Figure 2.7), identifying the component parts of society, the state, the family, institutions of learning, the economy and so on, and treating their combined functioning as akin to the relationship between the organs in the human body. These metaphors had strong evaluative connotations, for a stable society could be portrayed as healthy and normal whereas a society in conflict or a less developed society could be defined as primitive, pathological or abnormal. In addition, subordinate groups within societies could be defined as contaminated and, in some cases, described as cancers to be removed surgically. The eugenics movement in the late nineteenth and early twentieth centuries defined the lower classes in racial terms, recommending a range of solutions for social degeneracy, from birth control advice to sterilization and transportation to colonial societies. Even though the eugenics movement, with its dubious morality, has been discredited and has largely disappeared, the treatment of social relations as functioning systems is still prevalent in contemporary social science, although the

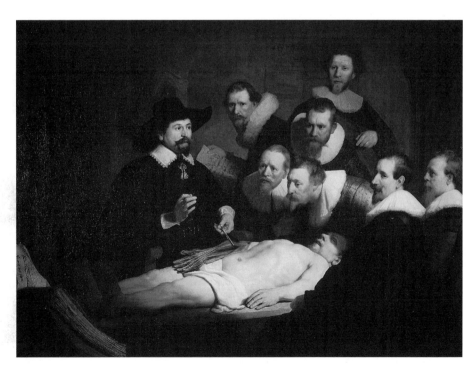

Figure 2.7 The anatomy class: science as precision.

The idea of studying social anatomy, in the manner of surgeons using precise instruments to dissect and explore the body, was a potent message. This demonstrated the potential of the early social scientists to reveal the hidden secrets of social organization.

metaphors used now are drawn from cybernetic systems and information flows (with the heavy use of the language of computing). An illustration of this is seen in Figure 2.8.

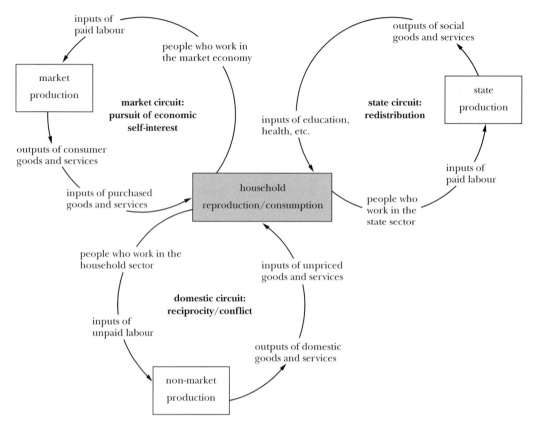

Figure 2.8   Cybernetic systems: the affinity of society and electronic systems. Many of the recent models of social life draw upon systems analysis for a way of thinking about relations and processes as flows and forces within circuits.

One of the most important ideas connected with science is the idea of progress. This is present in two senses. First, science is itself assumed to involve an accumulation of knowledge. This means that science is seen as generating progress in the level and in the depth of knowledge and understanding of the natural world as well as of ourselves as social beings. Second, progress also refers to the benefits which people have gained as a result of scientific knowledge, both in the application of science to the development of technology and in the level of specialization, complexity and diversity of people and their institutions. This second meaning of progress is also drawn from evolutionary biology, with its presupposition that all things move from a state of simplicity to a state of complexity as members of a species specialize, to occupy all the different niches which offer the potential for a sustainable existence. So evolutionary progress takes the form of a funnel or a cone with each step from the centre of the funnel seen as a move towards a superior state of existence, leaving all previous stages characterized as inferior and primitive. The idea of progress is a difficult one to challenge and attempts to do so often meet with ridicule,

The attractiveness of science depends upon its capacity to deliver 'progress' in terms of the accumulation of knowledge and the organization of society for human benefit.

especially if they are associated with what are often seen as non-scientific ways of thinking, as demonstrated in Figure 2.9 which represents a typical 'scientific' response to creationism in the USA.

Figure 2.9
Nobel scientists discover the missing link. The cartoon demonstrates the attitude of some scientists to religious belief.

However, we also need to question what sort of progress the history of science involves. One of the things that you will notice about the ideas covered in this chapter is the invisibility of women in the emergence of scientific thinking and the definition of progress. The history of science and most of social science is the history of the male perspective on the natural and social worlds (see Figure 2.10). When examining any

Figure 2.10
Evolution of man ... and woman. This ironic cartoon representation demonstrates the way that science delivers progress within a particular historical and social location. In hierarchical and unequal societies the benefits of progress can be unevenly distributed.

knowledge claim, ask yourself the question: for whom does science deliver progress?

More significant, especially in the twentieth century, is the use of mechanical and experimental metaphors, along with a desire to emulate physics as the purest form of scientific activity. In the natural sciences, the labels of experimental method and scientific method have often been used synonymously. Let's consider two examples of the experimental method in a little more detail before examining its legacy in the social sciences. Newton's experiments with prisms on the composition of light and Lavoisier's use of chemical experimentation to demonstrate the existence of oxygen are both characterized by the mechanical view. Mechanics assumes that the aim of science is to break things down into their various component parts, to understand how they work and, as a result, to master the natural forces of the world for human benefit.

The technique of the experimental method was most effectively demonstrated by Isaac Newton (1642–1727) in the study of matter, motion and light. By looking at one of Newton's experiments with light, through the use of prisms and pieces of white card, we can see how the experimental method can generate new scientific knowledge. In *Opticks* (1704), which is often portrayed as the model of experimental practice in physics, Newton set out to observe how light responds to being passed through a prism. He observed and noted how this created a spectrum of colour against a white surface (in the manner of a rainbow), as illustrated in Figure 2.11. Newton observed that rays of sunlight break down into bands of coloured light corresponding to different angles of refraction in the prism.

> The scientific study of things as if they are machine-like is the consequence of the success of the experimental method.

Of course, Newton could have concluded that this was a distorting effect produced by some imperfection in the prism. Instead, he explored whether it was possible to think about light in a new way – previously, light was seen as something which could not be broken down into smaller components. To assess this, he had to reconstruct and modify his original experiment with a single prism. Newton had to find a way of isolating the angle of refraction of a particular band of colour if he was to be able to demonstrate his findings more conclusively. He went on to construct a double prism experiment whereby a band of the spectrum of colour produced from the original experiment could pass through a second prism. In Figure 2.12 you can see how, by creating a hole in the white card, the colour band passes through a second prism at the same angle of refraction demonstrated in the original prism. Newton concluded that white light was, in fact, composed of a spectrum of bands of different colours each characterized by a distinct angle of refraction.

> Natural scientific experimentation demonstrates how it is possible to manipulate objects in order to create new knowledge.

We can see from this experiment how it is possible to take a single piece of evidence and, step by step, build an account of how light operates in general. The initial observation raised questions about how light had been understood in the past. Newton was developing the method of **induction**, by using observations of particular conditions as a foundation for constructing a general theoretical account of light. Little was known about light until scientific experimentation was used in this way.

> The method of induction is elaborated in Chapter 3, section 4.

At this time too, chemists were only beginning to understand gases, liquids and solids. For instance, it was not yet understood that water is composed of the elements of hydrogen and oxygen. Antoine Lavoisier (1743–1794)

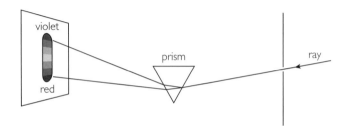

Figure 2.11
Newton's single
prism experiment.

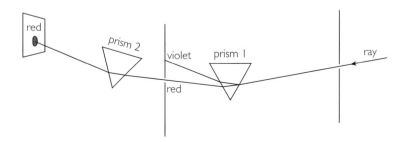

Figure 2.12
Newton's double
prism experiment.

used the experimental method to demonstrate the existence of a new gas, oxygen. In experimental conditions, chemists had observed that, following combustion, the weight of heated substances such as mercury or sulphur had decreased. They took this decrease in weight to be evidence of the release of a substance (which the chemist Joseph Priestley (1733–1804) had given the name 'phlogiston'). Without having any awareness of the existence of oxygen, the idea of sulphur consuming a gas when heated would have seemed to run counter to what they observed. Lavoisier discovered that when sulphur or mercury was heated it formed a 'calx' (which was, in fact, a combination of the element with oxygen, forming an oxide). When the calx was, in turn, intensely heated within the enclosed space of the laboratory apparatus, the gas given off could be collected and subjected to investigation (as illustrated in Figure 2.13 overleaf). It was discovered to be non-poisonous and to be flammable when kept in a pure state.

While Lavoisier's research went on to identify oxygen as the 'breath of life' and this subsequently led to a better understanding of water, Priestley had previously conducted a similar experiment and concluded that the same gas had been 'dephlogisticated air' and did not follow up the investigation. This scientific experiment, and later work, allowed Lavoisier to establish the scientific law of the conservation of matter: 'That within chemical reactions matter is neither created nor is it destroyed'. The findings of Lavoisier and Priestley clearly show that scientific experiments produce empirical evidence which can be interpreted in different ways. These interpretations depend upon the assumptions held about the characteristics of the things being experimented upon. Both Lavoisier and Priestley saw their work as a step in the direction of scientific progress although, in time, Lavoisier's discovery of oxygen was seen to have contributed more to scientific knowledge.

What do experiments, such as those carried out by Newton and Lavoisier, tell us about scientific investigation of social objects of analysis? Well, experiments like this work effectively because they are not set in natural conditions. An experimental situation is artificial and places things together which probably would not occur outside this situation. It simplifies a

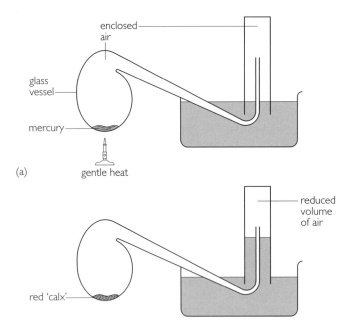

(a)

(b)

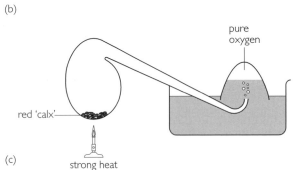

(c)

Figure 2.13 The discovery of oxygen (Lavoisier's mercury calx experiment). Lavoisier's experiments demonstrated that combustion allowed metals or sulphur to combine with the oxygen to form a 'calx' (in this experiment the metal is mercury and the red calx is 'mercury (II) oxide'). By subjecting the calx to intense heat, the oxygen was released and could be collected in a pure form.

situation in order to establish clear-cut relationships between things and creates a context where we can begin to manipulate the conditions to learn a little more. Although the effects of Newton's prism are manifested naturally when we see a rainbow, we cannot establish the angle of refraction of the bands of colour without the help of the experimental situation. In addition, an experiment enables us to establish the basic elements of a given situation. In the examples of those scientific experiments conducted by Newton and Lavoisier, we discovered that observable things were much more complex than appearances suggested (in these instances, that light and water were not indivisible but made up of more basic elements).

The experiments of the early natural scientists provided a model of inquiry which breaks things down into their smallest components in order to understand them.

So, to begin to answer the question of why this matters for social scientists, we can see that by creating a context within which only certain objects of analysis and their relations could be studied, both Newton and Lavoisier had, in their different fields of knowledge, effectively created a closed system. In the next section we examine these closed systems and how the conditions of closure that make natural scientific experiments so effective raise problems in the social sciences, where open systems exist. By understanding the experimental situation, it is possible to identify what it is that social scientists are doing when they adopt the assumptions and methods of the natural sciences in order to study people.

Summary

Scientific visions are transmitted through analogies and metaphors, such as 'nature as a machine' or 'society as an organism or body', and they have an impact upon scientific models to the extent that they are considered to be plausible, useful and accurate in a given time and place. More generally, they all offer the hope of progress.

The idea of science is associated most strongly with the experimental method and the manipulation of definite things (chemicals, matter, light and so on) in order to identify how they work. The aim of the method is to reduce such things to their basic components and establish what relationships can take place between them.

2.2 Closed systems and open systems

You may already be thinking that observations beyond the context of experiments are possible in science – experiments are, after all, artificial situations created for a human purpose. In astronomical physics, the movements of planets and stars operate in such a way as to provide reasonably predictable sequences of celestial events without human help. It is possible in astronomy to gauge the alignment of particular planetary objects with high degrees of accuracy. The object in this case, the solar system, provides an example of an object as a naturally occurring closed system (as demonstrated in Figure 2.14). Within a **closed system** it is possible to:

Elsewhere this sign will direct you to the glossary, but revisit this section if you need to.

- identify a limited number of variables;
- observe their behaviour, the frequency of changes in one variable in relation to another;
- account for, or avoid, any interference from unexpected external forces.

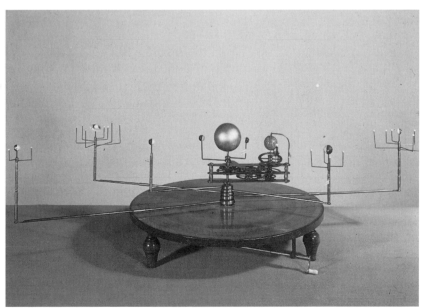

Figure 2.14
An orrery: a mechanical model of the solar system. This 1860 representation of the solar system as a clock-work model demonstrates the tendency to look for smoothly functioning systems in the natural world. From left to right are: Neptune, Saturn, Mars, Venus, the Sun, Mercury, Earth, Jupiter, Uranus (Pluto was still to be discovered).

Natural sciences have taken the condition of closure as their starting-point for developing scientific knowledge in situations where these distinct conditions do not hold. The scientific experiment is a way of artificially replicating the idea of a closed system. It is assumed that a scientist can dispassionately observe the experimental situation, and note all the changes within the system in response to carefully measured alterations in the combination of variables and/or the conditions of experimentation. Identifying simple relationships between discrete things would, then, enable a scientist to understand and explain events beyond the experimental situation. This enables scientific researchers to isolate the objects they wish to investigate from all the other objects which would confuse the picture. In science education, common experiments include subjecting magnesium ribbons to intense heat (which results in an incandescent flare) or depriving plants of certain life-giving properties, such as water or sunlight, in order to demonstrate photosynthesis. Such experiments have their uses in demonstrating the capacity of objects to behave in different ways from those observable in natural (non-experimental) conditions.

The scientific experiment is an artificial closed system.

Now let's examine the implication of closed system analysis for the scientific method in the social sciences, that is, in the study of people within social relationships and institutions. In the social sciences, a variety of techniques have been used to attempt to create closed systems and use observational evidence to construct theories and scientific laws. Indeed, the idea of closure has been an important part of all disciplines which have sought to establish **objective** knowledge. The assumption that closure can be achieved, whereby extraneous variables can be excluded in order to achieve an 'interference-free' zone for identifying clear-cut relations (conjunctions between empirical variables) is extremely popular as a technique. The application of this model in different social scientific disciplines is closely related to the nature of the object of analysis in each case. We turn to the implications of this now by examining three ways in which closure has been achieved in the social sciences: experimental closure, theoretical closure and statistical closure.

The experimental method is replicated in the social sciences directly through laboratory experiments and also through theoretical modelling and statistical techniques.

Experimental closure, such as in psychology, involves the physical separation of human beings from their normal context and their insertion into an artificial setting where they are subjected to a particular empirical treatment (stimulus). As you will recall from the previous sections, this involves the direct application of the assumptions and methods of the natural sciences to the study of social relations and processes. The point of the whole activity is to establish what form of responses follow from such treatments (stimuli) in the absence of all the other possible influencing factors which are normally present. So, just as natural scientists conducted experiments in artificial situations to concentrate on a limited range of things and the relationships between them, social scientists too can isolate people from the usual wide range of experiences. By doing this the people being studied respond directly to particular experiments in a way which is uncomplicated by the complex relations of everyday life. Let's examine the laboratory setting for the Bandura experiments (Bandura et al., 1963) on children's imitative or 'copycat' behaviour when exposed to controlled bursts of aggression. In the experiments, four groups of young children were placed in an environment which closely reflected the context of a playgroup. Each group was provided with a range of educational toys, including a mallet and a self-righting inflatable doll, a 'bobo doll'. Three

Closed systems in the social sciences come in three forms ...

• Experimental closure

groups were subjected to the experience of the doll being hit repeatedly with a mallet by an adult and one group was not, as a control against which the others could be compared. The first of these groups experienced the event in the flesh, the second viewed a film of the same act while the third experienced a cartoon version of the event. Before comparison, each group of children experienced the withdrawal of a portion of the toys, inducing a degree of frustration. The results revealed high levels of copying behaviour in all but the control group, with slightly lower levels of copying in the second and third groups, who had not experienced the attack on the doll directly but mediated in some way. This study has been used extensively as evidence in favour of the censorship of children's television, without much consideration of the highly artificial nature of the conditions in which the results were obtained. Real life is much more complex and simple causes are hard to identify.

Theoretical closure, such as within econometric models, poses similar problems. The replication of the economy as a series of variables and relationships in a computer program raises interesting issues about the way in which the variables and the relationships are themselves defined. The variables in economics include growth measures, the money supply, manufacturing output, employment levels and prices, all of which are open to alternative definitions. The relationships between the variables are conceived in terms of the susceptibility of one variable to changes in the others, such as the extent to which price inflation follows from increases in the money supply, which is an issue of intense dispute. The success of each model is measured in terms of its utility in forecasting the future. The variety of models on offer reflects the diversity of economics as a discipline and of the wide range of assumptions at the level of microeconomics. All models have been successful in accurately predicting some variables, although they may be very inaccurate on others. For instance, the Liverpool University model, based on monetarist assumptions and close to the Thatcher administration in the UK in the 1980s, is accurate on inflation. This model assumes that the rational expectations of actors in the economy should be integrated into the model. However, the Cambridge University model, based on Keynesian assumptions about the potentially positive consequences of state intervention, is more accurate on unemployment levels. In each case, the assumptions which make the models accurate predictors of some measures of economic performance undermine their accuracy on other measures. No model, however elaborate, can mirror or replicate the uncertainties and complexities of the real economy, although they can tell us useful things about certain aspects of the economy.

Statistical closure involves a situation in which quantitative numerical data sets are processed in order to identify correlations. This technique is particularly popular in economics and psychology, although it has also been applied in other disciplines such as political science. For example, the study of voting behaviour, psephology, involves the examination of electoral results and opinion poll questionnaire responses in an attempt to identify how and why people vote for particular political parties. The evidence here is based largely on the degree of correspondence or correlation between voting in a particular way and the particular characteristics of the voters under consideration. The relevant variables often highlighted by psephologists include occupational class, locality, gender, age and ethnicity. These served as useful indicators of likely voting

- Theoretical closure

These two approaches in economics are discussed in greater detail in Chapter 5.

- Statistical closure

intentions from the 1950s until the early 1970s. But over the last twenty years in the UK, the strong identifications between groups and political parties have weakened, forcing political scientists to question their assumptions. Some have identified evidence which suggests that individuals assess political parties according to perceived self-interest, whereas others have pointed to affiliations with the public or private sectors in terms of transport use, housing types or even provision of sports facilities (Butler and Stokes, 1974; Himmelweit et al., 1981; Heath et al., 1985). However, these attempts to predict voting behaviour are much more cautious than is generally the case for statistical closure analysis in economics.

Activity 2.2

Now turn to Reading A, 'The development of emotions: using experimental methods', from *Understanding Emotions* by Keith Oatley and Jennifer M. Jenkins (1996).

Try to identify the key features of this illustration of closure in experimental psychology by considering the following questions.

- What are the main variables under consideration?

- What has been excluded from consideration?

- Which conclusions would you consider to be plausible and which implausible?

What do you think are the uses of, and also the limitations on, this sort of experimental method when applied to the development of children? Here you should think about whether experimental closure provides the kind of evidence which can help us to understand childhood development beyond the experiment.

The use of the experimental method in the study of people has often been criticized for its artificiality and the subsequent problems of taking experimental results as a good indication of what happens throughout society. You may also have some reservations about the study of children's emotional development by psychologists using the experimental method. Nevertheless, such studies appear to highlight relatively clear-cut relationships and raise potential explanations about emotional development. You should consider too whether or not the children's responses to such artificial situations would occur in exactly this way in everyday life, where all sorts of factors come into play. There is a genuine problem in assuming that results from experimental research can be applied in situations beyond the laboratory. In everyday life, conditions are complex, changing, uncertain and involve individuals who have intrinsic properties which lead them to respond differently in real life compared with their behaviour in the artificial conditions of experimental closure. This raises the more difficult question of whether, with sufficient experimentation of a range of simple relationships, we could ever come close to replicating such complexity.

Social scientific knowledge produced within conditions of closure analysis produces theories and evidence which are difficult to apply beyond the context in which it was created.

As soon as the complexity of social life is acknowledged in social research, these techniques for simulating closure are problematized and the status of causal laws produced in this way is dramatically altered. The adequacy of developing simple accounts which exclude relevant variables becomes open to question. This problem is accentuated if it is accepted that social objects have an internal complexity and structure. If social life involves **open systems**, including objects with intrinsic properties, as defined in Table 2.1, then the conception of causal laws based entirely on empirical regularities between distinct variables established within a **closed system** is no longer tenable. This does not mean that we have to reject causal explanations but it does suggest that we have to think very carefully about what they mean.

Table 2.1   Summary of closed and open systems.

	Closed systems	Open systems
Simplicity and complexity	A limited number of measurable variables is involved to increase the possibility of identifying and predicting clear relationships.	A state of complexity is acknowledged as the condition of one's objects of analysis and the relations between them.
External boundary	Exclusion clauses ensure that the confusing mass of possible influences are screened out (such as the *ceteris paribus* clause, that, holding all other things constant, *x* will lead to *y*).	No external boundary is assumed to exist so that each object can be part of multiple causal relations and that one cannot predict an outcome with any degree of certainty.
Intrinsic properties	All objects of analysis are taken at face value so that the intrinsic properties of an object are not considered.	It is recognized that all objects have intrinsic properties and structures which affect their performance in different conditions.

Causal laws constructed in closed systems are usually less effective in situations which are more complex and uncertain, that is, in open systems.

Significant problems are generated in the translation of results from experimental situations to field research, or from econometric or policy modelling to examining real economic and political processes. For instance, in the psychological example involving the imitation of aggressive behaviour, field studies have been unable to reproduce the clear-cut results of the laboratory experiments conducted by Bandura's team of psychologists (Bandura et al., 1963). This raises questions not just about the experiments themselves but also about assuming that the experimental approach is the most useful. Such studies (for example Himmelweit, 1958; Eron, 1963; and Belson, 1978) demonstrate the difficult issues faced by social scientists, for the clear-cut connections which experimental studies had appeared to support could not be identified beyond the laboratory. The problems with closed systems have been well expressed by Robert Dahl, an American political scientist who gradually came to realize that his earlier attempts to create a closed system, in which political decision making could be observed, measured and explained, had severe limitations. In *The Dilemmas of Pluralist Democracy*, Dahl argues:

> The boundaries around an account of why Beta does x are not rigidly fixed by some palpable phenomenon revealed by our senses, like a chain-wire fence around a factory. Instead the boundaries are creations of the human mind – more like the boundaries the ancients drew around the constellations they saw in the heavens on clear nights.

Where one decides to draw boundaries around a causal system that is intended to explain human actions seems to depend in a significant way on many factors, including one's curiosities, purposes, and prior judgements as to the usefulness of a particular bit of additional knowledge ... Where one stops in the search for conclusive answers will depend on contestable judgements as to what one thinks it is crucial to explain, and how far outward in time and social space one wants to explore in search of a satisfactory account. To be sure, one may finally arrive at a boundary where the causal system is closed, in the sense that no further factors need to be taken into account in order wholly to explain the outcome. But when significant human actions are to be accounted for, complete closure is sure to require a vast system.

(Dahl, 1982, p.25)

Despite all of these reservations about applying scientific approaches to the social world, there is no doubt that these scientific attitudes and metaphors have had a profound impact on the ways in which human beings have viewed the natural and social worlds over the last three centuries.

Summary

The most important legacy of the early developments in scientific knowledge for the social sciences is the use of closed systems from the experimental method in the natural sciences. Closure involves the practice of holding other variables constant, in order to establish clear-cut relationships between objects of analysis which are to be taken at face value.

When studying human beings, closed systems simplify social relations to make the study of different aspects of social life more manageable. However, this may undermine the claims of social researchers to be accurately reconstructing a more complex reality in which open systems exist and it may also neglect the importance of interpretation in social research.

3   Science and modernity

In the previous sections you discovered how closed systems have had an impact upon many areas of social scientific practice. You have also begun to explore how this relates to the analogies and metaphors of natural scientific practice. If we are to stand any chance of understanding how these work today we have to turn our attention towards the way in which such approaches came to be established as well as recognize the hopes attached to the scientific approach. Considering the 'story of science' and the historical context in which science as a 'system of knowledge' emerged enables us to piece together how science came to be seen as authoritative knowledge. Similarly, the social sciences came to be established in a particular period in human history when social structures were undergoing enormous economic, political and social changes. At this time, new groupings of teachers, scholars and researchers began to develop radically new conceptual tools to deal with the challenges which they faced. A great deal that had been familiar for centuries was swept away with the emergence of modern societies. Indeed, the desire for knowledge which is universal and true but also human-made (rather than a product of divine revelation) is a direct product of the emergence of science in the modern condition. As we reflect on the challenges we face, perhaps we can also learn something about our own predicament today by looking back at the past.

Science is most effectively understood in terms of its connections with the other elements in the circuit of knowledge characteristic of 'modern' societies.

The remainder of this chapter traces the early development of the emergence of science in the context of the modern world, showing how this came to fruition in the Enlightenment during the eighteenth century when the intellectual foundations of the modern social sciences were established. The emergence of scientific thought and the experimental method from the seventeenth century involved a revolution in the creation of knowledge. The three parts of this section explore the scope and dimensions of this unfolding revolution.

- Section 3.1 considers the emergence of scientific thought in relation to the study of the natural world. It explains how a particular framework of scientific assumptions came to be accepted because of its plausibility in a broadly religious social context.

- Section 3.2 provides a brief outline of the social transformations in the early modern period and identifies how these changes produced new social, political and economic objects for which there was no adequate explanation.

- Section 3.3 explores the ideas of the Enlightenment, which applied the new forms of scientific thinking to the study of these new social objects – the economy, the state, society and the human mind – in various ways.

As the social sciences emerged, they were moulded through the application of the methods and assumptions of the natural sciences to the study of these new social objects. This chapter concludes with a brief discussion of the contradictory legacy of the Enlightenment period for the social sciences.

3.1 Science, observation and experimentation

See Chapter 1, section 3.1, for an introduction to situated knowledge.

One of the themes throughout this book is the usefulness of identifying the historical and social location of the various methodological approaches available to a social scientist. It is noticeable that the successful approaches (with success measured in terms of persuasiveness in the periods in question) are often treated as the logical culmination of earlier success stories. This intergenerational success story suggests an inevitable progress in scientific knowledge. The history of scientific thought is one of the most important success stories, with the lineage of scientific thinkers often drawn out in the manner of a family tree, as if the succession is natural or preordained. Such a conventional account is aptly described as a 'history of the present', whereby a march of progress is already implied in the construction of a **narrative** or a plausible story of scientific development (Dean, 1994). It is useful to focus upon some of the ancestors in the scientific family tree without treating them as foundations in the **canonical** sense. It is important to situate these foundational figures in order to illustrate how all forms of knowledge are themselves grounded in particular historical and social circumstances. This may help us to decide which ideas and research methods we should use to understand our own condition and those which no longer serve as a useful reference point.

More specifically, this section of the chapter looks at the intellectual foundations of Western science in more detail and provides an introduction to the ideas of three early scientific thinkers: Francis Bacon, Pierre Gassendi and René Descartes. While their ideas differed in some respects and there are many others whom we could have chosen, these three have been selected because between them they provide the central assumptions which were taken up by the founders of social science from the Enlightenment onwards. Bacon and Descartes have been selected because of the significance of their ideas for the way in which we have constructed knowledge in Western societies. Gassendi, on the other hand, is less well known today but in the period of the emergence of science was just as important. He has been included to help illustrate why Bacon and Descartes came to be regarded as the 'founding fathers' of science. To the audience for scientific work in the early modern period, their ideas were more plausible than Gassendi's contributions. In some respects, Gassendi offered a different model for thinking scientifically and helps us to imagine what the history of science might have looked like if things had been different. This is important because, if science could have been different, then perhaps social science might have been different too.

The account which follows is not a complete picture but simply picks out some of the distinctive features of the early scientific methods and assumptions about the natural world which were to have a lasting effect. Nevertheless, the approaches of Bacon and Descartes were the ones which shaped the emergence of science in the context of a world still largely governed by religious concerns. Thus, this section also identifies what made their ideas plausible to largely religious academic communities at that time. Rather than seeing science as a replacement for religious thinking, the earliest successful models for scientific inquiry, which set the ball rolling, were those which were compatible with the prevailing religious viewpoints four hundred years ago. That is, they could be accommodated within social structures with deeply embedded religious assumptions.

The models of scientific inquiry which came to dominate were those which were most plausible in the context of religious social structures and social agents.

The features of the Western scientific mentality, particularly the search for truth through observation, can be seen particularly clearly in the writings of Francis Bacon. In *The Advancement of Learning* (1605) and *Novum Organon* (1620), Bacon identified the key activity of science as one of demystifying existing false and irrational interpretations of the world around us, in order to establish the truth. He argued that the truth was often obscured by four delusions – idols – and that it could only be established by a combination of careful observation and logical inquiry. The illustrations which Bacon developed to convey the purpose of scientific activity

Science became understood as the 'search for truth' through the scientific writings of Francis Bacon.

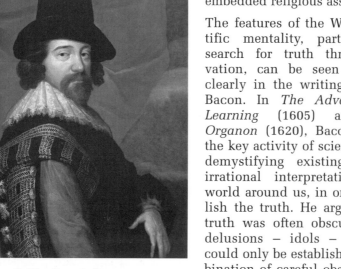

Figure 2.15 Francis Bacon (1561–1626) promoted the scientific method of observation and experiment.

had a tremendous effect on the subsequent development of scientific practice. By taking the objects apart in order to establish their working components or interrogating an object in order to reveal some hidden truth, he demonstrated things which no one had spotted before. This is reflected in the predominance of mechanical metaphors in scientific thought, such as the treatment of nature as analogous to the intricate and delicate workings of the mechanical parts of a clock.

According to Bacon, however, there were four idols which were, by definition, false and irrational and which had to be discarded in the relentless pursuit of truth:

For Bacon, the scientific method was the only route to truth ...

- *idols of the cave*, where we have become so focused upon particular instances that it is no longer possible to develop generalizations;

- *idols of the tribe*, where we rely upon customary habits and traditions or when we let our passions rule our heads, undermining the rational pursuit of the truth;

- *idols of the theatre*, where the myths of the past dominate without any clear empirical basis for their acceptance in the present;

- *idols of the marketplace*, where the language involved in everyday human relationships is seen to present an obstacle to scientific explanation.

This placed the relationship between science and truth as a key feature in the circuit of knowledge identified in section 1.2 of this chapter (see Figure 2.5). In addition, Bacon placed a special emphasis upon breaking down objects of analysis into their smallest possible component parts. In seventeenth-century France, there was a similar movement towards philosophical atomism as a way of thinking about natural things. **Atomism** involves the treatment of matter as if the physical objects we observe are composed of randomly moving particles (or atoms) which, through their constant re-arrangement, produce the variations in form observed by scientists. (Atomism is discussed further in Chapter 3, section 1.)

The *social agents* in this situation (teachers, theological scholars and scientists) placed a strong emphasis upon the role of 'human reason' in scientific practice, introducing a third important component in the circuit of knowledge. Right from the very start, the relationship between truth, reason and the experimental scientific method became a key feature of modern scientific thinking. However, the idea that truth came from human beings rather than from God raised significant problems in convincing the existing academies, which were by and large within the control of religious authorities. Bacon's stress upon observation and experiment prevented him from directly challenging religious authority. The position of Gassendi and Descartes in posing human reason as the source of scientific truth, however, was more difficult for the logical scholars to accept.

... whereas for Gassendi and Descartes, this could not be achieved without human reason.

The links between science, truth and reason were established through the writings of Gassendi and, especially, Descartes.

Let's look first at Pierre Gassendi, a mathematician, philosopher and scientist. Gassendi used a linguistic metaphor to account for the existence of particles in a vacuum. He suggested that these particles held (God-given) powers of attraction which enabled them to form groupings or corpuscles (molecules) from which 'things' emerged. For Gassendi, this operated in much the same way as letters combined to form words and sentences.

This was in direct opposition to beliefs about the existence of an eternal order in the universe, founded upon the 'basic elements' of earth, air, fire and water, a doctrine which had become intertwined with Christian theology. While Gassendi had found a place for God in the creation of all things, he questioned the established Christian beliefs about the principles of astronomy and physics and so met with a hostile audience. Earlier religious knowledge systems had posed the existence of a 'great chain of being' within which all things were connected. To question these established principles about the nature of matter was tantamount to questioning the 'true faith' of the Roman Catholic Church. Gassendi acknowledged and expressed the scepticism about traditional religious assumptions which was to emerge as a distinct feature of the period but which also generated some resistance to his contributions.

Figure 2.16 Pierre Gassendi (1592–1655), a less celebrated figure, pioneered the mechanical view that the world consists of atoms.

While Gassendi's work served to make the atomistic characterization of objects of analysis much more acceptable, it was the approach of René Descartes, a philosopher and mathematician, which captured the wider imagination of the period. It is useful to think about why it was that the 'Cartesian' vision (after Descartes) became an important foundation of science. A significant factor was the degree to which Descartes offered a mechanical approach to explain the formation of natural objects in a way which was compatible with the established religious **knowledge systems**. This had significant consequences for the scientific tradition. Like Gassendi, Descartes advocated atomism, but did so in a way which did not raise such fundamental objections from the church authorities.

Descartes' method involved the use of doubt as a critical tool, probing every idea for its weaknesses and stripping down ideas to their essentials. In particular, he drew a dividing line between mind and body (between thought and sensation), as two definite things, in order to establish human consciousness as the centre of rationality with the principle of *cogito ergo sum* (I think, therefore I exist). Reason came to be seen as the source of truth and the guarantor of progress. Descartes also developed a philosophical defence of God's existence using human reason alone. As a starting-point, it was assumed that God was, by definition, perfect, and human beings imperfect. This was tied to the idea of existence: human beings are mortal creatures whereas God is not subject to the laws of the life cycle (Gods are immortal, they always exist). Therefore, a God which did exist was somewhat more perfect than a God which did not. By logic alone, it could be demonstrated that God did exist! The rationality of this argument involves the practice of working towards a conclusion purely on the basis of a

Figure 2.17 René Descartes (1596–1650) promoted the use of human reason to establish the truth.

given premise (that of God being perfect). It is possible to question the status of the truth of the premises, but nevertheless this account of divine things was the first to establish a secular (non-religious) basis for faith. If it was possible to explain God's existence through human reason, then anything could be explained in this way.

The Cartesian vision of science was compatible with the belief in God and the doctrines of religious institutions. Therefore he did not challenge the prevailing attitudes of the academy.

Within his rational system of knowledge Descartes left some other issues unresolved which lent themselves to theological reinterpretation by his contemporaries in church institutions. Theologians who wished to reconcile emerging scientific thought with the *social structure* based upon religious values found that this approach to scientific knowledge was compatible with the Christian religion. However, the Cartesian separation of mind and body provided little basis for understanding how they worked together in practice and posed a peculiar problem for theological scholars. Descartes had argued that some connection between mind and body could be facilitated through the pineal gland attached to the brain, although he was unable to demonstrate this precisely (Figure 2.18).

 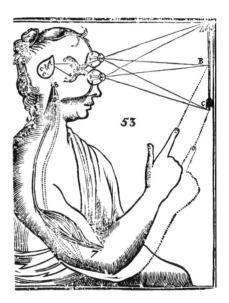

Figure 2.18 Descartes' demonstration of the role of the pineal gland in the reception of sense impressions – an important part of the emergence of scientific thought was its visual communication.

This problem became the most important reason for the acceptance of the Cartesian approach. It was Nicolas Malebranche (1638–1715), a practising priest with an interest in philosophy, who performed an important role in popularizing these principles. Malebranche resolved the problem from a theological point of view by arguing that the links between the mind and the body could only be brought together through the direct intervention of God. This emphasis upon divine intervention in all acts of sensory perception secured a much wider audience for the Cartesian approach, particularly among the clergy. Hence the Cartesian model offered a more plausible intellectual account of the scientific method than the alternatives within seventeenth- and eighteenth-century European societies. The Cartesian approach provided a means of using scientific discoveries without throwing the role of the clergy into doubt. In this way the clerical interpretation of the role of God and the rational scientific method could coexist rather than contradict each other.

Now, we can think through some of the implications of this. While Gassendi sought to maintain links with classical science, Descartes had broken with the past to establish a rational system of logic which could be used to judge all forms of knowledge. In both approaches, however, the basis for making universal judgements was man-made rather than a matter of divine revelation, reinforcing the importance of reason in constructing scientific knowledge. Perhaps more significantly for Western scientific development, while Gassendi attempted to maintain a closely integrated relationship between the study of science, history and philosophy, Descartes initiated the breaks between them from which disciplinary specialization emerged. This division and redivision of knowledge into more and more focused and specialized fields was in part a reflection of similar tendencies at work in other social spheres. One of the distinctive characteristics of the modern world has been the compartmentalization of social life and this is reflected in our knowledge of social life. Gassendi's approach was consigned to the dustbin of history because it could not reconcile the differences between the religious knowledge system and the emerging ideas of science. By contrasting Gassendi and Descartes, we can see how these different accounts of science have different implications for the later development of natural scientific and social scientific knowledge. One possible future was an interdisciplinary one, with the integration of science, philosophy and history. The other was a disciplinary future based on specialized ring-fenced fields of knowledge with little in the way of attempts to build bridges between them. For the last four hundred years we have followed the second path, leading to the compartmentalization of knowledge into narrower specialisms.

Descartes' scientific vision emphasized disciplinary specialization – Gassendi stressed the importance of interdisciplinary work.

Why then did the scientific vision which came to dominate Western thinking draw more from Bacon and Descartes? On the one hand, Descartes established the central place of human reason within the modern world but it was only because his academic audience could use the new knowledge in a way which was compatible with religious beliefs. On the other hand, Bacon sought to avoid the dangers of questioning matters of faith by constructing instead an account of the rules of experimentalist method. This enabled him to make observations within specified conditions and to make useful generalizations. The scientific method of experiment and observation presented observable evidence and left it up to the readers to make up their own minds. However, Bacon did not dispense with the role of human imagination, as is illustrated by the following extract from *Novum Organon*:

> The men of experiment are like the ant; they only collect and use;
> the reasoners resemble spiders, who make cobwebs out of their own
> substance. But the bee takes a middle course, it gathers material
> from the flowers of the garden and of the field, but transforms and
> digests it by a power of its own.

> (cited in Kearney, 1971, p.91)

As an early advocate of the method of **induction**, Bacon argued that it was possible to construct scientific knowledge simply through accumulating observational evidence. He was also one of the first to identify the role of science in delivering human progress. The common foundations of these emerging scientific approaches can be identified as:

- the shared belief that human progress could only be delivered through a root and branch transformation of human knowledge;

- the recognition of the human subject as the foundation for establishing the truth;

- the success of a branch of scientific knowledge depended on its capacity to combine with the religious ideas of the period in order to avoid accusations of heresy.

Consequently, the links between the scientific method, truth, reason and progress in the **circuit of knowledge** became stronger and were increasingly communicated to a wider audience in the institutions of learning which exercised some degree of power and influence.

By the late seventeenth and eighteenth centuries, human beings were increasingly accepted as the source of knowledge and the mechanical vision of matter as 'corpuscles in motion' had been given greater weight by the experimental work of Robert Boyle (1627–1691) in chemistry and Isaac Newton (1642–1727) in physics. Boyle developed the use of experimental techniques to demonstrate the existence of chemical elements; he also suggested that in alchemy the belief that all metals could be reduced to lead and hence changed back into gold was false. As you saw earlier, Newton's use of observations produced by experimental procedures, in order to generate and to test hypotheses about the laws of motion and the seven constituent bands of colour which made up white light, served further to confirm the view that progress in knowledge is achieved through the scientific method.

Scientists demonstrated that human progress was only feasible within a circuit of knowledge which effectively integrated science, truth and reason for human progress.

It was this creative mix of precise observation and scientific detachment from one's object (derived from Bacon) and the assumption of human consciousness as the source of knowledge (derived from Descartes) which had such a tremendous effect upon those who attempted to construct a scientific vision of society. Early social science was itself shaped by this potent combination of human consciousness of an external reality as the source of truth and the practice of science defined as taking objects apart in order to facilitate our understanding of the mysteries of nature. This profoundly affected the early development of social science and can be identified most clearly in the nineteenth-century **positivism**, from which all the existing social sciences are, in some way, derived. These approaches were 'positive' in the sense of offering an **objective** and true account of nature and society.

The early versions of the social sciences shared the same assumptions as these positivist approaches towards natural science.

With the benefit of hindsight, it is possible to identify how the positivist social sciences were remarkable in two ways: for their faith in the explanatory powers of human reason, and for their ability to translate their own cultural values and prejudices into objective facts. One notable feature of this can be traced in the misinterpretations of 'race' and sex in the period, whereby prejudicial common sense often crudely masqueraded as scientifically validated truth. The history of racism is littered with appeals to science as a means of making its claims more acceptable. This is more systematically explored in Chapter 3, where the impact of positivism on the social sciences is outlined and assessed through a case study on scientific racism.

It is useful at this stage to situate these 'founding fathers' of science in terms of their own taken-for-granted assumptions and prejudices. You may have already noted that the emergence of science was a very masculine affair. Mies and Shiva (1993) have identified strong patriarchal assumptions in this work, for instance, Descartes established the distinction between mind and body which, in the context of the gender assumptions of the period, relegated women's concerns as closer to nature than to culture and science. In addition, the metaphors utilized by Bacon that nature should be controlled, subordinated and 'forced by torture to yield her secrets, like a bad woman who keeps her treasures avariciously to herself and withholds them from her … sons' (Mies and Shiva, 1993, p.44) served to reinforce the gendered nature of science throughout the modern period. From this viewpoint, science is seen as an extension of the witch hunts in the sixteenth and seventeenth centuries.

It is also seen as deeply implicated in the naturalization of femininity in this period, whereby masculinity becomes associated with culture and learning and femininity becomes associated with nature. Throughout this period as well, femininity became more and more associated with animal drives and instinctual passions while masculinity became more associated with the civilized pursuits of art, culture and literature. To some extent, women were portrayed as corrupting influences on virtuous men, undermining their rationality. Feminist interpretations of these processes have suggested that the institutional exclusion of women from culture, art and literature, as well as the natural sciences, can also be related to the emerging modern distinction between the public sphere (where power and autonomy are defined) and the private sphere, regarded as the sphere of consumption, leisure and personal relations. Where femininity did exist within scientific discourse during the nineteenth century, it was almost invariably in the form of an object and, as such, reduced to passivity in response to biological and/or social determinants. There is a close relationship between this scientific objectification of femininity and the increase in the moral regulation of the private sphere.

Scientific knowledge in this period and since was androcentric (male-centred), which reflected the exclusion of women from academic life.

Common to all these developments is the gradual shift from theological ways of understanding and constructing knowledge to the establishment of the modern outlook by the 1800s. In the traditional societies of western and central Europe, it was widely believed that the world in all its manifest complexity was created by God; this led to the view that the place of human beings was to describe and clarify God's creation and certainly not to criticize the orthodox teachings of the Roman Catholic Church. Intellectual inquiry could lead an individual scientist into the questioning of 'eternal truths', as Galileo (1564–1642) discovered in 1633 when placed on trial by the holy Inquisition. Galileo had proposed the physical reality of the astronomical system (along the lines established in the mid sixteenth century by Polish astronomer and mathematician Nicolas Copernicus) whereby the Sun, and not the Earth, was at the centre of the universe. Galileo's treatment by the holy Inquisition, in his seventieth year, led Descartes to withhold from publication his own endorsement of the Copernican model. Dissent was thus channelled through the debates on the literal and symbolic meanings of the scriptures. The theological scholars involved in these debates had to tread carefully to avoid charges of heresy and the consequent punishment of death. Even Galileo recanted and denounced his own work in order to avoid such a penalty. So far, we have traced the emergence of science in providing a plausible account of nature within European societies dominated by religious values. The emergence of science served also to undermine these social orders and can be seen as an important part of a wider process of change involved in the development of the modern world.

Summary

The scientific method associated with Bacon, Gassendi and Descartes provided the framework for modern scientific knowledge in the natural and social sciences. Much of the philosophy of the social sciences involves various attempts to understand the relationship between the study of observable evidence and the role of human reason.

The accounts of the scientific method by Bacon and Descartes were successful because they were compatible with religious accounts of the natural world and human consciousness. The plausibility of these visions of science (as the search for truth) overshadowed the interdisciplinary alternative in the work of Gassendi and helped to initiate the process of disciplinary specialization in knowledge.

The story of science, with its stress upon the emergence of human reason as the basis for organizing and making sense of experience, masks the tendency to substitute male rationality for all forms of human knowledge. There is a close relationship between the emergence of scientific rationality and the exclusion of women from the institutions involved in the discovery and transmission of knowledge. If science could tell us its story, it would have the voice of a man.

3.2   The historical context of the Enlightenment

This section explores the links between the idea of science and the social structure which served as the context for the Enlightenment. In particular, during this period the emergence of new objects of analysis led those who were trying to make sense of their own experiences to pose the need for new explanations. The emergence of science is often portrayed as a slow but inexorable process which, once initiated, continues under its own momentum. This leaves the emergence of both the natural and social sciences as disembodied processes without regard for the complex historical and social conditions in which science as a practice took place. While a comprehensive account of these conditions is inappropriate here, it is useful to identify the broad shifts in social development which are associated with the transition from the premodern to the modern world. In the premodern or traditional world, both the natural and social worlds were conceptualized as the result of divine will. As you will recall, in this situation the role of intellectuals was simply to describe and clarify God's creations. Critical inquiry into the basis of political authority, the relations of ownership and control, or the role of religious institutions in interpreting the natural and social orders was tantamount to heresy, as you saw in the persecution of Galileo at the end of the last section. This had such a dramatic impact throughout Europe that even Descartes was reluctant to publish findings which were likely to stir up theological controversy. The social order was therefore seen as God-given, and the debates which were permitted operated within the framework established by the scriptures.

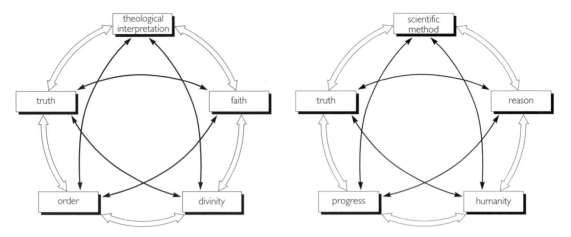

The theological circuit of knowledge   The scientific circuit of knowledge

Figure 2.19   The theological circuit of knowledge alongside its successor.

In the modern world, however, human beings have come to be regarded as the sources of knowledge. This changes the way in which systems of knowledge relate to social existence. In modernity, the production of scientific knowledge involves more than description and clarification. Modern thought also offers the possibility of critical inquiry as well as the potential for the transformation of social existence. Thus, modern knowledge, of which science is a part, offers greater opportunities to question even basic assumptions. With this in mind, we now turn to the massive social transformations with which the first social scientists were presented. By focusing briefly upon the changes of beliefs, the economic transformations and the emergence of the state, we can get a little closer to imagining how these early social scientists began to understand and define their objects of analysis. We do this now by examining the four major transformations: religious, intellectual, economic and political.

The first two transformations are very closely related. In the case of *religious beliefs*, the questioning of the Catholic faith across Europe and the emergence of diverse forms of Protestantism, each interpreting the scriptures in new ways, led initially to widespread division, persecution and war. Nevertheless, the social exhaustion produced by this discord led to the acceptance of a degree of tolerance for new ideas. There is a close relationship between the recognition that each individual could find their own personal salvation and the second transformation, the emergence of the principle of *free intellectual inquiry* in other fields of knowledge. As you saw in the previous section, the emergence of rational science and the rigorous pursuit of the methods of experiment and observation led to the belief that reason could be employed to grasp the inner workings of all objects. In relation to society, a notable consequence of the faith in reason to deliver progress can be seen in the attempts to establish the 'Age of Reason' by the revolutionary leadership during the events of the French Revolution. They attempted to wipe the historical slate clean by changing

The emergence of modern societies produced a transformation in the system of knowledge, and revealed knowledge gave way to human-made knowledge.

To understand the emergence of the social sciences we have to appreciate the challenges faced by early social scientists.

● The religious transformation

• The intellectual
transformation

all institutions, measures and laws. Even the calendar was restarted from scratch. The 'Age of Reason' placed an enormous emphasis upon the capacity of human beings to reshape the world they inhabit, whether natural or social. Scientific knowledge came to be seen as an instrument for securing control over the human condition and for making it better.

Third, the transformations in the *economy* meant that the traditional relations between noble lord and bonded serf or peasant were giving way to commercial pressures. Agrarian capitalism emerged, establishing contractual relations between landlords and tenant farmers and between farmers and agricultural labourers. As common lands were taken into

• The economic
transformation

private ownership, competition for wages in the countryside hastened the departure of large numbers of individuals and families to the towns in search of work. The emergence of capitalist markets in labour, goods and services transformed the production, distribution and exchange relations of the economy. Correspondingly, individuals were increasingly valued in terms of their place within the market, rather than their ascribed status as part of a social group or community.

Finally, the fourth transformation is the political one, the emergence of the *modern nation-state*. The first steps towards political liberalization were witnessed well before the French Revolution. The opening up of politics to competition between factions or parties within oligarchic parliamentary

• The political
transformation

systems and the shift of power from monarchies towards legislative assemblies marked the emergence of a new form of social cohesion. The brute force and punishments inflicted by traditional, supremely powerful monarchies gave way to government by consent and rule by law. However, this remained the consent of the propertied few (male electors) until the late nineteenth and early twentieth centuries.

Activity 2.3

In Chapter 1 (section 2) you considered the various challenges facing social scientists today. Three big transformations were highlighted – globalization, the environment and the communications revolution. Now try to imagine what it was like to be around when modern societies were emerging. It may help to read again quickly the four transformations identified above. Try to answer the following questions.

- What do you think were the challenges facing a social scientist at this time?
- What were the 'new' objects of analysis?
- Which ideas would you say were outdated?
- What were the obstacles to achieving a better understanding of these changes?

There are no perfect answers to these questions. However, you should think about the way in which changes in the social structure have an impact on the way in which social scientists think about the things they study and how they study them. You may also find it interesting to consider the parallels between the dilemmas facing social scientists then and now.

Together, these four transformative processes can be seen as crucial in creating the conditions for the emergence of economic, political, religious and intellectual individualism characteristic of the modern industrial era. In addition, these transformations were accompanied by demographic and cultural changes as the agrarian orders in western Europe gradually gave way to advanced and largely urbanized social relations. A final dimension to consider in the development of these processes is the global dimension. With the expansion of trade and the establishment of colonial empires, the social relations established in Europe had an impact well beyond the European continent. In this way, Western rationality and scientific knowledge are themselves defined in opposition to the cultural belief systems of the colonized peoples. Scientific knowledge is often portrayed as the mark of a civilized culture. However, it is only possible to define civilization by contrasting it with 'barbarism' and primitiveness. Consequently, scientific knowledge is, by definition, implicated in the cultural justifications of imperialism from the sixteenth to the twentieth centuries.

Summary

The complex and contradictory processes which modernized the Western world removed the institutional arrangements of premodern belief systems and allowed the secular scientific vision to become the dominant framework for constructing authoritative knowledge and for building new social institutions.

The transformations initiated by the modernization process transformed the social landscape in such a way as to make all the mental maps of previous modes of thinking flawed or redundant. New objects developed which demanded attention, such as the market economy, the nation-state, ideology, the individual mind and new forms of culture.

3.3 The Enlightenment, progress and social science

Having established the social transformations with which the early social scientists were confronted, it is also important to briefly explore the approaches which emerged during the Enlightenment in the late eighteenth century. The Enlightenment represents the culmination of the rational logic unleashed by Bacon and Descartes and applied to the study of humanity and society. You should bear in mind that Bacon emphasized careful empirical observation while Descartes emphasized the use of human reason to achieve a true account of nature. So whereas the early use of reason had only been accepted to the extent to which it was compatible with Christian beliefs, the experimental sciences had been tolerated to the extent that religious issues were avoided. The contributors to the Enlightenment, however, tackled religion head on and promoted an explicitly secular vision of scientific knowledge. In Roy Porter's account of *The Enlightenment*, this period 'saw the emergence of a secular intelligentsia large enough and powerful enough for the first time to challenge the clergy' (Porter, 1990, p.73). This shift is well expressed in the slogan coined by Kant, *sapere aude* ('dare to know' or have courage in your own understanding). In this

Transformations in the social structure and systems of knowledge coincided with the emergence of scientists, teachers and researchers who created new ways of thinking about nature and society.

way, the term 'enlightenment' represents not so much an immediate awakening from a deep sleep of ignorance and superstition, but rather an unfolding process of emerging self-consciousness as well as a historical progress towards the truth.

It is this preoccupation with self-consciousness which led to the characterization of the Enlightenment as one of a break or rupture with the past rather than as part of a process of gradual change. In addition, the main intellectual protagonists were seen as *philosophes*, 'men [*sic*] of letters as well as free thinkers', as cosmopolitan intellects with humanity in mind. This speaks volumes in indicating their pretensions to create and use universal knowledge for the benefit of humankind. The incredible certainty of belief in the benefits of scientific knowledge is a key feature of the Enlightenment. This movement in ideas coincided with the transformations in the social structures and social agents identified in the previous sections. Together, they ensured that the emerging circuit of knowledge within which science was understood came to fruition. The Enlightenment ensured that science, truth, reason and progress came to be seen as grounded through their role in serving the needs of humanity. In modernity, the new scientific **circuit of knowledge** came to be fully integrated.

In such a rapidly changing context, the traditional ways of doing things and the certainties of the past disappeared. The scientific goal of creating a universal system of human knowledge seemed to offer an alternative framework for the consolidation of knowledge. The tendencies towards the professionalization of knowledge fostered by Enlightenment thinkers hastened the process of disciplinary specialization as each field of knowledge was divided and subdivided. This process of professionalization also excluded women from authoritative positions in areas of life where they had previously been able to develop expertise, such as medicine. This chapter concentrates on those Enlightenment contributors who are directly relevant to the developments in social scientific practice identified in the following chapters. Particular attention is devoted to the ideas of Hume and Kant, who continue to serve as reference points in the social sciences today.

The emergence of scientific professions marks the start of the process of institutional and disciplinary specialization – hence scientific knowledge became fragmented and compartmentalized.

The Enlightenment drew upon the knowledge of mechanics in the scientific work of Bacon and Newton, as well as the empiricism developed during the previous century, outlined by the early modern philosopher John Locke (1632–1704). Locke's *Essay Concerning Human Understanding* (1690/1990) is not only the starting-point for the process which initiated the Enlightenment, for his writings also provide a foundation for the epistemological tradition of **empiricism** which has dominated much of social scientific thinking until the late twentieth century. The *Essay* is a relentless attack upon metaphysical arguments. **Metaphysics** literally means posing the existence of objects which cannot be established through observation (that is, objects which exist 'beyond the physical' realm). Metaphysical approaches also tended to endow natural objects with human properties. For instance, in experiments with liquids and pressure, early scientific texts suggested that 'nature abhors a vacuum' when explaining how vacuums could repel a mass. From this critique of metaphysics, two assumptions in the empiricist approach stand out:

- all ideas are derived from experience;
- no proposition (defined as a sequence of ideas) can be known to be true without reference to experience.

On the first assumption, Locke systematically approached each key idea in the study of humanity (such as identity, power, equality) in order to demonstrate that they were derived from experience. This ensured that, within Locke's system of ideas, any a priori propositions (that is, any ideas prior to experience) were merely trivial. Substantive knowledge, on the other hand, produced descriptions of the 'real empirical world'. This proved to be the foundation for the analytic/synthetic distinction within the twentieth-century approach to the philosophy of science known as 'logical positivism', which we explore in the next chapter. This approach assumed that **analytic** truths were true by definition, without any need to refer to experience, whereas **synthetic** truths could only be known through observation.

Don't worry about this distinction yet, just note its importance.

As in the natural sciences, there was some disagreement as to how to proceed in the development of scientific knowledge. Actually, it is useful to think about two Enlightenments, one which placed a greater emphasis upon the rational reconstruction of society (the Continental European or French Enlightenment) and another which stressed the importance of critical inquiry and had greater sense of doubt in the capacity of human beings to construct deliberately the 'good life' (the Scottish Enlightenment). The Continental Enlightenment popularized the new empirical scientific mentality through the use of human reason to create a better life for humanity. Therefore, the first owes more to Descartes and the second, with the emphasis on experience, is closer to Bacon.

The Enlightenment contained two broad traditions: the bold confident belief in the power of human reason in the continental Enlightenment and the critical cautious approach of the Scottish Enlightenment.

The co-ordination of the emerging empirical sciences was achieved through the work of Denis Diderot (1713–1784), who sought, with others, to catalogue the existing state of human knowledge by constructing what they hoped would be an indisputable reference point, the *Encyclopédie* (first published in 1751). Enlightenment sentiments often expressed the desire to combine the scientific method with anti-religious motivations and, in some cases, the expression of republican sympathies against the despotic absolute monarchies of Europe. Hence, from the start of the Continental Enlightenment, it was assumed that the use of reason and empirical knowledge would ensure that human progress was fostered and that the consequences of injustice and cruelty would be ameliorated. Above all, the Enlightenment made it possible to question and critically examine everything. Having said this, the Enlightenment thinkers did not themselves criticize certain foundations such as gender inequality, racial supremacy or the desire for objective and true knowledge. So they were quite selective in their choices of objects of analysis as well as in the foundations of knowledge that they sought to question.

Activity 2.4

Now turn to Reading B, 'The *Encyclopédie*', by Michael Bartholomew, Stephanie Clennell and Linda Walsh (1992). As you make your way through this reading about one of the most significant works during the Enlightenment, make notes in response to the following questions.

- How was knowledge classified in the *Encyclopédie*?

- Why did the contributors to the *Encyclopédie* (the *philosophes*) encounter resistance to their ideas?

When working through this reading you should focus upon the aims of the *philosophes* and how they placed human reason at the centre of their analysis (as well as what was pushed to 'the margins'). In particular, make notes on how they understood the idea of progress.

After answering these questions try the following exercise. Imagine that you are the editor of the *Encyclopédie* today. Allow yourself ten minutes to sketch out, in the same way as Figure 1 in the reading, a diagram which conveys the system of knowledge in the present as you see it. Think of ways of dividing and categorizing the forms of knowledge with which you are familiar. Remember, this does not have to be perfect but it should make you think.

Having done this, consider the following questions:

- What are the differences between your representation of human knowledge and the classification devices in the *Encyclopédie*?

- Have you organized the types of knowledge in a hierarchy and, if so, why? Does this suggest that one type of knowledge is more important than another type?

- Which types of knowledge have you grouped together? What characteristics do they have in common?

- Where have you distinguished between types of knowledge? Why are these different?

Finally, if you have not considered this in relation to the above questions, where have you placed the social sciences? Have you distinguished them from each other or placed them together with other forms of knowledge, such as natural science, the life sciences, ecology, the humanities and the arts? Consider your reasons for doing this.

The Enlightenment marks the final break between premodern and modern knowledge, for it transformed the way in which the system of knowledge related to the social structure and social agency. The operating principles of modern knowledge, as demonstrated in Figure 2.5 (the scientific knowledge circuit), were, from this point on, reinforced by a professional intellectual class in Western societies. This, in turn, was to modify progressively and at times transform the social structures of these societies. The theological values and beliefs, which had dominated for centuries, were gradually pushed to the margins and the authoritative knowledge which followed took on a more secular form as human reason replaced faith in divine truths. One word of caution before we fall into the trap of implying a march of progress: it is important to recognize that the transition was partial, uneven, patchy and, even today, incomplete. Indeed, the whole modern project itself has now become deeply questionable. Now, let's turn to the second strand of Enlightenment thought which emphasized a little more caution in considering human reason.

We return to these doubts and questions about modernity in Chapter 7.

Not all Enlightenment thinkers had such faith in the capacities of human reason to resolve all human problems. Others suggested that careful observation and a healthy sense of doubt in the capacity of humankind to identify the truth were much more important to scientific progress. In the Scottish Enlightenment, David Hume (1711–1776) extended the scepticism at work in Locke's empiricist approach to challenge the tendency of empiricists themselves to fall back upon ordinary and moral beliefs. For Hume, these beliefs were the products of psychological processes which created problems in the ways that causal relationships should be identified. He suggested that we can never be certain in assuming that the relationships in one set of particular instances, for which we have some empirical support, will be evident in circumstances which we have not yet experienced. In his *Enquiry Concerning Human Understanding* (1748/1984) he argued for a reconceptualization of the treatment of relations of cause and effect, suggesting that a correspondence or constant conjunction of two observable events, sustained over time, is a contingent occurrence and does not imply any necessary relationship between the two variables, nor is it based upon their properties.

Let's take an example of where a regular sequence of variables has been identified, such as the discovery that chimney-sweeps in the nineteenth century had a greater likelihood of developing lung cancer. Hume's position suggests that we should limit our explanations to a description of the association and not present this relationship as a natural necessity. Over time, the relationship between chimney-sweeps and lung cancer was sustained and corroborative relationships were identified with other industrial occupations, such as mining, or recreational pursuits, such as smoking. Nevertheless, Hume would insist that the scientific method should limit itself to claims that the relationships in question had been demonstrated only in so far as they had been empirically observed over time and in particular situations. For Hume, the uncertainty about our own knowledge is a condition of our existence. This uncertainty does not disappear when we either adopt an explanation based upon probability or when we resolve this in everyday life by simply expecting things to be predictable. For Hume, knowledge should never be taken for granted and scientists should always maintain a healthy sense of doubt. The most significant legacy of Hume's approach (even more so than with Locke) is the strong move against **metaphysics** as speculative and meaningless, as the following extract reveals:

> Does it contain any abstract reasoning concerning quantity or number? No. Does it contain any experimental reasoning concerning matter of fact and existence? No. Commit it then to the flames: for it can contain nothing but sophistry and illusion.
>
> (Hume, 1748/1984, p.173)

The consequence of this approach was to treat the use of human reason as somehow completely distinct from the observable evidence drawn from our senses. This obscures the important continuities between the positions involved. Immanuel Kant (1724–1804) attempted to steer a middle course between the two positions of **rationalism** and **empiricism**. In *Critique of Pure Reason* (1781/1987), he shows us how the imaginative constructions of the human mind are used to organize experience. For Kant, perceptions and impressions only make sense when placed within mental frameworks. Reason and observations work together. For Kant, the Enlightenment is a process of becoming enlightened. Even here, there is some ambiguity because the spirit of critical inquiry fostered by this transformation is in constant struggle with the dogmatic tendencies of the same processes which are part of the search for truth. These dogmas emerge from the belief that the latest scientific ideas must be true and, as such, cannot be questioned.

The Enlightenment is double edged for it contains a critical spirit and the aim of achieving certainty in one's own knowledge. Many Enlightenment thinkers believed that it was possible to use scientific knowledge to engage in social engineering. This was grounded upon the conception of popular sovereignty in Rousseau's account of the 'common good' in *The Social Contract* (1762), that it was possible to construct and reconstruct societies until we get it right. On the other hand, in the Anglo-American liberal tradition, which draws on the Scottish Enlightenment, there is a critical awareness of the limitations of human knowledge. This doubt about the rightness of one's own prescriptions created a preference for 'piecemeal' reform. Small changes in a step by-step-manner were seen as safer and easily rectified if something went badly wrong.

Activity 2.5

Now work through Reading C, 'What is the Enlightenment?', an extract from Robert Hollinger's discussion of Kant and recent interpretations of his legacy from *Postmodernism and the Social Sciences*. What do you consider to be the ethos of the Enlightenment?

You should focus on the conflicting legacies of Enlightenment thinking and how they relate to the construction of objective knowledge.

Early Enlightenment figures had engaged in the demolition of knowledge systems which depended upon faith rather than reason – later thinkers began to construct new ways of thinking about and understanding the social world.

The last phase of Enlightenment philosophers, notably Adam Smith (1723–1790), Adam Ferguson (1723–1816) and the Marquis de Condorcet (1743–1794), participated in the development of disciplinary boundaries between political economy, sociology and legal studies. Smith provided an account of the dynamic tendencies of the market economy. Ferguson established the idea of civil society as a legitimate object of analysis and Condorcet outlined the rational principles which operated in the legal system. All of these intellectual interventions represented an attempt to make sense of a new human condition. For these reasons, and as a consequence of the transformative processes identified earlier, the familiar objects of the social sciences (the market economy, the state or polity, civil society and the individual) came into academic discourse (Lukes, 1973b). This tendency was most vividly expressed in the proliferation of a wide range of seventeenth-century specialist journals and an active printing industry producing everything from the Bible to political pamplets and sex manuals. This ensured the emergence of a wider readership. It also indicates an improvement both in the living standards and in the level of literacy during the period. This period, too, witnessed the growth of the secular academic professions which developed and transmitted the new forms of knowledge. These male institutional groupings saw themselves as the custodians of the new system of knowledge and, as their confidence grew, came to replace the role of the theological scholars of the premodern societies.

Nevertheless, while the intellectuals and scientists of the Enlightenment popularized the rational acquisition of knowledge and the gathering of empirical evidence, there was no effort to separate the description of events from normative concerns (about what ought to be). While on the one hand they acknowledged the importance of distinguishing theory from observation, on the other hand the separation of facts and values (a distinctive feature of positivist conceptions of science) was more problematic. This was particularly the case for those in the continental European wing of this intellectual movement, for they embraced rationalism more wholeheartedly. The rationalist tendency assumed that scientific knowledge provided a solid foundation for the transformation of social institutions and the rational reconstruction of the social fabric in periods of change and dislocation. The legacy of the Enlightenment in the social sciences is a complex and contradictory one. On the one hand it established that human beings were the source of self-knowledge and generated a sense of the importance of certainty in our explanations. On the other hand, the ethos of the Enlightenment suggested that, in the name of critical inquiry, we could challenge the existing dogmas and preconceptions. It is the tension between these imperatives which have shaped the social sciences ever since.

The Enlightenment legacy is a contradictory one – it offers the possibility of absolute certainty (truth), but only through the continual criticism and questioning of all ideas and theories.

Summary

The Enlightenment enabled the study of social life to break away from religious interpretations and establish human beings as the active agency in constructing scientific knowledge.

The framework established by Bacon and Descartes, in which science sought to reconcile observation and reason, resurfaced in the debates over empiricism and rationalism, with Kant attempting a synthesis of the two.

The Enlightenment period established the foundations of the social scientific disciplines with which we are now familiar and had a formative effect upon their assumptions and methods.

Important differences remained between the confident optimism of the continental Enlightenment (Rousseau) and the more cautious sceptical approach developed during the Scottish Enlightenment (Hume and Smith).

The legacy of the Enlightenment is a contradictory one and established not only dogmatic conceptions of scientific inquiry but also the spirit of critical inquiry.

4   Conclusion: questions from the Enlightenment

The themes which constantly create difficulties for social scientists (at least those who treat their own research work uncritically) deserve a little further elaboration before moving on to the next chapter. Throughout this book, a great deal of emphasis is placed upon the problem of acknowledging both *theory* and *observation* in social research. A number of responses to this problem leap to mind. One could be emphasized to the exclusion of the other, reducing theory or observation to the status of a residual category, a passive concept with no independent role to play. For extreme rationalists, observations should not interfere with rational logic. For extreme empiricists, all thoughts are simply reflections or pictures of observed experiences and perceptions. Another common response is agnosticism, when social scientists simply pretend that it does not matter or suggest that it is impossible to know if observation comes before theory or vice versa. Such a 'chicken and egg' response is often used as a way of avoiding the issues raised rather than thinking them through. Finally, we can acknowledge some form of synthesis between human reason and empirical evidence. Again, the range of possibilities in attempting such a compromise is huge and the emphasis on the respective roles of the human imagination and empirical observations can vary.

These issues are often closely related to what has been called the 'mousetrap' of social scientific methodology, the fact–value controversy. We should ask ourselves, as social scientists, why it is important to study 'facts' and keep 'values' to one side. Is it because it helps an approach to sound 'authoritative', to be telling the 'truth'? Perhaps so, but is it realistic – are we just persuading ourselves that we can separate description from values and norms we hold about the social world? The examples of both value-free (or rather value-blind) research and explicitly normative approaches abound in social science. In some cases, normative approaches have succeeded in selling themselves as value free over long periods of time (as if they were simply describing the facts of the situation). This is demonstrated in Chapter 3 through a range of examples drawn from the history of social research, when attempts were made to portray social inequalities (along the lines of class, gender and ethnicity) as natural and inevitable.

Philosophers of social science have pinned high hopes on what knowledge can deliver. For some, science can provide a basis for gradual modification of social life, whereas others believe that scientific knowledge of the inner workings of society will prepare the way for wholesale social transformation and human emancipation. Both of those visions of the purpose of scientific knowledge are distinctly modern and have their roots in the complex social transformations and ideas we associate with the Enlightenment. In this chapter we have seen how transformations in the systems of knowledge have been closely related to changes in the social structure as well as to the transformation of the social agents who produce and transmit scientific knowledge within social institutions. Of particular note is the emergence of a system of knowledge composed of an integrated circuit of science, truth, reason, progress and humanity. In the next chapter we explore the ways in which social scientists put this approach into practice and, in so doing, find a way of negotiating the relationship between the dogmatic belief in certain knowledge and the spirit of critical inquiry.

READING A
The development of emotions: using experimental methods

Keith Oatley and Jennifer M. Jenkins

Let us now consider what information babies have and how early they perceive emotions in other people. What effects do other people's emotions have on the baby?

One of the challenges of developmental research is to find whether infants know something – when they are little one cannot ask them directly. A well-established method has been to use habituation, based on the finding that infants look at new patterns for longer than familiar ones. So if infants are presented with a happy face they look at it for a long time, then turn away. If presented with another happy face we might expect them only to look briefly because the expression is not new. But if they are now presented with a sad face, we might expect them to look at it for a long time, as this expression would be new for them. We are able to tell from this methodology what kinds of discrimination infants are able to make about emotions.

Field et al. (1982) used this method to see whether new born babies could discriminate emotional expressions. Infants who were 36 hours old saw an adult who made expressions of happiness, surprise, and sadness. The infant first habituated to one expression, then saw a new one. When the infant had habituated to the second expression, a third was presented. Infants did habituate and dishabituate to the three different expressions. They also showed some ability to imitate the expressions they saw. They showed more widening of the mouth and of the eyes in response to the adult's expression of surprise, more pouting of the lips in response to the adult's expression of sadness, and more widening of the lips in response to the adult's expression of happiness. ...

The conclusion was that before much opportunity for learning has occurred infants can discriminate among emotions shown by the same adult, and they can imitate some aspects of them. This implies a genetically specified mechanism of recognition and production of expressions. ... Remember too how subtle is the cue distinguishing a real smile involving contractions of the muscles round the eyes from a phony smile in which only the mouth moves.

Caron, Caron, and Myers (1985) have demonstrated that young infants probably cannot differentiate emotional expressions as such. They presented four- to seven-month-old infants with pictures of women showing angry and happy, toothy and non-toothy expressions [see Figure 1]. Infants could discriminate the toothy from the non-toothy faces, but if both angry and happy expressions showed teeth, they could not discriminate between them.

Figure 1   Stimuli used in the experiment of Caron, Caron and Myers (1985); children habituated to toothy anger did not dishabituate when new faces (on the right) showed toothy smiles.

Source: Professor A. J. Caron

Thus infants can recognize salient features of the face, but these features need not correspond to those that discriminate among emotions. ... When the experimenters investigated further by removing the voice and just showing the adults' faces, the five-month-olds could still discriminate happiness from sadness, but even at seven months they could not discriminate happiness and anger from faces alone. Hence, babies do not discriminate different emotional expressions made by different people before four months, and they probably discriminate emotion in the voice before they can make the same discrimination visually.

The voice is important for emotional communication, and Fernald (1989) has shown that adults use a different voice in talking to infants than in talking to adults. Infants pay more attention to this special voice of 'motherese' and show more positive emotion during speech intended for them. From five months they can discriminate affective messages indicating approval or prohibition, either in their parents' language, or in a language their parents do not speak. Infants showed more positive affect to approvals, and more negative affect to prohibitions (Fernald, 1993). ...

What is clear is that within their first few months babies do have skills of expression and perception suitable to their interpersonal needs. They can signal distress from the beginning, and soon afterwards they can signal happiness. They can also recognize aspects of their parent's emotional state, particularly from tones of voice. The stringent requirement that recognition must be demonstrated across several people is not necessary to most babies who have just one or two primary caregivers. ... By one year of age skills have developed that allow infants to take part in complex interactions. ...

The role of emotion in regulating interactions between mothers and young babies has also been demonstrated experimentally. Cohn and Tronick (1983) established the important role of emotion in mother–infant interaction by examining what happened when mothers showed no emotions to their babies. Twelve baby girls and twelve baby boys took part. The mother sat face to face with her infant who sat in an infant seat. In one condition (called flat affect) mothers were asked to direct their gaze at their infant, speak in a flat uninteresting monotone, keep their face expressionless, minimize body movement, and not touch their infant. This was contrasted with three-minute periods of the mother acting normally. Babies were videotaped. When mothers demonstrated flat affect, infants showed more wary expressions, made more protests and showed more brief positive expressions, were much more disorganized, and were more likely to enter a negative state. ... Emotions are communications: the infant signals to the parent, the parent signals to the infant, each alters behavior accordingly. ...

The sophistication in the communicative process can be seen in how anger is expressed in the first year. Sternberg and Campos (1990, pp. 247–82) examined where infants targeted their angry expressions. One-, four-, and seven-month-old babies were placed in an infant seat. To elicit anger, one investigator sat on one side of the child and restrained the child's arms. The mother sat on the child's other side. When the babies' arms were restrained, only the four- and seven-month-olds showed angry expressions. Whereas the four-month-olds look more at their restrainer or at the restrainer's hands, the seven-month-olds looked at their mothers after making facial expressions of anger. This suggests that the older infants were developing some notion of anger being used as a communication to their mothers. Vocalizations followed arm restrain immediately, before the negative facial expressions, as if vocal expressions were being used to capture attention. So, the expressions are not just read-outs of inner states: increasingly they are targeted towards specific people. The sequence of vocalizations and expression suggests that infants try to get the attention of the mothers, and then signal their distress.

In the first year not only do babies change their emotional signals as their relationships develop, but they acquire skills of using information from caregivers to alter their own actions, for instance if there is something ambiguous in the environment. These skills have been called 'social referencing'. For instance Sorce et al. (1985) exposed one-year-old babies to a visual cliff adjusted to a height that did not evoke clear avoidance. Seventy-four per cent of babies crossed the cliff when mothers showed a happy expression, but none crossed when their mother showed a fearful expression. [See Figure 2 overleaf.]

Infants older than 10 months, as compared with six- to nine-month-olds, are more likely to look at a parent's face for emotional information than at other parts of the body, and it is only the older babies who look at a parent before taking action ... Thus from the end of the first year babies begin to alter their own behavior on the basis of their parents' appraisals and emotions, and this influences how they themselves appraise and react to the world.

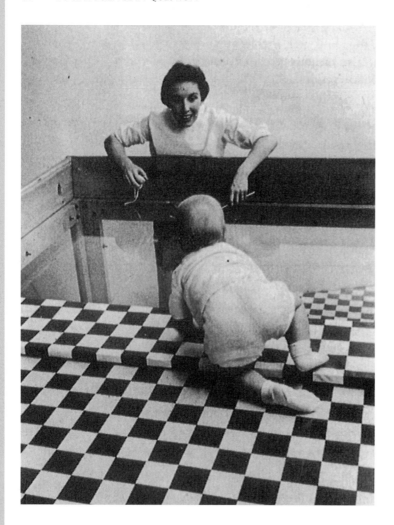

Figure 2 Picture of the visual cliff. What appears visually to the baby is a steep drop – notice the finer grain of the chequer-board pattern to the right of the baby's right knee – but a plate of thick glass supports the child safely when it crawls towards its mother (Gibson & Walk, 1960).

References

CARON, R.F., CARON, A.J. and MYERS, R.S. (1985) 'Do infants see facial expressions in static faces?' *Child Development*, **56**, pp.1552–60.

COHN J.F. and TRONICK, E.Z. (1983) 'Three-month-old infants' reaction to simulated maternal depression', *Child Development*, **54**, pp.185–93.

FERNALD, A. (1989) 'Intonation and communicative intent in mothers' speech to infants: Is the melody the message?', *Child Development*, **60**, pp.1497–1510.

FERNALD, A. (1993) 'Approval and disapproval: Infant responsiveness to vocal effect in familiar and unfamiliar languages', *Child Development*, **64**, pp.657–74.

FIELD, T., WOODSON, R., GREENBERG, R. and COHEN, D., (1982) 'Discrimination and imitation of facial expressions by neonates', *Science*, **218**, pp.179–81.

GIBSON, E.J. and WALK, R.D. (1960) 'The visual cliff', *Scientific American*, **202** (April), 65. Photo by William Vandivert.

SORCE, J.F., EMDE, R.N., CAMPOS, J. AND KLINNERT, M.D. (1985) 'Maternal emotional signaling: Its effects on the visual cliff behaviour of 1-year-olds', *Developmental Psychiatry*, **21**, pp.192–200.

STERNBERG, C.R. and CAMPOS, J.J. (1990) 'The development of anger expressions in infancy' in STEIN, N., LEVENTHAL, B.and TRABASSO, T.(eds.) *Psychological and biological approaches to emotion*, Hillsdale, N.J., Lawrence Erlbaum.

Source: Oatley and Jenkins, 1996, pp.166 (Figure 2), 171–6.

READING B
The *Encyclopédie*

Michael Bartholomew, Stephanie Clennell and Linda Walsh

If the spirit of the Enlightenment had to be represented by a single work, that work would be the seventeen volumes of text, and the eleven volumes of plates, of the *Encyclopédie*, published in France between 1751 and 1772. This vast encyclopedia was not a repository of safe, uncontentious information. On the contrary, it was polemical, tendentious, and sometimes scandalous. Its thousands of entries combined to promote a programme for the rational, scientific reconstruction of knowledge and of society. The man who launched the undertaking, Denis Diderot, summed up the bold programme:

> All things must be examined, debated, investigated without exception and without regard for anyone's feelings ... We must ride roughshod over all ancient puerilities, overturn the barriers that reason never erected, give back to the arts and sciences the liberty that is so precious to them.
> (Diderot, 1755)

Diderot was part of a remarkable intellectual movement which emerged in mid eighteenth-century France, and which was centred on Paris. The members of this loose, informal movement have become known as the *philosophes* [which] ... signifies a range of interests much wider than we would today recognize as philosophy. The *philosophes* were interested in politics, law, science, medicine, technology, religion, the arts, and public affairs generally. The *Encyclopédie* is the embodiment of their ideas. ...

All writers, rich and poor alike, had to be aware of censorship. By 1741 the royal government was employing 76 censors – 10 for jurisprudence, 10 for medicine, 10 for theology, 8 for mathematics, 2 for surgery, 1 for prints and the remaining 35 for literature, history and related subjects. By 1789 there were 178 censors. ... But the royal censors were not the only watchdogs; the clergy and the *parlements* (law-courts) also insisted on their rights to protect society from subversive literature. On several occasions, they persuaded the government into taking repressive action. ...

Why were the censors worried? The answer will emerge if we list the concerns of the *philosophes*. The list will show that while some of their activities posed no threat to the activities of the régime, the spirit of critical inquiry and the hatred of injustice that ran through their work gave no comfort whatsoever to church and state authorities.

First, and to the obvious annoyance – and sometimes fury – of the Catholic Church, the *philosophes* tended to be anti-clerical. They had no time for the church and its works [and] ... campaigned vigorously on behalf of victims of religious persecution. ...

Secondly, *philosophes* tended to regard knowledge based on experience as the best form of knowledge (as opposed to knowledge derived simply from authority, or from intuition or faith). They favoured explanations that ruled out the operation of immaterial agencies, be they 'the soul', or God. They recommended 'materialist' explanations of phenomena – explanations that derived from the conviction that the universe is composed simply and wholly of particles of matter, endlessly redistributing themselves, according to fixed scientific laws. The *philosophes* believed that science, which had received a tremendous boost from the work of their hero, Sir Isaac Newton, at the beginning of the century, would be a force for enlightenment and progress. In many ways, the *philosophes* regarded scientific knowledge as the supreme sort of knowledge: truths established by observation and experiment were secure. This confidence in the methods of science led to the belief that scientific methods could, and should, be applied not just to enterprises like astronomy and physics, but to medicine, the economy, the analysis of the human mind, to law, to the study of society and to practical technological enterprises. Above all, they were confident that the universe, including human beings, is explicable: it is not inherently mysterious, but susceptible to methodical, rational investigation.

Thirdly, *philosophes* were enthusiasts for technological and medical progress. They saw scientists, inventors and doctors as the curers of society's ills. The *Encyclopédie* has many articles on industrial machinery and processes, and on disease and surgery. ...

Fourthly, the *philosophes* were interested in legal and constitutional reform. They tended to be critical of the French absolutist régime and to be full of admiration for the British constitution with its entrenched liberties. ...

Fifthly, the *philosophes* championed reason, liberty and tolerance. Sometimes they spoke of equality, but it was of a theoretical sort: they were not democrats. They had no plans for the wholesale, egalitarian political reconstruction of society. ...

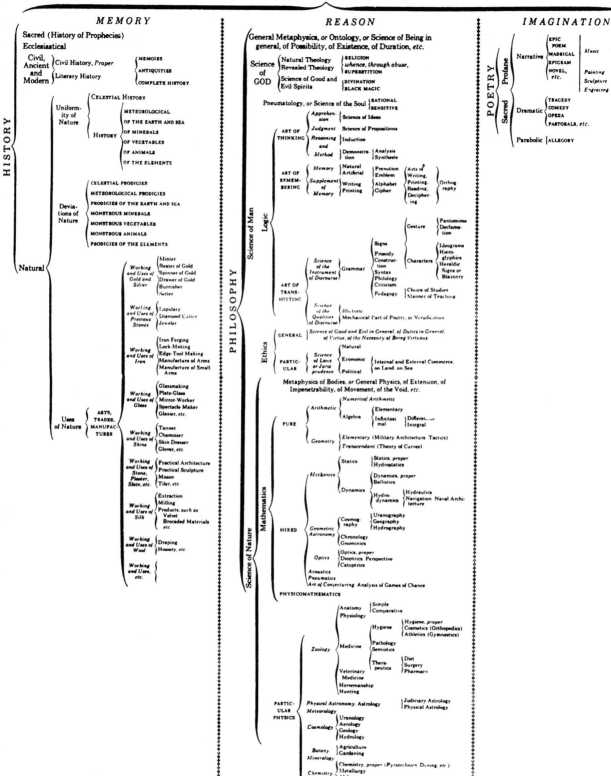

Figure 1   The knowledge system of the Enlightenment

Source: Roger Viollet

The *philosophes* were constantly in trouble with the authorities, and because of state censorship, had to be careful, in the *Encyclopédie*'s articles, to disguise their more radical opinions. For all that we must not think of the *Encyclopédie* as an 'underground' enterprise. It was launched with royal approval; and though it soon lost this approval and twice at least was officially suppressed, it always had strong supporters at court and was felt to be an important asset to France, both from a financial and a prestige point of view. ...

The *Encyclopédie* is arranged alphabetically, but in addition, as in any encyclopedia, some system of dividing up the various branches of knowledge was required. A highly elaborate diagram was printed, aiming to show how knowledge is acquired and stored [see Figure 1]. The system produces some peculiarities: 'History' for example, becomes a sub-branch of 'Memory', and biography is excluded. Shakespeare appears only in the entry on 'Stratford'. But the system does succeed in making the questions of the acquisition and classification of knowledge – principally 'knowledge of nature' and 'knowledge of Man' – central. At the same time, and here the *philosophes*' hostility to religion reveals itself, it pushes all theological questions out to the margins. In medieval classifications of knowledge, theology is at the centre: in the *Encyclopédie*, it is at the margin. ... Diderot, in his important article *Encyclopedia*, describes the *Encyclopédie* as intended to survive a revolution – to be a work from which, should some cataclysm overtake the world, all human knowledge could be reconstructed. And he says that any work of this type needs to be produced by a group of private individuals, 'a society of men of letters and artisans'.

Reference

DIDEROT, D. (ed.) (1755) *Encyclopédie*, vol.5, Paris.

Source: Bartholomew et al., 1992, pp.12–17.

READING C
What is the Enlightenment?

Robert Hollinger

The European Enlightenment of the 18th century marks a high point in Western history. Although its roots go much farther back in Western history and it continued to develop long after the 18th century, a program for improving human life was worked out. The *Enlightenment project*, as it has recently been called, is based on the assumption that ignorance is the basic source of all human misery and that the elimination of ignorance, and its replacement with scientific knowledge, would pave the way for endless human progress.

The basic ideas of the Enlightenment codified major developments in early modern European thought and provided a rallying point for future cultural and political struggles. The Enlightenment project can be expressed in several claims.

1. The epistemological unity of humankind is the claim that everything worth knowing can be unified into a set of beliefs that all human beings can rationally assent to and rationally accept on the basis of a universally valid set of methodological assumptions.

2. The moral unity of humankind is the claim that universal rational moral principles are binding on all rational beings everywhere and provide guides and standards for conduct and judgement.

3. Any beliefs, values, claims, or factors that contradict or impede these two (connected) goals is an obstacle to human progress and happiness. Only a society based on science and universal values is truly free and rational; only its inhabitants can be happy.

4. The truth shall make us free. The more we know about ourselves and the world, the better human life will become, because ignorance is the cause of unhappiness and immorality.

... Nietzsche criticizes the idea that truth, knowledge, and rationality are more important than anything else. When carried to extremes, this idea destroys what is most important in life, even life itself. Indeed, what is most important and valuable may not be 'provable' by science. Science itself may rest on faith. Nietzsche believes that the Enlightenment can be very destructive, perhaps even irrational, if it destroys everything that fails to meet its own standards, especially if those standards cannot themselves be proven.

Thus, there are two conflicting perspectives: The view that Enlightenment's goals are rational and enhance human life versus the view that the Enlightenment's goals are matters of faith that destroy life and all that we hold dear and can do nothing but destroy. What is of most value may be what cannot be proven, and what is most important is rooted in those very factors that the Enlightenment sees as the source of misery: culture, traditions, customs, myths. Is one of these views right? Are both of these views wrong? Are they both too one-sided? ...

Kant's seminal essay 'An answer to the Question: "What is Enlightenment?"' has become the canonical text of recent discussions. ... [This] focuses on the idea of 'maturity', which is glossed as the use of reason. 'The motto of Enlightenment is therefore *Sapere aude*! Have courage to use your own understanding!' Kant believes that the masses have not yet developed to the point where they can make use of this advice; hence, we do not live in an enlightened age but rather in an age of Enlightenment. Education of the masses by the few 'guardians' who have thrown off the 'yoke of immaturity' and achieved the proper level of 'understanding' define the ethos of the times as one of Enlightenment, even though society has a long way to go to achieve progress ...

Modernity as a philosophical concept

Bacon's notion of knowledge as power, of putting nature on the rack, marks a significant point of departure from the ancients, for whom knowledge of nature consisted of passive understanding of a world that cannot be changed. For Bacon, knowledge is tantamount to control and prediction, so knowledge can increase only as humankind's power over nature does. Bacon's idea that knowledge exists to promote the relief of the human estate is the first step in the direction of technocracy, scientific utopianism, and social engineering; the reduction of the practical and moral to the technical; and thus, arguably, the beginning of modern instrumental or technological rationality. ...

Descartes was the architect of the modern idea that 'method' is the road to knowledge and truth. He canonized Galileo's notions of objectivity and subjectivity for the modern world. One of the ramifications of this view is the idea of value freedom in the social sciences: Whatever can be known must be proven by a 'rational, objective' method. Value claims cannot be so proven; therefore value judgements do not constitute knowledge or belong in the realm of science. ... Distinctions between types of value judgements were made by later writers. The outcome is that ... value judgements [of one type are] subjective and belong outside the sciences, even the social sciences. Strictly speaking, according to this view, interpretations ... are also subjective, or at least untestable, and they, too, have no place in science. ...

For Descartes, the 'objective' is essentially that part of the world that can be described in what he calls 'nature's language', the language of mathematical physics. Nothing else is objective. Perceptions, values, interpretations, perspectives, and all other mental languages cannot describe objective reality. ... Objective reality, ... causes our individual perceptions, which are subjective and vary from person to person. Only the quantifiable data of physical reality are objective. To discover the truths about this reality, we need a method, which must itself be rational and objective, where objective now means disinterested, not tainted by values, interpretations, perspectives, or psychological or other factors. ...

For Descartes, only rigorous methodological objectivity permits the acquisition of objective knowledge and truth. But to achieve this result, the human enquirer must become objective, and the human body and all subjective qualities must be set aside in the process. Objectivity requires a God's-eye view of the world and ourselves. ... Descartes thinks that one can salvage religion, morality, and even social customs and traditions from total destruction, but his arguments reflect internal inconsistency, if not disingenuousness. Later writers have fewer qualms about eliminating customs and values that could not be reduced to science or scientific method. Despite Kant's valiant efforts to reconcile science, religion, morality, and ... nature, attempts within modernity to unify human experiences have failed. The dualisms of facts and values, the objective and subjective, science and the rest of culture, and reason and emotions have persisted.

Source: Hollinger, 1994, pp.7–9, 21–5.

Chapter 3
The Emergence of
the Social Sciences

Contents

1	Introduction	75
1.1	Defining positivism	77
2	**Positivism and the foundations of the social sciences**	**78**
2.1	Comte and the positivist philosophy	78
2.2	Positivism, utilitarianism and human happiness	82
2.3	Durkheim and the positivist science	83
3	**The normal and the pathological: positivism in practice**	**85**
3.1	Science and 'race'	86
3.2	Science and crime	92
4	**Positivism, language and science**	**97**
4.1	The logical positivist approach	97
4.2	Practical implications of logical positivism	101
4.3	The standard positivist approach	102
4.4	Practical implications of standard positivism	104
5	**From the problem of induction to the falsificationist alternative**	**105**
5.1	Situating Popper	106
5.2	Conjectures and refutations: Popper's falsificationist solution	107
6	**Positivist and empiricist approaches on the economy**	**112**
7	**Conclusion: the common foundations of empiricism**	**116**

Reading A
    The positive philosophy and scientific laws *Auguste Comte*   119
Reading B
    The principle of utility *Jeremy Bentham*   120
Reading C
    Samuel George Morton – empiricist of polygeny *Stephen Jay Gould*   121
Reading D
    The intelligence of American negroes *Hans Eysenck*   123
Reading E
    The young delinquent *Cyril Burt*   124
Reading F
    The professional stranger *Eileen Barker*   126

I   Introduction

As you saw in Chapters 1 and 2, the creation of objective knowledge has been a central goal of science for quite a while. This chapter explores attempts by social scientists to create 'objective knowledge' about the social world. A special emphasis is placed upon the way in which our assumptions about the construction of knowledge have implications for the collection and interpretation of empirical evidence. There are seven sections in this chapter. The first two examine the ideas associated with positivism, particularly the six general assumptions which underpin this approach. We see how positivism played an important role in generating claims about objective knowledge in the social sciences. Most significantly, the positivist approach draws a great deal from the Enlightenment thinkers outlined in Chapter 2, especially in the way in which they placed a stress upon the search for certainty and universal explanations. Section 3 focuses upon how the construction of objective knowledge or 'hard science' has been, and can be, misleading. Two case studies, on scientific racism and positivist criminology, are used to demonstrate how the values and prejudices of social scientists can masquerade as social facts in scientific accounts of social differences and in the relationship between normal and abnormal behaviour.

In sections 4 and 5 we see how important it is to distinguish positivism from the broader approach of empiricism, by focusing upon the differences between the positivist approaches in the twentieth century and the falsificationist method developed by Karl Popper. Section 6 explores one social science discipline, economics, in order to demonstrate how the empiricist approaches identified in this chapter appear within a particular field of human knowledge. Economics is a good example; first, because of its associations with objective accounts of social relations and, second, because of the clearly identifiable positions which exist within economic methodology. Finally, in section 7 we return briefly to the six general assumptions of positivism to highlight the differences between empiricism and positivism.

Positivism develops ideas established during the Enlightenment, but ...

In Chapter 2 we looked at the origins of scientific thinking and the ways in which these ideas were applied to the study of social phenomena during the Enlightenment. In this chapter we consider the legacy of the Enlightenment in explaining and understanding social life. The most significant feature of social science in the last two centuries has been the rise to dominance and the subsequent fall of the positivist tradition. Positivism has been increasingly questioned since the middle of the twentieth century. Even if positivism is something that many social re-

... take care, positivism means different things to different social scientists.

searchers would like to forget, it is hard to imagine any social scientific approach which does not, even now, draw from or develop its ideas in opposition to the positivist approach. The label of positivism has been applied to a wide variety of approaches in the social sciences, all of which claimed to offer a 'scientific' or **objective** picture of the social world and its constituent parts. As a result, the term 'positivism' has become very ambiguous and often contains different assumptions for different people. To make matters worse, 'positivism' is often used as a synonymous term for 'empiricism', but it is important to recognize that empiricism is a broad church and that it is possible to be empiricist without being positivist.

	Definition	**Implication**
Naturalism	Positivists are committed to naturalism, the idea that it is possible to transfer the assumptions and methods of natural sciences to the study of social objects, often referred to as the 'unification of method'.	This means that you would study behaviour, institutions and society in much the same way as studying, for example, chemical processes, hydraulic systems, geological structures. The closed system of a scientific experiment is often taken as a model for knowledge production in the social sciences.
Phenomenalism	Phenomenalism is the assumption that only knowledge gained through observed experience can be taken seriously. If something cannot be directly experienced it is said to be **metaphysical** – beyond our physical senses.	If we cannot touch it, see it, hear it, taste it or smell it, then an object cannot be said to exist except in so far as it is an idea of something. For example, 'happiness' is something which exists only in people's minds and cannot be directly physically experienced.
Nominalism	Nominalism shares with phenomenalism the argument that concepts must be based upon experience, but it also asserts that concepts have no use other than as names. Words are seen as pure reflections of things. It is, of course, very difficult to do this because the words we use are usually far more than simple descriptions.	All concepts or ideas which are not directly experienced through the senses are meaningless. In a strict sense, concepts such as the 'unconscious' and 'capitalism' are all names for things which we can't directly experience through our senses. Therefore, by this criteria, such concepts are meaningless.
Atomism	Atomism is a particular approach to the definition of objects. Atomism states that the objects of scientific study are discrete, that is, the objects cannot be broken down into any smaller parts. These objects act as the foundations of a scientific study. Collective objects are thus the sum total of their smaller atomic components.	When approaching any field of study, atomists look for the smallest observable units which cannot be broken down any further. When studying a society the most discrete unit is often taken as the individual. Atomistic explanations of society would start with the individual and regard society as no more than a collection of individuals.
Scientific Laws	The purpose of science is to develop laws. To develop a scientific law you start from the observation of a particular set of objects and look for regularities. The regular appearance of two or more things together, or in some kind of sequence, can be called an **empirical regularity.** This is sometimes described as a constant conjunction of events. You then explore whether the same regularities occur in other similar circumstances. A scientific law is a general statement which describes and explains empirical regularities which occur in different places and at different times.	The search for scientific laws involves finding empirical regularities, such as the well known example of smoking tobacco and developing lung cancer. Social scientists adopting this assumption would look for empirical regularities between, say, • poverty and crime, • the money supply and price inflation, • school class sizes and literacy levels, • gender and earnings, and so on. In practice, one is usually taken as the cause of the other. For instance, high levels of poverty are seen as a causal factor in crime levels.
Facts/Values	Facts and values are seen as distinct. Only facts can be regarded as scientific. Facts can be empirically verified, that is, observed, measured and explained by reference to observational evidence. Values involve subjective assessments and claims about what ought to be. Thus values cannot be observed, measured or explained.	Social scientists accepting these assumptions would distinguish scientific statements, which describe what is the case, from unscientific value-laden statements. For example, a measure of the number of homeless is often viewed as a fact whereas the statement that homelessness is a social evil is a value statement.

assumptions of positivism

| naturalism |
| phenomenalism |
| nominalism |
| atomism |
| scientific laws |
| facts/values |

When this box appears, the shaded portions will indicate which assumptions are at work.

Figure 3.1   The six general assumptions of positivism.
The terms in bold are also defined in the glossary.

As a result, the potential for conceptual confusion is very large, so this chapter offers a guide to the issues raised by the positivist and empiricist approaches within the social sciences.

1.1 Defining positivism

In Chapter 2 you discovered that the idea of science is closely associated with authoritative knowledge. Positivism is, perhaps, the most important attempt to generate authoritative knowledge about the social world. Actually, it is possible to define 'positivism' in many different ways. Nevertheless, it can be argued that there are three generations of positivists within the social sciences, as the social theorist William Outhwaite has usefully suggested:

See sections 2 and 3.

- the positivist traditions established in the nineteenth century (Auguste Comte, Herbert Spencer and some interpretations of Émile Durkheim);

See section 4.

- the logical positivism of the Vienna Circle (A.J. Ayer and Rudolf Carnap) in the early twentieth century;

- the 'standard positivist account', developed in the post-war period in the West, (associated with Carl Hempel) which emphasized the importance of value freedom, hard facts and prediction as a basis for offering policy proposals for governments, businesses and other private institutions.

(adapted from Outhwaite, 1987, pp.5–8)

Although there are three generations of positivist thinkers, it is important to establish what they hold in common. Norman Blaikie in *Approaches to Social Enquiry* (1993) suggests that certain shared assumptions can be identified without overlooking the significant differences between them. These six general assumptions, presented in Figure 3.1, are not solely associated with positivism but only positivism puts them together in this unique way. In particular, positivist science has a preference for empirical data which can be observed and measured so that the various component parts can be compared for their relative frequency. On the basis of such quantitative evidence, it is possible to generate law-like regularities which may then be generalized to other situations. Each of the six assumptions is explored in the sections that follow by reference to different forms of positivism.

Summary

Positivist approaches to the social sciences claim the label scientific, for they assume things can be studied as hard facts and the relationships between these facts established as scientific laws. For positivists, such laws have the status of truth and social objects can be studied in much the same way as natural objects.

2 Positivism and the foundations of the social sciences

As you will be aware from Chapter 2, the Enlightenment introduced new ways of thinking about the natural and social worlds, and that, after the Enlightenment, the world could no longer be explained as a manifestation of some divine plan in which the Church provided an authoritative account of both the natural and the social worlds in the name of God. Human beings were seen increasingly as the originators of knowledge. This means that instead of simply describing and clarifying what God had created, knowledge was seen as human-made and constantly open to question. Critical inquiry came to be seen as essential to human progress. The social transformations of the seventeenth and eighteenth centuries also produced a whole series of new objects of analysis, including 'society', the 'economy', the 'mind', the 'modern state', the 'individual' and the 'realm of ideas', and these objects have become the focus of analysis for the social sciences.

Post-Enlightenment knowledge is increasingly seen as human-made, rather than divine in origin.

The commitment to science as a means of promoting human progress is evident in the writings of Antoine Destutt de Tracy, a French rationalist philosopher working in the midst of the French Revolution. De Tracy proposed the foundation of the discipline of 'ideology' as the 'scientific study of ideas' as early as 1797. In this way, it was argued, science could reveal how society worked and, with this in mind, a rational social order could be sketched out, planned and implemented. Science, defined as the pursuit of truth, offered a means of social engineering so that social evils, such as conflict and war, could be eliminated and human progress achieved. Thus the choice of progress or catastrophe was seen as resting in human hands. In the context of the maelstrom of changes accompanying the emergence of the modern world, it was not altogether surprising that the certainties of religious faith were replaced by the belief in the certainties of science.

Rational scientific knowledge of human societies raises the possibility of improving the human condition.

This section highlights three approaches from the nineteenth century (Outhwaite's first generation of positivists) which have had an impact on contemporary social science. The positivism of Auguste Comte, the evolutionary utilitarianism of Herbert Spencer and the study of the social facts advocated by Émile Durkheim, each in their different ways, linked science to progress. You should bear in mind that each of these earlier positivist approaches illustrates some, but not all, of the six general assumptions of positivism identified in Figure 3.1.

2.1 Comte and the positivist philosophy

The most influential early positivist was Auguste Comte (1798–1857). Comte was a 'man with a mission', for he believed it was possible to reconstruct human knowledge in order to build a better society. He brought together the search for truth (from modern science) with the faith in progress which has been a key feature of Western thinking since the Enlightenment. For Comte, the Enlightenment was the last step in clearing away the mistaken assumptions of premodern knowledge systems. In so doing, human beings were placed at the centre of knowledge production.

Comte

naturalism
phenomenalism
nominalism
atomism
scientific laws
facts/values

However, Comte believed that one task remained, the construction of a new system of knowledge which could offer new certainties and new truths. Although Comte seems to have been associated more often with sociology, his work was also a crucial step in the development of both economics and political science.

For Comte, knowledge was characterized by change and development. He argued that earlier fictitious or religious forms of knowledge, based upon superstitions, were in decay. In fact, they had already given way to philosophical criticisms which were to stimulate the Enlightenment. Comte defined this critical stage as the period of metaphysics, but he argued that it was destructive rather than constructive, for although the Enlightenment had usefully challenged the prevailing way of thinking, it did not provide a suitable alternative to religion in a way which secured the stability of the social order. He proposed his own brand of scientific certainty to fill the vacuum left by the collapse of traditional and religious ideas. In order to find a replacement for 'divine truths', Comte looked to the natural sciences to establish a new foundation for objective knowledge. To emphasize this, he called his approach to the study of society 'social physics' and believed that it was possible to discover the scientific laws that governed social life in just the same way as laws had been identified in Newtonian physics, such as the physical laws of motion and light.

Through the use of the scientific method, as he defined it, Comte sought to restore order to his own society, and heal the wounds of the war, destruction and disorder which had characterized Europe since the French Revolution of 1789. When so much was uncertain, science seemed to provide a new way of establishing fixed and solid knowledge which could act as a means of reassurance. By looking at Comte's scientific vision we can see that the emergence of the social sciences was closely tied to his beliefs about what constituted a civilized society. Indeed, Comte envisaged that *social physics* could fill the gap left by the decline of faith and provide a new force for social cohesion or 'civic morality'. Figure 3.2 demonstrates how Comte saw each stage in the development of knowledge as grounded in a particular social order.

Scientific knowledge was seen as a way of identifying new foundations and new certainties in modern societies.

Comte is adopting the assumption of naturalism.

See Chapter 2, section 2.1 on Newton's view of science.

Comte sees science as a way of addressing human needs.

	I	II	III
Stage of knowledge	fictitious knowledge	metaphysical knowledge	scientific knowledge
Foundation of beliefs	faith and custom	philosophy	rational logic
Social base	family	state	humanity

Figure 3.2 Comte's three stages of scientific development and the corresponding bases of the social order.

With the passing of the social orders based upon the authority of the household and the authority of the state, the time was ripe for a new social order which could deliver the needs and desires of humanity as a whole. In the same way, fictitious and metaphysical knowledge would give way to science (Bryant, 1985). Positivism has now all but disappeared, but the link between scientific knowledge and meeting the needs and wants of human beings is its most tangible legacy.

Comte sought to build upon the established disciplines of the natural sciences constructing a hierarchy of disciplines which reflected the degree to which the forms of knowledge in question had succeeded in overcoming pre-scientific stages of development (stages I to II in Figure 3.2). He argued that astronomy, physics, chemistry and physiology had already moved through these stages. For example, in astronomy the fictitious stage can be seen in the belief that the Earth was the centre of the universe, the meta-physical stage endowed the planets with emotional qualities, and scientific astronomy marked a definite break by providing objective scientific laws which explain the solar system. Comte believed that his own project of social physics represented the beginning of just such a movement in social science taking it from the second to the third stage. In this way, he believed that the processes at work in society could be understood and explained with the same clarity as the scientific theories of planetary orbits around the Sun. For Comte, social science should attempt to emulate the progress of the natural sciences and develop scientific laws.

Comte is assuming that scientific laws are the goal of intellectual inquiry, and that science involves moving beyond metaphysics.

Activity 3.1

Turn now to Reading A, 'The positive philosophy and scientific laws', which is an extract from Auguste Comte's *The Positive Philosophy* (1853/ 1871). Make notes on Comte's account of the emergence of the positive science and try to answer the following questions:

- How does Comte see 'progress' in relation to scientific knowledge?
- What is the role played by statics and dynamics in the study of social facts?

You may find it useful to glance back at the circuit of knowledge in Chapter 2 (Figure 2.5) and look for the connections which Comte emphasizes as important when studying society.

Social scientists often distinguish between the analysis of social structure and the analysis of social change and, in Comte's work, we can see how this came about. Comte's positive science sought to identify the laws of *social statics* and of *social dynamics*. Once we identify these laws, he argued, social engineering was a real possibility. The *laws of social statics* were an attempt to draw upon the closest natural science to human existence, the study of human anatomy. The comparison of society to a living body served as a powerful analogy during the early development of social science. In doing this, Comte provided a way of identifying the internal operation of an existing set of social institutions and the conditions which generated co-operation. The *laws of social dynamics* offered a means of accounting for evolutionary change and the complex processes at work in the development of European societies.

See Figure 2.7 'The anatomy class' in Chapter 2.

Positivism established the tendency to view scientific laws of change as separate from scientific laws of social relations.

The most important conceptual legacy of Comte is this distinction between *statics* and *dynamics*: social, political and economic structures and relations at a given time are different from the processes which impact upon these structures. Fitting these two dimensions together is still a problem for contemporary social scientists. For instance, the models of economics are often static models which do not recognize process and change except as a series of time-slices (a sequence of static states). This can be seen in the case of the concept of equilibrium in a market (where supply and demand for a specific commodity are balanced at a given price). This model of the market is limited because it assumes that the values of given products (i.e. prices) do not change over time, making the model unrealistic and raising questions about its usefulness as a representation of the economy. Any approach which attempts to explain the working of the real economy (or any other object in social science) is subject to severe limitations unless it succeeds in integrating both of these dimensions. Similarly, in psychology, the treatment of the personality as having fixed characteristics which do not evolve in response to experiences and social interaction is likely to prove inadequate when applied to the study of human beings throughout their lifespan. It is not just in the so-called 'hard' social sciences that we find this issue. In the field of cultural studies a great deal of emphasis is placed upon the study of language. The key foundational work in the study of language is Ferdinand de Saussure's *Course in General Linguistics* (1916/1959). This emphasizes the distinction between synchrony (the structure of language at a moment in history) and diachrony (the processes through which meaningful language systems change) – a direct application of the static/dynamic distinction to the form and development of language systems.

You will come back to this when you read Chapter 6, section 2 on the relationship between structure and language.

So far we have concentrated upon the legacy of Comte's positivist approach for contemporary social science. Nevertheless, it is also interesting and useful to look at how Comte analysed his own society. By situating Comte, that is, by locating Comte's work historically and socially, we can see how he was responding to a particular set of problems and issues, namely the 'disorder' of European societies in the late eighteenth and early nineteenth centuries. While this does not invalidate the uses of Comte's ideas, it should raise questions about why we find elements of his works within the social sciences today. We can gain a better insight into the implications of this approach by looking at the way in which he characterizes the laws of statics and dynamics in European societies. Comte concentrates upon the role of military conquest and the annexation of territory in accounting for the laws of *social dynamics*. In addition, when defining his object of analysis in the laws of *social statics*, he treats humanity as if it is solely constituted by the 'white race'. Such arguments are a reflection of Comte's own cultural values and the broader cultural assumptions of European societies in the nineteenth century. The focus upon conquest and annexation between nations was central to this period in a similar way to the way in which concern about globalization affects social scientific research today.

The exclusive focus on the 'white race' was also a common feature of early social science, although this was often left as an implicit assumption. Since the standard of living in European societies in Comte's lifetime was grounded in colonial conquest, it should not be surprising that the knowledge constructed, in many subtle ways, not only justified but actually celebrated the dominance of European societies over other societies. This

Eurocentric orientation, and the exclusion of non-European peoples from explicit consideration, reveals the historically and socially specific content of Comte's work. We address this issue in more detail in section 3 when we consider scientific racism. The impact of Comte's positivism can be seen in the assertion that it was possible to study facts independently of values, even though he clearly undermines his own claim to have achieved this in his own work. Nevertheless, the distinction between facts and values was to have a profound effect on the development of social scientific disciplines, regardless of whether Comte's adoption of the organic analogy (treating society as if it worked like a body) offered a feasible working model. While Comte made an explicit link between knowledge and human progress, he left one question unresolved: how was it possible to measure human progress? This is the concern of the next section.

In positivism, values were often portrayed as facts even though this approach claimed to eliminate values, prejudice and common sense from scientific knowledge.

2.2 Positivism, utilitarianism and human happiness

In the later nineteenth century, the organic analogy was more systematically developed by Herbert Spencer (1820–1903). Spencer was a Victorian liberal who drew upon both the ideas of utilitarian liberalism and Charles Darwin's evolutionary theory to provide a scientific explanation of the industrial and trading success of Britain during one of the most sustained periods of high growth in Western history. Spencer's legacy can be seen in the association of positivism with justifications of inequality. Spencer based his approach upon the utilitarian ideas of Jeremy Bentham (1748–1832), who had constructed a way of measuring human **progress**. So, to understand Spencer we must first explore the ideas of utilitarianism in a little more detail.

Spencer

naturalism
phenomenalism
nominalism
atomism
scientific laws
facts/values

Bentham devised a means of calculating the consequences of various courses of action in terms of utility – that is, the satisfaction of our preferences. The assumptions underlying this model are revealing. Bentham characterized human beings as essentially pleasure seeking or pain avoiding. He also endowed them with the capacity to make rational choices which would maximize pleasure and minimize pain (which he referred to as the 'felicific calculus'). This is the foundation of the framework which social scientists now call cost–benefit analysis and which established the guiding principles of contemporary economics, political science and some branches of psychology. In addition, Bentham provided a powerful and compelling basis for relating social science to policy making.

Human progress is understood here as the consequence of changes which overall produce more benefits than costs.

Using Bentham's felicific calculus, it was then possible, once the likely consequences of a policy were established, to advise politicians on which policy would promote 'the greatest good for the greatest number'. By securing the goals of human happiness and collective welfare, this approach also offers a way of delivering human progress. Because of its focus upon effects rather than causes, utilitarianism is often described as consequentialism. In addition, this approach treated collective bodies as if they were simply the aggregate (the sum total effect) of the observable actors involved. The economy is thus an aggregate of individuals, firms and households; the political process is the aggregate of voters in elections, and parties and pressure groups (which are aggregates of their members) in between elections; and so on.

The utilitarian approach places special emphasis upon the assumption of atomism. Spencer adopts the general assumptions of positivism, except for nominalism.

Turn to Reading B, drawn from 'Of the principle of utility' from Jeremy Bentham's *An Introduction to the Principles of Morals and Legislation* (1824/1987).

• Identify the first seven principles of Bentham's calculus for ensuring that the common welfare is maximized. You may also wish to consider how accurately this approach describes human decision making.

This reading is something of a manifesto for establishing how to go about the activity of social inquiry as well as how human knowledge fits into the needs of policy makers. Remember that social science has always existed with the purpose of making social conditions better. The question you should ask yourself is whether this is the best way of doing so. (Whatever your response, also ask yourself why you made this judgement.)

Further uses of utilitarianism are developed in Chapter 4.

There are many ways of applying this approach; for the moment we concentrate on Spencer's use of utilitarianism. Spencer portrayed the market system, through which individuals made their pleasure-seeking and pain-avoiding choices, as an evolutionary mechanism operating along the lines of Darwin's principle of natural selection. So, Spencer argued that the organization of society can only be analysed in terms of the consequences of human actions, and that the flow of benefits and costs in society reflected the 'survival of the fittest'. We can trace the consequences of these assumptions in Spencer's approach to social inequalities. The hierarchical organization of society becomes the logical consequence of competitive processes in the market economy, implying that those at the top are the fittest and those at the bottom are the least fit. It was also common in this period of imperialist expansion to categorize social groups in racial terms, both externally in the colonies and internally when considering the lower classes, the peasantry or marginalized ethnic groups. Thus, in the same way as Comte, Spencer's work can be seen as a rationalization of the eugenicist concerns with racial degeneration rather than with the objective study of facts. When we situate social scientists and philosophers of social science, we can then begin to see how the cultural values of the time and place flow into academic writing.

Durkheim

naturalism
phenomenalism
nominalism
atomism
scientific laws
facts/values

2.3 Durkheim and the positivist science

Now we return to an old favourite. The social scientist most often given the label of positivist is Émile Durkheim (1858–1917), although it is far from clear that his approach can be categorized so easily. For the time being, let's treat him as a positivist to keep things straightforward. Above all, Durkheim argued that each discipline had its own distinctive (set of) object(s) of analysis and that these objects could be studied in the same way as the natural sciences, as 'social facts'. In particular, Durkheim pioneered the careful and systematic study of empirical evidence, which we tend to attribute to scientific approaches in the study of society. In *The Rules of Sociological Method* (1895/1982), Durkheim recognized that the way in

which the object of analysis in each discipline was defined had an important effect on the way the discipline was constructed, and how this limited
the scope of inquiry, that psychologists should stick to the mind, economists to the economy, and so on. In the case of sociology, with society as the
object, he argued that the complexity of social relations demanded greater
care in the treatment of empirical evidence than was common in his day. He
attempted to establish relations of cause and effect between variables which
tend to occur in the same place and time (empirical regularities). In *Suicide*
(1897/1952), Durkheim employed the comparative-historical method:
suicide rates were compared for different countries and regions and across
different social groups, as well as over time. This enabled him to establish
the correlations or **empirical regularities** which could be taken seriously in
a scientific account of suicide.

There are considerable problems in trying to establish relations of cause and
effect between things which tend to correspond in a regular way. How we
draw connections depends upon whether we find an explanation convincing or plausible. Durkheim argued that the study of suicide offered a way of
clarifying this problem. Suicide rates are relatively consistent over time in
different locations and different groups. Since, in each year, suicides involve different people, Durkheim argued that it was safe to assume that an
explanation could be found by looking for an external cause which tended
to coincide with the suicide rates. Conventional wisdom at the time placed
the causes of suicide (defined as an irrational act) within the constitution of
the individuals concerned. Unlike crime, where the same people can com-
mit the same action again over time and with the same motives, in the case
of suicide the same people cannot take their own lives twice. As a result,
suicide has been described as the ultimate dependent variable, for once the
effect (suicide) is established then there is only the task of specifying definite causes which explain its occurrence. Thus the study of suicide provided a useful means of demonstrating the potential for Durkheim's
scientific approach. In addition, this allowed Durkheim to challenge the
prevailing moralistic and religious approaches – which attributed suicide
to sin, madness, personal defects and abnormalities – as speculative and
lacking empirical substantiation. He accepted that psychology could explain the motives of a specific individual but not provide a general explanation of suicide as a 'social fact'.

Durkheim's chosen sources of empirical data also helped in the identification of relevant and plausible independent variables. The statistics were
derived from death certificates which also contained relatively accurate evidence of religious affiliation, location and family dependency. From this
evidence, Durkheim identified and eliminated variables, such as climate
and mental illness, which had featured heavily in accounts of suicide at
the time. For instance, he identified that while members of the Jewish
faith had a high recorded rate of mental illness, they nevertheless had low
levels of suicide – disproving the link between mental health and suicide.
He concluded that three variables should be taken seriously: membership of
religious groupings such as Catholic, Jewish or Protestant faiths; the
location of members of society in towns and in the countryside; and
whether there were dependants who would suffer from such an event.
Durkheim was careful to limit his claims to the examination of the propensities of groups to contribute 'definite quotas of voluntary deaths', rather
than suggesting that such relationships were automatically evident in

Durkheim developed
a strong case for
the identification of
empirical regularities
as the basis for
establishing
scientific laws in the
social sciences.

Durkheim saw
suicide as a clear-
cut 'effect' of some
other cause – by
looking for empirical
regularities he
hoped to isolate
the causes.

individual cases (or there would be, for example, no unmarried Protestants left alive in towns).

Durkheim also used the medical and organic metaphors in describing social facts as manifestations of normal or pathological conditions, a common feature of positivist approaches in this period. In the next section, we consider two examples of how social scientists contributed towards the definition of subordinate groups in society as abnormal and pathological. As you saw in Chapter 2, the use of analogies and metaphors is a consistent feature of scientific knowledge. However, this raises immediate difficulties in accepting such scientific approaches as free of cultural values. You also need to consider what science means and to whom is it meaningful whenever you explore an approach in social science.

Social facts were categorized as either normal or abnormal (pathological).

Summary

Positivism was, in part, a response to the disorder and chaos witnessed within European societies in the early nineteenth century. It also offered a confident vision for the production of objective knowledge as a basis for reconstructing social life. The optimism expressed by such approaches made positivist science a plausible framework for social science as western Europe prospered in the later nineteenth century.

The study of social facts and scientific laws became the common feature of social scientific practice; values remained unacknowledged, rather than absent, from social science.

Early positivism represented more of an attitude to social life than one agreed method. This allowed it to be combined with other approaches (such as utilitarianism) and to become an adaptable set of tools for policy making.

3 The normal and the pathological: positivism in practice

So that you can see how science conveys powerful meanings and associations, this section explores two case studies which demonstrate the implications of early positivism when applied to social objects – the emergence of scientific racism and positivist criminology. The study of the abnormal in order to establish the normal operation of social and cognitive processes is a common technique in social scientific investigation. For economists and political scientists, crises in the running of a society provide an opportunity for reflection upon basic principles and often reveal new features which had previously been overlooked. In psychology, it has been argued, the study of unusual and 'dysfunctional' cases can reveal processes in cognition and the development of personalities which had previously been taken for granted. In particular, the use of the distinction between normal and pathological (or abnormal) led to the construction of objective categories within which individuals were placed and defined.

The construction of objective categories as definite types or as clearly distinct pigeonholes is a common device for simplifying complex evidence. This technique enables the researcher to begin to compare and contrast their experiences of different forms and processes. However, there is a downside to this technique because placing people in pigeonholes may result in treating these types as real things rather than as useful organizing devices. When this happens, human beings come to be defined only by the qualities relevant to the categorization devices used. The definition of complex human beings as manifestations of one or two underlying categories or types involves a process of **objectification**, for their identities become fixed by reference to some highlighted ascribed characteristic, such as 'race' or sex or criminality, without recognizing that these characteristics are complex constructions in themselves. When this is combined with the distinction between normal and pathological states, then the behaviour of the people subject to this process can be categorized as abnormal or degenerative. In this way, certain social groups come to be identified as, for example, more or less intelligent or more or less criminal than other social groups.

In 'scientific' racism, the process of objectification was achieved through classification according to national citizenship, affiliations with a particular culture, and physiology. In the study of the causes of criminality, the association of certain social and physical characteristics with a high propensity for crime led to the use of psychological categories as devices to identify criminal tendencies in advance of the criminal act. In addition, the emergence of the social sciences alongside the development and institutionalization of medical knowledge gave the social sciences both principles to emulate and the opportunity to have an impact upon the lives of fellow human beings. In both of the following case studies, the relationships between the establishment of scientific knowledge, the objectification involved in the process of attributing abnormal conditions, and the treatment and potential cure of individual or social 'disorders' are very difficult to disentangle.

Studying abnormal cases or situations can highlight the relations and processes we take for granted because of their normality.

The establishment of medical knowledge provided a model of inquiry for social science – if the problems of society could be diagnosed, they could be treated or cured.

3.1   Science and 'race'

Let's examine, first, the implications of using concepts such as 'race' or 'racial difference'. There are dangers in treating the idea of 'race' as somehow fixed and definite, and especially in treating human beings as instances of the categories used. Immediately, we are faced with the problems of using categories which are themselves shaped by cultural values. You may want to consider why we use the concept of 'race' at all. The word itself is full of meaning and can be interpreted in various ways. When we think of 'race', certain associations are common in Western culture, such as the idea of racial hierarchy and its implied relations of superiority and inferiority. When we think of 'racial difference', we face the problem of defining otherness. These associations are embedded in our culture and in the very words we use to define and describe our own culture and identities. We start from the assumption of how others are different from some idea of ourselves. When we combine the ideas of hierarchy and otherness, we are only a short step away from suggesting that 'racial groups' are 'naturally' different and that some are better, or more important, than others. In the case of scientific racism, these tendencies are given greater credence through the addition of the label 'science'. The use of concepts such as 'ethnicity', which expresses cultural difference without recourse to biological differences or the idea of hierarchy, offers an alternative to the use of concepts such as 'race' (just as 'gender' is a useful alternative for 'sex'). Given these problems in making basic distinctions in the social sciences, it is important to consider a more fundamental issue: when we engage in the choice of concepts such as 'race', we are drawing upon cultural values in the identification of 'facts'. Either we treat this as a violation of the requirement to separate facts and values or, more problematically, we recognize that all so-called facts are really an expression of values.

The history of the concept of 'race' provides a powerful example of how values can be camouflaged as facts.

To demonstrate these difficulties we need to explore scientific explanations of 'racial differences' developed by the Social Darwinist and eugenicist movements. Scientific racist movements applied livestock principles to human development, that 'breeding matters', in the hope that a particular society could develop a 'pedigree', or at least avoid degeneration. Scientific racists often assumed that strong 'races', and hence strong cultures, developed in competition with one another. The focus of their concerns was largely fixed upon the rapidly growing urban population, whose high fertility and propensities for drunkenness and crime appeared to demonstrate the dangers of a population imbalance. The middle classes in this period experienced a sharp decline in fertility and a significant proportion of their offspring were emigrating, particularly from the UK to the colonies. These factors contributed towards a climate of anxiety over the biological make-up of Western societies which helped to promote the uncritical acceptance of scientific racist ideas.

In the USA, a society constructed through waves of migration, the concerns were directed more towards the possibility of intermarriage between ethnic groups – what scientific racists labelled 'miscegenation' – and the creation of a 'hybrid society'. Even after the American Civil War, scientific work was often directed towards the justification of deep ethnic inequalities as a natural product of biological/racial differences. In addition, some states possessed enough autonomy to pursue a sterilization programme of children taken into care, on the grounds that they were the 'feebleminded' offspring of degenerate lower-class white families. Segregation based on racial differences remained a significant political issue in the southern states until civil rights were secured in the 1960s. The cultural legacy of this racism remains a difficult issue and a source of conflict in contemporary American society. Recent research on the relationship between criminal behaviour and diabetes caused considerable controversy, and the sensitivity of these issues was highlighted when it was realized that the highest incidence of diabetes was found among the African-American community. Spokespersons from the black communities in the USA saw this as yet another attempt to fix the identity of the 'black American' with the attribution of physiologically based criminal tendencies, part of a long history of 'pathologizing' in the West.

In the early nineteenth century, the scientific study of racial difference centred on whether it was possible to establish the origins of racial groups in a single source (the monogenetic theory), or whether human 'races' had different physiological origins, (the polygenetic theory). The existence of 'racial difference' and social hierarchy went unquestioned. Much of the discussion focused upon whether it was possible to identify racial differences from external physiological characteristics, such as skin pigmentation and form of physique, or whether to concentrate upon cultural differences. In each case, there was a common presumption that it was possible to treat human beings in much the same way as any other natural objects, artefacts or physiological specimens, in the taxonomic fashion of Victorian natural history museums. Members of different cultures were categorized and classified in terms of intelligence, capacities for social organization and tendencies towards war or passivity. Underlying this process, those lower down the scale were seen as primitive and those at the top as civilized.

The ideas of 'racial difference' and 'racial hierarchy' fitted neatly with the Victorian natural history tradition of categorization and classification.

It is also important to note that these debates took place in the context of Western imperialist societies. One of the most significant ways in which the relations of power between colonizer and colonized was justified was through representations of the so-called 'natural inferiority' or 'childlike' qualities of colonized peoples. In this way, colonial powers saw it as their duty to govern the colonized for their own good in much the same way as parents were seen as 'guardians' of children. In *The Races of Men* (1850), John Knox argued that 'race' was the foundation of all cultural, literary and artistic achievement. Any 'races' which could not demonstrate such achievements were, in the eyes of this movement, inferior. Count Gobineau's *The Inequality of Human Races* (1854) reinforced these categorization devices through his distinction between 'culture creators, culture bearers and culture destroyers'. For Gobineau, the original noble white 'race' possessed a monopoly of beauty, intelligence and strength. Racial dilution, he argued, had created hybrid societies which were 'beautiful without strength' or 'strong without intelligence' or 'intelligent but weak and ugly' (Banton, 1967, p.32). These accounts attempted to demonstrate that each racial group had its own local origin and that the biblical Book of Genesis simply told the 'origin story' of the Adamic 'race' (white Europeans).

In societies where slavery was a way of life, science was often enlisted to justify the existing state of affairs. Samuel George Morton's *Crania Americana* (1839) was a systematic attempt to develop a polygenetic account from measurements (using lead pellets) of his extensive collection of skulls. By comparing the size of the cranial cavities in skulls from different cultures, Morton sought to demonstrate how racial difference and racial hierarchy were a function of 'natural differences' such as brain size. Recent measurements of the same skulls by Stephen Jay Gould have revealed considerable inaccuracies suggesting that Morton was clearly so convinced of his own approach that he overlooked conflicting evidence from his own measurements (Gould, 1981). Gould also notes that Morton drew no implications from the sex or stature of the skeletons belonging to the skulls. In particular, replication of his experiments suggests that the only way in which Morton could have achieved the recorded results of the white skulls would have been through very vigorous shaking in order to ensure the lead pellets used settled into all the crevices, creating space for more pellets and increasing the measured weight of 'white skulls'. While these issues may appear odd and archaic in the light of our own moral standards, the impact of scientific racism upon Western societies should not be underestimated. By way of illustration, Figure 3.3 suggests that the

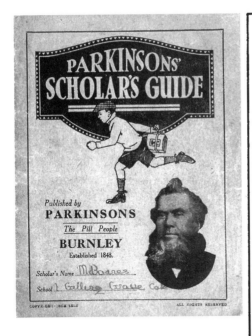

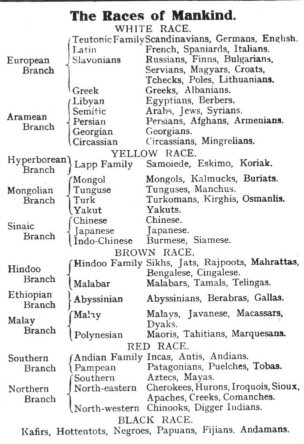

The Races of Mankind.

		WHITE RACE.
European Branch	Teutonic Family	Scandinavians, Germans, English.
	Latin	French, Spaniards, Italians.
	Slavonians	Russians, Finns, Bulgarians, Servians, Magyars, Croats, Tchecks, Poles, Lithuanians.
	Greek	Greeks, Albanians.
Aramean Branch	Libyan	Egyptians, Berbers.
	Semitic	Arabs, Jews, Syrians.
	Persian	Persians, Afghans, Armenians.
	Georgian	Georgians.
	Circassian	Circassians, Mingrelians.

		YELLOW RACE.
Hyperborean Branch	Lapp Family	Samoiede, Eskimo, Koriak.
Mongolian Branch	Mongol	Mongols, Kalmucks, Buriats.
	Tunguse	Tunguses, Manchus.
	Turk	Turkomans, Kirghis, Osmanlis.
	Yakut	Yakuts.
Sinaic Branch	Chinese	Chinese.
	Japanese	Japanese.
	Indo-Chinese	Burmese, Siamese.

		BROWN RACE.
Hindoo Branch	Hindoo Family	Sikhs, Jats, Rajpoots, Mahrattas, Bengalese, Cingalese.
	Malabar	Malabars, Tamals, Telingas.
Ethiopian Branch	Abyssinian	Abyssinians, Berabras, Gallas.
Malay Branch	Malay	Malays, Javanese, Macassars, Dyaks.
	Polynesian	Maoris, Tahitians, Marquesans.

		RED RACE.
Southern Branch	Andian Family	Incas, Antis, Andians.
	Pampean	Patagonians, Puelches, Tobas.
Northern Branch	Southern	Aztecs, Mayas.
	North-eastern	Cherokees, Hurons, Iroquois, Sioux, Apaches, Creeks, Comanches.
	North-western	Chinooks, Digger Indians.

BLACK RACE.
Kafirs, Hottentots, Negroes, Papuans, Fijians, Andamans.

Figure 3.3 Racial classification system from *Parkinsons' Scholar's Guide*.

taxonomic approach to 'race', with its implicit ordering of 'racial types', was widely accepted as a scientific fact well into the twentieth century.

The taxonomy of the 'races of mankind' in Figure 3.3 was placed in a booklet designed for schoolchildren in the inter-war period and sponsored by a manufacturing chemist from Burnley. The table of racial types is portrayed in a factual way alongside a guide to arithmetic, imperial to metric conversion tables, basic geometry, corrections of grammar and spelling, and notes on etiquette. In other words, the context gives it the status of truth. Although this taxonomy is simplistic and contradicts other accounts of racial differences in the inter-war period, it demonstrates the ways in which scientific accounts were reproduced for public understanding and how racial difference, however defined, was accepted as a matter of fact (McClintock, 1995).

The plausibility of scientific racism declined as social values changed in relation to the welfare of the lower classes and the poor.

The arguments in favour of scientific racism began to abate only in the 1920s and 1930s as it became clear that the categories developed were arbitrary and in many cases untestable. At the same time, the cultural climate was altering. Rather than justifying the condition of the poor and marginalized as a product of their own weaknesses, it was increasingly accepted that social reform was feasible and that the human condition of all members of society could be improved (Barkan, 1992). The experience of the Holocaust made eugenicism a taboo subject for social scientists, although the tendency to treat ethnic groups as definite objects has remained a feature of post-war social science. The controversial debates initiated by Hans Eysenck and Arthur Jensen on the relationship between educational performance, intelligence (measured through IQ tests) and membership of ethnic groups are in many ways an heir to these earlier debates.

Eysenck's *Race, Intelligence and Education* (1971), an attempt to popularize the research of Jensen, is founded upon the assumption that IQ tests provide an objective basis for comparing the inherited innate ability of individuals, and hence different ethnic groups. This approach also assumes that 'racial difference', based upon the ideas of otherness and hierarchy developed above, is in some way incontestable. Eysenck attempts to demonstrate that the mean IQ score of white American children is significantly higher than that of black American children. In order to outmanoeuvre a simultaneous opposing critique (which suggests such differences can be explained by environmental factors, such as urban deprivation), Eysenck introduces selective comparisons with other ethnic minorities, for instance, he chose Mexican Americans, who perform at different levels but whom he assumes experience similar environmental conditions as black American children. For Eysenck, this is a sufficient basis for believing that IQ differences are inherited according to 'racial group' membership. Neither side in the opening salvos of this debate took adequate account of the ways in which the test was constructed. Nor did they consider how the scores reflected pupils' ability to respond to particular forms of assessment and to utilize specific linguistic and cultural conventions, which are an implicit part of some cultures and not others. IQ tests have been increasingly recognized as skill-based tests, rather than an objective measure of innate ability. So, based upon the intelligence measures suggested here, the results are a reflection of the cultural training of members of the culture or subculture in question.

Activity 3.3

Turn to Reading C, Stephen Jay Gould's critical account of 'Samuel George Morton – empiricist of polygeny', from *The Mismeasure of Man* (1981).

- At which points in Morton's arguments would you identify his values interfering with his identification of facts?

- Does this have any implications for separating facts from values?

Bear in mind that Morton's evidence was widely accepted in the nineteenth and early twentieth centuries and that it is only with hindsight that we can identify the prejudices and biases involved.

When you have completed these questions, turn to Reading D, 'The intelligence of American negroes', from Hans Eysenck's *Race, Intelligence and Education* (1971), and consider the following questions:

- How does Eysenck's work differ from the studies of racial difference in the scientific racist approach?

- In what ways would you say that Eysenck's work is similar to that of Morton?

When social scientists start to explore the issues raised by cultural identity, they tread on difficult ground. You may wish to think about why some social scientists try to identify a biological basis for social behaviour. Is it simply the pursuit of 'truth' or does this conceal the cultural values for ethnic differences of the researcher?

In recent years genetic research has again pushed these kinds of 'issues' up the social science research agenda — whether genetics explains crime, dietary habits, sexual preference and so on. Whenever you see an example of this, ask yourself why this research is done, whom does it serve, what consequences are likely to follow from the conclusions of such studies.

Social research on 'race', ethnicity and intelligence has been the source of much controversy, and it is worthwhile considering some of the reasons for this. The attempt by Gould to demonstrate the inadequacies of the research techniques of early scientific racists, such as Morton, reveals some of the dangers of becoming too convinced about the anticipated results of one's own research. This raises a key problem in understanding scientific accounts, for what may appear to be a cast-iron certainty in one specific time and place may be deeply questionable in another. Nevertheless, there are deeper issues at stake than whether or not Morton consciously falsified his figures. Is it simply a matter of whether the scientific method is being deployed for value-laden purposes, *or* do we need to think through the way that Morton (or for that matter Eysenck) was situated in a particular time and place, *or* perhaps even the very idea of a value-free science should be in question? Actually, Eysenck's work demonstrates that it is possible to measure inequalities based upon 'race' and ethnicity without violating the norms of scientific method. This, in turn, raises difficult issues about the role of scientific categories and methods in representing cultural values.

For positivists, facts and values should be kept separate. Positivists do not see any reason to question whether the fact/value distinction itself is feasible or desirable.

So, what does evidence of this kind demonstrate? On the one hand, it is possible to treat the work of Morton and Eysenck as 'bad science' for allowing 'subjective values' to shape the definition and discussion of what should be regarded as 'objective facts'. In this interpretation, it is not the scientific method which is at fault but the social scientists themselves for letting personal prejudice interfere with the acquisition of knowledge. This also raises the problem of how we prevent our taken-for-granted assumptions from being expressed in 'scientific research', and whether this is indeed possible. So, on the other hand, it is arguable that the **fact/value distinction** is itself part of the problem. If any attempt to specify racial or ethnic difference is made, this will inevitably raise the problematic character of separating cultural values from the formation of concepts. If conceptions of 'race' always involve the value assumptions of otherness and hierarchy, then clearly the treatment of such concepts as factual definitions involves a process of **objectification**. In this way, individual identities are categorized as expressions of a type based, say, upon the colour of one's skin. Of course, a scientist could argue that categories matter, that research is impossible without them, but people matter too.

3.2 Science and crime

In this second case study we turn to the development of positivist studies of criminal behaviour and its causes and, more specifically, the process of objectification in the identification of normal and abnormal behaviour. The study of criminality is characterized, in the tradition of criminology, as the identification of causes, treatment and, when possible, cure of criminal behaviour. In this area, the legacy of positivism remains alive today and has an effect upon contemporary criminal justice policy. Whereas in the scientific racist studies external factors such as skin colour provided scientists with a way of demarcating types of people, the identification of 'criminal types' was to be much more problematic; consequently, attempts to separate the non-criminal from the potential criminal were more complex. In practice, criminality was often attributed to some ethnic groups. 'Race' was, at this time, understood as a much more flexible concept for it included what are today often referred to as 'lower-class' groups in society. Nevertheless, the application of the (positivist) scientific method to the problem of crime raised huge expectations that an answer to the 'problem' would be found. In *Pedagogical Anthropology* (1913), Maria Montessori states:

> The phenomenon of criminality spreads without check or
> succour, and up to yesterday it aroused in us nothing but repulsion
> and loathing. But now that science has laid its finger upon this
> moral fester, it demands the cooperation of all mankind to
> combat it.

(Montessori, 1913, p.8)

The foundational source of positivist criminology most frequently cited is Cesare Lombroso's *L'Uomo Delinquente* (1911) – the criminal man – which attempted to relate causally the physiological features of individuals in prisons to types of crimes and which claimed to offer a means of predicting criminality in the general populace. In his study of the crania of 383 dead and 3,839 living criminals Lombroso, an Italian physician, placed a great deal of stress on the 'atavistic' features of criminals (that they possessed characteristics which revealed their closeness to earlier steps in the process of human evolution). This approach combined phrenology (the study of the shape of the skull) with other 'anatomical stigmata' (physiological features which differed from the norm), such as webbed feet, large jaws, large ears, dark skin, thick hair, flat nostrils, extra nipples, the inability to blush and diminished sensitivity to pain. More specifically, he attributed criminality and moral degeneracy to epilepsy, which ensured that this particular condition became the object of intense interventions by eugenicists. In terms of gender, Lombroso and his assistant, Ferrero, were at pains to identify the physiological basis of female prostitution through the anatomical stigmata of prehensile feet (with the big toe widely separated from the other toes), a physiological feature which they attributed to a throw-back to the apes. As in the scientific accounts of 'race' in this period, physiological differences were taken to be an indicator of criminal and abnormal tendencies, as can be seen in Figure 3.4.

In positivist criminology, physiological differences were taken as indicators of potential criminality.

The atavistic assumptions within Lombroso's biological determinist approach were deeply contested by the prevailing 'classical school', which

Figure 3.4   A panoply of criminal faces from Lombroso's
Criminal Man. According to Lombroso: A are shoplifters,
B, C, D and F are swindlers, E are German murderers, G are
fraudulent bankrupts, H are purse snatchers and I are
burglars.

held that criminals were fully responsible for their own actions and that the
punishment should fit the crime and not the criminal. The supporters of
Lombroso's approach were often progressive social reformers, many
involved in left-wing politics, who recognized the humanitarian intent in
this work. Rather than recommending the treatment of criminals in terms of
the specific offence committed, that 'the punishment should fit the crime',
Lombroso and Ferrero recommended that the punishments of criminal justice should vary between occasional and inborn criminals. They argued that
criminals who could not be reformed by the prison system should be
transported to a place where they could do no harm (by which they meant
the colonies). While the biological determination of crime became

increasingly questionable, the tendency of criminologists to search for the determinate causes of criminality has continued in much the same way, with social causes supplementing or replacing biological ones.

A particularly useful example of this can be found in criminal psychology which attempts to explain the incidence and form of pathological behaviour in human subjects. Cyril Burt, prior to his pioneering development of the eleven-plus examination, spent his early years working on criminological psychology, with a particular focus on juvenile delinquency. With the publication of *The Young Delinquent* (1925/1961), Burt was to have a profound effect on both criminology and the criminal justice system. Burt contended that juvenile delinquents who demonstrated 'chronic recidivism' (in today's terminology, 'persistent offenders') could be explained by a combination of hereditary and environmental factors. This approach combined biological and social causes, and considered their effects upon the personality of young individuals. The biological or hereditary factors, Burt argued, could be established through the study of criminal pedigrees, the number and type of criminal tendencies of one's parents and grandparents (see Figure 3.5). He suggested that genetic traits, in line with Mendelian genetics, 'may skip a generation' (Burt, 1925/1961, p.45). Burt related hereditary conditions to the physical, intellectual and temperamental characteristics of 'delinquents'. The environmental conditions he identified as having a causal effect, ranged from poverty and urban deprivation, 'defective' family relationships and discipline, to peer group influences, working conditions, gambling and going to the cinema.

> Positivist criminology involves the search for definite causes of criminality, either within the individuals, or in the environment they inhabit.

Activity 3.4

Now turn to Reading E, an extract from Cyril Burt's *The Young Delinquent* (1925/1961) and consider the following questions.

- What do you think are the assumptions which lie behind Burt's positivist account of juvenile crime? Make a list of these assumptions.

- Identify how persistent young offenders have been characterized, using your own experiences and interpretations.

- Compare and contrast Burt's descriptions and your own interpretations and experiences (either personally or through media representations). You may wish to consider whether it is possible to separate the scientific characterization of criminality from popular beliefs about the causes of crime.

Before you read on, look at Figure 3.5 and have a go at constructing your own criminal pedigree using the key to symbols developed by Burt. You might be surprised by how many so-called 'pathologies' are present in most families.

The construction of 'objective categories' of character traits, family background and environmental conditions of various kinds as a basis for defining, predicting and assessing criminal behaviour reveals some of

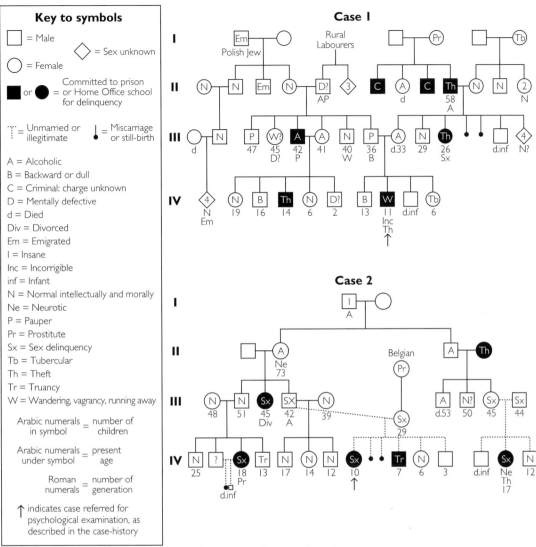

Figure 3.5 Burt's 'Pedigrees of Juvenile Delinquents': two case studies.

Summary of case-histories

Case 1. Boy, aged eleven. Charged as incorrigible. Wanders away after school; steals from maternal uncle with whom he lives. Weak health. Intelligence below average, but not definitely dull or backward (mental ratio, 90). Unstable, irritable temper.
Father, illiterate, in workhouse. Mother, married at eighteen, drunkard, died nine months ago.
Father's family: Paternal grandmother descended from a Polish Jew, five of whose descendants have emigrated. Paternal grandfather, a drunkard and pauper, apparently feeble-minded. Their descendents show tendencies to alcoholism, pauperism, and vagrancy, several being dull or borderline defectives. One paternal cousin is in an industrial school for theft.
Mother's family: Maternal grandfather, a heavy drinker, imprisoned for theft; two of his brothers have also been in jail. Their mother is said to have been a prostitute. The boy's maternal aunt has been in jail for theft, and is at present the mistress of a Chinaman. There is a tubercular strain on this side of the family.

Case 2. Girl, aged ten, illegitimate. Charged with sex offences.
Father, a heavy drinker, married to a respectable and intelligent woman; their legitimate children are normal in character and intelligence. Mother, a Belgian waitress; has had four children by this man, the first before she was nineteen.
Father's family: Paternal great-grandfather said to have been alcoholic and insane. Neurotic and alcoholic tendencies appear in several of his descendants. Every one of his female descendants has shown sexual misconduct, one being a prostitute from the age of sixteen. A hysterical girl of seventeen, who was later referred to me for repeated theft and sex delinquency, proved to be a member of this family: the only son of the great-grandfather had married a woman who had constantly been in jail for stealing; her daughter in turn had three illegitimate children, of whom this child was one. Later, a brother and a paternal cousin of the girl originally brought to me were reported for truancy.
Mother's family: Maternal grandmother a prostitute from Brussels.

the underlying problems in all social research. In particular, social scientists should take care to reflect upon whether they are simply translating commonsense prejudices on criminality and its causes as statements of fact, rather than as a feature of the situated knowledge of the culture in question. This is even more difficult to disentangle if the research itself becomes the principles by which individuals are evaluated in the institutional organizations of social life, as occurred in the case of Burt's study, which became an established reference work in the criminal justice profession. Burt's writings on the causes of crime came to be seen as a way of defining and classifying 'abnormal' or 'deviant' behaviour. In such situations, the experts in this objective knowledge become the means by which individuals in the criminal justice system are evaluated and processed. The individuals subject to such attention have no voice themselves, except through the voices of these same experts, the judges and legal representatives, the psychiatrists, social workers and so on. Ultimately, the judgements of these experts become the basis for decisions and the criminal justice system operates according to such decisions. Social researchers investigating the criminal justice system are in part providing an account of crime and its causes which, as a profession, they have also helped to construct.

From the two case studies of scientific racism and positivist criminology, it is possible to gain valuable insights into the effects of positivism on the study of social objects. In each case we can now see how cultural values were an important, if implicit and unacknowledged, part of the research process. At the time that such studies were conducted, many of these problems went unrecognized because the relations and issues raised appeared to be matters of fact. Such approaches appear to us now to be deeply contestable. Research today contains assumptions which are just as problematic, only we do not recognize them as such. At this point, it is useful to reconsider the question of whether this kind of social research is simply 'bad science', that such work simply violates the criteria for establishing objective knowledge.

The research by Eysenck, in conforming to the criteria of the scientific method, suggests that the problem is more deep-seated than this and that we should regard all concepts and ideas in social research as expressions of culturally specific meanings. If this is the case, then the **fact/value distinction** is itself in doubt. In particular, such research reveals that the development of scientific explanations is never neutral or innocent. Values creep into social scientific work in the choice of the field of investigation, the problems identified, the research techniques selected, the collation of results of empirical investigations and their use in causal explanations which, in turn, can affect the objects under study. This is certainly the case in Burt's account, which is still accepted as common sense by many in the penal system today. Whether studies like Burt's simply reflected popular common sense on crime and/or actually changed the way in which juvenile delinquents were treated is much more difficult to establish. We should always be aware of how the values of social researchers, or even organized communities of social scientists, have a shaping effect upon the way that knowledge is constructed. Even statements which appear to be simple descriptions can conceal important normative assumptions.

Cultural values, and the institutions within which these values exist and make sense, are the unacknowledged conditions of scientific explanations of crime or inequality.

Summary

The case studies of scientific racism and positivist criminology demonstrate the ways in which human beings can be constructed as objective categories. In both cases the prejudices of social scientists were portrayed as social facts and were received as such by the academic audience. For positivists, facts are clearly separate from values.

The central problem in establishing how the values of a particular culture come to be translated into social scientific facts is whether this is simply a matter of the scientific method becoming contaminated, that it needs cleaning up, or that the assumption of the separation of facts and values is itself untenable.

The individuals who were categorized as having abnormal or pathological features were treated along medical lines and the role of social scientists was to establish a cure. The voices which remained unheard in these studies were those of the objectified individuals, who were reduced to a position of powerlessness.

4   Positivism, language and science

Carnap/Ayer logical positivism

In this section we examine probably the most influential form of positivism in the twentieth century, logical positivism. This approach drew upon the techniques of formal logic in order to create an objective account of human knowledge; to achieve objectivity, every sentence and every statement had to be the direct expression of observable things and all speculative ideas removed. We also explore how, in the post-war period, some positivists developed a more practically oriented approach, which came to be known as standard positivism. These approaches dominated empirical social science in the 1950s and 1960s. This was because they appeared to be able to generate objective or 'authoritative' knowledge which could be relied upon to identify the 'facts of a given situation' and thus could be used for social planning.

Logical positivists endorse all six assumptions and seek to remove all traces of metaphysics from scientific knowledge.

4.1   The logical positivist approach

Logical positivism places an exceptional emphasis upon sensory perception and the role of observation in research as the foundation of knowledge. For this reason, logical positivism is often seen as an 'extreme' version of the positivist approaches for it attempts to eradicate **metaphysics** completely from the production of scientific knowledge. Scientific statements are seen as pictures or snapshots of the things they refer to, like reflections in a mirror. The two case studies you encountered in the previous section demonstrate the extent to which values interfered with the claims of positivism to eliminate speculation and subjective viewpoints. The stated aim of the logical positivist approach is to cleanse scientific knowledge of speculative thinking, for it is not tied in a direct and demonstrable way to experience.

The origins of this approach can be identified in Bertrand Russell's and Alfred Whitehead's *Principia Mathematica* (1910–13/1935) and the work of the young Ludwig Wittgenstein, *Tractatus Logico-Philosophicus* (1921/1961). The logical positivist approach was promoted by the Vienna Circle, a group of philosophers, intellectuals and scientists who clarified the logical positivist approach and sought to develop these anti-metaphysical ideas in the 1920s. Although, in common with the earlier nineteenth-century positivists, they sought to eradicate speculative metaphysics from science, they were well aware of the way in which speculative assumptions had actually prevented earlier positivists from achieving this goal. In other words, the earlier positivist approaches had simply not managed to live up to the standards of science. Logical positivism advocated an approach to the generation of new knowledge and human progress whereby sense experiences were taken as the starting-point for all ideas.

Following Wittgenstein, the logical positivists accepted that statements should reflect the atomic facts of the world and for them the world is made up of such separate irreducible atomic objects and their configurations. To each object, they argued, corresponds a definite statement which provides an accurate picture of that object. In this **mimetic** approach words should be a simple mirror reflection of things. This approach was popularized by Rudolf Carnap in *The Unity of Science* (1932/1995) and A.J. Ayer in *Language, Truth and Logic* (1936/1990). Such texts had a profound effect on the practices of social scientists in the mid twentieth century, until Karl Popper published his alternative approach to scientific method in English in the late 1950s. For Rudolf Carnap (1891–1970), a member of the Vienna Circle who was to have an enormous effect on the interpretation of the natural sciences in post-war America, this approach can be best described as **physicalism**. It was believed that, since there was only one set of physical things to study, a common language could be developed to encompass all human experiences. Carnap saw the physical language as the universal descriptive language which could be applied to the study of all things. The various specialized vocabularies of the sciences, he argued, could all be related back to the same set of 'physical determinations'. Therefore it was possible to unify the sciences into one common body of knowledge, although he added that this was simply physics.

From the opening sections of this chapter you will recall how early positivism was extremely ambitious in its claims about establishing objective knowledge. However, unlike the earlier positivist efforts of Comte, logical positivists were concerned to be much more cautious about what it was possible to claim before a statement acquired the status of truth. In order to achieve this, they took the form of language used in the construction of scientific knowledge as a much more serious issue. The logical positivists developed their approach in an attempt to ensure that human values and metaphysical speculation did not interfere with the acquisition and accumulation of objective knowledge. In particular, they drew upon the use of the linguistic distinction between **analytic** and **synthetic** statements in order to demonstrate how an empiricist science could be developed. This distinction was a key element of empiricism before and after the Enlightenment. The use of this distinction led many to refer to this new approach as the 'linguistic turn' in the philosophy of the social sciences. Analytic statements are seen as true by definition, such as the classic example of 'All bachelors are unmarried'. Synthetic statements, on the

Logical positivists adopt the position of atomism – see Figure 3.1.

For positivists, scientific statements should be simple pictures of the observable world.

other hand, are based upon observation and, as such, can be seen to be contributing new knowledge, such as 'London contains more bachelors than any other part of Britain'.

The aim of the logical positivist movement was to eliminate all the so-called analytic statements in science which were speculative synthetic statements. If it had been held to be true that all single men tend to drink too much, we could construct a statement such as 'All bachelors are drunkards'. Of course, this statement is inaccurate in synthetic terms, for observation would reveal the existence of unmarried teetotal males, and we would have to replace it with something like 'Some bachelors are drunkards on Friday nights'. It is not an analytic statement because being a bachelor simply means being an unmarried male, it does not by definition alone mean that the person in question drinks too much alcohol. Consequently, the claim in the statement 'All bachelors are drunkards' involves a speculative rather than a true claim about the behaviour of all unmarried males, and implies certain things about the behaviour of married males. A synthetic claim which conforms to the criteria established by the logical positivists could be 'On average, males consume more alcohol than females in a given year even taking into account differential body weight'. However, such a claim would not be true by definition, only in terms of its accuracy as a picture of observed experience. In other words, the truth of such statements can only be established by reference to observable evidence and if behaviour changes then the statement would have to change.

Logical positivists use the distinction between analytic and synthetic statements to clarify the idea of objective scientific knowledge – you may find it useful to look back at the emergence of empiricism (see Chapter 2, section 3.3).

The social sciences are packed full of claims which purport to be true, but which in fact violate the distinction between analytic and synthetic statements. For instance, the claim that 'All men are instrumental and all women are expressive' acts as an important foundational assumption – sometimes explicitly stated – in many areas of work on the family or in studies of working patterns. Nevertheless, in terms of the criteria established by the logical positivists, this conflates the analytic statement 'All men are human beings of the male sex' with the synthetic statement 'In the situation x, males tend to behave in ways which are instrumental'. The extent to which men and women are instrumental and expressive is a matter for empirical assessment; it would have to be demonstrated through observational evidence that the statement was an accurate one. If the central aim of logical positivism is to eliminate statements which conflate the analytic with the synthetic then, following this process of elimination, we would be left only with those analytic statements which were 'true by definition' and synthetic statements which were 'true by reference to empirical evidence'. In this way, through the careful application of the scientific method, logical positivists would hope to accumulate more accurate knowledge of social behaviour.

Statements which violate the distinction between analytic and synthetic are seen as meaningless.

The logical positivist approach uses the method of **induction** which involves collecting observational data and building theories to explain the observations. It is assumed that we experience our perceptions and impressions without any prior sets of theories to organize them. In short, we soak up sensations in the way that sponges absorb water. Supporters of induction also assume that, through repeated experiences of the same phenomena within particular instances, the phenomena will operate in much the same way in other such instances of which we have no experience. This then has the status of a general law. Thus the method of induction involves two movements simultaneously: a movement from the particular to the general; and a movement from observed events to theoretical reconstructions (see Figure 3.6). In practice, these are hard to separate; for instance, general laws are just well established theories which help us to understand other theories which relate to a single or limited number of situations.

Figure 3.6   The method of induction.

In logical positivism, the method of induction is combined with the **verificationist** approach to testing scientific explanations, whereby the scientists seek out similar observable conditions to demonstrate the validity of the general laws so far established. For instance, imagine you interviewed 150 married men who had purchased the services of a prostitute over the last twelve months so that you can identify their motivations for acting in this way. As the interviewing progressed you would tend to note the recurrence of certain characteristics in each case. For some of the men, the reasons for these actions may have been explained through sexual frustration, whereas for others it was the element of risk or the need to dominate a sexual partner. In addition, once the actions had been initiated more than once, for some of the men there may have been a strong feeling that this behaviour is addictive. All of these motivations have been identified in research studies on the clients of prostitutes (Høigård and Finstad, 1992; McKeganey and Barnard, 1996). On the basis of experiences in the research study on these men, the verificationist approach to testing would lead you in future to search for similar sorts of information, and the questions you would then ask are likely to reflect this. In other words, this brand of positivism tends to encourage the search for confirming evidence rather than offering a critical appraisal of existing knowledge. As a consequence, verificationism has often been dubbed as 'confirmationism' and 'justificationism', for simply providing evidence with which social scientists feel comfortable. Certainly, within a short time, it became clear that the theoretical statements developed within the confines of this approach did not provide consistently accurate predictions to support the explanations devised.

Now, let's return to the two movements involved in induction and relate them to this research study of the 150 men. On the basis of your 'observation' of the behaviour of these men, in relation to the 'particular instances' in which they act in this way, we can begin to formulate 'hypotheses' to explain the behaviour. In time the hypotheses may develop into 'theories' about frustration, risk, power or addiction, and these may be taken as manifestations of a **general law** that the theory applies to all particular instances where such conditions hold, such as 'Men are promiscuous regardless of their marital status'. Clearly, it would be very contestable for such a statement to have the status of a 'general law'. However, if we now engage in the search for confirming evidence with these theories in mind, general laws such as these may become part of a discipline and remain unquestioned.

4.2 Practical implications of logical positivism

In social situations where there is considerable uncertainty, positivists use probability statements to indicate the likelihood that their statements are true.

See statistical closure in Chapter 2, section 2.2.

One way out of these difficulties created by proposing general laws on the basis of limited observational evidence was to adopt a **probability model**, while at the same time assuming that the inductive method provides the best basis for inquiry. The use of probability explanations in the social sciences is common where social scientists wish to adopt the inductive method but the conditions are marked by uncertainty of outcome. In effect, it is a means of constructing a closed system, with the proviso that a small chance of disproof is possible. In accounting for the likelihood of actors to behave in certain ways, probability estimates are useful for, say, identifying why people buy particular goods in supermarkets, vote for particular parties, or choose to break off from talking if they hear something repellent in a conversation. Useful examples of these techniques in practice can be seen in studies of voting behaviour which draw upon statistical evidence. Strong statistical relationships are identifiable between owner-occupation in housing, the use of a private car, the possession of shares and employment in the private sector, and the propensity to vote Conservative. Similarly, there is a higher probability that council house tenants who use public transport and are members of a trade union in the public sector will vote for the Labour Party. For a logical positivist, these empirical regularities can be taken as an indication of a general law (on the relationship between social cleavages and voting behaviour).

In positivist research, empirical regularities have the status of scientific laws.

Such **empirical regularities** can be invaluable in estimating the outcome of a particular election and, when combined with evidence about the changing patterns of use of public and private services, can also provide an indication of future electoral outcomes. However, if you engage in such comparisons, this takes you no closer to explaining why such things occur. To take a more specific example, in order to plan for the health service it is useful to predict the probability of smokers contracting lung cancer. However, this is not the same as developing a scientific explanation of the causal relationships involved in the development of cancer, and neither does it offer an adequate explanation of the role of tobacco-based products in relation to the range of carcinogenic substances (such as radioactive substances or toxic chemicals) which could have produced the same end result.

The strength of induction is that all statements refer directly to observed experiences and can be immediately recognized.

The key weakness of induction, therefore, is that it assumes we passively absorb sense experiences.

To summarize so far, the method of **induction** refers to the logical process of constructing knowledge about observed relationships between variables in particular instances (usually a set of controlled conditions). This can be taken as a basis for making universal generalizations about such relationships in other, as yet unobserved, particular instances. The strength of induction also lies in its appeal to data collected through human senses, as a means of validating propositions (which follows from the anti-metaphysical assumptions of this tradition). This is combined with the assumption that a scientist gathers evidence in order to infer general laws. Hence the 'truth' of a statement is confirmed through the accumulation of evidence, that is, verification. The explanatory power of this approach is seen to rest upon its predictive uses (the extent to which the statements are verified or confirmed in evidence collected in new circumstances). However, the key assumption that sensations are the basis for arriving at theoretical ideas is open to question. Induction has been criticized for assuming that there are no differences between observers in terms of their interpretations of the same sense-data. Inductive approaches tend to treat the act of observation as if the observer plays no constructive role in the act and simply absorbs information, and so treat the mind as a passive receiver of sense-data, soaking up information, to which it responds in a predictable way. These are unrealistic assumptions which we examine again when we look at Popper in section 5.

See section 5.

4.3   The standard positivist approach

In response to these problems some positivist philosophers, such as Carl Hempel (1905–1997), place a greater stress on the deductive process to explain the steps involved in theory construction. Hempel's work modifies the arguments of the logical positivists to take account of the way in which scientists usually start with a set of general laws and theories before directly engaging in empirical research. His emphasis upon deduction came to be regarded as the model for the post-war standard positivist account of the scientific method. **Deduction** refers to the mental process through which valid conclusions can be logically deduced from valid premises, that is, a generalization or universal law. Deduction is used to establish a series of logical steps in the process of forming a theoretical statement about the world. Usually, a general claim is made and this is applied to a particular case or instance with a definite set of conditions. Finally, a conclusion is posed and the scientist engages in research to establish whether the predicted outcome is indeed the case. The truth value of the premise acts as a guarantor of the truth value of the conclusions, for the conclusions do not go beyond what is already contained within the premises. Let's look at two examples of deductive reasoning to illustrate the relationship between premises and conclusions.

Example A	Example B
1 Heavy people leave deep footprints.	1 All children are cruel.
2 This person makes deep footprints.	2 This person is a child.
3 This person is heavy.	3 This person is cruel.

The starting-point in deductive reasoning is theoretical (although the theory may have been established through induction at some point) and then observation serves as a basis for testing statements (regardless of how the statements are derived). In this general sense, deductive reasoning is compatible with all kinds of approaches to **knowledge construction** and does not of itself stand or fall as a logical technique, even if the initial premises are false, as Example B demonstrates, for not all children are cruel. In this case, logical consistency (alongside predictive success) is an important feature of a scientific explanation. It is important to recognize, as did Hempel, that the strict limits placed upon the scientific method developed by the Vienna Circle were too restrictive for science to be an innovative process.

The logical positivists had argued that a statement is either cognitively significant (in describing the world as it is) or it is simply meaningless. However, Hempel recognized that the empirical content of a theoretical statement could only be considered to be meaningful when the theory is placed within its 'interpretive system'. As with the logical positivist approach, Hempel is concerned to identify the empirical regularities which are significant in definite situations. Empirical regularities are not only seen as necessary for establishing a causal law, they are sufficient; that is, all you need for a law statement is 'if A then B'.

So, within the standard positivist approach, scientific explanations involve a particular way of developing a logical argument. We can see this when we look at how deduction was viewed as a process through which valid conclusions are deduced from valid premises in order to ensure logical consistency, as in Examples A and B above. In this model of scientific inquiry, one proceeds from general law statements (within specific conditions) to explain and predict particular cases. The combination of the laws and specified conditions (the premises) are often defined as the explanans statement and the conclusion is described as the explanandum statement (Hempel, 1965; but for a quick introduction see: Keat and Urry, 1982, pp.12–13; Hacking, 1983, pp.2–6). With this approach, providing that it is possible to identify the operating laws at work and the conditions within which these laws operate, then it should be feasible to predict the outcome accurately. The emphasis on the role of prediction implies that there should be complete symmetry between predicting something and explaining it. Successful prediction in this model is the same as providing a satisfactory explanation. So, in practice, if a scientific theory appears to predict an outcome accurately, then it must be true.

An example of this way of thinking can be seen in the study of human behaviour, developed by the psychologists B.F. Skinner and J.B. Watson, in the development of the concept of 'operant conditioning'. This approach, which became known as **behaviourism**, focuses upon the ways in which individuals respond to various stimuli and/or conditions in ways that maximize rewards and minimize punishments. One of the theoretical premises of this approach is the assumption that human beings are passive recipients of external pushes or pulls and that they modify their behaviour accordingly. The behaviourist approach also rests upon the assumption that it is misleading to speculate about the inner states or human creativity in explaining social life. In this way, it is plausible to construct a scientific statement, starting from a series of principles or laws (for example, operant conditioning) which are accepted as the motivation for certain forms of human behaviour, and examine an activity which demonstrates these laws in specific conditions, such as obedience or disobedience in schools. By establishing the conditions in which obedience is reinforced and/or disobedience deterred, it is possible to explain the level of order or disorder in certain schools. The success of this explanation would be measured in terms of its ability to produce the predicted results in the conditions of an experiment (to remove the possible influence of other variables in the empirical evidence); that is, a **closed system**. Of course, this whole approach rests upon the implicit assumption that the organization of school life can only be studied through the observation of the actual behaviour of the individuals involved – teachers, head, pupils, governors and so on.

Standard positivists put a special emphasis on the symmetrical relationship between explanation and prediction.

Behaviourism is covered in more detail in Chapter 5.

4.4   Practical implications of standard positivism

Standard positivism was committed to value freedom, that scientific explanations could be constructed without reference to the value positions of scientists. This was partly possible because of the emergence of a dominant set of assumptions within post-war Western societies. These assumptions reflected growing agreement about what sort of society should exist, and hence also about the purpose and focus of social science. The liberal social theorist Raymond Aron expressed this well when he suggested that 'in both East and West, debate was suppressed', while others were led to proclaim the 'end of ideology' and the emergence of 'consensus politics'. In this period of consensus in the 1950s, social scientists worked within a relatively solid framework with well established social goals. The main effect upon social science was the growth of empirical research with a relatively low level of theoretical sophistication and a fairly clear set of policy applications. This meant that values appeared to be less important, because there were relatively few fundamental disputes among social scientists until the later 1960s. Debate and disagreement focused upon how problems were resolved, rather than questioning which problems existed in society. Broadly speaking, social science was geared towards the primary goals of the post-war welfare state and the managed economy.

This suited the needs of post-war governments and large corporations, who were concerned with identifying problems, finding solutions and anticipating the practical difficulties or unintended consequences of various courses of action. Empirical research following the guidelines established by Hempel and the positivist assumptions of this scientific method went largely unquestioned. A great deal of research that you might encounter on social problems in sociology, human geography, economics and psychology can seen as policy oriented in this way. For instance, social research conducted by both psychologists and sociologists on the educational performance of different groups in society (largely in terms of class and, later, in terms of gender and ethnicity) assumed that low attaining groups suffered from 'cultural deprivation'. The main differences among researchers lay in their recommendations for resolving the problem, rather than questioning whose culture is referred to in the concept of 'cultural deprivation'. Broadly speaking, this research did not consider whether it was the form of knowledge which was responsible for low levels of educational attainment by working-class children. Instead, 'educational failure' was attributed to some flaw or defect in the child, the family structure and patterns of child-rearing, the characteristics of the neighbourhood and culture, and so on. In this way, the relationship between normality and pathology which characterized earlier forms of positivism resurfaced in the use of categories such as 'educational subnormality'.

Social researchers simply assumed that the criteria for success or failure in education should be the extent to which the working-class pupils displayed conventional signs of attainment within an educational system which favoured the standards and forms of knowledge associated with the already successful middle classes. They did not question whether these standards themselves were part of the problem. The 'causes' of educational success or failure were identified as parental interest, poverty in cultural and material terms, the ways in which teachers labelled pupils and/or the presence or absence of a positive school ethos. Few of these social scientists made their

Standard positivism served as a useful framework for policy-oriented research where there was broad agreement on the character and form of social problems in the post-war consensus.

positivist credentials explicit, because they did not feel the need to pro-claim what was obvious to them as good practice. In examining the existing sources of any field of human knowledge, it is important for you to inquire about what kind of questions are being asked as much as the nature of the evidence which social researchers produce. In the next section we examine an approach which challenged this uncritical use of a model of scientific inquiry, and which cast doubt upon the aspirations of science to attain the 'truth'.

Summary

Positivists in the twentieth century attempted to use careful analysis of language to distinguish between scientific knowledge and speculative metaphysics. The aim was to produce a body of knowledge composed of observation statements and tautologies, with theory playing no creative role except as a reflection of empirical evidence.

The logical positivist approach placed a greater emphasis upon induction and verification, while exponents of the post-war standard positivist view (such as Hempel) stressed the importance of deduction, although within strict empirical constraints. In all approaches, it was assumed that there was a clear separation of facts from values and that it was possible to 'discover' general laws.

5   From the problem of induction to the falsificationist alternative

g

Falsification makes a virtue out of being systematically sceptical about all knowledge claims.

By the middle of the twentieth century many philosophers of natural and social science were beginning to criticize the assumptions and aims of posi-tivism, especially the tendency to treat ideas as true pictures of the real world. In this section we explore **falsificationism**, an approach which places positivism and the search for truth in question although it maintains the commitment to the accumulation of knowledge as a means of securing human progress. This section is in two parts. The first establishes the con-text in which the inductivist approach was questioned and focuses upon the problems of induction. Particular attention is devoted to those issues raised by Karl Popper and the insights he draws from David Hume's scepti-cal attitude to truth in the Enlightenment as a way of questioning the logical basis of the logical positivist approach. The second part outlines Popper's alternative falsification approach to scientific method and provides some illustrations of the application of this method to the social sciences.

5.1 Situating Popper

Many of the familiar ideas we hold about natural and social scientific method were initially developed within one or other tradition in Vienna in the early twentieth century. You have already encountered one of these approaches, logical positivism, in the previous section. Vienna was a cosmopolitan crossroads through which the peoples of Europe flowed. They brought with them a wide range of ideas, adding these to the mix of German philosophical traditions which were already well established (we examine the impact of these traditions on the social sciences in the next chapter). The events in Europe in the 1930s (the rise of the Nazi regime and the spread of anti-semitism) were to lead to an intellectual diaspora. Whole scientific communities fled from Nazi persecution either for 'political crimes' or because they were Jewish. Many of the most influential natural and social scientists in the twentieth century took refuge in the USA and, as a consequence, the philosophical sensitivities of central Europe came into direct contact with the empirical techniques of American social science. This was to produce an explosion in theorizing about the assumptions and methods of the social sciences from the 1950s onwards. One particular approach, that of Karl Popper, was to have a profound impact on social scientific method in the West after World War II.

Popper (1902–1992) wanted to rescue the idea of the scientific method from the emerging criticisms of positivism and believed that there was a better way of resolving the problems involved. He concentrated on examining induction, which, as you will recall, emphasizes the importance of starting with observations of particular instances and then moving towards constructing theories and laws which explain what is happening in more than one of these particular instances. For Popper, the inductive method simply cannot sustain the explanatory weight placed upon it. He raises two problems with induction, the 'psychological problem' and the 'logical problem'.

- The 'psychological problem' involves finding an answer to the question of why 'reasonable people' expect new situations to operate in the same way as ones they know from experience. For Hume, the psychological problem is resolved through 'custom' or habit, which enables us to function in our everyday lives.

- The 'logical problem' involves the question of whether we are justified in leaping from statements about situations we have experienced to statements about situations we have not experienced. You saw in the previous sections how central to the positivist approaches was the shift from particular instance to general law.

For Popper, science should not operate by the rules of everyday common sense whereby we simply assume that a new situation will be the same as the situations we already know and understand. Popper asks us to focus upon the logical problem of not knowing what is going to happen in a new situation and accept this condition as something we scientists simply have to live with. Rather than expecting our knowledge to be confirmed, he developed a methodology around the possibility of refuting our existing

Popper empiricism

naturalism

phenomenalism

nominalism

atomism

scientific laws

facts/values

Values are part of the research process, but they must be strictly controlled through reference to empirical evidence.

Popper starts from the assumption that we can never be certain that an explanatory statement about one set of conditions will work just as well elsewhere.

theories. He argued that we cannot expect statements about situations we have not experienced to be true (Popper, 1972, pp.1–31). This also led him to rethink the concept of 'truth', not as an absolute (that a statement is simply true or false), but rather as a matter of degree (he defined truth as 'verisimilitude'). Actually, there is a deeper foundational problem with induction, most clearly identified by P.F. Strawson (1952). Many scientists adopted induction on the grounds that it worked, that it was possible simply to observe, measure and explain, and that, over time, the principle of induction had, through observation, become accepted. However, in logical terms, the principle of induction is exactly that – a theoretical principle established prior to experience. Hence at the heart of the induction approach there is a contradiction, in that the operating principle violates its own rules.

Induction violates its own rules, for it is still a theoretical principle prior to experience itself.

Popper's view was that, if we believe a particular approach can be confirmed and gather evidence accordingly, we are left in a position where we are unlikely to make 'scientific discoveries'. This would mean that we simply reinforce what we already know rather than finding new ways of stating and solving problems (Popper, 1959, pp.269–76). Popper attributed this insight, in part, to Albert Einstein's self-critical attitude towards his theory of relativity. Rather than treating his work as the establishment of a new set of truths to replace the Newtonian truths which had been established for more than two centuries, Einstein regarded his own theories of physics as tentative steps on the road to a general theory. He also attempted to specify the conditions in which his account could be disproven (rather than indicating ways in which his arguments could be confirmed). For Popper, it was precisely this undogmatic 'attitude' towards science which came as a revelation, and not Einstein's theories of physics. In this critical attempt to apply the powers of reason, controlled through empirical tests, he was to make the claim that science could deliver progress even without truth. Thus we can never be conclusively certain of any of our statements about the world, for there is always the possibility of a 'disconfirming instance'.

Popper proposes that all explanations should be subject to empirical tests and that a healthy sense of doubt was crucial for the progress of knowledge.

5.2 Conjectures and refutations: Popper's falsificationist solution

Popper adopts naturalism, but changes the criteria for demarcating scientific from non-scientific knowledge.

It is important to distinguish Popper's approach from that of the logical positivists of the Vienna Circle. On the crucial question of the **demarcation criteria** between science and non-science, the logical positivists saw this simply in terms of whether a statement described the world as it was observed, or whether that statement was a metaphysical one and hence meaningless. For Popper, a statement is never meaningless, even if it is unscientific. In the development of his 'hypothetico-deductive model', Popper challenged the logical positivist demarcation criteria. The falsificationist method rests upon the assumption that the demarcation criteria between what is science and what is pseudo-science rests upon whether the statement involved is testable or not, rather than whether it is true or false. A pseudo-scientific statement is one which is tautologous, in that the conclusion is already implied in the premises and, as such, there is no possibility of falsification.

The origin of the hypothesis is unimportant for Popper, whether it is from a dream or a fanciful wish it remains useful so long as it can be submitted to an empirical test. Science is no longer the search for truth but, he argued, the careful and systematic use of the scientific method, that is, constructing statements about the world and testing them against the evidence. Thus Popper retained his commitment to the use of empirical evidence, but without the traps of positivism, such as the tendency to collect evidence which simply justified our existing beliefs and theories. This, he sugggested, would lead to stagnation in the accumulation of knowledge rather than progress (Popper, 1959, 1963). If you cannot disprove existing knowledge, then it will never change. Popper claimed to have solved the problem of induction. He argued that there is no way of arriving at a theory simply from experiment and/or observation. Without an original conjecture, one would not know where to start or which knowledge to seek in the first place.

Scientific hypotheses should be bold conjectures which could be tested against empirical evidence.

For Popper, **falsification** rather than **verification** becomes the criterion of science; in other words, scientists should find ways of disproving their working hypotheses and theories. The focus on refutation rather than confirmation prompts scientists to think harder about what they are doing and to innovate when the things they take for granted are questioned. Science becomes not the search for universal or objective truth, but a method, a set of logical procedures for the construction or testing of hypotheses, a process of 'trial and error'. Popper's approach specifies the means through which scientists can create progress rather than identifying the ends of knowledge. This approach is the only one compatible with Popper's liberal assumptions about what should constitute an 'open society', whereby each possible explanation of events is scrutinized in an open-minded and sensible way within an atmosphere of tolerance. For him, conjectures or hypotheses which survive attempts at refutation are seen as 'corroborated' but not confirmed (Popper, 1959, 1963). Popper asks us to be intentionally critical, to test ideas against the evidence to the limit and to avoid being dogmatic in research. Falsificationism, therefore, is as much an attitude to research as a set of methodological procedures.

Falsification is a set of procedures for scrutinizing existing knowledge claims and embodies the sceptical attitude proposed by Popper.

Activity 3.5

Now turn to Reading F, 'The professional stranger', by Eileen Barker, (1988) in which she discusses some of the problems encountered in her research into the Unification Church.

- Make notes on the steps involved in her research investigation and the choice of research techniques.

- Try to identify the working hypotheses of this investigation into a religious movement.

This is a fairly ambitious research project using quite a range of ways to gather evidence, yet it is all driven by a particular purpose. When you read social scientific research papers, you may find that the intention of the researcher is not immediately apparent – sometimes you have to read between the lines to identify what is going on. Don't worry if you find the second task quite difficult; if you read on you will find the answer.

For someone studying examples of social research in their chosen research field, there is a problem in trying to relate existing research sources to their own research practice. In particular, it is often difficult to disentangle the key working hypothesis from the broad set of issues examined in any individual study. Few studies clearly pinpoint one key idea or conjecture. In the case of Eileen Barker's research into the motivations which lead people to join a new religious movement, a whole range of issues immediately present themselves. Barker's research explores what it means to join the Unification Church – what motivates new recruits, how the sect introduces new members to the rituals and beliefs of the movement, what new members get out of the experience – as well as exploring how the Unification Church is viewed by people in the UK. However, there is an underlying hypothesis in this study which is a response to contemporary debates about new religious movements. Barker is responding specifically to newspaper accounts of the indoctrination and 'brainwashing' of new members in this and other religious sects. Therefore her key conjecture is:

The Unification Church 'brainwashes' its members.

During the course of her study, Barker actually discovered that most members left the movement after a short period of time, usually 'burned out' from excessively intense involvement (Barker, 1984). This meant that the key conjecture had been falsified, for brainwashed members simply would not leave. Consequently, she was able to move on from the widely held simplistic hypothesis and investigate more effectively the complex motivations involved. As a result, we now know a great deal more about what it means to join a religious sect, which reinforces Popper's argument that refutation leads to the accumulation of knowledge.

The falsificationist version of the 'hypothetico-deductive method' developed by Popper is the most widely respected and influential version of the deductive model. However, we should also note that Popper's approach is an idealized reconstruction of the process through which scientists construct their theories and weigh up their hypotheses against the empirical evidence (modelled upon physics). For Popper, scientific advance can only come through the testing and attempted falsification of hypotheses replacing them, if necessary, by modified or new ones. Scientific progress thus involves a continual process of conjecture and refutation.

For Popper, statements which cannot be empirically tested are pseudo-scientific, but they are not meaningless.

Statements which cannot be empirically tested are simply non-scientific or tautological, and theories composed of such statements are dismissed as 'pseudo-sciences'. Popper specifically identifies psychoanalysis, astrology and Marxism as such approaches, so that the claims made by Freud, 'Mystic Meg' and Marx all suffer from the same flaws. For instance, Popper suggests that Marx made categorical rather than conditional claims about the nature of capitalism. A categorical claim contains the assumption that the statement must be true in all circumstances where it is relevant. For example, Marx made the categorical claim that, within the capitalist system, the interests of capital always overcome the interests of the workers. For Popper, the evidence that workers' interests can overcome the interests of capitalists suggests that this depends upon precise empirical conditions. In addition, he argues, Marx made a series of predictions which have not been borne out by experience, regarding the laws of motion of capitalism and the historical inevitability of revolution in advanced capitalist societies. By Popper's account of the **demarcation criteria**, Marxism falls far short of a scientific theory because it ignores refuting evidence.

The testing of hypotheses in the social sciences (or the treatment of established theories as conjectures) is a common feature of post-war sociological research. In the research on *The Symmetrical Family* (1973), the work of Michael Young and Peter Willmott can be seen as an attempt to test the 'march of progress thesis' against empirical evidence in the early 1970s. This thesis was developed within functionalist sociology in the 1940s and 1950s and portrays the normal family as nuclear in form and increasingly democratic in its internal relations between marital partners and between parents and children. One critic referred to this as a picture of 'sympathetic spouses and well adjusted children'. In their sample of homes in the south east of England, Young and Willmott demonstrate the corroboration of this thesis in both middle-class and working-class households. Interestingly, the research of Ann Oakley in *The Sociology of Housework* (1974), using **qualitative** data (in-depth interviews with forty housewives), can be taken as a falsification of these results, since she reveals women's profound dissatisfaction with housework and persistent inequalities between husbands and wives.

Falsification can be achieved through a variety of research methods. It is not solely connected to survey evidence.

An example of falsification of a hypothesis can be seen in the research of John Goldthorpe et al. in *The Affluent Worker Studies* (1968–9) which attempts to test the 'embourgeoisement thesis' (the conjecture that the working class were becoming middle class), a theme of sociology since the late nineteenth century. They discovered in their examination of the personal lives, working lives and political attitudes of workers who moved to the 'new town' of Luton following World War II that, while the working class is not becoming middle class, but is certainly experiencing a period of change. The traditional class-conscious working class, it is argued, is being transformed into instrumental self-interested affluent workers. In this case, an alternative hypothesis was generated – which had previously not been considered, so creating new knowledge. On a more critical note, this whole venture rests upon the assumption that the working class was actually a homogenous, class-conscious and organized proletariat in the first place, which historical research has since thrown into doubt. The identification of complex divisions in the organization of the working class over the last century, in terms of skill differentials, forms of association and cultural values, raises fundamental problems with the view that a largely homogenous working class is becoming more divided and fractured.

Both the 'march of progress thesis' and the 'embourgeoisement thesis' can be taken as examples of a common tendency in the social sciences to form hypotheses that assume that progress has indeed taken place, that human relations are becoming fairer and more just, more democratic and egalitarian, and that generally the lives of all members of society are getting better and better. Conversely, you may also encounter hypotheses based upon the assumption that human relations are worsening, that the social fabric is collapsing and that a 'golden age' of order, tranquillity and stability has vanished. These assumptions reflect an alternative underlying value position that 'progress' means decadence and degeneration. This attitude was

Falsification highlights the danger in believing that progress or social decline automatically occur over time. For Popper, progress is knowledge achieved by demonstrating that something is untrue.

epitomized by the political rhetoric of Sir John Stokes when he claimed that 'The twentieth century is a grotesque mistake.' Many hypotheses developed in social research in relation to the decline of religious participation, the 'rising tide' of crime, the increase in divorce and single parenthood are often based upon this underlying assumption. Such blanket claims about progress and moral decline should be regarded with a great deal of care, if not suspicion.

The success of the supporters of positivism in establishing this approach as the model of scientific inquiry to take seriously has helped create a story-line which often treats the Vienna Circle as the 'only game in town' in the 1920s. Many versions of the story of science go on to trace the success of Popper, a fellow Austrian, in developing the cutting edge of scientific inquiry in the post-war period. Popper became so highly regarded that some saw him as the 'Kant of the twentieth century'. In addition, his presence at the London School of Economics in the 1950s gave him a pivotal position in influencing social scientific practice. Until the 1960s, half of all the UK's graduates in the social sciences passed through the LSE and many went on to take up the new social science lectureships created by the expansion of higher education in the 1960s and 1970s. This academic generation placed Popper's approach firmly on the agenda of most undergraduate programmes. In fact, a whole range of alternatives existed in the early twentieth century which have had, and continue to have, an impact on social scientific practice, and many of these had their roots in Vienna. These idealist approaches, which put a greater emphasis on the role of ideas in the organization of empirical experience, are explored in greater detail in Chapter 4. Even social scientists in the post-war period who used the falsificationist approach did so in a variety of ways. It is also fair to say that social scientists have often paid lip-service to Popper's falsificationism although in practice they have behaved as if they were verificationists. This means that we need to be careful when examining how existing research is constructed. You will have the opportunity to explore the relationship between formal, perhaps idealized, accounts of scientific method and the actual practices of scientists in Chapter 5.

As you have seen in the previous sections on the history of science, approaches to the scientific method come and go, and each 'true view' has been replaced by another. For Popper, then, truth was a matter of degree rather than an absolute, because there was no way of being certain that the theories and assumptions we presently hold are true for all time. Instead, Popper turned critical inquiry and scepticism into a virtue by linking progress in knowledge to the refutation of existing laws and theories. Popper saw the development of scientific knowledge as an endless journey in which we have to discard worn-out truths in order to move on.

Summary

The method of induction, while popular as a conventional tool among natural and social scientists, became increasingly associated with confirming established opinions in the twentieth century. In addition, Popper and others argued that induction was not only untenable but self-contradictory. For Popper, the demarcation between science and non-science was whether or not a conjecture was testable.

Falsificationism was developed as an alternative approach, to allow for the use of the scientists' faculties for critical reasoning in the context of strict guidelines on the need for empirical testing at all stages of inquiry. In particular, truth was sacrificed to ensure progress in knowledge. This approach was empiricist but also managed to avoid some of the problems associated with positivism.

6   Positivist and empiricist approaches on the economy

If we look at one social science discipline, in this case economics, we have the opportunity to explore the implications of each of the approaches discussed in this chapter so far. In particular, we focus on the positivist and falsificationist approaches in this field of knowledge. 'Positive economics' is an explicitly acknowledged label which many economists have taken to indicate the factual and scientific character of their work. The term 'positive' is taken to refer to the acceptance of a clear separation of facts from values, and hence positive economics is often defined in opposition to normative economics. Defined in this way, positive economics is descriptive economics, concerned with what 'is', whereas normative economics is value driven, concerned with what 'ought to be'. Positive economics has its roots in the advocacy of **induction** and **phenomenalism** by John Stuart Mill in *A System of Logic* (1843/1879) and the dominance of his *Principles of Political Economy* (1848/1970) in the teaching of economics in Britain in the nineteenth century. This did not go unchallenged, and deductivism was soon proposed as an alternative within economics. For much of the history of economics, the methodological pendulum has swung between these two positions. A useful example of the positivist attitude towards research can be found in Richard Lipsey's *Introduction to Positive Economics* (1963/1979), a standard textbook from the 1960s to the 1980s:

In economics, positivism is associated with descriptive approaches to the economy, demonstrating how it works through the use of empirical evidence.

> Very roughly speaking, the scientific approach consists in relating questions to evidence. When presented with a controversial issue, the scientist will ask what is the evidence on both sides. He [*sic*] may then take a stand on the issue with more or less conviction depending on the weight of the evidence. If there is little or no evidence, the scientist will say that, at present, it is impossible to take a stand. He will then set about searching for relevant evidence. If he finds that the issue is framed in terms of questions about which it is impossible to gather evidence, he will try to recast the questions so that they can be answered by an appeal to evidence. This approach to a problem is what sets scientific inquiries off from other kinds of inquiries. ... Experimental science such as chemistry and some branches of psychology, have an advantage because it is possible to produce relevant evidence through controlled laboratory

experiments. Other sciences ... must wait for time to throw up observations that may be used to test hypotheses.

(Lipsey, 1979, pp.7–8)

The effect of textbook statements such as these should not be under-estimated, for in any discipline we start to learn and become familiar with the material in a particular subject through standard disciplinary textbooks. This extract contains an uncritical approach towards the relationship between facts and values and does not even glance at the contentious issues surrounding the choice of topic and methods. Moral questions are treated as if they are of no concern to social researchers, in a way which is common in research within the natural sciences. This attitude expresses the view that science is the detached exercise of certain specified methods, regardless of the qualities of the objects in question. Human behaviour is seen as predictable in its responses to various stimuli; for instance, seasonal consumption patterns in the market place are quite predictable (we buy more toys just before Christmas, and tennis balls in June and July). Consequently, positive economics tends to treat explanations as useful only in so far as they make reliable predictions, preferably about large groups of individuals. In this context, a reliable prediction is one which is supported by repeated tests against empirical evidence.

Positive economics usually assumes that good explanations must be predictively successful.

As you saw in the quotation above from Lipsey, the importance of prediction is very closely tied to the desire to achieve some means of closure. Since it is not plausible to replicate the experimental situation when studying economic processes, positive economics has attempted to achieve this theoretically. This can be demonstrated by examining the theory of perfect competition, a set of assumptions about the operation of exchange relationships in markets. The acts of exchange in this model take place between firms and/or households. In the hypothetical state of perfect competition it is assumed that, at a particular price, the demand for goods or services will be balanced with the available supply of the same goods or services. The price in this condition is described as the equilibrium price. When we examine the assumptions about the actors involved, it becomes clearer how much this condition is an abstraction from real economic processes. The firms in this model are seen as 'price takers'; that is, they can respond to changes in prices by immediately altering their production rates. In addition, it is assumed that firms can enter and exit from different markets without difficulty. The consumers (or households) are assumed to have perfect knowledge of the goods and services and can alter their purchasing behaviour quickly and simply according to the principles of cost–benefit analysis. The behaviour of all the actors in this model is in terms of opportunity cost, that as individuals make choices to do things they prevent themselves from doing other things, as much as in terms of the satisfaction of their preferences through the action chosen. On the basis of this simple model then, complications are gradually introduced (such as the existence of monopolies, the presence of trade unions and restrictions introduced by the state) in an attempt to replicate the actual conditions of markets.

See Chapter 2, section 2.2 on experimental and theoretical closure in science.

Ultimately, the assumptions which underlie the rational behaviour of actors in the model are the weak point of the whole exercise, for human intentions, desires and interpretations are difficult to predict with the precision of a calculus. Much depends upon whether such theoretical devices are seen as heuristic devices for attempting to explain and understand complex social objects or as an accurate portrayal of real processes and events. While Lipsey raises the importance of refutations in generating scientific explanations and the impossibility of absolute proof, his account of theory construction and the collection of empirical evidence in economics is drawn from the 'covering law model' developed by Hempel which you explored in sections 4.3 and 4.4, as Figure 3.7 demonstrates. I must hasten to add that many contemporary economists would question the usefulness of this approach. I include it here simply as a useful example of the practical implications of constructing a positivist social science.

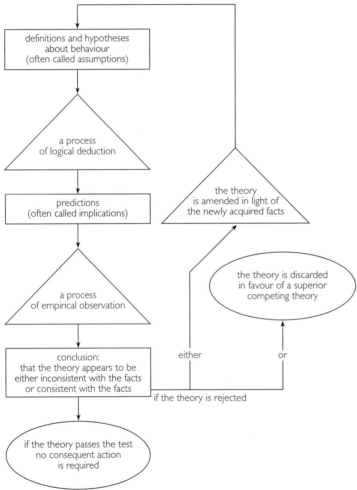

Figure 3.7   Richard Lipsey's version of the covering law model.

An interesting alternative approach, which still seeks to produce objective knowledge, can be seen in Milton Friedman's article 'The Methodology of Positive Economics' (Friedman, 1953). This approach has had a significant impact upon working economists as a guide to action in the processing of empirical data sets. Friedman argues strongly in favour of economics as an objective science. However, in some respects, his *methodological instrumentalist* approach differs from the covering law approach of Hempel. Unlike standard positivism, Friedman questions whether prediction should be the key criterion for establishing the authenticity of a theory. For

The instrumentalist approach in positive economics places less emphasis on prediction and sees all statements as guides to understanding.

Friedman, economic theories are instruments which cannot be seen in any way as true or false, and predictions hold no explanatory uses. Bruce Caldwell, an economist and historian of economic thought, suggests that these differences are instructive across the social sciences: 'Economists should not fall into the trap of believing that they have explained things when all they have done is predict accurately' (Caldwell, 1994, p.186).

Social scientists have often fallen into such traps by assuming that good predictors provide an explanation. Statistical correlations, where two variables reveal a common or similar frequency, are often used to good effect in identifying potential relationships. However, it is possible to achieve high correlations between variables where causal explanations are as yet undiscovered or are unlikely to be discovered. Some evidence exists of correlations between sunspot activity and particular weather systems. In contrast, the discovery of a high correlation between the growth of the stork population in western Europe and the human birth-rate can be seen as less plausible except for social scientists who believe in fairy stories.

With its emphasis upon prediction, economics is packed full of examples of statistical correlations which have been taken too seriously and transformed, inappropriately, into causal explanations. Economic policy makers in the early 1980s accepted Friedman's emphasis on the close relationship between the growth in the money supply in the economy and the inflation rate. Evidence suggested that when there was more money in circulation, following a time lag, prices increased, an argument supported by periods of hyperinflation such as in Germany in the early 1920s or in the first years of the Yeltsin administration in Russia in the early 1990s. However, this theory was applied in reverse under Thatcher's first administration of 1979–82, with the government limiting the money supply in order to deflate the economy and control inflation. In this situation, the predictive power of the theory was undermined. In the early 1980s the various indicators of the money supply suggested an increase in the supply, exceeding the targets suggested by economists, yet inflation declined. By 1985 the Bank of England expressed serious doubts about the money supply as a predictor and went on to question Friedman's analysis of the money–price relationship. In a more whimsical intervention, a Keynesian economist demonstrated that Scottish dysentery rates were a better predictor of inflation trends than the money supply. Others suggested that this was a good illustration of Goodhart's Law, which states that a theory works until it is applied as economic policy and affects the behaviour of those who are the object of the study. In this case, the change of government policy changed the processes at work in the economy and hence undermined the accuracy of the theory.

Economics contains evidence of significant progress through the falsificationist method to scientific knowledge.

Mark Blaug, whose work is largely responsible for the rebirth of interest in economic methodology since the late 1970s, suggests that the falsificationist approach developed by Popper offers a good description of what many economists do as well as a method which the remainder should adopt (Blaug, 1992). Blaug rests his case on the evidence of innovation and progress (both theoretical and empirical progress) in economics in the twentieth century, which he suggests emerged from the refutation of earlier approaches and the bold conjectures of economists which have survived attempts at refutation. Among his examples are the welfare economics of Antoine Pigou and Kenneth Arrow, the game theory of John von Neumann and Oskar Morgenstern, and econometrics (economic forecasting) by Paul Samuelson and others (Blaug, 1994, pp.109–36).

What is common to all the approaches you have encountered in this chapter, whether they are positivist or falsificationist, is their commitment to empiricism and the belief of their supporters that their method is applicable in all circumstances. Tony Lawson provides us with useful warning against attempting to impose a particular method regardless of the object in question:

> Imagine a situation in which an instrument of some sort has been found to be useful for a specific task. Let us suppose that a big stick is used successfully to beat and thereby to clean a dusty old mat. Imagine also that the inference is automatically made that if such an instrument is found to be useful for one job it must also be useful for any related jobs. Specifically, let us suppose that it is inferred from the success of the big stick in helping to clean the dusty old mat that it must also be of use in cleaning a dusty glass window – and that the window is duly beaten. No doubt many will find such an inference and act preposterous. But why? Presumably because we know enough of the nature of glass windows and big sticks to infer that (a) beating the window with a stick is unlikely to prove to be a successful way of cleaning it (to say the least); while (b) alternative more promising ways of cleaning the window can easily be devised. Imagine, furthermore, that the 'stick-cleans-windows' theory is put to the test and consequent upon the repeated instances of broken glass the inference repeatedly drawn is that it is necessary to 'try that little bit harder' – perhaps on the grounds that it is the wrong windows so far that have been beaten, and/or it is simply imagined that success is (always) around the corner. No doubt the perpetrator of the theory would be dismissed as a rather unreflective dogmatist. Certainly, he or she is unlikely to be retained for long as a window cleaner.

> (Lawson, 1994, p.258)

Lawson, a contemporary **realist** economist, believes that the things we study as social scientists have complex internal structures. This matters, he suggests, when we construct concepts and select methods to study our chosen objects. If this is the case – that one size does not fit all – then we need to be more flexible and innovative in our models of scientific inquiry.

Don't worry about realism yet, it's in Chapter 7.

7   Conclusion: the common foundations of empiricism

For much of this chapter we have explored a range of the key approaches which have all claimed to be able to generate objective scientific knowledge and the different ways in which they justify this claim. However, despite such wide differences regarding the relationship between theory and observation, the verificationist and falsificationist programmes have a great deal in common, especially their understanding of causality. For all these approaches an 'empirical regularity' is both necessary and sufficient for

g

establishing a **causal law**. This means that all empiricist approaches view closed systems as the means through which scientific explanations can be attained.

The battlefield between these competing approaches, rather than being strewn with dead bodies and mortally wounded scientists and philosophers, is more reminiscent of a ritual mock battle by the English Civil War Society – a great deal of smoke but very little real conflict. Ian Hacking, a philosopher of natural science, provides a neat summation of the differences between the positivist and verificationist assumptions of Carnap on the one hand and the falsificationism of Popper on the other. The differences between them can be seen as superficial when you consider the common foundations of each approach:

> Carnap thought that 'meanings' and a theory of 'language' matter to the philosophy of science. Popper despised them as scholastic. Carnap tried to explicate good reason in terms of a theory of 'confirmation'. Popper held that rationality consists in 'method'. Carnap believed in 'induction'; Popper held that there is no logic except 'deduction' ... whenever we find two philosophers who line up exactly opposite on a series of half a dozen points we know that in fact they agree about almost everything. They share an image of science.

> (Hacking, 1983, pp.4–5)

Despite the differences between the uses of induction and deduction, verification and falsification, there are common foundations.

Ultimately, in terms of what scientists actually do, there is not a great deal of difference between 'corroboration' and 'confirmation' except in terms of which formal logic such scientists adopt as their background frame of reference and mode of presentation. Even so, they agree upon the 'pretty sharp distinction between observation and theory', that 'scientific terminology is or ought to be precise', and that there should be a 'unity of science', that all sciences should utilize the same logic and methods (Hacking, 1983, p.5). On the big issues of the foundations of scientific knowledge and its role in generating human progress, it is impossible to slip a cigarette paper between them.

Activity 3.6

Now briefly return to the introduction at the start of this chapter and reread the six epistemological principles of positivism (Figure 3.1). Once you have completed this, make a list of the differences between the positivist approach and the more general empiricist position (as expressed by Popper, for instance).

So far, you have encountered a range of approaches which have been identified as positivist in some way or, more broadly, empiricist. Empiricism is often used as a synonymous label for positivism, but it also includes positions which can be described as post-positivist. Since Popper remains committed to empiricism and describes his approach as post-positivist, positivism can be categorized as a sub-branch of empiricism. Earlier, you saw how logical positivism subscribes to all of the six general assumptions of positivism. Empiricism involves the collection of observable empirical evidence of discrete variables or objects in order to test a hypothesis in a new situation as a way of generating new knowledge. Out of the six assumptions, **empiricism** unreservedly accepts the assumptions of **phenomenalism, atomism** and the possibility of general **scientific laws**.

Once we take Popper's falsificationist approach into account, we can also see it is possible to remain an empiricist without holding to the other three assumptions in the same way. In falsificationism it is possible to test value-laden statements which have no relationship to previous experience but which nevertheless remain open to (preferably simple) empirical test conditions. Thus in empiricism it is also possible to reject the principle of **nominalism**, for ideas are more than names for things we can experience. Postpositivist empiricism accepts that meaningful interpretations can play a legitimate part in science, which can cause problems in clearly distinguishing **facts** from **values**. However, this means that all statements, if they are to be regarded as objective in any sense, must be tied down by reference to strict empirical tests. Finally, falsificationism also qualifies our acceptance of **naturalism**, by accommodating different criteria for demarcating science from non-science. For some empiricists, science, it seems, is a set of methodological procedures rather than the identification of a true account of reality.

The differences between positivist and falsificationist approaches can be identified in terms of the origin and role of theories in the activity of empirical research. For Popper, there remains a need to control values and subjective assumptions in research, but to rule these out would be to eliminate valuable intuitions and insights which have been shown to work. It would seem that Popper has some sense of what scientists actually do. Certainly, while Popper rejects metaphysics in science, he, like the logical positivists, does not accept that this problem can be eliminated by restructuring the formal language system of science, nor does he see metaphysical statements as meaningless. Despite the assumptions held in common among empiricists, there are substantial differences in their accounts of the imagination involved in theory construction. For logical positivists, ideas should be a simple reflection of our impressions and perceptions, and that the words on a page should mean the same thing to whoever reads them. Popper accepts that ideas do not always emerge from observation, but also from hunches, guesswork, even those 'eureka' moments when we receive a flash of inspiration. However, if the ideas are not able to be independently tested against experiences they cannot be trusted. For Popper, theories are still separate from observations, so the way we imagine the world is still separate from our sensations, perceptions and impressions of it. It is to the role of the human imagination in constructing social scientific knowledge that we now turn in the next chapter.

Popper
empiricism

| naturalism |
| phenomenalism |
| nominalism |
| atomism |
| scientific laws |
| facts/values |

Values are part of the research process, but they must be strictly controlled through reference to empirical evidence.

READING A
The positive philosophy and scientific laws

Auguste Comte

In order to understand the true value and character of the Positive Philosophy, we must take a brief general view of the progressive course of the human mind, regarded as a whole; for no conception can be understood otherwise than through its history.

From the study of the development of human intelligence, in all directions, and through all times, the discovery arises of a great fundamental law, to which it is necessarily subject, and which has a solid foundation of proof, both in the facts of our organization and in our historical experience. The law is this: that each of our leading conceptions, each branch of our knowledge, passes successively through three different theoretical conditions: the Theological, or fictitious; the Metaphysical, or abstract; and the Scientific, or positive. In other words, the human mind, by its nature, employs in its progress three methods of philosophizing, the character of which is essentially different, and even radically opposed: viz, the theological method, the metaphysical and the positive. Hence arise three philosophies, or general systems of conceptions on the aggregate of phenomena, each of which excludes the others. The first is the necessary point of departure of the human understanding; and the third is its fixed and definite state. The second is merely a state of transition.

In the theological state, the human mind, seeking the essential nature of beings, the first and final causes (the origin and purpose) of all effects – in short, Absolute knowledge – supposes all phenomena to be produced by the immediate action of supernatural beings.

In the metaphysical state, which is only a modification of the first, the mind supposes, instead of supernatural beings, abstract forces, veritable entities (that is, personified abstractions) inherent in all beings, and capable of producing all phenomena. ...

In the final, the positive state, the mind has given over the vain search after Absolute notions, the origin and destination of the universe, and the causes of phenomena, and applies itself to the study of their laws, that is, their invariable relations of succession and resemblance. Reasoning and obser-vation, duly combined, are the means of this knowledge. ...

The first characteristic of the Positive Philosophy is that it regards all phenomena as subjected to invariable natural *Laws*. ... Our real business is to analyse accurately the circumstances of phenomena, and to connect them by the natural relations of succession and resemblance. ...

Before ascertaining the stage which the Positive Philosophy has reached, we must bear in mind that the different kinds of our knowledge have passed through the three stages of progress at different rates, and have not therefore arrived at the same time. The rate of advance depends on the nature of the knowledge in question, so distinctly that, as we shall see hereafter, this consideration constitutes an accessory to the fundamental law of progress. Any kind of knowledge reaches the positive stage early in proportion to its generality, simplicity and independence of other departments. Astronomical science, which is above all made up of facts that are general, simple, and independent of other sciences, arrived first; then terrestrial Physics; then Chemistry; and, at length, Physiology. ...

Nothing was said of Social phenomena. Though involved with the physiological, Social phenomena demand a distinct classification, both on account of their importance and of their difficulty. They are the most individual, the most complicated, the most dependent on all others; and therefore they must be the latest. ...

Statics and dynamics

The philosophical principle of the science being that social phenomena are subject to natural laws, ... we have to ascertain what is the precise subject, and what the peculiar character of those laws. The distinction between the Statical and Dynamical conditions of the subject must be extended to social science; and I shall treat of the conditions of social existence as, in biology, ... anatomy; and then of the laws of social movement, as in biology of those of life, under the head of physiology. The distinction is not between two classes of facts, but between two aspects of a theory. It corresponds with the double conception of order and progress: for order consists (in a positive sense) in a permanent harmony among the conditions of social existence; and progress consists in social development; and the conditions in the one case, and the laws of movement in the other, constitute the statics and dynamics of social physics. ...

That statical study of sociology consists in the investigation of the laws of action and reaction of the different parts of the social system ... in mutual relation, and forming a whole which compels us to treat them in combination. ...

Passing on from statical to dynamical sociology, we will contemplate the philosophical conception which should govern our study of the movement of society. ...

Though the statical view of society is the basis of sociology, the dynamical view is not only the more interesting of the two, but the more marked in its philosophical character, from its being more distinguished from biology by the master-thought of continuous progress, or rather, of the gradual development of humanity. ...

The true general spirit of social dynamics then consists in conceiving of each of these consecutive social states as the necessary result of the preceding, and the indispensable mover of the following, ... *the present is big with the future.* In this view, the object of science is to discover the laws which govern this continuity, and the aggregate of which determines the course of human development. In short, social dynamics studies the laws of succession, while social statics inquires into those of coexistence. ...

One consideration remains, of the more importance: ... I mean the consideration of Man's action on the external world, the gradual development of which affords one of the chief aspects of the social evolution ... In short, all human progress, political, moral or intellectual, is inseparable from material progression, in virtue of the close interconnection which, as we have seen, characterizes the natural course of social phenomena.

Source: Comte, 1853/1971, pp.18–21, 24–6, 31–2.

READING B
The principle of utility

Jeremy Bentham

I   *Mankind governed by pain and pleasure.*
Nature has placed mankind under the governance of two sovereign masters, *pain* and *pleasure*. It is for them alone to point out what we ought to do, as well as to determine what we shall do. On the one hand the standard of right and wrong, on the other the chain of causes and effects, are fastened to their throne. They govern us in all we do, in all we say, in all we think ... *The principle of utility* recognizes this subjection, and assumes it for the foundation of that system ...

II   *Principle of utility, what.* ... By the principle of utility is meant that principle which approves or disapproves of every action whatsoever, according to the tendency which it appears to have to augment or diminish the happiness of the party whose interest is in question: or, what is the same thing in other words, to promote or to oppose that happiness. I say of every action whatsoever; and therefore not only of every action of a private individual, but of every measure of government.

III   *Utility, what.* By utility is meant that property in any object, whereby it tends to produce benefit, advantage, pleasure, good, or happiness ... or ... to prevent the happening of mischief, pain, evil, or unhappiness to the party whose interest is considered; if that party be the community in general, then the happiness of the community; if a particular individual, then the happiness of that individual.

IV   *Interest of the community, what.* ... The community is a fictitious *body*, composed of the individual persons who are considered as constituting as it were its *members*. The interest of the community then is, what? – the sum of the interests of the several members who compose it.

V   It is in vain to talk of the interest of the community, without understanding what is the interest of the individual. A thing is said to promote the interest, or to be *for* the interest, of an individual, when it tends to add to the sum total of his pleasures: or, what comes to the same thing, to diminish the sum total of his pains.

VI   *An action conformable to the principle of utility, what.* An action then may be said to be conformable to the principle of utility ... (meaning with respect to the community at large) when the tendency it has to augment the happiness of the community is greater than any it has to diminish it.

VII *A measure of government conformable to the principle of utility, what.* A measure of government (which is but a particular kind of action, performed by a particular person or persons) may be said to be conformable to or dictated by the principle of utility, when in like manner the tendency which it has to augment the happiness of the community is greater than any which it has to diminish it. ...

Source: Bentham, 1824/1987, pp.65–6.

READING C
Samuel George Morton – empiricist of polygeny

Stephen Jay Gould

Morton's fame as a scientist rested upon his collection of skulls and their role in racial ranking. Since the cranial cavity of a human skull provides a faithful measure of the brain it once contained, Morton set out to rank races by the average sizes of their brains. He filled the cranial cavity with sifted white mustard seed, poured the seed back into a graduated cylinder and read the skull's volume in cubic inches. Later on, he became dissatisfied with mustard seed because he could not obtain consistent results. The seeds did not pack well, for they were too light and still varied too much in size, despite sieving. ... Consequently, he switched to one-eighth-inch-diameter lead shot 'of the size called BB' and achieved consistent results that never varied by more than a single cubic inch for the same skull.

Morton published three major works on the sizes of human skulls – his lavish, beautifully illustrated volume on American Indians, the *Crania Americana* of 1839; his studies on skulls from the Egyptian tombs, the *Crania Aegyptiaca* of 1844; and the epitome of his entire collection in 1849. Each contained a table, summarizing his results on average skull volumes arranged by race. ... They represent the major contribution of American polygeny to debates about racial ranking. They outlived the theory of separate creations and were reprinted repeatedly during the nineteenth century as irrefutable, 'hard' data on the mental worth of human races. Needless to say, they matched every good Yankee's prejudice – whites on top, Indians in the middle, and blacks on the bottom; and, among whites, Teutons and Anglo-Saxons on top, Jews in the middle, and Hindus on the bottom. Moreover, the pattern had been stable throughout recorded history, for whites had the same advantage over blacks in ancient Egypt. Status and access to power in Morton's America faithfully reflected biological merit. How could sentimentalists and egalitarians stand against the dictates of nature? Morton had provided clean, objective data based on the largest collection of skulls in the world.

During the summer of 1977 I spent several weeks reanalyzing Morton's data. (Morton, the self-styled objectivist, published all his raw information). ...

Morton's summaries are a patchwork of fudging and finagling in the clear interest of controlling a priori convictions. Yet – and this is the most intriguing aspect of the case – I find no evidence of conscious fraud; indeed, had Morton been a conscious fudger, he would not have published his data so openly.

Conscious fraud is probably rare in science. It is also not very interesting, for it tells us little about the nature of scientific activity. Liars, if discovered, are excommunicated; scientists declare that their profession has properly policed itself, and they return to work, mythology unimpaired, and objectively vindicated. The prevalence of *unconscious* finagling, on the other hand, suggests a general conclusion about the social context of science. For if scientists can be honestly self-deluded to Morton's extent, then prior prejudice may be found anywhere, even in the basics of measuring bones and toting sums. ...

Conclusions

Morton's finagling may be ordered into four general categories:

1   Favourable inconsistencies and shifting criteria: Morton often chose to include or delete large subsamples in order to match group averages with prior expectations. He included Inca Peruvians to decrease the Indian average, but deleted Hindus to raise the Caucasian mean. He also chose to present or not to calculate the averages of subsamples in striking accord with desired results. He made calculations for Caucasians to demonstrate the superiority of Teutons and Anglo-Saxons, but never presented data for Indian subsamples with equally high averages.

2   Subjectivity directed toward prior prejudice: Morton's measures with seed were sufficiently imprecise to permit a wide range of influence by subjective bias; later measures with shot, on the other hand, were repeatable, and presumably objective. In skulls measured by both methods, values for shot always exceed values for the light, poorly packing seed. But degrees of discrepancy match a priori assumptions: an average of 5.4, 2.2, and 1.8 cubic inches for blacks, Indians, and whites, respectively. In other words, blacks fared poorest and whites best when the results could be biased toward an expected result.

3   Procedural omissions that seem obvious to us: Morton was convinced that variation in skull size recorded differential, innate mental ability. He never considered alternate hypotheses, though his own data almost cried out for a different interpretation. Morton never computed means by sex or stature, even when he recorded these data in his tabulations – as for Egyptian mummies. Had he computed the effect of stature, he would presumably have recognized that it explained all important differences in brain size among his groups. Negroids yielded a lower average than Caucasians among his Egyptian skulls because the negroid sample probably contained a higher percentage of smaller-statured females, not because blacks are innately more stupid. The Incas that he included in the Indian sample both possessed small brains as a consequence of small body size. Morton used an all-female sample of three Hottentots to support the stupidity of blacks, and an all-male sample of Englishmen to assert the superiority of whites.

4   Miscalculations and convenient omissions: All miscalculations and omissions that I have detected are in Morton's favor. He rounded the negroid Egyptian average down to 79, rather than up to 80. He cited averages of 90 for Germans and Anglo-Saxons, but the correct values are 88 and 89. He excluded a large Chinese skull and an Eskimo subsample from his final tabulation for mongoloids, thus depressing their average below the Caucasian value.

Yet through all this juggling, I detect no sign of fraud or conscious manipulation. Morton made no attempt to cover his tracks and I must presume that he was unaware he had left them. He explained all his procedures and published all his raw data. All I can discern is an a priori conviction about racial ranking so powerful that it directed his tabulations along preestablished lines. Yet Morton was widely hailed as the objectivist of his age, the man who would rescue American science from the mire of unsupported speculation.

Source: Gould, 1981, pp.50–60, 68–9.

READING D
The intelligence of American negroes

Hans Eysenck

African negro children (and American negro children as well) show highly precocious sensorimotor development, as compared with white norms. Thus most of the African negro babies who were drawn up to a sitting position could keep head erect and back straight from the very first day of life; white babies typically require six to eight weeks to sustain these postures! It is implausible to assert that socio-economic differences or other extrinsic variables (particularly in so far as these disfavour negroes) could have produced this astonishing difference; the observed precocity lasts for about three years, after which time white children overtake the black ones. These findings are important because of a very general law in biology according to which the more prolonged the infancy, the greater in general are the cognitive or intellectual abilities of the species. This law appears to work even with a given species; thus sensori-motor precocity in humans, as shown in so-called 'baby-tests' of intelligence, is negatively correlated with terminal IQ. ...

When we turn to the direct measurement of intelligence, we are almost entirely restricted to work with American negroes; only there do we have a sufficiently uniform background to make comparisons between blacks and whites fruitful. This proposition is of course hotly contested by environ-mentalists who declare that we are dealing here with a sub-culture so different from the major (white) culture that no realistic and meaningful comparisons can in fact be made. ...

It is sometimes suggested that negro children are less highly motivated, or respond to different motivations; this is not borne out by such research (admittedly inadequate) as has been reported. Money and candy rewards only led to small improvements in the performance of negro children, and in their pattern of reaction to different types of incentive they did not notably differ from white children. ...

One very carefully chosen sample of white and black men was studied in order to see whether equating them on a large variety of background data, personality measures and test-taking attitude would eliminate the observed differences. Matching was done on age, education, occupation of parents, income of parents, geographical area of childhood home, army rank, number of years in the service, marital status, urban or rural background, and plans for re-enlistment, as well as on the personality and test-taking variables. Very significant differences of 10 to 14 points were again found, in spite of these efforts to eliminate socio-economic differences and 'intellectually defeating personality traits' from the comparison. ...

American Negroes on the average score something like 15 points of IQ below whites, with the southern negroes showing a greater gap, and the northern negroes a slighter one. These differences are sometimes expressed in terms of 'overlap', and it may be useful to introduce this concept into our discussion. By overlap is meant the percentage of negroes' scores that equals or exceeds the mean test score of the compared white group, i.e. the pro-

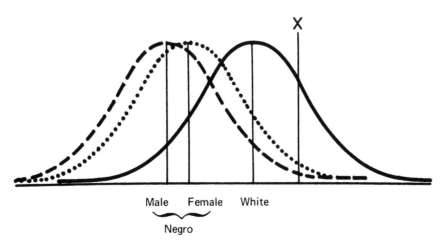

Figure 1 Diagrammatic distribution of IQs of whites, black males and black females. X marks some arbitrary minimum ability point on the IQ scale for college admission or similar qualifications. [Eysenck suggests that the distribution of IQ scores can be seen as variations on the normal distribution.]

portion of negroes having scores on IQ tests equal to or above the white mean. For school children, the average over-lap is approximately 12% (primary schools); for high school students (secondary school) it is approximately 10%. At the college level, overlap is 7%. This gives us an average over all groups of 11%, with overlap steadily decreasing as higher levels of scholastic attainment are being reached. Thus about one in ten negroes scores as high or higher than the average white. ...

This particular statistic has been criticized by several writers, on the grounds that it exaggerates the inferiority of negroes' scores. Unsophisticated readers are likely to run away with the impression that the curve of distribution of negroes' scores overlaps with that of whites' scores only to the extent of some 10%, and this of course is quite untrue. After all, if some 90% of negroes score below the white average, so do some 50% of whites! Consider ... the actual distribution of IQs for whites and a southern negro sample, i.e. a sample which shows a greater difference than would be found with northern, or mixed northern and southern negroes. The 'overlap' as defined in the preceding paragraph is obviously very small, amounting to less than 10%, but the overlap in the sense of distribution coincidence is quite large – only a minute proportion of negroes score lower than the lowest white, and only a small proportion of whites score better than the highest-scoring negro. It would seem that the term 'overlap', used in its technical sense, is indeed misleading and gives an impression of negro inferiority in no way justified by the facts. Of course writers are entitled to use descriptive statistics in any way they like, but there is no obvious advantage to the 'overlap' concept as compared to the much more widely used standard deviation, and the very name 'overlap' clearly misleads the casual reader who is unacquainted with statistical detail, and gives an erroneous impression. The facts regarding white and black comparisons on IQ scores are serious enough without exaggerating the observed differences in this manner. The excuse that the term is in fact usually carefully defined before being used is not good enough; simple statements about overlap being only 10% are often repeated in newspapers and other sources without careful definition, and many readers will therefore obtain quite the wrong view. Writers on the subject would seem to have a social duty to guard against misrepresentation, as well as being accurate in their statements; in this sense facts in a socially sensitive area are undoubtedly different to facts in other, not so sensitive areas where the use of arbitrary statistics, provided they are properly defined, is less dangerous.

Source: Eysenck, 1971, pp.84–99, 109–11.

READING E
The young delinquent

Cyril Burt

The cinema

The cinema, like the 'penny dreadful' before the advent of the film, has been freely censured and abused for stimulating the young adventurer to mischief, folly, and even crime. Among those who criticize it on this ground, the most credible are teachers of wide experience and magistrates of high standing; but perhaps none is so eager to advocate this view as the young culprit himself, who frequently sees, or thinks he sees, in such a derivation of his deeds to deflect blame and attention from his own moral laxity to that of the producer of films.

I have noted an excessive passion for the cinema among over 7 per cent of my delinquent boys – the child visiting the cinema on an average two or more times a week. In a few rare cases I have had to rank it as the principal cause of crime. An equal passion appears more seldom among the girls, namely, among only 1.4 per cent – these, unlike the male habitués, being all above school age. ...

It is alleged, in the first place, that what is called his 'faculty of imitativeness' renders the child peculiarly prone to copy whatever he witnesses upon the screen. 'Crook-films', it is said, are as popular as detective novelettes; the topic of crime has a special appeal to the young imagination; and if a boy or a girl has seen a representation of a cracksman breaking into a house, or a hooligan battering the police, or an adventuress proffering her love as the price of giddy pleasures, then, it is supposed, the child may be irresistibly inspired to re-enact in real life the fictitious example set before him. But how far, in point of fact, are children influenced in this way? On sifting the evidence ... adduced by those who express these fears, it is plain that both their inferences and their psychological assumptions are by no means free from fallacy. Nor are their facts better founded. They have between them hardly one well-attested instance from their own first-hand knowledge, hardly a single analysed case to put forward in proof. That certain children at certain ages are highly suggestible and imitative, I am far from wishing to dispute; and, beyond doubt, the peculiar conditions of cinematographic reproduction heighten this natural susceptibility still further by artificial means. The darkened hall, the atmosphere of crowd-excitement, the concrete vividness of visual presentation, the added realism due to movement and to the play of facial change, and, above everything, the intensely sensational character of the emotional scenes portrayed – all are calculated to increase the child's suggestibility, and to stamp upon the impressionable mind graphic images and lasting recollections. Mental pictures, so deeply imprinted, may sometimes issue in obsessions haunting and irrepressible – recurrent thoughts and impulses bound from their very persistence and strength to work themselves out by action. All this is not to be denied. Yet, of the ensuing acts, how much is crime? Most of the characters and situations rehearsed by film-smitten children are as innocent as those of any other piece of childish make-believe. ... The direct reproduction of serious film-crimes is, in my experience, exceedingly uncommon: and, even then, it is usually the criminal's method rather than the criminal's aim that is borrowed: the nefarious impulses themselves have been demonstrably in existence beforehand.

Four or five authentic instances I have, indeed, encountered, where a crime seemed directly inspired by the cinema; but they have been confined almost exclusively to the dull or the defective. ...

The attraction of the cinema, therefore, can be counted as a direct incentive, only where the child has acquired an overpowering habit, an inveterate taste and craving, for that particular form of diversion.

It is chiefly among boys that the picture-craze and the cinema-habit rise to this inordinate pitch. The commonest and most excusable instances occur when the child has been following week by week some absorbing film in serial form; and, money or no money, his eagerness to finish the concluding episodes is a passion too strong to overcome. ...

The main source of harm, however, has been as yet unmentioned. It is in the general and more elusive influences that the real danger of the cinema lies. Throughout the usual picture-palace programme, the moral atmosphere presented is an atmosphere of thoughtless frivolity and fun, relieved only by some sudden storm of passion with occasional splashes of sentiment. Deceit, flirtation, and jealousy, unscrupulous intrigue and reckless assault, a round of unceasing excitement and the extremes of wild emotionalism, are depicted as the normal characteristics of the everyday conduct of adults. The child, with no background of experience by which to correct the picture, frames a notion, altogether distorted, of social life and manners. The villain or the vampire, though outwitted in the end, has nevertheless to be portrayed with a halo of fictitious glamour, or interest would flag: he does wrong things; but he does them in a smart way, with daring, gallantry, and wit. It is true that, in most of the plays, the scoundrel is infallibly unmasked and eventually requited. But the hollow and factitious character of this pseudo-poetic justice seldom deludes the most youthful spectator. ...

The social dramas and the pictures of high life, with a force as subtle as it is cumulative, stir the curiosity, heat the imagination, and work upon the fantasies, of boys and girls of every age. They provide models and material for all-engrossing day-dreams; and create a yearning for a life of gaiety – a craze for fun, frolic, and adventure, for personal admiration and for extravagant self-display – to a degree that is usually unwholesome and almost invariably unwise.

Source: Burt, 1925/1961, p.143–9.

READING F
The professional stranger

(some methodological problems encountered in a study of the Reverend Sun Myung Moon's Unification Church)

Eileen Barker

The initial problem or impetus for carrying out research into the Unification Church (UC hereafter) was comparatively simple: why did people join and why did they stay in the movement? The problem was fairly sharply defined by the fact that ... people outside the UC ... could see no obvious attraction in what appeared by all accounts to be a bizarre, authoritarian sect, which held strange beliefs and whose members were ruthlessly exploited by a Korean gentleman who gave nothing but took all.

Immediately the basic problem was posed, it became necessary to turn to methodological considerations. What should the answer to my questions look like? Did I want to seek an explanation of the membership in terms of the members' social backgrounds or their psychological make-up? Might the explanation lie in the contemporary scene – the society which the Church and the members rejected? Or would it be more fruitful to assume the clues lay hidden in the UC itself, in its beliefs and practices and, especially, in the methods of recruitment which it employed? Were members the victims of social or psychological forces over which they had no control? Was I to assume *anyone*, given a particular social context, could be a Moonie (was this brainwashing?), or could I sort out a potential pool of converts from other, 'no-way', types? Was I myself to remain objective, scientific and uninvolved or did I need to immerse myself in the 'world view' of Mooniedom and share the subjective feelings and experiences of a 'Moonie trip'?

There is in sociology a time honoured dichotomy between those schools that focus on interpretative understanding and those that stress more behaviourist, positivistic or scientific approaches. What was to be my approach? Should I perhaps become an ethnomethodologist and investigate the taken-for-granted Moonie world, or should I regard Moonies as rats and dispassionately watch them running about their mazes, dismissing from my mind any notions of meaning or conscious purpose that could not be covered by stimulus/response or the more sophisticated operant-conditioning models of behaviour? Or perhaps I should forget about individuals as such and search only for structures and functions at a societal level? Would I adopt a philosophical anthropology that assumed we are

complicated but nonetheless determined, reacting robots: or are we free, initiating creators, capable of self determination? Whom would I believe when it came to descriptions of the Unification Church? Who was the more trustworthy, the brainwashed Moonies themselves or the sceptical critics? Would I learn more as an outsider or an insider? What was the true reality and how could I get to know about it? Was I to be guided by fact or theory or both? But which theory, and how was I to get the facts?

I began to realize that there could be no one answer. Several of the perspectives seemed to be necessary while none was sufficient for my purposes. I was convinced that without having a methodology as scientific as possible one would be unlikely to produce a sociological contribution that would add anything to all the claims and counter-claims which already existed. But it also seemed that without verstehen, or in other words some kind of emphatic understanding, one could not hope to find one's data in the first – or in the last – place. ...

In the end I decided on three main lines of approach: in-depth interview, participant observation and questionnaire. From the interview I hoped to understand the individual as an individual. Just over thirty interviews were carried out on the basis of a random sample of the membership. They were tape-recorded and usually lasted for between five and nine hours. The longest lasted for twelve hours. From the participant observation (that is, from living in UC centres and attending various courses), I hoped to observe the interpersonal level, and from the questionnaire I hoped to see patterns and relationships that I might suspect existed but about which I could only generalize from a large number of respondents. All the British members and several European and American members were given a forty-one page questionnaire containing both 'open' and 'pre-coded' questions. The response rate was surprisingly high and around 450 cases were fed into the computer for analysis. Added to these were over 100 responses to a similar questionnaire, filled in by a control group, that is by non-UC members who were similar in age and background (class, education and religion) to the UC membership. This was a methodological necessity if I were to be able to assess the extent to which the phenomena I was analysing were peculiar to the UC members. A further 'sub-control' of around 1,000 cases was [from those] interested enough to attend the Church's workshops but did not ... join the movement. In the event these control groups produced some of the most interesting data of the study.

Source: Barker, 1988, pp.5–11.

Chapter 4
Imagination and Complexity
in the Social Sciences

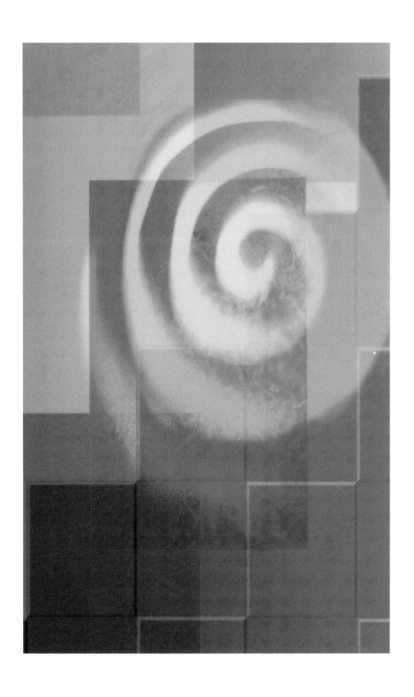

Contents

1	Introduction	129
2	The conceptual organization of experience: Kant's legacy	133
3	Understanding complexity	140
3.1	The emergence of neo-Kantianism	141
3.2	Facts, values and relevance in social science	144
3.3	Using ideal types	146
	Geographical Models 1	151
4	Rational choices and human action	155
4.1	Game theory	156
4.2	Problems in rational choice theory	158
5	Meaning and subjectivity	161
5.1	The self-concept and social interaction	162
5.2	Phenomenology and intersubjective meaning	164
5.3	Ethnomethodology and tacit knowledge	165
	Geographical Models 2	167
6	Conclusion: taking imagination seriously	171
Reading A		
	There is more to seeing than meets the eye *Norwood Hanson*	174
Reading B		
	Race relations in the city *John Rex and Robert Moore*	175
Reading C		
	The tragedy of the commons *Garrett Hardin*	177
Reading D		
	When rationality fails *Jon Elster*	178
Reading E		
	Normal rubbish: deviant patients in casualty departments *Roger Jeffery*	179

1   Introduction

In the earlier chapters we focused upon empiricist approaches in social research and considered how they applied natural scientific methods to the study of social objects. All of these accounts were primarily geared towards providing scientific explanations of distinct social objects rather than attempting to understand the meaning of social relationships and processes. As you will recall from Chapter 3, in the empiricist approach, theory and observation are treated as distinct things. Chapter 4 now challenges this assumption by arguing that it is not possible to separate theory and observation in this way and by examining the important role played by the human mind in the organization and interpretation of these observational experiences. While you will find that the approaches to social research covered here disagree about the precise role of imaginative interpretation of experience, they all agree that it is impossible to separate observation from the mental constructs we use to organize and understand our perceptions. Without such constructs in place, it is suggested, we simply cannot make sense of the complex world around us. For the sake of convenience, and to distinguish them clearly from empiricism, from this point onwards these approaches are labelled 'idealism'. There are many definitions of idealism, but in this chapter we are using the label to identify approaches which see knowledge as the use of ideas to organize experience.

Let's explore how different idealist approaches are from those of empiricism. For a start, they suggest that we should pay closer attention to the concepts and constructions which we invent and use as social scientists and recognize that we only come into contact with the 'real world' through these constructions. Moreover, as idealists reject the idea that observation is theory free, the clear separation of facts and values, which characterized empiricist social science, no longer holds so much weight as a key assumption of social science. Idealist approaches attempt to find a way of resolving the relationship between the development of scientific explanations and the role of interpretative understanding and cultural values. It is these very issues and problems that led empiricists to reject the formative role of values in scientific research in the first place. So, while empiricism tried to sidestep the issue, idealism takes this bull by the horns.

You may want to have a glance back at both Figure 3.1 and section 6 in Chapter 3.

We know from Chapter 3 that all empiricists are committed to **phenomenalism**. This assumes that the validity of a statement derives from the way it refers to empirical evidence. In short, empiricists assert that observations are the raw material from which we fashion theory. Positivist and empiricist approaches to the scientific method treat the role of interpretations, constructs, models and the human imagination as secondary factors in, if not irrelevant to, the study of empirical evidence. For instance, in logical positivism theoretical statements about observable evidence are treated as pictures of a definite state of affairs or, if they attempt to do more than this, they are seen as flawed by metaphysical assumptions. For empiricists, interpretative skills are seen, at best, as a necessary evil which must be constantly constrained by reference to empirical evidence. In Popper's case, scientific guesswork and hunches are constrained through repeated attempts at falsification. In the pursuit of **objective knowledge**, whereby facts and values are seen to be distinct, any attempt to bring subjective assessment into scientific research is regarded as a suspicious and poten-tially dangerous practice which tends to give rise to bias, distortion and prejudice.

In this chapter we also examine the problems involved in understanding the relationship between explanations and predictions. Idealist approaches enable us to account for **complexity** in social scientific research, as well as the simpler relationships established within the experimental setting. This means we will be considering accounts of social life which attempt to gen-erate explanations which do not depend upon a **closed system** of variables that can be clearly observed and measured. If it is recognized that social life is too complex to reproduce through experimental, theoretical and statisti-cal closure, then we should consider the role of the imagination of social scientists in putting together meaningful and plausible accounts of social relations and processes. In the following sections we look at four ways in which the role of imaginative thinking within natural and social scientific research is taken much more seriously.

See Chapter 2, section 2.2.

Each section addresses one of the four approaches (see Figure 4.1) which attempt to integrate the human imagination with scientific research, but reach different conclusions on how this should be done. In section 2, on the conceptual organization of experience, we briefly revisit the contri-bution of the Enlightenment thinker Immanuel Kant. In particular, we trace the role of interpretation and imagination in the organization of im-pressions and perceptions in both the natural and social sciences. Understanding Kant's position will enable you to gain a better sense of the three approaches in contemporary social science which are considered in the subsequent sections.

Idealism questions the assumption that only closed systems offer a basis for scientific laws and raises the possibility of social science using open systems – see Chapter 2, section 2.2.

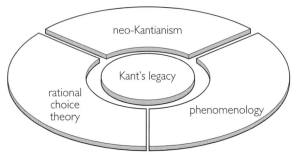

Figure 4.1   Imaginative approaches in the social sciences: the chapter structure.

As in Chapter 1, this sign helps you to keep track of your progress through the approaches.

In section 3 we explore the neo-Kantian approaches which have had a sig-nificant role in defining the problems familiar to the disciplines of the social sciences today. Here, we look at the use of 'ideal types' as a way of simpli-fying complex evidence. Ideal types are concepts which exaggerate aspects of social life in order to demonstrate the mechanisms through which social existence is produced. For instance, Max Weber developed three ideal types to characterize the dynamic patterns of behaviour in any interaction situation – habitual action, emotional action and rational action. None of these types actually exists in a pure state, but they serve as useful devices for organizing evidence and building a useful account of empirical reality. At this point, you will find the first of two sections on geographical models. Geographical Models 1 demonstrates how the neo-Kantian approach has been developed in one social scientific discipline.

Section 4 examines rational choice theory, a standpoint which differs, in some respects, from the other approaches considered in this chapter. Rational choice theory regards human beings as purposive rational actors and explores the ways in which the treatment of individuals as purely rational and self-interested can generate insights into human behaviour. This rational calculating individual is often characterized as a 'minimaxing' actor (for making decisions which minimize costs and maximize benefits). In addition, this approach is often portrayed as one which offers the possibility of general laws. You will be expected to consider whether this characterization of human action is an accurate one and to identify some of the problems in making unrealistic assumptions about human actors and the organization of social relations.

See Chapter 3, section 2.2, on Bentham.

See Chapter 1, section 4.1.

Finally, in section 5 we return to some of the themes raised briefly in Chapter 1 by considering the meaningful construction of social life. This section explores approaches developed by phenomenological or interpretive accounts of natural and social science. As you saw in Chapter 1 in Schütz's story of the person on the street, the cartographer and the stranger, this approach attempts to bridge the gap between subjective everyday experiences and objective explanations in social science. At the close of section 5, you will find the second part of the disciplinary case study. Geographical Models 2 explores how these phenomenological approaches can be applied in a particular social science. At any point in this chapter, to help you build a picture of the range of contemporary approaches in social research considered here, you may find it useful to refer to Table 4.1, which

Table 4.1 A quick guide to idealist approaches to knowledge construction.

	Varieties of Idealism			
	Neo-Kantian Idealism	**Rational Choice Theory**	**Hermeneutics and Phenomenology**	**Empiricism**
Theory and Observation	The complex empirical world is 'organized' through the use of mental constructs for comparing and contrasting evidence.	Theoretical work involves the reconstruction of rational decisions within definite constraints on the basis of calculations of costs and benefits of various courses of action.	The problem facing social science is the gulf between the everyday experiences of social actors and the detached accounts of social life produced by social scientists.	The scientific method involves a clear separation of theory and observation.
Facts and Values	The social sciences should be relevant to the problems of a particular society in question at a specific time.	Facts can only be identified through the subjective values and the intentional choices of individuals.	Scientific facts are the commonsense assumptions of the social scientists, for values remain unacknowledged in concept formation.	Facts and values are treated as separate to eliminate from scientific knowledge the researchers' subjective biases.
Explanation and Prediction	An empirical regularity beween variables is necessary but not sufficient for establishing a causal law. The complexity of causal factors in any empirical situation makes it difficult to make accurate predictions. Rational choice theory applies the same formal model across different situations.		Social settings only exist through the intersubjective relations of the actors involved as the product of meaningful communication.	For empiricists, successful predictions are effective explanations. Empirical regularities have the status of scientific laws.

provides a quick guide to the key assumptions, similarities and differences between idealist approaches, as well as a comparison with empiricism. A more detailed version of this table can be found in the conclusion to this chapter, once you have become more familiar with these approaches and what they mean in practice.

Before we look at these approaches more closely, we should consider what it is they attempt to address. All of these approaches consider the problems of thinking about experience and argue that the human imagination is a powerful tool which enables us to sift and sort the mass of sensory perceptions, impressions and experiences we constantly encounter. This enables us to establish patterns and formulate guidelines for our own choices and actions. In the study of natural objects, the role of the human imagination can be seen in the tendency to read social qualities or human sentiments into natural processes, that is, **anthropomorphism**. For instance, it is common to read what Western societies conventionally regard as feminine qualities into the forces of nature. Weather systems can be described as tempestuous and unpredictable, the product of mysterious forces. Within Western culture, this involves an implicit contrast to scientific attempts to observe, measure, dismantle and tame nature. For feminist interpretations of science, this is another reflection of the androcentric (male-centred) assumptions of the dominant culture of Western societies.

Let's explore the way in which the human imagination can lead us astray by taking a clear-cut example, that of media representations of animal behaviour. You may have noticed in natural history programmes that studies of primates reveal strongly subjective currents by identifying human qualities in the behaviour of various species of apes and monkeys. The popular science of Desmond Morris in *The Naked Ape* (1969) and *The Human Zoo* (1970) provides a good example of the problems of thinking about instinctive drives in human behaviour. Morris uses social qualities (such as 'male promiscuity') to define animal behaviour. Then, when explaining human courtship and sexual behaviour, the human male role is portrayed as a product of natural tendencies demonstrated by primates. For Morris, these natural tendencies always resurface in human behaviour when moral norms do not keep such 'animal passions' under control. In short, Morris has attributed social characteristics to animals, only to read them back into human behaviour as instinctual, in the process implying that male promiscuity is natural.

Even when describing natural things we need to take care – the words we use are always packed full of meaning.

You may have also noticed how such representations ignore the way that concepts such as 'promiscuity' can only be understood within a cultural setting. In this case, 'promiscuity' makes sense where there are moral and legal limitations on the number of sexual partners – something which cannot be identified in animal behaviour. Such imaginings, far from being neutral pictures of the world, are loaded with culturally specific values which involve complex sets of assumptions about permissible and impermissible behaviour. If such problems arise in the exploration of the relationship of society and nature, it should not be surprising that similar issues exist in the study of social objects. The remainder of this chapter provides you with some tools for unpacking the kinds of problem associated with thinking through the relationship between interpretation and observation, as well as continuing to explore the role of cultural values in social scientific practice.

2   The conceptual organization of experience: Kant's legacy

This section considers imaginative thinking in scientific knowledge. In Chapter 2 we saw how Immanuel Kant characterized the Enlightenment as a process containing the ethos of the critical spirit, that we should question all assumptions. To achieve this, he established a compromise position between **rationalism** (reason will lead us to the truth) and **empiricism** (observation and experimentation will lead us to the truth). Kant's approach emerged as a response to the inadequacies of both of these positions, although each approach had strengths as well as weaknesses (see Caygill, 1995). Empiricism, you will remember, had a solid foundation in sensory experience; however, it oversimplifies the relationship between theory and observation, for it treats the mind as a blank slate as if it is empty before receiving physical sensations. Rationalism, on the other hand, emphasized the important role of human reason in developing theories about the empirical world, but it also tended to neglect the role of observational evidence as a way of testing the validity of theoretical statements. Kant's compromise between these two positions sought to emphasize the strengths of each. For Kant, it is only through a 'synthesis' of both rational thinking and observable experiences that we can comprehend the world. In short, without reason we cannot make sense of our experiences and without observation we have nothing on which to employ our capacity for rational thought. It should be stressed that this is a synthesis, not a way of fitting the evidence conveniently within one's own theoretical model. This compromise became the basis of the range of approaches which attempted to place human imagination more clearly at the centre of social scientific inquiry.

Kant found a compromise between reason and observation by claiming that it is impossible to have one without the other – they should be seen as a synthesis.

It is useful to reconsider empiricism in a little more detail to gain a better sense of what Kant had in mind. This will help us to understand how he challenged the distinction between **analytic** and **synthetic** statements which came to be so central for the logical positivists. For the positivists, only analytic statements (that is, those that are true by definition) can be known through reason alone rather than through human experience. Such analytic statements are logically true by virtue of the meanings of the words they contain. Consider the statement 'Roses are flowers'. If we already understand what roses are, then this statement has the same logical status as 'A short man is a man'. It does not tell us anything new, for we already know this to be true by definition. The truth of all other statements rests upon observation, such as 'These roses are yellow and fragrant'. Statements like this are synthetic, for they express in ideas the textures, colours, sounds, odours, tastes and motions of the objects of our experiences. Kant was inspired by the clear thinking and conceptual tools developed by empiricists like David Hume, but he argued that empiricists were not asking the most appropriate questions.

It is often said that before we can recognize the right answers we have to ask the right questions. Empiricism asks us to consider the question, 'What objects do we experience?' – and consequently finds answers to human problems in the observable relations of human life. Let's think through what it means in practice to ask the empiricist question. If you ask yourself,

Empiricists ask the question: what can we experience?

'What did I experience yesterday?', then you are likely to respond with a fairly descriptive survey of your own perceptions, feelings, sensations and impressions in relation to specific events for a given amount of time. Kant's critical philosophy seeks an answer to a very different question, a *transcendental* question about *what can be known?* A transcendental question, therefore, involves asking, 'What are the conditions of possibility of (something)?' – in this case, identifying what must be in place for our knowledge of observable things to be possible. Let's apply this to your experiences of yesterday. A transcendental question here would involve something like, 'What prior concepts do we need to make sense of and organize our experiences yesterday?' For the sake of illustration, let's assume that you went to work and you had a 'horrible' time. Your boss or line manager was inconsiderate, rude and, at times, even abusive. So the question is, 'How do I make sense of and organize these experiences of working yesterday?' We do this through mental constructs which exist prior to these observed experiences. In this highly specific example, we can draw upon our prior conceptions of 'considerateness' and 'horridness' in human behaviour, and this may serve as a useful way of making sense of the events and for making a judgement such as 'My boss shouted at me at work and behaved badly. I hate my boss!' However, in such situations there will also be a range of alternative prior concepts that are relevant. Ideas of 'consideration' tend to be culturally specific. So, to make a comparison across cultures, we could draw upon prior concepts such as 'self-orientation' and 'collective-orientation'. For instance, you may judge that the 'boss' was only behaving in this way to serve the interests of the organization in question (treating the business as the collective) rather than having purely self-interested motives. Your account of the situation might then take the form of the statement 'He was only doing his job. In any case, all bosses are b******s!' Even here, such ideas may apply only to a limited range of societies which clearly distinguish the self from the collective order, so broader categories could be used. While Kant had categories in mind that were much more abstract, such as quality and quantity, examples like this reveal how difficult it is to separate perception and imagination.

Kantians ask the question: what do we need to make sense of experience? Answer: mental constructs.

Now, let's look at an example which draws from everyday experiences but is also relevant to social scientific explanations of the relationship between the built environment and the rural environment. For instance, you might decide to take a walk one day in the countryside and record your feelings about the environment and natural objects and then, on the following day, record a walk within a declining inner-city environment. According to an empiricist, the different accounts generated would be simply a picture of senses and impressions for the two walks. However, for a Kantian, we can only make sense of these experiences in terms of the mental frameworks and assumptions we already have in place about the nature of urban and rural environments. So we could describe our country walk in terms of open spaces, clean air, relaxed pace of life, friendly relationships and our closer affinity with nature, while the urban environment we might describe as more hemmed in, polluted, hectic, involving anonymous human relations and feeling somewhat divorced from the natural setting of the previous day. These oppositions are themselves part of our historical and cultural tendencies to contrast the countryside with the town in ways which oppose the values of 'community' (involving long-held

Mental constructs are the conditions of possibility of observed experiences, for if they were not in place prior to experiences, we could not make sense of our impressions and perceptions.

particularistic relations between individuals) to the more instrumental, impersonal relations involved in 'association' (see Figures 4.2 and 4.3). Of course, there are many other ways of thinking about urban and rural environments. Nevertheless, for a Kantian, such perceptions and impressions can only make sense within mental frameworks, however defined, and the concepts, categories and judgements they involve. Such conceptualizations can surface in all sorts of ways and may emerge within social scientific explanations of a range of issues. For instance, the urban environment is often described as being more prone to criminality than the rural environment, either without question or through the uncritical use of crime statistics.

Figure 4.2   Urban life representation.   **Figure 4.3**   Rural life representation.

When Kant's basic standpoint was introduced above, you saw how the 'phenomenal world' of appearances is the product of our experiences of the objects of analysis and the mental constructs which give shape and a logical form to these experiences. The objects are seen as 'things-in-themselves' or 'noumena', existing beyond our cognitive faculties. The concept of 'noumena' does not tell us anything substantive about the objects or things. It only indicates that the world of things is so complex and difficult to understand that we cannot simply reproduce it in our thoughts in the manner of a picture. All we can do is develop constructs, concepts and models which make experience intelligible. Thus perceptions and sensory impressions are arranged in 'space' and 'time' in a way which allows us to 'compare' and 'contrast' and consider one piece of data as the 'cause' of another (Russell, 1912/1959, Chapter 8). At this point, you should just note that, in order to make sense of your perceptions, you already engage in the use of whole sets of taken-for-granted assumptions and you have quite a range of mental constructs to choose from.

Idealist approaches identify simple ways of organizing, interpreting and explaining complex empirical evidence.

Whether we are reflecting upon yesterday's experiences or are engaged in social research, we always depend upon a variety of prior concepts to make sense of our experiences. This recognizes the mind as a creative agent in the production of knowledge, whereas empiricism tends to treat the mind as passive in relation to perceptions and sensory impressions. Nevertheless, this approach does not seek to go beyond the boundaries of our senses.

Let's look at an example, this time from contemporary social scientific research, such as the study of the causes and consequences of crime. At first sight, the study of crime appears to offer a clear-cut example of a field of research where **analytic** and **synthetic** statements can be clearly identified. Among the typical analytic statements in this area (that is, statements which are true by definition) would be:

Statement A   Criminal actions involve behaviour which breaks the law.

A synthetic statement (generating new knowledge from empirical evidence), an empiricist would argue, would involve statements such as:

Statement B   In regions within the UK which have experienced an above average rise in unemployment, a corresponding increase in the crime rate can be identified.

Traditional criminological research (within the disciplines of both psychology and sociology) tends to assume that the objects in question (in this case, the crime rate and the unemployment rate) can be clearly identified. This also assumes that a useful comparison can be made between the two variables. Actually, crime is typically related to a wide range of measurable variables based on age, class, gender, ethnicity, location and so on. However, this still ignores a range of significant issues about the definition of crime rates and the complex institutional processes within the criminal justice system through which criminal statistics are produced. The range of possible factors in accounting for crime is huge and each variable identified is difficult to disentangle from the available evidence. Definitions of crime are located within the institutional environments of law-enforcement agencies such as the courts and police force, and shaped by a series of authoritative decisions made by individuals who occupy significant positions within these criminal justice agencies. Crime statistics focus upon reported crime, criminal charges and criminal convictions and can be taken as indicative of different stages or snapshots of a process. For an action to become criminal, it has to be recognized as a breach of the law and taken seriously by the police. Subsequently, this action may be investigated and sufficient evidence collected to sustain a case so that an individual can be charged, and only in the case of criminal conviction is the final statistic realized. All of these factors involved in the production of crime statistics point to the complexity of the social processes involved. Any attempt to develop a social scientific account of the causes and consequences of crime is inevitably shaped by the debates and concerns of the criminal justice system and the moral climate on crime and punishment. Consequently, the relationship between theory and observation is a problematic one in so far as the empirical evidence is shaped through both the complex interpretations of the actors involved in the criminal justice system and the interpretations and values of the social researchers themselves. Just as social researchers use ideas to organize evidence, so too do the people being studied.

As you can see from the examples in Figure 4.4, experience can only be conceived in spatial, temporal and causal terms, and knowledge cannot

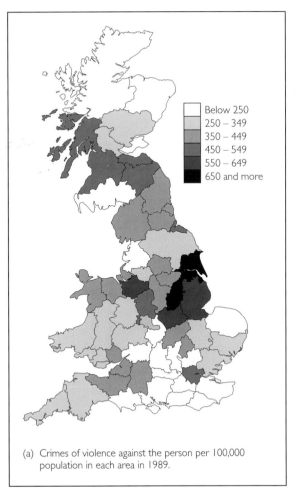

(a) Crimes of violence against the person per 100,000 population in each area in 1989.

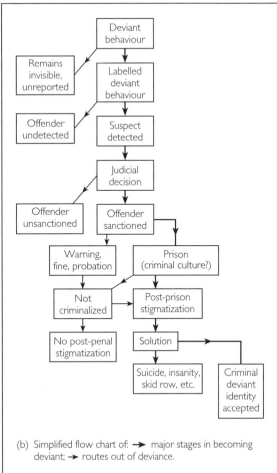

(b) Simplified flow chart of: → major stages in becoming deviant; → routes out of deviance.

Criminal damage >£2000	16.5 : 1
Offences under the Public Order Act 1986	17.0 : 1
Offence by prostitute	0.01 : 1
Drunkenness	16.5 : 1
Common assault	7.0 : 1
Assault on constable	5.5 : 1
TV licence evasion	0.5 : 1
Taking and driving away	33.0 : 1
Other	9.5 : 1

(c) Ratio of male to female offenders found guilty of non-motoring summary offences: England and Wales, 1993.

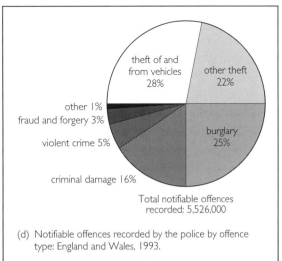

(d) Notifiable offences recorded by the police by offence type: England and Wales, 1993.

Figure 4.4   Interpreting crime.

be constructed without the concepts that allow us to think about our experiences. Hence, it is possible to think of statements – such as the examples above – which are both synthetic and contain concepts which were known prior to experience.

Let's revisit the synthetic statement on crime above. The statement as it stands identifies an empirical regularity between unemployment and criminal behaviour: a rise in unemployment is associated with an increase in the recorded incidence of criminal actions (along the lines of: if A, then B). But how do we make sense of such a statement? In order to understand this statement, we must also possess a set of assumptions and preconceptions of what motivates human conduct, whether this is material greed and acquisitiveness, social pressures, the denial of opportunities for self-improvement, or more generally a culture based upon materialism. Kant described any statement with these qualities as a **synthetic a priori statement** in a clear attempt to distinguish his approach from the empiricist distinction between analytic and synthetic statements. It is this conception of the human subject as a creative and purposive agent in the construction of knowledge which marks Kant's legacy to social science. When we recognize that there is no unmediated contact with the real world, that sense experiences are not reflected in an automatic fashion in our ideas and concepts, then we are forced to confront questions about the relationship between theory and observation, which empiricism avoids. In particular, we need to be aware of the way in which constructs can be uncritically imposed upon empirical evidence to create the patterns which we take for granted (as you saw in the case of scientific racism in Chapter 3). Kant's concern to explore the conditions of possibility and the limits to human knowledge has been a source of inspiration to a variety of approaches. It is these approaches which we consider in the following sections of this chapter.

Kant provides a way of dealing with the inter-relationships between rational thought and empirical evidence.

Before we focus upon the role of the human imagination in the social sciences in any more detail, we should briefly consider what happens when we apply these insights to the conceptual organization of our experiences of objects in the natural sciences. The problems of interpretation can be illustrated by drawing upon Norwood Hanson's work on the conceptual foundations of science in *Patterns of Discovery* (1958). Hanson, a philosopher of natural science, attempts to raise questions about the nature of perception as conventionally understood by philosophers of science in the 1950s. Hanson draws upon Wittgenstein's later work, *Philosophical Investigations* (1953/1967).

You may recall that Wittgenstein's early work influenced the logical positivists by seeing statements as pictures of the world. In his later work, Wittgenstein viewed language as a series of games, each with its own rules. In effect, he undermined any distinction between the real world and language. Wittgenstein argues that problems of philosophy arise not from the world but from language, with our concepts defining our experiences. Rather than seeing the world as something which we can approach through language, he saw the world as existing only within language. For Hanson, scientists may observe the same visual data but this is not the same as *seeing*, for 'People, not their eyes, see' (Hanson, 1958, p.6). Hanson demonstrates that biologists may see different things from the same observation by comparing two interpretations of observing an amoeba under a micro-

See Chapter 3, section 4.1.

scope. For one biologist, the amoeba is a '*single-celled* animal' (analogous to other forms of cells with a wall, cytoplasm and a nucleus) whereas for the other, it is a 'non-celled *animal*' (analogous to other whole animals which ingest and digest food). In either case, 'these data are moulded by different theories or interpretation or intellectual constructions' (Hanson, 1958, p.5).

Activity 4.1

Turn to Reading A, 'There is more to seeing than meets the eye', from Norwood Hanson's *Perception and Discovery* (1969).

- What are the different ways of 'seeing' and 'observing' in the argument developed by Hanson?

In this extract, the objects observed are either geometric or sketches of physical objects. When we apply Hanson's ideas to the study of social life, further complications arise. Think of any recent event you have experienced with someone with whom you have regular contact. Make notes on the event and then contact the person and discuss it with them – you might be surprised at how much your interpretations differ. You should ask yourself why these interpretations are different.

Identical evidence can be interpreted in very different ways, depending upon the assumptions in each approach.

In a more striking example from the history of the natural sciences, Hanson contrasts the different interpretations placed upon the observation of the morning Sun rising in the east by two early astronomers, Johannes Kepler and Tycho Brahe. Both astronomers observed the same physical stimuli, a yellow disc emerging from behind a green land surface against a blue sky, yet they saw very different things. For Kepler, the Sun was stationary and the Earth moved, whereas for Brahe, the Earth was stationary and the other planetary objects moved around the Earth. The question here is not only the accuracy of each account, but the extent to which we can interpret the same observations in a variety of ways. This example is useful in demonstrating the difficulties of interpretation. However, when we look at the problem encountered in the social sciences where the observer is not distinct from the object but is actually part of it, then the difficulties multiply.

As you work through this chapter, you will see that the approaches developed assume that the models used in social research are simplifications of a more complex (and, some would argue, incomprehensible) reality. For experience to be intelligible, we have to simplify. These approaches also raise important issues about the relationship between subject (researcher) and objects of analysis within the social sciences. The scientific approaches you encountered in Chapters 2 and 3 assumed that it was possible to deploy the same method in the study of human life as had been used in the study of natural objects. In the natural sciences, it is plausible to treat objects of analysis as distinct from the researcher. In the social sciences, however, the researcher is part of the object under investigation. There is a clear difference between studying physical matter or biological species and studying thinking, creative, interacting, unpredictable human beings. As social researchers draw upon the stock of knowledge and the language system of their own societies, this also means that the concepts and models developed are inevitably part of the object as well. Thus, in the study of social life there is no easy separation of subject and object.

Any attempt to impose the methods and assumptions of the natural sciences upon the study of social life, according to Peter Winch in *The Idea of a Social Science* (1958), is a mistake because the understanding of natural objects is completely different from understanding social objects. Winch recommends that the study of social objects should involve the recognition that all human behaviour is meaningful and involves both rule-governed and rule-following behaviour. In the social sciences, it is harder to establish whether human beings do observe the same things in the same way. In addition, as we saw earlier in the example of studying crime, the objects under observation are themselves much more difficult to define. Certainly, they are not as clear-cut as defining an amoeba or the sunrise. In the social sciences, we are in fact observing and contemplating ourselves as complex creatures living in conditions of uncertainty. So, as social scientists, we face the most difficult task of any scientific activity. It is to the issue of understanding complexity that we turn in the next section.

The application of the assumptions and methods of natural science within social research tends to ignore the important differences between studying things and studying people.

Summary

Perception and sense impressions are organized in meaningful ways only through the mental frameworks and associations which are taken for granted. These mental frameworks act as a means of sifting and sorting the mass of sensory experiences into some recognizable shape and order.

There are different ways of 'seeing' and this accounts for the ways in which human beings can interpret the same evidence in very different – and sometimes opposed – ways when they attempt to imagine social life.

3   Understanding complexity

Empiricists tend to see the observation of variables as the basis for establishing causal explanations. For idealists, the empiricist starting-point is deficient in two respects. First, the social world is much more complex than the use of **closed systems** can allow for. Second, observations only make sense through the use of prior concepts. In this section we explore the relationship between causal explanations and interpretative understanding. Explanations are more often associated with the natural sciences, while understanding is usually seen as characteristic of the arts and humanities. The natural sciences are said to be able to generate universal law statements which apply across space and time, while the arts and humanities only represent unique events in a particular time and place. The social sciences carved out their own space between these two traditions and have had to straddle these two modes of inquiry. Over the last century and a half, an intellectual and scientific movement has emerged which explicitly attempted to use Kant's ideas in order to study social relations and historical change. This approach came to be labelled neo-Kantianism. Although there remained considerable variation within this movement, there has always been a common concern to resolve the dilemmas raised by attempting to reconcile the tensions between hard facts and cultural values, between theoretical constructs and empirical observations and between explanation and understanding. Neo-Kantian debates about what would be the most appropriate methods for social science originated in economics, but they also had important implications for the subsequent development of sociology, psychology, geography and political studies. These approaches are so influential that they often remain unacknowledged. They have become such an integral part of social scientific inquiry that few feel the need to acknowledge them. They are simply part of the conceptual landscape of social science.

3.1 The emergence of neo-Kantianism

The neo-Kantian approach attempts to do two things. First, it attempts to resolve the dilemmas posed by accommodating both objective truth and subjective values in the same approach. Second, it attempts to find a way of addressing the thorny question of cultural values and their relationship to the generation of cultural and historical knowledge. Two key figures in this school, Wilhelm Windelband and Heinrich Rickert, both criticized positivism in the study of social life. Windelband's work provided us with a way of thinking about our methodological options, while Rickert (considered in more detail in section 3.2) raised interesting issues about the relationship between facts and values. In this section we focus upon Wilhelm Windelband, whose *History and Natural Science* (1894) regarded both the natural sciences and the human sciences as the study of empirical reality. Nevertheless, he distinguished between studying natural things and studying people and their institutions. For Windelband, there was a methodological difference between two forms of scientific thought:

Elsewhere this sign ***g*** will direct you to the glossary, but revisit this section if you need to.

- **nomothetic** – involving the construction of generalizing models and the identification of general laws;

- **idiographic** – the individualizing method of the cultural sciences concerned with the detailed depiction of particular circumstances.

This made it possible to distinguish between the study of natural objects in establishing objective knowledge and the important role played by the values and interests of the researcher in the study of social life. In the social sciences the objects are other subjects – thinking, creative and communicative beings. Scientists have different interests in their objects of analysis and define them in different ways. In the natural sciences, Windelband argued, the objects (physical matter) remain constant, allowing for the development of a 'science of laws', whereas in the social sciences the objects involved are 'unique configurations of events'. He argued that history and the humanities involve the use of individualizing or 'idiographic' method, while the natural sciences aim to produce general laws, the 'nomothetic' method. Within the nomothetic framework, values are seen as the product of an evaluative procedure and as such are subjective and cannot serve as the objective basis for establishing general laws. The social sciences are thus caught between two approaches to the study of social life, with one approach emphasizing the importance of scientific general laws and the other treating each set of social circumstances as unique. This helps to explain the competing options faced by social scientists.

In the remainder of this section we explore how this innovative distinction had an impact on the emergence of economics and psychology. The relationship between nomothetic and idiographic positions can be illustrated by briefly considering the *Methodenstreit* (the debate over method), which originated in Germany in the late nineteenth century. This was primarily focused upon which key organizing principles should act as a foundation for economic research and for social research in general. It had become widely accepted that it was appropriate to study the economy idiographically, understanding the complexities of each economic system rather than in terms of discovering general universal laws. By focusing upon actual economic conditions, it was hoped that the social scientific knowledge produced would deliver human progress and the social improvement of the condition of the working classes through the actions of the state. This established the idea that state policy and social scientific research could work hand in hand. One of these early economists, Carl Menger, was concerned that this focus on social problem solving would lead to 'economics without thinking'. So, in *Problems of Economics and Sociology* (1883/1981), Menger developed a nomothetic account of the general relations of economic phenomena rather than describing economic processes in a particular time and place. He suggested that it was possible to

For neo-Kantians, social scientific explanations offer a choice between developing general laws and attempts to understand unique events.

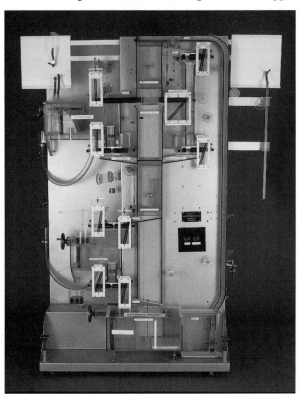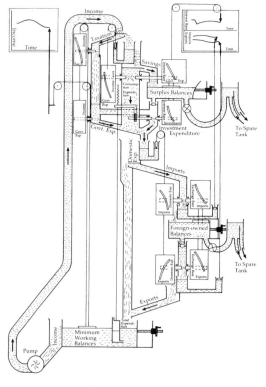

Figure 4.5   Representation of macroeconomics – the economy as a machine.

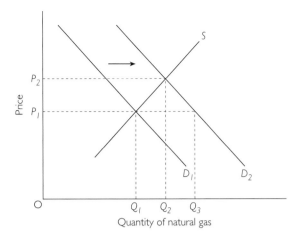

Figure 4.6   Representation of microeconomics. Alterations in the price of a particular commodity, in this case natural gas, relate to the quantity consumed. This is a fairly typical example of the way economists see the relationship in a market between price and the level of supply and demand for goods and services.

view the branches of economics (economic history, economic theory, economic policy and public finance) as each having its own distinctive forms of theory and method.

This was to have a profound effect on twentieth-century economics. For Menger, the appropriate method for economic theory involved two steps: first, break down phenomena into their smallest elements and, second, use these to deduce the development of more complex social phenomena. Thus a 'market' was no more than the sum total of consumer choices and the relations between them operating as a function of the individual actions which produced them. This approach to studying social life was to become known as **methodological individualism**. Menger was to establish a line of argument which rejected the aggregate concepts of macroeconomics in favour of microeconomics, which focused upon individuals, households and firms as decision makers (see examples in Figures 4.5 and 4.6).

In many social sciences, the difference between nomethetic and idiographic approaches came to be institutionalized in the branches of disciplines, such as the difference between theory and applied research work.

There was clear disagreement about which scientific method (nomothetic or idiographic) the discipline of economics should follow. In psychology, we find examples of both idiographic and nomothetic approaches living side by side. The emergence of experimental psychology enabled psychologists to develop a clearly nomothetic approach to scientific method. In particular, the technique of experimental closure was developed by the physiological psychologist Wilhelm Wundt, who established the first psychological laboratory in Leipzig in 1879 in order to demonstrate the interrelationships between sensory physiology and the 'mind'. Wundt, like all neo-Kantians, rejected the empiricist treatment of the mind (as a blank page for impressions) in favour of an active consciousness which could be selective in making discriminating judgements about our experiences. For Wundt:

> scientific investigation has three problems to be solved. ... The first is the analysis of composite processes; the second is the demonstration of combinations into which the elements discovered in the analysis enter; the third is the investigation of the laws that are operative in the formation of such combinations.

> (Wundt, 1897, p.25, cited in Manicas, 1987, p.183)

In this way, by clearly defining an object of analysis, psychologists began to carve out a space for their discipline, although the way in which the object of analysis, the mind, was defined in psychology was to change again with the emerging dominance of positivism. In particular, by focusing upon closed systems in the positivist way, the discipline of psychology was to lose its sense of the empirical complexity of social relations. However, in both psychology and economics the neo-Kantian framework came to be widely accepted. One of the legacies of this approach is the establishment of the distinction between theoretical and applied study in economics, psychology, geography, sociology and social policy.

Summary

The debate on method centred on what form social scientific inquiry should take – idiographic approaches study concrete social processes in a particular time and place, whereas nomothetic approaches attempt to construct accounts of general laws in some branches of the social sciences along the lines of the assumptions and methods of the natural sciences (especially physics).

Differences remained unresolved among the various alternative models emerging in the social science disciplines. Nevertheless, the debate triggered an increased awareness of the distinctive problems of social science posed by the role of cultural values in social research.

3.2 Facts, values and relevance in social science

The relationship between facts and values has generated a huge amount of heated discussion in the social sciences. As you saw in Chapter 3, taking their cue from logical positivism, many social scientists have been concerned to keep values out of scientific research. The contribution by the German philosopher Heinrich Rickert on the relationship between values and social science is the key starting-point for all the debates since. Rickert distinguished between the logical methods of the natural and the social sciences but also raised the possibility of differences between them because of the way in which the objects of analysis in each science are related to the values of those engaged in research. In the natural sciences, physics is formally nomothetic for it attempts to identify general laws and the objects concerned (atoms, neutrons, etc.) are not related to values. However, Rickert argued that some forms of natural science were formally idiographic (that is, concerned with unique situations), rather than nomothetic. For instance, in some areas of biology attempts have been made to establish the unique characteristics of earth-bound species, even though biologists have the same relationship to their objects as physicists.

In the social sciences, the objects of analysis are defined as value laden and culturally meaningful. Nevertheless, economics still concentrates upon developing general laws from the identification of recurrent patterns of events (as do many branches of sociology, psychology and political science). Rickert suggested that other approaches in the social sciences, influenced by history, are concerned much more with unique events and particular conditions. This helps to explain the variety of approaches in the social sciences.

Nomothetic and idiographic approaches coexist in both the natural sciences and the social sciences.

Sociology has often been described as containing two traditions, with one attempting to generate causal explanations in general terms and the other concerned with interpreting and understanding social life. These differences have also been developed into the methodological criteria of reliability and validity. **Reliable knowledge** can be defined as evidence which is supported through repeated testing under the same conditions, while **valid knowledge** (if difficult to replicate) is often defined as being true to life in a particular place and time. Nevertheless, in each case there is a clear attempt to represent reality even if there is considerable disagreement about what should be done. Both criteria claim to produce authentic knowledge, although they do so in different ways.

Identifying the values and purposes of social scientists raised problems which were to become known as the value judgement debate. Neither the nomothetic method nor the idiographic method provide us with clear criteria for deciding *what* we should actually study. Rickert suggested that it is possible to define objects and form concepts about them by following the criteria of **value relevance**. This means that, for a social scientist, the objects of analysis would be defined in such a way that they would already connect with the cultural values of the society in question and hold some meaning for the members of that culture. Therefore, it was argued, we should treat all social scientific concepts as expressions of the values of a given community and the conventional standards of morality considered to be universal within that community. The principle of value relevance means that concepts should be relevant to the problems of a particular society at a particular time. This also means that value judgements are the concern of philosophers in that time and place and cannot be established for all time.

Values are always involved in social research – this should be acknowledged so that social scientific knowledge is related to specific social and historical conditions.

Earlier in this chapter, we explored some of the problems involved in studying crime. In terms of the issues raised by value relevance, it is possible to identify important shifts in the study of criminality over the last forty years. The study of crime can be said to have moved through three stages:

- an attempt to establish the objective cause of criminality;

- a period concerned with processes through which crime was viewed as constructed by the criminal justice system itself;

- more recently, greater attention focused on the consequences of crime in terms of the experiences of victims and the development of crime prevention strategies.

Each phase of empirical research and theorizing can be related to the prevailing social issues at the time that the research took place. In the first phase, crime was attributed to definite causes, with some types of individuals identified as having criminal dispositions. This is often referred to as the positivist approach to crime. In the second phase, it was seen as a product of decisions by people in the criminal justice system. This phase emerged in the 1960s and 1970s when many social scientists were concerned with the ways that the police and courts constructed criminality. In the last phase, crime has been understood as something all rational individuals are capable of doing unless there is the possibility of being caught. This phase has been influential since the 1980s, with a move to more crime prevention measures. Each phase connects to a different set of concerns within Western societies.

3.3 Using ideal types

We noted previously, in the introduction, the use of ideal types in social science. This technique was popularized in social scientific research by Max Weber, who adopted an explicitly interdisciplinary approach using sources from economics, sociology, psychology, political studies and history. He was not concerned to demarcate the different forms of scientific method but, instead, wanted to bring them together in a coherent and unified approach. For Weber, this would provide a bridge between the interpretative understanding of human action and the scientific explanation of the causes and consequences of a particular relationship. To do this, Weber used the ideal type, a device which had been developed by Menger's economic theory. An **ideal type** is a theoretical device for generalizing beyond a particular situation, but one which accepts the complexity of social relations. It does not have the status that empiricists attribute to general laws for, in idealist approaches, it is assumed that closed systems are inappropriate for studying people. Ideal types are simplistic and exaggerated categories providing a yardstick against which it is possible to compare and contrast empirical evidence.

An important pair of ideal types in economics is the 'command economy' and the 'free market'. In terms of these 'ideal types', free markets are largely self-regulating systems for distributing goods and services, with a minimal state involvement ensuring that grievances are resolved and trust is maintained. Command economies have extensive state involvement in both producing and distributing goods and services as well as in fixing prices. They are portrayed as polar opposites in terms of the level of competition and degree of free choice displayed by the actors involved. In the free market these actors are assumed to be completely rational creatures operating according to opportunity cost (that we make purchasing decisions in markets fully aware that our choices always mean that we have to deny ourselves something else). In fact, although each ideal type is often used to describe empirical reality, neither can be said to actually exist. In practice there is no such thing as a perfectly free economy or a command economy for, as Figure 4.7 indicates, all actual economies can be located in between these types. In some cases, we can use these ideal types to identify how economies change, as in the transformation in post-communist Russia. For these reasons, Weber saw ideal types above all as useful devices for simplifying and identifying patterns in a concrete and complex empirical reality.

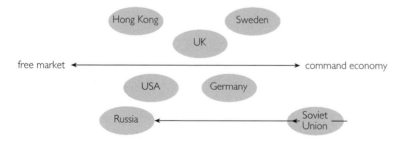

Figure 4.7
A use of ideal types in economics.

So, we can use the ideal type as an organizing device through which it is possible to establish the patterns of activity involved across social and economic institutions. By focusing upon patterns, these devices offer no final answers but allow for the development of useful models of human activity. Weber used them throughout his own research; for example, the

Ideal types simplify and allow for the identification of patterns of social relations within complex empirical evidence.

ideal types of traditional authority, charismatic authority and rational-legal authority. Authority relations are defined as ways of making power relations legitimate. Each of these, in turn, derives from Weber's more abstract ideal types of human action (that is, idealized in three ways: habitual, emotional and/or rational).

In order to understand the usefulness of this approach, imagine that Weber was alive in the 1980s in the UK and was faced with the social and political phenomenon of 'Thatcherism'. Using Weber's authority types, it is possible to develop a coherent and suggestive, if incomplete, picture of the Thatcher administrations in the UK which serves as a useful foundation for further research. The Conservative administrations in the 1980s consistently drew upon and reinvented 'traditional national' values as well as engaging in debates about the decline of moral values. Thatcher, as a 'charismatic' political figure, cultivated a populist appeal whereby she was able to draw upon the support of individuals within groups, such as trade unionists, whose interests are often seen as opposed to the Conservative agenda. The programmes for privatization, for taxation reforms and for the reform of the Civil Service can be seen as a return to a conception of bureaucratic administration that could be regarded as closer to the ideal type of 'bureaucracy as an efficient and rational machine for getting things done' which Weber would have seen as most suitable for a liberal democracy. In this way, the use of such ideal types provides a means of organizing the mass of empirical evidence about politics in the 1980s. This enables us to make sense of a more complex reality and even to deal with the evidence that appears to be contradictory. For instance, Thatcherism involved a 'strong state' (less freedom) in many areas of moral concern such as law and order, but also a considerable increase in personal freedom in the economy. By considering the 'strong state' as a strategy for maintaining traditional authority and the 'free market' (minimal state) policy as a means of generating popular support (through tax cuts and council house sales), we can see both as attempts to legitimate power in the way that Weber suggests. Of course, such an account only provides a partial picture of one brief period in British history. Nevertheless, it is a useful demonstration of neo-Kantian research practice.

Activity 4.2

We have just seen how ideal types can be used to help us understand social life. As you will have noticed, there are differences in the level of abstraction and simplicity of ideal types – such as the difference between the three *types of action* and the more concrete three *forms of authority*. Weber himself pointed to three levels of ideal type:

- ideal types which can be used in a particular historical and cultural context (such as the concept of 'considerateness' examined in the early part of section 2);

- purely imaginary ideal types serving as a basis for more general explanations (such as the three *types of action* – habitual, emotional and rational).

- ideal types which can be used in a variety of historical and cultural contexts (for instance, the types of self- and collective-orientation *or* the three ways in which Weber identifies these *forms of authority* as traditional, charismatic and rational-legal);

Even the identification of variables, such as class and status, involves a degree of simplification and abstraction, for there are always alternative ways of defining variables.

The following three variables of class, income and education (which are low-level abstractions) have been combined and analysed in enormous numbers of studies. Most have tried to explain the different educational attainment levels of children from different groups in society. Figure 4.8 shows a variety of ways in which these variables can be placed in sequence or in combination. The chains present examples of different causal relationships; each chain tells a story about a relationship between cause and effect. The arrow indicates which is the independent and which is the dependent variable. Look at the story in the first chain. Here, we can see that class position has been taken as the independent variable, and education and income are dependent upon this (that is, our class positions will shape our income levels and what educational qualifications we are likely to achieve). You can read this in a materialist way where class is just an economic term, but this depends upon how you define class. So, you will see that each story can be read in different ways.

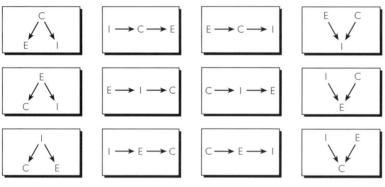

Figure 4.8   Causal chains.

- Work your way through the various possible sequences and combinations of the three variables. Think about the problems associated with the addition of further variables.

- Try to define these variables in different ways. For instance, there are different ways of measuring educational performance.

- What other variables would *you* introduce here? Identify the causal chain which fits with the explanation that *you* feel is most plausible compared with the others. You may also find it useful to attempt to translate each of these causal chains into a hypothesis about the way the world works.

The use of mental constructs to create competing accounts of the same empirical evidence is an important part of the process of research in the social sciences. Each of the relationships identified in the activity above is a simplification of the processes involved in the actual experiences of human beings. This demonstrates the capacity of human beings to interpret the social world, of which they are a part, in very different ways (even if they sometimes agree on what evidence is important). This is as much a feature of social science as it is of everyday life. In the process of identifying the twelve sequences and combinations represented by the causal chains in Figure 4.8, it is possible that you were drawn to one of the sequences as more plausible in comparison with others. It is worth reflecting upon why some relationships are more or less plausible. The choices we make when selecting one from a range of possible relations are closely related to our own values.

The Weberian model has been very influential in the social sciences, especially in sociology, although it represents only one way in which the neo-Kantian approach has developed. Durkheim's account of scientific method, so often described as positivist, also draws from Kantian insights on the relationship between interpretation and observation. Like Weber, Durkheim's work is misleadingly characterized as purely sociological yet it also displays many interdisciplinary features. However, Durkheim's neo-Kantian model is different from Weber's approach in one essential respect. Whereas Weber starts from the premise that all collective objects are the sum total of the components within them (just as the economy is the sum total of firms and households), for Durkheim, society has its own independent reality and can have a causal effect upon the components. There are two types of neo-Kantian approach – **voluntarist** and **determinist** – as you can see below.

Elsewhere this sign
g will direct you
to the glossary, but
revisit this section
if you need to.

Voluntarism

In this approach the causes of phenomena are located in the actions of individuals and groups (Weber's approach).

Determinism

This approach locates causes in social relations which exist as an external constraint upon individual choices (Durkheim's approach).

See Chapter 3,
section 2.3.

Durkheim clearly attempted to distance himself from the 'naive optimism' and 'positivist metaphysics' of Comte. There is much dispute about how to place Durkheim within the debates in the philosophy of social science, for he has been labelled a positivist, a neo-Kantian and, more recently, a realist (to which we return in Chapter 7). Thus we can use these different ways of reading Durkheim's social research as a way of highlighting the differences between approaches in the philosophy of the social sciences. In his own accounts, Durkheim explicitly identified his approach within neo-Kantianism and saw himself as steering a middle course between empiricism and rationalism (Lukes, 1973a). This involved the acceptance of the role of mental constructs in organizing and making sense of experiences. This clearly differs from the positivist emphasis upon the scientific reading of facts as if mental frameworks are absent or value neutral.

As you saw earlier, in *The Rules of Sociological Method* (1895/1982) Durkheim recognized the way in which the object of analysis in each discipline had an important effect on the way the discipline operated. He argued that each social science should have a clear focus which marked it off from other disciplines (for example, the economy in economics and the mind inpsychology). In terms of sociology, with society as the object, the complexity of social relations demanded more careful treatment of empirical evidence than was common in his day. For Durkheim, it remained possible to establish relations of cause and effect between variables which tend to occur in the same place and time. However, unlike empiricists, he regarded the identification of such relations as insufficient in themselves to provide a complete explanatory account of the processes.

The creative and interpretive role of the social scientist was crucial. Durkheim used the comparative-historical method to establish a simple set of identifiable variables in the study of suicide. He had concluded that, if suicide rates were stable over time, there must be some form of external constraint which accounts for this stability in the levels of suicide in different groups within society. For Durkheim, the empirical world could only be organized within a conceptual framework which emphasized the degrees of 'integration' and 'regulation', both of which are mental constructs which cannot be empirically identified. He used these constructs to specify the types of suicide in traditional and modern societies (fatalism, altruism, egoism and anomie). He was careful to examine the propensities of groups to contribute 'definite quotas of voluntary deaths' rather than suggesting that such relationships were always evident in particular situations. By acknowledging social complexity and the difficulties of interpretation, he limited his claims to the prediction of patterns rather than particular instances (Durkheim, 1897/1952). A former student of Durkheim, Maurice Halbwachs, went on to study the same kinds of evidence, but in *The Causes of Suicide* (1930/1978) he identified a different causal explanation. While Halbwachs established similar patterns of evidence between religion, location, dependency and suicide, he attributed the role of causal variables solely to location (in terms of the difference between urban or rural) and treated all the other variables as effects.

> For Durkheim, social scientific inquiry involves more than identifying social facts, it also involves the interpretation and organization of evidence in conceptual frameworks.

> Even if the empirical regularities remain constant, different social scientists will construct very different explanations from the same evidence.

Activity 4.3

Now turn to Reading B, 'Race relations in the city', from John Rex and Robert Moore's study *Race, Community and Conflict: a Study of Sparkbrook* (1967).

• Identify how Rex and Moore attempt to strike a balance between nomothetic and idiographic forms of social inquiry.

When reading through this extract look for the way in which Rex and Moore identify strengths and weaknesses in both the **nomothetic** and **idiographic** approaches.

In a later study drawing upon neo-Kantian ideas, Rex and Moore attempted to examine the relationship between housing markets and ethnic minority membership in Birmingham in 1964. The explicit attempt to bridge the gap between identifying general laws and providing an accurate empirical account of a particular time and place is characteristic of Weber's own position. In addition, in the formation of concepts, Rex and Moore adopt a Weberian approach by defining housing classes in terms of the common market position, whereby groups of individuals can be classified in terms of their access to private or public housing, owned or rented accommodation and so on. In terms of explaining the relationships involved, Rex and Moore sought to identify the causes and consequences of racial discrimination in housing in this inner-city area of Birmingham in the late 1950s and early 1960s. They established that a combination of low income and ineligibility for council housing drove new migrants into high-interest mortgage arrangements which could only be financed by the subletting of the properties involved to other migrant families. This led to a significant growth in multi-occupation households among ethnic minorities in this period and generated discrimination from, and conflict with, other residents and the local council. This, in turn, led to the isolation of the ethnic minority communities within Birmingham which reinforced cultural divisions.

Summary

The debate on the role of value judgements in the social sciences has focused upon the formal differences between social scientific methods and the differences which occur between the ways that the cultural values of researchers are related to the definitions of objects of analysis. One way around this problem is to follow the principle of value relevance, the notion that concept formation should be relevant to the problems of the time and place in which they are understood and used.

A particular problem is the identification and establishment of guidelines on what should constitute the 'proper' focus of analysis in each social science. For neo-Kantians, the objects of analysis are the product of the concerns of social researchers and the relevant problems in society at large, the context of the research.

The strategy of using ideal types is a means of organizing perceptions of empirical evidence in order to overcome the differences between nomothetic and idiographic accounts of social scientific method. This allows for the interpretation of 'hard facts' in various plausible ways.

GEOGRAPHICAL MODELS 1

Now for something a little more practical - in Geographical Models 1 you can see how neo-Kantian approaches are translated into practice.

There are two sections on geographical models in this chapter, each developing more practical applications of some of the approaches covered. Geographical Models 1 deals with the way in which neo-Kantian thinking has had an impact within the discipline of geography. Geographical Models 2 considers the ways that social scientific knowledge can be connected to everyday life in geography by focusing upon the development of theoretical modelling in the study of human populations and urban life. But first, in the examples here, we concentrate on how ideal-type models are constructed in order to organize and make sense of complex empirical patterns and relationships.

An example of the construction of ideal types to build models of complex social relations can be seen in central place theory. Central Place Theory was developed by Walther

Christaller in *Central Places in Southern Germany* (1966) and popularized by William Bunge's *Theoretical Geography* (1966). Christaller argued that it is possible to identify an 'ordering principle' which governs the number, sizes and distribution of human settlements. In effect, he created an ideal-type model founded upon economic factors as the basis for urban development. This involved the following set of idealized assumptions.

- Demands for facilities are made by a homogenous population distributed on an isotropic surface (an unbounded uniform plane).
- Such demands would be satisfied by central places.
- Each central place contains a complementary set of goods which can be categorized into high, middle and low orders (high-order goods are specialized and scarce, lower-order goods are more ubiquitous).
- Demands for goods take place within given catchment areas.
- Larger central places would carry high-order goods as well as lower-order goods, while smaller central places would only distribute lower-order goods.
- The size of a central place would be governed by its importance to the surrounding region (establishing its centrality).

Using these idealized assumptions, Christaller then engaged in a series of geometric steps to construct an idealized model of complementary regions comprising large, medium and small settlements servicing a range of goods with different orders, resulting in a hexagonal (or honeycomb) pattern, as the diagrammatic steps in Figures 4.9 and 4.10 illustrate. Each step (we only include two here) makes the model more complex in order to establish the likely patterns of human settlement. So we can see, although the empirical world, with all its variety as well as its susceptibility to change, cannot be reproduced in a mirror-like way, the theoretical model developed here is an attempt to provide a rough guide to what's going on in human settlement patterns. Even Figure 4.10, which looks complex enough, is still a far cry from actual settlements. The whole point of the model is to work from simple abstract ideas and gradually introduce more and more complexity into the account so that it becomes feasible to plot patterns of human activity. This enables us to make a judgement as to how these human activites are likely to have an impact on the organization of social life. At the end of the day, we only need a rough guide to anticipate problems and make decisions to resolve them.

Spatial models, such as these, enable geographers to compare and contrast empirical evidence of different settlement patterns, regardless of the location. In turn, this creates the possibility of producing general explanations of the distribution of human settlements and the development of urbanization. Empirical work in this area tended to focus upon the variety of goods available in different locations, the categorization of settlements in terms of the prevalent orders of goods, the identification of different spatial patterns in

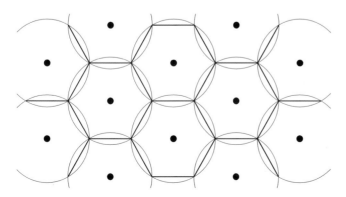

Figure 4.9 Central places on an isotropic plane combined with overlapping hexagonal complementary regions.

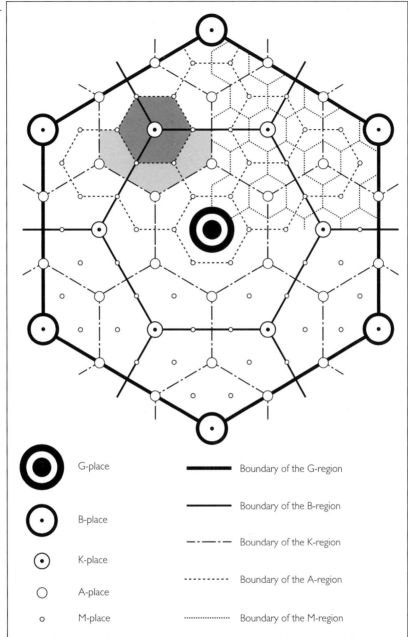

⊙ (G-place symbol)	G-place	▬▬▬	Boundary of the G-region
⊙ (B-place symbol)	B-place	───	Boundary of the B-region
⊙ (K-place symbol)	K-place	─·─·─	Boundary of the K-region
○	A-place	---------	Boundary of the A-region
∘	M-place	··········	Boundary of the M-region

The complementary region of each higher order centre is partitioned into the equivalent of three complementary regions of the next lowest order. By way of illustration, the complementary region of one K grade centre in the top left of the figure has been shaded to show that it contains the equivalent of three complementary regions of the next lowest order (i.e. A grade).

Figure 4.10 Model of interlocking complementary regions with five grades of central place.

the landscape and the identification of flows of goods between central places (defined as nodal flows). In Figures 4.11 and 4.12 (overleaf), we can see representations of central place theory in practice, representations which demonstrate spatial patterns and nodal flows in southern Germany and Wales.

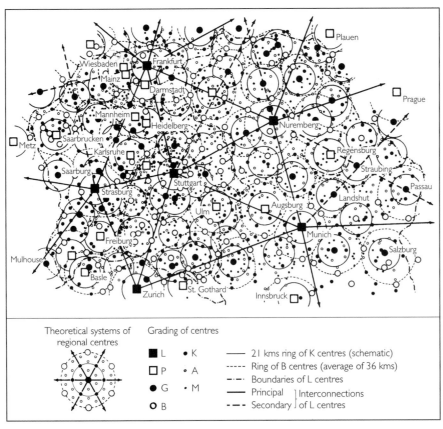

Figure 4.11
Empirical application I: human settlement patterns showing central places in southern Germany.

In effect, these models cannot convey the complexity of real life. Nevertheless, they offer useful tools with which to identify the patterns between actual human settlements. Evidence that does not match the expected pattern prompts further research into the reasons why. So the development of ideas is the product of an ongoing synthesis of empirical experience and the flexible use of mental constructs.

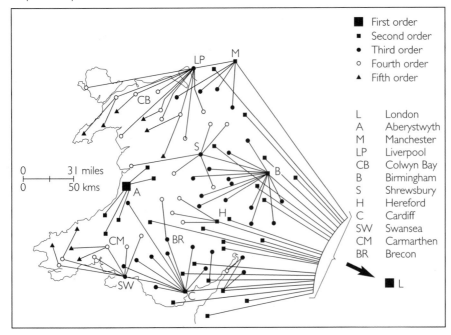

Figure 4.12
Empirical application II: telephone flows to establish nodal regions in Wales.

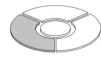

4   Rational choices and human action

In this section we explore one of the most influential idealist approaches in recent social science, rational choice theory. This approach sees all social phenomena as the sum total of individual choices involved, no more and no less. All forms of interaction are portrayed as exchange relations in the manner of a marketplace and all human choices are seen as the product of rational decision making. The attempt to develop models of social relationships and intentional actions based upon rational choice calculations has been a strong current in social sciences since the 1960s. This arose as a response to dissatisfaction with the attempts by positivist economists to establish general laws simply through the testing of predictions.

The problems within empiricism prompted a re-evaluation of the relationship between explanation and prediction.

Economists had discovered that, because their predictions were rarely accurate, they faced the choice of either rejecting reasonably solid theories without a clear idea of what could replace them or introducing a *ceteris paribus* rule. This rule requires 'holding other things constant' in order to ensure that it is possible to identify testable relationships between a limited number of variables. This involves placing the particular relationship within a closed system. However, in practice, this also means that empirical evidence which is contrary to that which is expected can be interpreted as either a refutation of the statement or as a failure of the *ceteris paribus* conditions used in the test. Consequently, statements which would have been shelved if Popper's criteria had been adopted can survive empirical falsification when the *ceteris paribus* rule is used.

Rational choice explanations start from the premise that all social phenomena are the products of intentional decision making.

One response to these problems was developed by Austrian economist Ludwig von Mises, whose influence on contemporary social science has generally been indirect but important. Mises attempted to establish a purely **nomothetic** science of human action which he labelled praxeology. He was concerned with establishing universally valid knowledge which could be taken to exist prior to experience and which could be identified through reason. The focus upon the intentional and purposeful nature of human action within economic life prepared the way for contemporary rational choice theory. In *Theory and History,* Mises argued, 'There are no judgements of values other than those asserting I prefer, I like better, I wish' (Mises, 1957, p.22). Therefore, the value of all things can only be identified through the subjective preferences of the actors involved, in this case, actors involved in the processes of economic calculation based on money prices within the conditions of market exchange.

Once social complexity is acknowledged, social scientists should limit their aspirations to identifying the prediction of patterns rather than specific outcomes.

By questioning the foundations of economics, Mises identified how the relationship between explanation and prediction needs to be rethought. In situations of social complexity, where scientific theories cannot be taken as simple pictures of the processes they attempt to represent, the empiricist assumption that explanations and predictions are the same thing becomes an ineffective tool of inquiry. Mises distinguished between the role of 'quantitative predictions' within the natural sciences and 'qualitative predictions' in sociology and economics. He argued that it is impossible to predict specific outcomes in social science with any degree of accuracy and that, instead, social science should concern itself only with the prediction of patterns. Praxeology, therefore, develops 'imaginary constructions' through which all human beings can comprehend these patterns. The main difference between everyday life and science, he argued, is that whereas commonsense constructions are 'more or less confused and muddled, economics is intent upon elaborating them with utmost care, scrupulousness, and precision' (Mises, 1957, p.237).

4.1 Game theory

The rational principles of the praxeological method were developed for more general use in the social sciences by Oscar Morgenstern (a student of Mises) and John von Neumann, in *The Theory of Games and Economic Behaviour* (1944). This approach has only become popular as a research approach across the social sciences since the 1960s. Game theory provides a means of describing and explaining social relationships in contexts where actors make rational choices in rule-governed situations. It is assumed that all participants in a 'game' understand the possible choices or 'moves' open to all players and their likely outcomes. Applications of this analogy have been very wide ranging – from decisions on family planning, criminal behaviour, voting behaviour and electoral campaigning, to the Cuban missile crisis and the environmental impact of overgrazing on commonly owned land. The actors in this approach are assumed to have certain characteristics; in particular, they are considered to be 'minimaxers' in their behaviour (a label for describing the tendencies of rational actors to minimize their perceived costs and maximize their perceived benefits).

Game theory enables social scientists to identify rule-governed patterns of behaviour within which all choices are made by purely rational and self-interested players.

This can be illustrated by focusing upon two of the well known games applied to non-economic situations. In the game of 'chicken' (an American teenage dare game with cars), two actors race their cars towards each other in the certain knowledge that, unless one of them moves out of the way, both may be seriously injured or worse. The object of the game is to test the nerve of participants and the likely outcome is that one of the vehicles will veer away, leaving both unscathed but one of the actors shamed in the process. Allison (1971) has applied this game to the superpower confrontation in 1962 between Khrushchev and Kennedy following the deployment of Soviet nuclear missiles in Cuba within easy range of the American mainland. As the confrontation intensified, Kennedy called the bluff of the Soviet leadership by threatening nuclear confrontation, and as a result the Russian navy withdrew. Allison argues that these events can be explained as a complex game of chicken involving very high stakes, with the ultimate victors being the Americans, especially because of the increase in prestige for Kennedy, and the recognition by the Soviet leadership that they had severely underestimated the resolve of the American leadership.

In a more complex game, prisoners' dilemma, the capacity of actors to make rational choices which generate unanticipated consequences is addressed. This game is most often illustrated through an imaginary sketch in which two partners in crime have been taken for questioning by the police. The police inspector is well aware that there is very little substantive evidence with which to take the case to court and that a successful prosecution depends upon the statements of the two suspects to provide the necessary evidence of wrongdoing. The suspects are faced with a choice of either telling the truth about the crime, in the anticipation of receiving a lenient penalty, or keeping quiet, without knowing whether the partner will do the same and not confess. Since the two suspects are separated from each other, this game is based upon each one's trust in the other partner and their perceptions of which choice would serve their self-interest. In terms of the consequences of their actions, if both refuse to confess they are unlikely to receive a harsh punishment and may avoid any penalty. If one confesses and the other does not, then the suspect who remains silent is likely to receive a harsh punishment and the confessor a suspended sentence for cooperating with the authorities. If both confess, then both are likely to receive a moderate to harsh punishment. The scores involved in such choices are represented in Figure 4.13.

Figure 4.13   One variation of the prisoners' dilemma game. The lowest score produces the best outcome; the highest score produces the worst outcome.

When we examine the aggregate consequences of these choices in numerical terms, it is clear that the combined choices of both not to confess would produce the best outcome, a score of 2. The worst outcome of 8 follows from both confessing. A minimaxing individual in this situation would resolve to choose the outcome which minimized the risk of a harsh punishment and which took into account the lack of trust in the other partner. From the point of view of each individual the minimax decision would be to confess in the hope that the other partner did not, and so escape harsh punishment. However, if both actors in this situation applied this rational decision to their situation and opted to confess, the aggregate outcome would be the worst outcome. In this way, game theorists argue, it is possible for rational individuals to act in ways which appear to be the best in the light of the circumstances and yet the unintended consequence of their individual actions is to produce the worst outcome for all involved.

In prisoners' dilemma, the rational decisions of the actors produce the worst possible outcomes for all the players involved.

This rational choice framework has been adapted for the study of electoral politics by James Buchanan and others in developing public choice theory (see Buchanan et al., 1978; Buchanan and Tullock, 1981; Green, 1987). The focus on public or political choices as rational decisions has led to it being labelled the 'economics of politics'. Buchanan's approach is interesting in its attempts to examine the interrelationship between the rational choices of voters and of political leaders, and how their combined decisions had effects on public policy (Buchanan et al., 1978). For Buchanan, the electorate is composed of individuals who behave like consumers in the marketplace and the votes they cast in elections are the same as purchases. Consequently, voters are seen to vote for the party which offers them the most in terms of their perceived self-interest. This approach to voters in the 1960s and 1970s seemed to provide a means of explaining the decline of voting according to party loyalty and class background and the rise of issue-based voting alongside the increase in electoral volatility more generally. It is assumed that voters overall would prefer to have lower taxes at the same time as greater public spending on services such as health, education and social services. For political leaders who, as rational actors, attempt to bid for votes in order to win power, these apparently contradictory demands by the electorate lead them into a situation where they can only keep themselves in power by increasing state intervention without passing on the costs to the taxpayer.

The consequence of such a policy, according to Buchanan, is increased public debt and the undermining of wealth creation sectors (private business) by state regulation and higher corporate taxation. Buchanan was associated with New Right or neo-liberal demands for 'rolling back the frontier of the state' under Thatcher in the UK and Reagan in the USA. He adds that the rational choices of members of the bureaucracy also lead to an expansion of the state, supposedly in the interests of the citizen, but really to serve the self-interest of the administrators in expanding their own power and rewards. In this case, as in prisoners' dilemma, the rational self-interested choices of those involved lead to a situation where everyone suffers in the long term. Buchanan argues that the expansion of the state undermines the economic growth upon which the social programmes depend because the tax base shrinks.

Activity 4.4

Now turn to Reading C, an extract from Garrett Hardin's *The Tragedy of the Commons* (1968), and Reading D, 'When rationality fails' (1989), by Jon Elster.

- Identify how Hardin follows the game of prisoners' dilemma identified above.
- Make a list of what you consider to be the strengths and weaknesses of Hardin's extract.
- Identify the main themes of Elster's account of the limits of rational choice explanations.

As you read through the extract by Hardin you may be struck by the way that certain premises and assumptions can lead you to certain conclusions. As you read through Elster, you should think about whether Hardin's assumptions about people are really true.

4.2 Problems in rational choice theory

The assumptions of game theory are open to criticism on a number of grounds, which all hinge on the extent to which the models used are realistic. In particular, a great deal of doubt can be cast upon the definition of the concept of rationality in rational choice theory; this has, in turn, raised questions about when the model can usefully be applied and when it would be inappropriate. To address these problems it is worthwhile to consider what it means for behaviour to be rational or irrational.

Rational choice theory works well when life is reasonably certain and predictable and the issues are kept simple – however, most situations are uncertain, unpredictable and complex.

The relationship between our choices and desires is often less clear-cut than the advocates of rational choice theory suggest for, in some situations, human beings act against their desires or experience conflicting desires. Since all decisions in the market involve these sorts of choices, it may not be accurate to characterize economic choices as rational calculations of costs and benefits. The characterization of rationality also depends upon the situation in which it takes place. What appears to be rational behaviour in one context may seem irrational in another situation, so that a universal principle of rational choice is unlikely to be established. Our personal attachments, traditional beliefs and even wishful thinking also play an important part in the formation of choices. The rational choice model assumes that, even if human beings are rational 'minimaxers', they make choices with full and perfect knowledge of the possible end consequences of their decisions and of the various means for achieving the same results. It can be argued that all of these assumptions are unrealistic. For instance, the behaviour of stockbrokers during a crash in the investment markets does conform to the rational model in that they sell stocks and shares in order to avoid further loss of value. However, in conditions of normal trading this profession operates by rules of thumb, intuition and hunches even though their occupational description would suggest the purely rational pursuit of profit taking.

The philosopher and economist Friedrich Hayek began to address some of these difficulties and became deeply critical of attempts to develop purely rational accounts of social life. In particular, he argued that the social scientific method should take proper account of the complexity of social phenomena within open systems. For Hayek the problem is **scientism**, which involves any claim to know the most appropriate way of investigating a social phenomenon before considering it (Hayek, 1952). Hayek warns against obstacles to the further advance of modern science, such as:

- the belief that ideas of things, such as 'laws', 'causes' and 'social order', possess some reality (that by analysing ideas we learn about the attributes of reality);

- the tendency of human actors to interpret external events after their own images;

- the attribution of a designing mind to the objects in question.

He was particularly concerned to counter the belief that it was possible to reconstruct the real world in social scientific theories and use this knowledge rationally to reconstruct actual societies (which he associated with the social engineering of fascism and communism). Hayek suggests that it is impossible to comprehend collective entities such as 'capitalism', 'society' and the 'economy', for:

> The concrete knowledge which guides the action of any group of people never exists as a consistent and coherent body. It only exists in the dispersed, incomplete and inconsistent form in which it appears in many individual minds, and the dispersion and imperfection of all knowledge are two of the basic facts from which the social sciences have to start.

(Hayek, 1952, pp.49–50)

Hayek also starts from a position of **methodological individualism**. However, unlike in rational choice theory, people are not treated as discrete atoms but are seen as engaged in mutual discovery through relationships. The examples Hayek has in mind include the long-term evolution of a system of language or the emergence of a system of monetary exchange. These evolving systems are seen as the unintended and unanticipated consequences of all the shared experiences of exchange.

> The way in which footpaths are formed in a wild broken country is just such an instance. At first everyone will seek for himself what seems to him the best path. But the fact that such a path has been used once is likely to make it easier to traverse and therefore more likely to be used again; and thus gradually more and more clearly defined tracks arise and come to be used to the exclusion of other possible ways. Human movements through the region come to conform to a definite pattern which, although the result of deliberate decisions of many people, has yet not been consciously designed by anyone.
>
> (Hayek, 1952, pp.70–1)

While the nomothetic method which identifies 'recurrent events of a particular kind' (Hayek, 1952, p.118) predominates in natural science in relation to social science, Hayek sees idiographic explanations of particular or unique situations as playing as important a role as that of generalization. He suggests that the role of theory is to constitute the wholes through recognizing the importance of the related parts and comprehending the intentions, shared experiences and tacit knowledge of subjective individuals. In the next section we turn to those approaches which focus upon the roles of tacit and subjective knowledge in social science.

Methodological individualism breaks things down into their smallest components and uses this to reconstruct more complex relations.

Summary

Rational choice approaches resolve the problems of cultural values by focusing upon the 'subjective preferences' of rational individuals. In praxeology and game theory, the rationality of individuals is established at an abstract theoretical level prior to empirical research and typically adopts a 'minimaxing' approach to decision making.

The imaginative use of games to identify the process of decisions made by individuals in complex and unpredictable situations provides social scientists with a means of identifying the similarities in decision making in very different contexts, highlighting the rule-governed nature of social life.

The assumption of rationality in these approaches provides a useful indication of the problems created by wishful thinking in social scientific research. In such cases, social scientists imagine an object (such as society, the economy, the mind, or the polity), treat it as a thing in itself and neglect the very processes by which such objects are constructed in the first place.

5   Meaning and subjectivity

For neo-Kantian idealists, general explanations have a useful role in social science even if they are only part of the whole picture; rational choice theories raise the prospect of a purely rational or 'minimaxing' approach to human decision making. However, the third group of idealist approaches, which we examine now, embraces the subjective dimension of social life wholeheartedly. They regard the existence of objects of analysis that we think of as real, as the product of our interpretations. In addition, individuals are not viewed as atoms bouncing off each other, but as having a sense of the shared existence through which identities are constructed. This does not mean that such 'objective things' have no effect – if we believe something to be real, it is real enough in its consequences for we behave as if it does exist. This section is concerned with a variety of approaches which have come to be known as forms of hermeneutics or phenomenology and which contain some useful insights into the problems of social science. We focus upon the interpretive approaches and their exploration of the self, interaction and meanings. The aim of hermeneutics is to make the obscure clear and plain, by identifying the processes and context of all approaches which attempt to understand society and culture. To do this, we should place ourselves inside the mind of the author or the social actor under consideration. The concept of **subjectivity** used in this approach is not the calculating machine of rational choice theory but, instead, it involves the meaningful interpretation of unpredictable relationships in everyday life.

Hermeneutics and phenomenology seek to understand the subjective and meaningful construction of the complex social world.

The emergence of contemporary hermeneutics, defined as the theory of the interpretation of meaning, can be traced to Wilhelm Dilthey's *Introduction to the Human Sciences* (1883; for brief extracts see Rickman, 1976). Dilthey's main concern was to identify a distinctly 'human science' which did not treat the study of society and history as the automatic play of objective forms and processes. For Dilthey, the natural sciences presented an inappropriate analogue for social science because natural objects cannot meaningfully interpret and construct their own cultural environment, whereas human beings can. Therefore, the study of society and history involved very different ground rules from those of natural scientific research because all human values, ideas, concepts, purposes and desires are seen as an inescapable part of understanding social life. This means that while human beings acted *upon* the natural environment, they also acted *within* the social environment. So the social and cultural forms taken as the objects of the social sciences were the expressions of the mind rather than external to the mind. The 'lived experiences' of individuals are thus the source of understanding. To deal with this, Dilthey argued, we have to recognize the problem of the *hermeneutic circle*: 'The whole of a work must be understood from individual words and their combination but full understanding of an individual part presupposes understanding of the whole' (Dilthey, 1896, cited in Bryant, 1985, pp.66–7). A common metaphor for explaining this idea is the sentence analogue, whereby the meaning of a word is identified by reference to its place in a sentence and the meaning of the sentence is established through the meaning of the individual words. Thus all mental constructions are historically and socially specific and hence prone to change as part of the web of cultural forms. There is, therefore, a crucial

Hermeneutics focuses upon the lived experience of human beings in their social and historical context.

difference between the approaches here and all the other approaches considered so far in this chapter. Here, there is no 'knowing subject' above and beyond the experiences of those being studied. In the following sections we look at ways in which this approach has been developed in the social sciences, particularly psychology, sociology and geography.

5.1   The self-concept and social interaction

The approaches considered in this section start from the assumption that the 'real world' is actively constructed by human beings, even though social scientists tend to behave as if it is independent of our knowledge. The first grouping we should consider, interactionism, draws from the philosophy of **pragmatism**. This is concerned with the way in which meanings and interpretations are the product of the 'pragmatic concerns' of practical problems and purposes of social life. The mind is treated as a tool for solving problems encountered in everyday life. This problem-solving approach has had a profound impact upon the interactionist approach in psychology (sometimes labelled humanistic psychology or sociological social psychology) and in sociology.

Pragmatic approaches treat social inquiry as a form of problem solving closely related to the concerns of everyday life.

Interactionism treats social actors and their small face-to-face interactions as the basis of all social life, so that the meaning of any concept or idea (personal, political, philosophical or scientific) can only be located in the experiential consequences which it produces. On the basis of this, the pragmatist William James distinguished 'knowledge about' from 'knowledge of' (James, 1890). 'Knowledge about' – that which is acquired through textbooks – is conveyed in abstract general principles which can be learned and memorized. However, 'knowledge of' – practical knowledge acquired through experience in everyday life – is established through trial and error and can take an unconscious or tacit form. This treats the concept of the mind as a 'thinking process' always in development, rather than as a fixed thing. In this way, individuals can define objects and their context, identify sensible courses of action or modes of conduct, imagine the consequences of these choices and, finally, select an appropriate course of action.

Practically adequate knowledge is derived through a process of trial and error.

Other forms of interactionist thinking, like that of psychologist and sociologist George Herbert Mead, focused more upon the social context in the shaping of choices. For Mead, in *Mind, Self and Society* (1934), meaning can be identified in the actual behaviour of the actors and the development of the mind as an unfolding process can be seen in the activities of children. In the *play stage* children play out roles and characters in order to be someone else, such as cowboys and Indians, doctors and nurses, etc. In the more advanced *game stage* the child learns to develop an inner conversation with the 'generalized other', which enables the child to predict the behaviour of others. The prediction of the routine habitual practices of others and responding in similarly predictable ways enables the everyday social interaction of human beings to take place while avoiding conflict. In Mead's own words:

For Mead, the concept of self is not fixed but the changing product of an ongoing process of interaction.

> in a game where a number of individuals are involved, then the child taking one role must be ready to take the role of everyone else ... [and] must have the responses of each position involved in his [*sic*] own position. He must know what everyone

else is going to do in order to carry out his own play. He has to take all of these roles. They do not all have to be present in consciousness at the same time, but at some moments he has to have three or four individuals present in his own attitude, such as the one who is going to throw the ball, the one who is going to catch it and so on.

(Mead 1934, p.151)

Often the things we know about can help us understand situations of which we have little or no experience.

This can be demonstrated through the example of the metaphor of the *looking glass self*, whereby other people act like mirrors for an individual's imagination. This is based upon three steps: the individual imagining how he or she looks to others; the imagination of how others judge the individual; and the emotional reaction of the individual to the imagined judgement. In this way, we constantly monitor ourselves at the level of our own imagination and, consequently, an adequate social science should attempt to address the existence of these processes (Cooley, 1902). Social interaction can be seen as an ongoing process, rather like the changing patterns of a kaleidoscope, instead of following a definite fixed plan. The search for patterns can be seen in the identification of 'career' patterns in different situations. It is possible to identify similar patterns in occupational careers, criminal careers (Becker, 1963) and the moral career of a mental patient (Goffman, 1987, pp.117–56). In criminal and non-criminal career patterns we would expect the rewards and respect to fit their place in the career ladder; Goffman reminds us that careers can be brilliant but also disappointing. A career in this approach is defined by the relationship between the internal processes through which we define our concept of self and the external processes through which we understand our social positions, lifestyles and institutional locations. It also helps us to see that labelling someone as criminal, or as mentally ill, matters. Goffman suggests that these moral aspects of careers can help us understand the relationship between the self and social institutions in the treatment careers of 'mentally ill' patients. Nevertheless, this approach is limited to considering what we can empirically observe rather than attempting to identify the assumptions upon which these actions and interactions are based.

Activity 4.5

If we consider identities to be social locations, it is worthwhile thinking through what it means to ask yourself the question 'Who am I?' before engaging in social research. Various dimensions of your identity should come to mind, such as your age, gender, ethnicity, social class, marital status and so on. You will consider some of these to be more important than others.

- Make a list of the relevant dimensions for your own identity.
- Organize this list in terms of their importance.
- Which of these dimensions has changed in importance and why?
- Quickly list the areas of social science which really interest you. Are these related to the dimensions of your identity? If so, in what ways?

5.2 Phenomenology and intersubjective meaning

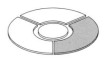

Phenomenology asks us to dig deeper than in previous approaches, in order to explore the taken-for-granted assumptions of social research. The German philosopher who established contemporary phenomenology, Edmund Husserl, asks us to reconsider the idea of the 'objective world', and the way that some approaches treat subjectivity as a pale reflection of some deeper or more authentic state of affairs. As you saw in Chapter 2, Descartes started with 'I think therefore I exist' as a foundational principle. However, for Husserl, the starting-point always involved an intention, 'I think something'. This means that the act of describing experience actually creates the object of analysis. Therefore, the distinction between 'surface appearances' and some 'underlying reality' is no more than a convenient fiction for positivist scientists. To get around this problem, Husserl argued, we have to 'bracket' the objective. This means that we should suspend our belief in the existence of the objective world and abstain from making judgements about whether the world does or does not exist. This process has been characterized as the peeling away of the layers of ideas to identify the pre-scientific forms of experience of the *Lebenswelt* (life-world), rather like peeling away the layers of an onion.

Phenomenology treats the distinction between surface appearances and reality as the product of the conscious mind.

Schütz developed this in a more practical way. In *The Phenomenology of the Social World* (1932/1967), he argued that it is through the condition of **intersubjectivity** that the individual actors involved are able to grasp each other's consciousness and construct their life-world. By sharing time and space, the two or more individual actors involved in communication could engage in a process of understanding which involves the discovery of what is going on in the other person's mind (Schütz, 1932/1967, pp.112–13). Although Weber had developed the use of ideal types as a theoretical tool against which empirical evidence could be compared, this still treated the evidence as factual even though it was open to various interpretations. Instead, Schütz argued that there were no hard facts, only interpretations – that facts are intersubjectively constructed. As you saw in Chapter 1, Schütz sought to establish connections between the second-order constructs of social science and the first-order constructs of everyday life (Schütz, 1953). At the heart of Schütz's approach is the sociological formulation often described as 'cookery-book' or 'recipe' knowledge, the notion that we do not need to understand the origins of a particular set of practices in order to select the ingredients, bake the cake and 'eat and enjoy it' (Schütz, 1943, p. 137).

Phenomenology sees consciousness as the product of the intersubjective relations between actors engaged in communication.

Schütz suggests that we need to identify the recipe knowledge of social scientists as well as everyday life.

Two points should be highlighted here. First, the social world is constructed by actors who possess free will and who can and will behave in spontaneous ways not anticipated by the 'fictitious consciousness' of the scientific model. Second, scientists employ the same procedures of typification as actors in everyday life. For Schütz, in the natural sciences it is plausible to collect 'facts and regularities', but, when faced with the problem of understanding social existence, we need to account for the motives, the means and ends, the shared relationships and the plans and expectations of human actors. In the next two sections we explore some of the ways in which this approach has been applied.

Social scientific practice should find ways to connect the 'first-order' constructs of everyday life and the 'second-order' constructs of social scientific knowledge.

5.3 Ethnomethodology and tacit knowledge

While phenomenology offers a useful philosophical critique of social scientific knowledge, the sociologist Harold Garfinkel developed this into a viable research programme which attempted to reconstruct the 'taken-for-granted' commonsense assumptions (tacit knowledge) of people in their everyday lives. This became known as ethnomethodology (literally, 'people-method'), combining Schütz's insights with the empirical research strategies of symbolic interactionists (Garfinkel, 1967). The interactionists used ethnographic research techniques, such as in-depth interviews and participant observation, to attempt to reconstruct social life in a way that was as true to life as possible. However, they limited their evidence to the relationships they could observe, even if they didn't see observation in quite the same way as empiricists did.

Garfinkel wanted to delve deeper into the lives of his subjects and aimed to reconstruct the tacit knowledge that they could not even express (which Schütz had labelled 'cookery-book' or recipe knowledge). For Garfinkel, human actors continually create and transform their social existence, so that the supposedly objective contexts in which we live are fragile and transitory. Garfinkel suggests that actors are constantly attempting to make sense of the mass of sensations they experience. To do this, actors draw upon their stock of stories and meaningful interpretations. The moment that the evidence seems to suggest the application of a particular story, the sensory evidence is transformed into a support for the story. Garfinkel labels this technique the 'documentary method', involving a constant reciprocal process of interaction between the story-lines and evidence. Consequently, the stock of stories itself undergoes renegotiation and transformation as identities are reinvented.

Some of Garfinkel's research strategies bordered on the unethical, for they deliberately disturbed 'normal' relationships to see what would happen. For example, he engaged in the disruption of conversations to identify how much the respondents would adapt. He would play chess in seminars with new students and, after a period of following the rules, would then violate minor rules to see how far his students would adapt. Taken by surprise in this way, the students would accommodate the rule changes in the game and play accordingly. More controversially, he trained a number of his students to pretend to be lodgers in their own homes when they left the university for the vacation. These students simply behaved politely at home as they would have done when visiting a distant relative, yet the minor changes in behaviour provoked considerable familial conflict and disorientation. In these ways, Garfinkel was able to identify the tacit assumptions of games, conversations and family life, and reconstruct the complex processes by which the 'objective world' only appears as such because we construct it in that way. Similar investigations have been carried out by Aaron Cicourel in *The Social Organisation of Juvenile Justice* (1976), which examined the taken-for-granted assumptions of the police and courts in defining and processing 'juvenile delinquents' in two comparable Californian cities. The differences in delinquency rates, Cicourel argued, were the product of the different judicial cultures in each city. In another example, Robert Bellah drew upon this strategy in his inves-

Ethnomethodology seeks to find ways of locating and reconstructing the taken-for-granted commonsense assumptions of social practices.

Ethnomethod-ologists demonstrate that the rules of social life are more flexible and fragile than is often assumed.

tigation of new religious movements. Bellah used a range of qualitative research techniques to identify the commonsense assumptions of religious people in their everyday lives to establish the intensity of belief and the extent of their commitment to religious values (Bellah, 1976). These different studies have different objects and are responding to very different debates; nevertheless, they all have a common concern to establish the taken-for-granted commonsense assumptions (or recipe knowledge) of the people involved.

Activity 4.6

Turn to Reading E from Roger Jeffery's 'Normal rubbish: deviant patients in casualty departments' (1979).

- Make notes on the forms of taken-for-granted typifications used in the treatment of patients in the casualty department and how they are used to place a value on the patients.

- Consider in which other ways you would engage in the study of casualty wards. In what ways would you say that Jeffery's approach has limits?

In this reading you should note the strengths and weaknesses of this kind of social scientific practice. Does Jeffery identify things that other social scientists overlook?

Summary

A common theme in hermeneutic and phenomenological accounts of social life is the identification of the meanings, intentions and context of the author of a text or the social actor in his or her natural setting. The focus of analysis is the social and historical conditions in which a specific set of ideas or actions is located.

Interactionist and ethnomethodological approaches sought to draw upon these insights in developing an active research programme into the self-concepts and/or tacit assumptions of everyday social life.

Schütz made a distinctive contribution to social scientific method by attempting to overcome the tendency towards detachment associated with the application of natural science methods to social objects. In order to prevent social scientists imposing their own typifications upon objects in social research, an adequate approach should seek to ensure that the concepts used are also intelligible in everyday life.

GEOGRAPHICAL MODELS 2

In Geographical Models 2 you can see how it is possible to establish stronger connections between social scientific practice and our constructs in everyday life.

Throughout this chapter, you have seen how the imaginative organisation of our experiences is a central feature of the way in which social scientists construct their accounts of the social world. However, social scientists who adopt the neo-Kantian approach or rational choice theory tend to look at the world through their own conceptual spectacles and assume that the frameworks they devise are the best way of looking at the world. Social scientists within the phenomenological and ethnomethodological approaches are more inclined to draw upon the everyday experiences of the people being studied in order to construct their theoretical frameworks. Of course, phenomenologists were not the first to do this, as you can see in the first example here, drawn from the study of town planning at the start of the 20th century. In this section we consider an example from Ebenezer Howard, a leading contributor to understanding urban geography and the built environment, in his attempts to make connections between social scientific models and lived experience. This is followed by a more explicit attempt to apply phenomenology to studies of the landscape, drawn from the work of Yi-Fu Tuan. In Geographical Models 1, we looked at ways in which the ideal types used could organize complex empirical evidence. These ideal types remained detached from the actual experience of the people under investigation. In the examples developed in this section, the models demonstrate how it is possible to establish connections between the problems and issues of everyday life and the concepts developed to study human relationships. Howard's model of harmony between town and country demonstrates the construction of a meaningful model which can act as a flexible framework for creating a healthier environment for human beings (Howard, 1898/1985). This model was set up in response

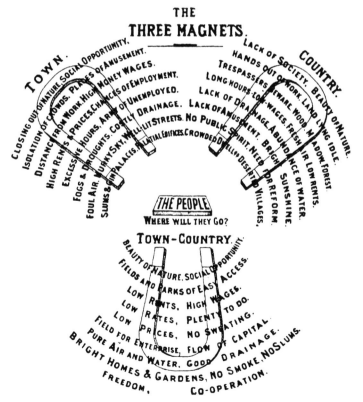

Figure 4.14 'The Three Magnets', demonstrating Howard's attempt to bring together town and country.

to the social problems generated by the deteriorating urban slum conditions of the late nineteenth and early twentieth centuries and the increased awareness of the relationship between squalor and disease. In particular, it was recognized that the increase in infant mortality rates in the 1880s and 1890s related to social conditions. Howard's model

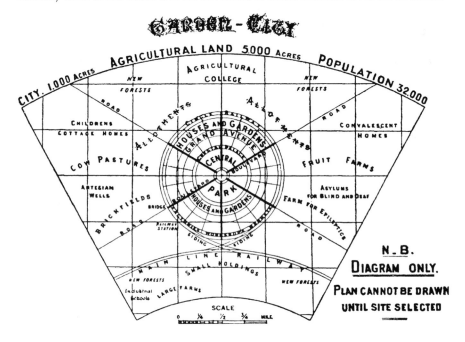

Figure 4.15 Howard's model of the ideal garden city.

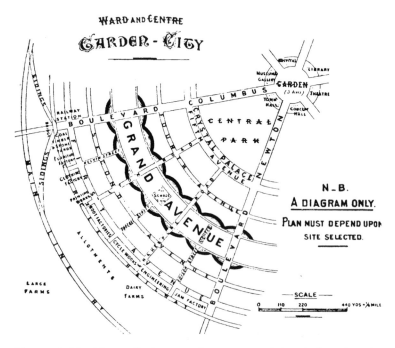

Figure 4.16 Howard's diagram of a segment of the ideal garden city.

is based upon the assumption that the possible solution would be to combine the amenities of the town with the recreational facilities and clean environment of the countryside. This model, demonstrated in Figures 4.15 and 4.16, was used in the development of the 'garden cities' such as Welwyn Garden City and, on a smaller scale, the leafy garden suburbs of Hampstead Heath. In particular, the model emphasizes the importance of the opportunities to use amenities through the construction of reliable and economical transport links.

While Howard demonstrates the ways in which planners and social scientists can organize the built environment for human benefit, in the next example we look at an explicit attempt to develop an account of the meanings of space for those who actually live within it. In Tuan's *Topophilia*, mapping can be seen as a complex cultural product (Tuan, 1974). Topophilia (literally, 'sudden encounter with the landscape') is described by Tuan as the 'love of place' and the work focuses upon the aesthetic dimension of the experience of historically and socially specific landscapes. By drawing upon the phenomenological and pragmatic approaches (alongside evidence from cultural anthropology to the role of language as a system of meaning), Tuan demonstrates that the environment plays a vivid role in the cultural imagination. For the geographer Denis Cosgrove, this provided a useful remedy for the detachment and abstraction of theoretical and quantitative geography (Cosgrove, 1986). Tuan examines the organization of the phenomena of the landscape by human minds in different cultural settings in order to establish the terms of reference for interpreting the forms and, in some cases, the harshness of conditions of different landscapes. For Tuan, the sense of place involves the use of meaningful constructs which enable human beings to orient themselves towards their surroundings. He divides these into three groupings (shown in Figure 4.17).

Biological and Social	Geographical	Cosmological
life–death	land–water	heaven–earth
male–female	mountain–valley	high–low
we–they	north–south	light–darkness
	centre–periphery	

Figure 4.17   Tuan's groupings of meaningful constructs.

Tuan argues that the human interpretation of space and place is closely related to the ethnocentric orientation of most human cultures. Drawing upon comparative cultural evidence, he shows how the mapping of space often reflects cultural beliefs about the centrality of one's own culture, as demonstrated in Figures 4.18–4.20 (overleaf).

We'll come back to this when we look at cultural geography in Chapter 6.

Tuan's approach can be seen as a form of idiographic response to the nomothetic tendencies in geography, although in this case it was also informed by phenomenological insights into the meaningful construction of the landscape. However, unlike other examples of phenomenology in this chapter, the focus is the relationship between human beings and their meaningful interpretations of the natural environment (modified by human construction and ecological damage). Tuan's account of space and place provides an indication of how it is possible to draw upon the beliefs and values of different cultural locations in order to understand the ways in which the environment is meaningful. This approach is an important precursor to the emergence of cultural geography in the 1980s, which also explores the production of meaning in relation to

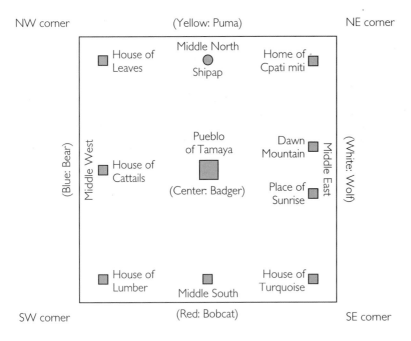

Figure 4.18 Ethnocentric mapping I: the Keresan Pueblo Indians, New Mexico.

space and place. However, from the standpoint of many contemporary cultural geographers, Tuan's approach retains too strong an attachment to the idea that there is an empirical world awaiting discovery and still treats representation in a simplistic way, an issue we revisit in Chapter 6, section 4.2.

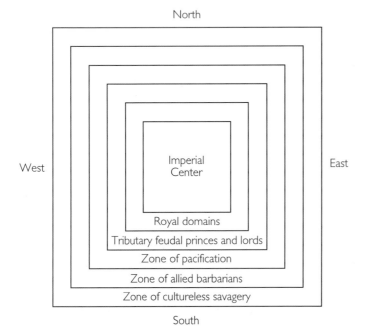

Figure 4.19 Ethnocentric mapping II: traditional Chinese world view.

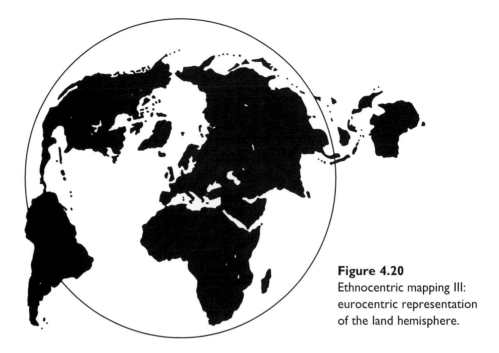

Figure 4.20
Ethnocentric mapping III:
eurocentric representation
of the land hemisphere.

6   Conclusion: taking imagination seriously

Let's briefly summarize the idealist approaches considered in this chapter.
They fall into three broad categories.

- Various forms of neo-Kantianism which, in different ways, attempt to
  explain or understand, or both explain and understand social life. They
  can be differentiated in terms of how they see social science – as
  nomothetic or idiographic, voluntarist or determinist.

- Approaches which place a special emphasis on rationality as a basis for
  human decision making, such as praxeology and rational choice theory.
  These tend to emphasize explanations of social behaviour but at the
  expense of understanding. As a result, there is a danger of making the
  evidence fit the model.

- Hermeneutic and phenomenological accounts of the meaningful
  construction of the social world which seek to understand how
  individuals interact and make sense of the world.

Earlier in this chapter you considered the quick guide to idealist
approaches to knowledge construction (Table 4.1) which offered a bold initial comparison of these approaches and how they differed from the empiricist approach to knowledge construction in Chapter 2. In particular, you
were asked to think about how the various idealisms can be compared and
contrasted in the ways that they understood the relationships between theory and observation, facts and values and explanation and prediction. Now
in Table 4.2 you have the chance to go through these steps again, but in a
little more detail, taking into account the key ideas developed throughout
this chapter.

Table 4.2   Varieties of idealism.

	Varieties of Idealism			
	Neo-Kantian Idealism	**Rational Choice Theory**	**Hermeneutics and Phenomenology**	**Empiricism**
Theory and Observation	Theoretical statements identify relationships between variables. Complex empirical evidence is 'organized' by ideal types (exaggerated characteristics of social life) as devices for comparing and contrasting. Ideal types provide a bridge between *understanding* human action and *explaining* social relations.	Theoretical work involves the rational reconstruction of principles and concepts which explain empirical relations. Theory reflects the capacity of individual actors to make rational decisions within definite constraints (such as the supply of resources like information). The key assumption is the 'minimaxing' individual making choices on the basis of calculations of costs and benefits of various courses of action.	The problem facing social science is the gulf between the everyday experiences of social actors (first-order constructs) and the detached accounts of social life produced by social scientists (second-order constructs). Scientific detachment results in social scientists imposing their conception of the way social processes operate upon the object in question. Detached science tells us more about the scientist than the object. *Understanding* is just as, if not more, important than explaining.	The scientific method involves a clear separation of theory and observation (although empiricists disagree about the relationship between the two). All theoretical statements must derive from (or are subject to repeated tests against) empirical evidence. Theoretical statements apply to all circumstances where the objects in question exist.
Facts and Values	Value relevance – concept formation in the social sciences should be relevant to the problems of a particular society in question at a specific time. Value judgements are the concern of the philosophers in that time and place and the values of the social researcher should be clearly stated.	Social scientific facts can only be identified through the subjective values and the intentional choices of individuals. Rational choice theories focus upon exchange relationships in a range of social settings. There is some question as to whether this approach is actually deeply value-laden in its advocacy of individualism.	Social science is deeply value laden, for the social scientists define their own identities through common stock of knowledge of the society they study. Scientific facts are the commonsense assumptions of the social scientists (values remain unacknowledged in concept formation). Social scientists need to be much more critically aware of their own taken-for-granted assumptions and make these clear to their audiences.	Facts and values are treated as separate things. It is important to ensure that the subjective biases of the researcher do not interfere with the account of empirical evidence. It is feasible and desirable to have a value-free social science. Some empiricists accept that there are problems in keeping values out of scientific knowledge.
Explanation and Prediction	An empirical regularity between variables (constant conjunction of events) is necessary but not sufficient for establishing a causal law. This acknowledges the complexity of causal factors in any empirical situation but raises problems in terms of making accurate predictions (*intelligibilty determinism*). It is possible to develop either nomethetic or idiographic accounts of social life. Nomothetic explanations identify general relations sustained over time. Idiographic explanations focus upon individual circumstances as unique and acknowledge the importance of interpretations in generating knowledge. Rational choice theory adopts a nomothetic account of explanation which applies the same formal model across different situations. Theories are useful and suggestive simplifications of more complex processes rather than perfectly accurate depictions of real life. Thus prediction in social science involves the identification of patterns rather than specific outcomes.		Social settings only exist through the intersubjective relations of the actors involved. Knowledge can only be understood in the historical and social situation in which it was produced. Social life is the product of the complex processes through which individuals and groups (re)negotiate their way through social life. The complexity of social life and the distribution of (often tacit) knowledge means that nomothetic approaches fail to account for events as unique concrete circumstances.	Empiricism assumes that there is a symmetry of explanation and prediction. Any explanation must be predictively accurate to be sustained. A constant conjunction of events is both necessary and sufficient to generate a causal law of social life (*regularity determinism*).

As you can see, there are considerable differences between these idealist approaches. In particular, they disagree about the precise ways in which social scientific practice should proceed. On the one hand, the rational choice theorists believe that an all-purpose theoretical framework can be devised to *explain* human decision making and behaviour. On the other hand, the phenomenologists argue that the choices we face are specific to each location, so the best we can do is to try to *understand* these situations. Neo-Kantians, however, try to juggle both preferences. They are divided over the choice of whether to develop general theoretical explanations of all situations (the nomothetic approach) *or* limit themselves to understanding all situations as unique (the idiographic approach) *or*, like Weber, try to find a way of generalizing in a looser way so that they don't have to explain the conditions of all situations in much detail.

Despite all of these differences, they are all critical of the empiricist account of what makes a causal relationship. While empiricists assume that an empirical regularity between variables sustained over time is in itself enough to justify the claim that a causal relationship is at work, for idealists these regularities have a much more tentative status. An idealist approach sees them as useful for indicating the patterns we should attempt to explain and understand, so that they become 'intelligible' to the people who study them. For this reason, a successful prediction like 'if x one day then y the next', is not enough to construct a causal law; it must also make sense within the existing body of conceptual knowledge through which we interpret our perceptions and experiences. In addition to this, idealists still hold in common certain distinctive features which can be highlighted as follows.

- The transfer of the assumptions and methods of the natural sciences (in conditions of closure) to the study of social objects in complex open systems is an inappropriate way to proceed.

- Any attempt to generate general laws should take into account the role of human interpretations and the lack of a clear separation between the subject and object in social science.

These approaches can be labelled idealist in the broadest sense. Idealism, as you will have noticed, is something of an umbrella label. However, it is possible to link all of these approaches by noting their emphasis upon the role of ideas and human imagination in organizing experience and constructing knowledge about the social world. Idealists tend to be anti-naturalist in considering empiricist accounts of the scientific method for studying social objects, believing that it is inappropriate to apply those assumptions and methods to studying people. Idealists emphasize the creative and interpretative characteristics of human beings and the impossibility of social researchers ever fully removing their values from the study of social relations and processes. Even Weber adopts the position of 'value relevance', that social research should be relevant to the problems of the day. Some idealists, by treating knowledge as a social product, reject both the separation of facts and values and the separation of theory and observation. So the key thing to remember is idealist approaches highlight the way in which observation is not as simple an activity as empiricists would have us believe.

READING A
There is more to seeing than meets the eye

Norwood Hanson

> There was a young man of East Bosham
> Who took out his eyeballs to wash 'em,
>   His mother said: 'Jack,
>   If you don't put 'em back,
> I'll jump on the beggars and squash 'em.'

The word 'observe' has many uses. Two of these must be kept distinct. ... 'Observe' sometimes serves in just the ways that 'look' and 'listen' serve, and it sometimes serves as 'see' and 'hear' serve. Thus we may speak of a man as a careful, systematic, industrious observer, or of his careful, systematic, and industrious observations. We may also, however, refer to his observations as his findings, his discoveries, what he has been successful in seeing. The word 'observe', then, is sometimes used to indicate what a person is doing, and sometimes used to signal the success of what he is doing. ... We know from common experience that the world does not go dark when we shut our eyes, nor do flowers lose their scent when we catch cold. So apparently we require ways of talking about what does go dark when I shut my eyes. ... We might talk about sensations ... by talking about *looks, appearances, glimpses, scents, flavors, sounds*, and so on. We say we see the sun. But all we really have to go on is the look of a brilliant yellow-white disc. We say we see a round penny, but the cash value of that in terms of sensation is just the appearance in our visual field of a copper-brown oval patch. We think we hear the telephone. But all we really hear is ding-a-ling. ...

The major mistake [is the] assimilation of the concept of *sensation* to the concept of *observation*. ... Visual sensations likewise are not *seeings,* though any case of seeing entails our having had at least one visual sensation. A visual sensation of a brilliant yellow-white disc is not itself a seeing of the sun, though any case of seeing the sun entails our having had at least one visual sensation of a brilliant yellow-white disc. ... In the strictest sense of 'see' what I see are two dimensional color patches; not the sun, the hills, and the trees, but only the looks or visual appearance of the sun, hills, and trees. The squinter may not see two candles, but he sees two bright somethings; these somethings are the candle-looks, the sense-data. The theory is not inventing fictitious entities; it is only drawing attention to our immediate object of sense, objects which we ordinarily ignore in favor of talking about common physical objects like candles, hills, trees, and the sun. ...

The conceptual organization of one's visual field is the all-important factor here. It is not something visually apprehended in the way that lines and shapes and colors are visually apprehended. ... It is rather the *way* in which lines, shapes, and colors are visually apprehended. I have been inviting you to consider a given constellation of lines and shapes (what psychologists call 'a stimulus pattern') and to consider further the different ways in which this given constellation of pattern can be apprehended visually, the different sorts of conceptual organization that can be accorded to that constellation. ... So while scientists are right in saying that they see physical objects ... we cannot leave things at that. For this would lead to some very uncomplicated ... views as to the nature of laboratory science, views to the effect that *seeing* is just an opening of one's eyes and looking; that *observing* is simply being in a position to watch when a phenomenon takes place, and the *facts* are just the things and situations in the world that we see when our eyes are open, the things we trip over when our eyes are closed. ... Wittgenstein said that 'we find certain things about seeing puzzling because we do not find the whole business of seeing puzzling enough.' ...

What follows is intended to show that the theories about seeing we have so far considered are too simple by far to be adequate. Consider first this well-known figure [Figure 1]. ...

We do not begin with the visual sensation and only then turn our theories and interpretations loose on it. In a most important way our theories and interpretations are in the *seeing* from the outset. *Figure 1* is seen as a box from underneath or from above, or as an octagon, or as a flat, flat-line drawing, or first one of these then another – but not all of them at once. ... Other figures to which all these remarks apply are these [Figure 2].

Figure 1

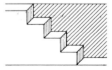

Figure 2

With each of these there are at least three possibilities open to us. We can see these figures in either a convex aspect or a concave aspect or as a flat-line drawing; or first one, then another – but not any two simultaneously. ...

Let us conclude with two well-known figures from experimental psychology [Figures 3(a) and 3(b)]. For those of you who see 3(a) as a duck, let me point out Bugs Bunny; and for those of you who see only a rabbit, let me point out Donald Duck. *Figure 3(b)* is complex in the same sort of way. Some of you will see an old, rather hag-like individual here; others will see a very young, stylish woman looking away. ...

Figure 3a   Figure 3b

Some people can *only* see these figures one way or the other; much as when we have at last solved the child's puzzle, having found the face in the branches of the tree, we can never see the tree any other way thereafter. The fact is always present in the tree. ...

Some will see [Figure 4] as a white cross on a black ground. Others will see this as a black cross on a white ground. ... If I drew for you exactly what I saw when I reported 'white cross on black ground,' how

Figure 4

would it differ from your drawing of what you see when you report 'black cross on white ground'? So too with Koehler's goblet [Figure 5].

Again, our retinas may react normally to this. But while I see a Venetian goblet, you may see two men staring at each other. Have we seen different things? Of course we have. And yet if I

Figure 5

draw my cup for you, you may say, 'By Jove, that is exactly what I saw, two men in a staring contest.' ...

Look back at Figure 3a, and then consider Figure 6. The context clearly gives us the clue regarding which aspect of the duck–rabbit is appropriate.

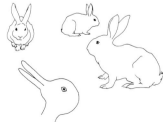

Figure 6

Source: Hanson, 1969, pp.61–97, 104.

READING B
Race relations in the city

John Rex and Robert Moore

The problem of race relations which confronted and perplexed the people of Birmingham in the early 1960s was one of immense practical political importance. ... It is important, therefore, that sociologists studying it should report their findings not merely to an academic audience, but to the widest possible audience of citizens. ... A sociological study of race relations must, in the first place, be distinguished from one which is purely historical and one which is psychological in its approach. This is not by any means to suggest that the historian and the psychologist do not have a considerable contribution to make to the study of race relations. It is to suggest, however, that neglect of the sociological dimensions of the problem could be disastrously misleading.

The inadequacy of historical explanation taken by itself rests upon the historian's inability to make explicit the general process which his explanation assumes. Very few historians, of course, confine themselves to reporting unique historical sequences of events. In their use of conjunctions like 'because', 'so', and 'therefore', they refer implicitly to general psychological and sociological laws. ... The prime virtue of the historian lies in the techniques which he has at his disposal for assessing the evidence as to what actually occurred. The explanatory laws to which he refers are for him a secondary matter. In the study of race relations his contribution will lie in his ability to record precisely what occurred in the situation of race contact. The interpretation of these occurrences is a task which falls to the generalizing, theoretical human sciences, above all to psychology and sociology. But psychology alone cannot explain the kind of problem with which we are concerned. If, for example, we are concerned to explain prejudice and discriminatory behaviour, the psychologist could only hope to show either that there was some universal human tendency towards behaving in these ways or that there was a deviant minority who were prejudiced because of their disturbed personalities. ...

It is also the case that a great deal of it was sufficiently explained, once we knew something of Birmingham's social structure and conflicts, and the constellation of interests and roles which was built into Birmingham society. At the very least it must be said that the universal factors and those having their roots in the individual personality could only be known if the factors arising from the social, economic, and cultural system were first sorted out. This point was emphasized for us by the feeling which we and many Birmingham people had about the race relations situation. This was the feeling that individuals were often acting in contradiction of their own ideals and sometimes of their own interests. They adopted discriminatory policies reluctantly, regretfully, and sometimes guiltily because they felt compelled to do so by circumstances beyond their control. Sometimes we felt that they acted as men possessed by some evil demon. But it is the task of sociologists to substitute casual explanation for demonology and what we have tried to do is to show that that which possessed them was not a demon, but the social system of which they were part. ...

False beliefs about an ethnic outgroup may serve to ensure that both an adherence to an ideal of social justice and a strong competitive position for one's group can be maintained. What we have to do is not merely to classify behaviour as prejudiced but to understand the part which customs, beliefs, norms, and expectations play in a larger social structure, be it the structure of an ethnic minority group or that of the overall urban society, marked as it is by diverse intergroup conflicts. Once we understand urban society as a structure of social interaction and conflict, prejudiced behaviour may be shown to fit naturally into or even to be required by that structure. Prejudice may be a social as well as a psychological phenomenon. ... Once we have grasped the idea of urban society as a number of overlapping and sometimes contradictory systems of social relations it soon becomes clear that the commonly used vocabulary of race relations which includes such words as 'assimilation', 'integration', and 'accommodation' is inadequate. Such vocabularies assume a 'host–immigrant' framework in which the culture and values of the host society are taken to be non-contradictory and static and in which the immigrant is seen as altering his own patterns of behaviour until they finally conform to those of the host society. ...

Several processes seem to operate. Firstly, class conflicts which are inherent in the situation because of shortage of facilities may cross-cut ethnic conflicts. Thus a tenant may come to see himself primarily as a tenant rather than as an Irishman or a West Indian. Or a landlord may come to put his economic interest as a landlord before his ethnic loyalty. Secondly, the children of a particular ethnic group may, through their school contacts, move into a different social world and so too may some adults. And, thirdly, since the available

means of association (for instance, churches and political parties) are not historically geared to the existing conflict situation, membership of these organizations may serve to blur the lines of conflict. ...

There are a great many different situations which might easily be confused under the too-restricted terminology of the sociology of race relations. We would wish to distinguish at least two variables: (1) the degree of the involvement in the legal, social, and moral norms of the host society on the part of the immigrants; and (2) the degree of conflict between the various ethnic groups. These are the variables which apply to the different groups. If we try a little artificially to put them in tabular form, our table might look something like this:

Degree of Involvement	Degree of Intergroup Conflict
(1) Anomie, lack of social orientation	(1) A free market situation between individuals competing for facilities
(2) 'Living in the colony'	(2) Mobilization of monopoly power by ethnic groups in a market situation
(3) 'Living in the colony' but accepting formal rights in the host society	(3) Use of violence and/or mobilization of political power
(4) Acceptance of some social norms governing relations with strangers, apart from legal norms	(4) Collective bargaining and temporary contractual agreement
(5) Abandonment of the colony except for reasons of retrospective sentiment	

What we have done ... is to employ some of the concepts which have been outlined ... in order to analyse the social system of an urban ward when immigrant lodging-houses have emerged and are thought to constitute a social problem. We show the various social pressures which have operated to produce this situation and the kind of social interaction which has been produced on a community level. But we do this not because we wish to say that this outcome is inevitable in an expanding urban society. Rather, we hope that by drawing attention to some of the determinants of the situation we may make its rational control possible.

Source: Rex and Moore, 1967, pp.1–3, 13–14, 17–18.

READING C
The tragedy of the commons

Garrett Hardin

Consider the problem 'How can I win the game of tick-tack-toe?' It is well known that I cannot, if I assume ... that my opponent understands the game perfectly. Put another way, there is no 'technical solution' to the problem. I can win only by giving a radical meaning to the word 'win.' I can hit my opponent over the head; or I can drug him; or I can falsify the records. Every way in which I 'win' involves, in some sense, an abandonment of the game, as we intuitively understand it. ... It is fair to say that most people who anguish over the population problem are trying to find a way to avoid the evils of overpopulation without relinquishing any of the privileges they now enjoy. They think that farming the seas or developing new strains of wheat will solve the problem – technologically. ... The population problem cannot be solved in a technical way, any more than can the problem of winning the game of tick-tack-toe. ...

Population ... naturally tends to grow ... exponentially. In a finite world this means that the per capita share of the world's goods must steadily decrease. ... It is clear that we will greatly increase human misery if we do not, during the immediate future, assume that the world available to the terrestrial human population is finite. 'Space' is no escape. ... We may well call it 'the tragedy of the commons,' using the word 'tragedy' as the philosopher Whitehead used it: 'The essence of dramatic tragedy is not unhappiness. It resides in the solemnity of the remorseless working of things.' ... The tragedy of the commons develops in this way. Picture a pasture open to all. It is to be expected that each herdsman will try to keep as many cattle as possible on the commons. Such an arrangement may work reasonably satisfactorily for centuries because tribal wars, poaching, and disease keep the numbers of both man and beast well below the carrying capacity of the land. Finally, ... the inherent logic of the commons remorselessly generates tragedy. As a rational being, each herdsman seeks to maximize his gain. ... The rational herdsman concludes that the only sensible course for him to pursue is to add another animal to his herd. And another; and another [and so on]. But this is the conclusion reached by each and every rational herdsman sharing a commons. Therein is the tragedy. Each man is locked into a system that compels him to increase his herd without limit – in a world that is limited. Ruin is the destination toward which all men rush, each pursuing his own best interest in a society that believes in the freedom of the commons. Freedom in a commons brings ruin to all. ...

In a reverse way, the tragedy of the commons reappears in problems of pollution. Here it is not a question of taking something out of the commons, but of putting something in – sewage, or chemical, radioactive, and heat wastes into water; noxious and dangerous fumes into the air; and distracting and unpleasant advertising signs into the light of sight. ... The rational man finds that his share of the cost of the wastes he discharges into the commons is less than the cost of purifying his wastes before releasing them. Since this is true for everyone, we are locked into a system of 'fouling our own nest,' so long as we behave only as independent, rational, free enterprisers. ...

The tragedy of the commons is involved in population problems in another way. In a world governed solely by the principle of 'dog eat dog', ... parents who bred too exuberantly would leave fewer descendants, not more, because they would be unable to care adequately for their children. ... If each human family were dependent only on its resources; if the children of improvident parents starved to death; if, thus, overbreeding brought its own 'punishment', ... *then* there would be no public interest in controlling the breeding of families. But our society is deeply committed to the welfare state, and hence is confronted with another aspect of the tragedy of the commons. ... To couple the concept of freedom to breed with the belief that everyone born has an equal right to the commons is to lock the world into a tragic course of action. ... We must now recognize ... the necessity of abandoning the commons in breeding. No technical solution can rescue us from the misery of overpopulation. Freedom to breed will bring ruin to all.

Source: Hardin, 1968, pp. 1243–8.

READING D
When rationality fails

Jon Elster

Rational-choice theory aims at explaining human behaviour. To achieve this, it must, in any given case, proceed in two steps. The first step is to determine what a rational person would do in the circumstances. The second step is to ascertain whether this is what the person actually did. If the person did what the theory predicted he would do, it can add the case to its credit side. Similarly, the theory can fail at each of the two steps. First, it can fail to yield determinate predictions. Second, people can fail to conform to its predictions – they can behave irrationally. ...

An action, to be rational, must be the final result of three optimal decisions. First, it must be the best means of realizing a person's desire, given his beliefs. Next, these beliefs must themselves be optimal, given the evidence available to him. Finally, the person must collect an optimal amount of evidence – neither too much nor too little. That amount depends both on his desires – on the importance he attaches to the decision – and on his beliefs about the costs and benefits of gathering more information. The whole process, then, can be visualized as depicted in Fig. 1. ...

Figure I

I shall explain how rational-choice theory can fail. ... Consider first indeterminacy of action. ... I am trivially indifferent between two identical cans of Campbell's soup in the supermarket. I want one of them, but it doesn't matter which. Less trivially, a manager might maximize profits in two different ways: by a low volume of sales with high profits per sale or a high volume with low profits per sale. What he does might be very important for the workers who will be laid off if he chooses the low-volume option, but if profit is all he cares about we will not be able to explain why he chooses one rather than the other option. ... Important decisions often involve incommensurable options. The choice, say, between going to law school or to a school of forestry, assuming that both attract me

strongly, is a choice of career and life style. If I had tried both for a lifetime, I might be able to make an informed choice between them. As it is, I know too little about them to make a rational decision. What often happens in such cases is that peripheral considerations move to the center. ... Perhaps I opt for law school because that will make it easier for me to visit my parents on weekends. This way of deciding is as good as any – but it is not one that can be underwritten by rational-choice theory as superior to, say, simply tossing a coin.

Beliefs are indeterminate when the evidence is insufficient to justify a judgement about the likelihood of the various outcomes of action. ... Consider a firm's decision about how much to invest in research and development. To decide rationally, the firm must estimate the probable outcome of the investment – how likely it is that its innovative activities will lead to a profitable innovation – as well as the investments made by other firms and the probable outcome of those investments. Now the outcome of innovative activities is inherently uncertain. The firm cannot foresee with any precision whether it will hit the jackpot or come out with empty hands. Against the background of a constantly changing technology, past records are not good predictors of future success. ... Under winner-take-all conditions, this is crucial. The more a firm invests in research and development, the greater are its chances of getting there first. If other firms invest a large amount, our firm has a poor chance of winning. The rational decision might well be not to invest at all. Other firms, however, are presumably going through the same calculations. If they all decide to invest little, our firm should invest heavily. But once again, this reasoning applies equally to the other firms, and if they all invest heavily, our firm should drop out. ...

Deciding how much evidence to collect can be tricky. If the situation is highly stereotyped, as a medical diagnosis is, we know pretty well the costs and benefits of additional information. In situations that are unique, novel and urgent, like fighting a battle or helping the victim of a car accident, both costs and benefits are highly uncertain. There is a risk of acting too soon, on too little information – and a risk of delaying until it is too late. ... Thus we just have to act, more or less arbitrarily. In between these two extremes fall most choice situations of everyday life. ... When rational choice is indeterminate, some other mechanism must take up the slack. That could be the principle of 'satisficing,' of choosing something that is good enough.

Source: Elster, 1989, pp.30–5.

READING E
Normal rubbish: deviant patients in casualty departments

Roger Jeffery

Casualty work amongst doctors has usually been couched either in terms of the poor working conditions, or in terms of the absence of a career structure within Casualty work. ... Prestige amongst doctors is, at least in part, related to the distance a doctor can get from the undifferentiated mass of patients, so that teaching hospital consultancies are valued because they are at the end of a series of screening mechanisms. Casualty is one of these screening mechanisms, rather like general practitioners in this respect. However, they are unusual in the hospital setting in the freedom of patients to gain entrance without having seen a GP first; another low prestige area similar in this respect is the VD clinic. One of the complaints of the staff is that they are obliged ... to see every patient who presents himself [*sic*], and this has hindered the development of a speciality in Casualty work.

... Moral evaluation of patients seems to be a regular feature of medical settings. ... In general, two broad categories were used to evaluate patients good or interesting, and bad or rubbish. ...

> We have the usual rubbish, but also a subdural haemorrhage.

... Good patients were described almost entirely in terms of their medical characteristics, either in terms of the symptoms or the causes of the injury. Good cases were head injuries, or cardiac arrests. ... There were three broad criteria by which patients were seen to be good, and each related to medical considerations.

(i) *If they allowed the CO [Casuality Officer] to practise skills necessary for passing professional examinations.* In order to pass [their] examinations doctors need to be able to diagnose and describe unusual conditions and symptoms. Casualty was not a good place to discover these sorts of cases, and if they did turn up a great fuss was made of them. ... The way to get excellent treatment was to turn up at a slack period with an unusual condition. The most extreme example of this I witnessed was a young man with a severe head injury from a car accident. A major symptom of his head injury was the condition of his eyes, and by the time he was transferred to another hospital for neurological treatment, twelve medical personnel had looked into his eyes with an ophthalmoscope, and an *ad hoc* teaching session was held on him. ...

(ii) *If they allowed staff to practise their chosen speciality.* For the doctors, the specific characteristics of good patients of this sort were fairly closely defined, because most doctors saw themselves as future specialists – predominantly surgeons. They tended to accept, or conform to, the model of the surgeon as a man of action who can achieve fairly rapid results. Patients who provided the opportunity to use and act out this model were welcomed. One CO gave a particularly graphic description of this:

> But I like doing surgical procedures. These are great fun. It just lets your imagination run riot really (laughs) you know, you forget for a moment you are just a very small cog incising a very small abscess, and you pick up your scalpel like anyone else (laughs). It's quite mad when you think about it but it's very satisfying. And you can see the glee with which most people leap on patients with abscesses because you know that here's an opportunity to do something. ...

(iii) *If they tested the general competence and maturity of the staff.* The patients who were most prized were those who stretched the resources of the department in doing the task they saw themselves designed to carry out – the rapid early treatment of acutely ill patients. ... The most articulate expression of this was from a CO who said:

> I really do enjoy doing anything where I am a little out of my depth, where I really have to think about what I am doing. Something like a bad road traffic accident ... It might be a bit sordid, the fact that I like mangled up bodies and things like this, but the job satisfaction is good.

Good patients, then, make demands which fall squarely within the boundaries of what the staff define as appropriate to their job. ... While the category of the good patient is one I have, in part, constructed from comments, 'rubbish' is a category generated by the staff themselves. ...

> It's a thankless task, seeing all the rubbish, as we call it, coming through. ...

> I wouldn't be making the same fuss in another job – it's only because it's mostly bloody crumble like women with insect bites. ...

> I think the city centre hospital gets more of the rubbish – the drunks and that. ...

Rubbish appeared to be a mutually comprehensible term, even though some staff members used other words, like dross, dregs, crumble or grot. ... In an attempt to get a better idea of what patients would be included in the category of rubbish I asked staff what sorts of patients they did not like having to deal with, which sorts of patients made them annoyed, and why. The answers they gave suggested that staff had developed characteristics of 'normal' rubbish – the normal suicide attempt, the normal drunk, and so on. ... In other words, staff felt able to predict a whole range of features related not only to [a patient's] medical condition but also to his past life, to his likely behaviour inside the Casualty department, and to his future behaviour. These expected features of the patient could thus be used to guide the treatment (both socially and medically) that the staff decided to give the patient. Thus, patients placed in these categories ... were treated as if they had such common characteristics. The following were the major categories of rubbish mentioned by staff.

(i) *Trivia*. The recurring problem of Casualty departments, in the eyes of the doctors, has been the 'casual' attender. ... Normal trivia banged their heads, their hands or their ankles, carried on working as usual, and several days later looked into Casualty to see if it was all right. Normal trivia drops in when it is passing, or if it happens to be visiting a relative in the hospital. Trivia 'didn't want to bother my doctor.' ...

> Trivia stretches the boundaries of reasonable behaviour too far, by bringing for advice something which a reasonable person could make up his own mind about. Trivia must find Casualty a nice place to be in, else why would they come? For trivia, Casualty is a bit of a social centre: they think 'It's a nice day, I might as well go down to Casualty.' ...

(ii) *Drunks*. Normal drunks are abusive and threatening. They come in shouting and singing after a fight and they are sick all over the place, or they are brought in unconscious, having been found in the street. They come in the small hours of the night, and they often have to be kept in until morning because you never know if they have been knocked out in a fight (with the possibility of a head injury) or whether they were just sleeping it off. They come in weekend after weekend with the same injuries, and they are always unpleasant and awkward. ...

(iii) *Overdoses*. The normal overdose is female, and is seen as a case of self-injury rather than of attempted suicide. She comes because her boyfriend/husband/parents have been unkind, and is likely to be a regular visitor. She only

wants attention, she was not seriously trying to kill herself, but she uses the overdose as moral blackmail. She makes sure she does not succeed by taking a less-than-lethal dose, or by ensuring that she is discovered fairly rapidly.

> In the majority of overdoses, you know, these symbolic overdoses, the sort of '5 aspirins and 5 valiums and I'm ill doctor, I've taken an overdose'. ...

(iv) *Tramps*. Normal tramps can be recognized by the many layers of rotten clothing they wear, and by their smell. They are a feature of the cold winter nights and they only come to Casualty to try to wheedle a bed in the warm for the night. Tramps can never be trusted: they will usually sham their symptoms. ... They are abusive if they don't get their way: they should be shouted at to make sure they understand, or left in the hope that they will go away.

Rubbish could be punished by the staff in various ways, the most important being to increase the amount of time that rubbish had to spend in Casualty before completing treatment. ... Good patients, in general being the more serious, could be seen immediately by being taken directly to the treatment area, either by the receptionist or by the ambulanceman. Less serious cases, including the trivia, would go first to a general waiting area. ... However, the staff could also delay treatment for overdoses, tramps and drunks in a more selective fashion. Patients in these categories could be taken to relative backwaters and shut into rooms so that they could be ignored until the staff were prepared to deal with them. Sometimes staff employed a deliberate policy of leaving drunks and tramps in the hope that they would get annoyed at the delay and take their own discharge.

The other forms of punishment used were verbal hostility or the vigorous restraint of uncooperative patients. ... Vigorous treatment of patients was most noticeable in the case of overdoses, who would be held down or sat upon while the patient was forced to swallow the rubber tube used. Staff recognized that this procedure had an element of punishment in it, but defended themselves by saying that it was necessary. However, they showed no sympathy for the victim, unlike cases of accidental self-poisoning by children.

Source: Jeffery, 1979, Vol.1, No.1.

Chapter 5
Paradigms, Conventions and Relativism

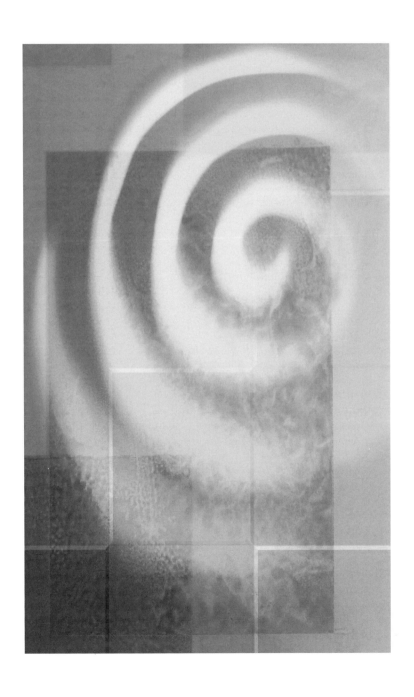

Contents

1	Introduction	183
2	Falsificationist escape clauses	185
2.1	Interpretation and observation in the natural sciences	185
2.2	Escaping refutation in the social sciences	188
3	Paradigms and conventions: the end of progress?	193
3.1	Kuhn's account of scientific change	193
3.2	Paradigms in the social sciences	198
3.3	Conventionalism beyond Kuhn 1: question everything!	204
3.4	Conventionalism beyond Kuhn 2: the sociology of knowledge and science	208
4	Rationality and relativism: keeping progress	214
5	Reassessing rationality and relativism: towards a conclusion	217

Reading A
The emotionally disturbed child as the family scapegoat
Ezra F.Vogel and Norman W. Bell 219

Reading B   Three social psychologies
Experimental social psychology   *Patrick McGhee* ... 220
Humanistic and experiential social psychology   *Richard Stevens* ... 221
Critical social psychology   *Margaret Wetherell* ... 221

Reading C   Theorizing the economy
Economic paradigms   *Howard R. Vane and John L. Thompson* ... 222
Economic crisis: the Marxist view   *E.K. Hunt and Howard J. Sherman* ... 223

Reading D
Methodological pluralism   *Bruce Caldwell* ... 224

Reading E
Two sociological perspectives on science   *Michael Mulkay* ... 225

Reading F   Bending the rules
Faking it to make it   *John Turney* ... 225
What if teacher is a cheat?   *Stuart Sutherland* ... 226

Reading G
The schizophrenia research programme   *Mary Boyle* ... 227

1   Introduction

In the earlier chapters we focused upon whether it is possible and desirable to apply the assumptions and methods of the natural sciences to study social objects of analysis. So far, these approaches have lined up either for or against **naturalism**. The positivist and empiricist answer to this issue is that we should adopt a naturalist position, while many idealists question whether we should study people in this way. Nevertheless, most of the idealist approaches considered in Chapter 4 tend to accept the positivist view of scientific method as an accurate description of natural science; they just do not see it as appropriate for studying social life. In contrast, many of the approaches considered in this chapter see natural scientific knowledge itself as situated in definite historical and social locations – as social products or conventions. For this reason, we use the label **conventionalism** to designate all of these views. These conventionalist approaches shook the foundations of natural scientific thinking, sometimes provoking considerable hostility. However, in addition to telling us more about natural science and natural scientists, they also opened up new possibilities for reinterpreting the history and the philosophy of the social sciences.

In the last chapter we saw how the same observations can be interpreted in various ways, whether we are observing natural or social things. So far you have worked through the debates on the relationship between interpretation and observation. These debates prepared the way for thinking through a new relationship between natural and social science. Rather than the social sciences trying to copy natural scientific methods, both have attempted to share their ideas about how knowledge works. The relationship is now two-way rather than one-way. Conventionalism raises important and difficult issues about the nature of the natural sciences themselves as well as the ways in which positivist or empiricist methods are applied to the study of social objects such as 'society', 'the economy', 'the state', 'the environment' and 'the mind'. These issues can be expressed in a series of closely related questions all of which are addressed in the following sections of this chapter.

- What is the relationship between approaches in the philosophy of science and the actual practices of both natural and social science? How realistic are these approaches in describing the scientific process of discovery?

- To what extent is scientific knowledge a social product or convention and what are the implications of this for the status of science? What is the role of the communities and institutions which produce scientific knowledge?

- Do accounts which portray the growth of scientific knowledge as a slow process of testing and accumulating evidence take adequate account of the role of hunches, guesswork and flashes of inspiration?

- If scientific knowledge changes periodically as scientific communities change, such that the status of science is *relative* to the cultures which produce it, is it possible to remain committed to the idea of progress in human knowledge?

- What are the implications of adopting either a relativist or a rationalist position in the social sciences?

- How are conventionalist accounts of scientific knowledge interpreted within the disciplines of the social sciences?

So, while in Chapter 3 we saw how there was already an increased resistance to the application of natural science methods to the social sciences, the studies raised in this chapter will actually challenge your understanding about what makes a natural science 'scientific'; that is, what makes it a true account of reality.

Before we address these questions, let's consider the structure of the present chapter (shown in Figure 5.1). In section 2 we focus upon the approaches which have generated an increased sense of doubt about empiricist accounts of knowledge. For empiricists, one of the key ways in which science is demarcated from non-science is whether it can be tested and falsified. However, we will explore how scientists build escape clauses into their theoretical constructs to avoid refutation. In section 3 we examine the arguments and evidence developed by Thomas Kuhn and others who, in their different ways, contributed to this crisis in the construction of knowledge. Kuhn was a historian of scientific thought and practice who initially set out to write about the unification of scientific method. In the course of his research, he became increasingly convinced that a universal and rational scientific method could not be established. In section 4 we return to the falsificationists to consider how they have responded to these arguments, focusing on the ideas of Imre Lakatos and how they have been applied. The empiricists suggested that conventionalism had given up on progress and offered no basis for making authoritative judgements about the world. Finally, section 5 explores the debate between empiricists and conventionalists in a little more detail by reassessing the relationship between rationality and relativism.

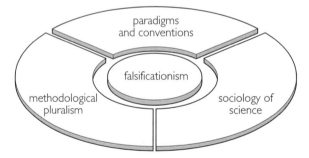

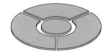

This sign will help you chart your way through the approaches in the chapter.

Figure 5.1   Conventionalist approaches in the social sciences: the chapter structure.

Before we address conventionalism, its applications and its critics, it is important to examine why empiricist theory and practice came to be questioned in the post-war debates on the philosophy of science. While the scientific method developed within empiricism offered a powerful rationale for conducting scientific research, by the 1960s it had become evident that there were serious problems with the falsificationist approach. In the social sciences, one of the main problems which emerged was the difficulty in disproving a proposition within the body of work from which it had been generated. In effect, it was possible in both the natural and the social sciences to build escape clauses from falsification into any scientific statement so that the critical edge of the approach was blunted.

2   Falsificationist escape clauses

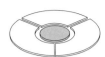

We start off with Popper, but come back to falsificationism again in section 4.

One of the most important problems in empiricist accounts of the scientific method is that of identifying a set of circumstances in which a scientific statement can be falsified through the acquisition of new empirical evidence. Statements and propositions attempting to explain the workings of the 'real world' do not exist in isolation but within complex theoretical systems. To begin, it is useful to distinguish between two types of theoretical statement.

Elsewhere this sign **g** will direct you to the glossary, but revisit this section if you need to.

- **Bedrock assumptions** specify the underlying assumptions within a particular scientific approach. These can be formally defined but can also be tacit, taken-for-granted rules and procedures which are rarely questioned. In short, they act as the 'bedrock' for building contextual hypotheses.

- **Contextual hypotheses** are generated when these bedrock assumptions are used within a definite context, producing statements which take into account the complex conditions of the objects in question. Contextual hypotheses also convey the combined operation of established laws working together within these conditions.

Scientists are often so busy testing statements about definite situations that they rarely consider their bedrock assumptions.

It has become increasingly apparent in the history of the scientific method that theories, hypotheses and propositions can continue to exist for some time despite the existence of conclusive evidence for their refutation. A good example of bedrock assumptions in the natural sciences can be seen in Newton's 'laws of motion'. In a similar way, the assumption that human beings are 'rational calculating individuals' is adopted in some branches of the social sciences. If it can be demonstrated that scientists evade falsification by introducing qualifications or by restricting empirical tests to contextual hypotheses rather than their bedrock assumptions, then how viable are the approaches? It is these issues which we consider in section 2.1. A Popperian response might be to describe this as bad science – a violation of the spirit if not the letter of falsificationism. However, Popper's approach applies to the testing of singular conjectures or hypotheses. In practice, empirical tests are conducted in the context of complex configurations of principles, laws, theories and previous empirical tests. This means that the conclusive refutation of a specific hypothesis can take place only within a reassessment of the whole body of theory concerned. But scientists become attached to specific bodies of theory, so are empiricist accounts idealized reconstructions of scientific method rather than an accurate and useful account of actual practice? This important question will be addressed throughout the chapter.

2.1   Interpretation and observation in the natural sciences

While the following sections explore the attachments and practices of natural and social scientists engaged in organized communities, here we consider the relationship between testing hypotheses and the theoretical systems in which hypotheses make sense, particularly what has become known as the Duhem-Quine thesis. In *The Aim and Structure of Physical Theory* (1914/1962), Pierre Duhem, a French philosopher and historian of

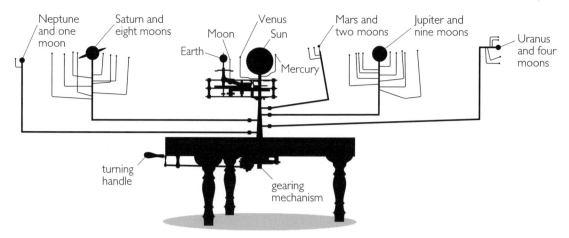

Figure 5.2   The orbital movements of the solar system: a clockwork model.

science, reassessed the history of physics from Newton onwards. He was concerned with the way scientific statements exist, not in isolation, but as part of complex hierarchies of theories and with reference to accumulated empirical evidence. So Duhem explored examples of situations where the available empirical evidence did not match the existing theories.

Astronomy provides a useful illustration of these problems. Until 1781 it had been assumed that the solar system consisted of six planets – Mercury, Venus, Earth, Mars, Jupiter and Saturn, ordered in terms of their distance from the Sun (see Figure 5.2). The discovery in that year of the planet Uranus, beyond Jupiter, created a new problem for astronomers. Using Newton's laws of motion and his law of gravity (as bedrock assumptions) in conjunction with a range of additional contextual hypotheses about the conditions within which the object existed (such as the various effects of other known planetary objects and taking into account their proximity and relative mass), astronomical scientists were able to plot a theoretical orbit for Uranus. For this example, it is important to note that planets exert gravitational pulls of varying strengths upon neighbouring planets. If we can estimate the gravitational effects of known planetary objects, then we should be able to plot their respective orbits around the Sun. However, the observational evidence of Uranus did not match the theoretical orbit established by the astronomers. This raised questions about the existing assumptions involved in the contemporary theories of astronomy. Two options exist in such a situation: either to question the bedrock assumptions and initiate a root-and-branch reassessment of the body of theory concerned, *or* to develop better contextual hypotheses but still founded upon existing bedrock assumptions.

New discoveries in scientific research often require a reappraisal of existing scientific theories.

In this example from natural science, the calculations of astronomers John Couch Adams and Urbain Leverrier (working independently in the mid 1840s) raised doubts about the contextual hypotheses developed on the orbit of Uranus; they raised the possibility of an additional planet orbiting beyond Uranus and exerting a gravitational effect on its orbit. The discrepancies between the theory and empirical evidence were, in this case, accurately explained in terms of their description of the mass and orbit of another planet (which was identified by telescope soon afterwards as the planet Neptune). So, in this example, by sticking to their bedrock assumptions and by making adjustments to the contextual hypotheses, Adams and Leverrier produced useful scientific knowledge. However, being loyal to your bedrock assumptions does not always work out so successfully. When attempting to explain unexpected features in the orbit of Mercury, Leverrier posed the existence of a planet closer to the Sun which was exerting a gravitational pull on Mercury. He labelled this planet Vulcan. This modification to contextual hypotheses was not to be so successful, for no such planet exists. This left an anomaly between theory and evidence which remained unresolved until the bedrock assumptions of Newtonian physics in astronomy were thrown into doubt eighty years later, when Einstein questioned these theories of gravitation.

Explaining new discoveries generates a choice between modifying existing theories or reassessing the foundations.

To revisit Bacon, see Chapter 2, section 3.1.

The Duhem thesis – an empirical test can never falsify an isolated hypothesis, it challenges the whole theoretical system of which it is a part.

The Quine thesis – an empirical test can never falsify an isolated hypothesis, it challenges the whole knowledge system of which it is a part.

Examples such as these led Duhem to question the standards of scientific theorizing. Francis Bacon had argued that 'true science' should involve the identification of all possible contending theories in the explanation of a specific phenomenon and the use of experimental tests to identify the inaccuracies and flaws in each theory until all but one of the contending theories had been eliminated and absolute certainty could be established. For Duhem, no such definitive test of a single hypothesis could be devised and applied. He suggested that it was possible only to examine **theoretical systems** against the available empirical evidence. When faced with a situation in which observations do not fit the existing theoretical framework, scientists must make a choice between the modification of bedrock assumptions and revision of contextual hypotheses. Whereas Duhem had related testing statements to theoretical systems, more recently Willard von Quine's essay 'Two Dogmas of Empiricism' (1953/1965) argued that such tests could throw whole **knowledge systems** into doubt. Rather than seeing scientific knowledge as just bundles of individual theories focused upon the same object of analysis and/or set of problems, Quine saw them as a 'sort of man-made fabric' woven together in complex ways. This means that when you start to unpick certain patterns in knowledge, the whole fabric can unravel. Therefore, empirical tests can also throw our view of reality into doubt. In Quine's account, it is the whole field of inquiry of human knowledge which is disturbed by the emergence of anomalies between empirical evidence and established theories, in much the same way as a stone can cause ripples on the surface of a pond. We see the full implications of this in section 4.

Quine's intervention is also important for highlighting the way in which scientists actually seek to avoid falsification by building escape clauses into their theories and explanations. They do this either by reformulating the contextual hypotheses or by making adjustments in the theoretical system in order to protect the bedrock assumptions from refutation (Quine, 1953/1965; Gillies, 1993). Such difficulties are not only a feature of natural science, they emerge in the social sciences as well. They exist regardless of the differences between the objects of analysis within the natural and the social sciences. In all areas where there is a fairly structured and extensive body of thought in a particular social science, we can witness a reluctance to question bedrock assumptions. In the next section we explore how these problems exist in the social sciences through two case studies, one drawn from political studies and the other from sociology.

Summary

The falsificationist method focuses upon the testing of single hypotheses. This runs into difficulty when put into practice in the natural sciences. Knowledge systems comprise different forms of theoretical statements which are defined in relationship to each other as well as in relation to empirical evidence.

Rather than reassessing the bedrock assumptions, scientists frequently test the contextual hypotheses generated from these bedrock assumptions. When these are found to be inadequate, then further contextual hypotheses are developed in the conduct of research without raising doubts about the underlying assumptions.

2.2 Escaping refutation in the social sciences

Now that you have explored some of the problems involved in falsification in natural science, let's look at how this affects social scientific practices. In the following two examples you will find that social scientists too have avoided falsification by introducing 'escape clauses' into their theoretical frameworks. In the cases of both pluralist political science and functionalist sociology, elaborate safeguards were developed to ensure that falsifying evidence did not undermine the bedrock assumptions. First, we consider the discipline of political science, which until the 1970s sought to explain the dynamic process of political choices and the exercise of power with the supposed precision of a natural science. Political scientists such as Robert Dahl and Nelson Polsby explicitly adopted the empiricist approach towards social research when constructing the pluralist model of the state and politics. Dahl presents a useful definition of his pluralist method: 'Based upon the study of individuals in political situations, this approach calls for the examination of the political relationships of men [sic] ... with the object of formulating and testing hypotheses concerning uniformities of behaviour' (Dahl, 1961, p.764).

Pluralists contend that a stable political system involves periodic elections and competition among pressure groups between elections. The concept of power is treated as an empirical regularity, whereby the behaviour of one agent causes uncharacteristic behaviour in another. Dahl characterized this as: 'A has the power over B to the extent that he can get B to do something that B would not otherwise do' (Dahl, 1957, pp.203–4). Individuals are taken as the basic unit of analysis, from which Dahl goes on to examine the personalities, groups, roles, offices, governments, nation-states and other aggregates of human individuals. This approach limits research on power to actual decision-making behaviour within situations where observable conflict of interests exists. The interests of the individuals or groups are defined as 'expressed policy preferences' (such as demand for change or support for the status quo), which are, in turn, revealed through political participation. This means that we should take what political actors say and what they do as a direct expression of their interests. By focusing upon the specific outcomes of observable behaviour, the pluralist approach is able to gather 'reliable evidence' (which has been subjected to further tests and

g

which produced the same or similar results). This usually takes the form of quantitative data in order to facilitate correlations between variables (statistical comparisons). Pluralists used statistical controls to simulate a **closed system** involving a limited number of simple variables (see Blalock, 1964).

If we consider Dahl's own use of this method, we can acquire a better view of what this means in practice. In *Who Governs?* (1960), Dahl examined observable concrete decision making in New Haven (USA), where he lived and worked. This involved studying the expression of policy preferences, the initiation of proposals and the casting of votes for, or against, formally sanctioned decisions. The key policy issues identified as objects of analysis in this study were urban development, public education and nominations for political office. Dahl concluded, on the basis of the empirical evidence collected in this way, that no one group dominated in all policy areas, all of the time. This evidence enabled him to argue that New Haven, while not an ideal democracy, was considerably more polyarchic (involving rule by the many) than oligarchic (involving rule by the few). In addition, Dahl concluded that the resources which contributed to the exercise of power were so dispersed and fragmented that direct political influence was limited (with most citizens having an indirect influence through use of the vote). According to Dahl, polyarchy was sustained between elections by the participation of pressure groups in the political process. The pluralist approach assumes that all individuals are willing and able to form and maintain a group when their own interests are affected, that all have equal access to an impartial decision-making process and that they will be mobilized to act on their own behalf. As demonstrated in Figure 5.3, the pluralist argument suggests that pressure-group politics involves a shifting balance of power among contending pressure groups engaged in political negotiations, with policy decisions achieved through compromise. With such assumptions built into the theoretical framework, the pluralists were likely to find the evidence they needed to reinforce their theories.

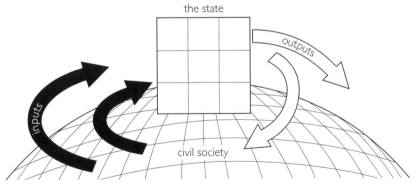

Figure 5.3
The pluralist model of state and society: a systems model.

In trying to establish the preconditions of political stability in New Haven, Dahl challenged the conventional explanations of what makes a political system democratic. Rather than just considering the basic rights, duties and procedures that serve to distinguish democratic from non-democratic systems, he placed a greater emphasis upon the importance of moral customs, laws and the physical, social and economic condition of the people. In other words, for Dahl, the relations of civil society are just as important as formal political constitutions. The conclusions of this study have been subject to intense criticism and evaluation, particularly on methodological grounds. The focus upon observed decision making inhibits the identification of other factors and is unrealistic in view of the fact that political decisions may be made behind the scenes in advance of the formal decision-making process in the political executive (in the UK, the Cabinet) or the parliamentary chamber. The pluralist approach ignored the way that decision making is based on an agenda, the processes involved in excluding some issues from the agenda, and the problems of equating the interests of a particular group with the public statements of those groups (their 'express policy preferences'). Pluralists have increasingly accepted that such problems have to be addressed in their research, although this has often been limited to the reformulation of the contextual hypotheses about the capacity of democratic political systems to contain undemocratic tendencies. They have not questioned the bedrock assumptions of this approach concerning political institutions or the empiricist research strategy which focuses on the collection of observed data from concrete decisions.

Social scientists also face the choice of modifying contextual hypotheses or reassessing their bedrock assumptions.

According to Jordan and Richardson (1987), recent work has clearly recognized the problems in the pluralist approach. The following contextual hypotheses have been challenged:

- the neutrality of the state;
- the separation of the state from civil society;
- the tendency for groups to balance each other;
- the view that policy making is the product of negotiation and compromise between contending interests.

Pluralists now accept that the institutions of the state can behave like interest groups, that groups may not have equal power even in the long run, that some significant groups remain disorganized (and hence are disenfranchised in pressure-group politics) and that some groups may colonize key departments of state to secure their interests and exclude the concerns of competing groups. Pluralists have accepted the importance of the formation of agendas in which decisions are made. They have also recognized that some issues can be excluded from the agenda. Nevertheless, they have not questioned the bedrock assumption that objects can be identified only through empirical evidence of actual observable decisions. This still means that pluralists use the express preferences of the various groups as an index of their interests. While this modified pluralist approach clearly recognizes the imperfections of democratic political systems, it does not lead pluralists to reassess the bedrock assumptions of their research programme itself.

Pluralists have developed elaborate safeguards to ensure that falsifying evidence does not undermine their bedrock assumptions.

For the second example of the use of falsificationist escape clauses in the social sciences, we turn to sociology. In the 1940s and 1950s a fairly well established body of theories in the basic principles of sociology came to be accepted. The theories were grouped together under the umbrella label of 'functionalism' and were most associated with the American sociologist Talcott Parsons. The effect of this distinct body of theory on the development of sociology was enormous for both supporters and critics. The underlying metaphors of the functionalist approach were derived from the **organic analogy**, in that society was compared to a human body with all the institutional parts functioning to ensure the health (or, in some cases, sickness) of the whole society which, in turn, was treated as more than the sum of its parts. The smooth operation of the social system, according to Parsons, depends upon the functional operation of the economy, the polity, cultural institutions and the kinship subsystem (Parsons, 1951). In addition, this theoretical system is founded upon the implicit normative assumption that the existence of social order and consensus is the normal state of affairs.

This theoretical assumption of social consensus as a normal condition, even in the relatively optimistic and prosperous conditions of post-war Western societies, was clearly at odds with empirical evidence on social conflict and became even more so by the 1960s and 1970s. Nevertheless, the response within the functionalist approach was to limit the damage of such evidence by constructing elaborate contextual hypotheses around the theme of 'strain' in the social system – leaving the bedrock assumptions of functionalism unchallenged. When addressing the effects of strains on individual behaviour, Robert Merton had argued (Merton, 1938) that dysfunctional criminal and deviant behaviour could be understood in terms of the relationship between individual choices and the value system (in this case, the key American value was material success). Merton distinguished between the legitimate and illegitimate means through which individuals could choose to attain the ends of material success and the degree of attachment that those individuals had towards the accepted goals of the American social system. This allowed Merton to identify the following five types of human response to the constraints of the norms and values of American culture.

- *Conformity* – positive commitment to the legitimate means and ends (the ideal citizen – this is quite hard to live up to).

- *Innovation* – negative on the means but a positive commitment to success (rule-bending to achieve status and wealth).

- *Ritualism* – positive on the means but negative on the ends, when people behave in an acceptable way without any commitment to, or hope of, achieving personal success (what most of us do most of the time).

- *Retreatism* – negative on both means and ends, whereby individuals seek to 'drop out' of society (but not create an alternative).

- *Rebellion* – a rejection of the established means and ends in favour of an alternative social order with its own ends and the identification of the means of achieving this (religious conversion or revolutionary activity).

Escapes from falsification can be achieved by constructing a theoretical framework whereby all types of evidence are taken to be a confirmation of the theories.

In this way, the existence of deviance and crime cannot be taken as a refutation of the bedrock assumptions of functionalist theory of what makes a healthy society, because such behaviour is explained as the consequence of a failure of integration into the established norms and values of the social system in question as well as a source of innovation and change. Thus cases of conformity and deviance are both covered by the theory through the use of different contextual hypotheses to explain different forms of behaviour and, in each case, the bedrock assumptions remain unchallenged. By building in these kinds of escape clauses, functionalism can have it both ways, for all evidence supports the framework in one way or another. Later versions of the functionalist account drew more explicitly upon cost–benefit approaches to establish the positive and negative aspects of forms of behaviour which go against the values of the social system. If the positive consequences of such cases outweigh the negative consequences, even 'maladjusted behaviour' can be seen as achieving a 'net positive functionality'. Evidence which appears, at first sight, to be a refutation of the functionalist view can be interpreted in a way which supports (instead of undermining) the framework. Rather than assuming that all relations are functional in a positive way, they can be seen as contributing to the social order as long as they have more benefits than costs.

Activity 5.1

Turn to Reading A, from Ezra F. Vogel and Norman W. Bell's 'The emotionally disturbed child as the family scapegoat' (1968).

- Identify the positive and negative functions of family relations in Vogel and Bell's account.
- Try to identify how Vogel and Bell evade falsification.

As you read this provocative extract, bear in mind the context in which it was written and how it relates to the cultural values in that location.

In the functionalist account of social systems, one of the most important institutions for constructing the moral fabric of society is the family unit. The family is portrayed as the key source of values, expressiveness and personal identity in an otherwise increasingly instrumental society. In the 1960s the structure of family life began to alter as the 'strains' of contemporary Western societies began to place increased pressure on the nuclear family unit. Both the changing structure of the family and the evidence of 'emotional disturbance' in otherwise 'functional family units' raised questions about the theoretical statements in the functionalist approach. When faced with the problem of questioning their basic principles or their contextual hypotheses, functionalists chose the latter. As in the case of Vogel and Bell, the consequences of the strains (here, increased divorce rates and single parent households) were seen by Parsons as bearable within the social system as long as the costs in personal lives did not undermine the role that such a flexible household unit played in other subsystems. In this specific example, the negative consequences for the children concerned were more than outweighed by the positive consequences in other areas of the social system. Clearly, few scientists would question their bedrock assumptions immediately and some exploration of new contextual hypotheses should be expected. However, in both of these cases from political studies and sociology, the substantive falsification of explanatory statements did not produce a critical reassessment of bedrock assumptions and the anomalies endured. We reconsider what we question and what we don't in social scientific practice when we explore the ideas of Lakatos later in the chapter.

Summary

In the cases of both pluralism in political science and functionalism in sociology, social scientists came to accept theoretical approaches based upon specific bedrock assumptions in explaining social life.

In both cases, when faced with empirical evidence which went against their expectations, the contextual hypotheses were modified in order to protect the bedrock assumptions involved. In short, falsification was limited to contextual hypotheses.

3   Paradigms and conventions: the end of progress?

If you want to revisit Popper, see Chapter 3, section 5.1.

In the middle sections of this chapter we explore approaches which consider scientific knowledge to be defined as a social product – as a convention which scientists and others hold to be true. As you saw in section 1, **conventionalism** has been used as a broad label to describe these approaches. To some extent, Popper's account of verisimilitude (that truth was a matter of degree, not an absolute) had prepared the way for this line of argument. However, with the conventionalists, this questioning of the foundations of knowledge was taken further to undermine the faith in 'rationality' and 'progress' as well. In *The Structure of Scientific Revolutions* (1962/1970), Kuhn developed an argument that is often identified as the cause of a 'crisis of rationality' in Western scientific thinking. He concluded that scientific knowledge does not produce an independently true account of the external world but reflects the organized activities of scientific communities. Kuhn was not the first conventionalist in the study of natural science, but his importance here is due to the role which his concept of **paradigm** has played in the social sciences since the 1960s. Now, before we consider how the idea of paradigm has been understood and applied in the social sciences, let's look at Kuhn's historical account of scientific change in a little more detail.

3.1 Kuhn's account of scientific change

The idea of paradigmatic change was a direct challenge to the idea of progress through the accumulation of knowledge.

Empiricist accounts of scientific knowledge had been committed to the idea of progress through the gradual accumulation of knowledge. Even though Popper had given up on the search for truth, the whole point of falsification was to build on existing knowledge in a cumulative way (rather like walking up a never-ending staircase). Kuhn's approach, however, suggested that it was not even possible to identify a progression in knowledge. Through a careful study of the ways in which natural science has developed and changed, Kuhn suggested that scientific knowledge went through long periods of stability interrupted by short periods of sudden transformation. In addition, instead of establishing a universal standard against which it was possible to compare all statements about the world, Kuhn argued that knowledge was a social product and, as such, changed as society changes. He described each phase of stability in the history of science as a period of **normal science**. This occurs when the rules of scientific method are well established and the role of scientists is limited to solving problems and puzzles without questioning the rules within which they work. These rules involve widely accepted **demarcation criteria** through which we can distinguish which forms of knowledge which are scientific and which are not. In the case of logical positivism, the demarcation criteria between science and non-science were such that if something could not be reduced to a simple observation statement and the theories could not be empirically verified, then it contained metaphysical components and was thus meaningless. These rules become part of the institutional life in which scientists work and their work is judged according to how closely they operate by the accepted principles of their disciplinary fields.

Kuhn developed the concept of 'paradigm' to characterize changes in the 'standards governing permissible problems, concepts and explanations' (Kuhn, 1970, p.106) within the context of a historical and sociological approach. The concept of paradigm is a matter of much dispute (which we come back to in section 3.2). However, the idea of paradigm in this context can be taken to mean the 'universally recognized scientific achievements that ... provide model problems and solutions to a community of practitioners' (Kuhn, 1970, p.viii) and therefore forms the implicit taken-for-granted commonsense assumptions of a scientific community. In this way, paradigms are more than sets of theories, they are scientific communities through which knowledge is produced and understood.

Each paradigm has its own demarcation criteria between which ideas and forms of evidence should or should not be taken seriously as scientific knowledge.

This historical account of scientific knowledge starts with a **pre-paradigmatic stage** in which a range of approaches compete for dominance although none is able to achieve it. Kuhn argued that the social sciences remain in this state, for they have not as yet achieved the maturity of one dominant set of rules. The natural sciences, he argued, have achieved this. For instance, the development of Newton's physics marked the emergence of a paradigm in physics, closely followed by paradigms in chemistry, biology and physiology. Kuhn described the dominance of normal science within which the activities of scientists can be characterized as puzzle solving within an established set of principles and methodological procedures. Newton's mechanics provided physics with just such a workable set of principles (rules of experimental inquiry and scientific laws of motion) for the development of further scientific laws and the identification of facts. However, by the middle of the nineteenth century a series of problems or anomalies emerged in the application of Newton's laws to astronomical objects which could not be adequately explained. By the 1890s these anomalies had accumulated to the point that physics was in a state of crisis and, with the emergence of an alternative set of principles, physics experienced a scientific revolution as a new paradigm emerged to replace the old one (see Figure 5.4).

This view of the history of science involving long periods of stability marked by sudden breaks draws from common narrative structure of historical story-telling.

Kuhn argues that a scientific revolution like the one from Newton's to Einstein's physics involves a 'gestalt shift'. This means that the scientists involved would have to go through a 'conversion experience' in order to move from the old paradigm to the new one. In the case of physics, Newton's mechanistic laws were replaced by Einstein's theory of relativity. However, many scientists were left behind in this process, unable to cope with the trauma of such a transformation. Kuhn agrees with Planck's view: 'a new scientific truth does not triumph by convincing its opponents and making them see the light, but rather because its opponents eventually die and a new generation grows up that is familiar with it' (Planck cited in Kuhn, 1970, p.151).

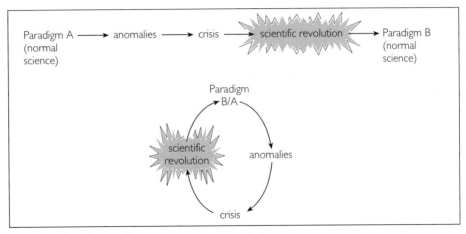

Figure 5.4   Kuhn's theory of scientific revolution.
The figure shows two ways of representing Kuhn's account of the transformations involved in a scientific revolution. Each representation tells a different story. In the linear one, the shift of paradigms implies a kind of progress (perhaps that Einstein's physics improves on Newton's). In the cyclical version, a paradigm shift sends us full circle – it implies that science changes but does not progress.

Paradigm shifts are intergenerational transformations in the bedrock assumptions of knowledge held to be true by scientific communities.

In practice, the shift takes place over a generation or even longer, for few of those who have worked their way up the academic career ladder are likely to question the theories upon which their research and careers are based. Each of these paradigms is mutually exclusive and the members of the scientific communities which construct each paradigm interpret their experiences so differently that they can be said to occupy 'different worlds'. In Chapter 3 you saw how experience could be interpreted in different ways, but nevertheless it was generally assumed that the interpreters had enough in common to communicate their interpretations effectively to each other. In Kuhn's account of paradigmatic differences, this would not be feasible. This can be seen when we look at examples of paradigm shifts. For instance, by the middle of the twentieth century, Einstein's theories provided the underlying rules for physics in the new normal science in much the same way as Newton's had in the previous paradigm. A physicist viewing the physical universe with the assumptions developed by Einstein would see a different universe from that of Newton. It is possible to see this as yet another addition to scientific knowledge, but the questions which Einstein raised struck right at the heart of the assumptions that had dominated physics for centuries.

Paradigms are incommensurable – the ideas generated by one paradigm cannot be used to judge the truth value of the ideas of another paradigm.

To suggest that members of different paradigms experience different worlds has further implications. Kuhn argued that each paradigm has its own way of demarcating science from non-science. Consequently, paradigms are **incommensurable**; in other words, it is impossible to use the criteria of one paradigm to judge the truthfulness of the theories of another. In effect, this means that there is no such thing as universally true knowledge, but it also means that paradigms do not progress, they merely change. Kuhn argued that because the standards of assessment are internal to each paradigm, then scientific revolutions involve a shift in the standards governing which explanations we can consider to be legitimate. Paradigms are seen as incommensurable, in that they involve mutually exclusive foundational assumptions. This is expressed in the different vocabularies of each paradigm.

During the tranquillity of periods of 'normal science', the scientific assumptions go unquestioned, with problems subject to the procedure of puzzle solving, whereby established theories are modified to maintain consistency with the evidence. Gradually, anomalies within a paradigm build up to the point of generating a crisis which precipitates a scientific revolution or paradigm shift, allowing a new paradigm to emerge through a form of conversion experience of gestalt shift (analogous to a religious conversion) rather than by a series of rational logical steps (see Figure 5.4).

Ian Hacking has written a useful summary of the key features of Kuhn's approach which helps us to differentiate the conventionalist position from the common foundations of empiricist approaches, and which relates closely to the conclusion of Chapter 3. You may recall that, for empiricists, theory and observation are distinct, science has a tight deductive structure, concepts should be precise, the sciences should be unified, the **context of discovery** is distinct from the **context of justification** and scientific knowledge provides, or should aspire to provide, universal explanations of things. Hacking highlights the way in which conventionalism provides a very different account of scientific knowledge because it disagrees with all the standpoints and assumptions on which empiricists are agreed. For Hacking:

You may find it useful to revisit section 7 of Chapter 3 where you met Hacking before.

> There is no sharp distinction between observation and theory.
> Science is not cumulative.
> A live science does not have a tight deductive structure.
> Living scientific concepts are not particularly precise.
> Methodological unity of science is false; there are lots of disconnected tools used for various forms of inquiry.
> The sciences themselves are disunified. They are composed of a large number of only loosely overlapping little disciplines many of which in the course of time cannot comprehend each other ...
> The context of justification cannot be separated from the context of discovery.
> Science is in time and is essentially historical.
>
> (Hacking, 1983, p.6)

However, this does not mean that Kuhn offered no basis for considering knowledge as good or bad. He became concerned that many portrayals of his ideas assumed that his account provided no basis for making judgements about knowledge. Consequently, he later identified five characteristics of good scientific theory, as a way of making these judgements:

Accuracy   that a theory should be accurate within its domain of inquiry

Consistency that a theory should be internally consistent as well as consistent with other theories

Broad scope that a theory should explain more than it set out to explain

Simplicity that a theory provides a clear and simple account of complex objects

Fruitfulness that a theory should identify new phenomena or previously unnoticed relationships between such phenomena

(adapted from Kuhn, 1977, pp.320–9)

The meaning of the concept of paradigm is open to question on two grounds. First, Kuhn himself was very imprecise as to how a paradigm

The imprecise definition of the idea of 'paradigm' has produced many and varied uses in the natural and social sciences.

could be defined. Margaret Masterman identified twenty-one different uses of the concept of paradigm in Kuhn's landmark text alone (Masterman, 1970). Kuhn responded in the second edition of his book with a sharper definition of paradigm as a 'disciplinary matrix' consisting of a strong network of commitments, theoretical, instrumental and methodological (Kuhn, 1970). Second, this conceptual confusion has led to different uses of the concept of paradigm between different disciplines and even different uses within each social science discipline. In the next section, we find it is often used loosely to mean a 'model' of the social world or to identify a school of thought, a tradition or a perspective. However, it is the many and varied uses of Kuhn's work which has made his approach so influential.

If we look at Kuhn's use of the term in his historical account of natural sciences, paradigms would have to dominate exclusively in a field of knowledge for a significant period of time. We can see something approaching this in sociology in the 1950s, when functionalism (considered in section 2.2) came close to exercising a dominance along these lines. Nevertheless, alternative approaches continued to coexist with functionalism in sociology and soon re-emerged in the 1960s. Actually, Kuhn only expected a paradigm to emerge in economics, so in terms of Kuhn's own use of the concept of paradigm the social sciences remain **pre-paradigmatic** (by which he understood them to occupy a pre-scientific phase of development). Kuhn's approach views scientific knowledge as a social product and the rules by which we judge knowledge to be scientific as merely conventions. Critics of Kuhn's approach, such as Karl Popper and Imre Lakatos, have argued that conventionalist approaches offer little hope for humanity. A defender of falsificationism, Lakatos suggested that, by giving up on the possibility of progress and by attributing scientific knowledge to the internal workings of communities of scientists, Kuhn's account was in fact the 'mob psychology' of scientific knowledge (Lakatos, 1970).

Summary

Thomas Kuhn situates scientific knowledge in the context of the historical and social practices which define natural science in a particular time and place. Consequently, the truth of a scientific statement is only relevant to those who share the belief system upon which such 'truths' are based.

Kuhn argues that each paradigm possesses its own demarcation criteria on what constitutes science and non-science. Paradigms replace one another through scientific revolutions and they are incommensurable. If one paradigm can never be used to judge another and the occupants of each paradigm are in 'different worlds', then progress is no longer a relevant term in the description of scientific knowledge.

If the way we think shapes the way we interpret evidence, we face substantial problems in distinguishing theories from observations and facts from values. This directly challenges the foundations of empiricist accounts of scientific knowledge.

3.2 Paradigms in the social sciences

How have these arguments been used to understand changes in the social sciences? Earlier it was argued that Kuhn's significance was a consequence of the widespread uses to which the concept of paradigm had been put in the social sciences. To make these changes comprehensible, these uses can be identified as falling into three broad categories.

- **Paradigm 1** – the strict sense identified by Kuhn in his account of the natural sciences, when a single dominant framework, disciplinary matrix or normal science exists and one demarcation criterion operates between science and non-science operates. In this case, paradigms are incommensurable and they are assumed to succeed one another rather than compete, although competition between alternatives may occur in the relatively short-lived periods of crisis and evolution.

- **Paradigm 2** – where the intellectual foundations of the community are such that to move from this paradigm to another would require reorientation of the type identified by Kuhn as a gestalt shift. In this case, we can identify a distinct scientific community with its own institutional foundation and academic career ladder existing within a particular field of knowledge. This use acknowledges the presence of competing paradigms in the same field of knowledge but requires them to be incommensurable.

- **Paradigm 3** – used to designate a school of thought, theoretical perspective or set of problems. This is the loosest but most common use, in which the term paradigm is seen as synonymous with a 'model' of a particular aspect of social life. This use does not require incommen-surability between different paradigms nor does it require a reasonably coherent scientific community with an institutional foundation in re-search and educational settings (although these features may be present and are usually necessary for the long-term survival of the approach).

Elsewhere this sign **g** will direct you to the glossary, but revisit this section if you need to.

We can explore the use of each of these conceptions of paradigm through two case studies, one from psychology and the other from economics. Within the social sciences, there are no perfect applications of Kuhn's original sense of **Paradigm 1**, where clearly identified foundational principles have replaced each other in quick succession, but we'll consider some examples which come pretty close. One of the nearest illustrations can be seen in psychology with the emergence of the behaviourist approach. Even here, the absolute dominance of one approach (of one world-view) implied by Kuhn is not apparent, for other approaches exist on the fringes of the discipline. However, behaviourism was influential in establishing psychology as a scientific discipline and, despite a great deal of self-criticism within the discipline, psychology is often identified as the closest of the social sciences to the natural sciences. This association of behaviourism with the dominant scientific method was also reinforced by the adoption of behaviourist approaches in sociology and 'political science' (including pluralism, ident-ified earlier in section 2.2). The behaviourist approach focuses upon observ-able behaviour and specifically excludes any reference to inner states or intrinsic qualities which, by their character, cannot be observed.

Behaviourism is largely concerned with the relationship between individ-ual human beings and their social and physical environment. This is partly a product of the origins of the behaviourist programme in the animal experimentation of John B. Watson. In his early studies of rat behaviour, Watson developed a theoretical framework which argued that consciousness was irrelevant to psychology and that, as a result, the introspective approach of Wundt, the dominant approach until the early twentieth century, was an inappropriate basis for establishing an objective science of behaviour (Watson, 1928). The rats in Watson's experiments were subjected to different environments within experimental conditions and to a range of rewards and punishments for their responses to various problems, such as finding food in a maze. (Figures 5.5 and 5.6 illustrate similar experimental work.)

See Chapter 4, section 3.1.

Figure 5.5 Scientists monitoring the behaviour of rats in a maze experiment.

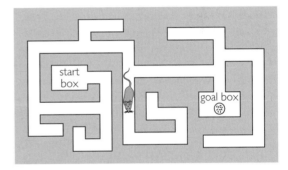

Figure 5.6 Diagram of the maze used in a behaviourist experiment.

The results of this experimentation established that rats could learn to respond to their environment and to various sanctions so establishing that their behaviour was not static but could be modified. Watson was at the forefront of arguing that the techniques developed in the objective study of animal behaviour could also be used within human psychology. This involved refocusing psychology towards the study of behaviour so that it could become a 'purely objective experimental branch of natural science'. Behaviourism required a move away from the study of the conscious mind, mental stages and images as subjectively defined. This challenged the existing approach of introspection which took subjective states as its starting-point. It is this difference in approach which marks off behaviourism from introspection and other earlier forms of experimental psychology, as a **Paradigm 1**. Since each approach operated through different demarcation criteria between science and non-science, there is no common basis for establishing objective knowledge or for judging between them. So introspection and behaviourism can be characterized as incommensurable.

In psychology, the shift from introspection to behaviourism is often seen as a paradigmatic shift.

It is worthwhile exploring this approach in a little more detail in order to highlight the ways in which psychologists have responded to behaviourism more recently. The central principle of behaviourist psychology is the explanation of the process of learning as one of **operant conditioning**. This assumes that behavioural modifications of individuals are a response to the consequences of their behaviour. The environment is assumed to react towards the individual in three ways – negative, neutral and positive – and that this reaction can act as a reinforcer (a reward) or as a punishment for the behaviour concerned. Of course, rewards and punishments can have a neutral effect, in that they may not alter behaviour. Nevertheless, there are four possible ways in which the modification of individual behaviour can take place.

Positive reinforcement – takes place when a particular form of behaviour produces pleasurable consequences for the individuals concerned and encourages similar behaviour in the future.	*Negative reinforcement* – takes place when an inhibiting or an aversive feature is removed, enabling the individual to carry out a particular form of behaviour and encouraging similar behaviour in the same circumstances.
Positive punishment – introducing (or the threat of introducing) an aversive stimulus in order to support or discourage particular forms of behaviour in the future.	*Negative punishment* – removing (or the threat of removing) a reward of entitlement which would otherwise provide pleasurable consequences in order to suppress or discourage particular forms of behaviour in the future.

Behaviourist psychologists have used this system of reinforcers and punishments to examine the processes of childhood socialization and to recommend therapeutic uses of behaviour modification where the behaviour of children was considered to be inappropriate or 'abnormal'. Similarly, in the treatment of criminality, solutions were sought in the modification of behavioural traits, rather than assuming that criminals would be deterred in future through the application of a particular standard form of punishment. If it were assumed that consciousness was not relevant to the study of behaviour then, when conducting research, it could be assumed that human beings are no different from non-human animals. All behaviour could be studied in experimental conditions, or through careful observation, in order to establish patterns of modification in learning behaviour. These studies could be replicated and the data verified to establish their authenticity, creating objective scientific accounts of human behaviour. The work of Watson became an important reference point for the generational shift from introspection to behaviourism in psychology. However, alternatives remained in existence, such as Gestalt psychology and psychoanalysis, although they remained marginalized in the discipline until the debates of the 1950s and 1960s which saw the reintroduction of the concept of the self as an intentional and purposeful social actor.

Introspection works from the subjective mental states of individuals, while behaviourism regards them as irrelevant for generating scientific knowledge.

In the behaviourist approach, a great deal of stress is placed upon the role of the stimulus–response relationship, whereby the behaviour of the individual is seen as an effect of external stimuli, with responses taking one of the four forms identified above. However, the same evidence can also be interpreted as an example of purposeful behaviour (or, if we are talking about animals, behaviour that appears to have a purpose) rather than as a conditioned reflex to a particular stimulus. The cognitive psychologist Edward C. Tolman (Tolman et al., 1946) argued that an alternative model of the learning process, whereby knowledge of past experiences is stored in a cognitive map of the environment, provided an account which could explain the variation of responses to the same stimuli in human and animal behaviour (in addition to the evidence explained by the behaviourist approach). Cognitive psychology assumes that the acquisition of information allows for 'rule-governed behaviour' but that these rules are flexible and adaptive in the light of subsequent experiences. There is some dispute as to whether cognitive psychology replaced the behaviourist approach in psychology as the most influential theory. In addition, Tolman's approach coexists with that of the later behaviourists, such as Burrhus F. Skinner, in a different disciplinary context where a range of new alternatives was also emerging. Human cultures are defined by Skinner as the composite of behaviours of the individuals who form a particular community. Skinner sought to purge any conception of individual autonomy and creativity. Like Watson, he was particularly concerned to challenge the conception of the 'autonomous man' within voluntarist approaches to social life (Skinner, 1953, 1971). For Skinner, it is not ideas, wants, values or desires which determine behaviour, for these can only be identified through the study of those aspects of social relationships and personal choices which, in a causal explanation, would be conventionally defined as effects (the dependent variables). In the field of social psychology, the emergence of a range of new approaches placed a greater emphasis upon the meaningful, personal and social aspects of the lived experience of social actors. Such humanistic and critical social psychologies focused on subjective experience as a foundation for knowledge and the role of social actors in actively constructing the social world, and moved beyond the experimental setting to draw upon a wider range of empirical research strategies.

Activity 5.2

Reading B includes three short extracts from *Theory and Social Psychology* (Sapsford *et al.*, eds, 1998): 'Experimental social psychology' by Patrick McGhee, 'Humanistic and experiental social psychology' by Richard Stevens and 'Critical social psychology' by Margaret Wetherell. Read these extracts now.

- Identify the differences between each approach and consider which of the three senses of paradigms adequately describes this area of social scientific knowledge.

You may also find it useful to think about how these different kinds of psychology lead to different approaches to research methods: defining the object of analysis differently may mean having to gather evidence in ways which match.

Psychology has now fragmented into those areas where one approach dominates in a paradigmatic way and those areas where contesting approaches coexist.

Cognitive psychology has, in time, become a scientific community in its own right with an institutional basis in research and teaching organizations separate from other approaches; in this context, it appears to exist in a paradigmatic way (in the sense of **Paradigm 2**) as a methodological framework in most of the areas of psychology, with the exception of social psychology. In social psychology, the influence of the cognitive framework is more limited. Here it has become known as psychological social psychology competing with a range of approaches from sociological social psychology. So, in the case of social psychology, the use of **Paradigm 3** would be more appropriate as a descriptive label for cognitive psychology (that is, psychological social psychology). The problems of applying the concept of paradigm to other social sciences are just as complex. In the case of economics, even Kuhn himself held out some hope of a singular mature science developing in the sense of **Paradigm 1**, although it should be added that his own perspective was coloured by the apparent success and widespread acceptance of Keynesian economic management strategies in the Western post-war boom from the 1950s to the early 1960s.

Activity 5.3

Turn to Reading C, 'Economic paradigms', on the Keynesian and monetarist approaches to the economy, from Vane and Thompson's *An Introduction to Macroeconomic Policy* (1982), and 'Economic crisis: the Marxist view' from Hunt and Sherman's *Economics: An Introduction to Traditional and Radical Views* (1981).

- Identify the key assumptions in each of the three approaches and consider whether these approaches are incommensurable.

- Identify which concept of paradigm best describes the differences between them.

As in the examples from psychology in Activity 5.2, you should look for clues as to the similarities and differences between these approaches.

In economics the contrast between Keynesian and monetarist approaches to the study of the economy has often been couched in Kuhnian terms. These economic theories represent opposing philosophies about the role of the state in the organization of production, distribution and exchange which are reflected in completely irreconcilable positions in policy terms. In substantive terms, Keynesianism presumes that the state can intervene in the free market in various ways with positive consequences in terms of employment, prices and growth. In this approach, the state ensures that the level of total aggregate demand is such that the economy does not fall into recession nor does it become overheated, causing inflationary pressure. This precarious state of affairs, where the state moderates the tendencies of the business cycle through fiscal and monetary fine-tuning, is achieved through the intervention of a benevolent state, which seeks to maximize the common good. This approach, then, assumes that the economy can be planned, or at least guided, towards certain common goals and that when the market fails (such as in the decline of an industrial sector) the state can intervene directly and take control of key sectors in the public interest.

Keynesianism and monetarism are often described as different paradigms in economics.

Monetarism, on the other hand, rejects the role of the state as a benevolent actor and assumes that an economy functions most efficiently when left to its own devices. The activity of the state is interpreted as a form of interference which damages exchange relations and diverts valuable and scarce resources from profitable uses (through taxation) by maintaining declining sectors of industry (through subsidies or state ownership). From the monetarist standpoint, the intervention of the state (by increasing the money supply) is the cause of both inflationary pressure and the perpetuation of inefficient sectors of the economy. In addition, the growth of state intervention creates a greater tax burden which further undermines incentives for wealth production more generally, as well as 'crowding out' private sector capital from the limited opportunities for investment.

With such well rehearsed arguments and the existence of institutional group-ings of Keynesian economists (for instance, at Cambridge University) and monetarist economists (for instance, at Liverpool University), it is easy to see how these two opposed approaches could be interpreted as different worlds. However, on closer examination the relationship between the two approaches is not so simple. The ideas of the economist John Maynard Keynes are often contrasted with the neo-classical economics which preceded them. Neo-classical economics assumed that the market would inevitably resolve any imbalances (slumps and booms) through the adjust-ments of the 'invisible hand' of the price mechanism whereby, according to Say's Law, the supply of goods will always find its own demand at a given price. The 'Keynesian revolution' was a revolution in the sense that it became possible to envisage the state adopting a proactive rather than a reactive relationship to the problems of the market. However, this is not the same thing as a scientific revolution, because the conceptual landscape remained much the same as before. Moreover, the object of analysis in both Keynesian and monetarist approaches remained the market, for it was de-fined as a set of exchange relations between firms, households and individ-uals. In addition, the values of commodities are identified in terms of exchange value. As to how they define their field of analysis, both approaches remain committed to identifying the same objects in the same way. Where these approaches disagree, then, is over the legitimate role of the state in the market as well as over the normative issue of whether it is poss-ible and desirable to create an egalitarian society.

Compared with the 'Marxist paradigm', Keynesian and monetarist economics have common foundations.

If, however, we contrast both of these approaches with Marxist economics, a different set of issues arises. For the Marxist economist, the object of analy-sis is not simply the exchange relations which characterize capitalist mar-kets but also the productive relations and the productive forces which together make up the economy. Exchange relations are treated as operating upon the level of surface appearances and present an 'ideological' obstacle to understanding the underlying real workings of the economy (preventing us from seeing the world as it really is). In the Marxist approach, the re-lations between capitalist and working classes are characterized by irrecon-cilable conflicts of interest which, at any given time, may or may not manifest themselves in visible social and political conflict. In addition, per-iodic economic crises are treated as the symptoms of underlying productive processes in a class-divided society. For Keynesians and monetarists, how-ever, 'capitalism' in the sense identified by Marxists cannot be observed and as such cannot be said to exist. Similarly, we can observe workers but not the proletariat, and individual businesses and firms but not capitalism. Clearly, different demarcation criteria are at work.

Now, let's see how these differences relate to the three senses of paradigm identified earlier. While the difference between Keynesianism and monetarism appears to illustrate **Paradigm 3**, the difference between both of these approaches and the Marxist theory of the capitalist economy seems closer to the meaning of **Paradigm 2**. The move from seeing the economy as a set of exchange relations to seeing the economy as constituted by definite productive relations could be seen as a movement between different worlds. Economics does not offer an example of **Paradigm 1**, and from this study we can see that a crisis in theorizing within a particular discipline does not constitute a revolution unless an alternative paradigm is emerging which is itself incommensurable with the paradigm it is replacing (Katouzian, 1987, pp.100–6).

The previous sections illustrated the ways in which definite approaches seem to emerge in the social sciences and can dominate in a particular discipline. However, the frequency of the turnover of theories and methods in the social sciences seems to ensure that such dominance is short-lived. One possible answer to the question of why this occurs could lie in the social conditions in which these dominant approaches in Western societies emerged during the 1950s (which produced behaviourist psychology, Keynesian economics, functionalist sociology, pluralist political science and quantitative geography). If scientific knowledge is a social product, it is interesting that periods of consensus within disciplines occurred simultaneously with greater social solidarity in the societies which produced this knowledge. This period witnessed a sustained period of economic growth, political stability and greater opportunities for wider sections of Western societies. Similarly, perhaps the social scientific discord which has occurred since is related to the decline of social cohesion in Western societies since the 1960s. If we take seriously the argument that knowledge is a social product, then it is possible to see Kuhn's work itself as a product of social conditions in the same way. In the following sections we focus upon the other main contributors to conventionalist interpretations from this period. These approaches raise important questions about Kuhn's description of the history of the scientific method.

> *Dominant paradigms in the social sciences tend to coincide with periods of greater social stability and consensus in the lives of the scientific communities involved.*

Summary

The application of Kuhn's concept of paradigm to the social sciences is common but inconsistent. Anything close to the strict use identified by Kuhn (**Paradigm 1**) has only been witnessed for brief periods where a particular approach has influenced a social scientific discipline (as in the case of behaviourism in psychology and functionalism in sociology).

The treatment of paradigms as incommensurable but not necessarily dominant (**Paradigm 2**) is particularly useful in identifying the bedrock assumptions of different theoretical systems in social science. This is often confused with the 'loose use' of paradigm as a particular 'model' or 'school of thought' in open competition with other models or schools (**Paradigm 3**).

3.3 Conventionalism beyond Kuhn 1: question everything!

So far, we have concentrated upon one example of conventionalism, Thomas Kuhn's historical account of science. Other conventionalists, such as Paul Feyerabend, place less emphasis upon fairly well defined periods of stability and change in the history of scientific knowledge. Feyerabend, perhaps more than anyone else, has challenged the tendency to look for

An approach associated with conventionalism is methodological pluralism.

order in knowledge. In *Against Method* (1975), he argued that the most important characteristic of scientific knowledge is its messy, accidental and discontinuous nature. This was directed as much against Kuhn's concept of paradigm as a period of normal science as it was against positivism. Feyerabend developed a standpoint which suggested that science was not rational, that no knowledge rules had operated effectively in any case, and that scientific knowledge could be oppressive rather than an instrument of progress. Further than this, he argued that rival theories themselves (rather than paradigms) are incommensurable, so that it was impossible to identify a basis for defining one form of knowledge as superior to another form at any point in time. For Feyerabend, to treat science as a rational and objective enterprise was a myth (that is, folklore for scientists). In addition, he portrayed the pursuit of rational scientific explanations (running from the positivists through to Popper) as undesirable because it substituted the accumulation of knowledge for the goal of emancipating human beings.

'Anything goes' – Feyerabend's view that the only defensible position is the idea that all ideas are equally valid.

Feyerabend was concerned that no ideas should be rejected just because they did not conform to a particular standard of useful or true knowledge. This principle of 'anything goes' earned him the label of 'epistemological anarchist'. The anarchistic vision he held was a positive one (in the sense that it referred to the positive condition of freedom from authority rather than a condition of chaos). Here, though, it was applied to knowledge systems rather than political systems. He never saw himself as a political anarchist, but more of a Dadaist who questioned our expectations. Kuhn and Feyerabend seem to offer different ways of thinking about the limits of truth, progress and reason. Feyerabend's conception of knowledge is relativist; he holds that all views are equally privileged, true and valid (Harré and Krausz, 1996). He hoped that it would be possible to live in a situation where all views could be taken seriously, that no ideas should be disregarded in case they become useful in another time and place. Feyerabend questioned the key principles of science just when it was reeling from the impact of Kuhn's work. Instead, he advocated the **principle of proliferation** as the alternative strategy to the imposition of one dominant view. The challenge that Feyerabend's approach presents can be seen in his comparison of scientific textbooks from the 1950s and the handbook for the Witchfinder General dating from the fifteenth century.

> In 1484, the Roman Catholic Church published the *Malleus Maleficarum*, the outstanding textbook on Witchcraft. ... It has four parts: phenomena, aetiology, legal aspects, theological aspects of Witchcraft. ... The aetiology is pluralistic, there is not just the official explanation, there are other explanations as well, purely materialistic explanations included. Of course, in the end only one of the offered explanations is accepted, but the alternatives are discussed and so one can judge the arguments that lead to their elimination. This feature makes the *Malleus* superior to almost every physics, biology, chemistry textbook of today. Even the theology is pluralistic, heretical views are not passed over in silence, nor are they ridiculed; they are described, examined and removed by argument. The authors know the subject, they know ... the positions of their opponents, they argue against these positions and they use the best knowledge available at the time in their arguments.
>
> (Feyerabend, 1978, p.92)

Feyerabend explicitly ties this critical questioning of established conceptions of authoritative knowledge to the desire to maximize the freedom
and realize the untapped potential of individual human beings. In terms of
the circuit of knowledge established through modern scientific thinking
(considered in Chapter 2), Feyerabend questions science, reason, truth and
progress in order to emancipate humanity, breaking the circuit in the process (see Figure 5.7). The existence of a single orthodox account of what
constitutes authoritative knowledge is portrayed as a form of oppression
and he raises the ways in which science can involve an increasingly diverse
range of theories with equal standing.

*Feyerabend
questions the
circuit of modern
scientific knowledge
established in an
integrated way
since the
Enlightenment.*

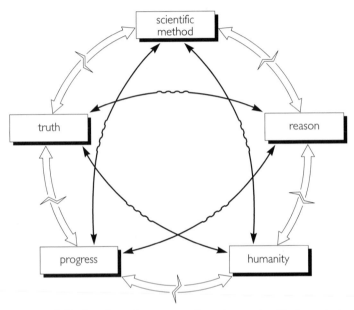

Figure 5.7   Breaking the circuit of modern scientific knowledge.

In a similar way, in *Deschooling Society* (1971) the radical social theorist
and critic Ivan Illich has identified and criticized the use of knowledge as
an instrument for promoting conformity and obedience. Illich distinguished
'education' (involving the process of learning and understanding) from
'schooling' which (through the practice of memorization and by instilling
obedience) destroys human creativity. This draws from the distinction between 'knowledge about' and 'knowledge of' developed by William James.
Illich suggested that the damaging effects of schooling on the realization of
the full potential of individuals could be identified within all educational
and academic institutions, ranging from the infant school to the university;
such institutions were designed to reward those pupils and students who
memorized and reproduced the authoritative knowledge rather than to encourage creative and free thinking. Illich's answer was to identify how a
plurality of ways of thinking could be fostered and monolithic knowledge
dislodged from its pre-eminence in the education system. This was to be
achieved through learning webs, where tutors and students could come
together around common interests and define their own curriculum, and
through skill exchanges, which would enable the practitioners in a particular field to pass on their skills and experience through practical applied
study.

*See Chapter 4,
section 5.1.*

Science should help make human beings free and not enslave them within a dogmatic set of methodological rules. **g**

Feyerabend and others, in the late 1960s and early 1970s, offered a radical way of challenging established conventions about scientific knowledge. In particular, they challenged the assumption that this form of knowledge, by virtue of its ability to distinguish truth and falsehood, could lay claim to a superior status over other forms of knowledge. In the place of one way of seeing the world, they advocated **methodological pluralism**. This approach is based upon the philosophical position of **relativism**, the view that no form of knowledge is more valid than any other. However, two examples of inconsistency have been identified in Feyerabend's work. First, while he does not believe that reason can lead us to the truth (he adopts an anti-rationalist stance), he still argues for the use of 'rules of thumb' in research which does not exclude the use of 'rational standards' in explaining phenomena. Second, Feyerabend continues to accept the possibility of progress in the development of knowledge which the rejection of a universal rational standard would appear to preclude.

Activity 5.4

Turn to Reading D, 'Methodological pluralism', from Bruce Caldwell's *Beyond Positivism* (1994).

- Briefly identify the steps in establishing methodological pluralism raised by Caldwell.

This is a practical manifesto for raising questions about the way a discipline is organized. Think about any discipline with which you are familiar and try to identify the broad approaches within it. Now think about the strengths and weaknesses of these approaches.

Sympathizers with this critique of the claims associated with scientific knowledge in the social sciences have embraced the idea of methodological pluralism, whereas critics, such as the social anthropologist Ernest Gellner, have warned against the relativism that this view implies. For Gellner, this means that social scientists cannot support or condemn any theoretical position – they are merely left standing on the sidelines of serious discussion. In particular, Gellner criticized Feyerabend for leaving us in a position where, for example, it is impossible to condemn events such as the Holocaust. In effect, Gellner was asking what is the point of social science if it does not have an impact on the organization of social life. Feyerabend responded by arguing that his approach was not relativistic in that sense. Gellner is addressing the issue of moral relativism, whereas Feyerabend is concerned with **epistemological** questions. At this point it is important to separate questions of truth (addressed by Feyerabend) from questions of 'the good' (raised by Gellner). Actually, in *Science in a Free Society* (1978) Feyerabend advocated that all knowledge should contribute to human freedom and not oppression, so it is clear that his values did motivate his approach to knowledge construction – even Feyerabend, then, links questions of truth to questions about 'the good'. The problem of the relationship between rationality and relativism is addressed in more detail in the final section of this chapter, but first we shall consider the role of explanations which adopt the position of social constructionism in the study of natural science.

3.4 Conventionalism beyond Kuhn 2: the sociology of knowledge and science

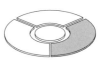

In this section you have the opportunity to go back to the issue of scientific practice by exploring approaches which consider the practical experiences of scientists. A common strand throughout all conventionalist approaches is the emphasis placed upon the institutional and cultural context of knowledge production. In the field of the sociology of knowledge and science, Barry Barnes in *Interests and the Growth of Knowledge* (1977) and David Bloor in *Knowledge and Social Imagery* (1976) have developed what they call the 'strong programme' to explain how the social context of research affects the development of knowledge in both the natural and the social sciences. Barnes and Bloor point to the variation in knowledge between groups, the variations in different individual interpretations of the same experience, and the role of the interests of scientists and researchers in maintaining deference to their expertise and their own personal advancement. In particular, they identify the disjunction between the tentative character of the evidence upon which scientific knowledge is based and the strong degree of certainty which the use of the label 'scientific' presumes. In this approach, all knowledge is mediated through a culture and language which scientists themselves inhabit. The label of 'strong programme' reflects an attempt to adopt the relativist position more explicitly compared with the weaker versions in Kuhn's and Feyerabend's approaches. Barnes's and Bloor's research identified that scientific knowledge is the product of a range of social factors within the academic, professional and industrial contexts in which the knowledge was generated. This approach, sometimes loosely called 'social constructionism', draws upon the insights of hermeneutics, phenomenology, ethnomethodology and cultural anthropology, because of the way in which all these approaches focus upon the situatedness of human knowledge.

See Chapter 4, section 5 and Geographical Models 2.

Such studies ask whether the social sciences should follow the formal procedures of scientific method when natural scientists do not do so themselves. The history of science is littered with useful accidents, such as the discovery of penicillin, or with informed guesswork, such as the discovery of DNA. In such cases, progress in the accumulation of knowledge was not delivered by the careful and rigid application of a particular scientific method. Kaplan's work had already prepared the way for this by pointing to the difference between the 'reconstructed logics' favoured by philosophers of science (that all philosophies are idealized stories of what should be done) and the 'logics in use' in the everyday practices of scientists where hunches, guesswork, leaps of intuition and accidents play an important part in the construction of knowledge. Kaplan is, in effect, distinguishing between what scientists do and what they say they do (Kaplan, 1964). Textbooks from the philosophy of science tend to present a highly formal account of the scientific method and tend to avoid the complex settings in which research takes place. In particular, they often focus upon the most successful examples of research rather than the ambiguous evidence of the work of scientists in general.

The sociology of science considers what scientists do, not just what they say they do.

In 1994, at the British Association for the Advancement of Science, Harry Collins (Professor of Sociology of Science at the University of Bath)

Science is a social product – it conveys the authoritative knowledge of the social and historical context in which it was produced.

presented a case for questioning the status of science as a superior form of knowledge. He raised the extent to which a scientific community depends upon trust. In particular, Collins focused upon the ways in which the results of scientific investigations are more ambiguous, the scientific theories are more flexible and that progress is more uncertain than most theoretical accounts of science suggest. In his view, what is regarded as 'science' is the end product of a complex process of legitimation in the identification of authoritative knowledge and is dependent upon the social context in which such knowledge is produced. Collins argued that the designation of particular forms of knowledge as scientific is dependent upon the plausibility of this knowledge for the scientific community involved. (See Figure 5.8.) He went further to say that, in the light of this, knowledge should not be subject to any universal standard. Collins concluded that scientific knowledge is a social construct and that science is tied to definite social and historical conditions, so that when conditions change so too does knowledge (Collins, 1994).

Figure 5.8   The mechanics of celebrity can be seen in the academic performance.
Scientific knowledge is produced and communicated in organized communities ... some large, some small. Jacques Derrida addresses the assembled academic congregation at the University of Sussex (1 December 1997).

The identification of variations in the forms of knowledge as if they were matters of cultural difference was derived from interpretative sociology and anthropology. This involved the careful empirical study of communities of scientists through in-depth interviews and participant observation in order to identify the taken-for-granted assumptions of scientists and to reconstruct the processes through which scientific knowledge was made. The distinctive contribution of anthropological insights to a discussion of natu-ral and social scientific method can be seen in the short story 'The Philosopher, the Scientist and the Anthropologist', related in Zygmunt Bauman's *Hermeneutics and Social Science* (1978):

> On one occasion Sir Karl Popper told his audience a story which had obviously shaken him. It concerned an anthropologist invited to join some other first-class brains in discussing an important matter in the methodology of science. At the end of long and heated arguments, to which the anthropologist listened in silence, he was asked to express his view. Much to the dismay of everybody present, the anthropologist replied that he paid little attention to the actual content of the dispute. The content was, he thought, the least interesting of what he saw and heard. Of incomparably greater interest were other things: how the debate was launched, how it developed, how one intervention triggered off another and how they fell into sequences, how the contributors determined whether they were in disagreement etc. Our anthropologist, presumably viewed the topic which aroused so much passion as just one of those 'native beliefs' whose truth or falsity is largely irrelevant for a scholarly study. This was why he was not particularly interested in the topic. Instead, he recorded with genuine interest the interaction in which the learned experts engaged. ... Sir Karl was, of course, indignant. For him statements are about something and are to be judged, in this way or another, by being tested against this something. ... He would try to extract from the sentence the message it contained, and then attempt to put the truth of the message to the test.
>
> (Bauman, 1978, p.172)

One way to try to understand what scientists (or even philosophers!) do is to observe them directly in their own environments, in the way that social scientists observe other small groups of people involved in communication and interaction.

Activity 5.5

Turn to Reading E, 'Two sociological perspectives on science', from Michael Mulkay's *Sociology of Science* (1991). Then consider the two journalistic extracts in Reading F: John Turney's 'Faking it to make it' (1989) and Stuart Sutherland's 'What if teacher is a cheat?' (1989).

• Identify which of the two approaches considered by Michael Mulkay is relevant for understanding the accounts of the practices of science given by Turney and Sutherland.

In this activity you should notice that each of the perspectives on science identified by Mulkay could be applied to the two journalistic accounts. However, you should also have noticed that the perspective adopted can lead you to look at them in very different ways and reach different conclusions. You may find it useful to to look back at Activity 3.3 in Chapter 3; again here the question is whether the research is evidence of 'bad science' or whether the way we see science itself needs to be rethought.

The scientific ethnographic studies of scientists, notably by Bruno Latour and Steve Woolgar (1979), Michael Mulkay (1972, 1991) and Karin Knorr-Cetina (1981), emphasize the differences between the informal and accidental dimensions of the research activity itself and the formal style of presenting results in scientific journals (Figure 5.9) and within the media as though a logical procedure had been followed from beginning to end of the research process. For sociologists of science, scientific communities are characterized by networks and forms of social interaction – like any other form of community. The interactions which take place are seen as governed by the same criteria of trust and credibility that obtain in other acts of exchange. In this case, the acts of exchange involve data, ideas and other forms of knowledge, whether the exchange is portrayed as an act of gift giving (Hagstrom, 1965) or as an investment in the collective body of knowledge which can be converted later into status, power and perhaps wealth by the investors (Bourdieu, 1975).

Figure 5.9 A measure of academic output.
The pressure to publish has become relentless – it's the only way in which academic work can be measured and performance compared. A snapshot of the *Economic Journal* in the 1940s and much more recently.

Scientific knowledge is the product of the complex social practices of scientific communities.

Latour and Woolgar compare scientific communities to markets in order to explain the social relationships and patterns involved. They are concerned to avoid general debates on whether science is a social construct and prefer to explore the process of research itself. They focus upon areas which they describe as 'hot' research, the cutting edge of research activity where scientists are more likely to meet unexpected problems and have to innovate to generate useful new knowledge. The research conducted by sociologists of science provides useful insights into the actual practices of scientists and the development of scientific communities. Such studies also focus upon the relations of communication and power which operate in scientific communities and the role of patronage and sponsorship (see Figure 5.10).

Figure 5.10   The master–disciple relationship in scientific work.
The recruitment process for joining an academic community is long, arduous and intensive (a doctoral student submits his research for scrutiny from his supervisor).

In a similar way, in the social sciences the success of a particular research approach is largely governed by social conditions such as:

- the compatibility of a research approach with existing evidence and research, or the extent to which the conclusions generated offer an 'acceptable' way of resolving an established problem;

- the support of academic colleagues who, through the process of peer review, can affect the reception of a particular piece of research (Figures 5.11 and 5.12);

- the relevance or usefulness of the social research in question for both the scientific community and wider society, particularly for the justification or questioning of policy making in a specific field of government;

- the contribution of the research to a currently exciting area of academic work rather than to a field of inquiry which is considered to be dormant or exhausted.

These four considerations have been portrayed in a favourable light. A critical interpretation would consider the success of a particular piece of research in the extent to which it does not challenge the orthodox interpretations of the field, and in the ways in which it attracts the patronage of established academics who sponsor or dismiss the work in question. Also important is the degree to which it serves the interests of those who control politics (and thus the financial basis for future research) and the extent to

Figure 5.11 Learning to use the tools of the trade.
A student tries to remember Kant's advice 'have courage in your own understanding'
when presenting a paper in a seminar conducted by Professor William Outhwaite.

which the choice of research topic and method reflects fashion and fad
rather than some other criteria for establishing the relevance and usefulness
of research. This approach highlights the dangers involved when social
research remains unquestioned, because it confirms the existing body of
opinion in a particular field and simply reinforces what is already taken
for granted.

Figure 5.12 Peer review: the exchange of ideas in an academic setting.
Contributing in a constructive way means that you stick your neck out and make your
views heard. But you should also expect your colleagues to be critical as well as
supportive.

Summary

Feyerabend presents a case for the acceptance of a proliferating diversity of competing scientific theories as a positive state for scientific and socially useful knowledge. This encourages greater tolerance and explicitly links the generation of knowledge to the development of human potential.

Sociologists of science identify the organization of knowledge in communities, the mechanics of celebrity and intellectual patronage and the relationship between knowledge and the interests of academic institutions as crucial factors in understanding the social construction of knowledge.

4   Rationality and relativism: keeping progress

The studies of scientific knowledge by Kuhn, Feyerabend and the sociologists of science provoked a crisis of rationality in the philosophy of science (particularly undermining the more positivistically inclined approaches). The sceptical treatment of truth by Popper and Lakatos ensured that supporters of **naturalism** and rational scientific methods in the social sciences could still draw upon a versatile approach. Lakatos usefully qualifies the Popperian approach and tries to draw some lessons from the work of the conventionalists. He draws upon the historical evidence produced by Kuhn on the ways in which knowledge is organized in communities of scientists and how academic and scientific organizations are as important as the methodologies adopted. However, his approach is committed to the principle that the gradual accumulation of knowledge should deliver progress. Popper and Lakatos are more often described as critical rationalists because they challenge empiricist assumptions about the role of ideas and theories. However, for both of them experience acts as the arbiter for testing scientific theories.

Lakatos, in his 1970 article 'Falsification and the Methodology of Scientific Research Programmes', argued that philosophers of science were faced with three alternatives: induction, conventionalism and falsificationism. He ruled out induction on the grounds that theories were not a direct reflection of experience. He rejected conventionalism for giving up on the accumulation of knowledge as a means of delivering progress, for this is the point of being a scientist in the first place. Regarding the last approach, he argued that it was important to distinguish various forms of falsificationist approaches. He gave the label **dogmatic falsificationism** to the scientists who interpreted Popper in too simplistic a way and immediately discarded any hypotheses which had been refuted. This position was to be distinguished from Popper's falsificationist approach, which accepted that a hypothesis, even if empirically refuted, may still be useful as a predictive statement in a different context. Such statements, Popper argued, should simply be shelved for the time being unless they had been comprehensively falsified. This was in part a recognition of the problems in conclusively falsifying scientific statements, which we explored when considering the Duhem-Quine thesis. However, because Popper's position remained

Through the work of Lakatos falsificationism learned something from its critics.

Defenders of falsificationism seek to draw upon the insights of conventionalism without losing the accumulation of knowledge as a source of 'progress'.

focused upon individual laws, theories and evidence on a particular problem, Lakatos labelled Popper's approach **naive methodological falsificationism.** Actually, it was Popper's focus upon individual theories and the importance of protecting individual freedom that prompted Lakatos to argue that Popper and Feyerabend had, in fact, a great deal in common.

In recognizing that theories do not exist in isolation, Lakatos addressed Kuhn's contributions on the way in which knowledge was culturally and historically located. However, unlike Kuhn, he argued that a viable methodology had to be both descriptively accurate and prescriptively useful (that is, it indicates what we 'should' do in scientific research). In developing **sophisticated methodological falsificationism,** Lakatos felt that he could account for the institutional life of scientists and offer a guide for further scientific research. Lakatos distinguished between the 'hard core' which held the key foundational assumptions of a scientific research programme, and the 'protective belt' of auxiliary hypotheses which could be tested and falsified at any point in time. This is very much the same distinction between bedrock assumptions and contextual hypotheses which we considered earlier in section 2.

Lakatos suggested that a scientific research programme (his alternative to the concept of paradigm) is governed by two sets of methodological rules. First, the *negative heuristic* dictates which research pathways cannot be studied. This protects the hard core from criticism: anyone who does this is often treated as a heretic or dangerous to the programme. For instance, behaviourist approaches which focus upon human actions as a series of effects resulting from various stimuli (such as pluralism in political science and political sociology) could not accept the existence of human beings as creative and reflective beings. You may recall that behaviourists reject the existence of inner selves as speculative and hold that such considerations are not the concern of science.

Now that we have established the grounds for excluding things from an inquiry, let's focus upon the second set of methodological rules, the *positive heuristic.* This indicates the research pathways which are legitimate and worthwhile. For instance, in the case of pluralism in political studies (considered earlier in the chapter) it is concrete decision-making situations which could be observed, measured and explained that are considered to be legitimate and worthwhile objects of analysis. For Lakatos, even if a set of theories and core assumptions has been falsified, as long as they continue to offer useful predictions, then it is worth keeping them. In addition, in the absence of a more adequate alternative, Lakatos suggests that it is better to hang on to a bad theory than to have no theory at all. He also makes a plea for tolerance with the emergence of budding research programmes. Overall, scientific research programmes, even if inadequate, can be identified as progressive or degenerating in the long term. This is a considerable way from Popper's falsificationism, yet it retains his commitment towards progress and the accumulation of knowledge. For instance, many sociological perspectives would fit this description. For instance, both functionalism and Marxism have encountered severe problems in explaining social life and have for a time appeared to degenerate. Nevertheless, with a reworking of their protective belt, both have bounced back at different times as neo-functionalism and neo-Marxism, taking into account some of the criticisms launched against them. In each case, the bedrock assumptions of both the

Negative heuristic – all theoretical systems contain assumptions about what it is not possible to study.

Positive heuristic – all theoretical systems contain assumptions about which pathways of research are feasible and which are likely to be fruitful.

old and new versions remain consistent. Neo-Marxism, for instance, retains its commitment towards defining the economy in terms of class structure and gives the economy a determinate role, in the long term, in explaining the development of capitalist societies.

In the social sciences, this defence of the idea of 'progress' developed by Lakatos continues to offer an attractive alternative to the relativistic assumptions of conventionalism. However, one of the difficulties in applying this approach is the problem of clearly identifying the hard core of bedrock assumptions which are taken for granted by the participants in a research programme. Another problem emerges when we attempt to find a means of distinguishing a progressive from a degenerating research programme. For Lakatos, a progressive problem shift takes place when the newly emergent theory accounts for the successes of the previous theory, contains a greater empirical content than the existing approaches, and has been subject to attempts at falsification and has been corroborated.

Scientists are usually considering the protective belt of the research programme, not the hard core of bedrock assumptions.

Activity 5.6

Now read the extract 'The schizophrenia research programme' by Mary Boyle (Reading G).

- Identify the hard core and the protective belt in this example of social scientific research. What is the evidence that the research programme is either progressing or degenerating?

Think about the issues which you explored in section 2 when you considered the differences between assumptions and contextual hypotheses. You should remember the ways in which scientists and social scientists, when they find their assumptions are challenged, dodge difficult questions simply by modifying the contextual hypotheses. Is the distinction between the hard core and the protective belt any different? In particular, ask yourself whether Boyle's evidence on the schizophrenia research programme leads you to question this as a particular example of a 'failed' programme. The survival of the schizophrenia research programme and its search for a biological explanation started in the early part of the twentieth century – perhaps even Lakatos is too optimistic about the capacities of scientists to discard ideas which have been repeatedly found wanting.

The Methodology of Scientific Research Programmes (MSRP) is particularly important in social scientific disciplines which retain a commitment to falsificationism and the application of the assumptions and methods of the natural sciences to social objects. While Lakatos draws upon Kuhn's account of the collective dimension of research, he does not reject the possibility of progress through the accumulation of knowledge in particular disciplines. He argues that it is rational to use some criterion to demarcate scientific knowledge from other forms of knowledge. However, the distinction between the hard core and the protective belt allows for the existence of unfalsifiable (that is, metaphysical) claims at the heart of the research programme. So, in some respects, his approach is at odds with empiricism as it is generally understood. Nevertheless, Lakatos found a way of maintaining a commitment to the accumulation of knowledge and progress while addressing the concerns originally identified by Duhem and Quine.

See section 2.1 of this chapter.

Summary

Lakatos establishes a compromise between the goals of progress that lie at the heart of the rational scientific method and the actual practices of scientists. This approach acknowledges the importance of studies of scientific communities, but also argues that the relativism and the treatment of scientific knowledge as a social product offer an inadequate foundation for identifying useful knowledge and for making progress.

5   Reassessing rationality and relativism: towards a conclusion

There is a tendency for critical rationalists (such as Popper and Lakatos) to be presented in complete opposition to relativists (such as Kuhn, Feyerabend and Collins). However, as we discussed in the last section, this oversimplifies the differences and similarities between their approaches to science. Consider Figure 5.13. All of the philosophers represented below disagree with each other about what science involves and what knowledge

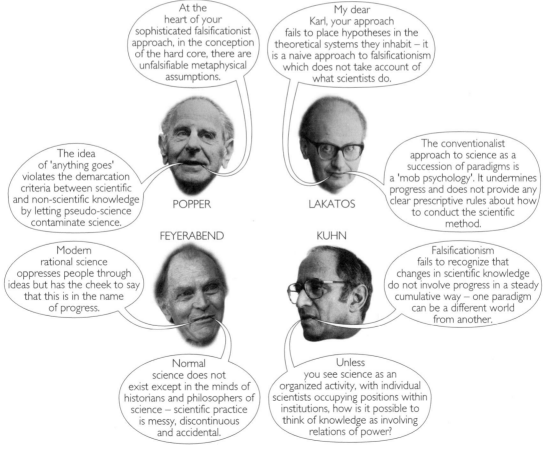

Figure 5.13   Philosophers like to argue a great deal ...

should be about. They disagree, in particular, on the role of falsification, whether progress is possible, the relationship between theory and observation, the role of scientific communities, and the relationship between science and freedom. Now consider Figure 5.14 on the connections between these positions. Actually, the disagreements only make sense when we consider the common terrain on which they stand (in other words, they agree on a great deal). Perhaps we need to reconsider the tendency to think of simple oppositional debates between rational science and relativism.

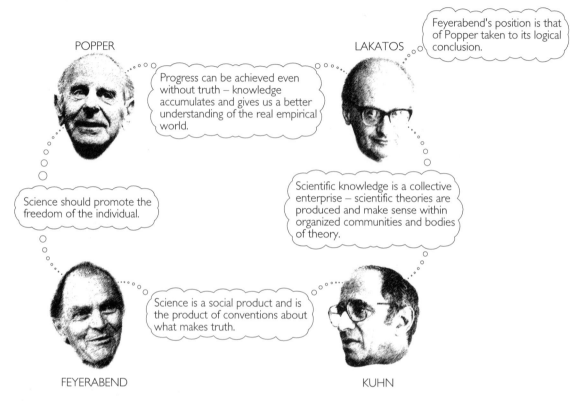

Figure 5.14   ... but we sometimes forget how much they agree.

So you can see that the tendency to set up Popper and Lakatos against Kuhn and Feyerabend misses a great deal. Rom Harré and Michael Krausz provide a useful alternative to the tendency to treat the difference between rationality and relativism as one of irreconcilable opposition. In *Varieties of Relativism* (1996), Harré and Krausz ask the question: is knowledge accepted as universal, objective and having definite foundations, *or* is it tied to particular social contexts, subjectively constructed and without firm foundations? For our purposes, let's accept the claim that there are no firm foundations to knowledge and that science is constructed within definite historically located cultures. Let's also accept the bold relativist view that this is a universal claim which applies to all forms of knowledge. We are still making a bold universal claim about science (the opposition doesn't work!). Once we have suspended our belief in the high status of scientific knowledge in Western culture, this leads us to question what social scientists have attempted to do. In particular, if natural scientists fail to live up to the standards of science, then why should social scientists try to copy them?

You can see how knowledge is situated by looking back at the examples of the scientific racist approach and positivist criminology in Chapter 3.

READING A
The emotionally disturbed child as the family scapegoat

Ezra F. Vogel and Norman W. Bell

The phenomenon of scapegoating is as old as human society. ... It is the purpose of this paper to examine the same phenomenon within families, by viewing an emotionally disturbed child as an embodiment of certain types of conflicts between parents. This pattern is a special case of a common phenomenon, the achievement of group unity through the scapegoating of a particular member. It is, perhaps, more widely known that a group may achieve unity through projection of hostilities to the outside, but there are also a large number of cases where members of a particular group are able to achieve unity through scapegoating a particular member of that group. Thus, the deviant within the group may perform a valuable function for the group, by channelling group tensions and providing a basis for solidarity.

The notion that the family is in large part responsible for the emotional health of the child is a compelling one in contemporary behavioural science. By and large, however, the research has focused largely on the mother–child relationship [and] the personality and developmental history of the mother. Recently an attempt has also been made to treat the father–child relationship, again largely in terms of the personality and developmental history of the father. While in clinical practice there is some awareness of family dynamics, in the literature, the family has largely been treated simply as a collection of personalities, and the child's personality development has been seen almost exclusively as a direct result of the separate personalities of his parents. Rarely is the interaction of parents treated as significant ... Even when broader cultural patterns have been considered, childhood development has been related to childrearing practices and socialization into the culture, with little consideration of the family as the mediating unit. Data for this paper are derived from the intensive study of a small group of 'disturbed' families, each with an emotionally disturbed child, and a matched group of 'well' families. ...

It is our contention that scapegoating is produced by the existence of tensions between parents which have not been satisfactorily resolved in other ways. The spouses in the disturbed families had deep fears about their marital relationship and about the partner's behavior. They did not feel they could predict accurately how the other would respond to their own behavior. Yet, the other's response was of very great importance and was thought to be potentially very damaging. The partners did not feel they could deal with the situation by direct communication, because this might be too dangerous, and they resorted to manipulations of masking, evading, and the like. ...

The Rationalization of Scapegoating

When a scapegoating situation was established, a relatively stable equilibrium of the family was achieved. However, there were difficulties in maintaining the equilibrium. Parents had considerable guilt about the way they treated the child, and when the child was identified as disturbed by neighbors, teachers, doctors, or other outside agencies, pressure was brought to bear for some action to be taken. ...

One way in which the parents rationalized their behavior was to define themselves, rather than the children, as victims. They stressed how much difficulty there was with coping with all the problems posed by their child. For example, mothers of bed-wetters complained about the problems of keeping sheets clean and the impossibility of the child staying over-night at friends' or relatives' homes. Such rationalizations seemed to relieve some of the guilt for criticizing the children and served as a justification for continued expressions of annoyance toward the children.

Another way was to emphasize how fortunate their children really were. For most of these parents, the standard of living provided for their children was much higher than the standard of living they enjoyed when they were children. One of the central complaints of these parents, particularly the fathers, was that the children wanted too much and got much more than the parents ever got when they were children. This was seen by the parents as a legitimate excuse for depriving their children of the toys, privileges, and other things they wanted and for refusing to recognize the children's complaints that they were not getting things. ... In general, these parents were reluctant to admit that their child had an emotional disturbance. ... Hence, what was needed, in their view, was not consideration, advice and help, but a 'lesson' in how to behave.

Functions and Dysfunctions of Scapegoating

... For the parents, scapegoating served as a personality-stabilizing process. While the parents of these children did have serious internal conflicts, the projection of these difficulties onto the children served to minimize and control them. Thus, in spite of their personality difficulties, the parents were able to live up to their commitments to the wider society, expressing a minimum of their difficulties in the external economic and political systems. Most of the parents were able to maintain positions as steady workers and relatively respectable community members. ...

While the scapegoating of a child is effective in controlling major sources of tensions within the family, when a child becomes emotionally disturbed, this leads to disturbing secondary complications. ... One dysfunction is that certain realistic problems and extra tasks are created for the family. The child does require special care and attention [and] the parents must expend time and money in providing this. [The child] may develop mechanisms of fighting back and punishing his parents for the way they treat him. Often the child becomes very skilled in arousing his parents' anxieties or in consciously bungling something his parents want him to do. ...

While the functions of the scapegoat within the nuclear family clearly outweigh his dysfunctions, this is typically not the case with the child's relationship outside the nuclear family. While the family gives the child sufficient support to maintain his role in the family, the use of him as a scapegoat is often incompatible with ... associations outside the nuclear family in relationships with peers and his teachers at school. It is at this time that many referrals to psychiatric clinics are made. While the child's behavior was perfectly tolerable to the parents before, his behavior suddenly becomes intolerable.

Source: Vogel and Bell, 1968, pp.412–4, 422–6.

READING B
Three social psychologies

Experimental social psychology

Patrick McGhee

Experimental social psychology is the dominant form of social psychology in North America and Europe ... The perspective of experimental social psychology is that the most scientifically efficient and intellectually rigorous method for understanding human social behaviour involves assuming that:

- social behaviour is objectively describable and measurable

- social behaviour does not just happen spontaneously, randomly, chaotically or mysteriously but is caused by a range of factors internal and external to individuals

- relationships between these factors and behaviour are regular (i.e. lawful) in a way which generally holds true for most people, most of the time.

It is further assumed that these relationships are only to be discovered through carefully controlled empirical investigations, preferably *experiments*. These 'laws' (though few experimental social psychologists would actually use the term in any unqualified way) are of the form 'Everything else being equal, increases in variable x (e.g. frustration) will lead to increases in variable y (e.g. aggressiveness)'.

Experimental social psychologists, however, do not believe that their scientific method is the *only* legitimate method, or that *all* social psychological questions can be answered by this method, or that human beings are *just* like machines, or that total objectivity is *ever* possible, or that people *always* tell the truth in questionnaires, or that structural and historical forces do *not* shape and constrain our social behaviour, or that their work is *totally* free from personal biases, or that it is *only* a matter of time before all the puzzles of our social being will be solved through experimental methods. The most compelling value of experimental social psychologists is that the scientific approach is *pragmatically* the best way of making definite progress in the study of social behaviour. ...

There is no progress without *some* common agreement on methods and evaluative criteria. Without controlled empirical studies, clear theories, specific testable hypotheses and laws, it is very difficult to enter into any intelligent dialogue about, say, depression and aggression. Non-experimental social psychologists can write very persuasively about subjective experiences, cultural trends and authenticity ... The problem is that, from the point of view of the experimental psychologist, these subjective interpretations of personal, public or cultural experiences are just too unreliable, too ambiguous and too untestable to use as the foundations for the systematic study of human social behaviour.

Source: McGhee, 1998, pp.7–8.

Humanistic and experiential social psychology

Richard Stevens

The concern of an experiential, humanistic social psychology is to ground the study of personal and social life in the actualities of lived experience. Our personal worlds, as we experience them, should be our starting point and the point to which we constantly return to check out the understanding we are developing. If that sounds obvious to you, it has not been the way that psychology has typically worked. ...

The use of scientific methods, such as experimentation, means that only certain kinds of problems can be investigated and that they have to be looked at in a special way. The behaviours concerned have to be isolated and expressed in some measurable way and as testable hypotheses. What comes out is the provisional and, usually, probablistic establishment of a causal link or effect. The problem, however, is that such results are usually far removed from people as we know them [and] encourages us to think of people as objects and to replace useful wisdom with esoteric jargon. ...

So how does experiential humanistic social psychology approach its subject matter: what does it do? Its starting point is not assumptions about what methods to employ but about the nature of the lived reality of experience, which, it argues, is quite different from the material world.

- This approach regards people's *experience* and the *meanings* they attribute to their actions and that of others as the core subject matter of social psychology. Behaviour always has to be interpreted to be made meaningful. So the idea of behaviour which is objectively observable and analysable is regarded as a myth. ...

- An experiential approach assumes that lived experience involves a greater or lesser degree of *active construction*. Although many factors influence and help to make us what we are, we are not simply the determined products of the forces that act upon us. A particular feature about the experience of being a person is that we are always in the process of becoming. We are never fixed or finalized: there is always the possibility of change, and we ourselves are the *agents* of change both for ourselves, others and the world around us. ...

- We are embodied beings: biological factors and unconscious influences both play a role in determining our feelings and actions. Our relationship with others and the culture in which we are immersed also affect both what we are and what we can become. We need to look at, and try to become aware of, the interplay of these varied influences in our reflexive experience of ourselves. ...

- Experiential social psychology acknowledges and respects individual uniqueness; no two of us are quite the same. Paradoxically, there is also a focus on fundamental aspects of being a person, such as our capacity for choice and our awareness of mortality – what are often called the *existential* issues of life. ...

The core of experiential social psychology is to develop a discipline which will help us to make sense of our conscious experience of personal being and relationships, and provide a basis for enhancing the ways in which we experience and live our lives.

Source: Stevens, 1998, pp.9–10.

Critical social psychology

Margaret Wetherell

Social psychology should be a social science, not an imitation natural science. We belong with disciplines such as sociology, politics and cultural studies rather than with physics, chemistry and astronomy. Our methods, research aims and theories should reflect the *particular* nature of social action, difficult though this is. We should work with and study the ambiguities, fluidity and openness of social life rather than try to repress these in a fruitless chase for experimental control and scientific respectability.

The social context is a vague term and sometimes, particularly in laboratory experiments, it is taken to mean just the presence of an audience or one or more bystanders in the person's environment. It should mean much more than this, in my view. Social influences are pervasive and inescapable. The social context is structured by power inequalities; it is an *organized* way of life which includes the material environment, technology and modes of economic production as well as language, meanings, ideologies and culture. Social psychologists should study not just the immediate effects of one person upon another, but relationships built up over time, family life, our broader communities, reference groups and the collective history of our society. ...

Social psychologists should be studying topics such as identity and the development of a sense of self in this social matrix. We should be looking at representations, stereotypes and cultural images and the way these act back and define people. Our research should have an immediate social relevance. We should be looking at gender, ethnicity and class and the way the structuring and organization of society (including conflicts between groups) directly impact on people's experiences, thoughts and feelings. ...

The term 'critical' suggests that social psychology should not stand on the sidelines of society. Research is a value-laden activity, from the choice of questions to investigate through to the interpretation of results. Social psychology should not just be a *moral* science, it should be a *political* science. Research is rarely neutral. We should not be afraid to be critical and see our work as part of a process of social change.

Source: Wetherell, 1998, pp.11–12.

READING C
Theorizing the economy

Economic paradigms

Howard R. Vane and John L. Thompson

In the 1930s the central problem facing economists was the need to provide an explanation of, and remedy for, the severe unemployment which prevailed at that time. ... Keynes put forward the view that unemployment reflected a state of deficient aggregate demand [total spending]. Since government expenditure is an important component of aggregate demand Keynesians believed that an increase in government expenditure would have a strong and direct effect in reducing the level of unemployment. ...

The revival of the belief in the potency of monetary policy that has occurred since the 1960s has largely been associated with ... (i) the importance of controlling the money supply and (ii) the need to follow a monetary rule in the conduct of monetary policy in order to avoid economic instability. During the 1950s through to the mid-1960s, instability in Western capitalist economies was largely reflected in the problem of inflation ... whereas in contrast many economies have experienced not only high rates of inflation but also high levels of unemployment since the end of the 1960s. ... Monetarists have argued that the inflation of the post-war years was stimulated by the widespread adoption of cheap-money policies and resulted from excessive money creation. Monetarists believe that most of the disturbances which affect the economy are monetary in origin. ... From this belief arises the first of two policy prescriptions central to monetarist analysis, namely that the authorities should seek to control the money supply. The second ... is that the authorities should follow a monetary rule rather than pursue discretionary monetary policy. ...

Although monetarism implies non-intervention in macroeconomic policies involving the management of aggregate demand, intervention especially on a micro basis is quite compatible with monetarist analysis of how the economy works. [For monetarists] the natural rate of unemployment is determined by the structure of ... the economy and by the institutional framework of the labour market. Monetarists argue that if governments wish to reduce the natural rate (i.e. achieve higher employment levels) they should pursue microeconomic policies towards improving the structure of the labour market in order to increase (i) the efficiency of labour markets and (ii) the occupational and geographical mobility of labour. ...

Keynesians argue [however] that the economy is inherently unstable and subject to fluctuations between long periods of unemployment and stagnation and periods of rapid expansion and inflation. [They] argue that (i) in the case of a disturbance the economy may take too long to return to the neighbourhood of equilibrium, and (ii) consequently discretionary demand-management policies are necessary to maintain the economy at a high and stable level of employment. ... The major issue dividing monetarists and Keynesians today concerns the role of macroeconomic stabilization policy whereas monetarists argue that the economy is inherently stable (unless disturbed by erratic monetary growth) and that policy should be carried out according to rules.

Source: Vane and Thompson, 1982, pp.307–12.

Economic crisis: the Marxist view

E.K. Hunt and Howard J. Sherman

It was this ceaseless drive to accumulate more capital that created many of the contradictions to capitalist development. The capitalist would begin with the acquisition of more machines and tools of the types that were currently being used. This would require a proportional increase in the number of workers employed in order to operate the new equipment. But the capitalist had been able to keep the wage rate at the subsistence level only because there existed what Marx called an 'industrial reserve army' of unemployed labor, which was living below the subsistence level and striving to take jobs that would pay a mere subsistence wage. Therefore, capitalists usually had no problem in keeping wage rates down. As the industrial expansion took place, however, the increasing demand for labor soon depleted the ranks of the reserve. When this happened, the capitalist began to find that he had to pay higher wages to get enough labor. ...

The most profitable course of action seemed to be changing the techniques of production by introducing new labor-saving machinery so that each laborer would then be working with more capital, and output per laborer would be increased. This labor-saving investment would enable the capitalist to expand output with the same or an even smaller work force [and] the reserve army was replenished by workers displaced by the new productive techniques. [The] concentration of wealth and economic power in the hands of fewer and fewer capitalists was another important consequence of capital accumulation. ... Competition between capitalists tended to create a situation in which the strong either crushed or absorbed the weak [and] to remain competitive, a firm would constantly have to increase the productivity of its laborers. ...

Business cycles or crises would occur regularly and with increasing severity as the capitalist economy developed. There would be a long-run tendency for the rate of profit to fall, and this would exacerbate the other problems of capitalism. Industrial power would become increasingly concentrated in fewer and fewer giant monopolistic and oligopolistic firms, and wealth would become concentrated in the hands of fewer and fewer capitalists. The plight of the laborer would steadily deteriorate. Given these increasingly bad conditions, the system could not be perpetuated. Eventually, life under capitalism would become so intolerable that workers would revolt, overthrow the whole system, and create a more rational socialist economy.

Source: Hunt and Sherman, 1981, pp.90–4.

READING D
Methodological pluralism

Bruce Caldwell

The approach to economic methodology advocated here is labelled 'methodological pluralism' because it takes as a starting assumption that no universally applicable, logically compelling method of theory appraisal exists. (Or, more correctly, even if it exists, we can never be sure that we have found it, even if we have.) ...

- The starting point of methodological analysis is the rational reconstruction of the methodological content both of the writings of economic methodologists and of the various research programs within the discipline.

- The next step is the critical assessment of the methodological content [to] highlight the strengths (if any) and limitations of the particular approach under examination. ...

A practitioner of normal science working in a well-established research tradition can safely assert that the choice problem is solved. Using the techniques he learned in graduate school, he busies himself doing substantive work in economics, applying those methods to various problems, solving puzzles in a good Kuhnian style. For such a scientist, explicit discussions of methodology seem utterly inane. When pushed to discuss methodological matters, however, the same scientist often responds that methodological debate is useless because the questions asked are unanswerable. 'No one ever agrees on methodological questions, so why waste time studying them?' he is apt to counter, 'And besides, only people working in fringe areas, like Institutionalists or Marxists, ever talk about methodology, and those people shouldn't even be considered scientists!'

When the research tradition in which this normal scientist works breaks down in a revolutionary period, he may briefly turn to methodology or to history to see what went wrong. What he wants to find is some definitive answer about the 'correct' method. What he discovers instead is a plurality of answers, each with its own weaknesses and strengths. This reinforces his prior autagonistic attitude toward methodological discussion, but luckily for him, it is not necessary to ruminate over the idiocy of methodology for too long. A new paradigm emerges, with its own accepted methods and procedures, he can happily busy himself with substantive work once more. This caricature of the normal scientist with anti-methodological biases is harshly drawn, but sadly enough, the general attitude attributed to him is not all that hard to find.

- [We should engage in] the critical discussion of the strengths (if any) and limitations of the rationally reconstructed methodological positions under examination.

- There are a number of research programs within economics whose epistemological and methodological foundations differ radically from those of mainstream theory. ... This approach ensures that novelty is promoted, that criticism is not dogmatic, and that a dialogue takes place among members of alternative research programs.

Answers to some possible objections

1 The initial assumption is wrong; methodologists should research for a universally applicable method of choice. A variation of this objection reads, 'Thus-and-so methodology (falsificationism, a priorism, instrumentalism, and so on) is the best methodology for economic science to follow.'

   The response of the methodological pluralist must be – convince me.

2 Methodological pluralism, if taken seriously, undermines all substantive work in economic science. How can a working economist try to make a contribution in his chosen field if he is always aware that the methodology he uses is open to criticism?

   The response of the methodological pluralists is that substantive work in economics need not halt; neither angst nor inaction are necessary byproducts of methodological pluralism. ...

3 Methodological pluralism, if taken seriously, leads to methodological anarchism, under which any particular methodological view could claim legitimacy.

   There are safeguards against this outcome. Simply put, methodological discussion is as much a form of persuasion as it is a means of ensuring that problems are viewed from different perspectives.

Source: Caldwell, 1994, pp.245–51.

READING E
Two sociological perspectives on science

Michael Mulkay

In the literature which considers the place of science within the sociology of knowledge, two contrasting perspectives are to be found.

Perspective one

Scientific knowledge is regarded as epistemologically unique – as consisting basically of observation statements which have been firmly established by the controlled, rigorous procedures of scientific method. The corpus of certified scientific knowledge is thought to represent, with increasing accuracy and completeness, the truth about the physical world. Because scientific knowledge is seen as an objective account of the real world, it is assumed that sociological analysis must stop when it has shown how the social organization of science enables scientists to observe and report the world objectively, with little sign of the bias and distortion which are thought to arise in other areas of cultural production through the impact of social and personal factors.

Within this perspective, the close analysis of the development of scientific knowledge can be left almost entirely to philosophers of science and to historians of ideas ... and social influences can intrude into the actual intellectual content of science only when science has been *distorted* by non-scientific pressures. Sociologists interested in the creation of scientific *knowledge*, as distinct from scientific error, have therefore come to concentrate, not on the intellectual content of science, but on the normative structure which is thought to make objective knowledge possible.

The norms of science have customarily been conceived as a defensive barrier, which protects the scientific community from intellectually distorting influences. ... General conformity to such normative principles as impartiality, emotional neutrality and, particularly, universalism, is seen as necessarily implied by the nature of scientific knowledge. ...

Perspective two

The procedures and conclusions of science are, like all other cultural products, the contingent outcome of interpretative social acts. It is argued that the empirical findings of science are intrinsically inconclusive and that the factual as well as the theoretical assertions of science depend on speculative and socially derived assumptions [for] the institutionalized norms of science are merely one part of a much broader repertoire of social formulations, which scientists employ as resources in negotiating the acceptance of specialized knowledge-claims. ...

Scientific research is never merely a matter of registering an objective world. It always involves the attribution of meaning to complex sets of clues generated by scientists' actions on the physical world; and such attribution of meaning is not carried out in a social vacuum. ... Instead, the propositions advanced by scientists are regarded, sociologically, as claims which have been deemed to be adequate by particular groups of actors in specific social and cultural contexts. ...

The second perspective on science does not lead us into intellectual chaos. We are not impelled to abandon all criteria of validity, nor to accept that all knowledge-claims are epistemologically equal. What we do have to accept is that criteria of validity are neither pre-established, eternal or universal. They are cultural resources whose meaning has to be re-interpreted and re-created constantly in the course of social life.

Source: Mulkay, 1991, pp.90–3.

READING F
Bending the rules

Faking it to make it

Jon Turney

Incompetence, plagiarism and fraud are all scientific sins, but the greatest of these is fraud. And while evidence that it is growing more common is contentious, it is certainly starting to get more serious attention. In the United States, a score or more of fraud exposures over the past 10 years have attracted public and political attention. Although the numbers are small in comparison with the thousands of papers pouring into journal offices each year, there are enough cases to raise serious concern about a multi-billion dollar industry with no effective quality control.

It is easy to understand the concern. New experimental results in science should face merciless criticism from the researcher's peers. A freshly published paper may be attacked for an implausible interpretation of data, for exaggerating their significance, for neglecting an obscure effect which explains them away, or for ignoring other results which contradict them. But whether the reported results concern low temperature nuclear fusion or a cure for the common cold, other researchers take it for granted that the experiments were done as described. So the smallest suggestion of fudging, trimming, sloppy recording, or even deliberate fraud makes waves far beyond the field concerned. It suggests contamination of a complex system which uses large sums of public and private money and a lot of creative energy. ...

At first sight this is curious. The number of scientific papers produced in British labs is second only to the US in most fields. And, after all, the most important scientific fakery this century ... was the work of a British scientist. The late Sir Cyril Burt believed so passionately that intelligence was inherited that he made up reams of data to prove it, and his talent for fiction was only revealed after his death. So are British researchers more honest than their US counterparts, perhaps because the pressure to publish is not quite so strong over here? It seems unlikely, with the recent growth in contract researchers all competing for a few secure jobs. Are any miscreants escaping detection? This would only be possible if the British were much less interested in uncovering fraud than the Americans – who have to cope with a larger country with attendant difficulties in checking credentials and references when researchers move around. Or are the cases of fraud which do occur simply dealt with, well, more quietly?

Evidence gathered recently by Dr. Stephen Lock, editor of the *British Medical Journal*, points firmly towards the last possibility. The results of a small survey he made last year confirm that misconduct is more common that is normally publicly acknowledged. Dr. Lock simply wrote to one professor of medicine and one of surgery in each of 29 medical institutions in Britain, plus 15 journal editors and a handful of others. Between them, their 79 confidential replies yielded 41 cases of misconduct – not an epidemic, but a worrying result all the same.

Misconduct in research, like corruption in the police force, tends to divide commentators into icebergers and body counters. Do the cases which come to light signify a huge concealed mass of malpractice, or are they the work of a few rotten apples in a clean barrel? The US experience suggests that politicians believe the system should respond to the iceberg hypothesis, while the scientific community naturally prefers body counting.

Source: Turney, 1989.

What if teacher is a cheat?

Stuart Sutherland

About 10 years ago a research grant was awarded to two professors of biology at an English university. One was to conduct experiments, the other to do the theoretical work.

The experiments were, in fact, carried out mainly by a research assistant, who one day approached the theoretician with a puzzled look and some notebooks full of carefully tabulated results. 'Look at these,' he said, 'I showed them to Professor X and he's altered some of the figures. Do you think that's all right?' The theoretical professor did not think it all right and the case went up to the Vice-Chancellor. One might think that the university would sack someone caught cheating in flagrante delicto, but not a bit of it. The delinquent professor was just told he could not apply for any more research grants and that he should try to be a good boy in future.

In the last 20 years, dozens of such cases of scientific fraud have been exposed in the US, but to my knowledge only two have been made public in Britain – Robert Gullis of Birmingham University, who fudged data on brain cells, and the notorious Sir Cyril Burt, who it now appears may not, after all, have been a complete fraud.

It is unlikely that British scientists are less prone to cheating than their American colleagues: indeed most senior British scientists know of cases of fraud that have never been exposed. This is more likely to be due to our harsher libel laws, to British reticence and decency, and to a reluctance to make trouble.

So how common is cheating in science? Surveys show that both in Britain and America, only about one in four scientists are prepared to provide their original data when requested. Unless there is something to hide, there is no reason for such refusal. One can only conclude that scientific fraud is extremely widespread. Moreover, it is not limited to minor figures: the verdict of history is that Ptolemy, Galileo, Newton, Dalton and Mendel all tampered with some of their data. ...

Why then do some scientists cheat? Not everyone, and perhaps not anyone, pursues science merely out of a quest for truth. At the best, people are heavily biased towards proving their own theories right, but they also want promotion, research grants and glory. Since all depend on publishing, the pressure to publish is enormous. It is obviously quicker to fake data than to run experiments and you can be sure of getting the desired result. The young researcher has to please his superiors, who want the glory of putting their names on his papers. If, however, the research worker cheats, his professor may get egg on his face, as happened in the Harvard case where the professor in question put his name to papers that were obviously false.

Cheating is particularly common in the following circumstances. Someone may be working on a problem and learn, either on the grapevine or by reading an unpublished copy of someone's paper, that it has been solved. In science, priority is all and if the other person's paper comes out first, he will get all the credit. The easiest thing to do is to invent your own research and publish them before the other fellow – you know they will be right because you have already seen his.

There is little risk of being caught ... except for the most important findings, little attempt is made to replicate there is no kudos in redoing someone else's experiments. And failures to replicate are usually never published, since few journals or readers are interested in negative findings. ...

Another extremely common way of cheating is to run an experiment over and over again until the desired result is obtained and then publish it, quietly forgetting the negative instances. Other scientists get things wrong, not by cheating but by unconsciously seeing what they are looking for even when it is not there – or failing to see what is there.

Source: Sutherland, 1989.

READING G
The schizophrenia research programme

Mary Boyle

We need, first, to identify the programme's 'hard core' – that part which the programme's protagonists have decided to treat as irrefutable. Second, we need to identify the major theoretical adjustments by which this core has been protected from anomalous and inconsistent data. And, third, we need to devise whether these adjustments represent progression or degeneration. I will argue that the schizophrenia research programme is in a degenerating phase. As it is in this phase, according to Lakatos, that a programme's hard core becomes vulnerable to challenges, I shall also briefly mention recent challenges to this hard core and some alternative research programmes.

Hard Core and Protective Belt

As Lakatos emphasizes, the hard core of a research programme will not be systematically recorded in the literature under the heading 'hard core'. Rather, we can discover what is a programme's hard core only by an analysis of the assumptions made by researchers; of their behaviour in relation to their research programme and those parts of the programme they explicitly or implicitly protect in the face of anomalous and inconsistent data. The traditional literature on schizophrenia suggests that many aspects of the programme are not seen as irrefutable. These include whether the outcome of the 'disorder' is good or poor; whether the 'age of onset' is invariably young; which particular brain sites or chemicals might play a major causal role; what are the cognitive characteristics of schizophrenia and the degree of overlap between schizophrenia and other psychiatric diagnoses. These then, can be seen as part of the programme's positive heuristic, of its protective belt, which may be changed to accommodate new data. What, it appears, has not changed since the introduction of the concept of schizophrenia ... is the belief in a recognizable pattern of abnormal phenomena which is symptomatic of brain dysfunction and which, perhaps with some adjustments because we are dealing here with mind and behaviour, can be conceptualized, diagnosed and treated in a manner similar to that of medical disorders. ...

Lakatos has emphasized that in every research programme, anomalies abound. It is therefore not constructive to list every anomaly or inconsistency in the schizophrenia research programme and to use these against the programme. Nor is it constructive to examine every theoretical adjustment ever made in the face of anomalous data and to banish the programme if any of these fail to meet Popper's criteria. What is important is to identify the major and persistent anomalies and inconsistencies and to examine the main strategies used to accommodate them. It seems reasonable to argue that the major and persistent anomalies in the schizophrenia research programme lie in its failure to produce a reliable definition of its major concept and in its failure to demonstrate, after nearly a century of effort, a reliable relationship between a diagnosis of schizophrenia and any aspect of brain structure and function, far less to demonstrate a causal relationship between brain abnormality and the behaviour of those with a diagnosis of schizophrenia. ...

Progressive or Degenerating?

Wing (1988) offers two major theoretical adjustments to protect the concept of schizophrenia and the biological assumptions which surround it. The first suggests that the goal of reliability is within sight: he describes 'hard won progress towards reliability and comparability ...' (p.327). This adjustment certainly cannot be seen as content increasing or progressive as it contains no novel theoretical or empirical information but merely bids us to be patient while researchers move towards the goal of a reliable definition of their major concept. ... It is rather as if researchers on a Newtonian research programme argued that we must retain as part of the hard core the axiom that the mass of bodies is constant, because even now researchers were working towards agreement on a definition of mass. ... It can be argued, then, that it is a contradiction in terms, at least in Popper's and Lakatos' terms, to posit as part of the hard core of a research programme a concept which implies that reliable observations have been made, and then to defend this hard core by arguing that we are progressing towards making those same reliable observations.

Wing's second theoretical adjustment is to suggest that it is the lack of non-invasive methods of studying brain function which is 'chiefly responsible for slow progress' towards establishing a reliable relationship between diagnoses of schizophrenia and brain structure or function (Wing, p.327). Lakatos has suggested that adjustments like this, which point to hoped-for technical advances should not always be regarded as representing degeneration although they do not really offer excess content or novel predictions ... Which aspects of brain structure and functions are to be measured and in what terms? How exactly will these relate to a diagnosis of schizophrenia? As Jackson (1990) has commented, virtually all lobes of the cortex – and various parts of the sub cortex – have been mentioned in 'schizophrenia' research. Similarly, many brain chemicals have been seen as holding the key to understanding this 'illness'. None of these brain sites or brain chemicals has found consistent empirical support. Nor is there good evidence that the majority of those diagnosed as schizophrenic has any brain dysfunction before drug treatment. If we add to this the implications of Wing's first adjustment – that researchers have not yet reliably specified which group of phenomena particular brain sites are to be associated with, then the scale of the problem becomes apparent. ...

It can reasonably be argued, then, that the major theoretical adjustments by which anomalous and inconsistent data have been accommodated within the schizophrenia research programme do not represent scientific progression ... It has been argued by Popper and Lakatos, however, that research programmes are not abandoned because they are degenerating or because their hard core is shown to be problematic. Rather, research programmes are abandoned because a 'better', i.e. content increasing, alternative becomes available. A number of alternatives to the schizophrenia research programme have in fact been suggested (see Boyle, 1990). ...

The final problem I want to consider which faces those advocating alternatives to 'schizophrenia' research, is that of the relationship between scientific progress and research methods. The traditional schizophrenia research programme has been closely modelled on research in the natural sciences, with its emphasis on quantification, measurement, objectivity, the separation of subject and experimenter and the creation of general laws. The protagonists of alternative programmes have not only challenged the concept of schizophrenia; they have argued variously for the need to pose different research questions, for the use of different methods and for the adoption of theoretical frameworks different from the traditional individualized, reductionist models.

References

BOYLE, M. (1990) *Schizophrenia – A Scientific Delusion?*, London, Routledge.

JACKSON, H.F. (1990) 'Are There Biological Markers of Schizophrenia?' in Bentall, R.P. (ed.) *Reconstructing Schizophrenia*, London, Routledge.

WING, J.K. (1988) 'Abandoning What?' *British Journal of Clinical Psychology*, 27, pp.325–8.

Source: Boyle, 1994, pp.401–4.

Chapter 6
Language, Discourse and Culture: Rethinking Representation in the Social Sciences

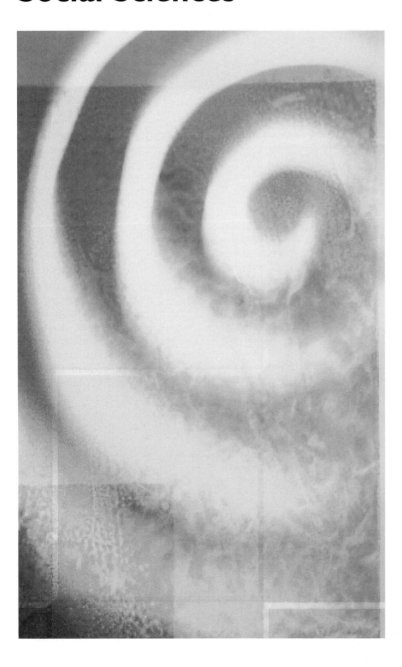

Contents

1 Introduction   231

2 Defining language: structure and meaning   234

2.1 Language and structure   234

2.2 Language and cultural representation   240

3 Language and discourse   246

3.1 Discourse and analysis in social psychology   247

3.2 Post-structuralism and discourse   252

4 Understanding culture   260

4.1 Culture as a way of life   264

4.2 Culture as a contested space   266

5 No conclusions, just some pointers   271

Reading A
    The uses of community   *Jonathan Potter and Margaret Wetherell*   272

Reading B
    Representation and discourse   *Stuart Hall*   273

Reading C
    Political discourse: homosexuality and its metaphors   *Anna Marie Smith* 274

Reading D
    Contested places, contested boundaries   *Doreen Massey*   275

1   Introduction

So far we have considered the story of science and explored a variety of approaches which have claimed to be scientific. We have also stepped back from these theories and begun to consider the overall story-line of social science. In particular, we have followed the impact of positivism, especially the claim that it is possible to study human beings in the same way as natural things and the responses this claim has generated. We have also considered how it has been contested on the grounds that human beings are different from natural things. The usual arguments against studying people in this way are founded upon the assumptions that people are rational, that they find meaning in what they do, that they communicate and that they can even shape the world. Whereas the positivist approach sees useful knowledge as a mirror reflection of things in the world, we consider now what it means to construct accounts of the world through language, discourse and culture. More specifically, we address the way in which ideas about social existence are seen as complex representations which have a cultural significance.

Rather than seeing language, discourse and culture as a set of tools or a bag of tricks, in this chapter we explore them as ways of thinking about 'representation' – that is, ways of producing meaning. In short, we examine the complexities of representation in social scientific practice. We begin with the more abstract concerns about what is involved in a language structure and how meanings are produced through the relations between words, before going on to consider how language is used to communicate meaning and how this is regulated through discourses. In drawing upon the techniques of discourse analysis, we are in a better position to understand the effects of the uses of language in concrete cultural conditions. I will argue that understanding language, discourse and culture is central to understanding people and that social scientists ignore these complexities at their peril.

In the last three decades of the twentieth century, all the disciplines in the social sciences have experienced a fundamental reappraisal of their basic assumptions, theories and methods. The most significant common feature of this reappraisal is the recognition that 'culture' deserves much more serious attention as an object of study in its own right and this has produced a reassessment of the linguistic, discursive and cultural conditions of social research. Social scientists have come to realize that many of the categories they use and apply make sense only within definite language systems and that academic communities themselves are involved in the construction and reconstruction of these language systems. This has been described as a discursive turn or 'cultural turn' in the social sciences. There remains a great deal of disagreement about what this cultural turn means: should we see culture as central to social science or perhaps just take the cultural dimension more seriously alongside other dimensions? In any case, it is clear that the social sciences have to come to terms with these developments. This chapter offers an introduction to some of the approaches involved in this cultural turn.

See Chapter 2, section 2.

In Chapter 2 we saw that, in order to understand the representations of science, we have to pay special attention to the analogies and metaphors involved in communicating scientific ideas. You already have, then, some experience of using the skills and techniques developed by the approaches covered in the present chapter. Of course, the meanings of culture and language are many, so later on you will also find a guide to some of the uses which are relevant to understanding social scientific practice. This chapter addresses the most crucial question in contemporary debates in the philosophy of the social sciences and social scientific practice: why is language so important to the study of the social sciences? In particular, this chapter explores the different ways in which language and the associated ideas of discourse and culture have been understood and what part they play in social scientific research.

You will have to reassess some of the things that were taken for granted by the scientific approaches to studying people that you considered earlier. In the previous chapters you were thinking primarily about the role of science in mediating the relationship between 'knowledge' and 'reality'. The approaches so far have taken for granted the existence of a distinction between knowledge and the real world, even if they disagree about the precise relationship between them or what the real world is like. This is a product of the way the human imagination has often been characterized as a barrier to knowing clearly what is going on. At times, philosophers have suggested that if we apply certain rules we can get closer to reality. A good example of this is the way the rules for knowledge construction were applied by logical positivists, who believed that their **synthetic** statements are a direct reflection of empirical experience. However, this demonstrates a simplistic understanding of what is involved in representation. In particular, it assumes that the meanings of words are fixed and universal, that values are separate from factual statements and that knowledge can be established as true. Even the **conventionalist** approaches considered in Chapter 5, which are much more cautious about truth, tend to assume that we can achieve a better account of scientific research by looking at the 'real' empirical activities of scientists at work rather than the ideal models of science proposed by philosophers.

Only through language can we make sense of the relationship between knowledge and reality.

See Chapter 2 on the story of science.

In this chapter you encounter ideas which challenge these assumptions and offer a better understanding of recent developments in the social sciences. In particular, you are asked to think of the fundamental building blocks of science – such as 'knowledge' and 'reality' – as linguistic categories. The next three sections each address the role of representation, although in different ways and with different conceptual tools (illustrated in Figure 6.1).

- Section 2 examines the implications of taking 'language' seriously in the social sciences. We see how meanings depend upon relations within a language structure and, in particular, consider the insights of structural linguistics and semiology.

- Section 3 explores the uses of the idea of 'discourse' in the social sciences. Here, the focus is upon the production and communication of meanings and we investigate two broad forms of discourse analysis, discursive psychology and post-structuralist discourse analysis.

- Finally, in Section 4 we consider the effect of the cultural turn in the social sciences by reference to just two ways of thinking about 'culture': culture as a way of life and culture as a contested space.

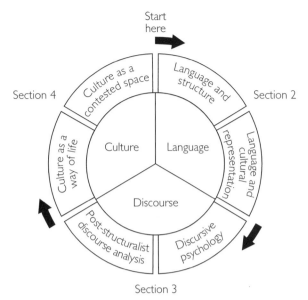

Figure 6.1   The structure of the chapter at a glance.

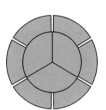

This will not only help you to keep track of where you are, but may also indicate where approaches to language, discourse and culture have something in common.

By exploring the role of language, discourse and culture in the construction of meaning, we can find that the things we take for granted are much more tentative and open to question than we have often supposed. For instance, the way we define society, inequality, culture, politics and so on have all changed significantly over time. We have only to look at Raymond Williams's *Keywords* (1983) to acquire a sense of the dramatic transformations of the meanings of the concepts which have been central to our concerns in this book (see his accounts of 'science', 'rational', 'empirical', 'society' and any others which catch your eye). For Williams, these transformations in the meanings of words are produced by the changes in the material relations of society. Some accounts of language, discourse and culture, as you will see, try to avoid establishing an external foundation or point of reference for the production of meaning. This raises the possibility that we are constantly reinventing ourselves within language, discourse and culture in quite complex ways.

In order to pursue this a little more, let's briefly consider the example of 'social inequality' in the social sciences. The meaning of inequality in the early twentieth century was often tied exclusively to class. In particular, a great deal of social research has been devoted to the meticulous reconstruction of the differences between social groups in terms of their occupational status. The occupational categories used to define class in social research (professional, managerial, routine non-manual, skilled manual, semi-skilled manual and unskilled manual) were constructed upon the general assumption that non-manual work indicated middle class and manual work indicated working class. We can see that this classification system reflected the view that working with your head was, on the whole, more highly valued than working with your hands. Of course, this is only one of many ways in which occupations have been divided. Other ways of distinguishing these groups have drawn upon evidence of differences in wealth, income, expenditure patterns, self-identity, political affiliations, lifestyle choices, housing type, education and family background, to name a few. Earlier studies even defined any household without a servant as working class; however, we wouldn't take this definition as particularly useful today.

So, although the changes in working lives have had some impact upon the way in which social researchers gave meaning to their evidence, these patterns have often emerged from the complex sets of distinctions and oppositions which allow us to make sense of social differences. For instance, the words 'upper class', 'middle class' and 'working class' are expressed – and only make sense – through the complex ways in which social differences of taste and cultural understanding are communicated. Thus we can see how cultural values have always been central to the social sciences, even if they have been unacknowledged. All social scientific knowledge is situated in particular cultures, and the categories which social scientists construct classify the world in ways which make sense for the people involved. So, the 'cultural turn' in the social sciences is not a completely new discovery but a rediscovery of something that was already there.

2   Defining language: structure and meaning

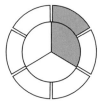

In this section we explore the ways of seeing language which have had an impact upon recent social scientific research. We concentrate upon the contributions of two linguistic theorists, Ferdinand de Saussure and Roland Barthes, in establishing the study of language as the 'science of signs'. While Saussure established the conceptual apparatus for studying language, Barthes developed these insights into a set of theoretical tools for understanding the meanings of cultural representations. We start, then, with Saussure, who wanted to place linguistics on the same footing as the natural sciences. Nevertheless, his work provides a basis for rethinking the relationship between science and language and for directly challenging the key ideas of positivist and empiricist approaches to scientific knowledge.

2.1   Language and structure

In the construction of language, human beings assign words to refer to definite things and ideas. This is possible even without speech, as demonstrated in the construction of sign languages by deaf communities. Language is both the product of speech and other acts of communication while, at the same time, serving as the precondition for speech and writing. This means that we cannot make sense of the spoken or written word without using a language system. Saussure provides us with a way of making sense of the process by examining how words become meaningful. This is exactly what science claims to be doing yet, as you have seen, scientific thought tends to assume that language is a mere reflection of things, a transparent medium depicting the truth of a situation. For Saussure, this was too simplistic a way of thinking about what people do with language.

Language systems provide the often unspoken and unwritten rules which enable people to communicate effectively.

Saussure was particularly interested in the ways in which the tacit system of rules of language enabled all participants in communication to understand each other. He distinguished **langue**, which refers to the underlying system of rules which enable us to make sense of speech, from **parole**, the utterances involved in speech. He suggested that language rules operate in much the same way as the rules for chess or Monopoly help us to make sense of the activities of the players. These rules govern the range of possible moves in a game and provide us with various clues about the intentions and strategy of the player. If we walk into the middle of a game we have no idea about what has happened before, but the rules immediately enable us to understand what is going on. Unlike chess and Monopoly however, in the language systems used in everyday life there are no clearly written rules demonstrating the concrete existence of the structure of language; we have to reconstruct this from the manifestations of speech. It is this focus on structured relations that has led to this approach being labelled 'structuralist linguistics' (Saussure, 1916/1959).

See Chapter 3, section 2.1.

Earlier, you considered the impact of the distinction between statics and dynamics in social scientific research; we find that distinction here as well. Traditional linguistics had focused on the evolution of language systems, the development of words and their gradual transformation. Saussure was concerned to challenge this exclusive concern with the study of change (diachronic analysis) and, in its place, proposed the careful and systematic study of the 'forms' and 'relations' between the constituent parts of language (synchronic analysis). To understand these relations and forms, Saussure viewed language as a 'total system' (see Hawkes, 1977, pp.19–28, for a straightforward introduction). Within a total system, the meaning of any word or utterance makes sense only in relation to the structure of the language system in question. This enabled Saussure to challenge the way language was studied as if it was made up of discrete objective things (such as nouns, verbs, adjectives) which could be observed and classified.

In order to begin to make sense of the uses of language in the social sciences, let's explore what tools Saussure offers. He starts with the images, words and sounds we use to identify things. He describes these sounds and words as signs. We often think of signs as uncomplicated ways of communicating meanings. Actually, they appear uncomplicated because, in everyday life, we already understand what they mean. For instance, if we consider traffic signs, we do not distinguish between the image we experience (like a hazard sign) and the meaning of the sign (in this case – take care, you are in danger!). However, Saussure is interested in how we come to produce meaning through signs. He argues that a *sign* is made up of two components, the signifier and the signified (see Figure 6.2).

Figure 6.2 The components of the sign.

Within the sign, the *signifier* operates as the medium, the recognizable word, sound or picture which attracts our attention and which communicates a particular message. The *signified* is this message or concept itself.

The process of communication involves an act of signification. If we concentrate on a relatively simple illustration first, we can begin to see what Saussure had in mind. When we compare the ways in which one object can be designated, we can begin to see the complexity involved, as here in the word, sound, image and gesture designating 'tree':

tree   tri:

You probably recognized the first three of these signs and you may also be familiar with the fourth. They make sense when we place them within patterns of meaningful contrasts and associations. For example:

spring   –   soil   –   tree   –   grass   –   butterfly

or within the terms of reference of a different language:

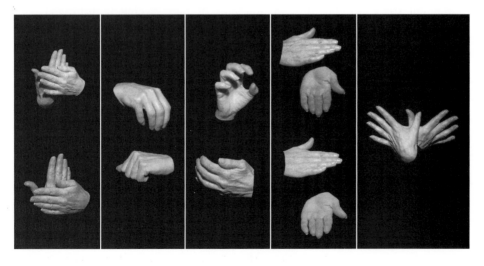

We can also consider them phonetically (a comparison of different sounds):

əˈgri: –   fli: –   tri: –   fri: –   gri:n

(agree)   (flee)   (tree)   (free)   (green)

... or visually through images:

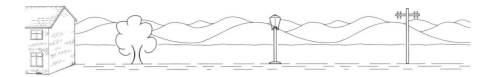

If we concentrate on the visual image of the concept of tree 🌳, without the contextual information provided above, this simple picture of the tree could also signify or represent a bush, a floret of broccoli, the back end of a sheep, a radioactive mushroom cloud, an audience's view of a cancan dancer and so on. In contemplating the relations of difference which allow us to understand the meanings of words, sounds and images, we can begin to acknowledge Saussure's main argument that 'Language is a system of interdependent terms in which the value of each term results solely from the simultaneous presence of the others' (Saussure, 1916/1959, p.114).

Saussure proposes that we should focus particularly upon two ways in which the relationships between words or signs can exist.

• Syntagmatic relations (horizontal relations), where we produce meaning by putting words together in chains.

• Associative relations (vertical relations), where words can stand in for one another; that is, they are different links which we can place in any syntagmatic chain. This still produces meaning even if the meaning is different.

If we look at a practical example, the difference between these types of relation becomes clearer.

The *monarchy* is in peril because of the collapse of public confidence.

> *royal family*
>
> *hereditary principle*
>
> *head of the sovereign state*
>
> *head of establishment*
>
> *legitimate ruler*
>
> *crown*

Within a language structure, the meaning of words is established through their relations with other words.

The meaning of the word 'monarchy' derives partly from its positioning in a succession of words (syntagmatic relationships) and partly from the relationship with other words which could operate in the same or a similar way (associative relationships). These associative relations can take the form of synonyms (identical meanings) or antonyms (opposite meanings: such as good/bad). The choice of words also eliminates other possible meanings, serving to define a word more clearly.

ACTIVITY 6.1

We have seen that any word, sound or image can mean anything – the relationship between the signifier and signified is an 'arbitrary' one. However, Saussure argued that there is one exception to this, onomatopoeia, where words such as 'plop', 'bang', 'cuckoo', 'bong' and 'swish' refer directly and unequivocally to a sound in a way which is fixed.

- Take this book and hold it in both hands. Drop it on a flat surface such as a desk or a table.
- Listen to the sound of the book making an impact on the surface and try to find at least one word which describes the sound.

You will probably describe the sound using words like 'bang' or 'slam' or 'bong' or 'flap'. Try repeating the activity just to make sure. Would words like 'plong', 'flop', 'pong', 'bing' or 'bomb' perform this task just as well?

- Now consider the following representation in Figure 6.3 of the ways in which bands of colour are understood in three different cultures.

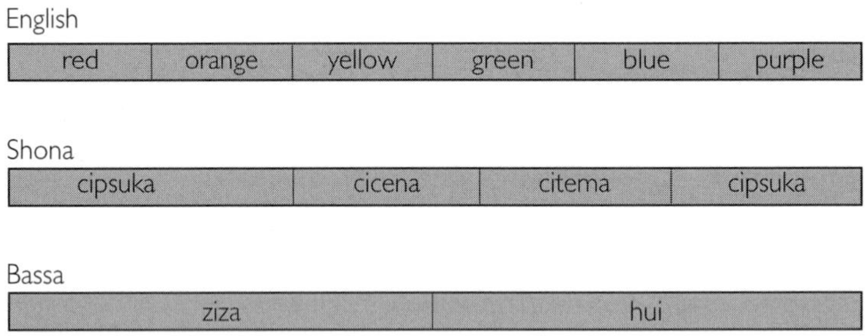

English

red	orange	yellow	green	blue	purple

Shona

cipsuka	cicena	citema	cipsuka

Bassa

ziza	hui

Figure 6.3

You can see that there is no necessary connection between the words we choose to designate a sound or band of colour and the messages which are signified to us. So Saussure's 'exception' can be seen as evidence supporting his general arguments about the way signs work (that the relationship between signifier and signified is always an arbitrary one). But there is more to think about in this example. When we use words like 'bang', 'slam', 'bong' we are usually referring to the actions involved when two objects come into violent contact. That is, we are making reference to something beyond language, but which we only make sense of through language. We return to this issue of 'reference' later in the chapter and in Chapter 7.

Once we accept that words do not reflect in the manner of a mirror the thing to which they refer, we are also led to reconsider the theoretical relationship between the signifier and the signified which make up the sign. It is the existence of the arbitrary relationship between signifier and signified within a sign which provides language both with its capacity to fix meaning temporarily (so that language appears to have a definite structure at any point in time) and to shift over time. On the one hand language systems are taken for granted by those who use them, yet on the other hand they are reproduced, modified and transformed through these uses.

There is no necessary link between a medium and a message – the relationship between a signifier and a signified is an arbitrary one.

This approach focuses our attention upon the structured patterns of differences involved in the language systems through which we represent the world. This places a particular emphasis upon the meaning of signs rather than the way in which signs are taken to refer to the world of things. It also tends to focus our attention upon the structure of language (langue) rather than the way we use language within everyday life (parole). The moment we start to consider how we use language, we also need to look at the role of cultural values. When we describe and categorize what we observe, when we classify things, we also make judgements about them. We can see something of the role of values if we move from considering 'tree' to a related but more difficult and ambiguous concept, 'nature'. Some of the implications of this can be identified when we recognize the way we see natural things and how we give them both a value and a status. When we give things a label, we also give them a standing, a position in a pecking order and an estimate of moral worth. As you may recall, the racial classification table from *Parkinsons' Scholar's Guide* demonstrates that scientific practice has involved the construction of complex hierarchies of superior and inferior states which are, in effect, the product of the values of a particular culture.

Chapter 3, section 3.1 including Figure 3.3.

If we turn to a specific example of how we see the relation between human and non-human things, such as the distinction between 'man and beast' which has prevailed in Western culture for centuries, we can see how this is full of evocative meanings. This distinction clearly attempts to separate human beings from other animals even though humans remain, of course, a particular form of animal. In this example, the word 'man' derives meaning, in part, from its negation of the word 'beast' (in addition to its other relations of cultural difference, such as the way the meaning of the sign 'man' is dependent upon its relation to the sign 'woman'). To be a 'beast', as conventionally understood, is to be savage; it has no moral constraints (is amoral) and is guided by instinct. The concept of 'man' has been defined as civilized, to know and understand moral constraints, as well as to use rational thought as a basis for communication and action. In this way, we place values on the things we talk about through the very words we use. In turn, these words only make sense within the systems of values we share within social communities. In the example of racial classification, the distinctions were used to designate certain peoples as being closer to a natural state. So the distinction between social and natural things makes sense only when we explore the ways in which it is actually used to organize people's lives. This also leaves the issue of reference unexplored: even if the way we refer to things changes, surely we still refer to something when we speak, write and create images?

This a good point in the argument to pursue the issue of reference. Throughout this section you may have been wondering how language can be seen as a way of referring to 'real' things beyond language. When we think of a word like 'planet' it seems to be more than a word; in the case of the Earth, we see it as something real which the human species inhabits and as something which exists regardless of whether human beings see it as flat or as a sphere. A common criticism of the Saussurian approach is that it fails to distinguish between the signified (the message within the sign) and the thing or object to which the sign makes reference. There are a number of responses to this problem. On the one hand, we could argue that if we never know what the thing is except through language and the idea of reference itself is a linguistic or discursive construct, it is not possible to move beyond language. Alternatively, we can see language as a reflection of the things to which it refers. Later, in Chapter 7, we consider one approach (realism) which tries to work between these alternatives – realists suggest that we are always using language to represent the world and yet we would not be able to do this unless there is something beyond language in the first place. If we go back to the earlier example, the Saussurian approach enables us to understand the ways in which we see nature. However, it can also be argued that this does not help us to identify the environmental relations and processes which constitute ecosystems in the real world and we still need to be able to grasp these if we are to do something about ecological damage from, say, industrial pollution (Smith, 1998).

This is as much as you need to understand about realism at this point.

So what does Saussure tell us? In contradiction to the positivist vision of scientific knowledge, his approach suggests that there is no simple or neutral act of perception. Every word we use to understand natural things is packed full of meaning. The way we distinguish human activity from natural relations and processes is a reflection of the values we hold in a situated location. These types of distinction reveal a great deal about the way in which Western societies demarcate culture from biology, masculinity from femininity, and how we see cultural differences. Other cultures, however, see the relationship between society and nature as one of friendship and respect. Saussure provided us with building blocks for the study of culture in the social sciences, but the theoretical framework needed further development. He envisaged that once his theoretical system had been refined, it would be possible to construct an account of signs – the science of signs, semiology – within social and cultural life more generally. In the following section, we explore the development of semiology, or semiotics as it is more often designated today, and the ways in which rethinking language transforms social scientific practice.

Since all perceptions are full of complex meanings, we should take the complexity of language more seriously.

2.2 Language and cultural representation

Semiology brings the study of language into contact with the study of culture, redefining what can be taken as a legitimate topic of study in the social sciences. In order to understand how language affects social scientific practice, the semiological approach highlights the need to take on the broader issues of how linguistic signs make sense within the cultural way of life of those interpreting them. Moreover, the concerns of semiologists range across the forms of representation which are part of our lives: from television programmes to magazine advertisements, from reading a novel to participating in mass spectator events and from the public understanding of science to the critical analysis of the role of soap operas in contemporary society.

In the cultural commentaries of Roland Barthes we can begin to identify some of the basic categories in this approach. Barthes is concerned with the ways in which 'mythologies' are generated through culture. Barthes does not define myths in the general sense of legend and folklore but in the more restricted sense of the capacity of a word, sound or image to generate meanings for those who read them. As a foundation, semiology draws upon Saussure's account of the sign. However, Barthes makes a distinction between how signs operate at the level of **denotation** and how these are transformed through **connotations**. Let's first consider what these two levels mean. To denote something is to identify what is widely accepted as a descriptive and factual account of the thing in question. For instance:

This is an oak tree:

In semiology, denotation describes the characteristics of the thing in question – connotation tells us what it means.

However, when we consider the meanings attached to the sign of an oak tree, we can begin to gauge the ways in which meanings are communicated. The oak tree is regarded within English culture as a symbol of organic growth, as an expression of working within a cohesive social order which has deep roots and solid foundations. The associations of 'Englishness' and 'traditionalism' with the oak tree mean that it can carry powerful connotations of strength, endurance, calmness, trust, steadfastness and protection against the hostile elements, but also of standing one's ground when others give way.

In short, within English culture the 'oak tree' is understood as a symbol of 'cultural strength' compared with the 'cultural weakness' of the 'non-English' (the other). What conclusions can we draw from this? Well, there is a reasonably clear understanding of the physical shape and properties of the oak tree: it is a perennial plant with a single supportive trunk. At the level of denotation (the first-order semiological system), this is not controversial; however, the moment we ask the question 'what does an oak tree mean?', a wealth of meanings are attached to the sign of 'oak tree'. According to Barthes, these new 'parasitic' signifieds transform the original sign into an empty signifier so that it can carry other messages. Whereas denotations operate at the level of language, connotations operate at the level of metalanguage, of myths (a second-order semiological system). Connotations are attached to the signs which exist in language, so transforming their meaning. Before we look at some examples, we can see the difference between language (Level I) and metalanguage (Level II) in Figure 6.4.

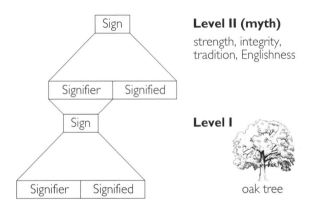

Figure 6.4 The construction of myths.

Earlier, we looked at the idea of 'nature' and focused upon the Western distinction between 'man' and 'beast'. We now return to this theme and explore what it 'means' to consume the flesh of animals. In *Mythologies* (1973) Barthes considers the role of meat in French cultural life and explores the connotations involved when we eat it.

> Steak is a part of the same sanguine mythology as wine. It is the heart of meat, it is meat in its pure state; and whoever partakes of it assimilates a bull-like strength. The prestige of steak evidently arises from its quasi-rawness. In it, blood is visible, natural, dense, at once compact and sectile. One can well imagine the ambrosia of the Ancients as this kind of heavy substance which dwindles under one's teeth in such a way as to make one keenly aware at the same time of its original strength and of its aptitude to flow into the very blood of man. Full-bloodedness is the raison d'être of steak; the degrees to which it is cooked are expressed not in calorific units but in images of blood; rare steak is said to be *saignant* (when it recalls the arterial flow from the cut in the animal's throat), or *bleu* (and it is now the heavy, plethoric, blood of the veins which is suggested by the purplish colour – the superlative of redness).
>
> (Barthes, 1973, p.62)

In this example, we can see how something which is a feature of ordinary everyday life is reconstructed in a way which identifies its complex connotative meanings. Although this example is located in a particular culture, similar connotative meanings are attached to 'eating meat' in all non-vegetarian cultures. We can also see how distinctions between human and non-human animals can be expressed in ways which convey the dominance of one side of the distinction (that is, human beings use other animals for their own purposes). Semiology, then, provides an opportunity to extend the scope of social science to include everyday life. In a second example from *Mythologies*, Barthes considers representations from the World Detergent Congress in Paris (1954), where the potent combination of consumerism and the 'appliance of science' produced a celebration of the benefits of soap powders and other cleaning products, which at the time was called '*Omo* euphoria'. In this short passage, Barthes contrasts:

The tools of linguistics help us to understand cultural representation and to widen the range of objects which social research can investigate.

> purifying fluids (chlorinated, for example) with that of soap-powders (*Lux*, *Persil*) or that of detergents (*Omo*). The relations between the evil and the cure, between dirt and a given product, are very different in each case. Chlorinated fluids, for instance, have always been experienced as a sort of liquid fire, the action of which must be carefully estimated, otherwise the object itself would be affected, 'burnt'. The implicit legend of this type of product rests on the idea of a violent, abrasive modification of matter: the connotations are of a chemical or mutilating type: the product 'kills' the dirt. Powders, on the contrary, are separating agents: their ideal role is to liberate the object from its circumstantial imperfection: dirt is 'forced out' and no longer killed; in the *Omo* imagery, dirt is a diminutive enemy, stunted and black, which takes to its heels from the fine immaculate linen at the sole threat of the judgement of *Omo*. Products based on chlorine and ammonia are without doubt the representatives of a kind of absolute fire, a saviour but a blind one. Powders, on the contrary, are selective, they push, they drive

dirt through the texture of the object, their function is keeping public order not making war. This distinction has ethnographic correlatives: the chemical fluid is an extension of the washerwoman's movements when she beats the clothes, while powders rather replace those of the housewife pressing and rolling the washing against a sloping board.

(Barthes, 1973, p.36)

We looked at the role of tacit knowledge in Schütz's phenomenological approach and in the ethnomethodology of Garfinkel in Chapter 4, sections 5.2 and 5.3.

In these two brief passages, we see the potential for taking cultural representations seriously. In each example, something ordinary and a part of everyday life is clearly shown to carry a wealth of meanings which we draw upon but barely acknowledge. There are striking similarities between the implications of taking such cultural representations seriously and the implications of adopting the phenomenological and ethnomethodological approaches. As you will recall, writers such as Schutz and Garfinkel are interested in the tacit or 'recipe' knowledge through which we make sense of each other and the things around us. Both semiology and phenenomology are concerned with the production of meaning in everyday life and stress the importance of making connections between the knowledge constructed and the people being studied, even if they use different toolkits.

Semiology or semiotics is now applied to a wide range of social practices and cultural artefacts (the objects through which meanings are transmitted): film and television, dress styles and fashion accessories, furniture and living space, music and associated artefacts (such as the Sony Walkman), advertising and the marketing of popular brand-names (such as Coca-Cola), to name just a few. Part of the reason for this growth of interest in artefacts and our uses of them is the increased recognition of the importance of consumption practices. Processes and relations in production and consumption are interconnected in complex and uncertain ways – which means that, as social scientists, we should pay closer attention to how people consume and what this means to them. So semiology is well placed to help us think through how the 'mundane' things we use matter in the invention and reinvention of identities. In the study of 'material cultures', Daniel Miller provides us with a way of thinking through the question of why things matter: 'the term "matter" tends to point in a rather different direction from terms such as "importance" or "significance". [It] is more likely to lead us to the concerns of those being studied than those doing the studying' (1998, p.11).

Recent work on the way shopping is conducted and understood, provides us with an important reminder of the ways in which social science has neglected many aspects of social existence. For instance, Alison J. Clarke's studies (1997, 1998) of 'shopping from home' – through tupperware parties, catalogues or magazines such as 'Loot', which offer opportunities for buying and selling of goods with 'histories' – demonstrate how studies of consumption which focus on established retailers only offer a partial account of the rich and varied social practices involved. Yet it was through claims to completeness that such accounts came to be seen as authoritative in the first place. By studying the things around us, such as irons, hoovers, music systems and televisions, which are standard features of most households (or for that matter, the kinds of dwellings in which we live), we can identify the ways in which production and consumption are interconnected. In the study of material cultures, we can see how useful and fruitful it can be to combine the ethnographic research strategies associated with phenomenology and anthropology with the semiological sensitivities to the complexities of cultural representation. Once we realize that people matter, then we are led to recognize that things matter too.

ACTIVITY 6.2

Concentrate briefly on the passages about eating meat and the use of soap powders from Roland Barthes's collection of cultural commentaries, *Mythologies* (1973), and look at the images in Figure 6.5.

- In each case, identify how denotation differs from connotation.
- Identify the myths involved in the soap-powder advertisements below (Figure 6.5). You may also wish to consider how gender is portrayed by Barthes compared with soap-powder advertisements today.

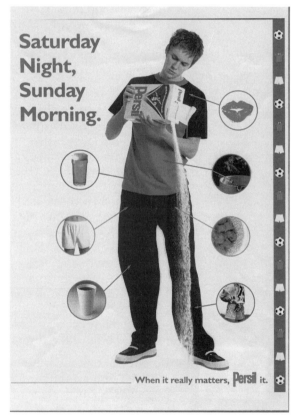

Figure 6.5 Selling soap powders, then and now.

- When you read the passage on eating meat from *Mythologies* on page 242, you may have thought that consuming meat holds a special place in French culture. How does your own culture consider meat eating? Do other myths come to mind?
- Return to the images of scientists in Figures 2.1–2.4 in Chapter 2 (section 1.1) and try to establish the connotations involved in these four representations of the embodiment of science.

If we consider contemporary representations of cleaning products (for instance, television advertisements for soap powders) we can see how many features identified in Barthes's description still operate, even though his original commentary is now over forty years old. Advertisements can carry the messages of 'killing germs' or pushing out the dirt from the clothing and leaving the material 'as good as new' or 'whiter than white'. At the level of denotation, the steak dinner is a 'nutritious meal' while soap-powders 'clean our clothes'. However, in the example of soap powders the language used connotes a campaign for purity and hygiene, suggesting that if we are to be liberated from dirt we must engage in a war with germs and use all the scientific techniques at our disposal to do so. The identification of myth, at the level of metalanguage, indicates the way it signifies an underpinning set of distinctions and rules, which have to be in place if the signs are to be recognized and understood. More than this, semiological analysis helps us to understand how meanings are produced through our social practices, whether we are social researchers engaged in the collection of evidence or whether we are making lifestyle choices in our personal lives.

Figure 5.5 in Chapter 5 shows scientists working on a behaviourist experiment.

Semiology also offers a useful way of examining the representations of scientific work which you considered in Chapter 2. There are quite complex myths involved in the representation of science. If you consider the images of white-coated social scientists and think through what kinds of practices they're engaged in, you can see how the conventions of experimental science are translated into behaviourist psychology along with the myths of science, such as the search for truth. In short, semiology highlights the complex ways in which we construct meanings about everything we encounter, but which we barely acknowledge. The two passages by Barthes reveal how consuming meat or cleaning clothes hold a symbolic importance which we usually take for granted. However, semiology also demonstrates that in order to decode the myths associated with these practices, we draw upon complex cultural conventions which are as essential to producing meaning as the rules of language are for recognizing the form that a sentence can take. Two issues should be highlighted here.

- Semiology leads us to consider new kinds of objects for investigation in the social sciences; things which we often pass over as ordinary, such as the consumption of food, the cultural artefacts in our homes, or the messages in advertisements, are very important for understanding social life.

- Semiology sensitizes social scientists to the problems and complexities of representation, both in the ways they conduct their research and in the ways they communicate their findings.

These aspects of communication and the production of meaning have not been regarded as a matter for serious attention by many social scientists. Some have seen them as trivial concerns compared with the so-called 'big issues' of social science. As you may recall, even the approaches identified in Chapter 4, which place a special emphasis upon the human imagination, tend to assume that there is something definite and real about experience before social scientists have a chance to interpret it in various ways. In the next section, we explore an approach which attempts to develop these ideas in a way which takes more seriously the uses of language as part of the process of conducting social research.

Summary

Scientific thought tends to assume that language is a mere reflection of things, a transparent medium depicting the truth. There is no simple or neutral act of perception, as positivists have suggested. Every word we use to understand the world is packed full of meaning.

Language systems are the taken-for-granted conditions of social practices and they are also reproduced, modified and transformed through the ways in which they are used. Structuralist linguistics focuses our attention upon the structured patterns of differences involved in the language systems through which the world is represented.

Semiology provides a way of thinking about cultural representations in order to demonstrate that ordinary things in everyday life carry a wealth of meanings which we barely acknowledge. This means that we must reassess which objects of analysis we take seriously in social science.

3   Language and discourse

So far we have concentrated upon the role of linguistics in the question of representation; let's now consider what this means for social science. Earlier, we focused upon the role of language as a structure and identified the role of relations within language as important for the production of meaning. Here we examine how language is used by people and how meanings are communicated. This section brings the idea of 'language systems' back into contact with lived experience and explores the implications of considering language as 'discourse'. The idea of 'discourse' is a matter of dispute. You will find that some ways of defining discourse are similar to the way conventionalists considered the role of scientific language within organized academic communities. However, where the advocates of discourse analysis differ from **conventionalism** is in the emphasis they place upon the role of active communication to produce meanings and the way in which the character and concerns of a discourse can change very rapidly.

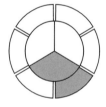

In this section we look at two types of discourse analysis: discursive psychology and post-structuralist discourse. In the first type, discursive psychology, we look at discourse as a product of the ways in which people produce meaning by drawing upon the rules of language; for example, conversational analysis explores the relations between speakers, their surroundings, their shared experiences and intentions, the event of which conversation is a part and so on. This approach views discourse as the activity of talking and writing. We will look at the concrete example of the discursive psychology of Jonathan Potter and Margaret Wetherell, who combine the insights from semiology with the **ethnomethodological** and **conventionalist** approaches considered in Chapters 4 and 5. In contrast,

These are two broad types of discourse analysis – one looks at the empirical experience of communication and the other focuses more upon the interaction between readers and writers.

the second example draws upon post-structuralist approaches to discourse. This type of discourse analysis acknowledges the complexity of 'texts' in two ways: every writer in social science is a reader first (so that each text brings together a whole range of ideas and arguments) and every meaning is produced through the activity of reading. It is useful to contrast these two types of discourse analysis, for the first is concerned with empirical expressions of language within communication (seeing speech and writing as an activity), while the second is more concerned with the theoretical components of discourses. These two approaches are really looking at different sides of the same coin of discourse. Both, however, are concerned to stress that representation is a complex process.

3.1 Discourse analysis in social psychology

In *Discourse and Social Psychology* (1987) Jonathan Potter and Margaret Wetherell attempt to find ways of developing discourse analysis in the field of social psychology. In their study of identity and social interaction they bring together three distinct approaches. You have already considered two: ethnomethodology and semiology. These two approaches are concerned with the conditions in which communication can take place. However, Potter and Wetherell also wanted to demonstrate that communication involves human agency, that is, purposeful human actions. So they combined ethnomethodology and semiology with a third approach, the 'speech act' theory developed by the philosopher John Austin. This approach provides a better understanding of agency in speech by considering words as deeds. Whereas structuralist understandings of language concentrate on what Saussure defined as **langue**, this approach concentrates more on **parole**. Potter and Wetherell argue that one of the key characteristics of the uses of language is the way it involves doing things, that it has purposes and intentions, as well as its role in describing the character and form of things.

Quickly re-read section 5.3 on ethnomethodology in Chapter 4. Semiology is discussed in section 2.2 of this chapter.

Language is therefore not simply a matter of truth and falsehood, an abstract system which reflects the world as it is; it is also a lived activity and, as with all human acts, it involves intentions and meanings. For a logical positivist, a statement is scientific by virtue of its ability to reflect observable reality. Potter and Wetherell suggest that the scientific demarcation criteria developed by logical positivists to distinguish between meaningless statements and true statements is a pointless one, because sentences do a range of things. For a discourse analyst, scientific statements are rhetorical devices for making claims look authentic and authoritative – they do a great deal more than describe the world. For Austin, a sentence such as:

Statements about the world are more than simple descriptions, they involve intentions and meanings.

See statements A and B in Chapter 4, section 2.

> I am reading this book.

can be seen both as a 'doing' and a 'stating' sentence. The things, people and events involved in this statement all have meaning. In addition, the way in which the utterance of this statement is made (as an assertion, an order or a question) can affect how it is received. Finally, the statement can elicit a range of very different responses. We know this can happen from our own experiences, but this aspect of language is ignored in many approaches to the construction of scientific knowledge. Austin's approach sees language as an activity which enables human beings to get things done and to communicate through a series of speech acts (Austin, 1962).

If science involves language, then it is also an activity, a way of doing things. If we invoke the claim that a statement is scientific, we are also engaging in a speech act – we are saying 'This is true, believe me!' Combining this account of speech acts with the assumptions of ethnomethodology reveals how certain types of speech act can follow in sequence to create rule-governed situations in which conversations can take place. As you will recall from Chapter 4, these rules are not universal ones, fixed for all time, they are flexible and subject to constant renegotiation and reconstruction. The existence of rules for talking, acting, co-operating and even for conflict is not at issue. It is the reflexive character of human activities which ethnomethodologists demonstrate so effectively.

Scientific statements are both describing and doing statements.

ACTIVITY 6.3

Turn back to Reading E in Chapter 4, 'Normal rubbish: deviant patients in casualty departments', by Roger Jeffery.

- Make careful notes on what the casualty officers 'say' in this reading.

- Reconsider the statements made by the casualty officers as speech acts. What are these acts doing?

- Try to identify the connections between these speech acts and the rules of conduct being constructed in the casualty department.

Earlier you would have focused on the stereotypes and labels used by casualty officers as taken-for-granted assumptions – here they should also be seen as actions or deeds (labels do things).

Once we recognize that rules of conduct offer a flexible way of responding to the uncertainties involved in human activities, this helps us to understand the ways in which language is actually used. Language systems are constantly reproduced through the activities of those who draw upon them in order to communicate, and they make sense only within a particular historical and social location. In short, speech acts take place within rules of conduct, and even then only make sense within the conditions of meaning identified through the use of semiological analysis (see Figure 6.6). It is the embeddedness of speech acts, rules and even myths within a particular location which leads us to conclude that, since scientific thought involves speech acts, rules and myths, then science too is a situated practice. So, for Potter and Wetherall, although speech act theory, ethnomethodology and semiology each highlights an aspect of existence which should be acknowledged in social research, they provided a one-sided account of research practice. To construct a research strategy for discourse analysis which could integrate these levels, Potter and Wetherell turned elsewhere.

Speech and writing are governed by rules of conduct and both exist within the more general conditions of meaning identified by semiology.

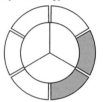

Here we can see how the semiological approach to language is used in an account of discourse.

In order to develop a discursive social psychology which counteracts the assumptions of the behaviourist and cognitive psychologists (see Chapter 5), Potter and Wetherell use an approach known as **ethogenics**. A significant exponent of this approach, Rom Harré, draws upon the distinction between 'competence' (which refers to our knowledge of a language system) and 'performance' (which refers to the uses of language such as speech). This operates in a similar way to that between **langue** and **parole**. Competence involves having a command of a particular language system, knowing its rules of conduct and working within them in order to communicate with others. For those who possess competence, there is a vast number of ways in which communication can be performed. At the same time, when we accept that communication is achieved by following a set of rules, this also imposes certain limits on what can be performed, because any breach of these rules will prevent effective communication taking place (Harré and Secord, 1973; Harré, 1979; Harré and Gillett, 1994). By drawing upon ethogenics in their approach, Potter and Wetherell account for the way communication works through discourse and so ensure that stronger connections are established between their three levels of analysis (see Figure 6.6).

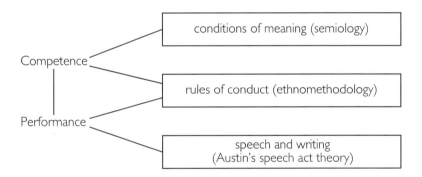

Figure 6.6   The levels of analysis in discursive psychology.

Even if values are situated in communities, language systems are more loosely associated with particular communities.

The idea of an interpretative repertoire draws upon the more recent work of Michael Mulkay which we explored in Chapter 5.

Nevertheless, in one crucial respect they go beyond the ideas developed in approaches to knowledge construction by both **idealists** (in the sense of 'idealist' identified in Chapter 4) and many **conventionalists** (considered in Chapter 5). Unlike that of the idealists, their approach sees representations as playing an active constructive role in the formation of the world, rather than just being one interpretation among many of some definite thing. Moreover, unlike that of the conventionalists, their approach does not fix representations to predefined communities. This means that groups can be used to define the scope of the conventions and representations with which we are concerned, but they do not match in such a neat way. In order to provide a more open-ended and flexible approach to discourse and representation in relation to the uses of language, Potter and Wetherell develop the idea of an 'interpretive repertoire'. These interpretive repertoires are the collections of ideas, concepts and terms which are used to define and evaluate experiences and events, so they fulfil much the same explanatory role as conventions. Interpretative repertoires are organized through the relations which linguists refer to as 'tropes' (such as metaphor and metonymy).

Tropes are departures from literal language which convey meaning. They are seen as established within language rather than as a simple expression of community identity.

In the discussion in this chapter (especially Activity 6.4), we focus upon metaphors as a type of trope. Metaphors involve the imaginative application of a word which conveys the character of something else but still leaves them clearly distinguished, such as 'The king is a tower of strength'. However, you should also consider the role of other tropes, such as metonymy (where the name of one thing stands in for another) and simile (a more explicit comparison between the character of two separate things). To use the example of the statement on the monarchy in section 2.1 of this chapter, 'crown' is a metonymic stand-in for 'monarchy' just as, say, 'turf' stands in for 'horse-racing'. Tropes can be very powerful in communicating ideas; in the example 'The pen is mightier than the sword', the word 'pen' acts as a metonym for persuasion and discussion and the word 'sword' for open conflict and war. A simile, however, works like a metaphor but keeps the comparison explicit. For instance, the statement 'The baron wormed his way into the king's affections' involves the use of a metaphor, whereas 'the baron behaved like a worm' involves the use of a simile. Such imaginative uses of words are a feature of some of the most successful and memorable writings in social science. When we examine the construction of statements in social scientific practice, we can begin to see why some accounts are more persuasive than others.

Metaphors and other tropes illuminate ideas and make descriptions and arguments persuasive for their audiences.

ACTIVITY 6.4

Turn to Reading A, 'The uses of community', from *Discourse and Social Psychology* (1987) by Jonathan Potter and Margaret Wetherell, and consider the following issues.

*   How is the word 'community' used in the evidence collected in this study? Consider each of the statements in the reading as 'speech acts' – what are they doing?

*   Consider the different metaphors associated with the word 'community' and identify which metaphors are used in each of the two different interpretations of the events considered.

When looking at this reading, you should try to think about the ways in which the uses of metaphors are connected to quite different political views about the social order and the role of the police: such views are either trying to change the ways that things are done or seek to maintain the existing social relations and values which underpin them.

When we explore the representations of a particular event (such as the inner-city disturbances in Britain in the 1980s) using the techniques of discourse analysis, we can identify the ways in which the meanings of such events are deeply contested and open to reinterpretation. In the extract from Potter and Wetherell you have a strong contrast between two uses of the idea of community. How we understand this event depends upon how we define community. Whether we define it in a way which includes the police-force (so that it is part of the organic ties which bind a community together) or whether we see the police as an external and hostile force locked in conflict with the community (so that the community acts) has serious implications for what kinds of meanings are produced. The role of metaphoric associations in this example helps us to see how different stories can emerge in social scientific practice as well as in the mass media.

Let's begin to consider the implications of viewing the disciplines and sub-disciplines of social science as discourses. Even economics – the area of social research which many of its practitioners see as the most scientific – has witnessed a heightening of interest in the techniques of story-telling. In the field of economic methodology, Donald McCloskey has developed a similar line of argument to that of discursive psychology (McCloskey, 1983). McCloskey states that we should think of all forms of knowledge as examples of **rhetoric**, which he portrays as 'disciplined conversations' for the purpose of mutual inquiry. If we briefly explore the role of metaphors in another social scientific discipline, we can develop a greater sensitivity to the role of metaphor. McCloskey presents considerable evidence of the way in which economics uses metaphors and suggests that the successful approaches in economics are so persuasive because they tell good stories. For instance, in the approach of John Maynard Keynes the story of 'people digging and filling in holes' for no obvious purpose other than to earn and spend money is persuasive in demonstrating the importance of consumption (demand) rather than production (supply). The metaphor of the 'invisible hand' is more than just a useful label for the price mechanism in the market, for it conveys the way in which the interactions of supply and demand ensures the most effective distribution of resources and rewards for effort and thrift.

Social scientists should not only study the metaphors used in discourse, but also consider how they are used to communicate ideas within the social sciences.

Similarly, the metaphor of 'human capital', whereby the training of employees is portrayed as a form of investment bringing a long-term gain for the company or society concerned, also demonstrates how metaphors work to good effect. McCloskey goes on to argue that even mathematical reasoning is metaphorical.

> Consider, for example, a relatively simple case, the theory of production functions. Its vocabulary is intrinsically metaphorical. 'Aggregate capital' involves an analogy of 'capital' with something – sand, bricks, shmoos – that can be 'added' in a meaningful way; so does 'aggregate labour' with the additional peculiarity that the thing added is no thing, but hours of conscientious attentiveness; the idea of a 'production function' involves the astonishing analogy of the subject, the fabrication of things about which it is appropriate to think in terms of ingenuity, discipline and planning.
>
> (McCloskey, 1983, pp.505–6)

The main theme in studies of this kind is that social scientists should begin to think very carefully about how they communicate their ideas and evidence. In particular, as social scientists we should be more aware of the linguistic, discursive and cultural conditions of existence within which social scientific practice takes place. Most of all, social scientists should tell interesting and useful stories rather than preaching to the converted in a language which only those who are already in agreement can understand. These aspects highlight the relationship between the existing knowledge system, the practices of research communities and the language communities of the people being studied.

Summary

For discursive psychology, language is not simply a matter of establishing truth and falsehood, nor does it simply involve constructing an abstract system which reflects the world as it is; language is also an activity and, as with all human acts, it involves intentions and meanings which are governed by rules.

In considering the role of discourse and its uses throughout the disciplines of the social sciences, we can develop a greater sensitivity to the role of tropes. Successful approaches in social research are persuasive because they use metaphors and other tropes to tell good stories.

3.2 Post-structuralism and discourse

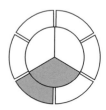

So far we have looked at discourse analysis through the lenses of those concerned with the uses of language as part of the way people communicate with each other. In addition, we have explored the role of the structure of language as a framework, as the conditions of meaning, within which people make sense of the world. However, the study of language has not stood still since the work of Saussure and Barthes; indeed, Barthes himself has contributed to a fundamental transformation in the way that language and discourse have been understood. So the study of language has moved beyond the study of language structure; it is now 'post-structuralist'. Whereas discursive psychology explores the lived experience of communication between people with intentions and purposes, post-structuralist discourse analysis explores the ways in which 'texts' are interrelated and places a special emphasis upon the interaction between the reader and writer. 'Texts' are defined much more broadly than their use in everyday language; they include talking, writing, posters, paintings, cartoons, computer-generated imagery, statistics, films, e-mails, web sites, computer games and even cyberpets – in fact, anything through which meanings can be produced.

What impact have these new studies of discourse had on social research? What are the philosophical implications for social science as a practice? We address these questions now. In particular, we examine the role of these views in undermining the assumption that knowledge has firm foundations in terms of some idea of truth, the use of human reason, the goal of human progress and even in terms of the lived experiences of social relations. These ways of grounding 'knowledge', which we have seen from positivism to phenomenology, are always of establishing some claim to authenticity. In the post-structuralist approach they are no longer seen as beyond discourse or as a point of reference against which we can compare and contrast our interpretations. Instead, these foundations are all treated as discursive constructs themselves and, as such, are open to continual reinvention and change.

So the approaches considered in this section are all anti-foundational. When we look at recent social scientific practice, three contributions stand out: the later post-structuralist writings of Roland Barthes, the challenging writings of Michel Foucault and the deconstructionist approach of Jacques Derrida. Of course, their ideas have been translated in various ways in the social sciences, but their main point is that all forms of representation can be rearticulated and transformed. If there are no firm foundations, then there can be no fixed rules for what makes a particular kind of knowledge authentic. This leads us now to the question of whether anything can be taken as an authentic representation. When you considered Barthes earlier in the chapter, your attention was directed towards the distinction between **denotation** and **connotation**. In his early cultural commentaries, Barthes assumed that at the level of denotation (the first order of signification) a sign conveys meaning in an incontrovertible way, but at the level of connotation (the second order) this sign becomes an empty signifier which can carry a whole range of meanings or myths, as in Figure 6.3 (Barthes, 1967, 1973). If we take the example of a 'box of chocolates', a distinction can be made between the definition of chocolates as a 'selection of sweets composed of sugar, fat and cocoa' and the connotations of love, romance, seduction, guilt and self-worth which are associated with chocolate. Nevertheless, the way we attribute meaning to sugar, fat and cocoa is itself tied into the complex and changing ways that we categorize the nutritional components of all foods and, furthermore, what we consider to be 'healthy' and 'unhealthy' lifestyles. So, following further exploration of the meanings of cultural representations, Barthes came to question the plausibility of even this distinction. All basic descriptive statements make sense only because of their place within frameworks which connote meanings.

The semiological distinction between denotation and connotation is not quite as clear-cut as we often assume – all descriptive statements actually connote meaning.

This raises questions about the role of discourse in communicating meaning. In particular, it undermines thinking about language as a transmission device for carrying the intention of the author. In his later work, Barthes explores the different ways in which texts can be read and suggests that this should lead to a reassessment of what it means to write or author a text. In *S/Z* (1970) he suggests that it is possible to place the reader of a text in a 'reactive' position or, alternatively, view the reader as a 'proactive' agent engaged in the production of meaning through the text concerned. In the first case, the example of **readerly** texts, it is assumed that the reader simply listens to an authoritative voice in the text and decides whether to

Post-structuralism asks social science to replace the role of the author as the authoritative voice with the interaction of writer and reader.

accept or reject this as an authentic view. As you may remember from the section on Feyerabend's methodological pluralism, some texts attempt to indoctrinate the audience by presenting one view as the truth. For Feyerabend, this is a common characteristic of scientific texts. Consider the anti-metaphysical story-line developed in the positivist tradition, for instance. One of the reasons why positivism is so hard to pin down to a definite set of assumptions is the substantial variation in the component parts of each positivist approach. Nevertheless, in each kind of positivism, there is always the authoritative voice claiming to possess the truth. Alternatively, in the example of **writerly** texts Barthes suggests that the reader can participate in the production of meaning, establishing their own connections, building their own stories. The connections between signifiers and signified are produced by the activity of reading itself and they do not exist prior to this. Barthes sees his role as ending the dominance of the 'Author-God' and so transforming the way that texts are understood. He concludes that 'the birth of the reader must be at the cost of the death of the Author' (Barthes, 1977, p.148), which means that rather than considering the products of social scientific research as reflections of the 'real world', we should redirect our attention to the relationship between the writers and audiences of social science (Barthes, 1976, 1977).

The idea that the author, the authoritative voice, is dispensable in social scientific thinking about the way in which people organize their lives has had a huge impact on recent social science. It undermines the belief that science can act as a **canonical** point of reference for explaining social relations and processes and says that social scientists should behave as 'writers' rather than 'authors'. So we need new ways of thinking about the role of representation and the reception of ideas, and we need to think very carefully about the way in which social science is conducted. The remaining part of this section addresses the contributions of Michel Foucault and Jacques Derrida, two such 'writers' who have had an impact on social scientific practice. They offer useful tools for developing a questioning and self-critical approach which social scientists could take on board.

At this point, we explore Foucault's views on representation and discourse, although we return to his contribution to the conduct of social and historical inquiry in the next chapter. Perhaps more than any other theorist of knowledge, Foucault placed the word 'discourse' on the conceptual landscape of the social sciences. He defined discourse as a system of representation which regulates the meanings and practices which can and cannot be produced. His terminology is distinctive and presents a challenge to anyone unfamiliar with his work, nevertheless the insights developed are certainly worth considering. Foucault, like the semiological approach, was concerned about the complexities involved in representation, but he also investigated the ways in which knowledge is produced within a shared social context and within definite historical circumstances. Discourse is made up, then, of rules of conduct, established texts and institutions. Thus Foucault's primary concern was the relationship between knowledge and the power relations of the location in question, rather than just establishing what representations mean (Foucault, 1970, 1972, 1980). If social science really is to understand representations, it has to acknowledge the complex processes through which meaning is produced.

Methodological pluralism was covered in Chapter 5, section 3.3 and Reading D.

For Foucault, discourse is a system of representation made up of rules of conduct, established texts and institutions which regulate what meanings can and cannot be produced.

ACTIVITY 6.5

Turn to Reading B, 'Representation and discourse' by Stuart Hall, and attempt the following activities.

- Identify the key components of discourse as a system of representation.

- Even positivism can be seen as a discourse, so why not try applying this kind of analysis to logical positivism as an account of scientific truth (see Chapter 3)? You may find it useful to note the rules of conduct, texts and institutions involved in the construction of logical positivism.

- Now identify the demarcation criteria between science and non-science in logical positivism. What role do these criteria play in positivist discourse?

You may also find it useful to apply this activity to behaviourism, discussed in Chapter 5. The key thing to remember when trying to understand the meaning of any approach in social science, is to think about the relationship between the practices developed and the social and historical conditions into which they emerge.

g

When we consider approaches in the philosophy of the social sciences as discourses we can gain some insight into how they operate in definite historical and social contexts. Positivism, falsificationism, neo-Kantian idealism, rational choice theory and so on can all be interpreted as discourses. They are all systems of representation which offer distinctive rules of conduct (the scientific method itself) about what sorts of theories and evidence are permissible (or not). These approaches can all be identified in definite texts and practices. In turn, these texts and practices exist within specific institutional contexts, primarily the academic and educational institutions of Western societies. For instance, in the case of logical positivism there are complex rules about what sorts of statements are acceptable (that is, **analytic** and **synthetic** ones) and these exist by virtue of the rejection (as simply meaningless) of any statements which do not follow this distinction. So, Foucault's account of discourse provides us with some of the tools for understanding how representations are situated. However, if we are to explore the complexities of texts themselves, we also have to draw upon ideas developed in literary studies.

You may find it helpful to re-read quickly Chapter 4, section 5.2 on phenomenology.

The idea that there is a firm foundation for knowledge is a convenient fiction which tells us more about the writer than any reality.

In the final set of ideas in this section we explore what it means to think of all things as discursive. Jacques Derrida drew upon phenomenology to demonstrate the impossibility of fixing the meaning of any concept. As you may remember, the basic starting-point of the phenomenological approach was the idea that we should suspend our belief in, or 'bracket off', the objective world. This 'bracketing' process, it was argued, demonstrated that conscious subjects had actively constructed the objective world. This still left the idea of a conscious subject as a firm foundation. Derrida questioned the idea that a single meaning of subject or object can hold for all time. Drawing from the phenomenological philosopher Martin Heidegger, Derrida suggests that rather than confronting philosophical problems for what they are,

Western philosophers had developed a technique for pretending these problems do not exist. This technique involves permitting a gap in understanding or giving a problem a name and slapping this name on the problem to cover it up (rather like applying a sticking plaster to a cut and then pretending it is made of skin). For Heidegger, the idea of 'Being' was just such a concept, for it had undergone so many transformations in meaning that it could not be used to demonstrate a universal meaning and yet, in the absence of anything better, it was still necessary to use it. Therefore Heidegger placed the word 'under erasure' to identify its ambiguous status:

~~Being~~

By drawing these lines across a word, he designated its status as inadequate yet necessary, simply because we have nothing better to express the problem. Derrida argues that concepts such as 'the subject' pose the same issues as 'being' and should be placed under erasure in the same way. This means that even the concepts of 'objective' and 'subjective' are themselves features of discourse rather than simply reflecting a feature of the world. Whereas the concept of 'knowledge' implies that we 'know about something', this approach suggests that the things we know only exist as discursive constructs. Thus even the distinction between 'appearance' and 'reality' exists only within discourse (Derrida, 1973, 1976, 1978).

Applying this critical technique, Derrida uses discourse analysis to destabilize the key ideas (objectivity, subjectivity, logic, truth and so on) upon which science is grounded. Derrida challenges the idea underpinning all the approaches considered in the first five chapters of this text, that some solid foundation exists for human knowledge (a foundation which he refers to as the 'metaphysics of presence'). Rather than searching for some underlying essence (as if we were mining for gold), he argues that we should map the conceptual landscape for the metaphoric relations which exist (in a similar way to McCloskey in the previous section). This technique of **deconstruction** involves the interrogation of a text in order to establish its organization around certain oppositions, such as true/false, rationality/irrationality, masculinity/femininity and same/other. We have already explored the first two oppositions in considerable detail, for they provide an important basis for scientific texts. In the remainder of this chapter, we hone in on the last two oppositions because they help us to understand cultural differences. We should be careful here. All post-positivists have questioned foundations (such as Popper's questions about truth), but in order to develop an effective scientific method they tend to replace one foundation with another (Popper replaced truth with progress).

See Chapter 3, section 5 on Popper.

In cultural studies, particularly studies of ethnic differences, the distinction between same/other is also used in the construction of identities. As with the other oppositions, one side is the dominant one. By charting the relations of equivalence (sameness) and difference (otherness) we can identify the ways in which cultural differences are constructed around the ideas of insiders and outsiders. If you retrace your steps to the account of scientific racism in Chapter 3, you can gain a sense of the way in which such cultural differences can be overlaid with other oppositions, such as rationality/irrationality. In gender studies too, a considerable amount of

See Chapter 3, section 3.1.

The production of meaning is organized through oppositions, such as true/false, with one more positively valued than the other.

research has been devoted to demonstrating how masculinity is positively valued in Western societies while femininity is regarded as secondary. This reflects the tendency of one side of the opposition between masculinity and feminity to dominate the other (just as in science, truth and rationality are put in a privileged position).

The post-structuralist reinterpretation of the categories of language leads us to think about the relationship between signifiers and signifieds in new ways. This approach assumes that any attempt to fix the meaning of a sign is doomed to fail, for there is always a surplus meaning – a 'supplement' – which leaves the meaning of a sign open to contestation. Derrida leads us to think of the idea of difference in two ways. First, there are relations of differences between words through which we make sense of the world. Second, there is the sense of deferral, that any attempt to finish the business of producing meaning is always provisional (Derrida, 1978, 1981). If we return to the issues raised by scientific racism in Chapter 3, we can see how these tools allow us to recognize that the construction of a stable 'white imperial civilization' is not an identity divorced from all other points of reference. Actually, it is possible to think of this identity only in terms of its difference from its opposition to 'black colonized primitiveness'. If we take the boundaries established between 'racial groups' identified in *Parkinsons' Scholar's Guide*, we can see how they involve an elaborate and complex set of relations in which a variety of oppositions work together in order to establish a relatively stable framework of meaning. Racist and sexist discourses (like that of Samuel Morton) try to fix cultural identity to a set of biological reference points, but using Derrida's approach we can see how such meanings are produced through discursive oppositions rather than by reference to physiological differences between human beings. Therefore it is only possible to identify the insider by reference to an outsider, and the boundaries between them only make sense through their relationship with each other. You can only draw a line in the sand if there is sand on both sides. So we can see in this example that the meanings of cultural identities are produced through relations of difference (as in the first sense identified by Derrida). However, this does not make racist or sexist discourses less dangerous or punitive for those who suffer because of their existence.

Difference has a double meaning – there are relations of difference through which meanings are produced as well as the sense of difference as deferred, that no meaning is ever finished.

See Figure 3.3 in Chapter 3.

Morton's work is discussed in Chapter 3, section 3.1 and Reading C.

Similarly, just as it is no longer possible to permanently fix the meaning of cultural identity, it is also no longer possible to think in terms of a single unified text, for each text exists by virtue of its relations with other texts. It is this relationship between texts which we refer to as the condition of **intertextuality**, where the meanings produced constantly change. (Figure 6.7, which you can find after the next activity, is an example of visual intertextuality and provides an opportunity for you to analyse how intertextuality 'works'.) Intertextuality involves no original source of meaning, only a flow of concepts which come together in a text and which can be combined in different ways with other concepts to construct new texts. Discourse analysis is particularly useful as a technique for exploring the role of identities and representations in the organization of social life but, more than that, it also highlights the way in which these identities and representations are constantly open to change, that they are always unfinished business. Now, let's turn to an example of the application of this approach to the political discourses of sexual identity.

ACTIVITY 6.6

Turn to Reading C, 'Political discourse, homosexuality and its metaphors', from Anna Marie Smith's *New Right Discourse on Race and Sexuality* (1994), which considers the political discourses on Section 28 of the Local Government Act, 1988, banning the 'intentional promotion of homosexuality' in the activities of UK local authorities. Smith charts the moral panic in the mid 1980s around the emergence of gay identity.

- Identify the metaphors associated with 'homosexuality' in the political discourses supporting Section 28.

- Which oppositions are being used in these political discourses?

Have a go at reading a recent headline story in this way. Look for the oppositions and how they articulated together. You might be surprised at how suggestive this technique can be.

In the discourse analysis developed by Anna Marie Smith, we can see how the post-structuralist approach can sensitize social research to the role of representation. Smith is concerned with the influence of racist and homophobic representations on cultural politics in Britain. As a result of her investigations, she concludes that these representations are a vital component in the broader forms of political mobilization involved in Thatcherism in the 1970s and 1980s. Thus discourse analysis can generate insights which lead to a reassessment of the dynamic forces at work in Britain at this time. More specifically, in the case of Section 28, which prohibited local government bodies from 'intentionally promoting homo-sexuality', Smith reconstructs the complex ways in which gay male sexual identities are rearticulated through the metaphors of 'invaders' and 'seducers'. She highlights the intimate connection between the meanings of racist and heterosexist discourses and the cultural assumptions and power relations of British society. In particular, she draws upon the analysis of the meanings of disease developed by Susan Sontag in *AIDS and its Metaphors* (1989), which considers the connections between fears of 'otherness' (particularly other, non-European, cultures) and the fears which are sometimes associated with disease.

In these political debates, Smith goes further to explore how the initiatives by local authorities in the 1980s to regard 'homosexual relations' as normal undermined the prevailing moral discourses, provoking an anti-gay backlash of which the campaign for Section 28 was a part. By doing this, she highlights the ways in which the oppositions of same/other, heterosexuality/homosexuality, rationality/irrationality, health/disease, safety/danger and so on can all be articulated together in ways which have dramatic consequences. Of course, critics of this approach would point to the problems of treating HIV/AIDS as a discursive construct, claiming that it has a 'biological reality' with definite consequences for many individuals and societies. Nevertheless, for social scientists, this does not undermine the importance of recognizing the complexities of representation in that we can understand this life-threatening illness more effectively when we are aware of the way in which it is represented and meaningful.

Cultural identities are established through relations of differences, but they are always unfinished and in process.

HARD TIMES, SOFT LOOKS.

The gentle lines of this hand-made Donegal tweed echo the romantic look of the Thirties. The suit £225, calf shoes £45, cashmere scarf £26, linen collarless shirt £37, pure wool tweed cap £28.

Quickly note what these pictures mean to you. What makes a photograph like that taken by Gloria Chalmers in 1983 (right) intertextual? For a start, it uses figures from the classic Kurt Hutton photograph taken during the 1930s depression (left) in order to make an ironic comment about life in the 1980s. You may not have noticed that the central adult figure on the right is actually wearing a 'Paul Smith original', an expensive designer outfit, and the children were just passing by. The Chalmers photograph demonstrates intertextuality in two senses: it reworks familiar representations in order to produce new meanings; and, as a representation, we can see that the way we read meanings into the image is both complex and open to contestation.

Figure 6.7   A visual illustration of intertextuality.

So what lessons can we draw from these post-structuralist approaches? One thing would be to consider how social researchers can enter into a dialogue with their readers. This means that they should treat the reader as a discerning and critical respondent rather than as a sponge to absorb the stories told by experts. We are also led to question the ideas of originality and authorship and to think about the key concepts of science – such as truth, progress and reason – as discursive constructs. Later in this chapter and in Chapter 7 we look at some of the implications of the post-structuralist approaches introduced here, particularly the technique of placing foundational concepts 'under erasure' in social science disciplines and how this opens up new opportunities for research. To do this, we explore in much more detail the ideas developed by Foucault (Chapter 7, section 2.2), whose epistemological insights were introduced earlier. In the substantive analysis of postmodernism (Chapter 7, section 2.1) we see how these insights were directed towards raising questions about the foundations of knowledge in the late twentieth century. Of one thing we can be certain: the emergence of cultural studies and the reappraisal of 'culture' across the social sciences have only been possible because of the development of the approaches described so far in this chapter. However, the way in which culture is defined varies enormously and so in the next section we consider the ways it has been understood in social science.

Summary

Post-structuralism considers the complexities involved in representation, but also investigates the production of knowledge in a shared cultural context and within definite historical circumstances. Discourses are systems of representation that regulate which meanings can and cannot be produced.

Post-structuralist discourse analysis undermines the idea that language is a transmission device for carrying the intention of the author, with the reader trusting an authoritative voice. If the author is no longer the authoritative voice of truth and authenticity, readers can be seen as participating in the production of meaning by constructing their own stories.

Post-structuralism challenges the idea that some solid foundation exists for human knowledge; rather it suggests that we should give up on the search for some underlying essence – suggesting that all the key ideas of science exist only within discourse.

4   Understanding culture

So far we have considered the role of language and discourse as an intimate part of social scientific practice. We have looked at how social scientists are trying to understand and explain the complex ways in which people communicate with each other. In addition, social scientists themselves are involved in communication and the production of meaning. So the issue of representation is a many sided one. Moreover, social scientists use similar interpretive repertoires to those used by the people being studied. In section 2 we saw how people act within reasonably stable conditions of meaning and that we have to agree (perhaps vaguely) on what most things mean before we can communicate with confidence. In section 3 we explored the ways in which people use language to communicate. However, this communication is neither haphazard, nor is it determined by an all powerful language structure. It is organized within certain rules of conduct and takes place within definite institutions; it is organized within discourse. The idea of 'discourse', Foucault suggests, enables us to think about how language is situated and constructed through the cultural values of a particular historical and social context. So, in this section, we concentrate on the way languages and discourses inhabit specific 'cultural locations'. Even if we understand how a discourse constructs the 'subject', if we are to stand any chance of understanding which 'subjects' are relevant in a particular time and place, or within a particular social scientific discipline, we have to find ways of understanding the cultures within which discourses operate as systems of representation. One way to represent the connections between language, discourse and culture can be seen in Figure 6.8. Bear in mind, however, that the meaning of culture is harder to pin down than is often assumed.

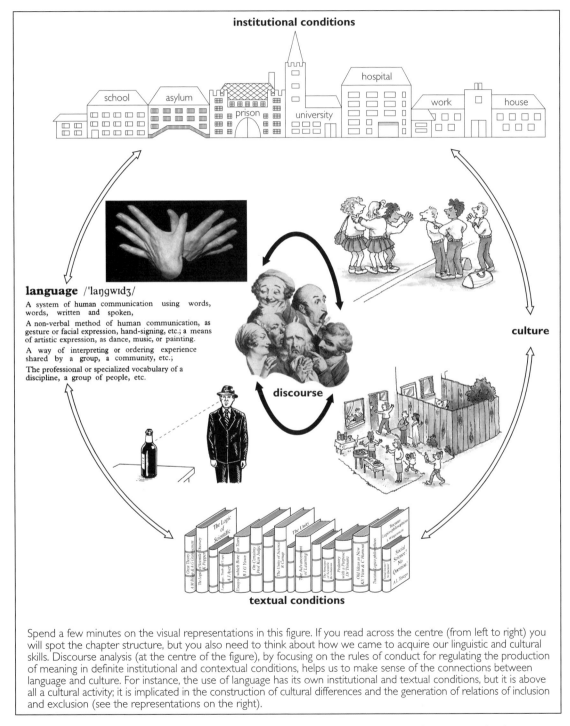

institutional conditions

language /'laŋgwɪdʒ/

A system of human communication using words, words, written and spoken,

A non-verbal method of human communication, as gesture or facial expression, hand-signing, etc.; a means of artistic expression, as dance, music, or painting.

A way of interpreting or ordering experience shared by a group, a community, etc.;

The professional or specialized vocabulary of a discipline, a group of people, etc.

discourse

culture

textual conditions

Spend a few minutes on the visual representations in this figure. If you read across the centre (from left to right) you will spot the chapter structure, but you also need to think about how we came to acquire our linguistic and cultural skills. Discourse analysis (at the centre of the figure), by focusing on the rules of conduct for regulating the production of meaning in definite institutional and contextual conditions, helps us to make sense of the connections between language and culture. For instance, the use of language has its own institutional and textual conditions, but it is above all a cultural activity; it is implicated in the construction of cultural differences and the generation of relations of inclusion and exclusion (see the representations on the right).

Figure 6.8   It is through discourse that we make the connections between language and culture.

When we think about the possible meanings and uses of the word 'culture', we walk into a maze of interpretations and associations. Culture is often used as a reference to the practices and lifestyles of the élite in a particular society, that is, high culture. In this sort of usage, it is seen as an expression and a measure of everything that is worthwhile in society. We can also think of culture as a representation of everyday life, as in 'working-class cultures', 'Asian cultures', 'street cultures' and even 'criminal subcultures'. Culture can be something to aspire to – such as the culture of books and learning or 'haute couture' fashion on the catwalks of Paris. We can be said to be talking in a cultured or uncultured way, whereby culture is associated with complex markers of dress, speech and gesture through which social status is communicated. For example, an individual who possesses this cultural knowledge can use the skills involved in the intonation and pronunciation of the spoken language to shape the reactions of those listening and engage in a dialogue. In this way, there are important similarities between the 'authoritative voice' of someone representing English literature, holding forth on Shakespearean tragedy or the romantic poetry of Wordsworth and Coleridge, and the prolonged ritual oratory of a chief of the Kayapó Indians in the Amazon basin (see Figure 6.9). In each case, an 'authoritative voice' is performing as the embodiment of the cultural heritage for a specific audience. In this sense, such cultural communication is a kind of performance which conveys meaning to an audience which possesses at least some of the skills to decode the messages, ritual and symbolism involved.

Melvyn Bragg chairs a discussion of authoritative voices on *Start the Week*, Radio 4 (*top left*); the chief of the Kayapó Indians performs ritual oratory to affirm the collective identity of his people (*top right*); Andrea Dworkin engages an audience in a discussion of the consequences of pornography (*bottom left*); Professor Paul Gilroy demonstrates that some of the most fruitful exchanges can take place over a cup of tea (*bottom right*).

Figure 6.9   Authoritative cultural voices can be heard everywhere – the radio studio, the community event, the academic performance or those brief moments of respite in academic conferences.

One of the ways in which culture can be understood is by organizing it into separate categories and giving each one a different value and status (just as scientific knowledge was classified in the nineteenth century). Many studies of culture devise complex ways of classifying cultural texts and practices. These are often defined quite separately from other areas of social research, as though the study of culture is divorced from the study of political institutions, the economy and so on. Of course, this sort of distinction is highly artificial and ignores the cultural dimension of these other areas of social inquiry. We can see some of the implications of treating cultural classification as hierarchical when we look at the literary and cultural commentaries of F.R. Leavis, who argued that the survival of intellectual refinement and high culture in the arts, literature and philosophy depended upon definite mechanisms for sustaining the distinction between high and low (or popular) culture.

The most important position was that of the 'critic', who acted as the custodian of all that was good and worthwhile in a culture. The role of custodian could only be given to those who possessed the ability and training for a 'discerning appreciation of art and literature' and who were in a position to make up their own minds about what was valuable in cultural terms. Leavis was particularly concerned about the effects of Hollywood movies in interwar Britain and targeted a range of examples of cultural representation as particularly dangerous for 'young minds', including the Tarzan novels of Edgar Rice Burroughs (Leavis, 1930). These kinds of arguments even crept into the social scientific accounts of the early twentieth century. In particular, Cyril Burt drew upon them in his account of juvenile delinquency (Burt, 1925/1961; see Reading E in Chapter 3). Only the custodian could decide whether a text was a 'great work' and whether an author merited **canonical** status. Everyone else, of course, lacked this capacity and had to accept the second-hand judgements of these custodians.

In this way, we can see a division between valuable culture, which should be preserved and passed on to future generations, and the rest of cultural experience, which was regarded as shallow and escapist entertainment undermining the active use of the mind. This attitude towards knowledge is, in many ways, similar to that adopted by scientists who wish to establish their version of events as the most authoritative. Of course, this model of knowledge is quite a crude one, which assumes that people are easily manipulated. In an era of mass communication and mass education, it is hard to support the cultural politics of this approach to knowledge. For Leavis, it was the 'intelligent few' who should make wise judgements for the 'unintelligent many'. As you have seen in this book so far, there are accounts of communication and knowledge construction which are much more complex than this.

When social scientific texts and their authors become widely established as authoritative, it is worthwhile thinking of them in these terms. Most disciplines in the social sciences have their canons, whether these are Adam Smith or John Maynard Keynes in economics or Max Weber and Émile Durkheim in sociology. These authors and their 'great works' come to be regarded as foundational in a particular discipline, and they become points of reference for making judgements about whether a particular study, method or type of statement can be taken on trust. In a fairly clear sense, the criteria according to which statements in science, art, literature and

Regarding scientists (like literary critics) as the custodians of knowledge, believing that they know best, undermines a critical and questioning approach.

Scientists and scientific roles in both the natural and social sciences can achieve canonical status, becoming the measure of what is considered valuable and useful research.

culture are judged to be of value, are broadly similar. Perhaps we have become so used to thinking about the social sciences straddling the arts and sciences as separate domains that we often overlook the similarities between them.

However, restricting the meaning of culture to the projection of a single viewpoint, or even placing limits on what counts as cultural knowledge (for example, the 'great novelist', 'serious composer' or 'scientific genius'), ignores a great deal of what is of interest to a social scientist. The role of 'popular culture', for instance, sometimes appears to have been trivialized and the idea that culture is just transmitted ignores the ways in which communication involves dialogue between the participants. Yet the cultural dimensions of human societies are the most significant areas of contemporary social research. Immediately, you can see some of the difficulties in thinking about and understanding culture within the social sciences. So to try to make sense of these complex areas, the following sections of this chapter focus upon two ways of understanding culture.

- The first explores the conception of culture developed by anthropology, which has been translated into cultural studies and, from there, the social sciences. This views culture as the 'structure of feeling' or 'design for living' and takes seriously popular culture (considered as a range of **texts** and **practices**) as a legitimate object of analysis. It explores how this has had an impact on the way in which social relations and processes have been understood and explained.

- The second examines the treatment of culture as a space or a terrain of contestation rather than as a thing in the sense of a definite object. This is a distinct break from the way in which objects were previously defined in social science. Rather than considering the object of analysis as a discrete thing which exists for the purpose of inquiry as separate from the inquirer, objects can now be seen as having a discursive existence. In particular, culture and social identities are seen as fluid and open to continual transformation.

While it is clear that we all experience and use cultural knowledge, it is very difficult to develop an effective understanding of one's own culture and how it should be studied. In the following sections we trace two of the ways in which this has been achieved.

4.1 Culture as a way of life

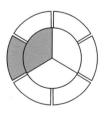

The idea that cultural studies should involve the exploration of the representations and lived experiences of everyday life owes its emergence, in part at least, to the discipline of anthropology. In particular, anthropology forces us to confront the obvious. By looking at the lived experiences of other cultures (Western and non-Western), their rituals, family structures, courtship patterns, transition from childhood to adulthood to old age, gift relationships and so on, we can identify what is so distinctive about our own culture. When we recognize that something can be different, this immediately highlights the things we take for granted. So cultural studies is carrying on the unfinished business of understanding our own social existence. Anthropology directs us to the study of culture as the everyday lives of a community, group or society. Nevertheless, this does not account for the development of the idea of culture. According to Raymond Williams, culture is one of the central 'keywords' in human knowledge generally, as well as in social science (1983, pp.87–93). Following his lead, let's now trace the changing ways in which culture has been understood, noting particularly how this ties into the account of the emergence of science.

As you saw in Chapter 2, the Enlightenment period effectively integrated the scientific circuit of knowledge (composed of the scientific method, truth, reason, progress and humanity). If we focus upon the meanings of 'culture' since this time we can begin to understand how the idea of culture only makes sense within definite social and historical locations. It is not only cultures themselves which are located – the very idea of 'culture' is situated as well. For instance, in the Enlightenment, culture meant 'civilization' and served as an important part of the project for establishing universal truth. In order to understand what civilization meant, these Western societies found themselves imagining 'other peoples' in ways which were directly opposed to the various components of the scientific circuit of knowledge (just as we can only think of 'night-time' when we establish its difference from daytime, twilight and dawn). Similarly, when we look at the accounts of the peoples of the Orient or the New World (the Americas) we can see immediately how these were shaped to provide the point of reference against which European identity could be constructed. As Derrida suggested, it is only through the construction of otherness that we are able to fix clearly but temporarily our own identities in the first place.

See the scientific circuit of knowledge in Chapter 2, Figure 2.5.

In short, 'civilization', and hence culture, was defined as the embodiment of the values of the western European societies, which defined themselves through the contrast between 'civilization' and 'barbarism' in the first place. Later, in the nineteenth century, the idea of 'culture' came to be associated with the study of the cultural forms of specific peoples, nations and societies. We have already explored this kind of account of historical-specific social relations in the **idiographic** approach of the neo-Kantian idealists (see Chapter 4, section 3). If we draw upon the same sources, the characterization of culture as open to universal definition – a prominent feature of the Enlightenment – can be described as a **nomothetic** approach. In addition, you have already considered the hierarchical accounts of culture (in the twentieth century). Now, in this section, we consider briefly the contribution of Raymond Williams to understanding the relations between culture and everyday life.

Culture has many meanings and uses, but it is always situated in a particular time and place.

When dealing with the contribution of a writer as seminal and as diverse as Williams, it helps to start with a summary. In *Common Culture* (1990), I think Paul Willis successfully manages to capture the contribution of Williams when considering the ordinariness of culture.

> It is the extraordinary in the ordinary, which is extraordinary, which makes both into culture, common culture. We are thinking of the extraordinary symbolic creativity of the multitude of ways in which young people use, humanise, decorate and invest with meanings their common and immediate life spaces and social practices – personal styles and choice of clothes; selective and active use of music, TV, magazines, decoration of bedrooms, the rituals of romance and subcultural styles; the style, banter and drama of

friendship groups; music-making and dance. Nor are these pursuits and activities trivial or inconsequential ... they can be crucial to the creation and sustenance of individual and group identities.

(Willis, 1990, p.2)

In this extract, we can see some of the key features of the study of culture as a way of life. For Williams, any attempt to study culture had to break with the tendency of élitists like Leavis to be dismissive of popular culture. In particular, this means that we should study 'ways of feeling and thinking' expressed within cultural institutions, such as the mass media, as well as high culture. This type of analysis goes much further than simply documenting the lives of ordinary people, for it also considers how it is possible to evaluate as well as reconstruct culture. In particular, Williams points to the need to recognize the 'structure of feeling' which underlies a particular culture, its shared values as well as the ways in which such values are expressed (Williams, 1961). In this way, it is possible to think about the shared experience of, for example, the working class or people from a particular region. Later proponents of this kind of approach extended this principle to the study of the 'structures of feeling' involved in the shared experiences through which we construct and reconstruct ethnicity and gender, alongside class differences. Whereas the cultural politics of Leavis was an attempt to defend the status quo and the role of the custodians of knowledge and values, the cultural politics of Williams was to embrace the lives of ordinary people and to value popular culture in a positive way, as part of a project of promoting a 'good life' for all people.

Culture is grounded in the lived social practices of people with complex identities.

So cultural analysis involves reading the lives of people in a particular way, to identify and interpret the social existence of the people under consideration and demonstrate how their values and stories make sense. This approach contains a respect for ordinary lives which is absent in much previous cultural analysis. It is possible to see many parallels between this approach and some of the approaches you have considered in the earlier chapters of this book. The phenomenological and ethnomethodological approaches also place a strong emphasis upon gaining entry into the lives of those being studied, to stand in their shoes and try to achieve a valid insight into their lives. These approaches also borrowed from anthropological research techniques. In particular, they developed **ethnographic** techniques, whereby the researcher becomes heavily involved in and shares the lived experiences of the group or community being studied. In a similar way, the approaches developed by the sociologists of science (considered in Chapter 5) can be seen as attempts to reconstruct the 'structures of feeling' of scientific research communities, treating science as a collection of cultural practices and texts. However, although this approach values culture (especially popular culture) more seriously, it still tends to view cultures as relatively unified. In the next section culture is considered as more heterogenous and flexible, as a terrain within which contestation takes place.

Culture as a 'way of life' has strong parallels with the assumptions of discursive psychology.

4.2 Culture as a contested space

When we think of culture as a way of life, it is easy to think of cultures as relatively fixed and stable around us. This is probably because we define our own identities through belonging to a culture and it is difficult to think about how identities and cultures change until after it has already

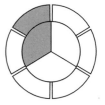

happened, when we realize we are no longer the same as we were. Cultures are always in a process of change, they are the product of competing ways of interpreting the world. In short, cultures are contested spaces. The impetus for this way of thinking about culture as a 'contested space' grew out of the concerns of the previous section. As research was conducted in the areas identified by Williams – especially on the cultures of class, youth, region and so on – it became more apparent that the notion of culture as simply an expression of some underlying set of conditions no longer made sense. In the work of the sociologist of culture Stuart Hall, we can see a particularly useful example of the way in which culture could be redefined.

See Reading D in Chapter 5 for a typical example of the Marxist paradigm.

Hall approached culture through the idea of hegemony, viewing it as a space within which struggles between social forces were conducted. Initially, for Hall, as with many who emerged from the Marxist tradition, the primary location of culture was the class structure. Hall challenged the idea that one should read cultural representation as a manifestation of some class interest. He regarded communication and cultural interpretation as an arena for the negotiation of meanings and defined popular culture in a relational way. Like the semiologists, discussed earlier, Hall asks us to recognize that the definition of cultural categories varies with the changing relations in the cultural field. Instead of defining popular culture as an inferior culture, he argues that its meaning depends upon its relationship with other categories; that is, the meaning of popular can only be understood by how it relates to categories such as high, élite and minority culture.

> For, from period to period, the *contents* of each category change. Popular forms become enhanced in cultural value, go up the cultural escalator – and find themselves on the opposite side. Other things cease to have high cultural value, and are appropriated into the popular, becoming transformed in the process. The structuring principle does not consist of the contents of each category – which, I insist, will alter from one period to another. Rather it consists of the forces and relations which sustain the distinction, the difference: roughly, between what, at any time, counts as an élite culture activity or form, and what does not.
>
> (Hall, 1981, p.234)

Before we examine what this means in contemporary social research, let's see how Hall managed to get around the problems involved in the Marxist analysis of culture. While he draws upon a range of approaches, we focus on just two of these in order to highlight the **articulation** of meaning. Marxism does provide an analysis of the social in terms of struggle and contestation; however, its treatment of cultural forms as an ideological expression of underlying economic interests was to prove unsatisfactory. Hall emphasizes those Marxist approaches which take culture and language more seriously.

Culture can be portrayed as a dialogic activity through which change can take place.

The first of these two approaches was provided by the Bakhtin Circle (named after the Russian Marxist, Mikhail Bakhtin), whose members explored the role of dialogue in communication. This approach recognizes that words have multiple meanings, that words and ideas never belong exclusively to the speaker or writer and are therefore open to many interpretations. For Bakhtin, meanings are constructed through dialogue. Like

Williams, the Bakhtin Circle viewed popular culture in a positive way but did so through the idea of the carnival. Cultural activities were characterized by excess and indulgence but could also challenge authority and change things through irreverence and vulgarity (Bakhtin, 1981). The second approach is drawn from the analysis of **hegemony** (developed by the Italian Marxist Antonio Gramsci). The idea of hegemony refers to the ways in which social forces are engaged in a constant struggle for political, intellectual and moral (if you prefer, cultural) leadership (Gramsci, 1971). Hegemony can thus be seen as a condition where one view of the world is dominant (you could reasonably say that standard positivism was hegemonic in Western social science in the 1950s), but it also assumes that such dominance can and will be contested (in the case of positivism, it certainly was).

Of course, as a Marxist, Gramsci was concerned primarily with class forces as well as with other categories, such as intellectuals. Hall recognized that other forms of social antagonism operated alongside class (for instance, differences in sexuality, gender, ethnicity and age). This meant that cultural contestation had to be understood as a looser process than was assumed by Marxists, who adopted an approach to culture based upon the logic of **mediation**. That is, Marxists had believed that it was possible to identify an example of cultural representation, say surrealist poetry, and trace its 'origins' back to some class interest as a fixed point of reference. So, for instance, surrealist poetry came to be seen as an expression of the *petit bourgeois* class (small shopkeepers).

The logic of mediation assumes that culture is a manifestation of some underlying foundation.

Hegemony, however, broke away from the idea of a necessary link between class and culture. Instead, it followed the logic of **articulation**, holding that culture is a product of fragile connections established between the various elements of language. Cultural representation is therefore contingent and constantly open to challenge (the elements can be disarticulated and rearticulated) rather than determined by an underlying structure. This directly challenges the structuralist accounts of language considered in section 2.1 of this chapter. Meaningful communication had been seen as the momentary expression of a fixed language system; this approach assumes that the construction of meaning involves the transformation of floating elements into definite moments (Laclau and Mouffe, 1985).

The logic of articulation assumes that there are no necessary links between ideas and that everything exists on the surface level of language.

This treatment of culture as contested fits particularly well with the post-structuralist understanding of discourse as an ongoing play of meaning without origin or end. If you look back in this chapter to Anna Marie Smith's study on political discourses on race and sexuality, you should notice that this combines a concern with social antagonisms (especially ethnic and sexual differences) with a recognition of the articulation of meaning. Here, we can see an ongoing struggle within cultural politics to establish the meaning of sexual identities, particularly through the opposition of same/other. Thus culture involves constant struggles for dominance and the generation of resistance. Identities are therefore accomplished through these struggles, but they are never complete for there is no closure of meaning. As you will recall from Smith's study, the construction of an identity involves the creation of a boundary which only makes sense when we consider the relations between the inside and the outside of that identity. In the area of social research now defined as cultural geography we can find similar arguments about the importance of the construction of identities in relation to defining places. The way we see ourselves in relation to

See Reading C and section 3.2.

the places where we live, work and play is a complex product of the construction of boundaries between ourselves and others. To give a place meaning, we also draw upon the kinds of oppositions discussed earlier, such as same/other, friend/stranger, security/danger, masculinity/femininity. In this way, we produce the meaning of places and the boundaries between them.

ACTIVITY 6.7

Now turn to Reading D, 'Contested places, contested boundaries' by Doreen Massey, and consider the following issues.

- Spend five minutes noting how Massey defines identity and boundaries.

- What oppositions are used to define the relationship between identities and places?

Think about your own experiences of moving from one place to another (whether this move was temporary or permanent). How did your identity change? If you returned some time later, did you find that the place had changed? If so, what did this mean to you?

Cultures, identities and the boundaries used to mark the differences between them constantly shift through the practices of human beings.

If we explore how cultures are themselves located in the shifting organization of space and place, we can gain a sense of the way in which culture is contested. In addition, we can see how the post-structuralist approach to discourse can help to generate new insights into a central concern in one social scientific discipline – the idea of 'place' in geography. When we say that cultures are contested, this does not mean that they are subject to perpetual transformation, but it does mean that we need to consider them as dynamic. Recognizing cultural contestation involves the identification of the complex forces and relations which can have an impact upon the ways in which human beings organize and reorganize themselves, as well as find meaning in what they do. We should be sensitive to the role of representation in the things we study as social scientists and we should also acknowledge that we ourselves are involved in an act of representation. That is, social scientists draw upon the existing repertoires of representation (within the academic communities and the wider culture they inhabit) if they are to make sense of their chosen area of study, to engage in the practice of conducting research and to present their findings in a way which holds meaning for their audiences.

So, right from the start, the social scientist is a cultural agent. If we recognize that social scientists study things using the skills provided by the cultures they inhabit, and that their chosen objects of analysis are defined and understood through cultural interpretations, we can begin to see what it means to read social research as a practice which produces meaning. More specifically, if we look at the arguments of Doreen Massey in her account of places and boundaries (Massey, 1995), we can see how careful research can highlight the ways in which places make sense only within boundaries, but that these boundaries make sense only when we recognize the complex, changing and uncertain patterns of social existence on both sides of the boundary. In this way, Massey comes to a conclusion which matches the ideas developed in the earlier section on post-structuralist approaches to discourse.

In tracing the role of oppositions within representations of place we can see how same/other and masculine/feminine work together to construct complex ways of defining identities in places. We can make sense of identities not by listing their attributes, but by seeing them defined through the relations between insiders and outsiders. In this way, places and boundaries as well as identities can also be seen as contested through the complex interrelations of discursive oppositions. How you read Massey's account also depends on how you produce meaning, how you view the oppositions in question (particularly which side of the opposition you value positively and which negatively) and how you use your own culture to make sense of the arguments raised.

Recognizing discursive oppositions enables us to make sense of the way that cultures, identities and places change – this should also highlight our own cultural values.

Critics of cultural studies have raised doubts about whether the social sciences should take such things seriously, implying that this kind of investigation is somehow less important than the study of the state, the economy and institutions such as the family. What this ignores, of course, is the important cultural dimension in all of these traditional objects of analysis within social research. The concern with culture in recent social inquiry is more than a shift of focus to new objects, it also means that social scientists have to reassess their own positions. For instance, understanding the operation of a democratic state depends upon recognizing the important part played by 'civic culture' in the construction of stable political systems and the complex forms taken by cultural politics. In a similar way, economies are locked into a complex set of relations with the cultural aspects of consumption. Recent social research on the economy is packed with references to 'enterprise culture', 'corporate culture' and the 'cultures of production'. This does not just mean goods being sold using cultural symbols and messages; it means that the cultural dimension is central to understanding actual economies and how things are made. In another illustration, the ways in which the family has been understood in recent social research directly connects to debates on moral values and the role of private life as a place of political contestation. Social scientists are not simply seeing culture as important, they are also recognizing that previous explanations had neglected the cultural dimension and subordinated it to economic and political explanations. Perhaps, even more importantly, they are starting to acknowledge their own role as cultural agents.

Summary

Culture can be said to be important in two ways.

- Culture is as much about ordinary lives as 'great works' and 'famous authors'. Cultural analysis involves reading the lives of people in a particular way, to identify and interpret the social existence of the people under consideration and to demonstrate how their values and stories make sense.

- Communication and cultural interpretation are a contested space for the negotiation of meanings. Culture involves constant struggles for dominance and the generation of resistance. Identities are therefore accomplished through struggle, but they are never complete.

The social sciences now face a process of reassessment in which culture is taken much more seriously. The question of whether they should consider culture as central to all social scientific accounts or as one of a number of dimensions of social inquiry (alongside politics, economics and so on) remains unresolved.

5   No conclusions, just some pointers

Since the implications of the approaches considered here are developed in the next chapter, this conclusion summarizes some of the key issues involved in using these studies of representation in the social sciences.

- While we can define the conditions of communication in various ways, we cannot escape the role of language, discourse and/or culture in constructing social scientific accounts. The question is: how do social scientists acknowledge these conditions?

- If we assume that social scientists are inevitably going to make judgements about the things they study, the evidence they collect and the explanations they consider, then social scientific practice will always contain values. This means that every social scientist is a cultural agent and we should try to spot the values involved in all interventions.

- Once we focus upon language, discourse and/or culture as key components of the way in which language is situated, both socially and historically (see Chapter 1), this leads us to question whether anything exists beyond discourse. This is the central concern of the next chapter.

On a more critical note, Hall suggests that there is a danger that approaches like that of Foucault 'absorb too much into "discourse", and this has the effect of encouraging his followers to neglect the influence of the material, economic and structural factors in the operation of power/knowledge' (Hall, 1997, p.51). This depends upon how discourse is understood. If you adopt the view that the only thing that can be defined as extra-discursive is speech, then there is a danger of falling into **textual reductionism**, which is just as much a trap as any of those identified in scientific thought. This means that rather than seeing, say, economic and political forces as real things, they are regarded as discursive constructs. When we consider the operation of authoritarian political regimes, for instance, I think we would view many forms of orchestrated violence and even the torture of political prisoners as more than simply discursive constructs. Similarly, the collapse of the market price for a global cash crop can create situations where people starve. Nevertheless, the way we represent such things has important consequences for the way we think about them. Think of the difference between the words 'dictatorship' and 'a state of national emergency', or between 'food shortages' and 'famine'. Perhaps a safer route would be to acknowledge the discursive dimension as a feature in all accounts of all things. It is to the issue of what makes things 'real' that we turn in the next chapter.

READING A
The uses of community

Jonathan Potter and Margaret Wetherell

In the spring of 1980 an event occurred in Bristol which came to be known as the 'St. Paul's riot'. Fighting took place between police and youths on the streets of the St. Paul's area of Bristol over a period of some hours. Several police vehicles and properties were destroyed, a number of police and civilians were injured – although none seriously – and the event dominated the next day's national news coverage and resulted in an emergency debate in Parliament. This seemed an ideal opportunity to look at the way social categories are used in the representation of conflict.

The study worked with an archive of documents: copies of reports and editorials from the local and national press, transcripts of television news and current affairs programmes, records of parliamentary proceedings, official reports and transcripts of interviews with people who were actively involved in the events. Since much of the time the discourse of conflict was addressed to defining the nature of the protagonists, it was an especially rich context in which to study people's use of categorizations, and in particular their use of the categorization 'community'.

The analysis was initiated by selecting out from the archive all instances of the term 'community' and its synonyms, and went on to identify the different predicates used with the term, along with the varying ways it was adopted to refer to the protagonists in the events. It was immediately apparent that certain sorts of predicates were repeatedly used, in particular predicates describing a certain cohesive style of social relationship: 'closeness', 'integration'

Sample predicates	Metaphors (where relevant)
Friendly Warm Happy Harmonious	
Close-knit Integrated Tight	Spatial
Grows Evolves Matures	Organic
Acts Knows Feels	Agency

Figure 1 Predicates and metaphors used with 'community'.

and 'friendliness', and those associated with certain metaphors: spatial ('close-knit'), organism ('growth') and agency (a community 'acts') – see Figure 1. Without exception, where the term 'community' was used with a strongly evaluative force it was positive: 'community' was seen as a good thing.

... In some accounts, for example, the 'community' had been 'disrupted' or even 'finished' by the 'riot'; in others the 'riot' was merely a sign of the cohesiveness of the 'community'. In some accounts the police were depicted as part of the 'community'; in others the disturbance was a conflict between the 'community' and the police. Variability on this scale has now become a very familiar phenomenon. Yet it represents an enormous headache for ... researchers bent on reconstructing exactly what went on, between whom, in the disturbance. ...

Contrast the following passages which illustrate two versions. The first is a statement by the then Home Secretary, William Whitelaw, made in the parliamentary debate which followed the disturbance; the second is from the beginning of a report in the newspaper *Socialist Challenge*.

> *Whitelaw.* As to what the Right Honourable Gentleman says about the community relations work of the police, it does so happen that a police officer in this particular area of Bristol, as I understand, has been very active indeed in the area of Community Council. ...

> [*Socialist Challenge*] On Wednesday 2nd April, the mainly black population of St. Paul's, a Bristol inner-city district, responded to police harassment by mounting a counter attack. ... Almost exactly a year after the police riot in Southall, the black community of St. Paul's fought back against police brutality and won.

Throughout the parliamentary debate the 'riot' was described ... as a problem of 'community relations' and the police were depicted as part of the 'community' ... If a *community* had been disturbed the problem will be one of fractured interpersonal relationships and trust. ... [However, if we see] the event as a riot triggered by ailing 'community relations' it is depicted as an open conflict, with the two sides explicitly characterized as the 'black community' and the police. ...

In accounts of this kind, the cluster of category-bound attributes and the positive force of 'community' contribute three consequences. First, the police are implicitly blamed; for 'communities' are not reasonable targets for police attack (unlike, say, 'thugs' or 'crazed rioters'). Second, actions against the police are legitimated. ... Third, any potential dismissal of people fighting with police as marginal and pathological is undermined.

Source: Potter and Wetherell, 1987, pp.133–6.

READING B
Representation and discourse

Stuart Hall

The first point to note, then, is the shift of attention in Foucault from 'language' to 'discourse'. He studied not language, but *discourse* as a system of representation. Normally, the term *discourse* is used as a linguistic concept. It simply means passages of connected writing or speech. Michel Foucault, however, gave it a different meaning. What interested him were the rules and practices that produced meaningful statements and regulated discourse in different historical periods. By *discourse*, Foucault meant 'a group of statements which provide a language for talking about – a way of representing – the knowledge about a particular topic at a particular historical moment. ... Discourse is about the production of knowledge through language. But ... since all social practices entail *meaning*, and meanings shape and influence what we do – our conduct – all practices have a discursive aspect' (Hall, 1992, p.291). It is important to note that the concept of *discourse* in this usage is not purely a 'linguistic' concept. It is about language *and* practice. It attempts to overcome the traditional distinction between what one *says* (language) and what one *does* (practice).

Discourse, Foucault argues, constructs the topic. It defines and produces the objects of our knowledge. It governs the way that a topic can be meaningfully talked about and reasoned about. It influences how ideas are put into practice and used to regulate the conduct of others. Just as a discourse 'rules in' certain ways of talking about a topic, defining an acceptable and intelligible way to talk, write, or conduct oneself, so also, by definition, it 'rules out', limits and restricts other ways of talking, of conducting ourselves in relation to the topic or constructing knowledge about it. Discourse, Foucault argued, never consists of one statement, one text, one action or one source. The same discourse, characteristic of the way of thinking or the state of knowledge at any one time (what Foucault called the *episteme*), will appear across a range of texts, and as forms of conduct, at a number of different institutional sites within society. However, whenever these discursive events 'refer to the same object, share the same style and ... support a strategy ... a common institutional, and administrative or political drift and pattern' (Cousins and Hussain, 1984, pp.84–5), then they are said by Foucault to belong to the same *discursive formation*. ...

The idea that 'discourse produces the objects of knowledge' and that nothing which is meaningful exists *outside discourse,* is at first sight a disconcerting proposition, which seems to run right against the grain of common-sense thinking. It is worth spending a moment to explore this idea further. Is Foucault saying – as some of his critics have charged – that *nothing exists outside of discourse*? In fact, Foucault does *not* deny that things can have a real, material existence in the world. What he does argue is that 'nothing has any *meaning outside of discourse*' (Foucault, 1972). ...

The main point to get hold of here is the way discourse, representation, knowledge and 'truth' are radically *historicized* by Foucault, in contrast to the rather ahistorical tendency in semiotics. Things meant something and were 'true', he argued, *only within a specific historical context.* Foucault did not believe that the same phenomena would be found across different historical periods. He thought that, in each period, discourse produced forms of knowledge, objects, subjects and practices of knowledge, which differed radically from period to period, with no necessary continuity between them.

Thus, for Foucault, for example, mental illness was not an objective fact, which remained the same in all historical periods, and meant the same thing in all cultures. It was only *within* a definite discursive formation that the object, 'madness', could appear at all, as a meaningful or intelligible construct. It was 'constituted by all that was said, in all the statements that named it, divided it up, described it, explained it, traced its development, indicated its various correlations, judged it, and possibly gave it speech by articulating, in its name, discourses that were to be taken as its own' (1972, p.32). And it was only after a certain definition of 'madness' was put into practice, that the appropriate subject – 'the madman' as current medical and psychiatric knowledge defined 'him' – could appear.

References

COUSINS, M. and HUSSAIN, A.(1984) *Michel Foucault*, Basingstoke, Macmillan.

FOUCAULT, M. (1972) *The Archeology of Knowledge*, London, Tavistock.

HALL, S. (1992) 'The West and the Rest', in HALL, S.and GIEBEN, B.(eds) *Formations of Modernity*, Cambridge, Polity Press/The Open University.

Source: Hall, 1997, pp.44–6.

READING C
Political discourse: homosexuality and its metaphors

Anna Marie Smith

Why was this expression of anxiety around homosexuality, in this particular form, at this particular juncture, so persuasive? Why did the conception of the erosion of the social order through the promotion of homosexuality seem to 'sum up' otherwise disparate concerns, concerns about disease, morality, children and the family, and the relations between central government and local government? Why did the devotion of extensive official discourse to this conception of homosexuality, at this particular time, appear to be a legitimate exercise?

In the late 1980s, discourse on homosexuality was thoroughly intertwined with discourse on AIDS. In terms of the Section 28 supporters' discourse, discourse on AIDS plays a key role in two different ways. First, the AIDS phenomenon is strategically interpreted so that homosexuality no longer appears to be one social element among many, but is represented as a threat to the very existence of other social elements. For example, Baroness Cox stated in the House of Lords, 'I cannot imagine how on earth in this age of AIDS we can be contemplating gay issues in the curriculum.' [Dame Jill] Knight states in the House of Commons, 'Some of that which is being taught to children in our schools would undoubtedly lead to a great spread of AIDS'. She also argues that Section 28 is necessary because 'AIDS starts with and comes mainly from homosexuals' and only spreads to others later. This interpretation of AIDS, so that 'homosexuality' appears to be equivalent to 'threat to others', is of course only one possible interpretation.

The AIDS syndrome does not live in an empirical group of people; indeed, the groundless equation, male gayness = AIDS, is an extremely dangerous strategy of denial by heterosexuals and lesbians of their own risks and responsibilities. The HIV virus associated with AIDS is transmitted by practices which cut across all social groupings, and an individual's imaginary location in a so-called 'low risk group' provides absolutely no protection from the virus. ... The search for the origin of AIDS is in turn nothing more than an attempt to ground this denial of the risks to heterosexuals; claims about the African and homosexual origins of AIDS are shaped more by racist and anti-gay fantasies than by reputable medical research.

Although the supporters of Section 28 engage in several strategic misinterpretations of the AIDS phenomenon, their statements on AIDS build up a legitimating structure which is fundamental to their homophobic discourse in general. The construction of the myth of the promotion of homosexuality is effective in part because it is preceded by the articulation, homosexuality = threat to other elements in the social. Statements on AIDS, both by officials like Knight and by the popular press, prepared the way for Section 28. However, discourse on AIDS is also re-represented in the discourse on Section 28. AIDS 'hysteria' has generated a great deal of hostility towards lesbians and gays, from everyday discrimination to 'queer-bashing'. Section 28 gives this expression of hostility an officially sanctioned and apparently disinterested form. Many individuals would not consider violent or hostile acts towards homosexuals as socially acceptable acts. By contrast, the act of agreeing with an elected official that 'our' children are being threatened by a campaign to promote homosexuality is more readily understood as a socially acceptable act ...

In her claim about AIDS, Knight appears to be expressing her fears about the threat of *illness* here. It should be noted that this expression is organized in terms of supplementary inside-outside metaphors. In Knight's discourse on AIDS and homosexuality, 'homosexuality' is represented as an element which is inherently opposed to the 'norm'. This opposition, however, is given a precise spatial and temporal structure. Homosexuality is equated with a disease which begins outside the 'norm' and later spreads into the 'norm' and contaminates the 'norm'. Her discourse therefore locates homosexuality both as a lethal medical threat and as a foreign invader. By representing homosexuality as an element which wants to cross the boundaries which protect the social order, however, the discourse of the supporters paradoxically creates a sense of a threatened space, the 'natural social order', the 'inside'.

Sontag demonstrates through historical research that the 'foreign invader' has been central to the medical response to disease for centuries. The bubonic plague and cholera were also depicted as foreign invasions. Xenophobic discourse in the late nineteenth century depicted the immigrant as the bearer of cholera, yellow fever, typhoid fever and tuberculosis. For Sontag, the representation of disease as a foreign threat is a basic element in European identity.

Part of the centuries-old conception of Europe as a privileged cultural entity is that it is a place which is colonized by lethal diseases coming from elsewhere. Europe is assumed to be by rights free of disease.
[Sontag, 1989, p.50]

When Tory MPs demanded HIV screening for immigrants travelling from the Third World in the mid-1980s, they were speaking within a well-established tradition.

The representation of disease as originating in foreign elements also mobilizes the ... discourse on immigration. ... [It] is a representation of the threat of subversion in the figure of the diseased gay male invader, and it offers compensation for anxieties about subversion by creating a sense of consensus.

It is taken for granted that a space of sexual normalcy exists as the primordial and natural space, and that, although that space is threatened by the homosexual invader, it remains for the time being uncontaminated. At the same time, however, the [Section 28] supporters' discourse is contradictory, for it contains a vision of the space of the sexual 'norm' as already thoroughly contaminated by queer otherness. In this second representation of the threat of subversive difference, homosexuality is not simply a threatening invader from the outside, but has taken on the properties of a seducer, a floating element whose corrosive effects are already experienced throughout the space of the 'norm'.

References

SONTAG, S. (1989) AIDS and Its Metaphors, New York, Farrar, Strauss and Giroux.

Source: Smith, 1994, pp.196–200.

READING D
Contested places, contested boundaries

Doreen Massey

It can be argued, that old – even rather romantic – notion of place may have within it many connections, if only implicitly, to the (unequal) construction of gender – of masculine and feminine – in current western society. There are a number of distinct threads in the series of arguments here.

To begin with, integral to ideas of places as stable and settled ... is often – explicitly or implicitly – a notion of place as 'home', as a haven of peace and quiet and of retreat. ... There are two elements to this way of thinking: first, there is the explicit analogy between the concepts of place and of home; second, there is the assumption that both are places of rest. Yet, as feminists have often pointed out, for many women home may be the place, not of rest, but of work. Neither is home necessarily a haven of peace and quiet: intra-family relations may be the source of just as much conflict as external social relations. ... The analogy with this notion of home, it is therefore argued, is an ill chosen one. Moreover, the same points can be made directly about places themselves. To imagine ... that the old English village is a place free of problems is to avoid looking at its reality. That whole notion of the settled, happy village as a place of retreat belies the fierce inequality of the social relations on which such societies were in fact built: between master and servant, between landowner and labourer. ...

Moreover, it is asked, who is it who has these romantic views of place (of the village, or of the region one comes from ...), if not those who have the ability to leave? ... In many cases it may be men who are more able to leave, and return to, a place; and women whose lives are enclosed there. Here again, though, there is variation: long distance migration is most certainly not an all-male affair ... in the past most labour migrations have indeed been male dominated; it is only recently that women have come to play a leading role in many migration streams. ... Moreover, it is not necessary to the argument for it always to be the case that men are more mobile in relation to place than women (Irigaray, 1987; Rose, 1993; Massey, 1994). The deeper point made by these critics is that this *way* of characterizing place as home, as an unchanging stability to be looked back on, to be returned to, is itself masculine. ... [W]hat is going on here is a much deeper and more general characterization of 'a place called home' in female terms, as Mother/Woman, as an unchanging point of reference from which one sets out on life. ... All of this in turn raises the issue of the power which can lie in voluntary mobility. The ability to leave, to travel, to return, may be as important in establishing an identity – especially a powerful and independent identity – as may be the attachment to place. ...

There are thus strong arguments for incorporating the interconnections of places into the way in which they are conceptualized. That is, at the same time as recognizing the individual uniqueness of each, places may be conceptualized as essentially open and porous, as interlinked. These arguments have been made ... from ... three positions: first, that current developments make a recognition of this interconnectedness simply impossible to evade; second, that in fact places have for long been open and porous even though it may only have been in more recent years that a recognition of the implications of this has been forced upon our theoretical consciousness; and, third, that there are anyway significant reservations to be made of any concept of identity (whether of person and place) which sees it as essentially bounded in the sense of closed off from outside. But ... places *do* have boundaries around them. There are nation-states and counties; there are the lines drawn around the European Union and there are the boundaries of the local parish. ... But there are a number of points to be made about boundaries.

First, the point which would be made by some ... that *these lines do not embody any eternal truth of places*; rather they are lines drawn by society to serve particular purposes. The county boundaries in the United Kingdom, or those of départments in France or Länder in Germany, do reflect long historical variations between different parts of their countries but they are also lines drawn for purposes of administration: for regional government maybe, or for the delivery of services. All of the boundaries, whether the national borders on the world atlas or the lines marking property and parish on a local map, are socially constructed. They are just as much the product of society as are the other social relations which constitute social space. ...

Second, boundaries inevitably cut across some of the other social relations which construct social space. The places they enclose are not pure. They gain, and have gained, their character by links with elsewhere.

Third, boundaries matter. Where you live in relation to them determines the level of your local taxes and the services you receive, where you were born in relation to them determines your nationality, determines which boundaries you may cross and those which you may not ... Boundaries, in a sense, are one means of organizing social space. They are, or may be, part of the process of place-*making*. And ... an enormous amount of effort may go into constructing a sense of identity within these bounded areas, whether it be national identity or the current moves towards the building of a European identity.

Finally, the drawing of boundaries is an exercise of power. This is true in the big issues of the determination of national boundaries but also in, for instance, the constant debates in the United Kingdom about what is the most appropriate shape for the units of local government. Boundaries may be constructed as protection by the relatively weak; they may also be constructed by the strong to protect their already privileged position. Boundaries are thus an expression of the power structures of society. They are one among the many kinds of social relations which construct space and place.

References

IRIGARAY, L. (1987) 'Sexual difference' in MOI, T.(ed.) *French Feminist Thought: A Reader*, Oxford, Basil Blackwell, pp.118–30.

MASSEY, D. (1994) *Space, Place and Gender*, Cambridge, Polity Press.

ROSE, G. (1993) *Feminism and Geography*, Cambridge, Polity Press.

Source: Massey, 1995, pp.64–9.

Chapter 7
Situated Knowledges:
Rethinking Knowledge and Reality

Contents

1	Introduction	279
1.1	Rethinking the challenges in the social sciences	280

2	Situating knowledge construction: postmodernism, genealogy and realism	281
2.1	Lyotard's report on knowledge	283
2.2	Using genealogy	288
2.3	Reinventing 'reality'	297
2.4	Thinking through knowledge construction	307

3	Situated knowledge: gender and science	311
3.1	Gender and empiricism	313
3.2	Gender and reality	314
3.3	Gender and representation	316
3.4	Reconsidering gender and science	318

4	By way of a conclusion: journey's end?	320
Reading A	Postmodern language games *Madan Sarup*	323
Reading B	The construction of homosexuality *Jeffrey Weeks*	324
Reading C	Abstractions, structures and mechanisms *Andrew Sayer*	326
Reading D	Challenging orthodoxies: gender, ethnicity and social science *Marcia Rice*	329

1   Introduction

In the previous chapters of this book we have explored a wide range of approaches with different assumptions and recommendations for the practices involved in the conduct of social scientific research. We saw how each of these approaches returns again and again to certain basic ideas, such as knowledge, reality, causality, imagination and values. However, each gives these ideas a particular meaning by defining them in a particular way, depending on how they are combined or articulated with other ideas. If you think back to Chapter 3, for instance, you will recall that each of the positivist approaches brings together some of the six general principles of positivism in quite distinct ways. So even with such 'scientific' approaches we can see the relational character of language at work. In this final chapter we explore these basic ideas one last time, especially the relationship between knowledge and reality, which has become the hot spot of debate in the last two decades of the twentieth century. We take this opportunity to rethink these basic ideas by using contemporary interventions in knowledge construction, such as postmodernism, 'genealogy' and realism, as well as the more substantive concerns raised by recent debates on the relationship between gender and science. There are close connections between the ideas developed here and our concern with language, discourse and culture in Chapter 6.

See Figure 3.1 in Chapter 3 and the associated marginal figures throughout chapter 2.

As you will remember, in Chapter 1 we explored the ways in which the approaches in the philosophy of social science can be situated in definite social and historical locations, a theme which has been emphasized throughout this book. Here, in the closing chapter (you can see the structure of the chapter in Figure 7.1), we can develop this a little further by situating the distinction between knowledge and reality in two different but interconnected ways: in terms of knowledge construction and in terms of its location. We look at each in turn.

- Section 2 considers the ideas of 'knowledge' and 'reality' within the terms of reference of three different approaches to epistemology and ontology. Epistemology involves the study of theories of knowledge, the questions we ask about how we know, whereas ontology involves the study of theories of being, the questions we ask about what can really exist. As part of this, we explore the postmodernism of Jean-François Lyotard and the genealogical method of Michel Foucault, as well as one approach which currently defends the idea of 'reality' in the social sciences, critical realism. Moreover, you have the chance to think through some of the overall arguments of the book by considering how realism differs from empiricism (Chapter 3) and idealism (Chapter 4) in social research.

- Section 3 returns to the concerns of situating knowledge in a definite historical and social location, but also considers the role of knowledge construction as part of this process. In this section, the epistemological and ontological questions considered in section 2 will be readdressed by examining the substantive issues raised in attempting to understand the relationship between gender and scientific practice. In particular, three feminist epistemologies help us to see how the approaches considered in this chapter and throughout the book make sense only when we examine their implications for social scientific practice.

Figure 7.1   The structure of the chapter at a glance.

These approaches and debates are still 'hot off the press' and any con-clusions which we can reach will be tentative at best. Nevertheless, each approach considered has already proved to be influential in recent social scientific practice. Your task in this chapter is to begin to think through the implications of viewing one approach as more plausible than the others. Of course, you still have to develop some criteria for making your own decisions on which of these approaches and associated ideas are useful, and you cannot rely on the history of science to tell you which approach is the most appropriate. More specifically, you should ask yourself which set of rules of conduct would suit your own kind of research. Think about the way you define your objects of analysis, the research techniques you think are most appropriate, their compatibility with the discipline or sub-disci-pline of social science within which you work, and so on. If you find one approach more plausible than any other, ask yourself not only why this is the case, but also why you reject other approaches.

Return to the questions in the opening section of Chapter 1.

1.1 Rethinking the challenges in the social sciences

You should remember how, in Chapter 1, we started out on this voyage of discovery through the philosophies of the social sciences by considering the challenges which face the social sciences today. Then, in Chapters 2 and 3, we saw how the social sciences developed as an attempt to under-stand the changes involved in the emergence of the modern world. In par-ticular, we explored how the theological circuit of knowledge gradually gave way to the scientific circuit of knowledge. The construction of the scientific circuit involved two kinds of interconnected intellectual re-sponses to modern conditions, which helped to define what social science was all about. First, it involved defining the form and content of the objects of analysis (society, the economy, the nation-state, the mind and so on) as real things, which we could only understand through the human senses (and not through divine revelation). Second, it involved the development of an account of knowledge construction in order to comprehend these 'real objects' through the conscious mind (described by Kant as the 'knowing subject'). This means that the social sciences tended to mimic the success-ful knowledges of the natural sciences. As the evidence in Chapters 2 and 3

Quickly re-read Chapter 1, section 2 regarding:
• the challenge of change
• the challenge of methods
• the challenge of terminology.

suggests, the most persuasive approaches applied models of analysis from physics, chemistry and biology.

Return to Chapter 2 and quickly re-read section 2.2 on closed and open systems.

In this way the social sciences emerged with a tendency to reproduce the closed-system model of scientific inquiry drawn from scientific experimentation and apply it to the study of people. To recap briefly, a closed system involves the artificial process of constructing a boundary between what you want to study and what you intend to exclude from your analysis. It assumes that your chosen objects are involved in simple relationships and that each object is discrete and has no internal complexity or structure. This model of inquiry also assumes that our knowledge of reality is an uncomplicated mirror reflection of the natural and social worlds (or that it could be, if we managed to eliminate the distortions and illusions associated with cultural values).

As you have seen, the remainder of this book has moved step by step to demonstrate the problems of viewing the 'real world' in such a simplistic way, through an exploration of the complexity, uncertainty and interconnectedness of the objects of analysis in social science. It also acknowledges the complexities of the way in which we understand these objects. In short, we have been exploring the difficulties of coming to terms with the subject–object problem in the social sciences. When people try to understand themselves and their own conditions of existence, it is not surprising that they become tangled up in knots. These conditions of existence play a crucial role in the activity of constructing knowledge in the first place. In this chapter we return to the problem of defining these conditions in order to begin to find ways of untying a few of these knots.

2   Situating knowledge construction: postmodernism, genealogy and realism

In Chapters 2 and 3 we saw how the emergence of science was part of a process through which modern societies came into existence. In a similar way, recent question-marks over the role of science and ideas, such as truth and progress, are part of a broader discussion about social transformations today. These discussions focus upon whether we are entering a new phase of social existence, the 'postmodern condition'. One of the concerns you will have at this stage is how to clarify the difference between the modern and postmodern. Indeed, a plethora of meanings and associations has been attached to the label 'postmodern' and it would be a major task (and distraction) for us to define here the roles that the postmodern condition has played in various disciplines (from art and architecture to sociology and political theory). However, we can identify two areas of concern. First, we can highlight those social transformations which are closely related to the need to rethink the process of knowledge construction. Second, we can consider the broad differences between viewing the present human condition as either 'late modern' or 'postmodern'. However, at the beginning of this section we focus our discussions and illustrations directly on the concerns of knowledge construction.

In Chapter 2 we explored the way in which the emergence of modern conditions was connected to certain processes of transformation in Western societies. To keep the focus on knowledge construction we noted four key transformations which highlighted the changes in the way that we know about the world (the intellectual and religious transformations) and the emergence of new concerns (such as the political and economic transformations). These transformations can be described as 'modernization' processes. However, modernity is more than just these processes; it also refers to the aesthetic response to such rapid changes and to how people coped with the loss of permanence in social existence. This new sensibility, sometimes described as 'modernism', was an expression of the feeling that the world was in perpetual flux and change throughout the nineteenth and twentieth centuries (Berman, 1982; Harvey, 1989). Modernity, therefore, refers to the combination of two things: the way that the people involved are affected by the social and historical experience of the processes of 'modernization', and the new ways of expressing this condition, 'modernism'. In the same way, recent debates on the relationship between modernity and postmodernity are concerned with both a new set of transformative processes and a new aesthetic response to these changes in art, litreature, politics and culture. You may have encountered some of these discussions on architecture, dance and in cultural debates.

> Modernity is the combination of the historical and social experience of both the processes of 'modernization' and their expression through 'modernism'.

In Chapter 1 we considered three interconnected dimensions of contemporary transformations – globalization, environmental change and the communications revolution. Of course, while we are fairly sure that changes are happening, social scientists are in considerable disagreement as to what they are and what they mean. What we can say is that social scientists have responded by rethinking some of the objects of analysis which have been part of the conceptual landscape of the social sciences since the Enlightenment. Let's quickly reconsider the challenges posed by two of these three transformations (we focus on the third one, the relations between the communications revolution and knowledge, in section 2.1). First, the recognition of global flows immediately challenges the ways in which we tend to locate governance within nation-states. It also challenges the tendency of economists to assume that the economy is a clearly defined object with definite characteristics (as in the study of national economies). Even cultural identities are being transformed through the growing interconnectedness of human societies (as represented in Figure 7.2). The recognition of global flows actually reinforces a theme running throughout this book, that the complexity and uncertainty of the things we study as social scientists should lead us to question the uses of closed-system models of scientific inquiry.

Second, the recognition that human beings can have dramatic unintended consequences upon the ecological systems they inhabit has re-emphasized how human activities are interconnected in complex and unpredictable ways with the natural world. This highlights the **anthropocentrism** (human-centredness) of much scientific knowledge and the tendency for social scientists to theorize the relationship between society and nature in an instrumental way (suggesting that natural things only have value in terms of their uses by human beings). The certainty of knowledge and the promise of human progress through the mastery of nature have both been challenged (Smith, 1998). These are just some of the ways in which the familiar categories, objects of analysis, and attitudes within social science are in question. We now turn to three attempts to think through the implications that this questioning process has for the way we construct knowledge. Just to

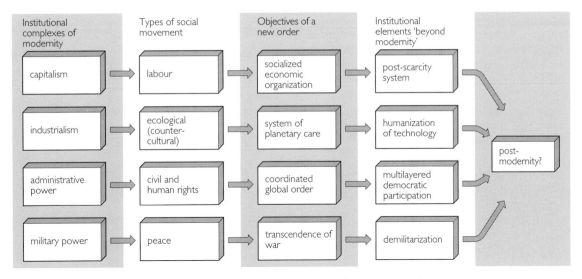

Figure 7.2   One attempt to represent the transformations of present social existence.

make things a little more complicated, remember that you have to take into account the way that each approach attempts to produce knowledge by drawing upon cultural values.

2.1 Lyotard's report on knowledge

In the first example of new approaches to knowledge construction, we consider Jean-François Lyotard's *The Postmodern Condition: A Report on Knowledge* (1984). This text sparked off the controversy in the social sciences about whether the West had entered a new phase of social development. The report, commissioned by the Canadian state of Quebec, originated as a study of the way we understand knowledge in the face of the impact of microelectronic computer technologies. This account synthesized the increased concern about language, discourse and culture *with* a consideration of the effects of the emergence of new information technologies and the communications revolution during the late twentieth century. Lyotard argued that the forces which had constructed the modern industrial social order were now giving way to new dynamic processes based upon information flows and digital processing. In this post-industrial society, Lyotard suggested, modern scientific knowledge was giving way to new conceptions of the role of knowledge: the mode of production had given way to a mode of information, with knowledge industries now driving the economy.

The view of knowledge construction within this account of the postmodern condition has influenced contemporary thinking on the links between knowledge and its location. Lyotard suggested that the **metanarratives** (or 'grand theories') of the modern world have given way to 'little narratives'. Metanarratives are presented as objective scientific accounts, all of which contain the promise that human beings can be emancipated from nature (or in the case of modern social movements like Marxism, emancipated from capitalism). In short, he argues that science no longer provides a useful account of the human condition. In addition, it has been increasingly realized that scientific knowledge does not provide a solution to all human problems and, in fact, can generate its own.

The microelectronic revolution has transformed the way society is organized – the knowledge industries are now the driving force.

Postmodernism attempts to challenge the foundations of the metanarratives of modern thought which underpinned industrial society.

To understand Lyotard's innovative argument, we have to consider how he applies Wittgenstein's theory of **language games** to these problems. In Wittgenstein's later work, *Philosophical Investigations* (1953/1967), instead of seeing sentences as pictures of the world (as in his earlier positivist writings), he came to view language as a series of games, each with its own rules. This undermines any distinction between the real world and language. Indeed, Wittgenstein argued that the problems of philosophy arise not from the real world but from language itself, with our concepts defining our experiences. Rather than seeing the world as something that we can approach through language, he saw the world as existing only within language. Each language game contains its own distinctive set of rules (or set of acceptable moves). Lyotard argued that Western scientific knowledge is really a peculiar language game which denies the relevance of a wide range of other games. In addition, science sets itself up as superior to forms of narrative knowledge, such as folklore, story-telling, common sense and myths.

Knowledge involves a series of language games, each with its own set of rules.

ACTIVITY 7.1

Turn to Reading A, 'Postmodern language games', from Madan Sarup's *An Introductory Guide to Post-structuralism and Postmodernism* (1993).

- What is the connection between technological change and the emergence of postmodernism?

- How does scientific knowledge attempt to separate itself from other forms of knowledge?

- Have scientists been successful in keeping other language games, each with different rules about what can be said and done, out of scientific knowledge?

Thinking back to what you have read so far throughout this book, can you identify one example in which a scientific account pretends that the other narratives are not present? Why not look at Burt's views on the young delinquent (Reading E in Chapter 3)?

Scientific knowledge is presented as the sole use of the 'denotative game', in which the rules are primarily concerned with distinguishing truth from false knowledge. We can see how this works when we think of the way empiricists are concerned to demarcate science from non-science, in terms of whether something can be observed by the senses or, in Popper's case, whether a statement is open to falsification. In the narratives of traditional folklore and story-telling there is still a place for distinguishing between true and false, but other games are often combined with the denotative game. These can include the technical game (governed by rules on what is efficient or inefficient, the best or worst way of doing things) and the prescriptive game (governed by rules on what is just or unjust). It is important to bear in mind that, just as there are different ways of distinguishing true and false, there are different ways of defining efficiency and justice too. Lyotard concludes that scientific knowledge attempts to keep these other

For Lyotard, modern scientific knowledge involves the sole use of the denotative game ...

... whereas narrative knowledge explicitly draws upon more than one language game.

games at bay. However, this is still bound to fail, for whenever the other games are excluded, they always emerge in unexpected ways.

We can see how this happens when values constantly sneak back into scientific accounts. As you know, in early scientific thinking it was common to treat natural objects as machines (for example, the early Cartesian view of chickens as machines for producing eggs). Human societies have been represented as operating either like gigantic engines or like evolving organisms (a feature of functionalism). Today, the analogies and metaphors of computer systems and cybernetics are often used to express social relationships. These kinds of representations of knowledge are vital for making the key ideas of science understandable and plausible. In effect, the reason why such accounts appear to be so plausible is as much to do with the other language games at work in a 'scientific account' as with the emphasis that scientists place on truth claims. Lyotard's approach treats science, and the objective knowledge it attempts to construct, as a metaphorical expression of the desire of scientists to establish their ideas as true.

You may wish to revisit these issues in Chapter 2, section 2.2 on representing science.

Let's now consider the impact of postmodernism on social scientific practice. The postmodern approach places a strong emphasis upon the role of story-telling in social research, as did the examples of discourse analysis in Chapter 6. It also considers how social scientists are often not aware of the way that their narratives combine language games. If we look back at the examples of positivist scientific research in this book, such as Burt's study of the causes of juvenile crime and Morton's attempts to fix the identity of racial groups through the measurement of skulls, we can see how the distinction between true and false alone is not the only game at work. More difficult to identify are examples of social research claiming objectivity when the values involved are not so different from our own. It is much more difficult to dispute the objectivity of arguments with which we agree – and especially when the evidence produced appears to be common sense.

While science attempts to play the denotative game on its own, other language games sneak back in.

See Chapter 3 for studies by both Burt and Morton.

ACTIVITY 7.2

Now return briefly to the readings in Chapter 1 by Peter Saunders, Jean Conway and Annabel Tomas and Helga Dittmar (Readings A, C and D).

- In what ways are they each attempting to produce a true account of their chosen objects of analysis?

- Try to identify any other language games at work in these studies. For instance, can you spot any conceptions of what makes a just society?

Remember to focus on whether these accounts play the denotative game alone or whether other games sneak back in.

By reconsidering these readings from Chapter 1, we can gain a better insight into the way in which Lyotard's account of knowledge construction enables us to identify the unspoken assumptions at work in social research. For a start, each reading attempts to bring out the 'truth' of a situation, whether this refers to the general empirical relationships between types of housing tenure and other patterns of social characteristics (such as social class), *or* whether this involves an attempt to investigate the 'true' depth of a housing crisis, *or* whether the research aims to provide a 'true' account of the lives of homeless people. In all scientific research you will find evidence of the writer playing the 'denotative game'. Some will pretend that other language games have been excluded, but watch out, other games are always at work.

Once we begin to look at how the other games operate in these examples we can obtain a much better view of the role of cultural values in social research. In the cases of Saunders and Conway, although it is hard to spot at first, there are very different views of justice at work. For Saunders, as a neo-liberal sociologist, justice is established through the ways in which individuals make voluntary agreements within exchange relations. Therefore, as long as all participants obey the legal rules at work in the housing market and voluntarily initiate the processes of buying and selling a home or renting and letting property, then, regardless of the collective consequences, the outcome is just. If we compare this with Conway, we can see an alternative criterion of 'social justice' at work, for she sees the collective consequences of these relations within the housing market as unjust. For Conway, the market should be assessed in terms of the happiness or suffering it produces for all members of society.

Here, we can identify a conflict between two ways of thinking about justice: Saunders uses a prescriptive language game based on individual justice whereas Conway draws upon a conception of social justice. There is also the language game based upon efficiency and inefficiency. Saunders stresses the way that private sector operations, where people are free to make their own decisions, are innately more effective than state intervention in solving these problems. Indeed, within the terms of reference of this approach, these issues are not even seen as **social problems** but as **personal troubles** (and as such they are a private matter). Conway, however, believes that this is a social problem and that a more efficient outcome can be achieved through public sector management and regulation of scarce housing resources. Even this brief contrast demonstrates how the use of language game analysis can tell us a great deal about how examples of social research can be better understood.

From examples like this, we can see that postmodernism is not just an account of knowledge, it also has implications for the conduct of social science. So let's now consider how a postmodern approach to knowledge can change the character of a social scientific discipline. In sociology, one of the key theorists responsible for developing the postmodern approach is Zygmunt Bauman, who makes connections between the consumer culture of contemporary capitalism and the emergence of postmodern societies. From Bauman's viewpoint, postmodern societies are composed of complex 'habitats' constructed around various forms and types of identities. These habitats are constantly changing, and with increasing rapidity. This presents a serious challenge to any sociologist attempting to explain social relations and processes, and it highlights the problems generated by sociologists who impose one grand model or theory upon the social world. From the postmodern viewpoint, each habitat contains its own sets of rules and one 'grand theory' or metanarrative cannot convey the diverse habitats of contemporary social life. Actually, Bauman's approach leans heavily on the ideas of the phenomenologist Alfred Schütz in order to make strong connections between his own social scientific practice and the lived experiences of

Social scientists like to play the denotative game, but it's useful to point out the way in which this is linked to prescriptive games.

Language games work together in all areas of knowledge – we can use them to identify the hidden assumptions of social scientific practice.

For an outline of Schütz's approach, see Chapter 1, section 4.1, and Chapter 4, section 5.2.

people today. In particular, Bauman draws upon Schütz's account of the **intersubjective** character of identities and attempts to ensure that his sociological concepts draw from everyday social life. However, Bauman's use of Schützian 'types' is altered by inserting them within the postmodern approach. For Bauman, the 'stranger' is a powerful metaphor, but it is a modern one and as such does not convey the fluidity of all identities in the postmodern condition. In its place, Bauman uses the 'type' of the 'nomad' to convey the aimless wandering and the loss of direction in our experiences of contemporary social life. He contrasts the postmodern 'nomad' with the modern 'pilgrim', who has a purpose and who knows where to go (Bauman, 1993).

Some postmodern theorists argue that it is no longer possible to distinguish fact from fiction – that we live in hyper-reality.

If we look at the cultural commentaries of Jean Baudrillard, we can see a similar kind of argument about the role of cultural transformation as part of the emergence of the postmodern condition. Baudrillard argues that it is no longer possible to distinguish between representation and reality in a conventional way, one which assumes that representation refers to something which really exists. For Baudrillard, all kinds of representation are just 'simulations' of the meanings which have been produced before. This condition, which he describes as *hyper-reality*, involves the blurring of the distinction between what scientists understood as 'fact' and 'fiction'. In hyper-reality meaning is not produced, it is reproduced through simulations, and simulations of simulations and so on. For example, according to Baudrillard, Disneyland is portrayed as a simulation of another simulation, 'America'. This serves to make 'America' look real when, he argues, all of America is Disneyland. Cultural meanings involve constant reinvention and bring together different aspects of representation in different ways, so that, in effect, there is no reality to represent (Baudrillard, 1983; Kellner, 1989). In this account the idea of **reference**, where it is believed that knowledge represents an independent reality, has disappeared completely. There is no reality to refer to.

These kinds of accounts of postmodernity stress the loss of certainty within knowledge, but also its loss in our everyday lives. For instance, if we look at sociological evidence on youth cultures in the 1980s and 1990s, we can find a good illustration of the increased pluralism and fluidity of social life which postmodern accounts suggest. In the 1960s there were still broad trends in fashion and group affiliation associated with a limited number of youth identities (such as hippies, mods and skinheads). Since then the identities have become less clear cut and the eclectic combination of styles and forms of music has become a feature of youth identities. In addition, just when a style seems to achieve a certain formula (and is in danger of becoming typecast) it implodes and a whole series of new styles and musical adaptations emerges. It is in this sense that youth cultures display the condition of **intertextuality**. What postmodernism seems to be suggesting is that we should distrust all attempts to establish fixed foundations in social science, for social forms and practices are changing so frequently and so unpredictably that we have to be much less confident about what we can know.

See Chapter 6, section 3. This is one of the ways in which postmodernism draws upon post-structuralism.

Certainly, the social sciences are now usually less ambitious and more likely to qualify new suggestions. Moreover, social scientific practice is more self-critical than it has been in the past. Yet there is still the presumption that scientific knowledge is the most important way of delivering progress in both knowledge and material terms. In the next section, when we consider Michel Foucault's approach to knowledge construction, we find that he is often placed within the postmodern approach because of his critique of modern knowledge, especially the idea of truth. However, his genealogical approach is different in some respects, for it linked the way we explain our present condition to how we explain the past. In addition, Foucault developed interesting studies of prisons, asylums and sexuality, so we can see what kind of research he was advocating. Above all, he considered the way in which scientific knowledge is itself embedded in the rules of conduct of certain institutions in society, that it is situated both socially and historically.

Summary

Postmodernism rejects the grand theories and metanarratives within modern science for attempting to construct universal explanations of social existence. It emphasizes the need for caution in the face of increased complexity and uncertainty.

Scientists attempt to keep cultural values at bay through the exclusion of all language games except the denotative game, which is only concerned with truth and falsehood; however, the other games re-emerge in all scientific knowledge.

Social scientists can use the language game analysis to highlight the other kinds of criteria which operate in social research (for example, efficiency and justice). It is the combination of language games which makes a piece of research or an argument plausible.

2.2 Using genealogy

In the last chapter, we began to look at Foucault's ideas by drawing upon his account of **discourse**. Foucault developed the idea of discourse by situating it historically. One of the weaknesses of semiological analysis had been its neglect of the way in which all discourses have a past. As a result, semiology tended to produce ahistorical accounts of the generation of meaning through representation. This means that an adequate account of the rules of conduct, established texts and institutions within a discourse would also account for the ways in which discourses as systems of representation are open to change and transformation. This does not mean that discourses are a reflection of the organizational principles of institutions. Nevertheless, Foucault suggested that these changes can only take place through the institutional context in which discourses regulate the production of meaning.

Foucault poses a difficult dilemma for science by asking the question: is it possible to establish 'true knowledge' when the concept of truth itself has had many complex and variable meanings? He identified the way that all ideas were historically specific, but that some concepts and ideas had come to be so widely accepted that they were taken as true. In *Madness and*

Semiology is discussed in Chapter 6, section 2.2.

Revisit 'Representation and discourse', Reading B in Chapter 6 – discourse is a system of representation made up of rules of conduct, established texts and institutions, which regulate what meanings can and cannot be produced in knowledge.

Civilisation (1967), he identified the emergence of the concept of reason, and its opposition to irrationality, in the events and social processes which created the asylums. He argued that the 'insane' were defined, identified and incarcerated in the buildings of the former leper colonies as part of the system which constructed social orders on modern rational principles. Without the emergence of scientific knowledge and rational explanations of the world, he argued, there would have been no mental illness as we understand it today; it would not have been appropriate to define forms of behaviour as rational or irrational or as normal or abnormal in the first place. The creation of 'madness' or 'insanity', like the construction of science, was the complex institutional product of the opposition between reason and unreason at the heart of the modern condition.

Scientific knowledge treats human beings as objects of analysis in a dispassionate and detached way ...

In time, academic disciplines emerged around the study of individuals defined as 'insane', with the emphasis on the treatment and cure of madness. Foucault argued that while this was justified with reference to humanitarian ideals, in practice it legitimized a range of harmful therapies and the intrusion of oppressive institutions into personal lives. Scientific knowledge made such practices more acceptable by treating human beings as objects of analysis who could be studied legitimately in a dispassionate and detached way. Individual cases became instances in a medical classification system. In this way, the human beings who had been classified were objectified and dehumanized. In addition, the people so classified lost their rights to participate in the discussion, for they simply became the matter to be investigated. So Foucault claims that scientific knowledge is used to intervene in personal lives in the name of human progress, yet it is also part of a project to control, dominate and keep people under surveillance. There are strong parallels between these arguments on the relationship between power and knowledge and those of Paul Feyerabend on science as oppressive (Chapter 5, section 3.3).

This link between the production of knowledge and the role of scientists in power relations can be seen in Foucault's *The Birth of the Clinic* (1973). Here, he charts the way that the methods of medical observation were transformed in the nineteenth century. Foucault provides a useful analysis of how medical accounts focused on the expressions of diseases in the human body, visible to the experts' detached scientific gaze – a gaze which dominates, a gaze which reconstructs hidden depths through observing symptoms. So, power relations can be seen in the ways that people are classified in knowledge, the ways in which the 'hidden depths' are charted as normal/pathological and the ways in which knowledge itself is classified. Foucault was highlighting how even the routine aspects of scientific practice involved 'power relations', for the very identity of the person being studied was invented and represented through the eyes of the scientist and, hence, scientists imposed their own presumptions and prejudices on the objects of analysis. At the same time, Foucault argues that scientists read the behaviour of the people being studied as manifestations of the categories which they have invented, so reinforcing the assumption that they are producing a true account. Scientific practice, he argues, is conducted within a definite location, so the kinds of knowledge which science generates have an enormous impact upon the lives of the people who inhabit these locations (a good introduction is McNay, 1994).

ACTIVITY 7.3

Imagine you are the parent of a child who has learning difficulties and you decide to consult an educational psychologist, who conducts a variety of tests to observe and measure the skills of your child. Your child responds to the tests in a variety of ways and the psychologist (the authoritative expert in this example) identifies a pattern and decides that your child is a 'dyslexic child'. As a parent, you breathe a sigh of relief and try to learn more about ways of helping your 'dyslexic child'. Now think about the following questions.

- Is the child any different after the diagnosis?

- Try to identify the ways in which the authoritative expert is considering the child objectively. It may help to think about the role of the tests, the use of the classification system, and the role of the authoritative expert in the treatment and cure of the 'condition'.

- How are the parents brought into the process of classification and treatment?

The approach developed by Foucault helps us reinterpret situations like this in which we tend to take the authority of experts for granted. Of course, psychologists disagree about what can be taken to indicate that a child has dyslexia; nevertheless, they all agree that the subject position of the 'dyslexic child' exists. When people are placed within a classification system such as this they are viewed differently by those around them.

In his later work, Foucault developed the **genealogical** approach to knowledge. This drew upon the critical techniques of Friedrich Nietzsche, who examined the way in which European intellectuals place a strong value on defining certain key ideas in a particular way. For Nietzsche, all the central values of western European societies are situated in definite social contexts and can be revalued through human action. Even ideas such as 'good', 'power', 'equality' were produced at a particular point in time within a particular culture (Foucault, 1977; for a recent interpretation, see Minson, 1985, or Dean, 1994). This means that it is possible to challenge even the key ideas of science and, according to Foucault, revalue them in ways which do not lead to oppression. Foucault was motivated by these concerns to participate in the politics of knowledge by joining the anti-psychiatry movements of the 1970s. He played a key role in the reform of mental care and helped to initiate the closure of asylums in the late twentieth century.

The 'human sciences' are therefore characterized by a complex process of constructing the identities of those they seek to study. In short, knowledge creates new 'subjects' and identifies what is normal and abnormal in relationship to them. The social agents of knowledge (scientists, doctors, teachers, social workers, police officers, social security officers – that is, anyone with the institutional power to define the identity of anyone else) are involved in activities which reinforce the powerlessness of members of a social order. They do this just by assessing people, using distinctions such

... however, in the process of objectification we can also see how scientific knowledge creates new 'subjects'.

as rational/irrational and normal/abnormal. These social agents are also moral agents, for they judge behaviour against cultural values and, in turn, these values only make sense within the discourses concerned. This reinforces the argument developed by Derrida that there is no single, universal subject in knowledge, because the 'subject' (like the object) can be so many things.

You may want to glance back to Derrida in Chapter 6, section 3.2.

Perhaps the best illustration of the way in which 'subjects' are constructed through knowledge can be seen in *Discipline and Punish* (1977), Foucault's own study of the emergence of the prison system in Western societies. Foucault attempts to account for the development of the carceral system of punishment in modern societies, not on the basis of any grand plan or design, but through the myriad applications of the rational principles at work within these societies. The emergence of the prisons corresponds to the emergence of new ways of thinking about the character and causes of criminality, so knowledge construction and institution building go hand in hand. In each approach developed within the history of criminology we can see the emergence of a particular kind of criminal subject, based upon the criminological discourse through which it is constructed. In utilitarian accounts of crime the 'criminal subject' is a rational decision maker, who responds to the legal punishment prescribed for each criminal action. However, the positivist 'criminal subject' is constructed with a disposition towards committing crime, but also with definite individual propensities for reform. In this positivist criminological discourse, where criminals have different ways of responding to different punishments, the punishment should fit the criminal rather than the crime.

In each social scientific discipline, we can find a range of 'subjects' constructed by the competing perspectives within each field of knowledge.

In each case, the 'criminal subject' is constructed in a way which matches the system of representation at work in the criminological discourses concerned, so that the people convicted of illegal actions are punished within the rules of conduct, established texts and institutions which make sense of the world through these discourses. Texts such as *The Young Delinquent* (1925/1961) by Cyril Burt became an indispensable reference point for the social agents of knowledge working in the British criminal justice system. If you compare the American illustration (Figure 7.3, overleaf), from William H. Sheldon's *Varieties of Delinquent Youth* (1949), with the illustrations from British criminology in Burt's research (Chapter 3, section 3.2 and especially Figure 3.5), you can see how, while there was considerable disagreement about what made a criminal subject, both Sheldon and Burt constructed the 'criminal subject' as if it was a product of both biological and social determinations.

For Foucault, the regulation of the production of meaning is closely tied to the regulation of behaviour.

In any account of Foucault's approach to knowledge, there is another feature of *Discipline and Punish* which should be included. The operation of power and knowledge at work in Foucault's account of punishment is seen as a manifestation of a wider set of processes. He argues that the **objectification** of subjects in knowledge is also connected to the **disciplinary** processes through which people are turned into 'docile bodies' in modern society. In particular, he draws upon the Panopticon diagrams sketched by the utilitarian philosopher Jeremy Bentham, which illustrate the best way of securing a docile prison population (see Figure 7.4). In this circular prison, where surveillance is maximized, the prisoners do not know when they are being watched and so behave as if they are observed at all times. In short, they regulate themselves in the way that the institution expects.

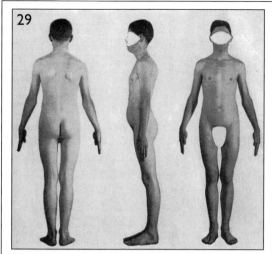

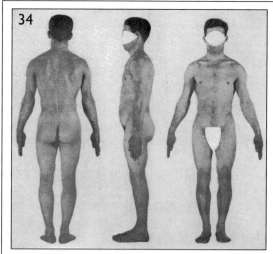

Description: A 16-year-old asthenic mesomorph two inches above average stature. Large, heavy face and neck. Comparatively weak, poorly developed chest and legs. Heavy bones throughout the body, with relatively poor muscling. Later he will fill out to become fat and paunchy. The facial expression has been described as a perpetual leer. Coordination good. He moves, throws, swims, and dances well. Cannot run well or fight well. The greatest weakness is in the legs.

Temperament: Highly energized, extroverted, dramatic, slap-happy sociability. He loves action, noise, crowds, confusion. Remarkably relaxed, greedy for food and for company. Generally described as a good-natured troublemaker. He has one of the loudest voices and filthiest vocabularies yet encountered.

Delinquency: Excessive truancy, persistent minor stealing, larceny, breaking and entering; robbery, destructiveness (as one of a gang), and juvenile racketeering. Identification entirely with 'gangsters'. Never a runaway, never a fighter. Always a fringer, or peripheral follower, in multiform mischief.

Origins and Family: Ninth of twelve, urban family. Father Irish and of average build, an irregularly employed artisan with several court appearances for alcoholism, nonsupport, and the like. Mother, Irish, had court records for larceny, breaking and entering, disturbing the peace. She died in her forties of cancer, when this boy was about 10. Boy then lived with relatives under agency support. At least seven of the siblings have been involved in court delinquency.

Mental History, Achievement: After two years of failure and incorrigibility in the first grade, sent to a disciplinary school. Long series of IQ reports fall between 60 and 67. He is 'feebleminded' yet within his own family was regarded as the smart, clever one. He has been considered a shrewd, successful thief, and 'good with the cops'. His breezy personality is disarming, this boy could hardly be called stupid. Rather gifted in music, and doubtless gifted as an actor, but no vocational plan or interest other than 'big-time crime'. A sociable, extroverted youth who flauntingly defies you to do something with him. Many have taken up the challenge, and he loves the game.

Medical: No serious illnesses or injuries. Many hospital referrals for minor matters and for psychiatric consultation. He can tell you of his ambivalences, his fears, his conversion hysteria, and his castration complex, not to mention his 'narcissistic libido'. This boy picks up Freudian and Christian profanity like a sponge.

Running Record: He had too much energy for us, was too profane, too destructive, too clever a thief, too mendacious. We lacked the disciplinary controls necessary for coping with him. He made no friends but was always a prima donna in the spotlight. Involved in a series of episodes of larceny, but instead of serving sentence was permitted to enter military service, as were many delinquent boys at that time.

Summary: Healthy, over energized asthenic mesomorph who is big for his age and will later be gross and fat. Moron intelligence; strongly delinquent outlook, second-order psychopathy.

Comment: Prognosis still in doubt. This case presents a nice problem in diagnosis. Is the boy feebleminded? We have accepted that label for him, but we shall be more embarassed than surprised if he turns up as governor of Massachusetts.

Description: A 21-year-old extreme mesomorph, an inch under average stature. Gnarled physique and excessively powerful for size. Features heavy, forbidding, asymetrical, badly molded. Coordination excellent he is lithe as a panther, fast, athletic, has perfect rhythm. A wrestling champion at his weight, and in demand as a jitterbug soloist.

Temperament: He is loud, demanding, has a hair-trigger temper, easily infuriated. A speech impediment interferes with articulation and failure on the part of anyone but an obvious 'superior' to understand him precipitates furious vocal exhibitionism. He loved to be nude. It was difficult to get him to cover his mesomorphic torso with a shirt except in cold weather. He was heartily unrestrained. For some reason, perhaps from long institutional life, he had deference for those in authority. Toward others he was a harsh tyrant or constant threat.

Delinquency: Frequent early runaway from a state school for the feebleminded. Often destroyed property during juvenile tantrums. A violent fighter at 13, described as 'not knowing his own strength'. In trouble as a vagrant between 18 and 21. No history of stealing and none of destructiveness or violence after 15.

Origins and family: Illigitimate, from a large city, nothing known of parents except that the father was an Italian laboror and the mother a 'feebleminded' Irish factory worker. The boy spent his first eight years in an orphanage and Church home, then lived in an institution for the feebleminded.

Mental History, Achievement: No grade school attendance. At our clinic his IQ was placed at 56, but he did well on tests of manual dexterity. He had a long-standing vocational ambition to be a cook. No athletic interests, despite great strength and despite having won a wrestling tournament. A very earnest, swarthy youth with the worst possible background and an apparently sincere desire to learn a trade. Also he commands the natural deference due to all extreme mesomorphs.

Medical: Normal birth and development. No serious illnesses or injuries. History of a severe speech impediment with a congenital defect, defective vision and excessively flat feet.

Running record: He was harsh, surly, impatient, difficult to manage. He was feared by other boys and by the staff as well. He seemed to demand restraint, punishment. To our knowledge he never touched alcohol or tobacco while with us. He kept within bounds sexually, did not steal, and although he had no control over his temper and over a surly hostility, he did exercise control over physical violence. He seemed to want, and to depend upon discipline and justice.

Summary: Healthy extreme mesomorph of nearly average stature; great strength, imbecile intelligence, violent temper. Apparently worst possible environmental background.

Comment: The outlook, so far as delinquency is concerned, is probably good. When he came to us he was already conditioned against essential misbehavior. Somebody or some institution had already accomplished this long before we saw him. Possibly it was because he never was mixed up in a 'family'. Perhaps we can abolish delinquent behavior by abolishing 'the family'. It may be that once the idea of father and mother is got rid of, an IQ of 56 will turn out to be quite adequate. Then some of us will have a chance.

Figure 7.3   Criminal subjects are constructed in social science as much as in the criminal justice system.

Similarly, Foucault argues that the same practices of surveillance combined with the careful use of punishment can be seen in all institutions in modern societies – schools, hospitals, housing estates, shopping centres, football terraces and so on.

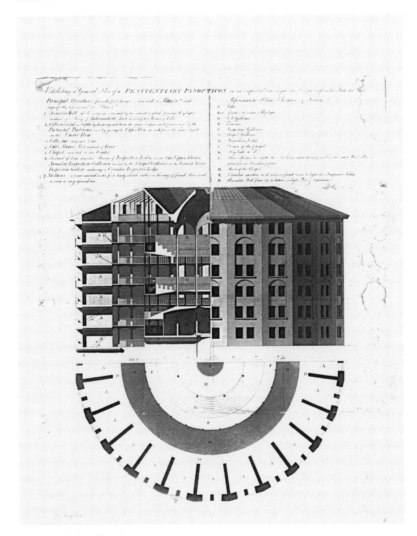

Figure 7.4 The Panopticon.

This means that the carceral practices of the prison system are part of a move towards a 'disciplinary' or 'panoptic' society. At the heart of these practices is the emergence of a new system of power, control and surveillance (operating through what Foucault describes as disciplinary technologies) within all aspects of the institutional life of modern societies. In Foucault's words:

> The carceral texture of society assures both the real capture
> of the body and its perpetual observation; it is, by its very nature,
> the apparatus of punishment that conforms most completely
> to the new economy of power and the instrument of the
> formation of knowledge that this economy needs. Its panoptic
> functioning enables it to play this double role. By virtue of its

methods of fixing, dividing, recording, it has been one of the simplest ... most indispensable conditions for the development of this immense activity of examination that has objectified human behaviour. ... I am not saying that the human sciences emerged from the prison ... it is because they have been conveyed by a specific and new modality of power ... a certain way of rendering the group of men docile and useful. This policy required the involvement of definite relations of knowledge in relations of power; it called for the technique of overlapping subjection and objectification; it brought with it new procedures of individualization. The carceral network constituted one of the armatures of this power-knowledge that has made the human sciences historically possible. Knowable man (soul, individuality, consciousness, conduct, whatever it is called) is the object effect of this analytical investment, of this domination-observation.

(Foucault, 1977, pp.304–5)

So you can see that we have returned to one of the key themes in Chapters 1, 2 and 3: the dangers involved in objectification and detachment. We find that knowledge creates the subject with which it is concerned and measures the evidence against its own definition of the subject. If you reconsider the readings by Stephen Jay Gould (on Samuel G. Morton) and by Hans Eysenck on the intelligence levels of different racial groups, you can see how the subject can be constructed in ways which draw upon and reinforce cultural differences.

See Chapter 3, Readings C and D.

Stuart Hall provides a useful way of thinking about the role of the 'subject' in the social sciences.

Foucault's 'subject' seems to be produced through discourse in *two* different senses or places. First, the discourse itself produces 'subjects' – figures who personify the particular forms of knowledge which the discourse produces. These subjects have the attributes we would expect as these are defined by the discourse: the madman, the hysterical woman, the homosexual, the individualized criminal, and so on. These figures are specific to specific discursive regimes and historical periods. But the discourse also produces a *place for the subject* (i.e. the reader or viewer, who is also 'subjected to' discourse) from which its particular knowledge and meaning most makes sense. It is not inevitable that all individuals in a particular period will become the subjects of a particular discourse in this sense, and thus the bearers of its power/ knowledge. But for them – us – to do so, they – we – must locate themselves/ourselves in the *position* from which the discourse makes most sense, and thus become its 'subjects' by 'subjecting' ourselves to its meanings, power and regulation. All discourses, then, construct *subject-positions*, from which alone they make sense.

(Hall, 1997, p.56)

You can see, then, that the way we construct 'subjects' takes place within discourse, and that the subject is often invented and reinvented through a succession of 'figures' such as 'delinquent youth' (Reading E in Chapter 3), 'problem families', the 'emotionally disturbed child' (Reading A in Chapter 5), and the 'black mugger' (Hall et al., 1978). However, this involves more than simply constructing stereotypes or typifications. For Foucault, it also means that the discourse within which the subjects are created regulates the production of meaning through reference to these kinds of figures. So, to discuss these categories and to produce meaning in an intelligible way within such a discourse, we end up reinforcing the preconceptions upon which these subjects are based. Similarly, you will find later in this chapter that subjects are produced in ways which draw upon particular conceptions of appropriate gender roles. The history of the social sciences is packed with examples where the opposition of normal/pathological is articulated with that of masculinity and femininity.

ACTIVITY 7.4

Now turn to Reading B, 'The construction of homosexuality' by Jeffrey Weeks, from *Sex, Politics and Society* (1989).

- In what ways is the subject position of the 'homosexual' identified by Weeks?

Quickly re-read Burt's account of the young delinquent (Chapter 3, Reading E) and Vogel and Bell's account of the emotionally disturbed child (Chapter 5, Reading A).

- Are there any differences between the way in which the subject is defined as a 'young delinquent' or 'emotionally disturbed child' and the way in which 'the homosexual' as a subject is understood by Weeks?

- You may also find it useful to compare the reading by Weeks with the reading from Smith's account of homosexuality in political discourse (Chapter 6, Reading C).

What conclusions can we draw from looking at these readings in this way? It can be argued that there was no grand design which existed behind the developments in question, and certainly no march of progress, but rather a series of coincidental changes. For Foucault, all accounts of knowledge are 'histories of the present' in that they involve the reinterpretation of the past in the light of present concerns. In effect, we should recognize that many social sciences often consider established social institutions as the culmination of social development, as the product of a **march of progress**. To avoid this, Foucault developed his own genealogical accounts of the emergence of prisons, welfare institutions and hospitals without identifying definite causes and without treating history as progressive. Indeed, in some respects, he argued that these institutions made things worse for those who had the misfortune to be placed within them.

Similarly, the story of the development of scientific knowledge since the Enlightenment has often been characterized, within historical accounts, as a series of logical and successive steps in the growth of civilization and away from primitiveness and barbarism. For Foucault, all such claims should be viewed with suspicion. Foucault concluded that all forms of knowledge are intimately related to power relations at all levels of social

g

Genealogy traces the changes in both knowledge construction and social institutions without attributing the changes to an underlying cause and without assuming that there is progress.

life. Jacques Donzelot applied these ideas in *The Policing of Families* (1979), where he suggested that the social services departments, which have proliferated in Western societies in the late twentieth century, justified their own existence by reference to the need to constantly monitor personal relationships within families. From this perspective, much of post-war sociology on the welfare state and on the deficiencies of families are implicated in the policing of personal life. Historical accounts tend to celebrate the welfare state as the end product of a civilizing process, transforming such intrusions and interferences in everyday life into a virtue. For Richard Rorty, although the conclusions which Foucault presents are certainly disturbing, they still provide the 'best account of the dark side of the human sciences' (Rorty, 1994). What Rorty means is that Foucault demonstrates how scientific knowledge can produce 'subjects' in such a way as to transform people into docile bodies and leave them in a position of powerlessness.

However, there is also a message of hope in Foucault's account. While he demonstrates how the power/knowledge links are very effective, discourses only work as systems of domination through the rules of conduct, texts and institutional practices where meaning is produced. Power always generates its own forms of resistance – and if meanings are produced, they can also be subverted and changed. However, this can be achieved only through a root-and-branch transformation of both the institutions concerned and the way in which subjects are constructed through knowledge itself. In the next section we consider the last of the three new approaches to knowledge construction, the realist approach, and here again there is a strong emphasis on the relationship between subject and object in social science, although in a very different way from that of Foucault. In addition, the realist approach believes that it is possible to transform the conditions in which people live, but only if you already know and understand what is really out there. So it is an approach which brings 'reality' back on to centre stage.

Summary

Genealogy offers an approach to the study of social relations which:

- integrates the study of historical change with a recognition of contemporary cultural values;
- attempts to avoid the tendency to assume that all changes have definite causes.

The discourses through which the meanings of scientific knowledge are produced constantly invent and reinvent 'new subjects' (such as the 'criminal subject', 'emotionally disturbed child' and 'madman') in a way which allows social researchers to identify the normality and abnormality and the rationality and irrationality of human behaviour.

Foucault places a special emphasis on the role of knowledge in power relations; he sees science as part of a process which produces 'subjects' and in so doing transforms people into docile bodies.

2.3 Reinventing 'reality'

In the previous section we saw how subjects and objects are closely interconnected. In this section we explore an approach which also takes the complexity of the subject–object problem seriously, but which attempts to identify what 'reality' involves as well. The new interpretations of social scientific knowledge covered so far have, through the recognition of language, discourse and culture, had an impact on social scientific practice. The arguments of conventionalists that knowledge is a social product and, more recently, the critical perspectives of Roland Barthes, Jacques Derrida, Michel Foucault and Jean-François Lyotard on the complexities of representation have all left the traditional claims of science severely undermined. The main contender in defending the existence of 'reality' and the role of knowledge in understanding it as part of social scientific practice is critical realism. The realist approach is deeply critical of positivism and falsificationism, but still attempts to use the methods and assumptions of natural science to study the social world. In addition, realism tries to take on board some of the insights of idealist and conventionalist criticisms of empiricist approaches. This may seem like a difficult trick to pull off in the light of the differences between the approaches outlined above. However, realists suggest that earlier forms of **naturalism** misunderstood science, for they viewed it as the sole use of a closed-system model of inquiry. Similarly, even the opponents of naturalism still see the closed system as the only way to think of science. Realists, instead, argue that science only makes sense in open systems. So both supporters and critics of naturalism misunderstand the natural scientific method.

See Chapter 2, Table 2.1 on the difference between closed and open systems.

Earlier (in Chapter 4), we explored the way in which the questions we ask have a big effect on the kind of answers we are likely to find. You saw how the empiricist question 'What do we experience?' leads to a concern with evidence from perceptions, impressions and sensations. The idealist approach, however, which you also considered in Chapter 4, asked the question 'What are the conditions of possibility of experience?' (that is, what do we need to make sense of the evidence we gather from our perceptions, impressions and sensations). The idealist answer to this question is that people use mental constructs in imaginative ways to organize this complex evidence, to give it shape and to identify connections and patterns. Realists, too, accept that we do have to use our perceptions, impressions and sensations and that we do imaginatively organize our experiences, but they also ask a different kind of transcendental question. The realist transcendental question is 'What are the conditions of possibility of science (or, rather, the scientific method)?'

Realists think about what the 'real world' must be like for the scientific method to be possible.

In doing this, they draw attention to the way in which we have concentrated too much on what scientists do (or what they say they do). Instead, this realist kind of transcendental question asks us to think about what the world must be like for 'experimental activity' (the imaginative understanding of complex evidence drawn from our senses) to be possible. They argue that experiments only work so effectively in identifying the properties of things because the things already have these properties in the first place. For a realist, then, this means that there are real things we do not know. Therefore, for the scientific method to have any intelligibility, the things we study have properties, dispositions and susceptibilities by virtue of their internal structure (regardless of the arguments that contend we can give meaning to them only through language, discourse and culture). By taking the example of an experiment, we can see how natural things are transformed in the experimental setting simply by changing the conditions. In the earlier examples of experiments (Chapter 2, section 2.2) we looked at the composition of light, the production of oxygen and the effects of combustion on magnesium strips. To take this last example, what the realist argument suggests is that magnesium always has the properties for producing an intense flare and that these properties are 'real' regardless of whether this would happen independently of the experimental situation. Similarly, water has the capacity to convert from a liquid into a gas at a given temperature, regardless of whether or not it is subjected to these conditions. Thus, for realists, all objects have intrinsic properties and structures and their capacity to act in certain ways exists by virtue of these properties.

Experiments are intelligible – that is, they make sense – because of the real existence of the properties and capacities of objects.

Whereas the empiricist identifies causal laws by identifying **empirical regularities**, a realist view of causality focuses on the structures of objects. The properties of objects continue to exist regardless of whether or not they are placed in the experimental conditions which produce observable results. Thus, according to realists, it is also possible to construct causal laws regardless of whether successful predictions corroborate the theories developed. Realists are concerned with the conditions of the real world rather than just with the existing body of knowledge. This does not mean that we can leap to conclusions about what those internal 'structures' involve. However, it does mean that we can assume that there is something out there which can be understood if we manage to identify the conditions that activate these structures, so creating an 'event' (a process which realists refer to as a 'generative mechanism'), as Figure 7.5 demonstrates. So realists are interested in what the real world is like (they ask ontological questions), as well as how we experience, come to know and understand this reality (involving epistemological questions). For a realist, reality has three levels (empirical, actual and real or deep), which have to be distinguished if we are understand how things work.

Causality concerns the structures of objects and how they produce events in different conditions.

In Figure 7.5 we can see how the 'empirical level' of perceptions, impressions and sensations is distinguished from the 'actual level' of events and states of affairs, which are the products of the imaginative practices of people making sense of the world in which they live. Events can be understood as something like the collapse of a liberal democratic regime, the response to the death of a significant public figure, or an increase in recorded crimes in a given year. When we identify an event, we are saying that it needs to be explained. We have already seen how recorded crimes, as in Figure 4.4 in Chapter 4, have been identified as events. However, each representation of the objects in question is quite distinct. A 'state of affairs' refers to the normal conditions within which such events take place, such as institutions of a liberal political system, the rules of conduct for behaviour at state funerals and the operation of the criminal justice system.

For the realist, there are three levels of reality, which are always out of phase with each other.

Many empiricists do not believe that it is possible to distinguish between the things we experience and the mental constructs we use to understand the empirical level and, in effect, they collapse these two levels together. This is a **flat ontology**, where perceptions (the empirical level) and events (the actual level) are indistinguishable. This approach also denies the existence of anything which cannot be observed. So the 'deep level' simply does not exist for an empiricist, because any attempt to think beyond experience

| **empirical** | perceptions, impressions, sensations |

| **actual** | events, states of affairs |

| **real/deep** | structures, mechanisms, powers/liabilities |

Realists tend to focus on the structures, mechanisms and powers/liabilities, which are defined below.

structures	the relations between the parts of an object give an object its characteristic properties and they exist independently of our knowledge of them
mechanisms	the way in which the structure of an object can, within definite conditions, generate an observable event
powers/liabilities	the particular structure of an object will ensure that the object has the capacity to do certain things in certain conditions *and* that it is susceptible to effects from the same or different conditions; these conditions are themselves made up of other structures and their mechanisms

Figure 7.5   The three ontological levels of reality: empirical, actual and real/deep.

You can revisit these different interpretations of Durkheim in Chapters 3 and 4.

is just speculation. Interestingly, one study which is taken as a classic example of how to apply the **empiricist** method can be interpreted as doing exactly this, of distinguishing the empirical from the actual. The research by Émile Durkheim on *Suicide* (1897/1952) had been seen as both positivist and idealist, and earlier I promised to return to this example. Recently, Steve Taylor has argued that Durkheim's analysis is actually realist. Taylor suggests that the empirical evidence in Durkheim's study, which demonstrates the relations between suicide, location, dependency and religious affiliation, is shaped by Durkheim's identification of two underlying forces, integration and regulation. This interpretation suggests that suicide is the empirical manifestation of excessive integration (altruistic suicide) or insufficient integration (egoistic suicide), and of excessive regulation (fatalistic suicide) or insufficient regulation (anomic suicide). These two forces are not observable and, it is argued, we can only comprehend their existence through careful abstraction (Taylor, 1982).

Since Chapter 4, you have seen how the empiricist approach has been repeatedly questioned. By recognizing that we can interpret experiences in different ways, idealist accounts highlight the way in which the 'empirical' and 'actual' levels are different. However, like empiricists, idealists still do not accept that there is a deeper reality than the things we experience imaginatively. In a similar way to idealists, realists accept that the empirical and actual levels are out of phase with each other, but they also pose the existence of a third deeper level upon which the other two levels are based. We can see from Figure 7.6 that, for realists, the empirical and actual levels are not possible without this underlying realm of structures, mechanisms and powers/liabilities.

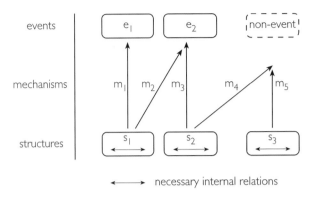

The idea of internal relations is explained in Reading C as part of Activity 7.5.

Figure 7.6 Structures, mechanisms and events.

Before we consider the implications of these arguments for social research, we also have to consider what this means for 'causality' – how we explain what is going on in the world around us. While some of these arguments may appear to raise the obvious, this approach highlights some of the simplistic aspects of many existing accounts of causality (of relations between cause and effect). At this point, we need to compare and contrast how empiricists, idealists and realists produce causal laws in their scientific explanations (see also Figure 7.7).

- *Regularity determinism* – empiricists argue that causal laws can be established simply by reference to **empirical regularities** (a constant conjunction of events between two variables; that is: if *x* then *y*). As you saw in Chapter 3, this means that a scientific explanation can be based simply upon evidence of two or more things happening in a regular way, although such regularities are taken more seriously if they fit our existing knowledge. Empricists also assume that facts and values are separate, that observation is separate from theory and that explanations are symmetrical with predictions.

You may find it useful to look quickly at Chapter 3, Figure 3.1, and Chapter 4, Table 4.1.

- *Intelligibility determinism* – idealists tend to assume that the imaginative way in which we make sense of the complex empirical world requires a different approach to causality. For idealists, an empirical regularity is a useful starting-point and a necessary part of any causal explanation, but it is not in itself sufficient for establishing a causal law. Idealists argue that the distinctions between facts and values and between observation and theory do not convey the way in which knowledge is produced. They also suggest that explanations do not have to predict specific outcomes to be useful, but only identify what patterns of evidence we would expect from a given cause.

- *Ubiquity determinism* – realists argue that an empirical regularity is neither sufficient nor necessary for establishing a causal law. The structures at work in a given situation, which can generate mechanisms in certain conditions are not always going to produce events for us to experience imaginatively. Sometimes a particular structure will generate an event in conjunction with other structures and mechanisms, and sometimes it will not, depending on the conditions.

In certain situations, the mechanisms generated from one structure may be cancelled out by those generated from elsewhere and therefore no definite event is produced.

The status of a constant conjunction of events is …	*necessary*	*sufficient*	… for a causal law statement
empiricism	✓	✓	regularity determinism
idealism	✓	✗	intelligibility determinism
realism	✗	✗	ubiquity determinism

Figure 7.7 Some you see and some you don't – three ways of defining causality.

So far, we have a useful set of contrasts between empiricism, idealism and realism, based on:

- the kinds of questions they ask;
- the kind of reality they think exists;
- the kinds of explanations they produce when answering their initial questions.

Realism does not dismiss the insights of empiricism and idealism but incorporates them within a broader concern to identify the properties of the 'real world'.

While empiricism takes experience seriously and idealism takes our imagination of experience seriously, realism takes the real structures of objects seriously. So the attempt to apply the assumptions and methods of the natural sciences to the social sciences now needs a thorough reassessment. If the realists are right, then the debate between **naturalism** and anti-naturalism has to be re-run. In particular, we should reassess the practices of natural science and explore what kinds of natural science offer useful analogues for studying people. A starting-point would be those natural sciences which recognize that uncertainty and complexity cannot be wished away. When we think of social objects, however, we still have to recognize that people are intrinsically different from rocks, plants and weather systems, and a realist social science has to accommodate this. As a first step towards thinking about what a realist social science would mean, we have to reconsider the subject–object problem one last time.

If we were to attempt to put into operation a positivist model of natural science, we would be considering the relationship between subject and object in the manner of Figure 7.8.

Figure 7.8 Four ways of seeing the subject–object relationship: step one.

See Chapter 4, section 2, if you need to remind yourself of the arguments of the idealists.

This assumes that the scientist and the object of analysis are clearly separate things, rather like a geologist studying a rock or a botanist observing plant growth. It also assumes that both subject and object are simple in their own composition, in that they possess no internal complexity. If we take on board the arguments of the idealist approaches, we can also see how it is possible to interpret the same empirical evidence in different ways. This problematized the simplistic vision of knowledge construction which underpinned positivist science. We know that scientists make sense of natural things through their location within organized communities, each with their own language, assumptions, methods and values, as we can see in Figure 7.9.

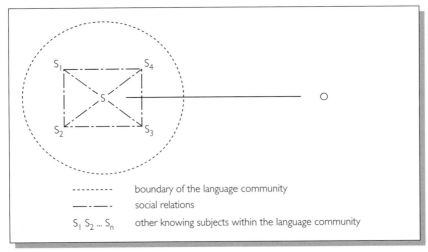

See Chapter 5, section 3.

Figure 7.9
Four ways of seeing the subject–object relationship: step two

In Thomas Kuhn's account, for instance, these communities were the institutional locations for paradigms and even had their own ways of demarcating scientific from non-scientific knowledge. The moment we move from the scientific study of natural things to studying people, there are further complications. In Figure 7.10 we can see how acknowledging the complexity of the objects of analysis changes the ground rules for thinking about scientific activity.

Even natural scientists make sense of what they do in organized communities using a common language.

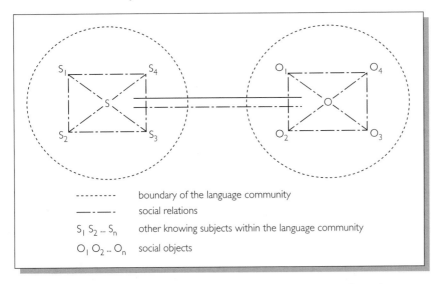

Figure 7.10
Four ways of seeing the subject–object relationship: step three.

One further complicating factor remains to be introduced. As you discovered in the opening chapters of this book, when we study people we are also studying ourselves. It is impossible to separate our own uses of language and cultural values from the language system and cultural values

There are important differences between studying natural things and studying people.

of the objects we study; as Figure 7.11 demonstrates, we are always part of the object, and any sense of detachment is always artificial.

When people study people, things become much more complicated.

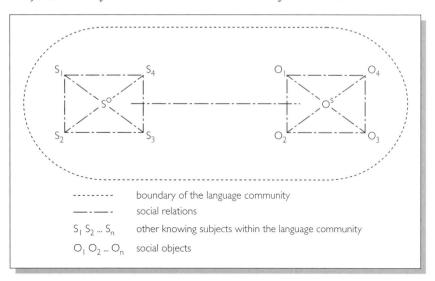

Figure 7.11
Four ways of seeing the subject–object relationship: step four.

It is this which makes the recognition of the role of language, discourse and culture so important to scientific practice. If we consider these four ways of thinking about the subject–object problem, then it is not surprising that social scientists have often rejected naturalism. However, as you have seen in this section, we do not have to define natural science in an empiricist way, as both the supporters and the critics of empiricism within the social sciences have tended to do.

The realist philosopher Roy Bhaskar suggests that any attempt to apply the methods and assumptions of natural science to the study of social relations must recognize that social structures and mechanisms operate in a different way from natural structures and mechanisms.

Don't worry about the terminology here, we'll come back to the difference between structure and agency before the end of the section.

- Social structures do not exist independently of the activities they govern.
- Social structures do not exist independently of the agents' conceptions of what they are doing in their activities.
- Social structures may be relatively enduring (they are situated in a particular space and time).
- Social structures are reproduced and transformed through social agents which are, in turn, dependent upon the relationship between structure and 'praxis' (Bhaskar's way of defining 'agency').

Let's look at the example of family structures, which are produced through relations between parents and children, between marital or cohabiting partners, between siblings, between close and distant relations and so on. The people who occupy these positions within family structures have, on the whole, a fairly good idea of what is expected of them. However, even though family structures may appear to have a solid form, they only remain in this form as long as the people involved accept the arrangements. Indeed, family structures can undergo fairly extensive transformations.

So realists do want to establish naturalism, but only in a way which acknowledges the complexity of open systems in both the natural and social worlds (Bhaskar, 1979, 1986). While realism rejects the application of positivist and empiricist assumptions (largely modelled on physics) in the social sciences, realists argue that there are alternative sources of natural science analogues for the social sciences, such as meteorology, palaeontology and seismology, which have the status of science but which recognize the complexity and unpredictability of their objects. In the study of weather systems in meteorology, scientists can predict patterns, but the failure of predictions does not necessarily undermine their explanations (tendencies) of the forces producing the weather. Similarly, seismology recognizes that earthquakes are quite unpredictable. These natural sciences accept that closure is absent and that objects exist in open systems.

ACTIVITY 7.5

Now consider Reading C, 'Abstractions, structures and mechanisms' by Andrew Sayer, from *Method in Social Science: A realist approach* (1992).

- In what ways does Sayer define structure? What is the difference between necessary and contingent relations?

- Think of a situation with which you are familiar, such as a school, workplace, community centre, law court or any situation which has an institutional basis. Try to make a list of the structured relationships at work in this situation and identify which relations are necessary and which are contingent.

For instance, in a law court the relation between a lawyer and a client is internally necessary, but the relation between this client and the other clients of this lawyer is a contingent one. To take another example, in a university a student will have a necessary relationship with a particular tutor and with the student welfare officer; however, the relationship between the tutor and welfare officer is contingent. Through this kind of analysis, we can begin to build a picture of the complex relations in any social situation.

So realist approaches to the social world attempt to identify the structures and mechanisms through which social events are understood. A structure is described as a necessary relationship which endures over time and space, such as those between employer and employee, landlord and tenant, parents and children, and teachers and students. The relations are necessary because each role exists only in relationship to other roles. For a realist, it is a nonsense to suggest that 'Everyone can be a capitalist by the year 2000' (as the British Conservative Party did in the 1980s). For a realist, there can be no capitalists without workers (just as there can be no tutors without students), so some people cannot be capitalists. Moreover, the very definition of what it means to be capitalist only exists through the relationship with workers. Similarly tutors without students no longer remain tutors, for the activity of teaching depends on sustaining this relationship.

Social structures involve necessary relationships which endure in time and space; necessary relationships are those in which each part depends on the other parts for its own existence.

We can see how realists ask very different kinds of questions from empiricists. For instance, empiricist social researchers would treat divorce and crime as discrete events and would assume that an empirical regularity between higher divorce rates and increases in crime suggests that a causal law is at work (usually that an increase in family instability is the cause of an increase in recorded crime). Realists, on the other hand, would attempt to explain the social structures which produce these complex empirical patterns. Empiricism provides a shallow account of crime and family instability, which ignores the complex structures and mechanisms at work in family life and the criminal justice system as well as other areas of social life. Moreover, realists emphasize the way in which structures can acquire a degree of solidity and apparent permanence, that we should recognize the legacy of the past in shaping our present concerns and desires.

In answering the question 'What are the conditions of possibility of social science?', realists answer that social structures, like natural ones, have definite properties.

The realist analysis of social life emphasizes the ways in which all social structures are ultimately related to the concrete practices of members of society (that is, social agency). According to Bhaskar, this relationship is often inadequately theorized and many social scientists fall into the trap of treating 'structure' as the active category and 'agency' as an empty and passive category. Alternatively, they can fall into the trap of seeing agency as active and the social structure as a passive outcome. This leads to what Bhaskar portrayed as the two errors of knowledge construction: reification and voluntarism.

- *Reification* – involves becoming too concerned with the unacknowledged conditions or unintended consequences of action. For example, in the functionalist sociology of Talcott Parsons, agency is reduced to the position of a passive carrier of social roles and this neglects the need to understand purposeful and meaningful action (Parsons, 1951).

See Chapter 4, section 4 for an account of rational choice theory.

- *Voluntarism* – focuses upon the intentions and purposes of actors, in that it ignores the unacknowledged conditions and the unintended consequences of action. An example of voluntarism can be seen in rational choice theories – social structure is the passive result of the total sum of individual actions.

A number of attempts have been made to overcome the one-sided nature of these approaches. Anthony Giddens attempts to overcome the view that social structure and the actions of agents are two different things, seeing them instead as two sides of the same coin. To understand human action, he argues, we must focus upon the duality of structure and agency (in Bhaskar's realist terminology, agency is described as 'praxis'). Giddens attempts to overcome these problems by viewing the properties of social structures as both enabling and constraining for human action and sees structure as both the medium and outcome of social agency.

Social structures are both the medium and the outcome of social agency.

To illustrate this, Giddens uses the 'language-analogue'. First, the language structure is a *medium*, such that all acts of communication generally conform to the rules of the linguistic game (involving the possession and the exercise of a range of skills) if they are to be understood. Second, the language structure is (simultaneously) the *outcome*, such that the practice of communication reproduces or transforms language just as voting and political group activity reproduces or transforms the political system, *or* being employed as wage-labour reproduces or transforms capitalism, *or* domestic servitude reproduces or transforms patriarchal family life. These examples illustrate the way in which the practical knowledge and capabilities which are necessary for everyday life are preconditions for social structure (Giddens, 1976, 1979, pp. 69–79, 1984). As a realist, Bhaskar adopts a similar approach but gives structure a stronger grounding by placing a greater emphasis upon the 'pre-existence of social forms'. For Bhaskar, **structure** is both the ever-present condition (material cause) and the reproduced/transformed outcome of human agency. Structural forms may operate as constraints for certain agents, while offering opportunities for others by giving them strategic advantage. For instance, when we look at employment opportunities in the labour market, especially the different opportunities for men and women, for feminist realists the structural forms of 'patriarchy' create opportunities for men but present obstacles, constraints and 'glass ceilings' for women. On the other side of this equation, **agency** involves the conscious production of social life and the, possibly, unintended and/or unconscious reproduction/transformation of structure (bearing in mind that the structures produced are also the future conditions of action). This complex relationship can be more clearly represented in Bhaskar's 'transformational model of social activity' in Figure 7.12.

Through the identification of structures as human constructions, realists hope to identify the ways in which it is possible to transform social life and secure the emancipation of human beings. This philosophy of social science has been used by a range of approaches in the social sciences which attempt to emancipate human beings from exploitative relationships, such as that of the Marxists (like Bhaskar himself), of radical and socialist feminists, of critical criminology and in some studies of ethnicity, such as Paul Gilroy's *There Ain't No Black in the Union Jack* (1987). All of these approaches are concerned with identifying the structures which oppress people and using this knowledge to change the way society is organized.

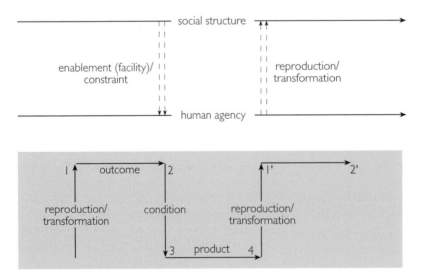

Movement of arrows from left to right is an indication of the passage of time.

1,1' – unintended consequences
  2 – unacknowledged conditions (properties of practices)
  3 – unconscious motivation
  4 – tacit skills (properties of agents)
1,1' – unintended consequences
1 and 2 place limits upon the individual's understanding of social life,
while 3 and 4 place limits upon one's understanding of oneself.

Figure 7.12 Transformational model of social activity.

For empiricist critics of realism, these structures and mechanisms cannot be taken seriously because they are not necessarily observable and the law statements produced cannot be taken as useful predictive tools. Concepts such as 'capitalism', in Marxist versions of this approach, are seen as speculative abstractions. Empiricists argue that we can only observe individual employers and employees, or business companies and people engaged in labour markets, and that we cannot observe the 'bourgeoisie' or the 'proletariat'. To empiricists, these approaches involve a pseudo-scientific attempt to camouflage political ideologies as science. However, realists would see themselves as scientific and view the empiricists as attempting to justify the status quo ideologically. The distinction between science and ideology, of course, depends upon your criteria for what constitutes science, or how you distinguish truth from falsehood. Perhaps it is better to see the difference between them as a paradigmatic one, acknowledging that they live in very different worlds. Alternatively, they could be seen as different versions of the exclusive use of the denotative language game, except in the realist case we see an implicit acknowledgement of the importance of emancipation to achieve a 'just' society. So, realism, if we think back to Lyotard's argument, brings together denotative and prescriptive language games.

Summary

Realist theories of science start from the premise that for science to be intelligible there are real things, with definite properties, for scientists to observe and experiment upon.

Realist social science attempts to identify the social structures which human beings inhabit, but also sees them as produced, reproduced and transformed through human agency.

Realism recognizes the importance of experience and imagination, but says that we should also try to dig deeper to find how things work.

2.4 Thinking through knowledge construction

So, even if we agree that things are changing, does this mean that we should think of the present human condition as a new stage of social existence or the continuation of what we have already experienced throughout modernity? This depends upon how we define modernity. If we think of the modern period, particularly the Enlightenment period, as a complete transformation from some kind of premodern existence, then the suggestion that we have now entered a new stage of existence seems more plausible. However, this depends upon thinking of modernity as characterized by the rational pursuit of universal knowledge and holding that all things should be studied in the manner of the natural sciences. It also assumes that the accumulation of knowledge brings us closer to the truth and that human progress is the most important objective of knowledge construction. In this way, the postmodern can be seen as a rejection of all these things. However, there is a danger in adopting this caricature of the experience of modern conditions, for it reduces science to a crude positivist impulse, the notion that we can be sure our latest conclusions must be true. The previous chapters demonstrate that things are much more complex than this.

The status of truth has been questioned by the philosopher Richard Rorty in *Philosophy and the Mirror of Nature* (1980). He suggests that the problems of explaining and understanding the world stem from the theories of knowledge (or epistemologies) themselves and their tendency to see the mind as a great mirror of reality. Like Lyotard, Rorty also drew upon Wittgenstein's later work to recognize the inadequacies of viewing language as a picture of reality, because this view of language as a reflection ignores the imaginative uses of language. For Rorty, scientific statements and laws are metaphors and stories (forms of rhetoric) rather than an objective representation of reality. In an article, 'Science as Solidarity', he says:

> In our culture, the notions of 'science', 'rationality', 'objectivity' and 'truth' are bound up with one another. Science is thought of as offering 'hard', 'objective' truth; truth as correspondence to reality, the only sort of truth worthy of the name ... We tend to identify seeking 'objective truth' with 'using reason', and so we think of the natural sciences as paradigms of rationality. We also think of rationality as a matter of following procedures laid down in advance, of being methodical ... Worries about ... 'objectivity' are characteristic of a secularised culture in which the scientist has replaced the priest.
>
> (Rorty, 1991)

While Rorty accepts that scientists do not see themselves as priests, he warns against the tendency of scientists to see themselves as the custodians of some ultimate truth or the technique of achieving it. In particular, this ignores the way that science is itself a contested space.

In the previous chapters we have seen how scientific thought, far from clearly indicating the certainty of knowledge, has often demonstrated evidence of reflexivity and a sensitivity to the complexities involved in understanding the world. You may also remember how the Enlightenment was double-edged, containing both a dogmatic tendency to take existing knowledge as true and a critical and questioning ethos which continually undermined this. In the writings of the social theorist Zygmunt Bauman we can find the suggestion that postmodern thinking is the questioning, critical and doubting dimension already at work in modernity and only now has it been set free from the dogmas of the Enlightenment (Bauman, 1992, 1993). Alternatively, if the 'postmodern' is an accentuation of characteristics within modern society, why do we need the prefix 'post' to signify a break with the modern? For Beck, Giddens and Lash, what we are now experiencing is late modernity – 'modernity coming to its senses' and undergoing an experimental phase as humanity becomes more aware of the limits on human understanding and the potential hazards of the human activities of the last four centuries (Beck et al., 1994).

Postmodernism is an accentuated dimension of the modern, so perhaps we do not need a 'post' at all?

See Chapter 2 if you need to refresh your memory on modernity.

However, all of these approaches rest upon one underlying premise, that there was a fundamental break between modern and premodern knowledge. Let's return briefly to the earlier contrast between the theological and scientific circuits of knowledge (Figure 7.13). While we can identify a substantive reorientation of the way the world is understood, there still remain strong continuities between the two circuits. In particular, both circuits

By destabilizing 'truth' the postmodern approach does more than go beyond the modern; it breaks with both the theological and scientific circuits of knowledge.

claim that the correct method establishes or paves the way to 'truth' and certainty. In this sense, then, we have never been modern or, as Umberto Eco has suggested, perhaps the period which we see as 'modern' would be better described as 'neo-medieval', with scientists replacing priests in carrying out the role of custodians of the truth, as Rorty suggests. So we can see how recent attempts to question truth, by writers such as Foucault, not only mark a break with modernity but indicate a shift in knowledge construction which runs much much deeper than this. This means that we have to recognize that there are both significant breaks and continuities in knowledge construction today.

Activity 7.6

Have a go at constructing your own circuit of knowledge. Quickly glance at Figure 7.13, which identifies how knowledge has been organized in the past, and think about where social scientific practice may be going in the future. You might find it useful to look back at your response to Activity 2.4 in Chapter 2, when you were asked to map out your own account of social science, like the encyclopedists during the Enlightenment. You should find the activity of constructing your own account of the circuit of knowledge a useful way of pinning down what *you* think social scientific practice should be all about. Remember, this is speculative but try to address the issues raised so far in this book.

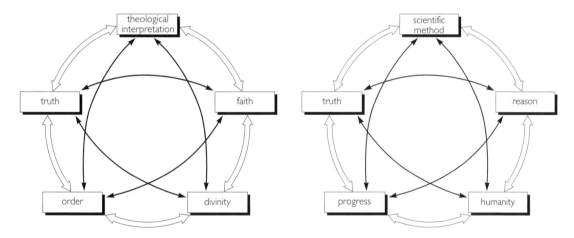

Figure 7.13   The theological and scientific circuits of knowledge.

In the previous chapters, I have used the circuit of knowledge to highlight some of the important connections between ideas in scientific knowledge and how they can be changed. In presenting an alternative circuit, the point is not to produce a fixed alternative but simply to plot some of the patterns in knowledge construction which seem to be emerging. While speculating about the future may be fun, we rarely manage to anticipate the complex outcome of present practices. My own attempt in Figure 7.14 (overleaf) remains, at best, a suggestive device and should not be read as a privileged account of knowledge construction. I found it a useful way of thinking through what it means to be a social scientist today.

Given these new kinds of approaches to knowledge construction (postmodernism, genealogy and realism), if we stuck our necks out and proposed a newly emerging integrated circuit of knowledge, perhaps it would look something like Figure 7.14. To begin, if we assume that social scientific knowledge consists of narratives or stories, we can view social scientific practice as one of reading, writing and talking in ways which are plausible for the audiences concerned. When these audiences interpret these stories in ways which make sense within the social and historical situations in which they are located, they are actively engaged in the production of meaning. We should recall that social scientists are readers first (they are part of the networks of audiences) before they are writers, talkers and performers. Recognizing this helps us to understand why social science is such a complex and uncertain practice which can be understood in different ways. The same process can be seen when (social and natural) scientists produce meanings within the terms of reference of authoritative knowledge and the institutions in which this corpus of knowledge makes sense.

Have a look back at Figure 6.8 on language, discourse and culture in Chapter 6.

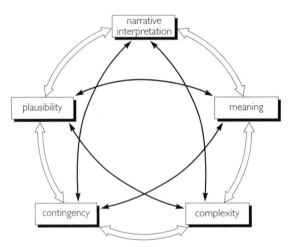

Figure 7.14   Rethinking the circuit of knowledge.

As you made your way through this book, you would have noticed that much of the history of social science is characterized by successive forms of authoritative knowledge, all of which have been understood to be true at some point. Since Chapter 4, you have had the chance to consider a variety of ways in which it is possible to question ideas like truth, certainty and progress. In this circuit, it is assumed that we should acknowledge the complexity and uncertainty characteristic of social relations, institutions and processes. This kind of approach can be uncomfortable for social scientists who believe that their views are privileged in some way. But then, one of the key lines of argument throughout this book is that social scientists should be more reflexive, less simplistic (that is, more willing to acknowledge complexity) and less convinced of the certainty of their own views than has hitherto been assumed to be the norm for their kind of practice. When we think about how things are classified by social scientific practices, even the various ways in which kinds of knowledge are classified, we should ask questions about the process of classification itself. Why are some kinds of academic work viewed as scientific or objective and others

Disciplinary knowledge has definite objects of analysis and ways of studying them, while interdisciplinary study draws upon a range of disciplines to present a more rounded picture – 'post-disciplinary' knowledge changes the rules of the scientific game, so we can be flexible in our construction of objects and methods.

not? Why are some forms of knowledge (such as disciplines) more valued than others?

Disciplinary knowledge is focused upon a precise set of objects of analysis and prescribes definite ways of studying them. Interdisciplinary knowledge construction offers opportunities for looking at different sides of an event or problem, drawing together the assumptions and methods of different disciplines. Post-disciplinary social science, which looks for the parallels in knowledge construction across the social sciences, throws such inhibitions out of the window and asks us to be much more flexible and innovative in the ways we define objects and the methods we use. In this way, it is possible to think of social scientific practices which go beyond knowledge disciplines and even beyond interdisciplinary social science – by devising alternative circuits of knowledge, we can find a way of thinking about social science in a post-disciplinary way.

3   Situated knowledge: gender and science

Throughout this book, we have considered and evaluated the ways in which scientific approaches have often attempted to portray themselves as universal and true, that we can depend on scientific research to tell us the 'factual' story of what is going on around us. One of the areas of social research where claims like this have been questioned is in the study of gender differences. In this section we explore what the study of gender has generated in the way of insights and warnings. In addition, the uses of the scientific method in the study of gender provides a useful way of following through the approaches which you have considered so far (especially postmodernism and realism). We will focus our attention on how the arguments of empiricism, realism and postmodernism have been developed through the studies of social relations and processes by various approaches in feminist social research. These approaches are very diverse and complex; here we concentrate on the way in which they see the relationship between knowledge and reality, the central story-line of this chapter. These accounts of knowledge construction provide a useful way of examining the consequences of adopting the positions identified in this chapter and earlier. Three main feminist epistemologies stand out: feminist empiricism, feminist standpoint approaches (we concentrate on those which draw upon realism) and feminist postmodernism. So in this section we consider realism and postmodernism in reverse order from section 2.

Feminist epistemologies challenge 'malestream social science' – that is, it is social science by men, on men and for men.

All of these approaches are in broad agreement on one thing, that Western rational knowledge is androcentric (male-centred). However, they disagree on what this means, on how knowledge should be constructed and on how to change this situation. In Western societies, much of social research is 'malestream' social research. This means that it is overwhelmingly 'social science on men, social science by men, and social science for men'. As a result, social scientists have focused upon institutions, topics and issues which are of greater concern to men, so neglecting women's issues and concerns. In addition, throughout much of the modern period most social researchers have been male and the evidence they have produced has supported a social order in which men benefit more than women. Furthermore, they have often regarded male experiences and interpretations as representative of the experiences and interpretations of all people in society. Hence, in many areas of social research, the concern was not just the way in which women were constructed, but also that women were 'invisible', as if their contribution to knowledge and society was of little significance.

Social researchers have often distorted women's experiences by interpreting their evidence through these kinds of assumptions. However, at the same time, they have also had an impact upon the organization of social institutions. Sometimes this has had dramatic consequences, such as the uses of social scientific evidence in relation to the planning of girls' schooling as national education strategies were devised in Western societies. The taken-for-granted assumptions or prejudices of a male-dominated or 'patriarchal' society were often translated into 'scientific facts'. Throughout the early twentieth century, social research on the supposed dangers for girls of studying maths and physics (incredibly, suggesting that these kinds of intellectual activities interfered with the functioning of female reproductive organs and created mental instability) was taken as a convenient justification for organizing male and female schooling along different lines. We don't take these 'dangers' seriously now, but the organization of schooling initially based on these assumptions continued until the late twentieth century. So here we can see how the life chances of half the population were dramatically affected by the way in which social scientific practices legitimated the attitudes prevalent in a patriarchal social order.

Malestream social science translates the prejudices of a patriarchal society into scientific facts – as such, they had real consequences.

Many would now write this off as a thing of the past. However, in many disciplines there are deep-seated gendered assumptions which inform the way we understand social relations. The difficulty is identifying them. In criminology, for instance, up till very recently, there have been some startling examples of these kinds of assumptions having a central place in accounts of female crime. In this discipline, we can find some of the most explicit attempts to claim that the evidence is factual and produced through scientific means. The basis of these claims is that they use criminal statistics as their source of evidence, or that the prison population can be studied as a way of reconstructing the causes of crime more generally. The recorded instances of female crime are low compared to male crime, although there are some types of crime which are considered more likely to be committed by women. Criminological investigations of crime rates from the 1950s through to the 1970s placed an emphasis on the way in which criminal men were more likely to be detected than criminal women. It was argued that women were, on the whole, better criminals than men because they committed more of the unsolved instances of crime. When we look at why this was felt to be the case, we can gain a better sense of the way cultural values were masquerading as scientific facts. In these studies it was consistently asserted that female criminals were able to use 'feminine wiles', that they were more cunning than men and that they had an innate predisposition to tell lies convincingly. More than this, female prisoners were assessed in terms of their demonstration of characteristics usually attributed to male criminals (for two representative examples of this kind of research, see Mannheim, 1965, and Pollak, 1961). Either they were condemned for being feminine or condemned for being too masculine. So, when considering just this one area in the social sciences, we can find a host of (often inconsistent) stereotypical assumptions in use within social research. In the late twentieth century the use of such crude stereotypical oppositions of masculinity and femininity have been challenged and recent social research has often been much more sensitive to these concerns. However, these examples do demonstrate the seriousness of the problem.

Now, these examples also raise another important issue for social researchers to consider. On the one hand, all social researchers are situated in a particular time and place. This means that social researchers such as Pollak and Mannheim, who lived in a culture which not only took gender inequalities for granted but also inhabited institutions which were grounded upon the importance of maintaining male dominance, are likely to produce accounts which draw upon these kinds of values and assumptions about what is normal and what is pathological. We should recognize that the androcentric criminology noted above, and even the scientific racism of Samuel Morton, are embedded in social relations where gender and ethnic inequalities are normalized and that all forms of knowledge are involved in these kinds of processes. Feminist approaches to knowledge construction, by recognizing that knowledge is connected to the power relations within social orders, are particularly important for helping social scientific practice think through these difficulties. In the following sections we explore three ways of responding to these problems. As you will see, this does not necessarily mean that we have to throw away the scientific method, but it does mean that social scientific practice should involve more careful reflection upon the role of values and norms. Indeed, each of the following sections is a kind of manifesto for changing the ways in which knowledge is constructed.

3.1 Gender and empiricism

Quickly re-read the section on Popper's account of the empiricist scientific method in Chapter 3, section 5.

For feminist empiricists, androcentric assumptions violate the key distinction between facts and values through which 'objective knowledge' is identified.

In this section we explore the feminist empiricist approach, which tries to find a way of holding on to the aims and objectives of the scientific method without falling into the problems involved in androcentric social science. The key question here is: how do we overcome male bias in social research? As you will recall, empiricism rests upon the principle that facts should be separate from values and that the treatment of values and norms as if they are facts is a form of metaphysics and not science. For feminist empiricists, malestream social science is simply bad science, for androcentric values, assumptions and prejudices are masquerading as an objective account of the social world. For instance, in addition to the examples from androcentric criminology in the first section, you may also wish to consider sociological research on the family, which you might expect to be a little more responsive to women's concerns than the studies of social institutions largely populated by men because of the exclusion and/or marginalization of women. However, until the 1970s many accounts of family life simply assumed that the stereotypical roles of rational and instrumental male breadwinners and emotional and expressive domesticated housewives were normal social relationships, which may imply that alternatives are abnormal.

According to the feminist empiricist approach, the principles of empiricism have been violated by the ways in which androcentrism creeps into social research. According to this approach, then, the scientific study of social life can be, and has to be, reformed if 'objective knowledge' is to be produced. But how is it possible to develop a reformist manifesto for science? We can find one answer in the essays brought together by Marcia Millman and

Rosabeth Kanter in *Another Voice* (1975). They argue that by applying the methodological rules of empiricist science, such biases and prejudices can be eliminated from social research. This means that facts and values have to be kept separate, but how is it possible to do this when most social researchers within an androcentric knowledge system are male? For Millman and Kanter, it is important to increase the number of women who occupy authoritative positions within social research communities. In this way the culture of research itself can be changed, they argue, for female researchers are much more likely than male researchers to produce objective (in the sense of unbiased) research evidence. You will find many similarities between the kind of critical use of empiricism developed by Popper and the arguments developed by feminist empiricists. In effect, both approaches are committed to the goal of a tolerant and open society in which all prejudice, bias and metaphysical speculation are overcome through the systematic use of the scientific method.

Some empiricists accept the fact/value distinction as an ideal rather than as a state of affairs – see Chapter 3, section 5.

While this may be one way of addressing the problem of androcentrism, there are other issues which feminist empiricism seems to ignore. Sandra Harding, in *The Science Question in Feminism* (1986), argues that the main problem with using the methodological rules of empiricism as a basis for cleaning up the social sciences is that empiricism focuses upon the **context of justification**, in which statements are tested and evidence collected and explained. This means that empiricists tend to ignore the **context of discovery**, in which the issues and problems to be studied are identified and constructed in the first place. Although feminist empiricism is concerned with the culture of social research, it draws upon an approach to knowledge construction which ignores the role of human imagination in organizing experience. A major obstacle in countering androcentric bias is to ignore the role of the imaginative understanding of experience at all stages of research. In particular, the crucial first steps in social research are ignored, because empiricists focus most of all upon the gathering of evidence. For example, social scientists have largely focused upon the problems defined in the spheres of social life where men's concerns predominate (such as the economy and politics), rather than the spheres of social life where women's issues are taken more seriously. So it is not just a matter of how we gather evidence, but how we identify the purposes of social research and how we define our objects of analysis. Indeed, there is a contradiction between the goals of feminist empiricism and the limits inherent within empiricism itself. In addition, this approach defines objective knowledge rather narrowly as simply knowledge which is free of bias, for it retains its commitment to detached explanations of universal scope.

Feminist empiricism focuses so strongly on the context of justification that it neglects the context of discovery.

3.2 Gender and reality

In the second approach to gender and science considered here, we can find a direct concern with the way in which objects are defined and the way in which problems of research are constructed. These feminist standpoint approaches are quite varied and include a range of radical and socialist feminist positions. They argue explicitly for a transformation in social relations but, in order to do this, many standpoint theorists point to the need for social research to identify the real social structures which need to be changed first. These positions have one thing in common: the conviction

that the experiences of women are shaped through social relationships which are oppressive, exploitative and dehumanizing. This means that social scientists should take the 'standpoint of the oppressed' as a basis for constructing 'objective knowledge'. However, the way in which these real structures have been defined also varies, although definitions usually refer to patriarchy or capitalism or a combination of the two. As a result, the links between these approaches and realism are very strong. All these approaches hold that the answer to the androcentric biases within knowledge cannot be located in scientific traditions, which are themselves part of the oppressive social order in question.

Before we move on to examine the implications of our second approach, let's consider in more detail the way in which these feminist standpoint approaches link knowledge to oppression. The answer, they suggest, can be found through a feminist reinterpretation of Hegel's master–slave relationship. For Hegel, masters are natural fearless dominators and slaves are fearful – and therefore subservient – individuals. Jane Flax (1983) argues that the standpoint of the 'male' master produces distorted and perverse understandings of the world, whereas the standpoint of the oppressed can act as a foundation for constructing an alternative vision of a non-patriarchal (or non-capitalist) society. This means that the standpoint of the oppressed offers a more objective account of knowledge and social life. This has been a strong theme throughout the radical feminist movement since the 1960s. In radical feminism the concept of patriarchy and patriarchal ideology plays a key role in explaining women's experiences.

Patriarchy can be defined as a set of social structures which govern social behaviour and within which oppression was made to appear normal. This approach viewed all existing social institutions, and the knowledge systems which sustained them, as part of the problem they were attempting to solve. The attempt to secure the emancipation of women from oppressive social relations depended upon mobilizing the women's movement to seek alternative forms of social organization. This involved non-élitist organization and awareness-raising around issues such as sexual violence and domestic violence, with a strong emphasis upon the subjective, personal experiences of women's everyday lives. This was in direct opposition to the androcentric focus upon detached and impersonal accounts of science, which placed men in a privileged position in Western knowledge. Moreover, like the realist approach to knowledge construction, it places a strong emphasis on the relationship between social structures and the way we think and act within them.

Feminist standpoint approaches focus upon the perspective of the oppressed in a patriarchal society in order to produce objective knowledge.

Patriarchy is composed of social structures which regulate appropriate behaviour for men and women, and within which women are constrained in certain social spheres.

Like realism, feminist approaches also combine the denotative and prescriptive language games – both see objective knowledge as a way of securing emancipation from an unjust society.

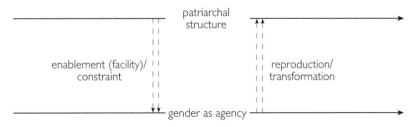

As in Figure 7.12, the movement of arrows from left to right is an indication of the passage of time.

Figure 7.15   The connections between feminist standpoint and realist approaches: a feminist use of the transformational model of social activity.

So whereas empiricism attempted to reform knowledge, we can see that this approach to knowledge construction was grounded in a social movement which attempted to secure social transformation and human emancipation. These standpoint approaches draw upon the realist account of the philosophy of social science by seeking to identify the structured relationships which make up patriarchal social orders and by finding ways of transforming rather than reproducing existing social relations. As you will remember, many of the realist accounts drew from the Marxist account of capitalism as social structure within which all participants are victims, whether they are the oppressor or the oppressed. Similarly, feminist standpoint approaches point to the distortion of the personalities of male oppressors and female oppressed. So, the only answer to androcentric knowledge is a complete transformation of both the social structures (of social institutions and practices) which knowledge systems inhabit. Nevertheless, although feminist standpoint approaches reject the account of science in feminist empiricism, they still make a claim to objective knowledge as a foundation (that is, from the standpoint of the oppressed). In the next set of approaches, we consider the way in which feminist postmodernism challenges the foundationalism which exists in all the approaches considered so far.

Whereas feminist empiricists try to reform scientific knowledge, feminist standpoint approaches try to transform knowledge and society.

3.3 Gender and representation

In the two previous approaches to the problem of androcentric knowledge, there is a common theme developing in the desire to establish some basis for objective knowledge, although there is disagreement on what this means and how this should be established. Here we consider the third set of approaches, which have been labelled 'postmodern feminisms'. In one fundamental respect, they differ from the previous approaches. In feminist empiricism there is one road to the truth, the scientific method, whereas in feminist standpoint approaches there is one universal feature of all social systems which defines their character, a single relationship which is experienced by all women: patriarchy. For postmodern feminists, there is no single unitary method nor is there a universal basis for women's experience; they argue that there are no universals in the world or in the way we construct knowledge about the world. I have jumped ahead a little here to highlight the contrasts between these approaches to gender and science. Yet, like the standpoint approaches, they place a strong emphasis on making connections between knowledge construction and the everyday lives of women and men. We need to consider first how these postmodern feminist conclusions came about and how they developed out of the standpoint approaches considered earlier.

By the 1980s, a range of new feminist perspectives had emerged which highlighted problems and questions about the assumptions in the standpoint approaches. On the one hand, standpoint approaches had posed the existence of a definite and universal experience for all women, yet, on the other hand, they argued that an objective account could only be achieved by drawing upon the experiences of women. So as feminist researchers began to explore the ways in which patriarchy worked through social institutions, they came to realize that everyday experiences were more diverse and complex than such an all encompassing model could explain. This questioning

Postmodern feminism challenges the modern ideas which claim that any scientific method can be established and that women can be emancipated from a universal form of oppression.

process within different branches of feminism was to spill over into many areas of the social sciences. For a start, the standpoint approaches had placed a special emphasis on the role of the family as the cornerstone of oppression and the source of all other master–slave relationships. For black feminists, such as Patricia Hill Collins in the USA, who were just as concerned with racist oppression as with gender, there was a particular problem with criticizing the family in this way. The family also served as a safe haven from, and site of resistance to, racism. Black feminism placed a stronger emphasis upon building alliances with men to challenge structures of oppression grounded in ethnic differences. In turn, this came into direct conflict with 'political lesbianism', which actively encouraged 'coming out' as a political act against the prejudices of one's own family. In addition, the use of scientific contraceptive technologies to sterilize black women in the USA, and the use of the female populations in developing societies to test birth-control techniques, prompted standpoint feminists to reassess the role of science in emancipating women from childbirth. What this highlighted was the important but simple realization that no one formula could account for the complex and diverse experiences of all women. As a result, no single answer could be identified (Collins, 1990; Mies and Shiva, 1993).

ACTIVITY 7.7

Now turn to the final reading in this book, Reading D 'Challenging orthodoxies: gender, ethnicity and social science', by Marcia Rice (1990). This reading attempts to highlight how contemporary research on gender, ethnicity and crime has investigated and exposed the myths associated with white female and black male offending. However, Rice argues that this research has neglected to carry out similar investigations into black female offending. She examines the reasons behind this problem and proposes a short manifesto for changing social scientific practice. After reading the extract, consider the following questions.

- On what grounds does Rice suggest that the relationship between gender and ethnicity presents a problem for feminism?

- Identify the ways in which Rice suggests that feminism is ethnocentric. You may also wish to consider the ways that feminism is actually being accused of falling into the same traps that it identifies in androcentric knowledge.

Since reading a text involves the production of meaning, this short extract can be read in different ways. Read it through again, but this time adopt the viewpoint of one of the three feminist epistemologies considered in this chapter. This may help you to evaluate the reading. For instance, you may find that the questions which Rice raises point to the need for a re-evaluation of all universal claims (a key postmodern feminist concern), or to the need to consider the complex combination of structured relations involved (a feminist standpoint or realist concern).

This questioning of earlier feminist arguments raised a significant problem for the claim made by standpoint approaches that patriarchy was universal to women's experience and was the source of all other forms of oppression. Many feminists increasingly felt that feminism had simply substituted one set of feminist universal rational categories for the problematic androcentric ones. In addition, black feminism raised the possibility that the theory of patriarchy represented the prejudices of 'colour-blind' white middle-class feminism. Ecofeminism also placed greater stress on representing the diverse experiences and concerns of 'women from the south' (that is, non-Western women), who are a majority of all women. The problem appeared to be the conception of modern scientific knowledge which had been endorsed as a solution, so many feminists began to construct a sceptical approach to the idea of objective knowledge (Mies and Shiva, 1993).

Postmodernism draws upon insights of post-structuralism to question the tendency of modern feminists to search for the foundations of knowledge (by placing such concepts 'under erasure' we can see all meanings as in process and unfinished).

So, in effect, there was no longer a single truth which could serve as the foundation for knowledge construction. As you remember from Chapter 6, one way to destabilize ideas like 'truth' or 'objectivity' is to place them 'under erasure'. This means that key ideas are no longer taken as the answer to a problem but are viewed as 'inadequate yet necessary'. In this case, postmodern feminists place 'patriarchy' under erasure:

~~patriarchy~~

This means that, for postmodern feminists, the ideas of science, reason, progress and emancipation associated with feminist standpoint approaches, are replaced by an emphasis upon pluralism, complexity, difference and diversity. There is no one feminist account which can accommodate all the experiences of women. Attention should be directed towards the relationship between the sexist, racist, ethnocentric, classist and heterosexist discourses which are involved in the formation of gender identities.

For feminist postmodernists, identities are not fixed but fluid and fragmented; they are always in process and unfinished. Some postmodern feminists draw more explicitly upon the genealogical approach of Foucault. In particular, they concentrate on the various ways in which the sciences have constructed the 'subject' of 'woman' in Western knowledge – for example, the 'hysterical woman' in the history of psychiatry (Showalter, 1987) or the 'deceiving woman' of criminology. In addition, the genealogical approach draws our attention to the ways in which social research should be focused upon historically and socially specific sexisms, racisms and so on, rather than searching for a single underlying cause. On a more critical note, the standpoint approaches (who still believe it is possible to have a single answer), suggest that postmodern feminism does not offer a political strategy for change and thus leaves the feminist approach without hope. They argue that if you cannot make a decision about what is fundamentally wrong in the world, then it is impossible to develop a strategy for changing it.

Postmodern feminists use Foucault's account of discourse to demonstrate how, in the construction of subject-positions, gender matters.

3.4 Reconsidering gender and science

At the start of this chapter, you were advised that you would consider two ways in which knowledge can be situated, in terms of knowledge construction and in terms of the social and historical conditions in which these approaches to knowledge construction make sense. In this section on gender and science we have explored three distinctive feminist epistemologies, all of which emerged within the social movements of the late twentieth century. Like all the other approaches to knowledge construction in this book, they had definite historical and social conditions of existence. By exploring the debates on knowledge construction in relation to gender, we can see how these three kinds of feminist epistemology draw upon the experience of the cultural values of Western societies and, in the case of postmodern feminism, the complex and diverse experiences of all women. As stated earlier, the sequence of approaches we have considered merely reflects the way these debates developed within feminist thought from the 1960s to the 1990s. Of course, there is much more of relevance in these debates than we can consider here. We are limited to looking at what it means to view knowledge as situated and to understand how different approaches can emerge from a concern with the same problem, in this case the problem of **androcentric** bias in social science. The key issues involved in this discussion are the status of objective knowledge, the everyday lived experiences of women and the questions of whether or how social science can be reformed or transformed.

What these debates demonstrate is the close connection between the ways in which knowledge can be constructed and the way in which all attempts to study social existence have a normative content, even though this may be hidden behind claims to objectivity. We can see, too, how each of the feminist epistemologies draws upon broader debates on the nature of knowledge construction, in this case empiricism, realism and postmodernism. As you have already seen, these all have their own conditions of existence, in that they themselves are the product of historically and socially specific practices. If we look at the normative component of these three approaches we can see why they served so well in the feminist arguments.

First, the empiricist approach tends towards description of the world as it is and sees itself standing against mixing science with normative claims about what the world ought to be like. Some empiricists, such as Popper, place a special emphasis upon theories; however, these are always strictly controlled by the scientific method in order to prevent values, bias and metaphysical distortion from creeping in. The point is to find out more about the way the world works and use the knowledge produced to secure human progress. For this to work all views must be tolerated, but they can only be assessed through empirical (that is, observable) evidence. So the concern of an empiricist is to make the world a better place, but in a piecemeal step-by-step way, without grand designs or dramatic transformations. In this way, individual freedom is secured and an atmosphere of toleration (one free of bias and prejudice) maintained.

Second, the realist approach digs below the surface level of observed experiences and tries to find out about the hidden workings of social existence. In this way, realism hopes to offer an authoritative account of the way in which exploitative and oppressive forms of social organization come about. To do this, realists seek to identify the structured relations relevant to a given situation, the conditions which activate the structures and the mechanisms which produce events. Moreover, they see social structures as the product of human agency and, as such, believe they can be changed. Thus they attempt to challenge the oppressive social structures themselves and take part in projects for emancipation (in Bhaskar's language, to transform unwanted forms of determination into wanted ones) in order to establish new social structures (Bhaskar, 1991, pp.70–7).

Third, postmodern accounts of knowledge construction place a special emphasis upon the role of representation. In this, they draw upon the insights developed in recent post-structuralist accounts of discourse and cultural differences. Rather than viewing representations as a reflection or manifestation of some underlying foundation, they concentrate upon the way in which cultural identities are the complex and unstable product of **articulatory practices**. As such, meanings are continually in process; they are always unfinished business. This involves a universal claim of sorts, that all meanings are potentially unstable and open to contestation. If this is the case, in science there is still remarkable stability in the production of meaning. The continued longevity of closed-system models of science, the idea of the figure of the scientist as the authoritative voice and the continual appeal of the search for truth (a 'heroic quest' which has been given fresh impetus in recent work on genetics) all point to considerable stability in scientific discourses. Postmodern feminism also draws upon the insights of genealogy. What Foucault offers is a way of understanding this stability as a product of the rules of conduct, the established texts and the way in which social institutions are effective settings for stabilizing meanings. However, this stability is always an achievement; it is temporary and can always be challenged. So postmodernism is normative in two senses: it challenges the truth claims of all custodians of knowledge (all people who set themselves up as a judge of someone else) and the classification process in which such judgements are made, and it highlights the way in which cultural differences have no essential foundations and so promotes the message of toleration and the acceptance of pluralism (of live and let live).

As a result, we can now see how each account of knowledge construction is appealing and plausible for the normative concerns of situated social scientists, whether this is the defence of individual freedom, the transformation of oppressive relations, or the promotion of the acceptance of a plurality of differences. When we say that knowledge is situated we are also acknowledging that it is always embedded in cultural values. This is a feature of approaches to knowledge construction as much as of the actual practices of social researchers.

4   By way of a conclusion: journey's end?

A consistent thread runs through the chapters of this book: if we are to find a way of constructing social science in order to understand how people communicate and organize their existence, then we have to take on board the different ways in which social existence is complex. The idea of complexity can be misinterpreted as simply something we do not understand. However, we always find ways of making sense of the world around us; acknowledging that something is complex is not just a matter of throwing our arms up in the air and saying we don't have a clue about what it means. What acknowledging complexity does mean is that we should always be open to the unexpected, that there are always different interpretations, that the things we take for granted are not universal, and that the way we see the world is just one way of producing meaning.

We have a strong preference for simplicity, for things to be definite and manageable, for wishing that the connections we establish between a simple cause and an effect are necessary and sufficient for establishing a scientific law, and that we have found the answer to our problems. This kind of preference can be seen in all attempts to use the closed-system model of scientific inquiry for studying people. Throughout this book you have encountered a range of approaches which have questioned different aspects of this closed-system model and have considered ways in which the assumption of simplicity is unhelpful for effective social research. So, when we think of complexity, a number of different kinds of complexity should come to mind.

- *Practical complexity* – involves recognizing that simple relations are artificial human inventions, for other factors always have a part to play when we are reconstructing social existence (the empirical world is always much more complex than we expect).

- *Imaginative complexity* – rather than seeing thoughts as a reflection of the things we study, it is important to recognize the way in which imaginative thinking organizes our perceptions, impressions and sensations (we simplify empirical complexity through imaginative thought).

- *Situated complexity* – all forms of knowledge, including scientific knowledge, are the complex product of the practices established in the historical and social locations in which they were produced. As such, they carry the cultural values upon which they were grounded, although they may be received and understood in other locations in different ways.

- *Representational complexity* – the production of meaning is itself a complex process, composed of linguistic, discursive and cultural elements, all of which can have dramatic effects upon how social scientists construct evidence and communicate arguments to others.

- *Structural or deep complexity* – in order to see science as an intelligible activity, the things we study must have real internal properties (real powers and liabilities), but we should not forget that our only way of expressing these things is through representation.

Each kind of **complexification** involves a step away from the conventional view of what it means to be scientific. If we accept that studying people means acknowledging these aspects of social complexity, then we must recognize that the adoption of a closed-system approach is inappropriate. However, you may find some kinds of complexity more convincing than others, depending on how you assess the alternatives to the closed-system approach developed from Chapter 4 onwards. At each step of the journey, you have considered the ways in which science itself is a contested concept – its meaning is slippery and often elusive. When we face an approach which claims the authority of being scientific, it is useful to ask questions that can help us to pin down exactly how this approach is using the word 'science'.

- How does the approach define causality?

- How does the approach consider the relationship between knowledge and reality?

- In what way does the approach define experience?

- How does the approach see the relationship between knowledge and values (that is, what kind of society does it want to deliver)?

Questions like these help us to identify the ways in which the 'social science' in question is addressing an audience and how it attempts to present a plausible account of social existence. Sometimes the terminology tells us what kind of approach is being developed, such as textual references to discourses rather than knowledge (and reality). In this way, by placing 'social science' in question, you can be better equipped to meet the challenges of the social sciences.

In a sense, you have been through a long and arduous journey, constructing your own conceptual map through the arguments and assumptions of a range of different approaches as you passed through them. You have probably spent a great deal of time and energy finding ways to understand each of the new conceptual landscapes you have encountered along the way. You will also have spotted that the approaches you have explored often have a great deal in common (such as a similarity in terminology), but that they agree and disagree on different issues. You will have found, as at the end of all long journeys, that you could not bring back with you everything you have encountered and you have had to be selective about what you could carry with you. You may find that you have changed your perspective on certain aspects of the world, simply by trying to understand things in a new way. Your long journey will have taken you full circle and you are now in a position to look upon the things you took for granted in a different way, rethinking the basic issues and problems of what it means to practise social science. As you return to these basic issues, you will probably find that the same problems you encountered before are still there, but at least you now know why there are no perfect answers to these issues and problems.

In the opening chapter, I raised the arguments of Alfred Schütz on the perspective of the 'stranger' in understanding the difficulties faced by social scientists when trying to make sense of a world of which they are a part and which they help to construct. Schütz has a way of thinking through what it means to leave a place with which you are familiar, and then return only to find that, while it all looks the same, both the place and you have changed. He calls this experience the perspective of the 'homecomer' (a **type** which works in a similar way to that of the stranger). Before you set off on this intellectual journey, you probably had some idea of what science involves, the relationship between knowledge and reality, and the implications of applying the assumptions and methods of the natural sciences to studying people. These issues will not go away and you will return to them constantly throughout your own experiences of social scientific research. All there is left to say is good luck …

… and, of course, welcome home.

READING A
Postmodern language games

Madan Sarup

Many people are aware that Western societies since the Second World War have radically changed their nature in some way. To describe these changes social theorists have used various terms: media society, the society of the spectacle, consumer society, the bureaucratic society of controlled consumption, post-industrial society. ...

In *The Postmodern Condition* Lyotard argues that during the last forty years the leading sciences and technologies have become increasingly concerned with language: theories of linguistics, problems of communication and cybernetics, computers and their languages, problems of translation, information storage and data banks.

The technological transformations are having a considerable impact on knowledge. The miniaturization and commercialization of machines are already changing the way in which learning is acquired, classified, made available and exploited.

Lyotard believes that the nature of knowledge cannot survive unchanged within this context of general transformation. The status of knowledge is altered as societies enter what is known as the postmodern age. He predicts that anything in the constituted body of knowledge that is not translatable into quantities of information will be abandoned and the direction of new research will be dictated by the possibility of its eventual results being translatable into computer language. The old principle that the acquisition of knowledge is indissociable from the training of minds, or even of individuals, is becoming obsolete. Knowledge is already ceasing to be an end in itself. It is and will be produced in order to be sold. ...

For Lyotard knowledge is a question of competence that goes beyond the simple determination and application of the criterion of truth, extending to the determination of criteria of efficiency (technical qualification), of justice and/or happiness (ethical wisdom), of beauty (auditory or visual sensibility), etc. Knowledge is what makes someone capable of forming not only 'good' denotative utterances but also 'good' prescriptive and 'good' evaluative utterances. But how are they to be assessed? They are judged to be good if they conform to the relevant criteria (of justice, beauty, truth and efficiency) accepted in the social circle of the 'knower's' interlocutors.

It is important to mention here that Lyotard, who has been greatly influenced by Wittgenstein's notion of language games, makes the following observations. Each of the various categories of utterance can be defined in terms of rules specifying their properties and the uses to which they can be put. The rules of language games do not carry within themselves their own legitimation, but are objects of a contract, explicit or not, between players; if there are no rules, there is no game. Every utterance is thought of as a 'move' in a game. Messages have quite different forms and effects depending on whether they are, for example, denotatives, prescriptions, evaluatives, performatives, etc.

Lyotard believes that language games are incommensurable. He distinguishes the denotative game (in which what is relevant is the true/false distinction) from the prescriptive game (in which the just/unjust distinction pertains) and from the technical game (in which the criterion is the efficient/inefficient distinction). ...

Scientific knowledge does not represent the totality of knowledge; it has always existed in competition and conflict with another kind of knowledge which Lyotard calls narrative. In traditional societies there is a pre-eminence of the narrative form. Narratives (popular stories, myths, legends and tales) bestow legitimacy upon social institutions, or represent positive or negative models of integration into established institutions. Narratives determine criteria of competence and/or illustrate how they are to be applied. They thus define what has the right to be said and done in the culture in question.

In traditional societies a narrative tradition is also the tradition of the criterion defining a threefold competence – 'know-how', 'knowing how to speak' and 'knowing how to hear' – through which the community's relationship to itself and its environment is played out. In the narrative form statements about truth, justice and beauty are often woven together. What is transmitted through these narratives is the set of rules that constitute the social bond.

Lyotard discusses the retreat of the claims of narrative or story-telling knowledge in the face of those of the abstract, denotative or logical and cognitive procedures generally associated with science. In the science language game the sender is supposed to be able to provide proof of what s/he says, and on the other hand s/he is supposed to be able to refute any opposing or contradictory statements concerning the same referent. Scientific rules underlie what nineteenth-century science calls verification, and twentieth-century science falsification. They allow a horizon of consensus to be brought to the debate between partners (the sender and the ad-dressee). Not every consensus is a sign of truth, but it is presumed that the truth of a statement necessarily draws a consensus. ...

The main difference between scientific knowledge and narrative knowledge is that scientific knowl-edge requires that one language game, denotation, be retained and all others be excluded. Both science and non-scientific (narrative) knowledge are equally necessary. Both are composed of sets of statements; the statements are 'moves' made by the players within the framework of generally ap-plicable rules. These rules are specific to each par-ticular kind of knowledge, and the 'moves' judged to be 'good' in one cannot be the same as those judged 'good' in another (unless it happens that way by chance). It is therefore impossible to judge the existence or validity of narrative knowledge on the basis of scientific knowledge or vice versa: the relevant criteria are different.

Lyotard argues that narrative knowledge certifies it-self without having recourse to argumentation and proof. Scientists, however, question the validity of narrative statements and conclude that they are never subject to argumentation or proof. Narratives are classified by the scientist as belong-ing to a different mentality: savage, primitive, underdeveloped, backward, alienated, composed of opinions, customs, authority, prejudice, ignor-ance, ideology. Narratives are fables, myths, legends fit only for women and children.

Here there is an interesting twist in Lyotard's argu-ment. He says that scientific knowledge cannot know and make known that it is the true knowledge without resorting to the other, narrative kind of knowledge, which from its point of view is no knowledge at all. In short, there is a recurrence of the narrative in the scientific.

The state spends large amounts of money to enable science to pass itself off as an epic. The state's own credibility is based on that epic, which it uses to ob-tain the public consent its decision-makers need. Science, in other words, is governed by the demand of legitimation.

Source: Sarup, 1993, pp.133–7.

READING B
The construction of homosexuality

Jeffrey Weeks

Most works on the history of sex tend to concen-trate on the major forms of sexual experience to the exclusion of the minority forms. This is not sur-prising given the centrality in our society of the great rituals of birth, maturation, pair-bonding and reproduction. But to ignore extra-marital, non-reproductive, non-monogamous, or even non-heterosexual forms is to stifle an important aspect of our social history. Nor indeed are they indepen-dent aspects. The regulation of extra-marital sex has been a major concern for the forces of moral order throughout the history of the West, whether through the canonical controls of the church over adultery and sodomy in the medieval period, or the state's ordering of prostitution and homosexu-ality in the modern.

Of all the 'variations' of sexual behaviour, homo-sexuality has had the most vivid social pressure, and has evoked the most lively (if usually grossly misleading) historical accounts. It is, as many sex-ologists from Havelock Ellis to Alfred Kinsey have noted, the form closest to the heterosexual norm in our culture, and partly because of that it has often been the target of sustained social oppression. It has also, as an inevitable effect of the hostility it has evoked, produced the most substantial forms of resistance to hostile categorisation and has, consequently, a long cultural and subcultural his-tory. A study of homosexuality is therefore essen-tial, both because of its own intrinsic interest and because of the light it throws on the wider regu-lation of sexuality, the development of sexual cate-gorisation, and the range of possible sexual identities.

In recent years it has become increasingly clear, first to sociologists, and belatedly to historians, that it is essential to distinguish between on the one hand, homosexual behaviour, and on the other homosexual roles, categorisations and ident-ities. It has been apparent to anthropologists and sexologists since at least the nineteenth century that homosexual behaviour has existed in a variety of different cultures, and that it is an ineradicable part of human sexual possibilities. But what has been equally apparent are the range of different re-sponses towards homosexuality. Attitudes towards homosexual behaviour are, that is to say, culturally specific and have varied enormously across different cultures and through various historical periods. What is less obvious, but is now central to any historical work, is the realisation not only that *attitudes* towards same-sex activity have varied but that the social and subjective meanings given to homosexuality have similarly been culturally specific. Bearing this in mind it is no longer possible to talk of the possibility of a universalistic history of homosexuality; it is only possible to understand the social significance of homosexual behaviour, both in terms of social response and in terms of individual identity, in its exact historical context. To put it another way, the various possibilities of same-sex behaviour are variously constructed in different cultures as an aspect of wider gender and sexual regulation. The physical acts might be similar, but their social implications are often profoundly different. In our culture homosexuality has become an excoriated experience, severely socially condemned at various periods, and even today seen as a largely unfortunate, minority form by a large percentage of the population. It is this that demands explanation.

The general tendency is still to assume that 'deviance', and especially sexual unorthodoxy, is somehow a quality inherent in the individuals, to which the social then has to respond. Over the past twenty years, however, it has been increasingly recognised that the social not only defines, but actually in part constructs the deviance. ...

The latter part of the nineteenth century, however, saw the clear emergence of new conceptualisations of homosexuality although the elements of the new definitions and practices can be traced to earlier periods. The sodomite, as Foucault has put it, was a temporary aberration. The 'homosexual', on the other hand, belonged to a species, and it is this new concern with the homosexual person, both in legal practice and in psychological and medical categorisation, that marks the crucial change, both because it provided a new subject of social observation and speculation, and because it opened up the possibility of new modes of self-articulation. It is precisely at this period that we see the development of new terms to describe those interested in the same sex. The adoption in the last decades of the nineteenth century of words like 'homosexual' or 'invert', both by sexologists and by the homosexuals themselves, marked as crucial a change in consciousness as did the widespread adoption of the term 'gay' in the 1970s. Changing legal and medical attitudes were important elements in this development. ...

Social regulation provides the conditions within which those defined can begin to develop their

own consciousness and identity. In the nineteenth century, law and science, social *mores* and popular prejudice established the limits but homosexual people responded. In so doing they created, in a variety of ways, self-concepts, meeting places, a language and style, and complex and varied modes of life. Michel Foucault has described this process in the following way:

> There is no question that the appearance in nineteenth century psychiatry, jurisprudence, and literature of a whole series of discourses on the species and sub-species of homosexuality, inversion, pederasty, and 'psychic hermaphrodism' made possible a strong advance of social controls into this area of 'perversity'; but it also made possible the formation of a 'reverse' discourse: homosexuality began to speak on its own behalf, to demand that its legitimacy or 'naturality' be acknowledged, often in the same vocabulary, using the same categories by which it was radically disqualified.

But this 'reverse discourse' was by no means a simple or chronologically even process. It is difficult to fit homosexual behaviour into any preconceived mould; on the contrary, it pervades various aspects of social experience, and as the recent work from the Kinsey Institute of Sex Research has indicated, despite the plethora of definitions and social regulations there is not a single homosexuality but on the contrary, 'homosexualities': 'There is no such thing as *the* homosexual (or *the* heterosexual, for that matter) and (that) statements of any kind which are made about human beings on the basis of their sexual orientation must always be highly qualified'.

It is the social categorisation which attempts to create the notion of uniformity, with always varying effects. The very unevenness of the social categorisation, the variations in legal and other social responses, meant that homosexual experiences could be absorbed into a variety of different lifestyles, with no necessary identity as a 'homosexual' developing. ...

In any study of homosexuality the important point to observe is that there is no automatic relationship between social categorisation and individual sense of self or identity. The meanings given to homosexual activities can vary enormously. They depend on a variety of factors: social class, geographical location, gender differentiation. But it is vital to keep in mind when exploring homosexuality, which has always been defined in our culture as a deviant form, that what matters is not the inherent nature of the act but the social construction of meanings around that activity, and the individual response to that. The striking feature of the 'history of homosexuality' over the past hundred years or so is that the oppressive definition and the defensive identities and structures have marched together. Control of sexual variations has inevitably reinforced and reshaped rather than repressed homosexual behaviour. In terms of individual anxiety, induced guilt and suffering, the cost of moral regulation has often been high. But the result has been a complex and socially significant history of resistance and self-definition which historians have hitherto all too easily ignored.

Source: Weeks, 1989, pp.96–7, 102, 108, 117.

READING C
Abstractions, structures and mechanisms

Andrew Sayer

Knowledge must grasp the differentiations of the world; we need a way of individuating objects, and of characterizing their attributes and relationships. To be adequate for a specific purpose it must 'abstract' from particular conditions, excluding those which have no significant effect in order to focus on those which do. Even where we are interested in wholes we must select and abstract their constituents.

In many accounts of science abstraction is assumed to be so obviously necessary that little is said about how it should be done. It is a powerful tool and hence also a dangerous one if carelessly used. Once we have become accustomed to a particular 'mode of abstraction' it is often hard to dislodge, even where it generates problems in research and applications. In contrast to some accounts, I therefore want to emphasize the importance of trying to keep in mind what we abstract *from.* ...

In popular usage, the adjective 'abstract' often means 'vague' or 'removed from reality'. The sense in which the term is used here is different; an abstract concept, or an abstraction, isolates in thought a *one-sided* or partial aspect of an object. What we abstract *from* are the many other aspects which together constitute *concrete* objects such as people, economics, nations, institutions, activities and so on. In this sense an abstract concept can be precise rather than vague; there is nothing vague about abstractions such as 'temperature', 'valency', 'gender', 'income elasticity of demand', or 'the circuit of money capital'. ... At the outset our concepts of concrete objects are likely to be superficial or chaotic. In order to understand their diverse determinations we must first abstract them systematically. When each of the abstracted aspects has been examined it is possible to combine the abstractions so as to form concepts which grasp the concreteness of their objects. ...

In making abstractions it is helpful to distinguish relations of different types. The term 'relation' is a very flexible one but there are some significant contrasts implicit in its various uses. A simple distinction can be made between *'substantial'* relations of connection and interaction and *'formal'* relations of similarity or dissimilarity. Houses are connected by roads and electricity cables, individuals may interact directly, but they may also bear a purely formal relation, lacking any interaction, as objects having similar characteristics. Clearly, things which are connected need not be similar and vice versa. ...

Another useful distinction can be made between *external* or *contingent relations* and *internal* or *necessary relations*. The relation between yourself and a lump of earth is external in the sense that either object can exist without the other. It is neither necessary nor impossible that they stand in any particular relation; in other words it is contingent. (Note that this sense of contingent is quite different from that common in everyday uses where 'contingent upon' means 'dependent upon'.) Although a relation may be contingent it may still have significant effects; thus people may break up lumps of earth or be buried beneath them – but the nature of each object does not necessarily depend on its standing in such a relation. By contrast, the relation between a master and a slave is internal or necessary, in that what the object is is dependent on its relation to the other; a person cannot be a slave without a master and vice versa. Another example is the relation of landlord and tenant; the existence of one necessarily presupposes the other. ...

The necessary/contingent distinction has nothing to do with importance or interest – either kind of relation may be insignificant or important; the relationship between British governments and North Sea oil is contingent in the sense that each could exist without the other, but the effect of North Sea oil revenues on the position of British governments is of considerable importance. The external relationship between the British government and my musical preferences is contingent and insignificant. Similarly, not all the necessary conditions of existence of people are of much interest to social science, for instance their need to breathe. ...

In any real situation there is usually a complex combination of these types of relation. The structure of a system of interest can be discovered by asking simple questions about such relations: What does the existence of this object (in this form) presuppose? Can it exist on its own as such? If not what else must be present? What is it *about* the object that makes it do such and such? These questions may seem simple ... but the answers are often complex and many errors of conceptualization and abstraction stem from evasions of them. Let us consider three examples, starting with an artificially simple one, concerning the relations between two people, Jones and Smith.

They may be employer and employee respectively and in this respect they are internally related, although in others, such as religion, attitudes or recreational activities, they may be contingently related. In other words, *unless we make it clear what aspect of Jones and Smith we are considering, the attempt to distinguish internal from external relations, or necessary from contingent conditions, of certain attributes or practices is liable to result in confusion.*

A more complex example which demonstrates the need for clear definition in assessing the nature of relations concerns the question of whether capitalism and patriarchy are interdependent. At the level of the most basic relation of capitalism – the capital/wage-labour relation – it is contingent whether capitalists or workers are male or female. At this level capital is 'sex-blind'. However, in their *concrete* forms, instances of the relation may be affected by gender, and less basic structures of particular capitalist societies, such as the British welfare state, may include practices determined by and reproductive of gender which 'interlock' patriarchal and capitalist structures. So even though in virtually every instance, capitalist social relations are gendered in some way, and even though patriarchy and capitalism take advantage of one another (though they can also cause problems for one another), we can argue that the relation between patriarchy and capital is contingent. For not only has patriarchy existed without capitalism but there seems to be nothing about class relations, exchange-value, production for profit, etc., which would make them dependent on the survival of patriarchy. Provided due care is taken in abstraction in deciding which *aspects* of the phenomena are being considered, illumination rather than confusion should result.

A third example illustrates the importance of asking qualitative questions about the nature of our objects. This concerns the explanation of why some industries are more strike-prone than others. Many social scientists would tackle this by proceeding quickly to a statistical analysis in order to evaluate possible independent variables such as union membership, size of establishment, gender composition, etc. But interesting though the results might be, this line of inquiry ignores our simple qualitative questions: e.g. What does strike activity presuppose? What is it *about* the size of establishments which affects propensity to strike? Is it just size *per se* in terms of numbers employed, or the nature of social relations and forms of management control associated with different sizes? Often, researchers stop short of such questions as if the revelation of statistical relationships were sufficient to

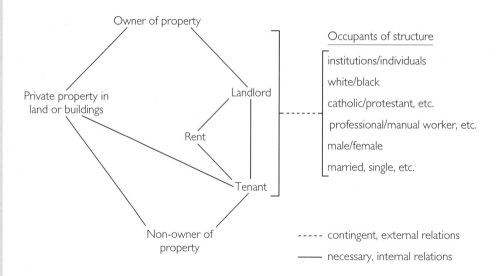

Figure 1   Necessary and contingent relations

explain things. Alternatively, they may be tempted to treat the answers to the questions as further 'independent variables' and run additional statistical tests, but whatever the results we will still need to arrive at a conclusion in answer to the qualitative questions. In turn, answering them again requires considerable attention to how we abstract and what we abstract from.

Abstraction is particularly important for the identification of *structures*. These can be defined as sets of internally related objects or practices. The landlord–tenant relation itself presupposes the existence of private property, rent, the production of an economic surplus and so on; together they form a structure (see Figure 1). Contrary to a common assumption, structures include not only big social objects such as the international division of labour but small ones at the interpersonal and personal levels (e.g. conceptual structures) and still smaller non-social ones at the neurological level and beyond.

Within social structures there are particular 'positions' associated with certain roles. It is particularly important to distinguish the occupant of a position from the position itself. One of the most pervasive illusions of everyday thinking derives from the attribution of the properties of the position, be they good or bad, to the individual or institution occupying it. Whatever effects result, it is assumed that particular *people* must be responsible; there is little appreciation that the structure of social relations, together with their associated resources, constraints or rules, may determine what happens, even though these structures only exist where people reproduce them. In such circumstances it is futile to expect problems to be resolved by the discovery of a guilty person and their replacement by a different individual. We may question individuals in a structure in the hope of finding someone to blame or credit for certain outcomes without ever finding one where 'the buck stops here'.

Source: Sayer, 1992, pp.86–93.

READING D
Challenging orthodoxies: gender, ethnicity and social science

Marcia Rice

Given the history and theoretical objectives of feminist criminology, one might have assumed that the monolithic, uni-dimensional perspectives employed by traditional theorists would have been abandoned for a more dynamic approach. But, almost without exception, feminist criminological research – from the late 1960s to date – has focused on white female offenders. Pioneering writings by Heidensohn (1968) and Smart (1976) and more recent writings by Carlen and Worrall (1987) and Morris (1987) have all adopted an essentialist position with regards to the construct of 'women' and have paid little attention to the relevance of race. Sexist images of women have been challenged but racist stereotypes have largely been ignored. ...

Since the 1970s, feminist criminologists have launched a critical attack on male-dominated theoretical premises in criminology. The basic point which they make is that these expositions are not theories of women's crime but stereotypes which perpetuate sexist ideologies of women. Feminists insist that many of the assumptions made about female criminals are incorrect – they are based on middle-class notions of morality and behaviour – and that the focus on biological and social pathologies to explain both crime and conformity is inadequate.

Central to these arguments is the belief that notions such as 'femininity' and 'sexuality' are constructs, not objective givens. But, this said, feminist writers have made little reference to the different cultural experiences and socialization patterns of black women. There is a failure to situate, for example, discussions of sex roles within a structural explanation of the social origins of these roles which are influenced by black women's racial and sexual experiences and their general position in society (Malson, 1983). Gender differences are assumed to be universal, irrespective of race (or class). ...

Black women, like most other women, experience some degree of sexual oppression. However, this fails to acknowledge the complexity of gender considerations ... [for the] unqualified focus on men's domination does not allow for the historical specificity of patriarchy which has meant that oppression is not experienced in the same way by all women or expressed by all men (Davis, 1981; Anthias and Davis-Yuval, 1983; Mama, 1984; hooks, 1989).

To take the first point. While accepting that relationships between black men and black women are likely to be as sexually oppressive as those experienced by white women, the historical experiences of black women compound their situation and produce a more complex mesh of struggles both within and outside the family. The experiences of black women as chattels under slavery and colonialism has meant that social relations were often mediated and bound up with economic as much as sexual reproduction. Thus, in order to understand the unique oppression of black women, we need to understand their experiences as black *people*.

We need to note also that black women do not comprise a homogenous group, although the majority share a similar class position. Black women are further subdivided in terms of ethnicity. For example, there are differences in histories and experiences between ... white women and white men; black women experience sexual and patriarchal oppression by black men but at the same time struggle alongside them against racial oppression (Davis, 1981; hooks, 1982).

With respect to the second point, the hierarchical relationship on which patriarchal oppression is premised assumes that black men naturally occupy a similar economically privileged position to white men. However, in Western industrialized countries black men have been socially and politically disadvantaged to an extent which has limited their power both in the family and in society in general.

One of the consequences of the employment structure in capitalist countries has been reliance on the labour of black women which has reduced their dependency on black men. This has contributed to the complex social and patriarchal relations in which black women are involved and stands in contradiction to the conception of the family which predominantly white feminist academics have endorsed. The traditional model of the family is based on ethnocentric ideals of the dependent married women with a male patriarchal head of the household. Black women's relationship to the family is then presented as deviant or pathological. This is reiterated in discussions of the black family in feminist theory where the dominance of black women is portrayed as both a cause of consternation and an explanation for structural weakness. ...

Hooks explains that white women may be victimized by sexism, but racism enables them to act as exploiters and oppressors of black women (and men):

> Black women are in an unusual position for not only are we collectively at the bottom of the occupational ladder, but the overall social status is lower than that of any other group. Occupying such a position we bear the brunt of sexist, racist, and classist oppression. Racist stereotypes of the strong superhuman black woman are operative myths in the minds of many white women, allowing them to ignore the extent to which black women are likely to be victimised in this society and the role that white women play in the maintenance and perpetuation of that victimisation.
>
> (1984, p.14)

Thus it is not just or simply that black women are subject to 'more' disadvantage than white women. Their oppression is of a qualitatively different kind. Women's experience of oppression in social or patriarchal relations cannot be reduced to those of white middle-class women. Ethnocentric feminist analyses are not adequate. ...

If feminist criminologists wish to take account of black women's criminality then they must think carefully about the framework which they are using to analyse women's involvement in crime. Feminists must not include black women solely to add an extra edge to the victimization or offending patterns of women. Black women do not represent a homogenous group and, as such, should not be grouped together and referred to as a common 'other'. ... I would suggest:

1   Theories of black women's criminality should not be based on ethnocentric models or racist stereotypes which construct an inaccurate picture and which ignore differences between female offenders.

2   Criminology should avoid the use of universal, unspecified categories of 'women' and 'blacks' in theoretical discussions and in research. Homogeneity cannot be assumed.

3   The significance of race and racism must be seen as integral to any analysis of (women's) criminality. ...

4   Comparative studies, on the basis of race, sex and class, should be carried out to determine how black and white women (and men) are dealt with in the criminal justice system.

5   [The] studies of (women's) offending should be situated in the wider political, economic and social sphere.

6   The experiences of (black) women should not be investigated in a manner which separates the researcher from the subject. There should be a dynamic exchange which involves participation and consultation at all stages in the research process.

References

ANTHIAS, S. and DAVIS–YUVAL, Y. (1983) 'Contextualising feminism – gender, ethnic and class divisions', *Feminist Review*, 15, pp.62–77.

CARLEN, P. and WORRALL, A. (eds) (1987) *Gender, Crime and Justice*, Buckingham, OUP.

DAVIS, A. (1981) *Women, Race and Class*, London, Women's Press.

HEIDENSOHN, F. 'The deviance of women: a critique and an enquiry', *British Journal of Sociology*, 19, pp.160–75.

HOOKS, B. (1982) *Ain't I a Woman: Black Women and Feminism*, London, Women's Press.

HOOKS, B. (1984) *Feminist Theory: from Margin to Centre*, Boston, Southend Press.

HOOKS, B (1989) *Talking Black: Thinking Feminist, Thinking Black*, London, Sheba Feminist Publications.

MALSON, M. (1983) 'Black women's sex roles: the social context for a new ideology', *Journal of Social Issues*, 39, 3. pp.101–13.

MAMA, A. (1984) 'Black women, the economic crisis and the British State', *Feminist Review*, 17, pp.20–35.

MORRIS, A. (1987) *Women, Crime and Criminal Justice*, Oxford, Basil Blackwell.

SMART, C. (1976) *Women, Crime and Criminology: a Feminist Critique*, London, Routledge and Kegan Paul.

Source: Rice, 1990, pp.59–68.

References

ALLISON, G.T. (1971) *Essence of Decision: Explaining the Cuban Missile Crisis*, Boston, Mass., Little Brown.

AUSTIN, J. (1962) *How To do Things With Words*, Oxford, Oxford University Press.

AYER, A.J. (1936/1990) *Language, Truth and Logic*, Harmondsworth, Penguin.

BAKHTIN, M.M. (1981) *The Dialogic Imagination: Four Essays*, Austin, Texas, University of Texas Press.

BANCROFT, J. (1974) *Deviant Sexual Behaviour: Modification and Assessment,* Oxford, Clarendon.

BANDURA, A., ROSS, D. and ROSS, S.A. (1963) 'Imitation of Film-Mediated Aggressive Models', *Journal of Abnormal and Social Psychology,* Vol. 67, pp.627–34.

BANTON, M. (1967) *Race Relations*, London, Social Science Paperbacks/Tavistock Publications.

BARKAN, E. (1992) *The Retreat of Scientific Racism: Changing Concepts of Race in Britain and the United States between the World Wars*, Cambridge, Cambridge University Press.

BARKER, E. (1988) *The Making of a Moonie: Choice or Brainwashing?* Oxford, Blackwell.

BARNES, B. (1977) *Interests and the Growth of Knowledge*, London, Routledge.

BARTHES, R. (1967) *Elements of Semiology*, London, Cape.

BARTHES, R. (1970) *S/Z*, London, Cape.

BARTHES, R. (1973) *Mythologies*, London, Paladin.

BARTHES, R. (1976) *The Pleasure of the Text*, London, Cape.

BARTHES, R. (1977) *Image–Music–Text*, London, Fontana.

BARTHOLOMEW, M., CLENNELL, S. and WALSH, L. (1992) 'The *Encyclopédie*' in Hall, B.P. and Lentin, A. (eds) *The Enlightenment*, Milton Keynes, The Open University.

BAUDRILLARD, J. (1983) *Simulations*, New York, Semiotext(e).

BAUMAN, Z. (1978) *Hermeneutics and Social Science: Approaches to Understanding*, London, Hutchinson.

BAUMAN, Z. (1992) *Intimations of Postmodernity*, London, Routledge.

BAUMAN, Z. (1993) *Postmodern Ethics*, Oxford, Blackwell.

BECK, U, GIDDENS, A. and LASH S.(1994) *Reflexive Modernization: Politics, Tradition and Aesthetics in the Modern Social Order*, Cambridge, Polity.

BECKER, H. (1963) *Outsiders, Studies in the Sociology of Deviance*, New York, Free Press.

BELLAH, R.N. (1976) 'New Religious Consciousness and the Crisis in Modernity' in Bellah, R. and Glock, C.Y. (eds) *The New Religious Consciousness*, Berkeley, University of California Press.

BELSON, B.A. (1978) *TV Violence and the Adolescent Boy*, Farnborough, Teakfield.

BENTHAM, J. (1824/1987) 'An Introduction to the Principles of Morals and Legislation' in Mill J.S. and Bentham, J. *Utilitarianism and Other Essays* (edited by Ryan, A.), Harmondsworth, Penguin.

BERMAN, M. (1982) *All That Is Solid Melts Into Air: The Experience of Modernity*, London, Verso.

BHASKAR, R. (1979) *The Possibility of Naturalism: A Philosophical Critique of the Contemporary Human Sciences* , Brighton, Harvester Press (the second edition, 1989, published by Harvester Wheatsheaf, Hemel Hempstead, contains a postcript addressing its critics).

BHASKAR, R. (1986) *Scientific Realism and Human Emancipation*, London, Verso.

BHASKAR, R. (1991) *Philosophy and the Idea of Freedom*, Oxford, Blackwell.

BLAIKIE, N. (1993) *Approaches to Social Enquiry*, Cambridge, Polity.

BLALOCK, H. (1964) *Causal Inferences in Non-experimental Research*, Chapel Hill, N. Carolina, University of North Carolina Press.

BLAUG, M. (1992) *The Methodology of Economics: or How Economists Explain* (2nd edn), Cambridge, Cambridge University Press.

BLAUG, M. (1994) 'Why I am Not a Constructivist: Confessions of an unrepentant Popperian' in Backhouse, R.E. (ed.) *New Directions in Economic Methodology*, London, Routledge.

BLOOR, D. (1976) *Knowledge and Social Imagery*, London, Routledge.

BOURDIEU, P. (1975) 'The Specificity of the Scientific Field' and 'The Social Conditions of the Progress of Reason', *Social Science Information*, No.14.

BOYLE, M. (1994) 'Schizophrenia and the Art of the Soluble', *The Psychologist*, September, pp.399–404.

BRYANT, C. (1985) *Positivism in Social Theory and Research*, Basingstoke, Macmillan.

BUCHANAN, J.M., ROWLEY, C.K., BRETON, A., WISEMAN, J., FREY, B., and PEACOCK, A.T. (1978) *The Economics of Politics*, Readings 18, London, Institute of Economic Affairs.

BUCHANAN J.M. and TULLOCK, G. (1981) 'An American Perspective from "Markets Work" to Public Choice' in Seldon, A. (ed.) *The Emerging Concensus?*, London, Institute of Economic Affairs.

BUNGE, W. (1966) *Theoretical Geography,* Lund Studies in Geography, Series C1, Lund, G.W.R. Gleerup.

BURT, C. (1925/1961) *The Young Delinquent* (4th edn), London, University of London Press.

BUTLER, D. and STOKES, D (1974) *Political change in Britain: The Evolution of Electoral Choice*, Basingstoke, Macmillan.

CALDWELL, B. (1994) *Beyond Positivism: Economic Methodology in the Twentieth Century* (2nd edn), London, Routledge.

CARNAP, R. (1932/1995) *The Unity of Science*, Bristol, Thoemmes Press.

CAYGILL, H. (995) *The Kant Dictionary*, Oxford, Blackwell.

CHRISTALLER, W. (1966) *Central Places in Southern Germany*, Englewood Cliffs, N.J. Prentice-Hall.

CICOUREL, A. (1976) *The Social Organisation of Juvenile Justice*, London, Heinemann.

CLARKE, A.J. (1997) 'Tupperware: suburbia, sociology and mass consumption' in Silverstone, R. (ed.) *Visions of Suburbia*, London, Routledge.

CLARKE, A.J. (1998) 'Window shopping at home: classifieds, catalogues and new consumer skills' in Miller, D. (ed.) *Material Cultures: Why Some Things Matter*, London, UCL Press.

COLLINS, H. (1994) 'Science is a Social Construct', *The Times Higher Education Supplement*, 30.9.94, p.17.

COLLINS, P.H. (1990) *Black Feminist Thought: Knowledge, Consciousness and the Politics of Empowerment*, London, Routledge.

COMTE, A. (1853/1971) 'The Positive Philosophy', in Thompson, K. and Tunstall, J. (eds) *Sociological Perspectives*, Harmondsworth, Penguin.

CONWAY, J. (1984) *Capital Decay: An Analysis of London's Housing*, London, SHAC Publications.

COOLEY, C.H. (1902) *Human Nature and the Social Order*, New York, Schribner's.

COSGROVE, D.(1984) *Social Formation and Symbolic Landscape*, London, Croom Helm.

COSGROVE, D. and DANIELS, S. (eds) (1988) *The Iconography of Lanscape*, Cambridge, Cambridge University Press.

DAHL, R.A. (1957) 'The Concept of Power', *Behavioural Science*, No. 2.

DAHL, R.A. (1960) *Who Governs? Democracy and Power in an American City*, New Haven, CT, Yale University Press.

DAHL, R.A. (1961) 'The Behavioural Approach in Political Science', *American Political Science Review*, No. 58.

DAHL, R.A. (1982) *Dilemmas of Pluralist Democracy: Autonomy versus Control*, New Haven, CT, Yale University Press.

DARWIN, C. (1859/1872) *The Origin of Species by Means of Natural Selection* (6th edn), Oxford, Oxford University Press.

DEAN, M. (1994) *Critical and Effective Histories: Foucault's Methods and Historical Sociology*, London, Routledge.

DERRIDA, J. (1973) *Speech and Phenomena*, Evanston, Illinois, Northwestern University Press.

DERRIDA, J. (1976) *Of Grammatology*, Baltimore, John Hopkins University Press.

DERRIDA, J. (1978) *Writing and Difference*, London, Routledge.

DERRIDA, J. (1981) *Positions*, London, Athlone Press.

DILTHEY. W. (1883) *Introduction to the Human Sciences*, see Rickman (ed. and trans.), (1976).

DONZELOT, J. (1979) *The Policing of Families*, London, Hutchinson.

DUHEM, P. (1914/1962) *The Aim and Structure of Physical Theory*, London, Atheneum.

DURKHEIM, E. (1895/1982) *The Rules of Sociological Method*, Basingstoke, Macmillan.

DURKHEIM, E. (1897/1952) *Suicide: A Study in Sociology*, London, Routledge.

ELSTER, J. (1989) *Nuts and Bolts for the Social Sciences*, Cambridge, Cambridge University Press.

ERON, L.D. (1963) 'Relationship of TV Viewing Habits and Aggressive Behaviour', *Journal of Abnormal and Social Psychology*, Vol. 67, pp.193–96.

EYSENCK, H. (1971) *Race, Intelligence and Education*, London, Maurice Temple Smith.

FEYERABEND, P. (1975) *Against Method*, London, Verso.

FEYERABEND, P. (1978) *Science in a Free Society*, London, NLB.

FOUCAULT, M. (1967) *Madness and Civilisation: A History of Insanity in the Age of Reason*, London, Tavistock/Routledge.

FOUCAULT, M. (1970) *The Order of Things*, London, Tavistock/Routledge.

FOUCAULT, M. (1972) *The Archaeology of Knowledge*, London, Tavistock/Routledge.

FOUCAULT, M. (1973) *The Birth of the Clinic: An Archaeology of Medical Perception*, London, Tavistock.

FOUCAULT, M. (1977) *Discipline and Punish*, Harmondsworth, Penguin.

FOUCAULT, M. (1980) *Power/Knowledge: Selected Interviews and Other Writings 1972-1977*, Brighton, Harvester.

FRIEDMAN, M. (1953) 'The Methodology of Positive Economics' in Friedman, M. (ed.) *Essays in Positive Economics*, Chicago, University of Chicago Press.

GARFINKEL, H. (1967) *Studies in Ethnomethodology*, Englewood Cliffs, Prentice-Hall.

GIDDENS, A. (1976) *New Rules of Sociological Method: A Positive Critique of Interpretative Sociologies*, London, Hutchinson.

GIDDENS, A. (1979) *Central Problems in Social Theory: Action, Structure and Contradiction in Social Analysis*, Basingstoke, Macmillan.

GIDDENS, A. (1984) *The Constitution of Society*, Cambridge, Polity.

GILLIES, D. (1993) *Philosophy of Science in the Twentieth Century: Four Central Themes*, Oxford, Blackwell.

GILROY, P. (1987) *There Ain't No Black in the Union Jack*, London, Unwin Hyman.

GOLDTHORPE, J.H., LOCKWOOD, D., BECHHOFER, F. and PLATT, J. (1968–9) *The Affluent Worker Studies*, Cambridge, Cambridge University Press.

GOFFMAN, E. (1968) *Asylums: Essays on the Social Situation of Mental Patients and Other Inmates*, Harmondsworth, Penguin. (The essay 'The Moral Career of the Mental Patient' was originally published in 1959 in *Psychiatry*, Vol. 22.)

GOULD, S.J. (1981) *The Mismeasure of Man*, Harmondsworth, Penguin.

GRAMSCI, A. (1971) *Selections From Prison Notebooks*, London, Lawrence and Wishart.

GREEN, D. (1987) *The New Right: The Counter Revolution in Political, Economic and Social Thought*, Brighton, Wheatsheaf Books.

HACKING, I. (1983) *Representing and Intervening*, Cambridge, Cambridge University Press.

HAGSTROM, W.O. (1965) *The Scientific Community*, New York, Basic Books.

HALBWACHS, M. (1930/1978) *The Causes of Suicide*, London, Routledge and Kegan Paul.

HALL, S. (1981) 'Notes on Deconstructing the Popular' in Samuel, R. (ed.) *People's History and Socialist Theory*, London, Routledge.

HALL, S. (1997) 'The Work of Representation' in Hall, S. (ed.) *Representation: Cultural Representations and Signifying Practices*, London, Sage/The Open University.

HALL, S., CRITCHER, C., JEFFERSON, T., CLARKE, J. and ROBERTS, B. (1978) or *Policing the Crisis: Mugging, the State, and Law and Order*, Basingstoke, Macmillan.

HANSON, N. (1958) *Patterns of Discovery*, Cambridge, Cambridge University Press.

HANSON, N. (1969) *Perception and Discovery: An Introduction to Scientific Inquiry*, San Francisco, Freeman, Cooper and Company.

HARDIN, G. (1968) 'The Tragedy of the Commons', *Science*, No. 162.

HARDING, S. (1986) *The Science Question in Feminism*, Milton Keynes, Open University Press.

HARRÉ, R. (1979) *Social Being*, Oxford, Blackwell.

HARRÉ, R. and KRAUSZ, M. (1996) *Varieties of Relativism*, Oxford, Blackwell.

HARRÉ, R. and GILLETT, G. (1994) *The Discursive Mind*, London, Sage.

HARRÉ, R. and SECORD, P.F. (1973) *The Explanation of Social Behaviour*, Oxford, Blackwell.

HARVEY, D. (1989) *The Condition of Postmodernity: An Enquiry into the Origins of Cultural Change*, Oxford, Blackwell.

HAWKES, T. (1977) *Strucuralism and Semiotics*, London, Methuen and Co.

HAYEK, F.A. (1952/1979) *The Counter-Revolution of Science: Studies on the Abuse of Reason* (2nd edn), Indianapolis, Liberty.

HEATH, A., JOWELL, R., CURTICE, J., FIELD, J. and LEVINE, C. (1985) *How Britain Votes*, Oxford, Pergamon.

HEMPEL, C.G. (1965) *Aspects of Scientific Explanation*, New York, Free Press.

HIMMELWEIT, H. (1958) *TV and the Child*, Oxford, Oxford University Press.

HIMMELWEIT, H., HUMPHREYS, P., JAEGER, M. and KATZ, M. (1981) *How Voters Decide: A longitudinal study of political attitudes and voting extending over fifteen years*, London, Academic Press.

HØIGÅRD, C. and FINSTAD, L. (1992) *Backstreets: Prostitution, Love and Money*, Cambridge, Polity.

HOLLINGER, R. (1994) *Postmodernism and the Social Sciences*, London, Sage.

HOWARD, E. (1898/1985) *Garden Cities of Tomorrow*, Eastbourne, Attic Press.

HUME, D. (1748/1984) *Enquiry Concerning Human Understanding*, New York, Bobbs-Merrill Co.

HUNT, E.K. and SHERMAN, H.J. (1981) *Economics: An Introduction to Traditional and Radical Views*, New York, Harper and Row.

ILLICH, I. (1971) *Deschooling Society*, London, Calder and Boyers.

JAMES, W. (1890) *The Principles of Psychology Vol. II*, New York, Holt.

JEFFERY, R. (1979) 'Normal Rubbish: Deviant Patients in a Casualty Department', *Sociology of Health and Illness*, Vol. 1, No. 1.

JORDAN, A.G. and RICHARDSON, J.J. (1987) *Government and Pressure Groups in Britain*, Oxford, Clarendon Press.

KANT, I. (1781/1987) *Critique of Pure Reason* (2nd edn), London, Dent .

KAPLAN, A. (1964) *The Conduct of Inquiry*, New York, Chandler Publishing.

KATOUZIAN, H. (1987) *Ideology and Method in Economics*, London, Macmillan.

KEARNEY, H. (1971) *Science and Change 1500–1700*, London, Wiedenfeld and Nicholson.

KEAT, R. and URRY J. (1982) *Social Theory as Science* (2nd edn), London, Routledge.

KELLNER, D. (1989) *Jean Baudrillard: From Marxism to Postmodernism and Beyond*, Cambridge, Polity.

KNORR-CETINA, K. (1981) *The Manufacture of Knowledge: An Essay on the Constructivist and Contextual Nature of Science*, Oxford, Pergamon.

KUHN, T.S. (1962/1970) *The Structure of Scientific Revolutions* (2nd edn), Chicago, University of Chicago Press.

KUHN, T.S. (1977) *The Essential Tension: Selected Studies in Scientific Tradition and Change*, Chicago, University of Chicago Press.

LACLAU, E. and MOUFFE, C. (1985) *Hegemony and Socialist Strategy: Towards a Radical Democratic Politics*, London, Verso.

LAING, R.D. (1960) *The Divided Self: An Existential Study in Insanity and Madness*, London, Tavistock.

LAKATOS, I. (1970) 'Falsification and the Methodology of Scientific Research Programmes' in Lakatos I. and Musgrave, A. (eds) *Criticism and the Growth of Knowledge*, Cambridge, Cambridge University Press.

LATOUR, B. and WOOLGAR, S. (1979) *Laboratory Life: The Construction of Scientific Facts*, Princeton, University of Princeton Press.

LAWSON, T. (1994) 'A Realist Theory for Economics' in Backhouse, R.E. (ed) *New Directions in Economic Methodology*, London, Routledge.

LEAVIS, F.R. (1930) *Mass Civilisation and Minority Culture*, Cambridge, Minority Press.

LEMERT, C. (1993) 'Social Theory: Its Uses and Pleasures' in Lemert, C. (ed.) *Social Theory: The Multicultural and Classic Readings*, Oxford, Westview Press.

LIPSEY, R.G. (1963/1979) *An Introduction to Positive Economics* (5th edn), London, Wiedenfeld and Nicholson.

LOCKE, J. (1690/1990) *An Essay Concerning Human Understanding*, London, Dent.

LOMBROSO, C. (1911) *L'Uomo Delinquente* (*The Criminal Man*), London, Penguin.

LUKES, S. (1973a) *Émile Durkheim: His Life and Work*, Harmondsworth, Penguin.

LUKES, S. (1973b) *Individualism*, Oxford, Blackwell.

LYOTARD, J-F. (1984) *The Postmodern Condition: A Report on Knowledge*, Manchester, Manchester University Press.

MANICAS, P. (1987) *A History and Philosophy of the Social Sciences*, Oxford, Blackwell.

MANNHEIM, H. (1965) *Comparative Criminology*, London, Routledge.

MASSEY, D. (1995) 'The Conceptualisation of Space' in Massey, D. and Jess, P. (eds) *A Place in the World*, Oxford, Oxford University Press.

MASTERMAN, M. (1970) 'The Nature of a Paradigm' in Lakatos I. and Musgrave, A. (eds.) *Criticism and the Growth of Knowledge*, Cambridge, Cambridge University Press.

McCLINTOCK, A. (1995) *Imperial Leather: Race, Gender and Sexuality in the Colonial Contest*, London, Routledge.

McCLOSKEY, D. (1983) 'The Rhetoric of Economics', *Journal of Economic Literature*, Vol. XXI, pp.481–517.

McGHEE, P. (1998) 'Experimental social psychology' in Sapsford, R., Still, A., Wetherell, M., Miell, D. and Stevens, R. (eds) *Theory and Social Psychology*, London, Sage/The Open University.

McKEGANEY, N. and BARNARD, M. (1996) *Sex Work On The Streets: Prostitutes and Their Clients*, Buckingham, Open University Press.

McNAY, L. (1994) *Foucault: A Critical Introduction*, Cambridge, Polity.

MEAD, G.H. *Mind, Self, and Society* (1934) (edited by Morris, C.W.), Chicago, University of Chicago Press.

MENGER, C. (1883/1981) *Problems of Economics and Sociology*, New York, New York University Press.

MERTON, R. (1938) 'Social Structure and Anomie', *American Sociological Review*, No.3.

MIES, M. and SHIVA, V. (1993) *Ecofeminism*, London, Zed Books.

MILL, J. S. (1843/1879) *A System of Logic*, London, Longman Green and Co.

MILL, J. S. (1848/1970) *Principles of Political Economy*, Harmondsworth, Penguin.

MILLET, K. (1970) *Sexual Politics*, New York, Doubleday.

MILLER, D. (1998) 'Why some things matter' in Miller, D. (ed.) *Material Cultures: Why Some Things Matter*, London, UCL Press.

MILLMAN, M. and KANTER, R.M. (eds.) (1975) *Another Voice: Feminist Perspectives on Social Life and Social Science*, New York, Anchor Books.

MINSON, J. (1985) *Genealogies of Morals: Nietzsche, Foucault, Donzelot and the Eccentricity of Ethics*, London, Macmillan.

MISES, L. VON (1957) *Theory and History: Interpretation of Social and Economic Evolution*, New Haven, CT, Yale University Press

MONTESSORI, M. (1913) *Pedagogical Anthropology* , New York, F.A. Stokes Co.

MORGENSTEIN, O. and NEUMANN, J. VON (1944) *The Theory of Games and Economic Behaviour*, Princeton, Princeton University Press.

MORRIS, D. (1969) *The Naked Ape*, London, Cape.

MORRIS, D. (1970) *The Human Zoo*, London, Cape.

MULKAY, M. (1972) *The Social Process of Innovation*, London, Macmillan.

MULKAY, M. (1991) *Sociology of Science; A Sociological Pilgrimage*, Buckingham, Open University Press.

OAKLEY, A. (1974) *The Sociology of Housework*, Oxford, Martin Robertson.

OATLEY, K. and JENKINS, J.M. (1996) *Understanding Emotions*, Oxford, Blackwell.

OUTHWAITE, W. (1987) *New Philosophies of Social Science: Realism, Hermeneutics and Critical Theory*, Basingstoke, Macmillan.

PARSONS, T. (1951) *The Social System*, New York, Free Press.

PLANCK, M. (1949) *Scientific Autobiography and Other Papers*, New York, New York University Press.

PLUMMER, K. (1975) *Sexual Stigma: An Interactionist Account*, London, Routledge.

POLLAK, O. (1961) *The Criminality of Women*, New York, A.S. Barnes.

POPPER, K. (1959) *The Logic of Scientific Discovery*, London, Hutchinson.

POPPER, K. (1963) *Conjectures and Refutations: The Growth of Scientific Knowledge*, London, Routledge.

POPPER, K. (1972) *Objective Knowledge*, Oxford, Clarendon.

PORTER, R. (1990) *The Enlightenment*, London, Macmillan.

POTTER, J. and WETHERELL, M. (1987) *Discourse and Social Psychology: Beyond Attitudes and Behaviour*, London, Sage.

QUINE, W.O. VON (1953/1965) 'The Two Dogmas of Empiricism' in *From a Logical Point of View: Logico-Philosophical Essays*, New York, Harper and Row.

REX, J. and MOORE, R. (1967) *Race, Community and Conflict*, Oxford, Oxford University Press.

RICKMAN, H. P. (ed. and trans.) (1976) *Wilhelm Dilthey, Selected Writings*, Cambridge, Cambridge University Press.

RICE, M. (1990) 'Challenging Orthodoxies in Feminist Theory; A Black Feminist Critique' in Gelsthorpe, L. and Morris, A. (eds) *Feminist Perspectives in Criminology*, Buckingham, Open University Press.

RORTY, R. (1980) *Philosophy and the Mirror of Nature* , Oxford, Blackwell.

RORTY, R. (1991) 'Science and Solidarity' in *Objectivity, Relativism and Truth: Philosophical Papers Vol. 1*, New York, Cambridge University Press.

RORTY, R. (1994) 'Method, Social Science and Social Hope' in Seidman, S. (ed.) *The Postmodern Turn: New Perspectives in Social Theory*, New York, Cambridge University Press.

RUSSELL, B. (1912/1959) *The Problems of Philosophy*, Oxford, Oxford University Press.

RUSSELL, B. and WHITEHEAD, A. (1910–13/1935) *Principia Mathematica* (2nd edn), Cambridge: Cambridge University Press.

SARUP, M. (1993) *An Introductory Guide to Post-Structuralism and Post-Modernism* (2nd edn), Hemel Hempstead, Harvester Wheatsheaf.

SAUNDERS, P. (1990) *A Nation of Home Owners*, London, Allen and Unwin.

SAUSSURE, F. DE (1916/1959) *Course in General Linguistics* , London, Collins.

SAYER, A. (1992) *Method in Social Science: A Realist Approach* (2nd edn), London, Routledge.

SCHÜTZ, A. (1943) 'The Problem of Rationality in the Social World', *Economica*, Vol. X, May, pp. 130–49.

SCHÜTZ, A. (1944) 'The Stranger: An Essay in Social Psychology', *American Journal of Sociology*, 49, 6, May, pp.499–507.

SCHÜTZ, A. (1945) 'The Homecomer', *American Journal of Sociology*, 50, 4, December, pp.363–76.

SCHÜTZ, A. (1946) 'The Well-Informed Citizen: an Essay on the Social Distribution of Knowledge', *Social Research*, Vol. 13, No. 4, pp.463–78.

SCHÜTZ, A. (1953) 'Common-Sense and Scientific Interpretation of Human Action', *Philosophy and Phenomemological Research*, Vol. XIV, No. 1, pp.1-38, and in SCHÜTZ, A. (1962) *Collected*

Papers I: Studies in Phenomenological Philosophy (edited by Natanson, M.), The Hague, Martinus Nijhoff, pp.3-47.

SCHÜTZ, A. (1932/1967) *The Phenomenology of the Social World*, Evanston, Illinois, North Western University Press.

SHELDON, W.H. (1949) *Varieties of Delinquent Youth*, New York, Harper and Brothers.

SHOWALTER, E. (1987) *The Female Malady*, London, Virago.

SILVERSTONE, R. (1997) *Visions of Suburbia*, London, Routledge.

SKINNER, B.F. (1953) *Science and Human Behaviour*, New York, Free Press.

SKINNER, B.F. (1971) *Beyond Freedom and Dignity*, New York: Knopf.

SMITH, A.M. (1994) *New Right Discourse on Race and Sexuality: Britain 1968–1990*, Cambridge, Cambridge University Press.

SMITH, M.J. (1998) *Ecologism: Towards Ecological Citizenship*, Buckingham, Open University Press.

SMITH, M.J. (1999a) *Rethinking State Theory*, London, Routledge.

SMITH, M.J. (1999b) *Situating Hayek*, London, Routledge.

STEVENS R. (1998) 'Humanistic and experiential social psychology' in Sapsford, R., Still, A., Wetherell, M., Miell, D. and Stevens, R. (eds) *Theory and Social Psychology*, London, Sage/ The Open University.

STRAWSON, P.F. (1952) *Introduction to Logical Theory*, London, Methuen.

SUTHERLAND, S. (1989) 'What if teacher is a cheat?' *The Observer*, 20 August 1989.

TAYLOR, I., WALTON, P. and YOUNG, J. (1973) *The New Criminology: For a Social Theory of Deviance*, London, Routledge.

TAYLOR, S. (1982) *Durkheim and the Study of Suicide*, London, Macmillan.

TOLMAN E.C., RITCHIE, B.F. and KALISH, D. 'Studies in spatial learning II, Place learning versus response learning, *Journal of Experimental Psychology*, Vol. 36, pp.221–9.

TOMAS, A. and DITTMAR, H. (1995) 'The Experience of Homeless Women: An Exploration of Housing Histories and the Meaning of Home', *Housing Studies*, Vol. 10, No. 4, pp.493–515.

TUAN, Y-F. (1974) *Topophilia*, New Jersey, Prentice-Hall.

TURNEY, J. (1989) 'Faking it to make it', *The Times Higher Education Suppplement*, 28.7.89.

VANE, H.R. and THOMPSON, J.L. (1982) *An Introduction to Macroeconomic Policy*, Brighton, Harvester.

VOGEL, E.F. and BELL, N.W. (1968) 'The Emotionally Disturbed Child as the Family Scapegoat' in Bell, N.W. and Vogel, E.F. (eds) *A Modern Introduction to The Family*, New York, Free Press.

WATSON, J.B. (1928) *Behaviourism*, New York, Harpers.

WEEKS, J. (1989) *Sex, Politics and Society: The regulation of sexuality since 1800*, Harlow, Longman.

WETHERELL M. (1998) 'Critical social psychology' in Sapsford, R., Still, A., Wetherell, M., Miell, D. and Stevens, R. (eds) *Theory and Social Psychology*, London, Sage/The Open University.

WILLIAMS, R. (1961) *The Long Revolution*, London, Chatto and Windus.

WILLIAMS, R. (1983) *Keywords: A Vocabulary of Culture and Society* (2nd edn), London, Fontana.

WILLIS, P. (1990) *Common Culture*, Buckingham, Open University Press.

WINCH, P. (1958) *The Idea of a Social Science – and its relation to philosophy*, London, Routledge.

WITTGENSTEIN, L. (1921/1961) *Tractatus Logico-Philosophicus*, London, Routledge.

WITTGENSTEIN, L. (1953/1967) *Philosophical Investigations*, Oxford, Blackwell.

YOUNG, M. and WILLMOTT, P. (1973) *The Symmetrical Family*, Harmondsworth, Penguin.

Acknowledgements

Grateful acknowledgement is made to the following sources for permission to reproduce material in this book:

Figures

Figures 1.2, 2.3, 5.8, 5.9, 5.11, 5.12 and 6.9 (bottom right): Mike Levers/Open University; *Figure 1.3:* Institute of British Geographers; *Figure 1.4:* London Transport Museum; *Figure 2.1:* Camera Press, London; *Figures 2.2 and 2.4:* Ronald Grant Archive; *Figure 2.6:* Mary Evans Picture Library; *Figure 2.7:* Mauritshuis, The Hague; *Figure 2.9:* Detroit Free Press; *Figure 2.10:* Dayton Daily News; *Figure 2.14:* Greenwich Observatory; *Figure 2.15:* National Portrait Gallery; *Figure 2.16:* Roger Viollet; *Figure 2.17:* Giraudon; *Figure 2.18:* Ann Ronan Picture Collection; *Figure 3.3:* Courtesy of Marjorie Nuttall; *Figure 3.4:* Frontispiece to the Atlas of Lombroso's *The Criminal Man*, 1911, Penguin Books Ltd; *Figure 3.5:* Burt, C. 1925, *The Young Delinquent*, 1961 edition, Hodder & Stoughton Educational, used with permission; *Figure 3.7:* Lipsey, R. G. 1979, *An Introduction to Positive Economics*, Fifth Edition, Weidenfeld & Nicolson, by permission of Oxford University Press; *Figure 4.2:* Sacha Lehrfreund/Format; *Figure 4.3:* Popperfoto; *Figure 4.4 a:* Rose, D. 1991, 'Crime: the facts, the figures, the fears', *The Observer Magazine*, 17 February 1991, The Observer; *Figure 4.4 b:* Box, S. 1981, *Deviance, Reality and Society*, Second Edition, Holt, Rinehart and Winston; *Figure 4.4 c:* Coleman, C. and Moynihan, J. 1996, *Understanding Crime Data: Haunted by the dark figure*, Open University Press; *Figure 4.4 d: Criminal Statistics in England and Wales 1993*, Crown copyright is reproduced with the permission of the Controller of Her Majesty's Stationery Office; *Figure 4.5 (left):* Science Museum, Science and Society Picture Library; *Figure 4.5 (right):* Economica 18 1950, © London School of Economics; *Figures 4.10 and 4.11:* Christaller, W. 1966, *Central Places in Southern Germany*, Baskin, C. W. (trans.), © 1966, reprinted by permission of Prentice-Hall, Inc., One Lake Street, Upper Saddle River, NJ 07458; *Figure 4.12:* Davies, W. K. D. and Lewis, C. R. in Carter, H. and Davies, W. K. D. (eds), *Urban Essays: Studies in the geography of Wales*, Longman; *Figures 4.17, 4.18, 4.19 and 4.20:* Tuan, Y-F., 1974, *Topophilia*, Prentice-Hall, Inc., One Lake Street, Upper Saddle River, NJ 07458; *Figure 5.5:* From Hebb, D. O. 1972, *A Textbook of Psychology*, W. B. Saunders, Philedelphia. Reprinted with permission; *Figure 5.10:* Science Photo Library; *Figure 5.13 and 5.14 (top left):* Getty Images; *Figure 5.13 and 5.14 (top right):* London School of Economics; *Figure 5.13 and 5.14 (bottom left):* © Serafino Amato; *Figure 5.13 and 5.14 (bottom right):* MIT Museum; *Figure 6.3:* From *Word Play* by Peter Farb. Copyright © 1973 by Peter Farb. Reprinted by permission of Alfred A. Knopf Inc.; *Figure 6.4:* Reprinted by permission of Sage Publications Ltd from Potter, J. and Wetherell, M. 1987, *Discourse and Social Psychology: Beyond attitudes and behaviour*, © 1987 Jonathan Potter and Margaret Wetherell; *Figure 6.5 (left):* OMO 1951, © Unilever UK; *Figure 6.5 (right):* Persil, © Unilever UK; *Figure 6.7 (left):* Kurt Hutton, Getty Images; *Figure 6.7 (right):* © Gloria Chalmers, Portfolio Gallery, Edinburgh; *Figures 6.8 (top right and bottom right):* © Heather Clarke; *Figure 6.8 (centre):* Lithograph by L. L. Boilly, *Thirty-five Heads of Ill Persons* in Clements Fry Collection, Yale, from *Seeing the Insane* by Sandor Gilman 1982, Brunner/Mazel Inc., New York; *Figure 6.9 (top left):* 'Start the Week', British Broadcasting Corporation; *Figure 6.9 (top right):* Sue Cunningham Photographic; *Figure 6.9 (bottom left):* Brenda Prince/ Format Photographers; *Figure 7.3:* Sheldon, W. H. 1949, *Varieties of Delinquent Youth*, Harper and Brothers Publishers. Reprinted by permission of Addison Wesley Longman; *Figure 7.4:* Bentham's design for a reformed prison: the Panopticon, 1791 Collection, University College, London; *Figure 7.5:* Lawson, T. 1994, 'Transcendental realism: An alternative conception of reality, science and explanation' in Backhouse, R. E. (ed.), *New Directions in Economic Methodology*, Routledge, by permission of Tony Lawson; *Figures 7.6, 7.8, 7.9, 7.10 and 7.11:*

Sayer, A. 1992, *Method in Social Science*, Second Edition, Routledge; *Figure 7.7:* Smith, M.J. 1999, *Rethinking State Theory: New State Theory*, Vol. 1, Routledge; *Figure 7.12:* Bhaskar, R. 1986, *Scientific Realism and Human Emancipation*, Verso.

Readings

Chapter 1

Reading A photograph: Jacky Chapman/Format.

Chapter 2

Reading A: Oatley, K. and Jenkins, J. M. 1996, *Understanding Emotions*, Blackwell Publishers Ltd, *Figure 1:* Professor A. J. Caron, *Figure 2:* Gibson and Walk, 1960; *Reading B Figure 1:* Roger Viollet; *Reading C:* Hollinger, R. 1994, *Postmodernism and the Social Sciences*, pp. 7–9, 21–25, copyright © 1994 by Sage Publications, Inc. Reprinted by permission of Sage Publications, Inc.

Chapter 3

Reading C: Gould, S. J. 1981, *The Mismeasure of Man*, W. W. Norton & Co; *Reading D:* Eysenck, H. 1971, *Race, Intelligence and Education*, Maurice Temple Smith Ltd, courtesy of Dr Sybil Eysenck; *Reading E:* Burt, C. 1925, *The Young Delinquent*, 1961 edition, Hodder & Stoughton Educational, used with permission.

Chapter 4

Reading A: Hanson, N. R. 1969, *Perception and Discovery*, Freeman, Cooper and Company; *Reading B:* Rex, J. and Moore, R. 1979, *Race, Community, and Conflict*, © Institute of Race Relations 1967, Oxford University Press; *Reading E:* Jeffrey, R. 1979, Normal rubbish: Deviant patients in Casualty Departments' in Kelly, D. H. (ed.) *Deviant Behaviour: A text reader in the sociology of deviance*, Blackwell Publishers Ltd.

Chapter 5

Reading A: Reprinted with the permission of The Free Press, a Division of Simon & Schuster from *A Modern Introduction to the Family*, edited by Ezra F. Vogel and Norman W. Bell. Copyright © 1968 by The Free Press; *Reading F:* Turney, J. 1989, 'Faking it to make it', *Times Higher Educational Supplement*, 28 July 1989, © Times Supplements Limited, 1989 (Cartoon by Ken Pyne) and Sutherland, S. 1989, 'What if teacher is a cheat?', *The Observer*, 20 August 1989, by permission of The Guardian; *Reading G:* Boyle, M. 1994, 'Schizophrenia and the art of the soluble', *The Psychologist*, September 1994, The British Psychological Society.

Chapter 6

Reading A: Reprinted by permission of Sage Publications Ltd from Potter, J. and Wetherell, M. 1987, *Discourse and Social Psychology: Beyond attitudes and behaviour*, © 1987 Jonathan Potter and Margaret Wetherell; *Reading C:* Smith, A. M. 1994, *New Right Discourse on Race and Sexuality, Britain 1968–1990*, Cambridge University Press.

Chapter 7

Reading A: Sarup, M. 1993, *An Introductory Guide to Post-Structuralism and Postmodernism*, Harvester Wheatsheaf, Simon & Schuster Group; *Reading B:* Weeks, J. 1981, *Sex, Politics and Society: The regulation of sexuality since 1800*, Longman. Reprinted by permission of Addison Wesley Longman; *Reading C:* Sayer, A. 1992, *Method in Social Science*, Second Edition, Routledge; *Reading D:* Rice, M. 1990, 'Challenging orthodoxies in feminist theory: a black feminist critique' in Gelsthorpe, L. and Morris, A. (eds), *Feminist perspectives in criminology*, Open University Press, by permission of Dr L. Gelsthorpe.

Glossary of key words

The glossary is designed to provide you with some of the tools for identifying how key words are used in different ways by different approaches to knowledge construction. Each glossary item provides a list of the chapters and relevant sections where these key words have been highlighted.

For instance: **2**, 3.1 means that you will find this key word in Chapter 2, section 3.1.

So don't worry about moving back and forth between the chapters and the glossary, or for that matter between the items in the glossary. This is what I expect you to do. Any words placed in *italics* indicate that these words are elsewhere in the glossary.

This is a relational glossary, not a list of dictionary definitions. It is relational in two interconnected ways. First, you can use it to retrace your steps through the book and clarify the ways in which the key words are used in social science. Second, all these key words are matters of dispute and contestation – that is, what they mean depends on the approach in which they are placed. This means you have to try to avoid assuming that the way a particular word is understood stands for all times, in all places and, crucially for us, in all approaches.

agency   **7**, 2.3
The concept of 'agency' is usually taken to refer to any social force which has an effect on the way things are organized – some social scientists see individuals as agents, others are interested in groups, organizations, institutions or, in the Marxist account social classes and their fractions are seen as *social agents*. How we define agency is closely connected to how we see *structures* – if we consider structures as determinant then agency is passive, a carrier of social roles, whereas a *voluntarist* view of agency sees structure as a casual effect of agents working in the world (as in rational choice theories in Chapter 4). Alternatively, we can see structures as simultaneously shaping (enabling and constraining) our actions as well as being the outcome of these actions, choices, purposes, behaviour – that agency reproduces and transforms structures (see Figure 7.12).

analytic   **2**, 3.1; **3**, 4.1; **4**, 2; **6**, 3.2
The concept of analytic is closely connected to *synthetic*. For a logical positivist, analytic statements are self-defining (they are tautologically true and cannot be refuted), such as 'All oranges are fruit' (because being an orange already means that it is a member of the class of fruit), whereas synthetic statements tell us something about the world, such as 'Oranges from Seville have no pips'. Thus a synthetic statement can be empirically tested – in this case, it can be empirically refuted. Any statement which violates the distinction between the analytic and the synthetic is a metaphysical one; for instance, the statement 'All oranges are sweet' rests on the false assumption that what defines an orange is, amongst other things, its sweetness, whereas, in fact, some oranges are sharp.

androcentric   **7**, 3.4
Androcentric statements are those which presume that all that is important can be ascertained from the masculine attitudes, *values* and *practices* of men and the institutional and textual conditions of *discourses* which privilege masculinity over femininity – androcentric social science is to a greater or lesser extent conducted by men, on men and for men. This can mean that social scientific knowledge ignores women's concerns, sees them as synonymous with men's concerns, represents women as passive objects, and/or is openly prejudicial against women. The dominance of the masculine can be seen in the history of many branches of Western knowledge, from art and literature to the natural and social sciences.

anthropocentrism   **7**, 2
Anthropocentric accounts of the social and natural world see natural things as existing solely for human uses (that they have an instrumental *value*). In anthropocentric *discourses* humanity is privileged over the natural, the needs of human beings over the integrity of ecosystems or the intrinsic *value* of other species. This is closely connected to androcentric accounts of the way that culture (in the West associated with masculinity, see *andro-centric*) is privileged over biology (associated with femininity).

anthropomorphism   **4**, 1
Anthropomorphic statements presume that things have social or human attributes or characteristics, but read such things as natural in order to explain social characteristics and behaviour as driven by natural forces or dispositions. We can see this not only in the way that hurricanes are named and

described as possessing human temperaments, but also when inequalities and cultural differences between human beings are understood as the product of essential natural differences between sexes or 'races'. It's not just how we attribute social characteristics to natural things, but how we see the natural in ourselves – we 'anthropomorphize' with a purpose.

articulation   **6**, 4.2
articulatory practices   **7**, 3.4
Unlike the wide range of foundational approaches which apply the logic of *mediation* (which assumes that all things can be traced back or reduced to their underlying causes), the logic of articulation is a way of understanding connections which does not presume any necessary links between the elements which make up social relations. Articulation assumes that such attempts to fix the production of meaning, articulatory practices, are transitory and the elements involved are open to re-articulation in different ways. Many branches of the social sciences which use the logic of mediation have read consumption *practices* as a necessary effect of productive relations (giving production an underlying causal status). Alternatively, social identities have often been given an essentialist foundation in, for illustration, biological differences. Social scientific research can be seen then as made up of articulatory practices which construct *narratives* and stories which are then taken to be authentic and authoritative accounts of social life within specific *discourses*.

atomism   **2**, 3.1; **3**, 7
This involves a particular set of assumptions about the way we should define the objects of analysis in the natural and social sciences, and is associated with *positivist*, *empiricist* and some *idealist* accounts of social relations and processes. An atomistic view of the way things work assumes that we should break down these objects (such as society) into their discrete component parts (such as individuals) in order to understand how these basic elements produce the events we can observe. Atomism emerged as part of the tendency of early scientific representations to view 'nature as a machine' and it came into social science through *naturalism*.

bedrock assumptions   **5**, 2
These are the basic theoretical assumptions which any scientific approach takes for granted. Bedrock assumptions are the taken-for-granted assumptions (the foundations) upon which scientific *practices* are based. They are described in different ways in different philosophies of science; for instance, Lakatos described them as 'hard core assumptions' to distinguish them from the protective belt of 'auxiliary hypotheses' (see Chapter 5, Section 4) which, unlike bedrock assumptions, scientists are

willing to discard when seriously challenged. Bedrock assumptions are often hard to reconstruct although some have been formalized as axiomatic principles, like Newton's laws of motion or Einstein's formula of $e=mc^2$, in physics. The assumptions of 'rationality' in economics or the 'cognitive structure' of the mind in many areas of psychology are good examples in the social sciences. According to Lakatos, these assumptions are subject to methodological rules about what it is NOT possible to study – the negative heuristic. From Foucault's perspective, this is a good illustration of the way *discourses* regulate what can and cannot be said.

behaviourism   **3**, 4.3
Behaviourism starts from the assumption that it is speculative and unscientific to study the intentions and motives of individuals. Behaviourist social scientists focus on the observable behaviour of individuals through an exploration of their actions in response to positive and negative stimuli. This approach to social science emerged from animal psychology in the early twentieth century and was applied throughout psychology until the 1950s. It also extended into political science (such as pluralism in the 1950s, see Chapter 5, section 2.2) and some branches of sociology. In psychology, behaviourism was so important, it had the status of a *paradigm* (Chapter 5, Section 3.2 has an extended discussion). See also *operant conditioning*.

canonical   **2**, 3.1, **6**, 3.2
When writers acquire canonical status in social science they are assumed to be a *reference* point of good practice – their works acquire the status of authoritative knowledge and the substantive claims are assumed to be authentic descriptions of the way the world is. In social science, for a shorter or longer time, the work of Adam Smith, John Maynard Keynes, John B. Watson, Talcott Parsons and Karl Popper, to name a few, have assumed the status of a canon, as a measure of all that is good and/or true in a field of knowledge. The canonization of writers and *texts* is part of the process of establishing *disciplinary* foundations – the key thing to remember is that these writers are rarely questioned and problematized, they are taken on trust. Post-disciplinary thinking seeks to undermine all canonical points of reference (for more on this, see *disciplinary*).

causal law   **3**, 7
See *scientific laws*.

circuit of knowledge   **2**, 3.1; **2**, 3.3
The circuit of knowledge is a device developed in this book to identify the assumptions which organize *knowledge construction* in different times and places. It is based on the logic of *articulation*

and attempts to demonstrate how even the most cherished *bedrock assumptions* about the foundations of knowledge only make sense through their relations with other words – such as the relationship between the scientific method, truth, reason, humanity and *progress*. These circuits map the meaningful associations through which we practise social science and they make sense in definite historical and social locations – as such, they are open to contestation although some may prove to be more resilient than others. The circuit is revisited in Chapter 7, Section 2.4.

closed system(s)   **2**, 1.2, 2.1, 2.2; **3**, 4.3; **4**, 3; **5**, 2.2
Closed-system analysis emerged in scientific thought as a model of good practice through which it was possible to establish authoritative knowledge. Closed systems can be identified in early models of astronomy and in scientific experimentation. To construct a closed system, you should identify a limited number of discrete variables (see *atomism*), exclude influences which you feel will confuse the picture and adapt the conditions of the experiment to establish which variables are causal and which are the effects. Closed-system analysis is associated with identifying *scientific laws* and explanations. In the social sciences, closure is simulated through theoretical, experimental and statistical devices. It has been criticized for ignoring the *complexity* of relations between things and the unpredictability of outcomes beyond the model, as well as for assuming that things have no intrinsic complexity or properties (see *open systems*).

complexity   **4**, 1
Acknowledging complexity can take a number of forms, all of which problematize the *closed-system* model associated with scientific knowledge. Complexity can be identified in the things which social scientists define as simple discrete variables – such as class, income, parental interest and educational attainment – as well as in the way that all sorts of factors or variables can have a role to play in events which social research has attributed to simple causes. In Chapter 7, section 4, you will find an overview of the ways in which the role of the imagination, the historical and social situation, the discursive representations and the internal properties or *structures* of things each add further dimensions to the processes of complexification which closed-system accounts could not think through (this section brings together the threads of the whole book).

complexification   **7**, 4
See *complexity*.

connotation(s)   **6**, 2.2, 3.2
Connotations are usually distinguished from *denotations* (words, sounds or images which work as simple descriptions of the characteristics of a thing). These things also connote meaning through the associations we have about them – see the connotations around the image of an 'oak tree' (page 241). For Barthes, these connotations can carry myths, meanings of the world which help us to make sense of what things do (see the long extracts from Barthes on meat and cleaning products in Chapter 6, section 2.2). One of the difficulties with this distinction is that when we look at simple denotations (like the box of chocolates, page 253) we discover that the way we classify and categorize things also connotes meaning – that all meanings are relational (see Chapter 6, section 3,2).

context of discovery   **1**, 2.2; **5**, 3.1; **7**, 3.1
This is concerned with the situation where the problems which deserve attention and investigation are identified and defined – the grounds for identifying such things are the product of a wide range of factors, such as the emergence of anomalies which don't fit existing knowledge, the recognition of holes in the research literature, and the *values* of the communities and institutions engaging in research. Cultural values are particularly important for thinking through the ways in which objects of analysis are defined – in *androcentric* and ethnocentric accounts of scientific knowledge values are often camouflaged as *facts* (see Chapter 7, section 3, for some of the different ways in which feminist research strategies have responded to this problem).

context of justification   **1**, 2.2; **5**, 3.1; **7**, 3.1
This is concerned with the actual conduct of research, of collecting evidence, testing ideas and hypotheses, and of interpreting, applying and evaluating the evidence. In practice, since research is a lived activity, it is often difficult to distinguish between the *context of discovery* from the context of justification. The way the context of discovery is defined shapes the way that research is conducted, what things are studied and, perhaps most crucially, what is left out of the research.

contextual hypotheses   **5**, 2
Contextual hypotheses are those statements which make substantive claims about how the world actually works and, as such, are open to empirical testing. They are developed by thinking through what *bedrock assumptions* would mean if they are in operation in definite contexts. In social science, if we assume that human beings are perfectly rational (as in rational choice theory) and we place this assumption within the context of an election, we can develop hypotheses about how we would expect people to behave and test this against the evidence by monitoring, for instance, their voting preferences. Lakatos suggested, in his own terminology, that these 'auxiliary hypotheses' form a pro-

tective belt around the 'hard core' (the foundations) of existing knowledge and follow the methodological rule of positive heuristics (that they follow the legitimate pathways which researchers are expected to consider within their field of knowledge or discipline).

conventionalism (-ist)   **5**, 1, 3; **6**, 1, 3, 3.1
Conventionalists assume that all knowledge (including scientific knowledge) is a social product, that it is the outcome of social relations and processes involved in organized communities of scientists. This is a major departure from views of knowledge which saw science in a *canonical* way, as a standard of truth or authoritative knowledge which could be held as *objective* regardless of the differing views and *practices* of scientists at any point in time. On the whole, conventionalists are concerned with people organized in groups for scientific purposes (which distinguishes them from *discourse* analysis considered in Chapter 6). This is as far as conventionalists agree, for they have quite different ways of thinking about 'the social' from which scientific knowledge is produced – for Kuhn, it is organized in *paradigms* whereas for Feyerabend it is disorganized and unsystematic (see *methodological pluralism*) – Chapter 5 takes you through these and other kinds of conventionalism.

deconstruction   **6**, 3.2
This technique in textual reading, drawn from Derrida, involves the identification of the ways in which a *discourse* works by mapping its configuration of oppositions and the construction of subject positions, and then attempting to destabilize the ways in which the oppositions place one side in a privileged position (for example, truth over falsehood). Deconstruction problematizes the essentialist and foundational claims through which the *discourse* attempts to construct its authenticity – in short, it highlights the ways in which some *values* and assumptions are given a privileged place in situated discourses (see *discourse* for some illustrations of oppositions and subject positions).

deduction   **3**, 4.3
This involves a particular form of abstract reasoning which takes us from a set of given premises, an established theoretical starting point, to a logical conclusion – much depends upon the validity of the premises, for instance:

1   Creatures with wings can fly.

2   This pig has wings.

3   This pig can fly.

Deduction is a way of working through logical first principles to generate useful statements about the world (see also *induction*). Clearly, this is not one of them because a valid conclusion has been drawn from an invalid premise, that is, the possession of wings does not automatically mean that something can fly (quite apart from the question of whether pigs can have wings).

demarcation criteria   **3**, 5.2; **5**, 3.1
The demarcation criteria in any account of what makes knowledge scientific are important indicators of the ways in which approaches to *knowledge construction* can generate statements which are seen as *objective*. The problem for those who believe that science offers authoritative knowledge is that different approaches demarcate the scientific from the non-scientific in different ways. For instance, logical positivists draw upon the linguistic distinction between *analytic* and *synthetic* statements to develop their own criterion: scientific statements should not be speculative but offer empirically verifiable accounts of observable things – simple observation statements. In adopting *phenomenalism*, they argued that if we cannot see it, touch it, taste it, hear it or smell it then 'it' does not exist. Alternatively, Popper was not concerned with truth or with the assumption that all useful scientific ideas sprang from observation but with *progress*, so he developed a demarcation criterion which assumed that a statement which could be empirically tested and was open to refutation was scientific and one which could not be tested and was not open to *falsification* not scientific. Where the idea originated – in the bath, in a dream or wherever, was not important; the question should be 'is it testable?' For Kuhn, these demarcation criteria help to pinpoint the development of *paradigms* for they indicate a basis around which organized scientific communities can coalesce and make judgements.

denotation   **6**, 2.2, 3.2
See *connotation*.

determinism (-ist)   **4**, 3.3
Determinist explanations of social behaviour assume that our actions are governed by social forces beyond our control, that we are like cogs in a machine determined by some kind of social hydraulics. You can find determinism in social scientific accounts when they presume that the best place to look for explanations of social behaviour, events, states of affairs, and so on, is in the social relations or *structures* which constrain our choices and decisions (see *voluntarism*).

disciplinary   **7**, 2.2
Disciplines are institutionally and textually defined areas of knowledge (see Figure 6.8) where a clear collective identity has emerged and research is conducted according to a broad set of rules of

conduct on how appropriate knowledge should be expressed – a discipline is in part defined by its style of expression but, crucially, it involves a broad agreement on the form and shape of the object(s) of analysis with which it is concerned. The problem with disciplines is that they can become very restrictive on innovation both in understanding and researching the things they consider to be relevant. Interdisciplinary research tends to focus on different ways of posing social scientific questions by borrowing from similar kinds of approaches in different disciplines. However, disciplines are, on the whole, resistant to such innovative developments and see themselves as the domains for the 'hard work' of rigorous focused inquiry. Post-disciplinary knowledge presents an opportunity for thinking through how the members of different disciplines can develop accounts of social relations and processes which acknowledge their *complexity*.

discourse(s)   7, 2.2
Discourses are systems of representation involving rules of conduct which regulate the production of meaning within the context of definite textual and institutional conditions – they regulate what can and cannot be said and read within historically and socially specific situations. Particular discourses are organized through the formation of imaginary symbolic figures or 'subject positions' (such as 'the criminal') which provide a focus for producing meanings through discursive oppositions such as the following: rational/irrational, same/other, justice/injustice, masculine/feminine, true/false, civilised/primitive, culture/biology, and so on.

dogmatic falsification(ism)   5; 4
See *falsification*.

empirical regularities   3, 1, 2.3; 7, 2.3
Empirical regularities are the constant conjunctions of events which scientists take seriously when formulating *scientific laws* – they consist of two or more variables which occur together (sometimes subject to a time-lag) in roughly similar conditions. Empirical regularities occur between many things and they do not automatically imply a cause/effect relationship. A scientific law involves a general statement which explains such regularities between the observed frequency of different variables and is associated with *closed-system* models of scientific knowledge. While we like to make connections between variables we need to be vigilant about the way we do this, for the history of social science is littered with many silly regularities and crazy correlations which have been taken seriously (for an example, have a glance at Morton's studies of skulls in Chapter 3). In particular, some have been used to legitimate and rationalise social inequalities organized around cultural differences

(as in Eysenck's work in Reading D; also in Chapter 3).

empiricism (-ist)   2, 3.3; **3**, 7; **4**, 2; **7**, 2.3
This approach to *knowledge construction* starts from the assumptions that scientific knowledge and laws should emerge largely or wholly through empirical evidence and that the activities of making theories and conducting observations are separate things. All branches of empiricism are committed towards *phenomenalism* but many (such as the *falsificationists*) do not adopt *nominalism*, for they are willing to accept that theoretical concepts are more than names or descriptive labels. Empiricism clearly distinguishes theory from observation and on the whole separates *facts* from *values* (although falsificationists are more aware of the problems). Nevertheless, all empiricists assume that explanation and predictions are symmetrical (that any explanation worthy of the name 'scientific' must be a consistently accurate predictor). So it takes experience seriously but ignores or underplays the role of the human imagination in organizing our perceptions, impressions and sensations in ways which makes them intelligible (an issue developed in chapter 4 on *idealism* and revisited in Chapter 7, section 2.3).

epistemological   5, 3.3
Epistemology is the study of *knowledge construction* and is distinguished from ontology, the study of reality. It is in the debates on what is an appropriate epistemology that many of the problems over representation start, for we can only think through what is real through the *knowledge systems* or *discourses* we have constructed.

ethnographic   6, 4.1
This involves the careful collection of *qualitative* evidence (that is, detailed evidence on a few people) through involvement in the lives of those studied. The point is to see them in the context in which their lives take place and try to reconstruct their experiences, beliefs, understandings from their own standpoint. This attempt at empathy is always fraught with difficulty, for the social researcher's experiences and conceptual frameworks are inevitably involved in the reconstruction of the events, relations and processes which are the focus of attention. Successful ethnography usually finds a balance between being inside and being outside the group.

ethnomethodological   6, 3
Ethnomethodology – 'people method' – involves the identification of the taken-for-granted common-sense assumptions (in phenomenology this is called 'cookery book' knowledge, see Chapter 4, section 5.2) through which we make sense of the social world. While it draws upon *ethnographic* research methods, it tends to delve deeper than inter-

actionist accounts of social communication (see Chapter 4, section 5.1) – it asks us to think about the rules of conduct and the shared cultural assumptions which enable communication to take place as a relationship of mutual discovery (see *ethogenics*).

ethogenics   6, 3.1

This approach to the investigation and analysis of social interaction emerged within social psychology as a reaction against the experimental method and behaviourist accounts. In particular, it focuses upon the conceptual schemes through which observations, attitudes and identifications are made (in a similar way to *ethnomethodological* research) and how this is co-ordinated in a way which is meaningful for those involved – it focuses on the ways in which belief systems work (beliefs about appropriate behaviour, about roles, about the *objectives* of the interaction) in definite situations; in short, it focuses upon rules of conduct and how they translate the possession of certain resources and skills into performances.

facts, fact/value distinction   3, 3.1, 3.2, 7

Facts and values are often portrayed as clearly separate – which was the goal of logical *positivism*. Usually facts are described as *objective*, in the sense of being defined without bias. The difficulty with this distinction is that social science has witnessed a succession of accounts which have claimed facticity but which have become questionable over time. Part of the problem in distinguishing facts from values is that many things which appear to have a factual basis are often things with which we agree, things we consider to be normal and part of the social landscape. Good examples of value laden approaches masquerading as factual accounts can be seen in studies of the family, gender differences, crime and other *social problems*. Remember that Figure 3.3, which presents a racial classification system, which was once regarded as factual description of the cultural order of the world rather than a product of the value-laden ways of classifying people in an 'Imperial' and ethnocentric culture. There are always ethical questions to raise in social scientific practice even when they are not as obvious to us as this.

falsification(ism)   3, 5, 5.2

Falsification was developed by Karl Popper to deal with what he saw as the inadequacies of *verification* procedures in the construction of scientific knowledge, which tended to search out confirming evidence for existing scientific theories and laws rather than asking more disturbing questions and seeking out refuting evidence. He suggested that verification tended to lead to stagnation in *knowledge systems* and that it was more worth-while to disprove things because that led to more useful questions and more challenging research practices. This did not mean that we should throw theories and evidence away at the first refutation in the manner of dogmatic falsification (for much falsified work has been demonstrated to have uses later on) but that it should be shelved and the search for a better explanation initiated. By setting up scientific theories in ways which made them systematically testable and trying to refute what we take to be true, Popper argued that we are much more likely to make new discoveries, accumulate new knowledge and, as a result, achieve scientific *progress*.

flat ontology   7, 2.3

Ontologies are theories of being or reality – they involve a set of assumptions of what can be taken to really exist (also see *epistemology*). A flat ontology is one which is unable to distinguish between our perceptions, impressions and sensations of things and the way we define events or states of affairs through the human imagination and is associated with the method of *induction*. A flat ontology cannot accommodate the ways in which mental constructs are used to organise the evidence collected through our senses into recognisable patterns. This is a problem within *empiricist* approaches to *knowledge construction* identified by both *idealists* and realists (see Chapter 7, section 2.3).

genealogical   7, 2.2

Genealogical analysis, developed by Michel Foucault, presents an account of historical change which avoids the tendency to construct a *narrative* in terms of a *march of progress*. It also avoids explaining these changes in terms of an underlying set of causes or foundational principles. Through the genealogical method we can explore the ways in which *discourses* change through the many and varied historically and socially specific situations in which they emerge. As a result, rather than celebrating the present as the logical culmination of the past, this offers a careful reconstruction of the ways in which power and knowledge work through definite institutions, *texts* and *practices* – in particular, how these are articulated through the discourses of clinical medicine, psychiatry, criminology and the social sciences.

general law(s)   3, 4.1

See *scientific laws*.

hegemony   6, 4.2

Hegemony has been defined mainly as a relation involving domination through the *articulation* of beliefs and cultural *values* around a common project. However, through the prison writings of Antonio Gramsci, it has acquired a second dimension – all attempts to dominate will be contested and are open to re-articulation within counter projects. It is this double *connotation* of an attempt to shape desires and of the ultimate impossibility of ever achieving such dominance that hegemony has been adopted in cultural analysis to demonstrate how cultures are contested spaces.

historical situatedness   1, 1
See *social situatedness*.

idealism (-ist)   6, 3.1
This approach to *knowledge construction* is united by its common acceptance of the different ways in which mental constructs shape and organize our perceptions, impressions and sensations. This means that, unlike *empiricists*, idealists do not see a clear separation of theory from observation nor of *facts* from *values*. It also raises questions about what it is possible to predict through scientific explanations – that it is only possible to predict patterns, not specific outcomes. However, despite these common assumptions, idealists can be *voluntarist* or *determinist*, *idiographic* or *nomothetic*, phenomenological or rationalist, and so on.

ideal type(s)   4, 3.3
Ideal types, popularized by Max Weber, are a common device used by *idealist* researchers when trying to organize complex empirical evidence – they are simplistic exaggerated categories which serve as a yardstick for comparing and contrasting events. Since these ideal types are mental constructs then they can be conceptualized at different levels of abstraction (see Activity 4.2 for an illustration of this). The selection of ideal types is governed by the concerns of practical problem solving in definite situations (see *value relevance*).

idiographic   4, 3.1, 3.3; 6, 4.1
Idiographic accounts of the social world, developed as part of an attempt to construct the cultural sciences and have been associated with historical analysis. They focus on a definite location such as a society, region, city, neighbourhood at a specific point in time and attempt to provide an informed account of the relations and processes involved – that is, they do not attempt to invest their explanations with the capacity to generalize beyond the events or states of affairs for which they were devised (see *nomothetic* and *idealism*).

incommensurable   5, 3.1
Incommensurability refers to the inappropriateness of making authoritative judgements as to the superiority or inferiority of one theory, *theoretical system*, *paradigm* or *knowledge system* using the *demarcation criterion* of another – in Kuhn's use of the term, it means that the criterion for truth or for *progress* in one paradigm should not be used to judge another. While such claims are frequently made in social science, they are devices for asserting the dominance of one approach over another and in themselves carry no foundational or universal status.

induction   2, 2.1, 3.1; **3**, 4.1, 4.2, 6
The method of induction involves a series of steps in moving from the observation of particular instances of, say, an *empirical regularity* within definite conditions, to making generalizations about the operation of this regularity in other situations with similar conditions – with the goal of establishing a *general law* (that 'if x, then y' in specific conditions). The problems with this method start when we acknowledge that it only works in *closed systems*, but also that it assumes that theories are not simple reflections of the things we see (see *idealism*).

intersubjective, intersubjectivity   **4**, 5.2; **7**, 2.1
This is drawn from the phenomenological view of human communication and interaction. Intersubjective relations exist through the ways in which human actors engage in processes of mutual discovery and, in so doing, their identities are in a process of continual transformation.

intertextuality   **6**, 3.2; **7**, 2.1
This idea developed within post-structuralist accounts of *discourse*, which argue that intertextuality can be seen in two ways: that all forms of representation are a configuration of elements which have been used in different ways before, but also that the reading of the text involves the production of meanings in complex and often unanticipated ways – intertextuality highlights the *complexity* and fluidity of representation (see Figure 6.7).

knowledge construction   3, 4.3
By thinking about knowledge construction rather than knowledge as a given, we are in a position to identify the institutions and textual conditions within which different *knowledge systems* make sense. This also draws our attention to the different ways in which we can think through what it means to construct knowledge and how this can be based on very different assumptions about what the world really is (although some approaches dispute even this and whether the 'real' exists), how we develop knowledge systems and *theoretical systems* through which we can make sense of it (for illustrations of approaches to knowledge construction see *empiricism*, *falsificationism*, *idealism*, *conventionalism* – you will find realism and postmodernism in Chapter 7).

knowledge systems   2, 1; **5**, 2.1
Knowledge systems are complex configurations of assumptions about *knowledge construction* and methodological rules which are plausible in a given historical and social location and serve as a grounding for *theoretical systems* – this book con-

tends that it is possible to conceptualize these knowledge systems through the device of the *circuit of knowledge* (see Figures 2.5, 2.19 and 7.14). Chapter 2 presents a *narrative* of the emergence of the knowledge system which emerged through the *articulation* and integration of the elements associated with the scientific method.

language games   7, 2.1
A language game, drawn from Wittgenstein but developed in Lyotard's conception of the postmodern condition, involves a set of rules of conduct for producing meaning. Such meanings are established through judgements as to what is true/false, just/unjust and efficient/inefficient and so on – different language games can be combined in various ways although science is distinctive in its repeatedly failed attempts to play the denotative game (of truth and falsehood) on its own.

langue   6, 2.1, 3.1
This is drawn from the writings of Saussure (actually, the lecture notes of his students) and refers to the language system which exists as the tacit structure (rules of grammar and syntax as well as the principles through which formal descriptions of a language are translated into the vernacular) which make communication possible. Speech is only possible because the language structure serves as its condition of possibility (see *parole*). The language structure can be understood as possessing a definite shape at any one point of time, but its reproduction is through use (by speakers and writers engaging in talking and writing) therefore the collective engagement in communication ensures that language structures change (in the same way as depicted in Figure 7.12).

march of progress   7, 2.2
See *genealogical*.

mediation   6, 4.2
See *articulation*.

metanarratives   7, 2.1
This term, developed by Lyotard, is used to designate theoretical claims which have the audacity to attempt to explain all of social existence (although many, like Marxism, attempt to explain the whole process of historical change as well). Metanarratives are grand theories with huge ambitions and enormous scope. For Lyotard, they are associated with the Enlightenment, the consolidation of modernity and the belief that human reason could be deployed to understand the human condition in all its *complexity*. In practice, this involved making simplistic claims and assuming that this was how the world worked – in short, they imposed these assumptions and concepts upon the objects of analysis.

metaphysics   2, 3.3; 3, 4.1
For *empiricists* (especially positivists), metaphysical claims are a problem, for they involve treating speculative assertions as if they were 'true' claims about the world (see *analytic/synthetic*).

methodological individualism   4, 3.1, 4.2
This is a version of *atomism* applied to human societies and other collective organizations. Methodological individualism assumes that the individual is the smallest possible component in social existence and that, in order to understand broader social processes, all we have to do is work out the collective consequences of these individual actions. One of the problems with this involves the assumptions made about what makes individuals act – for instance rational choice theory assumes that collective organizations are the sum total of all individuals making 'rational' choices and decisions. In addition, this approach, neglects the possibility that individuals have complex identities (a criticism from *discourse* analysis) or have complex cognitive structures (a criticism from psychology) or that they are engaged in an *intersubjective* process of mutual discovery, that they are constantly changing (a criticism from phenomenology).

methodological pluralism   5, 3.3
This approach to the various options facing social sciences emerged through the writings of Paul Feyerabend. He argued that attempts to impose one universal approach to *knowledge construction* were not only a mistake, but that this also flies in the face of the messy history of scientific knowledge. In the place of universalist accounts, he advocated the *principle of proliferation* – that 'anything goes' – to encourage flexibility and innovation in the development of scientific knowledge.

mimetic   3, 4.1
This approach towards meaning is a shallow one which allows for no *complexity* in representation (see Chapter 6 for a critique). Mimetic accounts assume that words are a mirror-like, transparent reflection of the things to which they refer – that words only work in a denotative fashion. This simplistic account of language fits all too neatly with the logical positivist vision of what *synthetic* statements should do (see *nominalism*). The relationship between reference and representation is, however, deeply contested (see *reference*).

naive methodological falsification(ism)   5, 4
See *sophisticated methodological falsification*.

narrative   2, 3.1
Narratives are sequences in the production of meaning which, on the whole, conform to what we expect in story-telling. Part of their plausibility is established through our expectations of what is

coming next in story-telling. Some approaches to narratives suggest that they are structured in familiar ways and that they make sense through operationalizing definite oppositions (which can take place in some well established and standardized genres, such as Westerns). However, this book views narratives as being more open to change and re-articulation in unexpected ways. Part of the pleasure of social science is the way in which, despite all of its attempts to build foundations and assert universal truth claims, it seems to be in a state of transformation – that story-telling in the social sciences is very inventive and increasingly so since the *canonical* status of some *references* has been acknowledged and questioned.

naturalism   **2**, 1.2; **3**, 7; **5**, 1, 4; **7**, 2.3
Naturalism is any approach to *knowledge construction* which assumes that the methods and assumptions of the natural sciences can and should be applied to the objects of analysis in the social sciences. The problem is that there are different assumptions about what natural science involves (see the differences between logical *positivism* and *falsification* in Chapter 3, but also compare these to the realist view of natural and social science in Chapter 7). Most forms of naturalism draw upon the *closed-system* model but realism adopts the view that natural and social objects of analysis exist in *open systems*.

nominalism   **3**, 7
This assumption about experience shares with *phenomenalism* the emphasis on the importance of perceptions, impressions and sensations as the basis for making concepts but goes further to see words as mirror-like reflections of the things they describe – that concepts have no other use except as names, that they are purely descriptive or denotative labels (see *mimetic*).

nomothetic   **4** 3.1, 3.3, 4; **6**, 4.1
Nomothetic approaches to the social world attempt to develop abstract theories so that the events and states of affairs which occur in one specific time and place can be compared and contrasted with events and states of affairs elsewhere – the point is to provide *general laws* which explain similar processes in different places (see *ideal types* and *idiographic*).

normal science   **5**, 3.1
This was developed by Kuhn in order to describe the long periods of stability between the scientific revolutions. Despite Kuhn's focus on normal science, it has been revolutions which have received all the attention when the idea of *paradigm* is borrowed and transformed in the social sciences. Normal science refers to the sustained periods of 'puzzle solving' in which many anomalies are worked through and made intelligible within the

paradigmatic framework. It is only when the framework of *knowledge construction* and the demarcation criterion appropriate to the paradigm is problematized that the relatively short crisis phase ensues and normal science breaks down. Feyerabend is very critical of this term as a description of what scientists have done or even how they actually do things today – he argues that science has been much less systematic and more disorganized, and that discoveries owe more to accident than design (see *conventionalism*).

objectification   **3**, 3, 3.1; **7**, 2.2
The process of objectification highlights one of the many difficulties in privileging what we believe to be true and universal with the label of *objective* knowledge – *objectification* can be seen in the ways in which the identities of people are fixed by *reference* to some ascribed characteristic. In the process, the *complexity* of identities evaporates as they become the personification of discursively constituted subject positions (usually these are derogatory accounts of subjects as pathological). The other side of this process is the way in which this normalizes those who are not so pathologized – it reinstates a principle of sameness for those who are 'not like that' – this is the trouble with normal. It is interesting to note the kinds of subject positions which are pathologized in this way: 'the homosexual', 'the black mugger', 'the emotional female employee'; never, or hardly ever, is it 'the racist', 'the sexist', 'the heterosexual male' – the processes of normalization deserve attention too.

objective   **1**, 3.1; **2**, 2.2, 3.1; **3**, 1
When we say that knowledge is objective we are making authoritative claims about its standing. Actually, objectivity is an essentially contested concept in the philosophies of science and the social sciences; it is usually invoked to convey a sense of truthfulness and to offer a cloak of legitimacy for a particular story – it is a mark of authoritative knowledge. At its simplest, objectivity refers to a lack of bias or prejudice, that is independent of human valuation. In this most common *empiricist* use of the term (including feminist empiricism in Chapter 7), it presumes that *facts* and *values* can be or should be separate from each other. Whether you interpret 'objective' as an accurate adjective for knowledge or not depends on whether you are affiliated with empiricism or with one of its many critics. More generally, objectivity has been associated with claims to universality, detachment, whether something exists and in these circumstances is construed as related to opposed versions of subjectivity – in short we should also recognize that objectivity/subjectivity is a discursive opposition which makes sense through the way it is articulated with other oppositions (like true/false) within situated *discourses*.

objective knowledge   **1**, 1; **4**, 1
See *objective* and *objectification*.

open system(s)   **2**, 2.2
While these are conventionally defined as the
absence of closure, this ignores the way that *closed
systems* are artificial human constructs (even
cosmological systems are less structured and
smoothly functioning than many early astronomers
had assumed). In open systems objects have complex internal *structures* and properties but also
that they exist in complex multiple relations with
other things with their own internal *complexity*.
This means that objects can display different properties depending on the presence or absence of
other things which make up the conditions. Until
recently it was assumed that the main argument
against *naturalism* was that closure could only be
seen as feasible in natural science and not in the
social sciences. However, realists claim than open
systems are a defining feature of both the natural
and social sciences. *Empiricists* stick with closure,
idealists recognize external but not internal complexity, while realists endorse both internal and external complexity.

operant conditioning   **5**, 3.2
This is a key concept in behaviourist descriptions
of the processes involved in behaviour modification. It involves the application of various
changes in the conditions which stimulate actors
into a response (negative and positive, reinforcing
and punishing) in order to achieve a change in
the way that people behave. So the animals or people involved associate behaviour which has been
categorized as inappropriate with aversive consequences and modify their behaviour accordingly
(a worrying application of this can be seen in the
aversion 'therapy' treatment of homosexuality).
Behaviourists seem to be completely oblivious to
the pathologizing tendencies of their work.

organic analogy   **5**, 2.2
The organic analogy is a rhetorical device in social
scientific story-telling – for a long time it provided a
convincing *narrative* that society worked in many
respects like the human body with various social
institutions resembling the different body parts
and organs (for example, with the state as the metaphoric stand in for the head of the social body). As a
narrative, it reinforced conservative views of the
symbiotic character of the social order and warned
against tinkering with the mysterious operation of
an evolving society (instead, radical views often
drew upon 'machinic' analogies through which society could be rebuilt). Today cybernetic research is
full of computer-based versions of these analogies.

paradigm(s)   **5**, 3
See *Paradigm 1*.

Paradigm 1   **5**, 3.2
Kuhn's account of scientific paradigms has quite
strict preconditions for the use of this word –
in Paradigm 1, there is a single dominant *disciplinary* matrix or framework within which *normal
science* is conducted. Such paradigms are *incommensurable* because they involve radically different assumptions about what makes knowledge
scientific and, therefore, useful. In this definition,
unlike *Paradigm 2* or *Paradigm 3*, the lack of a
dominant *disciplinary* matrix means that knowledge is in a prescientific or *pre-paradigmatic
stage* and, as such, does not operate by Kuhn's sequence of periods of stability and periods of transformation.

Paradigm 2   **5**, 3.2
This is a half-way house definition between
Paradigm 1 and *Paradigm 3*, which ignores
Kuhn's own prescription that a paradigm had to
be dominant although also views scientific communities in the same way as Kuhn. In this use
paradigms exist side by side but hold very different
assumptions about what the world is like and how
we know it. Nevertheless, like Paradigm 1, these
competing paradigms are still seen as *incommensurable*. Confusions arise and the explanatory
value of the concept is undermined when social
scientists conflate this definition of paradigm
with the looser use associated with Paradigm 3.

Paradigm 3   **5**, 3.2
This is the 'loosest use' of *paradigm*, where it seems
to be used for a model of the world, a school of
thought, a *disciplinary* perspective – as such it became a vague descriptive term for disagreements
within a discipline or field of knowledge with little
if any explanatory *value*.

parole   **6**, 2.1, 3.1
Parole (speech) involves the production of meaning
through the activity of speaking (see *langue*).

personal troubles   **7**, 2.1
See *social problems*.

phenomenalism   **3**, 6, 7
The assumption that useful knowledge can only be
identified through experience instead of through
metaphysical claims (which are portrayed by *empiricists* as scientific wishful thinking). However,
empiricists disagree about whether these ideas/hy-
potheses have a role independent of experience.
For Popper, theories have uses, but if they have
not emerged from experience they can only be
taken seriously when they have been submitted to
empirical tests and have been corroborated (see
positivism).

physicalism   **3**, 4.1
In some areas of positivist thinking there are
attempts to find an absolute foundation for all
sciences – by reducing human activities to psycho-

logical processes, down to biological functions, down to chemical combinations and finally down to the atomic *structure* of the universe – such that, ultimately, it would be possible to develop a basic universal language for describing all things. Carnap was especially fond of this idea, that there was one set of physical things to study – but as with all foundationalisms it was succeeded by others.

positivism   **2**, 3.1
Positivist approaches are united in their attempt to eradicate *metaphysics* and other hangovers from *rationalism* from scientific knowledge. In particular, they are strongly attached to grounding all our knowledge of things in perceptions, impressions and sensations as evidence of their tangible and observable existence (see *phenomenalism*). Many early versions simply translated their *values* into *facts* and it was this failure to separate theories from observation and facts from values that led logical positivists to develop their rigorous account of the need to separate *analytic* from *synthetic* statements and try to eradicate all speculation not derived from empirical evidence through the method of *induction*.

practices   **6**, 4
This refers to human activities which are conducted through the use of our capacities; they are situated historically and socially, and signify or produce meaning through the way they operationalize discursive constructs. Practices are a lived activity, yet they cannot be understood except through the *discourses* through which they are represented and which, in turn, they work upon and transform in the process.

pragmatism   **4**, 5.1
This approach is often mistakenly associated with the idea of 'muddling through', but it actually expresses a concern that any explanation or understanding of the social world should start with the features of a definite situation rather than from basic theoretical principles. This means that it starts within existing conditions – along the lines of the meaning of 'praxis' – although it also draws from Kant's account of practical knowledge. In pragmatism, human activities are a meshing together of unreflective and tacit habitual knowledge and creative energy directed towards goals, although these goals are solutions demanded by the problems evident in a given situation. This philosophy of situated action was influential on interactionist approaches and some areas of phenomenology (Alfred Schütz drew upon it in his later writings on 'the stranger' and 'the homecomer', 1945).

pre-paradigmatic (stage)   **5**, 3.1
Kuhn refers to any situation in which there is an absence of a single dominating *disciplinary* matrix

(see *Paradigm 1*) as a pre-paradigmatic stage in which knowledge does not deserve the name science. By this, *Paradigm 2* and *Paradigm 3* are not paradigms at all – and the social sciences are not scientific.

principle of proliferation   **5**, 3.3
See *methodological pluralism*.

probability model   **3**, 4.2
When *closed systems* appear to be very unrealistic options in social science, closure can be simulated through statistical models which organize evidence in ways which comes close to identifying an *empirical regularity*. This is a very common practice when dealing with complex evidence. In such models, it is possible to treat probability as the proportion of actual cases displaying an attribute or as a proportion of possible cases.

progress   **3**, 2.2
This component in the scientific *circuit of knowledge* usually conveys a forward movement or an accumulation of things and can be simply divided into forms of material progress and progress in knowledge. The *empiricist* approach to *knowledge construction* places a special emphasis on the accumulation of knowledge as a series of steps to the truth – in Popper's case, it is rather like moving up a never-ending staircase (for *falsificationists*, there is no end because we will never know if we have reached the truth – perhaps we missed it on the last landing?).

qualitative   **3**, 5.2
Qualitative evidence can be collected through a variety of research methods ranging from in-depth interviews to direct and participant observation as well as drawing upon textual evidence which contains extended and detailed evidence of the lives of the people being studied (for example, diaries, letters, emails, photographs and other personal documents). This kind of research strategy generates an informed and well illustrated account of the lived experiences of a defined group of people and the relevant contexts in which they produce meanings (also see *ethnographic*). However, it is difficult to compare and measure qualitative evidence; by contrast, quantitative research strategies involve the collection of evidence which is standardized, measurable and comparable. But, since this means that only a limited response comes from each respondent, it lacks the depth of qualitative evidence.

rationalism   **2**, 3.3; **4**, 2
This is an ambiguous umbrella label which, beyond the common emphasis placed upon human reason in providing a source for human knowledge, can mean many things – largely because this depends upon what rationalism is contrasted against. In social and political theory it is the opposite of tra-

dition, in theology it is the opposite of faith, in ethics (morality) it is the opposite of moral sentiments or feelings – in *knowledge construction* it is often seen as opposed to experience (with the strongest contrasts being between rationalism and *empiricism*). For positivists, rationalism was the source of metaphysical speculation and it undermined the healthy sense of doubt which *empiricism* was supposed to engender – many failed positivists were attacked for their rationalist leanings. But this fear of *metaphysics* gets in the way of recognizing the important role played by the rationalist tradition in scientific knowledge, either in Descartes' approach or Kant's synthesis of empiricist and rationalist concerns – even Popper has accepted the label of 'critical rationalist' for his brand of empiricism. As with all oppositions, they need careful thought.

readerly   6, 3.2
See *writerly*.

reference   7, 2.1
The idea of 'reference' is a contested concept in the social sciences because of the problems associated with the *subject–object problem*. In *mimetic* accounts of social science, where it is assumed that scientific statements are mirror-like reflections of things, then the objects referred to are seen in a very tangible way. Most accounts of social science recognize that words are attempts to portray the characteristics of things but that they will never be able to reflect it in all its *complexity* (both *idealists* and realists adopt this position). *Discourse* analysis, especially post-structuralist approaches to *knowledge construction*, presents a more serious challenge – the words 'reality', 'reference' and 'structure' can also be seen as rhetorical devices to bolster or shore up the status of truth claims in a particular account of the social world.

relativism   5, 3.3
When we use the label of relativism we should be careful about the different ways in which it is used – in Harré and Krausz's (1996) terms it has variety. Semantic relativism involves the way that the meanings of words are specific to languages and cannot be translated without a loss of meaning. Ontological relativism deals with the way that the existence of some things (such as God, sorcery, individuality) which are tied to conceptual systems (that they are real for some people but not for others). *Epistemological* relativism suggests that approaches to *knowledge construction* are best understood by locating them in the condition of their emergence, where they are plausible. Moral relativism suggests that the moral worth or ethical standing of things is tied to definite times and places. Aesthetic relativism suggests that beauty or aesthetic worth is tied to situated locations in the same way. Relativism is also invoked as a ne-

gation of all claims that one view of what is true, good, beautiful, or of what exists, can hold for all times and places. It counters all claims to universalism, all attempts to suggest that such claims are *objective*, that is beyond human judgement, and all attempts to establish foundations for these things. Nevertheless, many of the claims relativists make are also universal in scope.

reliable knowledge   4, 3.2
This kind of knowledge is the product of repeated empirical tests; it has survived repeated attempts at refutation – borne the tests of time and can be trusted. This does not mean that it is true, although some social scientists take it as such, it simply means that it has not been disproven, that it is corroborated (also see *valid knowledge*).

rhetoric   6, 3.1
The concern with rhetoric in social science is a product of the recognition that social science involves the construction of *narratives* and stories and that these only work if they are persuasive. Rhetorical analysis involves the study of the forms of expression and the use of devices such as analogy and metaphor in communication within the social sciences, in the production of meaning. In addition, we should recognize that all such devices can be read in different ways (see *intertextuality*). By focusing on the persuasiveness of social scientific story-telling for its varied audiences we have an opportunity to explore the complex relationships between writers and readers and the variety of ways in which meanings are produced in different situations. This undermines the idea that social science can be be engaged in the transmission of the 'truth'. In this book we have concentrated on rhetorical devices in social scientific *knowledge construction*, but it is also important to highlight the way that *discourse* analysis explores all forms of human communication as rhetoric.

scientific laws   1, 2.2; 3, 7
The development of scientific laws is seen as the ultimate goal of scientific practice – however, as with everything else there is considerable disagreement about what constitutes a scientific law. This is a consequence of different views on the process of causality. For an *empiricist*, the most you can ever know about the directly observable relationship between two variables is that an *empirical regularity* exists. As a result, the existence of a constant conjunction of events is enough in itself to justify the claim of a *causal law* (see Figure 3.1). However, *idealists* argue that, while we should use empirical regularities to construct laws, they are not sufficient in themselves; they also have to be intelligible (to make sense) in the existing theoretical knowledge through which we organize our experiences. Then there is the realist argument that causal laws can be made without empirical regularities

(see Chapter 7). Finally, scientific laws can be seen as discursive constructs, they are claims about the world which carry a high truth value and as such often remain largely unquestioned. What makes a causal or scientific law is a contested business – it depends on your approach to *knowledge construction*.

scientism   4, 4.2
Scientism involves an account which, before it has considered its object of analysis, claims to know what is the most appropriate way of investigating it. As a result, it does not take adequate account of the *complexity* of social phenomena within *open systems* in a way which could explain the unintended consequences or the unacknowledged conditions of their existence. Three main problems with scientism were identified by Hayek (1952). First, the belief that by analysing ideas we learn about the attributes of reality (sometimes described as conceptual realism). Second, the tendency of human actors to interpret external events after their own images. Third, the attribution of a designing mind to the objects in question i.e. an example of *anthropomorphism* (Smith, 1999b).

social agents   2, 1
See *agency*.

social problems   7, 2.1
Social problems are those aspects of social existence which occupy a place in the public domain and which are taken seriously by the state – they are seen as a problem for which society is responsible; that is, they warrant a social policy to ameliorate or resolve them. However, the boundary between the public and the private domain is a moving one, so that what is seen as a social problem in one particular time and place can become a personal trouble at another time and place. Good examples include poverty, unemployment, homelessness which were viewed as social problems in the 1950s and 1960s, but which were depoliticized in the 1980s, they became personal difficulties for which individuals were responsible instead of society. In other areas, such as 'child abuse', we have witnessed a politicization of the issues translating what were often seen as personal troubles into a major social problem. This highlights the ways in which the discursive *articulation* of social problems and personal troubles with the opposition of public/private can transform the way in which the meanings of such experiences are understood. The distinction of public and private through which we separate the concerns of civil society from those of the state is a deeply contested opposition which has been repeatedly challenged. For instance, feminist accounts argue that it rests on the assumption that the public domain is political (that it involves power relations) and the private is not. For many advocates of feminist analysis, the personal (the private) is political (see feminist standpoint approaches in Chapter 7, Section 3.2).

social situatedness   1, 1
When we think about how an example of social scientific practice is socially and historically situated, we are focusing on the way it makes sense in a definite culture with its own set of institutional and textual conditions. When identifying how knowledge is situated a number of dimensions are relevant:

- identification of the normative assumptions within social scientific *practices*;

- exploration of the *narratives*, stories and metaphors within a body of *texts* which make up the established points of *reference* (points that are taken as authoritative);

- placing social scientific *practices* in a definite cultural location;

- consider the institutional and textual conditions within which these social scientific *practices* are plausible (Smith, 1999a and 1999b).

social structures   2, 1
See *structure*.

sophisticated methodological falsification(ism) 5, 4
This approach is associated with Imre Lakatos, who critized Popper's account of *falsification* for focusing too much on the refutation of individual theories. For Lakatos, falsification should only take place within the context of a research programme. He drew some of his insights from Kuhn's account of paradigms but, like Popper, he felt that knowledge should deliver progress. As a result, Lakatos defined research programmes as made up of *bedrock assumptions* (which remained unquestioned most of the time) and contextual hypotheses where attempts at falsification were largely concentrated. He playfully labelled Popper's approach 'naive methodological falsificationism' (see Chapter 5, section 4) for not taking adequate account of what organized groups of scientists actually did.

structure(s)   7, 2.3
Structures refer to the conditions in which social agencies exist. They are organized in such a way that they enable certain things to happen but at the same time this places constraints on what can be done (rather like knee joints enable us to walk and run but, along with other constraints within the body structure, they make backwards movement difficult). Social structures involve necessary internal relations, that is, they are made up of components which are mutually defining, like the examples of landlord and tenant (see Figure 1 by Andrew Sayer, in Chapter 7, Reading C) and parent and child within the family. If we explore the latter example a little further we can see how this struc-

ture both enables and constrains parents and children. Children in Western societies are, on the whole, dependent upon their parents. On the one hand, they have the opportunity to have a prolonged education in which their potential (their capacities) can be developed and enhanced. On the other hand, they have definite constraints (many of which are legally defined and regulated by state authorities) on their freedom to, say, stay out late at night or to be economically independent through paid work. Both the enablements and the constraints follow from their position as the child (and they can differ when taking into account the gender of the child). Similarly, this structured relationship enables the parents to find fulfilment in various ways but it also places definite constraints on their capacity to do other things (like going out as often as they would like). These constraints can be formally prescribed, such as the legal responsibilities a parent has for their child, or they can operate informally, such as through the prevailing cultural expectations of how parents should act. These structures are reproduced or transformed through the practices of parents and children as well as other relevant social organizations (such as the state and the media). Institutions are configurations of structures which have become such a fixed part of the social landscape, they have acquired a solidity in time and space, that very fixed sets of norms and expectations are attached to them (remember that institutions are constituted within *discourses*). In the early to mid twentieth century, the roles of parents were more clearly defined and regulated; for example, parents were often instructed by health visitors to follow the Truby-King method of child-rearing (based upon the experiences of sheep farming), such as 'feeding by the clock', strict discipline and stringent limits on physical contact with children. Today the structured relations of families, between marital partners and their children, are much more open to variation and innovation. As Groucho Marx once warned, 'marriage is a great institution, but who wants to live in an institution?' (see *agency*).

subject–object problem 1, 2.2
This is a problem because it indicates the different ways in which social scientists have studied people. The subject–object problem focuses our attention on the relationship between the researcher and the things studied. It also highlights the way in which there are crucial differences between social science and natural science. Unlike geologists studying rocks, social researchers are actually part of the object of analysis which they attempt to explain and understand. In addition, social scientists are studying people through language systems which are themselves part of the object of analysis – raising interesting issues about the ways in which social research represents the social

world (see Figures 7.8–7.11 in Chapter 7). This raises questions about how we define the process of research – do we assume that our objects are separate from ourselves (a common feature of detached social science) or do we acknowledge that we are part of the very things we study? Not surprisingly, this means that social scientists often conflate the meanings of subject and object – we call our objects of analysis our subject matter and we often point to processes of objectification as responsible for the construction of subject positions – a recipe for genuine confusion.

subjectivity 4, 5
See *objective*.

synthetic 2, 3.3; **3**, 4.1; **4**, 2; **6**, 1, 3.2
Synthetic statements are descriptive statements about the empirically observable world which, according to logical positivists, are a *mimetic* or simple reflection of the things as they really are (see *analytic* and *synthetic a priori statement*).

synthetic a priori statement 4, 2
Idealists argue, drawing upon Kant, that in practice it is impossible to avoid entering any situation to make fresh descriptive statements without drawing upon prior mental constructs which we already hold in order to make the empirical evidence intelligible. Moreover, they claim that our approaches to *knowledge construction* should recognize this (a criticism of the *empiricist* distinction between theory and observation)

texts 6, 4
The idea of text or textual is usually too closely associated with the written text as a *reference* point for establishing true meanings. The use of text in this book challenges this in two ways. First, 'texts' include talking, writing, statistics (numbers are textual too), posters, television images, photographs, paintings, cultural artefacts, cartoons, museum displays, computer software and games, films, e-mails, web sites and so on – any representation through which meanings can be produced. Second, texts are seen as complex terrains or zones for the *articulation* and contestation of meanings; they are interrelated and involve interactions between readers and writers.

textual reductionism 6, 5
This is a criticism of some forms of *discourse* analysis which make a strong claim that 'reality' or the 'material world' do not exist except as discursive constructs. This critique suggests that such approaches only offer a partial or one sided account of the various dimensions of human existence and is often associated with the realist critique of poststructuralism. Also bear in mind that realists tend to neglect the *complexity* of representation. Nevertheless, there are some approaches which are sympathetic to discourse analysis which also

highlight this problem – such as the account of culture as a contested space developed in Chapter 6, section 4.2

theoretical systems   **5**, 2.1
Theoretical systems involve a body of *scientific laws* and associated *contextual hypotheses* formulated around a particular problem – such as the study of sub-atomic particles or the problems of persistent teenage offenders. As such, they exist through the *practices* of the communities of scientists oriented towards such problems and they emerge through the systems of representation, the *discourses*, through which scientists formalize their aims and objectives. The Lakatosian example of a research programme provides an example of a theoretical system (see Reading G in Chapter 5 for an illustration of a research programme on schizophrenia). Theoretical systems can coalesce, disintegrate, overlap but they exist within *knowledge systems*.

type(s)   **7**, 4
Types are stereotypical figures which we construct in our imagination in everyday life in order to make the behaviour of those around us intelligible and to some extent predictable. In *discourse* analysis, these types would be described as subject-positions but the idea of a type emerges from particular branches of *idealist* approaches to *knowledge construction*. Phenomenological, *ethnomethodological* and some postmodern social scientists have used types to establish stronger connections between social scientific knowledge and the lived experiences of everyday life. The types highlighted in this book are 'the stranger', 'the homecomer', 'the pilgrim' and 'the nomad'. This analysis of types raises questions about the tendencies of social scientists to use *ideal types* to impose their views upon their objects of analysis.

valid knowledge   **4**, 3.2
This refers to knowledge which has been authenticated in some way – that it is true to life or presents an accurate account of the lives of the people studied – that the researcher has found ways to empathize with the situated experiences of these people. It is often associated with *ethnographic* research strategies and the collection of *qualitative* data. Also see *reliable knowledge*.

values   **3**, 7
See *fact/value distinction*.

value relevance   **4**, 3.2
This is a compromise between the belief that social research is value free and being value laden or normative. It means that social researchers should engage in studies of the social world which are relevant to solving the problems of the social situation in which they are placed, and recognizes that these problems are connected to the cultural values of this context (also see *facts* and *idealism*).

verification (-ist)   **3**, 4.1, 5.2
The verification of a hypothesis, and occasionally a *scientific law*, involves subjecting it to an empirical test in order to justify its existence and, as a result, tends to produce confirming evidence that you can always find the evidence you want if you look hard enough (hence the use of the label confirmationism). Verificationism also equates the conditions of the meaningfulness of a statement with the conditions within which it can be empirically demonstrated. This approach to testing theories and hypotheses has been criticized for, in practice, it involves seeking those conditions where an established *empirical regularity* is likely to be seen again – in short, verificationism often resulted in confirming things we already knew. Popper proposed *falsification*, the active search for refuting evidence, as a more promising way of producing new evidence and the accumulation of knowledge. However, *idealists* argue that it cannot take adequate account of the role of mental constructs in organizing perceptions.

voluntarism (-ist)   **4**, 3.3
Voluntarism can be seen in social scientific accounts which presume that the best place to look for explanations of social behaviour, events, states of affairs, and so on, is in the motives and intentions through which we make our decisions – that is, it is assumed that our actions produce the social order. To understand how society works, all we have to do is imagine it as the aggregate total of all our individual activities. Also see *determinism*.

writerly   **6**, 3.2
Whereas *readerly* texts are assumed to be involved in the transmission of knowledge, that they attempt make the reader passive and reactive – they act as a *canonical* point of *reference* – writerly *texts* recognize that the relationship between readers and writers is a complex one. By engaging with a writerly text we engage in the production of meaning and find ways of adapting the *narrative* themes in unanticipated ways within definite situations. In practice, few texts have ever managed to pull off their readerly strategies without the systematic support of institutions, rules of conduct and a series of established textual references which direct the reader into a privileged way of reading – so that they embrace the text as authoritative knowledge. However, the success of some scientific accounts suggests that in the philosophy of science and of social science, at times, they came pretty close.

Index

abnormal/normal categorizations, and positivism 85–6, 92, 97, 104
Adams, John Couch 186–7
Age of Reason 56–7
agency, and structure 305, 306
agnosticism 65
alternative health therapies 13
analytic statements 98–9, 255
    on crime 136
    and empiricism 133, 138
analytic truths 60
anatomy, social science as a form of 35
androcentrism, and feminist epistemologies 311–17, 318, 319
animal behaviour, and anthropomorphism 132
anthropocentrism 282
anthropology 264–5
anthropomorphism 132
Aron, Raymond 104
articulation, and culture 267, 268
articulatory practices 320
associative relations in language 237
astronomical physics, as a closed system 41
astronomy
    and positivism 80, 119
    theory and empirical evidence in 186–7
atomism 49, 50
    and empiricism 118
    and logical positivism 98
    and positivism 76, 78, 83
audiences, and social scientific knowledge 310, 322
Austin, John 247–8, 249
authenticity, and scientific knowledge 28–31
authority relations, as ideal types 147
authors
    canonical 263
    and poststructuralist discourse 253–4, 259, 260
Ayer, A.J. 77, 98

Bacon, Francis 48–9, 52, 53, 54, 55, 64, 187
    and the Enlightenment 58, 59, 60, 72

Bakhtin Circle 267–8
Bandura experiments (children's 'copycat' behaviour) 42–3, 45
Barker, Eileen, 'The professional stranger' 108–9, 126
Barnes, Barry 208
Barthes, Roland 234, 240–5, 252, 253–4, 297
Bartholomew, Michael *et al*, 'The *Encyclopédie*' 60–1, 69–71
Baudrillard, Jean 287
Bauman, Zygmunt 210, 286–7, 308
bedrock assumptions 185, 215
    and falsification escape clauses 188, 190, 191, 192
    n the natural sciences 186, 187
    and paradigm shifts 195
    and progress in scientific research 215–16
behaviourism 103, 198–201, 204, 215
    and discursive psychology 249
    and semiology 245
Bell, Norman W. *see* Vogel, Ezra F. and Bell, Norman W.
Bellah, Robert 165–6
Bentham, Jeremy 82–3, 291
    'Of the principle of utility' 82–3, 120–1
Bhaskar, Roy 303, 305–6, 319–20
biology *see* evolutionary biology
black feminism 317, 318
black women, and crime 317, 329–30
Blaikie, Norman, *Approaches to Social Inquiry* 77
Blaug, Mark 115–16
Bloor, David 208
body *see* mind and body
boundaries, contested 270, 276
Boyle, Mary, 'The schizophrenia research programme' 216, 227–8
Boyle, Robert 53
Brahe, Tycho 139
Burt, Cyril, *The Young Delinquent* 94–6, 124–5, 263, 284, 285, 291, 295

Caldwell, Bruce 115
    'Methodological pluralism' 207, 224

Cambridge University model (on economic performance) 43
canonical status of authors 47, 254, 263
'career' patterns, and social interaction 163
Carnap, Rudolf 77, 98, 117
carnival, and popular culture 268
cartographer, perspective of the 16, 17, 18, 131
categorical claims, and Marxism 109
causal explanations
    and behaviourism 201
    and interpretative understandings 140–54
    and positive economics 115
causal laws
    in closed systems 44, 45
    and empirical regularities 103, 116–17, 298, 300
    empiricists, idealists and realists on 300–1
    and idealism 173
causal relationships
    closed systems 33
    in Durkheim 84–5, 150
    Hume on 62
    and ideal types 148–9
    and idealism 173
    and scientific knowledge 29, 30
causality, defining 322
central place theory 151–4
ceteris paribus rule 155
challenges in the social sciences 3, 4, 5–11
    change 5–6, 11
    methods 6–8, 11
    rethinking 280–1
    terminology 8–9
change, challenge of 5–6
'chicken', game of 156
children
    Bandura experiments on 'copycat' behaviour 42–3, 45
    emotionally disturbed 192, 219–20
    experimental closure in child development 44, 66–8
choice of research techniques 8
Christaller, Walther 152
Cicourel, Aaron 165
cinema, and juvenile delinquency 124–5
circuit of knowledge 308–10

alternative 309–10, 311
breaking the circuit 206
and Comte's positivism 80
and the Enlightenment 59, 61
integrated 65
scientific 32–3, 49, 53, 56, 59, 265, 280, 308–9
theological 56, 61, 280, 308–9
civic culture 270
civilization, and culture 265
class
and the embourgeoisement thesis 110
language, discourse and culture of 233–4
closed systems 33, 40, 41
and the *ceteris paribus* rule 155
compared with open systems 45
and complexity 321
and empiricism 117
experimental closure 42–3, 44, 66–8, 113, 130
and idealism 130
in the natural sciences 41–2, 46
and naturalism 297
and postmodern feminism 320
and psychology 144
in the social sciences 42–5, 46, 140
and standard positivism 103
statistical closure 43–4, 130
theoretical closure 42, 43, 113, 130
cognitive psychology 200–1
Collins, Harry 208–9
colonialism
and Comte's positivism 81–2
and scientific knowledge 58
and scientific racism 88
and utilitarianism 83
communication
and culture 260, 267–8
and discourse psychology 247–8
communications revolution 5, 6, 282
'community', metaphors associated with 250–1, 272–3
competence, in language systems 249
competition, theory of perfect 113
complexification 321
complexity
acknowledging 280, 281, 320–1
different types of 321

in Durkheim 150
and idealism 130
and postmodern feminism 318
understanding 140–54
Comte, Auguste 77, 78–82, 98, 149
'The positive philosophy and scientific laws' 80, 119–20
Condorcet, Marquis de 63
connotations, in semiology 241, 242, 244, 253
'consensus politics', and standard positivism 104
consequentialism 82
context of discovery 8, 196, 314
context of justification 8, 196, 314
contextual hypotheses 185, 215
and falsification escape clauses 191, 193
in the natural sciences 187, 188
and the schizophrenia research programme 216
contraception, and feminist epistemologies 317
conventionalism 183–4, 204–13, 232, 297
and discourse analysis 246, 249
and Kuhn's theory of scientific change 196
and paradigm 193–204
Conway, Jean, 'The homeless' 9, 10, 14, 232, 285, 286
Copernicus, Nicolas 54
covering law model 114
criminality
behaviourist psychology in treatment of 200
causes of 86
construction of the criminal subject 291, 292
and ethnicity 317, 329–30
and functionalist theory 191
and gender 312, 313, 317, 318, 329–30
interpretation of statistics 136–7, 140
and value relevance 145
see also juvenile delinquency
criminology, positivist studies of 75, 85, 86, 92–6, 97, 124–5
critical inquiry
and the Enlightenment 62–3, 65, 78, 308
Kant and 133
and Popper 111

critical realism 279
critical social psychology 201, 221–2
critics, as custodians of culture 263
cultural differences, and postmodernism 320
cultural geography 169–70, 268–70, 275–6
cultural identity
and boundaries 269–70, 275–6
transformation of 282
cultural representation
and language 233, 234, 240–5, 246
and Marxism 268
artefacts 243
cultural studies 259–60
and language 81
same/other distinction in 256
cultural turn 231, 232
cultural values
and language 240
and language games 288
and neo-Kantianism 141
and positivist criminology 96
and rational choice theory 160
and scientific knowledge 30, 85
and scientific racism 86
and social research 17, 132, 144, 145, 151, 286
and social scientific knowledge 234
and the subjectÄobject relationship 302
culture 231, 232, 233, 260–71
civic culture 270
as a contested space 232, 233, 266–70
custodians of 263
and discourse 260–1
high culture 262, 267
and language 260, 261, 271
popular 264, 266, 267, 268
possible meanings of the word 262–4
as a way of life 232, 233, 264–6
cybernetic systems, social systems compared with 36

Dahl, Robert 45–6, 188–90
Darwin, Charles 82
The Origin of Species 34, 35
deconstruction 256
deduction 117
and standard positivism 102, 105
deep complexity 321

demarcation criteria
  between science and
  nonscience 107, 110, 111–12,
  194, 195, 255
  and language 240, 247
  and Paradigm 1 198, 199
denotation, in semiology 241,
244, 253
denotative language game 284,
285, 288, 307
Derrida, Jacques 253, 254, 255–
6, 265, 297
Descartes, René 48, 49, 50–1,
52, 53, 54, 55–6, 64, 164
  and the Enlightenment 58, 60,
  72
detachment
  and the construction of the
  subject 294
  and social scientific research
  4, 15, 20, 27, 166
determinism
  and neo-Kantianism 149, 171
  regularity, intelligibility and
  ubiquity 300–1
diachronic analysis 235
diachrony, in language 81
dialogue, and the Bakhtin
Circle 267–8
Diderot, Denis, *Encyclopédie*
60–1, 69–71
difference, in poststructuralist
discourse 256–7
Dilthey, Wilhelm 161–2
disciplinary knowledge 311
disciplinary processes 291–4
disciplines of social science
  Durkheim on 83–4
  metaphors in 251–2
  and paradigms 197
  and social conditions 204
discourse 231, 232, 233, 322
  and culture 260–1, 271
  and language 246–60, 271
  see also poststructuralist discourse
discovery, context of 8, 196, 314
discursive psychology 232,
233, 246
Dittmar, Helga *see* Tomas,
Annabel and Dittmar, Helga
dogmatic falsificationism 214
Donzelot, Jacques 296
DuhemÄQuine thesis 185–7,
215, 216
Durkheim, Emile 77, 78, 83–5,
263

Rules of Sociological Method
83–4, 149–50
Suicide 84–5, 150, 299
dynamics, in Comte's positivism 80–1, 119–20

Eco, Umberto 309
ecofeminism 318
econometric models, theoretical closure in 43
Economic and Social Research
Council (formerly Social
Science Research Council) 20
economic transformation, and
the emergence of scientific
knowledge 57, 58
economics
  and the *ceteris paribus* rule 155
  and Comte's positivism 81
  and culture 270
  and general laws 144
  and ideal types 146
  and neoKantianism 142–3
  paradigms in 202–4, 222–3
  positivist and empiricist
  approaches to 75, 112–16
  and utilitarianism 82, 83
education
  gendered assumptions in the
  organization of 312
  and schooling 206
  social research on educational
  performance 104–5
Einstein, Albert 107, 194
Elster, Jon, 'When rationality
fails' 158, 178
embourgeoisement thesis 110
emotional development, experimental closure in 44, 66–8
empirical regularities 76, 116–
17, 298, 300
  in Durkheim's *Suicide* 84
  and logical positivism 101
  and standard positivism 103
empiricism 59–60, 62, 64
  and causal laws 300, 301
  and central place theory 152–4
  and the *ceteris paribus* rule 155
  common foundations of 116–18
  and conventionalism 183, 184
  and the denotative game 284
  and Durkheim 149, 150
  and falsificationism 108, 109,
  112
  feminist 280, 311, 313–14, 319
  and ideal types 146, 150, 151,
  164

and idealism 129–30, 131,
132, 171, 172, 173
and Kant 133–8
and knowledge construction
319
and Kuhn's theory of scientific change 196
and Lakatos 216
and logical positivism 98, 99
and neoKantianism 143
and Popper's induction
method 106, 107
and positivism 75, 117–18
and realism 279, 297–301,
303, 304–5, 307
and scientific knowledge 193
and social research 65
Enlightenment 20, 47
  Continental European or
  French 60, 64
  and culture 265
  and empiricism 59–60, 62, 64
  and the 'founding fathers' of
  science 48
  historical context of the 55–8
  and modernity 307
  Nietzsche's critique of the 71
  and the *philosophes* 59, 60–1,
  69–71
  and Popper's falsificationism
  105
  and positivism 75, 78, 79
  and progress 58–64, 71
  and rationalism 62, 64
  and scientific knowledge 59,
  60–1, 63, 64, 69, 71
  Scottish 60, 62, 63, 64
  spirit of critical inquiry 60,
  62–3, 65, 78, 133, 308
  and transformative processes
  56–8, 63, 78
environmental change 5, 6, 282
epistemological questions 207
epistemology 279
  and reality 308
ethnicity
  and the concept of race 87
  and crime 317, 329–30
  and positivist criminology 92
  social research on intelligence
  and 90–1, 121–4
  see also race
ethnocentric mapping 169–71
ethnocentricity, in social scientific research 14, 317
ethnographic 266
ethnomethodology 165–6, 167
  and culture 266

and discursive psychology 246, 247, 248, 249
ethogenics 249
eugenics movement 35, 83, 87, 90
Eurocentrism, and Comte's positivism 82
everyday life
    complexity of 6
    connecting the social sciences to 4, 15–20, 27
    and culture 264–6
    culture as a representation of 262
    and experimental closure 44
evolutionary biology
    and progress 36–8
    social sciences compared with 34–5
experiential social psychology 201, 221
experimental closure 42–3, 45, 113, 130
    in childhood development 44, 66–8
experimental method in science 33, 38–40, 41
    and behaviourist psychology 245
    as a closed system 42, 46
    'founding fathers' of the 47–55
    and positive economics 112–13
    and realism 297–8
experimental social psychology 201, 220–1
experts, authority of 290
explanation
    and idealism 130, 131
    and prediction 155
Eysenck, Hans, 'The Intelligence of American negroes' 90–1, 123–4, 294

fact/value distinction 64, 65
    and idealism 129–30, 131, 173
    and neoKantianism 131, 141, 172
    and positive economics 113
    and positivism 76
    and positivist criminology 96
    and postpositivist empiricism 118
    and scientific racism 87, 91
    in social science 144–5
falsificationism 75, 105, 108–11, 112, 129
    and the denotative game 284
    as a discourse 255

dogmatic 214
and empiricism 118
escape clauses 184, 185–93
and Lakatos 197
and the 'march of progress thesis' 110–11
naive methodological 215
and positive economics 115–16
and positivism 75, 105, 112, 118
rationality and relativism 217, 218
and realism 297
sophisticated methodological 215
and verificationism 116–17
families
    policing of 296
    structured relationships 303
    studies of 7–8, 110, 192, 219–20
femininity, scientific objectification of 54
feminist empiricism 280, 311, 313–14, 319
feminist epistemologies 279, 311–20
feminist interpretations of science 132
feminist postmodernism 280, 311, 316–18, 319, 320
feminist standpoint approaches 280, 311, 314–16, 317–18
Ferguson, Adam 63
Feyerabend, Paul 204–6, 207, 208, 214, 215, 217, 218, 253, 289
fictitious knowledge, and Comte's positivism 79, 119
flat ontology 298, 299
Flax, Jane 315
Foucault, Michel 297
    Discipline and Punish 291–4
    and discourse 253, 254, 255, 259, 271, 273, 288, 295
    genealogical method 279, 290–6, 318, 320
    Madness and Civilization 288–9
    and postmodernism 287–8
    on power and knowledge 289, 295–6
    The Birth of the Clinic 289
freedom, and standard positivism 104
French Revolution, and the Age of Reason 56–7

Friedman, Milton, 'The Methodology of Positive Economics' 114–15
functionalist sociology 204, 215
    falsification escape clauses in 190–2, 193
    and reification 305
functioning systems, social relations as 35–6

Galileo 54, 55, 72
game theory 156–8, 160
    see also language games
garden cities 167–9
Garfinkel, Harold 165, 243
Gassendi, Pierre 48, 49–50, 52, 55
'gay gene', and science as authentic knowledge 29–30
Gellner, Ernest 207
gender
    and contested places 275–6
    and the emergence of science 54
    and feminist epistemologies 279, 311–20
    and scientific practice 279
    and scientific progress 37–8
    see also women
gender studies 256–7
genealogical approach to knowledge 279, 280, 290–6
    and postmodern feminism 320
general laws 106
    and economics 144, 155
    and idealism 173
    and logical positivism 99–100, 101, 105
    and the nomothetic scientific method 141–2
    and rational choice theory 131, 155
    and standard positivism 102, 103
Geographical Models 1 130, 151–4, 167
Geographical Models 2 131, 151, 167–71
gesalt shift, and paradigms 194, 196, 198
Giddens, Anthony 305
globalization 5, 6, 282
    and Comte's positivism 81
Gobineau, Count, *The Inequality of Human Races* 88

Goldthorpe, J. et al., *The Affluent Worker* 110
Goodhart's Law 115
Gould, Stephen Jay, on Morton's *Crania Americana* 88, 90, 91, 121–2, 294
Gramsci, Antonio 268

Hacking, Ian 117, 196
Halbwachs, Maurice 150
Hall, Stuart 267, 268, 271
    'Representation and discourse' 255, 273–4
Hanson, Norwood 138–9, 174–5
happiness, utilitarianism and human happiness 82–3
Hardin, Garrett, *The Tragedy of the Commons* 158, 177
Harding, Sandra 314
Harré, Rom 218, 249
Hayek, Friedrich 159–60
Hegel, G.W.F. 315
hegemony, and culture 267, 268
Heidegger, Martin 255–6
Hempel, Carl 77, 102–3, 104, 105, 114
hermeneutic circle 161
hermeneutics 131, 161–2, 166, 172
historical situatedness 4
Hollinger, Robert, 'What is the Enlightenment?' 63, 71–2
'homecomer', perspective of the 322
homosexuality
    construction of 295, 324–6
    political discourses of 257–8, 274–5, 295
    and science as authentic knowledge 29–30
housing
    examples of research on homelessness and 9–11, 19–20, 21–4, 285–6
    and race relations in Birmingham 150–1, 175–6
Howard, Ebenezer 167–9
human consciousness, social science and 53, 280
humanistic social psychology 201, 221
humanity, and science 32, 33
Hume, David 59, 62, 64, 133
    and Popper's social scientific method 105, 106

Enquiry Concerning Human Understanding 62
Husserl, Edmund 164
hypheticodeductive model, and falsificationism 107–11

ideal types 130, 146–51, 164, 172
    in central place theory 151–4
idealism 129–32, 183
    and causal laws 300, 301
    and empiricism 129–30, 131, 132, 171, 172, 173, 299
    and hermeneutics 131
    meaning and subjectivity 161–6
    and phenomenology 131
    rational choice theory 131, 155–60, 167, 171, 172, 173, 177–8, 255
    and realism 279, 297, 301
    see also neoKantianism
idealists, and discourse analysis 249
identity, and boundaries 269–70, 275–6
ideology
    discipline of 78
    and science 307
idiographic scientific method 141, 142, 143, 150, 151, 171, 172, 173
    and culture 265
    in geography 169
    and rational choice theory 160
Illich, Ivan 206
imaginative complexity 321
imaginative interpretation of experience
    and idealism 129, 130, 132, 297
    and language 232, 245
incommensurable, paradigms as 195
induction method 38, 52
    and logical positivism 99–100, 101–2, 105
    and Popper 106–7, 111–12
    and positive economics 112
inequality, and positivism 82, 83
inflation, and the money supply 115
intellectual transformation, and the emergence of scientific knowledge 56–7, 58
intelligence, scientific racism and 90–1, 121–4

intelligibility determinism 300, 301
interactionism 162–3, 166
interpretation 130, 131, 132
    of crime statistics 136–7, 140
    in Durkheim 150
    meaning and subjectivity 161–6
    in the natural sciences 139–40, 185–8
    and observation 138–9, 149, 174–5, 183
interpretive repertoire 249–50
intersubjectivity 164, 287
intertextuality 257, 259
    and youth cultures 287
IQ tests, scientific racism and 90–1, 123–4

James, William 162, 206
Jeffery, Roger, 'Normal rubbish: deviant patients in casualty departments' 166, 179–80, 248
Jenkins, Jennifer M. *see* Oatley, Keith and Jenkins, Jennifer M.
justice, individual and social 286
justification, context of 8, 196, 314
juvenile delinquency 94, 124–5, 165, 263, 284, 285
    classification of 291, 292

Kant, Immanuel 58, 59, 62–3, 64, 72, 130, 133–6, 137, 280
    Critique of Pure Reason 62
Kanter, Rosabeth 314
Kepler, Johannes 139
Keynesian economics 202–4, 222–3
knowledge
    authoritative 310
    classification of in the *Encyclopédie* 61, 70, 71
    and Comte's positivism 79
    construction of subjects through 290–6
    'cookerybook' or 'recipe' knowledge 164, 243
    and culture 263
    disciplinary 311
    and falsificationism 105, 108
    Foucault on power and 289, 295–6
    genealogical approach to 279, 280, 290–6
    limitations of human 63

and poststructuralism 252–3, 260
and reality 279, 322
reliable and valid 145
sociology of 208–13
specialization of 52, 59
tacit 165–6, 179–80
and values 322
see also circuit of knowledge; scientific knowledge

knowledge construction
and empiricism 319
and Feyerabend 207
and postmodernism 281–2, 283–8, 307–8, 309, 320
and realism 319
and standard positivism 102–3

knowledge systems
and the emergence of scientific knowledge 50, 52
and the Enlightenment 63
in the natural sciences 187, 188
science and 27–8, 33
Knox, John, *The Races of Men* 88
Krausz, Michael 218
Kuhn, Thomas 184, 193–7, 198, 202, 204, 208, 214, 217, 218
and Feyerabend 205
and the subjectÄobject relationship 302

Laing, R.D. *The Divided Self* 8, 15
Lakatos, Imre 184, 192, 197, 214–16, 217, 218
language 231, 232, 233
and Comte's positivism 81
and cultural representation 233, 234, 240–5, 246
and cultural values 30
and culture 260, 261, 271
and discourse 246–60, 261, 271
and logical positivism 98–9
and reality 240, 308
relational character of 279
and representing science 33–4
and structure 233, 234–40
and the subjectÄobject relationship 302
Wittgenstein on 138

language games 284–6, 288, 307, 323–4

langue 235, 239, 247
late modernity 308
Lavoisier, Antoine, discovery of oxygen (mercury calx experiment) 38–9, 40

laws of social dynamics, in Comte's positivism 80–1, 119–20
laws of social statics, in Comte's positivism 80–1, 119–20
Lawson, Tony 116
Leavis, F.R. 263, 266
lesbianism, political 317
Leverrier, Urbain 186–7
linguistics 234–40
Lipsey, Richard, on positive economics 112–13, 114
Liverpool University model (on economic performance) 43
Locke, John 62
Essay Concerning Human Understanding 59–60
logical positivism 60, 77, 97–102, 105, 129, 133, 138
demarcation criteria 107, 194
and discourse 255
and Popper 105, 106, 107, 118
practical implications of 101–2
and scientific statements 247
and social science 144
and standard positivism 103
and synthetic statements 98–9, 232, 255
logical problem, with induction 106
Lombroso, Cesare, on criminality 92–4
London School of Economics (LSE) 111
looking glass self 163
Lyotard, JeanFrançois 279, 297, 308
The Postmodern Condition 283–5

McCloskey, Donald 251, 256
McGhee, Patrick, 'Experimental social psychology 201, 220–1
madness, Foucault on scientific knowledge and 288–9
Malebranche, Nicolas 51
mapping, ethnocentric 169–71
Marxism 215, 283
and culture 267–8
and economics 203, 223
as a 'pseudoscience' 109–10
and realism 306, 307

masculine/feminine, and cultural identity 256–7, 270, 295
master–slave relationship, and feminist standpoint 315
Mead, George Herbert, *Mind, Self and Society* 162–3
meaning, and subjectivity 161–6
meateating, cultural representation of 242, 245
mediation, and culture 268
medical knowledge, and the development of social science 86
Menger, Carl 146
Problems of Economics and Sociology 142–3
mental constructs
and central place theory 154
experience and 134–40
and hermeneutics 161–2
and ideal types 148–9
and idealism 297
and realism 298–9
Merton, Robert 191
metanarratives, and postmodernism 283, 286, 288
metaphors
of 'community' 250–1, 272–3
of computer systems and cybernetics 285
of economics 251
of homosexuality 258, 274–5
of postmodernism 287
and scientific knowledge 34–41, 85
as a type of trope 250, 252
metaphysical knowledge, and Comte's positivism 79, 119
metaphysics 59, 62
and logical positivism 97, 98, 105, 118
and phenomenalism 76
of presence 256
meteorology 304
methodological individualism 143, 160
methodological instrumentalist approach, to positive economics 114–15
methodological pluralism 204, 207, 224, 253
Methodology of Scientific Research Programmes (MSRP) 216
methods, challenge of 6–8
metonymy 250
microeconomics 143

military conquest, and Comte's positivism 81
Mill, John Stuart 112
Millman, Marcia 313–14
mimetic 98
mind and body
 Cartesian approach to 50, 51, 54
 and Chinese and Western medicine 13
minimaxers
 and game theory 156, 157
 and rational choice theory 159
Mises, Ludwig von 155–6
modernity 282
 and knowledge construction 307–9
 late 308
 as a philosophical concept 72
 transformative processes and the Enlightenment 56–8, 63
monetarist economics 202–4, 222–3
money supply, and inflation 115
Montessori, Maria, *Pegagogical Anthropology* 92
Moore, Robert *see* Rex, John and Moore, Robert
Morris, Desmond 132
Morton, Samuel George 285, 294, 313
 Crania Americana 88, 90, 91, 121–2, 257
Mulkay, Michael, 'Two sociological perspectives on science' 210, 225
myths, constructed through culture 240–5, 246

naive methodological falsificationism 215
narrative, of scientific development 47
natural sciences
 assumptions and methods of 6, 7, 11, 33, 183, 322
 and closure 42, 46, 173
 and realism 297
 bedrock assumptions in 185
 and causal explanations 140
 and Comte's positivism 79, 80
 emergence of scientific thought 47–55
 experimental method 38–40, 41
 idiographic and nomothetic approaches to 139–40, 144
 and linguistics 234

metaphors of 34–5
observation and interpretation in 139–40, 185–8
and open systems 304
and positive economics 112–13
preparadigmatic stage 194
understanding of 184
see also scientific knowledge
naturalism 33, 183, 214
 and positivism 76
 and postpositivist empiricism 118
 and realism 297, 301, 303–4
negative heuristic, in scientific research 215
neoKantianism 130, 131, 141–4, 151, 167, 171, 172, 173
 as a discourse 255
 and Durkheim 149–50
 and ideal types 147
neoMarxism 215–16
neomedievalism 309
new religious movements, studies of 108, 109, 126, 166
Newton, Sir Isaac
 and the Enlightenment 59, 69
 laws of motion and gravity 186
 and paradigms in physics 194
 prism experiments 38, 39, 40
 and progress in scientific knowledge 53
Nietzsche, F. 71, 290
nominalism
 and empiricism 118
 and positivism 76, 82, 83, 106
nomothetic scientific method 141–2, 143, 150, 151, 171, 172, 173
 and culture 265
 in geography 169
 and rational choice theory 155–6, 160
normal science 193–7
normal/abnormal, human beings categorized as 85–6, 92, 97, 295

Oakley, Ann, *The Sociology of Housework* 110
Oatley, Keith and Jenkins, Jennifer M., 'The development of emotions' 44, 66–8
objectification 86, 97
 and criminology 92
 and scientific racism 91

of subjects in knowledge 291, 294
objective characteristics, in social science 14, 20, 53, 75
objective knowledge
 closure and 42
 creation of 75
 and criminology 96
 and the fact–value distinction 129–30
 and feminist epistemologies 316, 318
 and logical positivism 98
 and neo-Kantianism 141
 and positivism 85
 scientific knowledge as 5, 14
objective world
 and phenomenology 164
 and tacit knowledge 165
observation
 and empiricism 133–5
 and idealism 129, 131, 172, 173
 and interpretation 138–9, 149, 174–5, 183
 in the natural sciences 139–40, 185–8
 and perception 135–9, 174–5
 and prior concepts 140
 in social research 65, 132
onomatopoeia 238
ontology 279
 and levels of reality 298–300
open systems 40, 45, 46
 and idealism 130, 173
 and natural sciences 304
 and realism 303–4
operant conditioning 103, 199–200
organic analogy 190–1
organic analogy of society 35
otherness
 and cultural identity 265
 in poststructuralist discourse 256–7, 258, 274
Outhwaite, William 77

palaeontology 304
Panopticon 291, 292
Paradigm 1 198–9, 202, 204
Paradigm 2 198, 201, 204
Paradigm 3 201, 203, 204
paradigms
 Kuhn's concept of 193, 194–7
 in the social sciences 198–204
 and the subjectÄobject relationship 302

parole 235, 239, 247

Parsons, Talcott 190–1, 192, 305

patriarchy, and feminist epistemologies 316–17, 317–18

perception, and observation 135–9, 140, 174–5

performance, in language systems 249

person on the street, perspective of the 16, 17, 131

personal experiences *see* subjective experiences

personal troubles 286

phenomenalism
and empiricism 118, 129
and positive economics 112
and positivism 76

phenomenology 131, 161, 164, 166, 167, 172, 173
and culture 243, 266

philosophes 59, 60–1, 69–71

physicalism 98

physiology
and criminality 92, 93
and scientific racism 87–8

places, and identities 269–70, 275–6

pluralism, and postmodernism 320

pluralist political science 204
falsification escape clauses in 188–90, 193
and the positive heuristic 215

police, and community 250–1, 272–3

political discourse, and homosexuality 257–8, 268, 274–5

political lesbianism 317

political objectives, in social research 9, 15

political science
falsification escape clauses in 188–90
limitations of closed systems in 45–6
and the positive heuristic 215
and public choice theory 157–8
statistical closure in 43–4
Thatcherism as an ideal type 147
and utilitarianism 82

political transformation, and the emergence of scientific knowledge 57, 58

Popper, Karl 75, 105, 106–8, 109–10, 111–12, 155
and conventionalism 197, 205
and empiricism 117, 118, 314, 319
and falsificationism 75, 105, 108–11, 112, 115, 117, 129
Lakatos on 214–15
violating 185
and induction 106–7, 111–12
'The 'Philosopher, the Scientist and the Anthropologist' 210
and rationality 217, 218
and truth 193, 256

popular culture 264, 266, 267, 268

Porter, Roy 58

positive economics 112–16, 155

positive heuristic, in scientific research 215

positivism 53, 64, 231
Comte and 77, 78–82, 98
and conventionalism 183, 205
and criminology 75, 85, 86, 92–6, 97, 124–5
defining 77
and discourse 253–4, 255
Durkheim and 83–5
and empiricism 75, 117–18
and the Enlightenment 75, 78, 79
and falsificationism 75, 105, 112, 118
and language 240
and neoKantianism 149
and postpositivism 117, 118, 256
and psychology 143–4
and realism 297, 303
and scientific racism 75, 82, 85, 86–91, 121–4
six general assumptions of 75, 76, 77, 78, 97, 117, 118, 279
and utilitarianism 82–3, 85, 120–1
see also logical positivism; standard positivism

positivist approach to crime 145

postdisciplinary social science 311

postpositivism 117, 118, 256

poststructuralist discourse 232, 233, 246, 247, 252–60
and culture 268, 269–70
and representation 320

postmodernism 280, 281, 283–8
feminist 280, 311, 316–18, 319, 320
and knowledge construction 281–2, 283–8, 307–8, 309
and language games 284–6, 323–4
and social scientific practice 285–8

Potter, Jonathan and Wetherell, Margaret
discursive psychology of 246, 247, 248–9
'The uses of community' 250–1, 272–3

power and knowledge
feminist approaches to 313
Foucault on 289, 295–6

practical complexity 321

practice, social science as a 4, 12–15

pragmatism, and interactionism 162–3

praxeology 155–6, 160, 171

pre-paradigmatic stage 194, 197

prediction
and explanation 155
and idealism 130, 131
and positive economics 114–15
see also standard positivism

Priestley, Joseph 39

principle of proliferation 205

prisoners' dilemma 156–7, 158

prisons, and the **genealogical** approach to knowledge 291–3

probability model, and logical positivism 101

professionalization, process of 59

progress
and the Age of Reason 56–7
and discourse 259
and the emergence of scientific knowledge 47, 52–3
and the Enlightenment 58–64, 69, 71
and falsificationism 105, 109
and Kuhn's account of scientific change 197
'march of progress thesis' 110–11, 295
and neoKantianism 142
and Popper 107, 218
and positivism 78, 119, 256
in poststructuralist discourse 252

questioning 206
and science 20, 32, 33, 36–8, 78
in scientific research 215–16, 217, 227–8
'pseudosciences' 109–10
psychological problem, with induction 106
psychological social psychology 201–2
psychology
cognitive 200–1
and Comte's positivism 81
discursive 232, 233, 246
Durkheim on 84
experimental closure in 42–3, 44, 45, 66–8
idiographic and nomothetic approaches to 142, 143–4
interactionist approach in 162–3
paradigms in 198–201
study of abnormal cases 85–6
and utilitarianism 82
see also **behaviourism**; social psychology
public choice theory 157–8
public/private spheres, and women 54

qualitative data, in social research 110, 166

race
changing concept of 92
and feminist epistemologies 317
and housing in Birmingham 150–1, 175–6
utilitarianism and racial categorization 83
see also ethnicity; scientific racism
radical feminism 315
rational choice theory 131, 155–60, 167, 171, 172, 173, 177–8, 255
rationalism 62, 64
and Durkheim 149
and empiricism 133
rationality, and relativism 183, 207, 214–18
readerly texts 253–4
readers, of social science texts 253–4, 259
realism 280, 297–307
and causal laws 300, 301

and empiricism 279, 297–301, 303, 304–5, 307
and knowledge construction 319
and language 240, 308
realist economics 116
reality
and gender 314–16, 319
and knowledge 279, 322
reinventing 297–307
and representation 287
reason
Age of 56–7
in Descartes' method 50–1, 52
and discourse 259
and empiricism 65
and the Enlightenment 59, 60, 61, 62–3, 71, 265
and the positivist social sciences 53
in poststructuralist discourse 252
questioning 206
and rationalism 133
and science 20, 32, 33, 49, 55
reference
as knowledge 287
in language 238, 239–40
refutation
accumulation of knowledge through 108, 109
of bedrock assumptions 187
escaping refutation in the social sciences 184, 188–93
regularity determinism 300, 301
reification, and realism 305
relativism, and rationality 183, 207, 214–18
reliable knowledge 145
religion
and Comte's positivism 79
and the emergence of scientific thought 47, 48, 49–50, 51–2, 54–5
and the Enlightenment 58, 60, 69
and scientific knowledge 28
studies of new religious movements 108, 109, 126, 166
and the theological circuit of knowledge 55–6, 61
religious transformation, and the emergence of scientific knowledge 56–7, 58
representation 232
and cultural contestation 269

and discourse 249, 254–5, 260, 273–4
and gender 316–18
language and cultural representation 233
postmodernism and knowledge construction 320
and reality 287
see also cultural representation
representational complexity 321
research approach, in the social sciences 212–13
Rex, John and Moore, Robert, 'Race relations in the city' 150–1, 175–6
rhetoric 251
Rice, Marcia, 'Challenging orthodoxies: gender, ethnicity and social science' 317, 329–40
Rickert, Heinrich 141, 144
Rorty, Richard 296, 308
Rousseau, JeanJacques 64
The Social Contract 63
Russell, Bertrand 98

same/other, and cultural identity 256–7, 270
Sarup, Madan, 'Postmodern language games' 284–5, 323–4
Saunders, Peter, 'Owning and renting houses' 9, 10, 11, 14, 21, 285, 286
Saussure, Ferdinand de 234–40, 252
Course in General Linguistics 81
Sayer, Andrew, 'Abstractions, structures and mechanisms' 304, 326–8
scepticism
and Popper 111
and the Scottish Enlightenment 62, 64
schizophrenia research programme 216, 227–8
Schütz, Alfred 4, 16–17, 19, 131, 164, 166, 243, 286–7, 322
science
as a contested concept 321–2
as a contested space 308
'founding fathers' of 47–55
and gender 311–20
and ideology 307
and knowledge systems 27–8, 33

and modernity 46–64, 307–8
practice of 208–13, 225–7
representing 33–46
see also experimental method in science; natural sciences
scientific knowledge
authenticity of 28–31, 33, 34
and civilization 58
closure in 42
and Comte's positivism 79–80, 119
and conventionalism 183–4
emergence of modern 46–7
and the Enlightenment 59, 60–1, 63, 64, 69, 71
Kuhn's account of change in 193–7
and logical positivism 97–100
and madness 288–9
metaphors of 34–41, 85
as objective knowledge 5, 27
and positivism 105
and postmodernism 283–8, 323–4
progress in 36, 47
questioning 204–7
rationality and relativism in 183, 207, 214–18
research and 3
as situated 4, 12–14
and social conditions 204
and social science 65
and technological change 283
and traditional ways of thinking 28
see also circuit of knowledge; natural sciences; social scientific knowledge
scientific laws 7, 28
and closure 42
and objective knowledge 5
and paradigms 194
and positivism 76, 77, 85, 118
scientific racism 75, 82, 85, 86–91, 96, 121–4, 138, 239
as discourse 256, 257
and gender 313
scientific research
fraud in 225–7
methodological rules of 215
professionalization of 34
progress in 215–16, 227–8
scientism 159
scientists
as custodians 308, 309
ethnographic studies of 211–13
representations of 30–1, 244, 245

scientific communities 194, 195, 198, 208–13, 217, 218, 225–7, 266
Scottish Enlightenment 60, 62, 63, 64
seismology 304
selfconcept, and social interaction 162–3
selfconsciousness, and the Enlightenment 59
semiology 232, 240–5, 246
and discursive psychology 246, 247, 248, 249
sexual identity, and political discourse 257–8, 268, 274–5
Sheldon, William H. 291
signifier/signified
in discourse 253, 254, 257
in language 235, 238–40
signs, in language 235–40, 253
situated complexity 321
situated knowledge, gender and science 311–20
situated practice, social science as a 4, 12–15
Skinner, B.F. 103, 201
Smith, Adam 63, 64, 263
Smith, Anna Maria, 'Political discourse, homosexuality and its metaphors' 258, 268, 274–5, 295
soap powder advertisements, cultural representation of 242–3, 244, 245
social agents
and the circuit of knowledge 49
and knowledge systems 27, 28, 33
social inequality, language, discourse and culture of 233–4
social physics 79
social problems 286
social psychology 201, 220–2
discourse analysis in 247–52
Social Science Research Council (later Economic and Social Research Council) 20
social scientific knowledge
and audiences 310, 322
and cultural values 234
as situated 12–15
and values and aims of researchers 10, 11, 14–15, 33
social scientists, as cultural agents 270

social situatedness 4
social structures
and knowledge systems 27–8
and realism 304–5, 319–20, 326–8
sociology
falsification escape clauses in 190–2, 219–20
ideal types in 149–50
of knowledge and science 208–13, 225
reliable and valid knowledge in 145
sophisticated methodological falsificationism 215
speech act theory 247–8, 249, 250
Spencer, Herbert 77, 78, 82, 83
standard positivism 77, 97, 102–5, 114, 268
practical implications of 104–5
statics, in Comte's positivism 80–1, 119–20
statistical closure 42, 43–4, 130
statistical correlations, and positive economics 115
stereotypes, in social scientific research 14, 16
Stevens, Richard, 'Humanistic and experiential social psychology' 201, 221
Stokes, Sir John 111
stranger, perspective of the 16–20, 131, 287, 322
'strong programme', in the sociology of knowledge 208
structural complexity 321
structuralist linguistics 232, 235, 246
structure
and agency 305, 306
and language 233, 234–40
structure of feeling, culture as 264, 266
structured relationships 303, 304, 326–8
subject positions 294
subject–object problem 7–8, 281, 297, 301–3
subject–object relationships, and idealism 139–40, 173
subjective experiences, of social researchers 8, 15
subjectivity, and meaning 161–6

subjects, construction of through knowledge 290–6
suicide, Durkheim's study of 84–5, 150, 299
Sutherland, Stuart, 'What if teacher is a cheat?' 210, 226–7
synchronic analysis 235
synchrony, in language 81
syntagmatic relations in language 237
synthetic a priori statements 138
synthetic statements 98–9, 232, 255
    on crime 136, 138
    and empiricism 133, 138
synthetic truths 60

tacit knowledge 165–6, 179–80
    see also bedrock assumptions
technological change, and postmodernism 283, 284, 323
terminology, challenge of 8–9
texts
    and **intertextuality** 257, 259
    in poststructuralist discourse 252, 253–4
textual reductionism 271
Thatcherism
    as an ideal type 147
    and public choice theory 158
theoretical closure 42, 43, 113, 130
theoretical systems, and the Duhem–Quine thesis 187
theory
    and empiricism 133, 138
    and idealism 129, 131, 172, 173
    and the practice of social science 12
    in social research 3, 65
Thompson, John L. *see* Vane, Howard R. and Thompson, John L.
Tomas, Annabel and Dittmar, Helga, 'The meaning of home' 9, 10–11, 24, 285
Tracy, Antoine Destutt de 78
transcendental questions 134
transformational model of social activity 306, 315
transformative processes, and the Enlightenment 56–8, 63, 78
tropes 249–50, 252
truth

analytic and synthetic truths 60
and Bacon's four idols (delusions) 48, 49
and the circuit of knowledge 32, 33, 53, 265, 309
and discourse 252, 259
and the Enlightenment 59, 71
and falsificationism 105, 112
and Kuhn's account of scientific change 197
and language 245, 246
and neoKantianism 141
and Popper's induction method 107
and positivism 78, 79, 256
in poststructuralist discourse 252
questioning 206
and science 20
and scientific communities 209
and scientific knowledge 28, 29
Tuan, YiFu, *Topophilia* 169–70
Turney, John, 'Faking it to make it' 210, 225–6
types, in everyday life and social scientific research 16–20, 322

ubiquity determinism 300, 301
United States of America, and scientific racism 87, 90–1, 121–4
utilitarianism 82–3, 85, 120–1

valid knowledge 145
value judgements 151
    and the Enlightenment 72
    fact–value controversy 64, 65
value relevance 145, 151, 173
values
    and knowledge 322
    and logical positivism 97
    in social scientific research 14–15
    and standard positivism 104
    see also cultural values; fact–value distinction
Vane, Howard R. and Thompson, John L., 'Economic paradigms' 202, 222–3
variables, and ideal types 148
verificationist approach
    and falsificationism 108, 111, 116–17
    and logical positivism 100, 105

Vienna Circle 77, 98, 102, 107, 111
Vogel, Ezra F. and Bell, Norman W., 'The emotionally disturbed child as the family scapegoat' 192, 219–20, 295
voluntarism
    and neoKantianism 149, 171
    and realism 305
voting behaviour
    and public choice theory 157–8
    statistical closure in studies of 43–4

Watson, John B. 103, 199, 200, 201
Weber, Max 130, 146–9, 164, 173, 263
Weeks, Jeffrey, 'The construction of homosexuality' 295, 324–6
Wetherell, Margaret
    'Critical social psychology' 201, 221–2
    see also Potter, Jonathan and Wetherell, Margaret
Whitehead, Alfred 98
Williams, Raymond 233, 265, 266, 267, 268
Willis, Paul, *Common Culture* 265–6
Willmott, Peter *see* Young, Michael and Willmott, Peter
Winch, Peter, *The Idea of a Social Science* 140
Windelbrand, Wilhelm 141–2
Wittgenstein, Ludwig 98, 138, 284, 308
'woman', construction of in Western science 318
women
    exclusion from academic and professional life 54, 55, 59
    research on homeless 9, 10–11, 21, 24
    treatment of women in social scientific research 14
working class, and the embourgeoisement thesis 110
writerly texts 254
Wundt, Wilhelm 143, 199

Young, Michael and Willmott, Peter, *The Symmetrical Family* 110
youth cultures 287